CELEBRATE!
Young Poets Speak Out

Heartland – Fall 2007

Creative Communication, Inc.

CELEBRATE!
Young Poets Speak Out
Heartland – Fall 2007

An anthology compiled by Creative Communication, Inc.

Published by:

CREATIVE COMMUNICATION, INC.
1488 NORTH 200 WEST
LOGAN, UT 84341

Printed in the United States of America

ISBN: 978-1-60050-154-8

Foreword

The poets between these pages are not famous...yet. They are still learning how language creates images and how to reflect their thoughts through words. However, through their acceptance into this publication, these young poets have taken a giant leap that reflects their desire to write.

We are proud of this anthology and what it represents. Most poets who entered the contest were not accepted to be published. The poets who are included in this book represent the best poems from our youth. These young poets took a chance and were rewarded by being featured in this anthology. Without this book, these poems would have been lost in a locker or a backpack.

We will have a feeling of success if upon reading this anthology of poetry each reader finds a poem that evokes emotion. It may be a giggle or a smile. It may be a thoughtful reflection. You might find a poem that takes you back to an earlier day when a snowfall contains magic or when a pile of leaves was an irresistible temptation. If these poems can make you feel alive and have hope in our youth, then it will be time well spent.

As we thank the poets for sharing their work, we also thank you, the reader, for allowing us to be part of your life.

Thomas Worthen, Ph.D.
Editor
Creative Communication

WRITING CONTESTS!

Enter our next POETRY contest!

Enter our next ESSAY contest!

Why should I enter?

Win prizes and get published! Each year thousands of dollars in prizes are awarded in each region and tens of thousands of dollars in prizes are awarded throughout North America. The top writers in each division receive a monetary award and a free book that includes their published poem or essay. Entries of merit are also selected to be published in our anthology.

Who may enter?

There are four divisions in the poetry contest. The poetry divisions are grades K-3, 4-6, 7-9, and 10-12. There are three divisions in the essay contest. The essay division are grades 4-6, 7-9, and 10-12.

What is needed to enter the contest?

To enter the poetry contest send in one original poem, 21 lines or less. To enter the essay contest send in one original essay, 250 words or less, on any topic. Each entry must include the student's name, grade, address, city, state, and zip code, and the student's school name and school address. Students who include their teacher's name may help the teacher qualify for a free copy of the anthology.

How do I enter?

Enter a poem online at:
www.poeticpower.com

or

Mail your poem to:
Poetry Contest
1488 North 200 West
Logan, UT 84341

Enter an essay online at:
www.studentessaycontest.com

or

Mail your essay to:
Essay Contest
1488 North 200 West
Logan, UT 84341

When is the deadline?

Poetry contest deadlines are August 14th, December 4th, and April 8th. Essay contest deadlines are July 15th, October 15th, and February 17th. You can enter each contest, however, send only one poem or essay for each contest deadline.

Are there benefits for my school?

Yes. We award $15,000 each year in grants to help with Language Arts programs. Schools qualify to apply for a grant by having a large number of entries of which over fifty percent are accepted for publication. This typically tends to be about 15 accepted entries.

Are there benefits for my teacher?

Yes. Teachers with five or more students accepted to be published receive a free anthology that includes their students' writing.

For more information please go to our website at **www.poeticpower.com**, email us at editor@poeticpower.com or call 435-713-4411.

Table of Contents

States included in this edition:

Arkansas
Kentucky
Missouri
Oklahoma
Tennessee
West Virginia

Fall 2007
Poetic Achievement Honor Schools

** Teachers who had fifteen or more poets accepted to be published*

The following schools are recognized as receiving a "Poetic Achievement Award." This award is given to schools who have a large number of entries of which over fifty percent are accepted for publication. With hundreds of schools entering our contest, only a small percent of these schools are honored with this award. The purpose of this award is to recognize schools with excellent Language Arts programs. This award qualifies these schools to receive a complimentary copy of this anthology. In addition, these schools are eligible to apply for a Creative Communication Language Arts Grant. Grants of two hundred and fifty dollars each are awarded to further develop writing in our schools.

All Saints' Episcopal School
Morristown, TN
Betty Golden*
Angie Smith

All Saints School
St Peters, MO
Carol Wegescheide*

Alpena Elementary School
Alpena, AR
Sherry Choate
Ginny Hulsey
Dawn Keys
Mr. Nichols
Mrs. Phillips
Ruthie Weidenfeller

Alpena High School
Alpena, AR
Annette Phillips
JoAn K. Rider*

Anderson County High School
Clinton, TN
Lori Price*

Annunciation Elementary School
Webster Groves, MO
Mrs. Kelly*

Audubon Youth Development Center
Louisville, KY
Myrna Marshall Brame*

Barret Traditional Middle School
Louisville, KY
Paulette Goetz*

Baylor School
Chattanooga, TN
Fontaine Alison
Tammy Burns
Amy Cohen
Bart Loftin
Sally Naylor*

Bearden High School
Knoxville, TN
Anna Marie Hughes*
Virginia L. Thurston*

Belle Isle Enterprise Middle School
Oklahoma City, OK
Paula Armstrong*

Benton County School of the Arts
Rogers, AR
LaVona Cerna*

Capital High School
Charleston, WV
Diane Ferguson*

Chelsea Jr High School
Chelsea, OK
Ms. C. Quinton*

Chickasha High School
Chickasha, OK
Jo Perryman*

Clarksburg School
Clarksburg, TN
Jeannine Stokes*

Coffee County Central High School
Manchester, TN
Joyce McCullough*

Dyer Elementary & Jr High School
Dyer, TN
Lee Hudson*

Elkton School
Elkton, TN
Teri Mize*

Family of Faith Christian School
Shawnee, OK
Jessica Harper*

Germantown High School
Germantown, TN
Billy M. Pullen*
Nancy Scott

Glenpool High School
Glenpool, OK
Rhonda Gantz*
Margaret Gibson
Phil Harriman
Barbara Wishart

Greenfield Jr/Sr High School
Greenfield, MO
Renée Burton*

Gresham Middle School
Knoxville, TN
Katye Clemmons*

Hartville Jr/Sr High School
Hartville, MO
Teresa Oliphant*

Hebron Middle School
Shepherdsville, KY
Trina Henn
Beverly Stangel

Heritage Middle School
Maryville, TN
Marie Richardson*

Highland Rim School
Fayetteville, TN
Dana Casey*

Hollis High School
Hollis, OK
Laurie Westmoreland*

Houston Middle School
Germantown, TN
Joye Phipps*

Jeffersontown High School Magnet Career Academy
Louisville, KY
Kimberly Messer*

Ketchum Jr High School
Ketchum, OK
Mary Davis*
Mrs. Herndon*
Trish McQueen*

Lee A Tolbert Community Academy
Kansas City, MO
Elizabeth Deardorff
Zanova Gasaway
Valerie Guy
Pamela King
Rayma Moburg
Cindy Salomone
Dana Tiller
Janice Yocum*

Leeton Middle and High School
Leeton, MO
Carole Smith*

Maury Middle School
Dandridge, TN
Rebbeca McGaha*

Mayflower Middle School
Mayflower, AR
Rhonda Smith*

McGehee High School
McGehee, AR
Larell Jones*

Meredith-Dunn School
Louisville, KY
Kathy Beck
Susan Prater
Nancy Stewart

Montgomery Central Middle School
Cunningham, TN
DeAnne Murphy*

Musselman Middle School
Bunker Hill, WV
Jennifer Grubb*
Linda Shaw*

Nettleton Jr High School
Jonesboro, AR
Cheryl Russell*

Newcastle Middle School
Newcastle, OK
Cindy Shaw*

Niangua High School
Niangua, MO
Joann Jirik
Sharon Rooney

Odessa Middle School
Odessa, MO
Leah Chamberlin
Linda Walsh
Lori Weddle

Our Lady Catholic School
Festus, MO
Brenda Fischer*
Mrs. Kempfer

Owasso 8th Grade Center
Owasso, OK
Kimberly Derby*

Owasso High School
Owasso, OK
Mrs. Arnold
Sallyanne H. Wallace*

Pigeon Forge Middle School
Pigeon Forge, TN
Laura Turner*

Prue High School
Prue, OK
Kari Garman*

Rock Bridge Sr High School
Columbia, MO
Jennifer Black Cone
Laura Overton
Joe Wilson
Denise Winslow

Rocky Comfort Elementary School
Rocky Comfort, MO
Liz Webster*

Seven Holy Founders School
Affton, MO
Karen Brandt
Joe Morice
Mary Wagner*

Slater High School
Slater, MO
Randolph Niswonger*

South Intermediate High School
Broken Arrow, OK
Kristin Gillespie
Mrs. M. O'Brian

Southern Reynolds County R-II School
Ellington, MO
Mona Huffman*

St Charles Homeschool Learning Center
St Peters, MO
Heather Nuehring*

St Francis Borgia Regional High School
Washington, MO
Chuck Bright*

St Gerard Majella School
Kirkwood, MO
Lorraine Behrens*

St Joseph Institute for the Deaf
Chesterfield, MO
Pat Watson*

St Mary of the Woods School
Whitesville, KY
Kay Howard*

St Mary's Episcopal School
Memphis, TN
Caroline Goodman*

Stuart Middle School
Louisville, KY
Diana Berger*

Union County High School
Maynardville, TN
Sherrie Collins*

University Heights Academy
Hopkinsville, KY
Faye Hendricks*

West Jr High School
Columbia, MO
Heidi Barnhouse
Susan Botkin*
Jeff Fagan*
Lisa Fullerton*
Michelle Jones*

White Station Middle School
Memphis, TN
Angela Davis
Helen C. Erskine*
Ruby Hubbard
Soo Scott
Mrs. Thompson
Robert Wade
Dwight Wade

Wilson Middle School
Tulsa, OK
Jeffrey Laymon*

Woodrow Wilson High School
Beckley, WV
Tammy C. McKinney*

Language Arts Grant Recipients 2007-2008

After receiving a "Poetic Achievement Award" schools are encouraged to apply for a Creative Communication Language Arts Grant. The following is a list of schools who received a two hundred and fifty dollar grant for the 2007-2008 school year.

Acadamie DaVinci, Dunedin, FL
Altamont Elementary School, Altamont, KS
Belle Valley South School, Belleville, IL
Bose Elementary School, Kenosha, WI
Brittany Hill Middle School, Blue Springs, MO
Carver Jr High School, Spartanburg, SC
Cave City Elementary School, Cave City, AR
Central Elementary School, Iron Mountain, MI
Challenger K8 School of Science and Mathematics, Spring Hill, FL
Columbus Middle School, Columbus, MT
Cypress Christian School, Houston, TX
Deer River High School, Deer River, MN
Deweyville Middle School, Deweyville, TX
Four Peaks Elementary School, Fountain Hills, AZ
Fox Chase School, Philadelphia, PA
Fox Creek High School, North Augusta, SC
Grandview Alternative School, Grandview, MO
Hillcrest Elementary School, Lawrence, KS
Holbrook School, Holden, ME
Houston Middle School, Germantown, TN
Independence High School, Elko, NV
International College Preparatory Academy, Cincinnati, OH
John Bowne High School, Flushing, NY
Lorain County Joint Vocational School, Oberlin, OH
Merritt Secondary School, Merritt, BC
Midway Covenant Christian School, Powder Springs, GA
Muir Middle School, Milford, MI
Northlake Christian School, Covington, LA
Northwood Elementary School, Hilton, NY
Place Middle School, Denver, CO
Public School 124, South Ozone Park, NY

Language Arts Grant Winners cont.

Public School 219 Kennedy King, Brooklyn, NY
Rolling Hills Elementary School, San Diego, CA
St Anthony's School, Streator, IL
St Joan Of Arc School, Library, PA
St Joseph Catholic School, York, NE
St Joseph School-Fullerton, Baltimore, MD
St Monica Elementary School, Mishawaka, IN
St Peter Celestine Catholic School, Cherry Hill, NJ
Strasburg High School, Strasburg, VA
Stratton Elementary School, Stratton, ME
Tom Thomson Public School, Burlington, ON
Tremont Elementary School, Tremont, IL
Warren Elementary School, Warren, OR
Webster Elementary School, Hazel Park, MI
West Woods Elementary School, Arvada, CO
West Woods Upper Elementary School, Farmington, CT
White Pine Middle School, Richmond, UT
Winona Elementary School, Winona, TX
Wissahickon Charter School, Philadelphia, PA
Wood County Christian School, Williamstown, WV
Wray High School, Wray, CO

Young Poets
Grades 10-11-12

Note: The Top Ten poems were finalized through an online voting system. Creative Communication's judges first picked out the top poems. These poems were then posted online. The final step involved thousands of students and teachers who registered as online judges and voted for the Top Ten poems. We hope you enjoy these selections.

Top Poem Grades 10-11-12

What If

I can see the pain in your eyes,
Memories of a fractured, broken paradise.
Of all the things that've been said and done,
The fights you've fought and could've won.

I know you know me, my friend.
I'll be the one to stay through the end.
Then can you look into my eyes,
And hear the silence of my desperate cries.

I know you feel like you've been beaten down,
But it's by the words of men who have no ground.
So tell me, which constitutes a harder fall,
To love and lose, or never love at all.

What if there's more to us than you and I?
What if there's a love that could never die?
What if there's an escape from scars and pain?
What if we lose that which is for us to gain?

Oh, won't you listen to my cries.
There comes a cleansing rain with stormy skies.
You'll never have to face that pain again.
You know I know you, my friend.

Levi Carey, Grade 11
Grove High School, OK

Top Poem Grades 10-11-12

Summertime

The bottle was opened, and carbonation overflowed
The sun was high; it was noon.
Sweet syrupy caffeinated substance rushed in
To wet the candy saturated taste buds
The driveway became a canvas
For ten different colored jumbo chalk pieces
And six little hands created masterpieces
Of hopscotch and portraits.
Soccer, basketball, football, volleyball
They were all possibilities.
Hours upon hours of swimming
To only wince in pain;
Of course no one applied sunscreen like Mom said to.
Staying still and watching for small flickers of light
To catch and release one, and do it over again.
The simplicities of a childhood summer day.

Kaitlyn Cornett, Grade 11
Germantown High School, TN

Top Poem Grades 10-11-12

Ways of the World

"Hello, good-bye," you said to me then;
I told you the same,
'Cause you seemed to be in
A great hurry just like the rest of the world;
A world in a hurry, with no time to spend.

We run and we run and we run oh so hard,
For what, no one knows,
Only those blessed with regard
For others, in much more unfortunate states;
A world in a hurry, with no time to spend.

Sometimes it's blurry; sometimes it's fuzzy,
And the ones with the memories,
Now they are the lucky;
The ones with the purpose and passion to live,
See this world in a hurry and make time to give.

Meredith B. Daniel, Grade 11
Woodrow Wilson High School, WV

Top Poem Grades 10-11-12

Whispers in the Fields

The cock-a-doodle-doo raised my eyes to the blue —
Tinted heavens above with streaks of clear dew
Gently tapping my shoulder and blades of grass
I skip through quickly, though the barn I don't pass.
Cuddled with chicks on a soft bed of straw
A brown cow was eating with her round, black jaw.
This place is in the middle of paradise,
Where my grandparents opened my hazel eyes
To the hills and dark woods I now truly love
Made from the calmest of hands up above.
Oh, this way of life, a constant place I am dreaming
On the wooden front porch, where I'm just 'a swinging.
A time of the past and of that to come
All with a single strand of hope to succumb.
With the same squeaky giggle and silly smile
Kick off your shoes and stay just a while.
Boundless hospitality, endless growing grins
Church-clothes worn every Sunday, wiping all sins.
Oh, this way of life, a constant place I am dreaming
On the wooden front porch, where I'm just 'a swinging.

Christina England, Grade 12
Merrol Hyde Magnet School, TN

Top Poem Grades 10-11-12

We the People

The land of the free and the home of the brave,
But what of the voices that cry from the grave?
With every day that we let freedom ring,
There is one more voice that will never sing.
One baby murdered is not much to lose,
For at least we have practiced our right to choose.
Strolling by idly, just smelling the roses
While a holocaust rages right under our noses.
O glorious land of the red, white, and blue!
How is true freedom understood by so few?
Freedom's streets are paved with red;
Our guilty hands stained by the blood of the dead.
We stand by and watch as each child dies
And close our eyes beneath the red sunrise.
Though all around us the Truth shines so bright,
Our blindfolds will not let us see what is right.
Day by day America limps on,
Never aware that her future is gone.
Amidst the echo of the silent scream,
We've lost the essence of the American Dream.

Emily P. Gandy, Grade 11
Heritage Academy, MO

Top Poem Grades 10-11-12

Broken

Daddy, please listen,
Please listen good.

I want to forgive you for leaving me,
And making me feel unloved.
For all the nights I stayed up crying
Wishing you would come back.
I want to forgive you for crushing,
The heart of a seven year old girl.
Breaking the biggest promise,
That little did you know changed my world.

I want to forgive you for doing
The stupidest thing in your life,
You lost your son and your daughter,
And most of all, your loving wife.
But Daddy, can you forgive me?

For not giving you a second chance.
For hating you, and thinking,
I won't ever get that "dance."
Little did I know, it also took a toll on you,
Because not only do you hurt,
But you lost someone you loved, too.

Caitlin Kelly, Grade 11
Owasso High School, OK

Top Poem Grades 10-11-12

Storm

Gray takes over the sky,
Trees begin to sway,
The sun slowly fades.
Aromas of sweet droplets fill the air,
A trickle moves in.
My heart begins to rush.
Chest begins to heavily beat
I lose all connection to my thoughts.
Gleaming droplets float down my flesh
A chill runs down my spine.
Sparks of light
Flash upon my face,
Roaring thunder
Whispers in my ear.
Surrounding sounds disappear;
Time stands still.
My cheeks begin to rise.
Something in me
Dreams this will never die.

Jessica Key, Grade 12
Cheyenne High School, OK

Top Poem Grades 10-11-12

Rural Life in the 1940's

A quiet life in the country sounds good,
But I wouldn't change, even if I could.
Can you imagine life without technology or microwave?
No emails, iPods, cell phones, electricity, running water — you'd be a slave.
Long empty roads,
No road kill, not even toads.
Fields of corn, tomatoes, watermelon and beans;
All worked by the local teens.
This was before the advent of the malls,
A boy's job was cleaning the stalls.
Work was from sunup to sundown.
Thrill of the week was going to town.
Household smells were of homemade bread,
Moms had plenty of mending with needle and thread.
There were hens to set and pigs to feed,
If a neighbor was sick, those around helped meet the need.
No wonder my Grandparents always smile,
They've enjoyed the best of both for a while.

Samuel Adam Phillips, Grade 12
Bixby High School, OK

Top Poem Grades 10-11-12

Semper Fi

We've died on shores across the globe,
For family and friends back here at home.

My brothers in arms that have gone before me,
All those I have never seen,
I love and revere all of them;
They are United States Marines.

They fought for what they thought was right,
They battled for greater good.
All just wanted to come back home,
But many never would.

It is my time now; I am called to duty,
With rifle in my hand.
I will not back down or cower;
This is my last stand.

From the halls of Montezuma,
To the shores of Tripoli,
I'm ready to die for country and home.
I'm a United States Marine.

John Syler, Grade 10
Niangua High School, MO

Top Poem Grades 10-11-12

Daniel O'Neil*

His last chord was in C minor.
The awkward apex of jumbling C, E flat, and G,
Trickling down guitar strings,
A chilling melodious waterfall
Constricting the coffee shop audience,
With a mocha autumn frost,
Into static ice crystals.
It wasn't a slip of his fingers
Or a malfunctioning microphone.
Simply an eerie cacophony of foreboding mood,
Storm clouds on the Monday horizon,
Written by the artist formerly known as O'Neil.
A stale note stinging over musician's graves,
Scaling people's spines into forlorn silence,
The Westminster chimes of a grandfather clock
In the abandoned hours of the late night.
However, this clock's a time bomb
That questioned the ability of defying fate in vain,
For suffering for his art
Is not the same as a bullet to the brain.
His last chord was in C minor.

A.J. Tirrell, Grade 12
Germantown High School, TN
**Dedicated to Daniel O'Neil,*
a victim of the Virginia Tech tragedy

My Light

There is a shimmer in the distance,
A light that guides me through,
A beacon of hope I call it
To remind me of what is true.

It lights my path in darkness,
It holds steady during the storm,
It is my strength on a cold, cold night,
It is the blanket that keeps me warm.

It is this light that watches over me
Each and every day.
It is this light that always protects me
As I saunter on my way.

I hold it dear and close to me,
For I shall never let it go.
This light is as precious to me
As winter's first fallen snow.

I know where I am heading,
Yet the journey is still in its prime.
Regardless, I know I am always safe,
For this light will always be mine.

Kirsten Lilly, Grade 10
Shady Spring High School, WV

The Leaves Fall Down

The leaves fall down,
Red, yellow, and brown,
The weather becomes chilly,
The leafless trees look silly,
It's easy to gain cash,
Just rake them up real fast,
It's not too bright,
It's a very pretty sight,
The wind picks up height,
Making it easier to fly a kite,
It starts most schools,
And closes the pools,
It marks two great holidays,
Halloween and Thanksgiving Day,
Halloween is cool,
With all the little ghouls,
Thanksgiving is satisfying,
Everyone is gratifying,
Oh, you will have a ball,
With the great season of fall.

Wesley Yarber, Grade 10
Powell High School, TN

Mountain

The mountain rises
Shadowing the cool river
Swiftly winds below

Brittany McDonald, Grade 10
Fort Towson Jr/Sr High School, OK

Color Blind

The palate I hold mixes colors indiscernible to your eye.
Like a newborn child, you fail to see my brilliant hues.
Swirling and spilling off my brush
my pen
my mouth.
Before you, lay a thick oil painting, rich with texture and depth.
Focused on the aesthetics, you rely merely on what your eyes perceive.
Isn't your mind screaming at you to think deeper,
To think at all?
No, you are a victim of measurable time.
Move on, move quick,
Shuffle that painting between your hands.
Place it under the shallow watercolors,
Those that lack the ability to bleed a substance of thought.
You may see my painting, but you don't know my art.

Andrew Reed, Grade 12
Louisville Male High School, KY

The Perfect City

It was a dark and stormy night under the ocean,
There lay the perfect city, a place to dwell peacefully,
One could say that it was a haven for those who became lost,
From the society that abandoned them.

When that dark and stormy night screamed woefully,
People died, unaware of what was truly going on,
A massacre occurred, one man did cause,
His experiments were the reason for their loss,
The end for these people, quickly it arrived,
Left a mark on the ruins of the perfect city when its inhabitants died.

This city, no one has found,
A place called Rapture, a bustling town,
For when this dark and stormy night loomed near,
The people would truly discover the real face of fear.

Steven Stribling, Grade 11
Anderson County High School, TN

The Fighter

I am a fighter
Lover of my family and friends
I belong to myself and no one else
When you see me on the street you see a strong willed woman
I have qualities to give to the world
I dream of a day when I no longer must be a fighter
In twenty years, you will see me as a mother who fights for her children.
My flaw is my kindness to people who don't deserve it
I could change the world if I just try
If you listen to me you will understand why I am a fighter
I will be remembered by my strong will to survive
If you believe in one thing believe in yourself, no one else matters
My name is Bethany
My soul is strong
I am a fighter

Bethany Flowers, Grade 11
Grandview Alternative School, MO

Be Happy...

The flower didn't like its shade,
Its large petals torn and grayed.
It looked at the rose by the tree,
Hopelessly wishing it was she.
The flower should not have been so sad,
It should've been happy with what it had.

Winter breathed its bitter breath,
Bringing with it the foreshadowing death,
Of our helpless little flower friend
Knowing its life was at an end.
It did not have to be joyous, but it should not have been sad.
It should have been happy with what it had.

Spring came with a sudden boom,
Lifting up the winter's gloom.
The flower opened its weary eyes,
To find its rose friend in disguise.
Her crimson petals now were sad,
The flower learned to be happy with what it had.

Christine Copelan, Grade 11
Anderson County High School, TN

Destiny

Human beings…the most carefully engineered,
Dominate among all creation
Granted on Earth, we live for a time.
Cherished by most…detested by some.
It is as delicate as a rose petal,
Perishable and perilous…or possibly
Fulfilling, satisfying, and gratifying.
Freewill binds the minds of all to none
For the paths taken are to satisfy one's self
A path ill traveled or a path so rarely uncommon.
Dreams fill them with excitement…
Fear…intensity…suspense.
Finally the end…the new beginning…
It is determined from our life on Earth,
Through that we sketch our destiny!

Elliot Bertasi, Grade 11
Germantown High School, TN

My Journey

Loneliness surrounds me everywhere I go
The emptiness that is in my heart must never show
I walk a dark path that is full of fear
Knowing not if the end is near
The burden I hold within my heart
I hope will one day soon depart
And though I walk on this shadowy road
I will one day lose this heavy load
Because the burden that I hold within
Will soon be gone so I can begin
On a journey I will go
To a wonderful place I do not know

Desirae Foreman, Grade 11
McMinn County High School, TN

Situations Like This

Have you ever been in a situation like this?
One where you know that there's no way
To end up with exactly what you want?
I know I should give up hope…
But I've never been very good at that.
There have been too many times where hope is all I've got.
I wish I could tell you exactly why
I'm so sure that this is what I want.
It just seems like it was meant to be.
But then again, who really believes in fate?
I'm one of those strange ones who thinks
That nothing worth having comes without a fight.
Have you ever been in a situation like this?
One where you're pretending that you don't want something
Because you're afraid of making a fool of yourself?
The words are playing in my mind,
Telling me to give up.
But I'm not ready for that yet.
I really hate situations like this;
The ones where you want more than anything to see the end;
But at the same time, you're afraid of how it might turn out.

Kat Weltha, Grade 11
Joplin Sr High School, MO

I Have Learned

I have learned to like myself
to appreciate who I have become
I have learned to be patient
My prince charming is out there somewhere
I just have not found him yet

I have learned to be thankful
that I have my whole life ahead of me
to find that special someone
I have learned to be grateful
for everything he has given me

I have learned to love others
for who they are inside
I have learned to love myself
for who I am inside
I have learned to love me for me

Katie Howe, Grade 10
Crowley's Ridge Academy, AR

Lost

Grandmas are good, but mine was the best.
When I would get tired, on her lap I would rest.
The times she felt good, we always had fun.
In her house I would play, and in her yard I would run.
Now her mind has quit, and it breaks my heart inside.
To see her sitting there, I can't help but to ask "why?"
She's nothing but a shell, lost in her own mind,
Searching for a way out, one which she'll never find.
Times that we shared are times I think of,
For it is my grandma, that I will always love.

Jessica Pack, Grade 10
Shady Spring High School, WV

Strawberries

Deep red
Sweet juiciness
Trickling down your lips
Yellow dots piercing its surface
Scarlet berry

Seguin Warwick, Grade 11
Union County High School, TN

Who Are You?

You make me think,
You make me blink,
You're on my mind
All the time.
You stop me from doing crimes,
Just at the right time.
You're tired of seeing me do time,
For little crimes.
You wish you could rewind,
Back the hands of time.
If you don't mind,
The decision is mine.
It's your time to shine,
I know you will do fine.
You're in the back of my mind,
All the time.
Who are you?
You weigh about the same as a
Chihuahua,
Ha ha!
Your name is the brain!

Gary H., Grade 10
Audubon Youth Development Center, KY

Someone Else

The mask is dawned,
The character created.
He becomes someone else again.
No one must know who he really is.
Instead they must see
A much different story.
He moves with such grace,
Interacting with the people
Of his own little world,
Questions arise to all
Who pass by this man:
Who is he, and what does he want?
Where is he going with this facade?
What is the meaning of the words
He shouts, so ardently,
So that all may hear?
What is this man's struggle?
The man does very well
What he has been trained to do,
But of his task, one must inquire.
Is this man a liar? No, an actor is he!

Thomas Vines, Grade 11
Owasso High School, OK

Fly Away

This town is small and filled with familiar faces.
There are so many memories in so many places.
I'm standing here in my cap and gown.
So many people all around.
You stand in front of me;
Your tears fall for all to see.
My car is loaded down.
My time has come to leave this town.
But, I promise you, I'll be back someday.
Now, you have to let me go so I can fly away.

We all stand up here together.
We've known each other for what seems like forever.
Now, our time has come.
Our adventure has only begun.
We're all so ready to leave this place.
The smile refuses to leave my face.
People are talking all around.
My feet refuse to touch the ground.
My friend, I promise you, I'll be back someday.
But now is the time that I start to fly away.

Since we promised you we'll be back someday; we'll spread our wings and fly away.

Kara Frauenfelder, Grade 12
Summersville Jr-Sr High School, MO

To: Unknown

I sit in my filth, coughing and cold.
I think I am dying, with no one to hold.
I will tell you my life, you're the only one who will listen.
As I progress, you'll see through my vision.

My school years were riddled with special needs classes.
Accompanied so well with bulletproof glasses.
I hold all the answers, none of which I can tell.
My mouth always failed me, never allowing me to yell.
My life led to nowhere, I'm left not feeling love.
I've never felt warmth, unless from above.
My body is able, but not able enough.
I live on my own, my life has been rough.

Although I am glad you are here with me, I fear you're too late.
I would have asked to come with you, but I am in an unmovable state.
You have done more than your part, leaving me in peace by my cart.

With one last scream, my body, it shakes.
So much pain, I wish it were fake.
I've finished my letter, and lie here unmoving.
My pen and my paper have made dying so soothing.

Mark Dewbre, Grade 11
Siloam Springs Sr High School, AR

The Hole

I jump off the bus,
excited about the upcoming weekend.
My journey home seemed almost like seconds,
when it generally takes a minute or two.
The door opens with ease,
and I walk in beaming.

It didn't hit me until I came upstairs.
There's her door,
never to be opened by her again.
Knowing I'd never see her anymore,
or in general hear her voice,
for the rest of my mortal life,
hurts.

In my world,
there's now a hole…

Tegan Thomas, Grade 10
Germantown High School, TN

When I Have Memories

When I have memories that may not die
Before my life has fulfilled its purpose,
Before nothing's left worth remembering
Some memories I'll take away with me;
Someday when I go to my dark cold grave,
Some shall never be remembered again,
And some may never come to mind again
But memories shall never die alone,
And when I die, new ones will come to be
I'll not forget the ones that brought me joy
Nor forget days that made me laugh out loud.
Nor forget the day that I was chased by
A little boy on the play ground in the
Kindergarten when we were six years old.

Sharlee Roberts, Grade 12
Colbert High School, OK

Invisible Children

In darkness, they walk for miles.
In daylight, they hide and sleep.
Their eyes watering from pain,
That from their legs and from their hearts.
For they ache to see their loved ones,
To feel the warmth of a hug, the everlasting moment of a kiss,
And to find a place that they can call *home*.
But guns and hatred surround them,
Engulfing the villages with fear.
Yet in groups they discover happiness,
With common goals to read and write one day.
And with almost nothing, they live on,
Shivering in the darkness,
Hoping the violence will cease.
But until that day,
They continue
As invisible children.

Arpan Prabhu, Grade 10
Morgantown High School, WV

Why Do I Say Those Words to You?

Why do I say those words to you?
Every morning I see you
I say I love you
Ever night I see you
I say I love you

Do these words mean anything at all?
Do people say out of lust or love?
Do people say it to make others feel better?
Do people even know the power that these words hold?

When people say
I LOVE YOU
Do they mean it?

You answer this question
WHY DO I SAY THOSE WORDS TO YOU?
If you think that someone truly loves you,
Don't let that someone go

Michael Hall, Grade 11
Alpena Elementary School, AR

Winter's Cold

You can feel it in the air
As the leaves begin to change.
You can sense it in the stillness
Provided by the dark blanket of night.
It seemed a long time coming,
But now that it is showing its face,
It will be gone before we know it.
As the days go forth
More and more of it is seen,
And we seek refuge from its effect.
The presence of friends and family
Is where this warmth is found.
They are the protectors when you start to feel
The chills of the season down your spine,
At the very moment you hit the air.
This long awaited thing,
From summer's heat we take on change
To the beloved winter's cold.

Sarah Hall, Grade 11
Germantown High School, TN

Country Boys

Workin' on cars,
and closin' the bars.
Drivin' Chevy trucks,
and getting stuck in the sticky muck.
Huntin' all the animals,
and eatin' like a cannibal.
Lovin' pretty women,
and helpin' them in the kitchen.
Being very sweet,
and makin' sure the ladies have a great treat.
Those are all the ways
that country boys will always stay!

Taylor Jones, Grade 10
Gibson County High School, TN

Night of the Harvest Festival

The leaves are changing colors.
The world around us flutters.
The night begins to chill.
The people dance in meadows browning
The bend upon which I am rounding.
Harvest moon is rising.
Couples dance the night away.
The children gently move and sway.
A wolf howls in the distance.
Tables piled high with sweets.
The women smell of peppermints.
I stand in the shadows.
Fireworks light up the sky.
The people "ooh" and "aah" and sigh.
They are filled with cheer.
Time grows short and people weary.
They return, their smiles merry.
I am not so lucky.
It is not a silly whim.
I am waiting just for him.
But he will never show.

Makala Carlile, Grade 10
Glenpool High School, OK

You

I love you with all my heart
I hope we never part
You are so very sweet
You sweep me off my feet
I'm so glad I met you
I hope I never forget you
This is a poem I wrote
From my heart I quote
I love you

Coco Lundy, Grade 11
Gibbs High School, TN

Fire's Eyes

The fire monster leaps,
What it touches, it keeps,
From its mouth comes a snarl,
Its prey it goes to gnarl,
Its fingers grope about,
Nothing it can't go without,
Its hunger is endless,
The world it must possess,
The monster grows in size,
Rising into the skies,
But luster in its eyes,
Is also in the guise,
Of the home's dozing kitten,
That with a close listen,
A soft snore may be heard,
The sound so much preferred.

Tyler Adams, Grade 11
Bearden High School, TN

Survivor

I am a survivor
Lover of my quiet time
I belong to all my battles
When you see me on the street, speak to me
I have qualities to give to the world that no one else has
I dream of just being a normal teenager, without any parental responsibilities
In twenty years you will see me on my own, just living the good life
My flaw is having to fight the same war every day
If I could change the world, teenagers could be themselves
If you listen to me, you might understand my struggles
I will be remembered by all the obstacles I had to face
If you believe in one thing, believe you can achieve anything
My name is Kendra Bobo
My soul is damaged
I am a survivor

Kendra Bobo, Grade 11
Grandview Alternative School, MO

Soccer Goal

I never worry about the score; we are out there for fun.
I refuse to sit down on the bench; I'm like a tiger pacing in a cage.
I won't tolerate a player that refuses to try, I want 110%.
I don't allow feelings of regret, which come after a loss.
I am not the greatest coach; I'm a rookie like my players.

I never pretend to be a pro, but I did learn from the best.
I refuse to cry about a loss, winning isn't everything.
I won't shout at the referee, that's what parents are for.
I don't want the boys to get hurt, but if they do, I come running.
I am not the greatest coach, but I hope to be someday.

I never say the word "can't," because I believe you can.
I refuse to spend time dreaming of trophies, I have goals to achieve.
I won't try to race my fastest player, not again.
I don't understand why kids don't like to practice.
I am not the greatest coach, but that's my true goal.

Megan Gosnell, Grade 11
Louisville Male High School, KY

Parents and Grandparents

Life is shiny
Life is sunny
Life is full of hope
Being around you makes me realize that I need to cope
With all the outside distractions running through my head
You have become a part of me
I mean everything I said
Death is gray
Death is dark
Death is pain and sorrow
Being without you through the night makes me pray for tomorrow
With the nightmares and scary monsters underneath my bed
I need you by my side
I mean everything I said

Sydney Kellams, Grade 10
Home School, MO

Undeniable Love

My love for her is undefinable
If she asked me about it, it would be undeniable
It started in the seventh grade
But it never will fade
I would have done anything to see her happy
It would kill me to see her feel crappy
There is a piece missing in my heart
That only she can fill
I always hate when we're apart
It hurts so bad, I don't want our friendship to part
That's why I'm so afraid to ask her out
If I only had the courage, I would do it without a doubt

Luke Cary, Grade 11
Hollis High School, OK

What's Stopping You?

The world is changing.
It's pushing, shoving, taking;
Your time, your space, your money.
Your giving, spending, buying;
For things you'll never need.
Your ideas are ignored by everyone —
No one has time to listen,
To what you have to say.
They're moving with the world
And what they think is most important.
If they would stop to think they'd realize:
Life is an opinion.
You think, you live, you breathe;
You have ideas you want to be known.
So what's stopping you?
Say them loud to everyone,
Stop the world in its own tracks.
Give it something to think about,
To ponder and to discuss.
You have the power to spread your thoughts —
So yell them loud and clear.

Ciera Fegel, Grade 11
Owasso High School, OK

A Heart at War

When your heart is heavy with guilt,
It is hard to stay calm.
The anxiety courses through your veins,
Faster than a jet breaking the sound barrier.

When your heart is heavy with guilt,
The struggle never ceases.
What's right, what's wrong?
Your conscience is always debating itself.

When your heart is heavy with guilt,
The dreaded mistake has already been made.
You have lost the battle,
But you can still win the war.

Christopher Range, Grade 10
Germantown High School, TN

Mother

Mother,
With your truthful eyes and clear smile,
You always care for me first.

When I'm talking to you,
I usually feel like I'm speaking with a friend.
Perhaps, you are my best friend.

When I feel tired,
You always stay next to me and give strength.
When I'm sick,
You would say,
"If I could, I would be sick instead of you."

You are an advisor and a supporter.
Moreover, you are my mother.
You gave me a life, raised me up,
And always supported me from behind.

With my whole heart, I want to say to you,
"Mother, thank you so much, and I love you."

Sun Ah Jung, Grade 12
Family of Faith Christian School, OK

God

Falling leaves,
A calming breeze,
Anything to put me at ease,
When I think of the past you come to mind,
You never left me behind,
You always took me with you so I could see a different view,
And I thank you,
You were always there when I needed you,
You never forgot about me,
I won't forget about you,
I could forget about you,
But I choose not to,
It's because you're someone that can't be forgotten,
You're the one who taught me right from wrong,
You're the one who always helped me,
I believe you're the only one who knew the truth,
I don't need proof to know you're there,
It's because I know you're everywhere.

Ashley Wade, Grade 10
Alcoa High School, TN

Summer Storms

Rain taps on my window,
like tears falling from the sky.
They are slow but steady,
as a muffled growl echoes in the background.
The wind howls at the rustling leaves,
gleaming with beads of wetness.
The air smells of drenched bark.
The birds wait calmly in their hiding places,
as crevices in the streets become streams of murky water.
These summer nights are therapy for my soul.

Jessica Brown, Grade 12
Jeffersontown High School Magnet Career Academy, KY

Love's Song

She hears it faintly
Barely a whisper
It grows with each step of her foot down the gravel road
And with each beat of her anxious heart
She knows what awaits her at the end of her path
(It is like a tub of hot water
She knows not whether to slowly sink in or quickly retreat)
The face and arms and smile — that rogue's smile — of a man
The man who placed the kiss upon her lips and the song within her heart
She hears it growing
Now more of a chorus
His figure is becoming more palpable at the end of the path in the dark in the fog
She is afraid to smile, to hope, to quicken her pace
She knows it is forbidden
Knows that this half hour's meeting could metamorphosize into eternity
An eternity that could commence all too soon
It's getting louder
Her heart's beating faster
But the resounding noise pulsing through her ears and throat turns suddenly into a question mark
The song's scream escapes from her mouth as she runs to where he lies, still smiling
That rogue's smile that's been painted red that ended the song within her heart

Kayla Bryant, Grade 11
McGehee High School, AR

Graduation

The big day finishes the writings, on the pages of a childhood near to end,
and a new book is just beginning with our whole life just around the bend.
The final notes are playing of our familiar high school song,
and once the music's over will we only remember the wrong?
Or will we be left with the happy snapshots, the memories of our lives…
yes they'll still remain.
We'll take them as we go though we know things will never be the same.
The book, the song, the snapshots are all that will be left to show:
the girl fights, the boyfriends, and the toilet papering nights,
the hard classes, the drama, and the Jr./Sr. fights,
walking down the hall,
the comforting smiles, and the shoulders late at night,
the pep assemblies,
the softball games, the football games cheering for the big red and white,
the friendships, the angry moments, the happy and the sad…
As we walk away that final day we will fondly remember the times that were always great — Class of 2008

Kali Westmoreland, Grade 12
Hollis High School, OK

Heaven Sent

Heaven must have sent you from above to be my one and only true love
The angels in heaven must have knew that you'll be the one to make all my dreams come true
In the beginning God created Adam and Eve so he must have created you just for me
One day you'll be my strong African king and I'll be your loving, caring, and beautiful black queen
When I met you all of my problems soon drifted away and if your ex knows what's best for her she'll stay out of my way because I'm here now and I'm here to stay
I know that these dudes out here wish that I was with them instead of you but they won't love me or treat me the way that you do
People say that I'm too young to know what love is but little do they know that I knew what it was when we shared our first kiss
If only they knew about the time together we spent then they would soon realize that you really were heaven sent.

SaLeia Aaron, Grade 12
World Revival Church Academy, MO

Families

Families today are falling apart
Over useless reasons that should not start
Not giving care to their kids
Just worried about their own bids
Not keeping the One above in mind
And leaving everyone else behind
Brother, sister, mom, and dad
Not talking because they are mad
Blood brothers for life or so they say
Until the day one cannot pay
We promise to love till death do us part
But when money gets tight we're torn apart
Holidays seem to disappear
Replaced by days that have no cheer
Trading kids every week
Because of the lifestyles that we seek
Respect for authority is not taught
Because we think good morals can be bought
On the outside life looks well
While on the inside life is hell

Brandon Kinkead, Grade 11
Centralia High School, MO

Untitled

Soothing, like quenching an ancient thirst,
The creative melody washes over me;
Vocals, notes, lyrical lines doth come first
And from my aching want I am now freed.
Serving as the cure for an itching cough
The instrumentals' tonics act as one.
Artists' empathy makes me cry and laugh,
Ending all misery when days are done.
Arrangements of notes still can make me swoon,
No words convey the passion felt by me
Or express my affair with any tune;
Adoration with happiness fills me.
As my one and only love in this life,
Music makes forgotten all my strife.

Lillie Blanton, Grade 11
St Mary's Episcopal School, TN

Memories to Last

What do you think when you hear retreat?
We gathered in an abbey for three days
So much fun at one time that is hard to beat
Bonding and hanging in so many ways
Thinking about memories of the past
We reflect on everything we have done
The memories we made are meant to last
Old and new found friends made it lots of fun
These lasting friendships I'll never forget
Even when we depart from each other
I'd remember anyone's name I'd bet
Without hesitation I'd call each brother
Because with a spirit that will not die
We are the brothers among Cov Cath High

Ryan Satek, Grade 12
Covington Catholic High School, KY

Ready, Set, Go!

This is where it begins —
Friday night football games
Saturday night parties
Sunday morning services
Monday morning classes
Days drag on endlessly
Nights fly by quickly
Afternoons seem nonexistent
Dawn only appears a moment —
I live for the nights I can't remember
With the people I will never forget.
Memories fade into the darkness,
Continuously replaced by new ones.
Just think,
College is next —
Peaceful protest
Self expression
Late night studying
Early morning classes
Altering the present to ensure a just future.

Bria Brown, Grade 12
Germantown High School, TN

Love and Think

Nobody will ever understand
what someone thinks or loves
but someone out in the world will understand
and tell someone that will never understand
who would understand what you think and love

Love is one thing nobody can live without
because someone who is heartbroken
will never heal from the pain love has caused
and the pieces missing will never return to normal
unless someone comes into your life
and tries to fill in the pieces
that were missing from your heart

Kyla Lowe, Grade 11
McGehee High School, AR

The Death and Ascent

She takes her last breath and blinks,
For she is on her death bed and cannot speak.
Into a great depression I sink,
For the time of death is getting to its peak.
I am going to miss all the good times,
Even when she drove me mad.
Her death should be a crime,
As I hold my dad.
Her life now is no more,
She went with our consent.
But she left our hearts with a big sore,
She begins her heavenly ascent.
Her job in life was to teach,
But now she can enjoy a vacation on a beach.

Quinton Settle, Grade 12
Covington Catholic High School, KY

Oblivion

Living on the edge,
Without any cause.
Sacrificing all the danger,
With no guaranteed life.
For some, it's a thrill,
For most, it's a job.
Serving for their country,
Or just for an everyday walk.
No one know what's coming,
Until it has already happened.
Death is just around the corner,
And it's creeping up behind you.

Will Hickey, Grade 12
White County High School, TN

Vampires Versus the Evil

Darkness fell upon the city.
The butterflies left,
and the bats flew in.
Transforming from wings to legs.
Bats to vampires.
Out to save the world,
from the Evil.

Midnight came,
the Evil came out.
The vampires were ready,
and the Evil was not.
He was tortured,
and then burned.
The same technique that he used.

The sun rose again.
The butterflies flew back in.
And the vampires left,
for good.

Lacey Floyd, Grade 10
Coffee County Central High School, TN

Those Days

Those days, you were mine.
We used to walk the paths
underneath the forest pine.
And in the creek, we took baths.

But that horrible thing called war
took those beautiful days away.
You were gone so long in the tour
that our young love decayed.

I walk alone now,
along that pine needle trail.
I have my sad head bowed,
close as ever to stop and wail.

Rachel Calloway, Grade 11
Woodrow Wilson High School, WV

Earning Happiness

Tears from depression
Tears from insecurity
Tears from rejection
And tears from frustration

So purposely she questioned hoping for God's ability to bless
But still shockingly she experienced no more than less
Without faith and hope she still was and was not going to contain anything
God wanted her to see first He needed to receive something

Appreciation
Dedication
Love and sacrifice
All these desires He was longing for had a special price

If she obeyed then all of her suffering and pouting would soon come to an end
He would then see that she was not doubtful; but fully woven within
All her tribulations were only the backbone to finding Christ
He figured that was the way to ordain her life

After continuous days of committing her life to God she found that her present life
Was what she had been searching for
Happiness Ease
Love Joy and Peace were the gifts from God that He wanted to grant her

Jasmine Gregory, Grade 11
McGehee High School, AR

Twist and Turn

We can be together for hours at a time.
Just sitting, laughing at the silly sunken site of her car.
It doesn't matter what we do.
We always make each other smile.
Having intelligent conversation isn't what we do.
We talk about the most random things to pass the time.
The way she lays with me at night.
Curled up tight, she holds onto me.
It makes me feel wonderful.
I know when she is sleeping the way her body twitches ever so gently.
So I tuck her in tight and give her a kiss on the cheek and say goodnight.
Rolling on to my side of the bed I feel her heart beating next to my back.
As we awake in the morning, her hair so soft to the touch
Her eyes shine from the little light, if any breaking through my little window.
When we go out with our friends, she brings life to the crowd which was calm.
She is always full of life.
Falling fast for fluttering emotions.
Better watch out or it could turn into just a commotion.
She makes me laugh when I am down, and make my frown turn upside down.
This is how she makes me feel, holding tight.
Butterflies in me flying around, all over turning and twisting.

Joey Sapone, Grade 11
Slater High School, MO

Trials of Sleep

I lie in bed at night, I look left, and then right,
tossing, turning, the images in my head.
I try and try to push them out,
but do I want them gone?
I never stop looking for advice, guidance…anything…
But the biased opinions of onlookers never help,
except for me to reach a state of confusion.
Oh, how I want them gone, out of my head. I think…
But no, I can't let them go, I still want them,
I hold them so close to my heart,
so close that they are tearing at it,
eating away at it. Killing me.
Not knowing what to do I just lie there,
sometimes for hours, wasted hours, without sleep
accomplishing nothing.
Finally, I drift off, success I think, but no…
Instead I enter my dreams,
filled not only with images,
but actual re-livings of my experiences.
When the night is finally through I am finish…
How I wish I could have rested…

Elijah Koyn, Grade 10
St Francis Borgia Regional High School, MO

Baby Boy

A boy was born on November 13th only to weigh just
U nder three pounds. He stayed in the hospital for
S everal weeks.
T he anxiousness of my mother waiting to
I ndulge me in soft hugs and wet kisses was too great.
N ow that day has arrived,

C hristmas day
O f 1990, her little soldier has
N ow arrived home. The
N ews to the family was the most
O bvious gift from God. To
R eceive me on Christmas day was the ultimate gift.

Austin Connor, Grade 11
University Heights Academy, KY

Wait

The wind gracefully dances among the trees,
Like beautiful butterflies in the air.
Slowly, one-by-one, the distant stars appear,
As if recovering from a long winter sleep.
You quietly wait, hoping "that someone" will discover you there.
Although it seems like you've waited forever,
Your heart insists "a little longer"
You patiently sit and wonder "is this worth it?"
Your mind says get up and move on,
But your heart says stay put and wait.
Everything inside of you suddenly screams "don't give up."
And at that moment, you make your decision.
You sit back down and wait.

Emily Pritchett, Grade 10
Salina High School, OK

The Hidden Message

The blue and yellow baby swing,
Hangs from a yellow rope.
It looks so insignificant,
As the big oak shadows down.

It seems so unimportant,
To notice such a little thing.
What would it change if I stopped to consider,
All the things I don't know and understand.

Is there a baby to go along with that swing,
And does the mother push her as she sings?
What is their life like,
And what songs does she sing?

I suppose their family could be just like mine,
Or maybe very different.
What could I learn if I took the time,
And even got to know them?

Everything has a story,
And so many memories attached.
If only I could look at things,
And understand the hidden message.

Diana Dorsey, Grade 12
St Francis Borgia Regional High School, MO

Thursday #937

6:56 my alarm goes off
7:05 it goes off again
11 seconds on the microwave
52 minutes for English, PE, and math
37 for lunch
3:22 the last bell

60 seconds, ten questions. Buzz Buzz Buzz
38 minutes, watch the clock

4,378 steps, eight laps, two miles, in. out. in. out.
35 seconds, hit the line.
10 black pentagons
2 touches, shot.

1/2 notes, whole, quarter and eighths
1 ee and uh two ee and
112 beats per minute, fortissimo
1-3-5-3 Do Me So Me

5:30 Silence. The counting stops until
10:42 alarm set, lights off

School, Quiz Bowl, Soccer, Piano, Thursday #937

Julia Lyon, Grade 12
Morrilton High School, AR

Breeze

I feel the breeze blowing in my face.
Blowing as if I were running a race.
Cool air blowing in my cheeks.
Summer air leaving after weeks.
September air blowing in my hair.
Feeling the breeze in my hair.
Harsh winds during the storm.
Winds start to take their forms.
Wanting the breeze like it was before.
As if it never disappeared before.

Drew Smith, Grade 10
Crowley's Ridge Academy, AR

Ode to Father Time

O you with the vice grip on the calendar,
O you with the eyes on the watch,

O spinner of seasons,
O ticker of tocks,

What are you racing against?
Whose life are you trying to beat?

O sucker of seconds,
Why dost thou patronize me?

O maker of moments,
O taker of twilight,

O hand of haste,
Why won't you pause
And just let me —
Breathe?

Nick Clark, Grade 12
Germantown High School, TN

Darkest Hour

In my darkest hour
a hero has come
come to save this worthless being
how dare you break into my dreams
forcing your terror on me
too bad my hero leaves you bleeding
memories trigger tears
nothing I need
my heart broken once too many
how dare you try to harm
such innocence lost to thee
a mistake made by hoping
hoping only to find
a false truth
In my darkest hour
a hero, my hero
has saved me
from a fate
so bleak

Amber Padgett, Grade 12
McClellan Magnet High School, AR

A True American Patriot

Two men in uniform came to the door.
They asked if our family had been waiting for a message from a soldier.
And as my father responded,
Their subtle expressions turned to those of sorrow.
Our family gathered together and we listened to them preach.
They spoke of my brother as brave and fearless.
They then conveyed their sympathy for many soldiers
Who had given their lives for our country,
They then began a story of a tragic accident that took the life of a courageous soldier.
This courageous soldier was my brother.
He gave his life for our freedom
And he will always be remembered as a true American patriot.

Kate Ryan, Grade 10
Germantown High School, TN

Time Flies When You Are Dying

I wonder why clocks tick
I wonder why clocks tock
I wonder why clocks are called clocks
I wonder why we have so little time here
I wonder why we are not fully immortal
They say our souls are
So why not our bodies?
I wonder why no one can know everything
I wonder why some of us never find time to do anything
I wonder why some of us never really live
I wonder why we just let the clock tick, tock away
I wonder who will be everlastingly remembered 100 years from now
And who will be forever forgotten 2 years from now

Joey Clark, Grade 10
Germantown High School, TN

Never Replaced

Having the bleak streaks ripped across your face
never knowing what hit you.
No one knowing the true meaning of resistance,
feeling like you're walking the walls of a black hole
with fairies trembling as you wipe your tears.
Can you picture yourself at the door with nothing to say?
Know nothing will be the same
The end of time asking you, did you?
He still says "I love you"

Music notes always off key,
hearts always broken, stars growing dull,
tears always falling with nothing, but
please don't make me pay for the promise that was meant to stay.

Wishing you could go back in time for the missed goodbye.
Thinking it's my fault even knowing we all die.
Confusion is a mind game that can't be played
like a nightmare that can't be erased.
Yet we take the pieces that are broken,
Pieces that can never be replaced.

Jaimie Ford, Grade 11
Colbert High School, OK

The Only Chance

It was one simple step to take
I might have held your hand
But I decided otherwise
On a different place to stand

Was it too late to win?
My time was all but spent
It would not go from me
Leaving my soul a dent

Darkness didn't drown out
What others now have seen
That undemanding attitude
Is still so distant from me

A smile that could kill
Deserved the best of mine
Rather, got what was the worst
Of what I believed was fine

I could have that dance
That chance to escape
The poor frame of life
I, alone, chose to take

But I walked away...

Matt Wright, Grade 12
St Francis Borgia Regional High School, MO

Who Am I*

I was a hearing person,
I remember when I lost my hearing,
I heard many sounds,
I saw what changed in my life,
I worried about what would happen to me,
I thought about me as a deaf person,
That used to be me.
I am confused,
I think I am in a dark, cold world,
I need to move on with time,
I try to talk to others,
I feel like I am lost behind time,
I forgive others who have treated me wrong,
Is this me?
I will be the same person as a hearing person,
I choose to do things differently now,
I dream about my future,
I hope to become successful,
I predict I will be no different from anyone else,
I know I will be ready for my future,
This is who I am.

Nathan Keaton, Grade 10
Capital High School, WV
**Based on "Freedom Writers"*

Friends

You are a great friend to me
More than what I figured a friend would be
You always make me feel so strong
You tell me what is right from wrong

Always when I have a problem
I come to you because you know how to solve them
I feel I can always come to you
No matter what you will put me through

You make me feel whole again
No matter what or even when
You are like a string and I'm the bead
You are there to hold me through every need

You are like an older brother
I know there will never be another
You have a special place in my heart
I feel that nothing will ever tear us apart.

Jessica Hackney, Grade 12
Union County High School, TN

Family

They are always there when you need them the most
Even when it seems they are not the best host
You are not alone in this world
You always have family
Even when things get twirled
They are always here for you timely

If you need them don't be afraid
Don't lie to them, don't make a charade
They really care about everything you do
Just keep them close
Keep them true.

Josh Weems, Grade 10
Jeffersontown High School Magnet Career Academy, KY

Minuscularity Complex

Prosperity's bosom lay not far off,
But that time is such from here.
Our dreams lead us to the right path.
The time, of course, a hundred year!

Memories are all that remain
Of disgust, the must, and disdain.
Poverty, Hunger, and War forgotten.
Toleration of race, belief, and gender,
A Utopian image I am forced to render!

But now is yet the time of strife and woe.
It appears like forever until they will all go,
For we are minuscule, dots on the paper.
OH NO, LOOK OUT, HERE COMES THE ERASER!

We must not give up, must not give in.
Toleration of ignorance is the Devil's sin.

Zachariah Koyn, Grade 11
St Francis Borgia Regional High School, MO

Imagine

Walking outside,
feeling a blast of cold air.
The river rapids dragging,
you away.
Dreaming out loud,
in front of the whole world.
Building your dream family
in your dream home.
Taking a walk to the
grocery store.
Spending a fortune
with the little money you have.
Giving your all for
an unworthy team.
Dreaming of the perfect death
but not ever dying.
Giving your entire life
to a dream,
of your imagination

Heather Shaw, Grade 11
Mountain Home High School, AR

Ginger

Once I had a little dog.
She was as pretty as could be.
My brother named her Ginger.
I loved her and she loved me.
At night she snuggled very close
To me upon my bed.
I would say, "Goodnight Ginger,"
And pat her on the head.
Ginger got so excited
To see us come home each day.
After school we had fun.
We would play and play and play.
We don't have Ginger anymore.
It was time to say goodbye.
She was my special little dog.
Sometimes I still cry.
Even though she's gone away,
I still hold her in my heart.
In my life she'll always be
A very special part.

Mandy Lovelady, Grade 10
Grove High School, OK

Strong Love

Touch Me,
like I'm a breakable object.
Kiss Me,
like its the last day ever.
Hold Me,
like we're going through a war zone.
Love Me,
like no one else ever has.

Angel Hester, Grade 10
South Intermediate High School, OK

The World to See

Life is a long-loved story by the way you live it:
Bloodshed, tears, hurt, and pain,
But in the end life can be played like a game
My story is a very particular one of them all
Being different in life from what I recall
Dad never around, mom struggling to hold me down.
A woman can't raise a man to be a man is what I'm hearing now
People making me frown, but I'm trying to keep my head up
Feet stay on the ground, I've learned never to let up.
Friends, family, and many more people telling me I don't have to hurt any more
It can be the good life or it can be bad —
It can be the happy life or it can be sad —
Music changing, people slanging,
Trying to make quick money but it's not easy.
Is anybody out there anymore?
Can anybody see the heart that's so tore?
Mind, body, and soul is what I stay focused to
Pay attention to it don't let anything slip away
The world we live in, to see the future, knowing it will be ok.
Struggles and more but I just look forward —
Keep moving along my goals I'm coming toward.

Tre Hicks, Grade 10
Capital High School, WV

Stay to the Right

I watch them walk by, everyone putting on an act
Some smiling, some frowning, some changing their mind with the weather
Setting their mind only on trying to exceed you
I've been looking in all the wrong places for something that isn't there
Sitting back and listening with a blank stare
They have something I want, something I used to have, how can I get it back?

"It's all right, you're better than them"
How hard this is to make herself believe
For they have the happiness, and I only have the need
They made me this way, hopefully the end will draw near
If I stay on the right then I'll be out of their way
Maybe by this I'll learn more

It's here…It's there…I lost it again
No surprise, no big deal, I'm used to it all
Who's acting now, me or them? Is happiness even real?
It's merely mortal things that make them happy
Something that won't matter in the long-run
But why would I want that? Why even bother?

Stay to the right you'll eventually end up stronger
Show them you're different
Don't put on an act, for the play here on Earth eventually ends

Olivia Noland, Grade 10
Chickasha High School, OK

Running

Running from all of the memories,
What have I become to be?
Probably just a young and reckless teen
Living no life, having no dreams,
Getting into a few fights,
Telling a couple of lies,
Hoping that I don't lose my head.
It's creating a world of dread.
Have I become to life a disgrace?
How, oh how, did I end up in this awful place?
All the memories driving me insane,
I'm still running,
Running from the pain.

Christina Hansche, Grade 10
Caney Valley High School, OK

What If

What would happen to the world if liars spoke truth?
If oldness became youth?
If the weak became strong?
If people chose right over wrong?
If people thought of others?
If the nations loved each other like brothers?
No sadness.
No tears.
No one in the world lived in fear.
One person can change it all.
No thought nor dream is too small.
This person is you.
Make our old world new.

Megan Payne, Grade 12
Beit Israel School, OK

Second Chance

Second chances — Another try
To forgive and forget
Is it really possible
To forget all the hurt you've left me in
Is it really possible
To let it all go and start fresh
I miss the way it used to be
But we all know that could never happen again
There is no trust
And there is always that doubt
There is always that 50-50 shot
That you will do the same thing to me again
Should I really put myself out there once more
With the chance to get hurt
You have done things you don't even realize
You have done so much wrong
But I think I will give it another shot
I'm not all in, but I will give you a chance
Please prove me wrong
It's in your hands
Please be my friend

Sarah Ramsay, Grade 11
Owasso High School, OK

Sadness

I saw sadness clearly.
It was tired and ragged.
It turned and crept slowly.
I saw its grey skin and saggy blue eyes.
And I heard it mumble, it was almost a whisper.
And I felt depressed.

Chase Lanpher, Grade 12
Madison High School, MO

Hearts

There it was, in your hands
My heart, so fragile and frail
Yet somehow, so strong and unwieldly
I gave it to you
In hopes that you would protect it
Such was not the case
You did so much more.
You saved it from the pain others caused it,
You stitched up the tattered edges
Never did you bruise it
Never did you break it
All you ever did was love it
You gave me yours not so long ago
With yours, I tried to do the same
The loving part is easy, but the protecting,
I can't seem to do
I always seem to come too late to save it
So in the end, if ever I give it back, it will be
Battered and bruised
Torn and stitched
But still beaming with all the love from mine

Jessica Evans, Grade 11
New Covenant Academy, MO

The Black Widow

The black widow
is a widow by choice
such a lonely little spider
Spider tell me why you are alone
what makes you want to be on your own?
Spider how do you just carry on?
How are you happy when he is gone?
How do you still look so pretty?
Spider why didn't you drown in self pity?
You wear black...
is it because you want him back?
Spider what's your secret?
Do you live with no regret?
Spider do you ever cry?
Do you ever feel like you want to die?
What about your heart
isn't it cold and torn apart?
Spider how can you act like he never existed?
How can your mind be so twisted?
Tell me little spider...
I want to know your secret

Kristin Montgomery, Grade 11
Viola High School, AR

Sugar, Spice, and Everything Nice

It was as if Dionysus himself looked down
On those transient days of simplicity and naiveté.
Days during which cookies and milk were shared amiably
Days during which hair was braided and expectorating contests were held
Days during which the obsequious children glowed like the golden stars on their chests
Those were the days when imagination soared as far as Icarus could fly
Days when it stretched across the abyssal sky,
Expunging the dreary predilection of tomorrow
As the radiant rainbows shot out like Cupid's arrow
On children who like the Tin Man found their vehemence
On children who like the pusillanimous Lion found their valor
On children who like Dorothy found their castle in the sky.
It was truly as if Circe herself had divulged her magic
On those ephemeral days of Kindergarten.

Akshitha Yarrabothula, Grade 10
Germantown High School, TN

But Why?

Why is it so hard to get up once you've hit rock bottom?
Is it then you realize that there's no one really there to help you get up?
When you try to get up you're only pushed back down when you realize that your focus is still off.
How can you forget the pain? End the sorrow?
Trying to remember who you are and living each day as if there's no tomorrow.
How can you breath a little easier? Retaliate a little less?
Try to remain calm, give your all, do your best.
How can I stop the vomiting, the unbearable pain in my chest?
Why can't I jus' quit it all…sit down and take a rest?
Why is God making me suffer? Did I do something wrong?
I thought I learned the game of life, but now I'm singin' a new song.
I can't stop walkin'. I can't give up hope.
I have to remain faithful, even though at times I'm being provoked.
The devil is toying with my mind. I'm ready to shake him loose.
I'm trying to forget the past, trying to be brand new.
I'm making God the center of my attention cuz' I know the impossible can't be done by me or you.
I'm tryna' regain my focus. The one I had before it was distorted by this crazy world.
I'm tryna' get back on God's team…be His main girl.

Kassondra Price, Grade 12
Pine Bluff High School, AR

Confined to the Wall of Life

Like a picture trapped in a frame, I feel confined to this wall called life. You see me, but yet I cannot speak. Fortified by those who have hung me here, I reflect and hold a story that no one will ever know, held tight, with such preciseness; transparent to all it seems but you. I long for the moment you become conscious of this. Take me down slowly and embrace my features; outline the elaborate border of my existence. But of course you won't. The light tends to seize my color and terminates the beauty. Forced to restrain against a white blank barrier of society, where I have illustrated and projected the "perfect" image. With each step you take, I become more apprehensive. I count the seconds while you cross the room. Inches from me, you extend your hand, almost as if the reflection is blinding. Unbearable imprison causes all emotions to detonate. Terrified I weep, feeling humiliated. For the first time I am recognized. Tears stream down, smearing everything they encounter, simmering at the foundation of my penitentiary wanting desperately to escape. Instead I scream inside united as one, your flesh burns me. I somehow manage to disregard the reality. All at once the burden of being counterfeit emerges. Exhaustion, hitting full force. Effortlessly and nonchalantly, I detach myself, collapsing into the anonymous unknown, evaluating my duration as I descend colliding with the humanity of hell. Pieces, strewn in chaos, assembling by magnetism into their place. My obligations are finalized, concluding the complete emptiness, and finally feeling content, free to linger aimlessly, until remains of life are swept away and a new picture is replaced only to be trapped in a frame, confined to the wall of life.

Kelsi Little, Grade 10
South Shelby High School, MO

The Peasant's Heart

Come my dear, and sit with me
So that I can confess my love for thee!
Oh, for our love, what a pleasant night
So that we can be one in His holy light.
To deny my love would be a lie
But to confess it in the streets I'm much too shy.
If only you'd confirm and lighten my soul so lonely
Then could I confess my love so boldly.
The garden bed is not your place
For the flowers would be dull compared to your face.
But your beauty alone have I not sought
For I remember the lessons that God has taught.
The value of your soul is far greater than any gem
For you're truly the greatest of gifts from Him.
The beasts from my fields and my lord's zoo
Would all I give for an eternity with you.
I work day and night in the field
I know for my love will the harvest yield
If only you'd sit with me beneath the great tree
And spend the rest of your days with me
Then I could confess my love for thee!

Brad Morris, Grade 12
Diamond High School, MO

A True Star*

When things don't seem to go your way
And everything feels like it's falling apart
You don't want to wake up to another day
For fear of another broken heart.

You cannot give up! Just stay strong
When people doubt you and say you can't
That's just more motivation to prove them wrong!
Hold your ground. Don't break your stance!

Keep your head high and you know you will.
Come hell, or high waters, make your dreams come true.
No matter how rocky that mountain or steep that hill
You were born for a purpose and they can't define you!

You have your dreams and you have your goals
Don't let them stop you from finding yourself
You know who you are, just look into your soul
Your priorities and your future belong on the top shelf.

Don't listen to them, they're know-nothing twits
One day you will realize how special you are
And once you understand yourself and your wit
You will see what I have seen all along.

You're a true star!

Kayleigh E. Hunt, Grade 11
Mulhall-Orlando High School, OK
**Dedicated to my best friend, Lauren (Lo)!*

Dear Alpaca

O dear alpaca thine picture I saw
That great day in a wooden picture frame.
Alpaca, thoust caught my eye in a claw —
My life so changed can never be the same.
Like the beard of Zeus is thy fur yellow
That maketh one a sock or a blanket.
Oh so soft I would give up my pillow
And let my arm go out of its socket.
Like many sapphires in a treasure chest
Do thy eyes glimmer in the darkest night
So all can see — even a tiny nest —
But none look except at thy pretty sight.
Thoust will brighten all my days forever.
My alpaca, nothing will this sever.

Elizabeth Anderson, Grade 11
St Mary's Episcopal School, TN

Dumb Poem

Down in the garden
Where you smiled at me
I came again to find you
Having conversations
With tiny flowers
You held romance
In the palm of your hand
I asked you about dandelions
And impatiently you replied,
"I don't know nothin' bout no dandelions."
And then
I swear I saw that romance fly
Like a scared hummingbird
From your hand

Jessica Withers, Grade 12
Monterey Jr-Sr High School, TN

One and Only

How did it come to this?
How did it come to where you'd be the one I'd forever miss?
How did it come to where you and I are together?
That we are to be forever.
How did it happen?

That it was you who took me by the hand.
You who said not to be afraid, making it clearly to understand.
Being without you, would just kill me inside.
When I am with you, my feelings I don't have to hide.

What can I say? You're my whole world.
But most of all, you're my baby girl.
Having you hold me in your arms,
Lets me know that my heart is never going to break.
And it is only yours to take.
Hearing your soft, sweet voice. Telling that you love me.
It makes me feel so alive, never having to feel empty.
We belong together, and I hope we always will be.
For you my darling, are my one and only.

Jayde Coblentz, Grade 11
Enid High School, OK

In the Little Black Box

Recall the day,
When it was first made,
Tears were laid,
Full of rejoice they came.
Your hand was what I longed for,
That Golden token of affection
A spinning symbol and reflection,
Of all we have to love and offer.

It was mine to keep and hold,
To be a reminder,
That our love could only grow stronger,
That Our days would last forever.
Through its course,
It may have turned color,
And faded as we grew older,
Yet break, it could never.

You never saw it leave my finger,
I held onto it like a child,
Cherished it and thought only of you,
For it was the promise kept,
Everlasting love I'll never forget.

Katie Bain, Grade 11
Owasso High School, OK

Seasons of Life

Seasons of life have bundles of joy,
Sadness will come with it too.
Flowers of life will bring the joy,
Death of fall brings sadness too.

Seasons of life they all will bring,
Summer, fall, winter, spring.
Seasons of life are here to sing,
Songs of sad and joyful things.

Summer shows the heat of life.
Sunshine pierces like a knife.
It pierces dark and gloomy day.
Don't fear for summer is here.

Fall brings what has been sown,
Things brought forth from spring.
Whether good or bad things they bring,
Things that are worthy to be shown

Winter seems sad and lonely too.
Depression may bring forth soon,
But not to fear for spring comes soon,
Following that summer comes too.

Josh Willmore, Grade 11
Silverdale Baptist Academy, TN

The Price for Freedom

Project Iraqi Freedom,
that is its name.
Sending our people to war
for peace is what we aim.

Our men and women are dying,
and leaving their families behind.
It's on the news every day,
so why are we still blind?

The world is crumbling
right under our feet.
The question is
can America be beat?

Right here in America
not on our land but in our heart,
are we getting stronger,
or are we falling apart?

That's the price we all pay.

Kristen Keyser, Grade 12
Mount View High School, WV

Outsiders

Prosecuted for nothing,
For an accused sin.
They're all in control,
Being the leaders' kin.

We're not giving in,
We will stay strong.
Their land of the free
Is interpreted wrong.

We are completely different,
Causing them fear.
None of us are leaving.
We'll always be here.

In spite of our beliefs,
They seem to shoot them down.
We are kept silent,
Never to make a sound.

A few of us resist,
But it is shown fatal.
Here, we have our rights,
But it seems none at all.

Garrett Shields, Grade 11
Grove High School, OK

Organized Chaos

Few understand
The clutter that she is.
An enjambment of thoughts;
yet all so poetic.
The pieces for her puzzle
don't seem to fit
as she appears to lose one each day.
Yet as it crumbles,
she still stands,
standing tall,
a giant among most,
with the heart of a child.
She floats away every now and then,
relishing in the only consistent factor
in her equation called life.
The unknown reality,
the sad hidden truth
lies behind brown portals
seldom revealing anything at all.

LaRonda Mitchell, Grade 12
Germantown High School, TN

The Onlooker

A sense of vengeance felt
Throughout the ranks
Of an army of rogues

Traveling side by side
Eyes darting here and there
Watching, for that treasonous blow

With Daggers drawn
Threads of suspense,
They grow thin

A breeze in the trees,
A ruffling of leaves,
A raindrop felt on a head

A thrust and a leap,
Hands covered in blood,
With chaos following its lead

Overlooking the scene
A lone man and his hound
Bordering on the edge of life

A torrent of knives
A storm of blood
A night that shan't be forgot.

Kjartan Kennedy, Grade 11
Owasso High School, OK

How Can This Happen

How can this happen?
Everything came so fast.
Never expecting this time to come,
now wonder how long it will last.
How are we breathing,
as he lies there asleep.
He makes no moves,
everyone weeps.
A soul ripped from the hands of fate,
amazing how life can fly by so fast and irate.
Never again awakening or being able to say goodbye,
all we can do is sit here and cry.
We need him here,
just as Good needs him there.
Wanting him back
with no breaths to spare.
His life on earth is done,
but his spirit remains.
Life will move on,
but there will always be pain.
In loving memory.

Niki Kruger, Grade 10
Slater High School, MO

Interception

You line up behind your center,
The whistle blows and the clock starts.
Ten seconds left in the game,
Your team down by three,
You hike the ball,
Drop back three steps,
Your number one receiver is open down the line,
You pull back and fire the ball.
Through the air the ball soars,
But wait,
The safety comes out of nowhere,
Interception, interception,
You've just thrown an interception.
The clock hits zero and the home team cheers
And just like that the game is over and your team lost.

Alex Blair, Grade 10
Jeffersontown High School, KY

Clutter

Four towels hanging on the wall
Clothes on the floor
Dirty sinks
Smells of different colognes combining
Claustrophobia taking over
One by one the towels are gone
The dirt removed
The smells have faded
One towel is left
The smell of perfume consumes the room
Not a speck left in sight
Loneliness creeps in

Allison Lauderdale, Grade 12
Woodward High School, OK

Burning Peace

Descending down into the fiery pit
Of a hell bride and her crimson Sinner
Who know no concept of judicial writ
Within these blazing gates lies no winner.

Oppressed, struggling to breathe, small gasps for air
The heat dries up the trail of dripping tears.
Here there is no ear for cries of despair
And all around you lay your deepest fears.

But devilish creatures dwell in all hearts
Kindness is the only check and balance
For goodness should not become an art
As Intolerance's first step is abhorrence.

To everything let kindness know no bounds
And the peace of Earth will ring in all sounds.

McKenzie Fields, Grade 11
St Mary's Episcopal School, TN

Graduation

Graduation is upon us. Fast-paced minds. And hectic times.
Great time for ACT and SAT. College visits and applications.
Students looking in mailboxes, to see if they got into their
dream college. Rushing rushing to make everything right.
Then the day is upon us. It's a wonderful and nervous feeling
when your name is called. Then finally hats are tossed up.
Afterwards, hugging. Crying with joyful noise. Students
realizing they're adults now not just high school students but
high school grads. Then they leave on their own new paths.

Shantae Peace, Grade 12
Concord Academy, TN

Words

They breed wars,
They split up families,
They ruin marriages,
They break hearts,
They tear you down,
They bring death.

They bring life,
They bring joy,
They bring peace,
They build you up,
They mend families
And they heal.

What are the things that can decide one's fate?
They are something we use every day.
Those powerful "things" that bring life and death,
Joy and peace,
Pain and comfort,
Damage and healing are…

Our words.

Morgan Webb, Grade 10
Family of Faith Christian School, OK

I Hide

There's a certain side of me
that you do not see
it's hidden from the human eye
it's just the real me you cannot find
I've got a past that no one knows
and that part of me will never show
I fear of what people will see
if you see the real me
I'm not what you expect
deep down inside
and that part of me
I can't help but hide
I hide from the world
in fear of rejection
not knowing what to do
If you figure out who I am
I am not as simple
as I seem to be
but that's apart of me
you will never see

Amy Petersen, Grade 12
Tahlequah High School, OK

Ode to Matters of the Heart

To the heartfelt
Feelings inside me melt
The anger inside
With which I cannot subside
My mind at ease
For I fell on my knees
And gave it away
So I could say
I love you
And then to
Say today is my day
I shall not run away
For He is here
Whispering these things in my ear
To keep my spirits
Without fear it is life.

Natashia Jones, Grade 12
Union County High School, TN

Contradiction

He works hard in practice
He works hard in school
He thinks he is the best on the team
The coaches think otherwise
They never let him play
He decides he will quit
But then he got a chance
He scored 40 points
And lead them to a win
He played the rest of the year
And never sat again

Sam Jones, Grade 10
Capital High School, WV

Green [With Envy]

"Ignorance is bliss…"
This hypocritical statement trickles from our mouths,
Like the saccharine juice of a ripe slice of watermelon.
The last time I checked,
Bliss is a feeling of tranquility and living without inhibitions.
Ignorance is a ludicrous attribute of society we cannot cleanse from our hands.
How is one to learn if one refuses to acknowledge and accept?
How is one able to experience bliss if one refuses to tolerate?
Ignorance runs maliciously in the blood streams of the narrow-minded.
The jealousy of not being as superior, as accomplished, as intelligent, as attractive
Only suppresses the change needed for the world.
Let it be cliché for one to fancy the idea of the world holding hands,
Because it is a minute matter if it can cure the green coursing through our veins.
We live in denial. We tread coveting what we do not possess.
Ignorance is envy.

Allison Yu, Grade 11
Germantown High School, TN

Here I Stand

I learned not to cry when I saw your face,
Learned not to hold my breath,
Learned not to pay attention
To the promises that aren't kept.
Learned to take chances,
And lessons well learned,
Can't confuse misery
With shame that's well earned.
I'm no angel,
But I'm no ordinary dream,
I'm just trying to get by in this nightmare
And it seems no one can see me,
Even though I'm standing tall,
I'll always be the one you can call on!
Hold onto me as we fall,
Don't stop believing, cause it's not wrong.
You said I would make it to the end…
Pulled from the wreckage of the pain that pulled me down,
Here I stand.

Sarah Bellis, Grade 11
Center for Distance & Independent Study - University of Missouri, MO

The Climb

As infants,
We were placed
At the bottom of one
Steep, jagged set of stairs
And told to climb until we reached
The top. The mission seemed impossible;
The stairs were too high! Yet we began that
Long journey, aided by a parent's love and warmth.
Our steps were tiny at first; as we grew, they did, too,
From crawling, to toppling, to walking, to running. We climbed
Up that staircase, nothing left behind. Now, we sit at the very tip top
On our graduation day, ready to tackle a more ominous staircase — maturity!

Lyssa Prince, Grade 12
Hollis High School, OK

I Have Feelings Too

No matter how hard I try,
The more I seem to fail.
I can only take so much
My emotions are very frail.

I'm sorry,
I didn't exceed your expectations
But all we do is bicker and argue
And that causes more frustration.

Every time I come home,
Someone's gotta start a fight.
Then someone's gotta cry
It's the same thing every night.

The more you tell me about my mistakes,
The more I want to scream so loud I grow hoarse
This anger is like a virus,
Like a sickness that keeps on getting worse

I know life isn't fair,
But it's not always about you.
If only you'd stop and realize
That I have feelings too.

Amanda Cooper, Grade 10
Preston High School, WV

Fire

It is blazing all around me,
Burning every earthly possession I own,
Inching closer and closer to me.
I can no longer see the door,
The window is covered with flames.
I have no way out.
I want it to stop.
I want it to leave.

It is eating and destroying everything in its path.
It is yelling so loudly,
crackling in my ears.
I cannot even hear myself screaming,
Nor can I hear the wail of sirens on my front lawn.
It is an angry lion,
Devouring all it sees.
It is a train,
Blazing through with deafening noise,
Not stopping for anyone,
Not even me.

All I see is flames.
All I hear is fire.

Laura Sadler, Grade 11
Owasso High School, OK

The Changing of Life Situations

Everything changes as life progresses,
From stuffed animals to high school prom dresses.
The way you see the world differs by day,
Trying not to let peer pressure get in your way.

Saying 'No' becomes harder to things you know are wrong,
And when you get caught you say, "Well they do it mom."
Not knowing the effect it will have in the end,
And not being strong enough to not give in.

Girls getting pregnant still being a kid,
Wondering how long they can keep it all hid.
Being scared to death not knowing what to do,
It could've all been prevented if it was just thought through.

Best friends, break ups, drama between us all,
Never knowing who to talk to, or who it is to call.
Fights, homework, cheats, and lies,
And these are supposed to be the best years of our lives?

Cortney Mearse, Grade 10
Coffee County Central High School, TN

Love

Love is inside you
Like a burning candle
Trying to stay lit
But sometimes you can't get a handle

You hope to find someone
That you can hold on to
Usually that only happens once
And you keep them until the end of time

Yearning to see them
Day by day
You call them up every second they're gone
Sometime just to say hey.

Thomas Gill, Grade 11
Woodrow Wilson High School, WV

The Farmer

The farmer wakes at the first break of dawn,
He is the reaper of God's given land.
God's chosen one he is pure like a fawn.
Dutifully he obeys God's command.
Strong as a rock; most self-disciplined man.
Reaps what he sows, wasting nothing at all.
Man of the land his skin's bronzed with a tan,
Great in stature, he is so very tall.
Jefferson praised this humbled type of lad,
He said farming is the most honest work.
In farming there is something to be had.
None exist that are known to be a shirk,
High above the city skyscrapers stand,
Stealing our God-given men and their land.

Michael Wurzbacher, Grade 12
Covington Catholic High School, KY

Tell Me What Love Is

Forty degrees outside,
Chills going down my spine.
It's not the cold that chills me,
It's what I see in his eyes.
He stares at me, I melt.
He doesn't know I'm weak.
I hold up my defenses.
He thinks I am the strong one.
When he kisses me my knees weaken.
The thought of him keeps me on my feet.
We are polar opposites.
He is one person, I am another.
We become one when we are together.
He treats me like a queen.
No matter what others think.
We have our two separate worlds.
They don't always mix as we do.
"Is it love?" you ask
It's far too soon to tell.
But if I stay with this one,
The possibility is real.

Shelby L. Ward, Grade 11
Spring Valley High School, WV

The Hard Stuff

Add, subtract, multiply, divide.
I don't want to do it. Do you?
It all sounds so easy,
Until Algebra II.

I didn't think it would be
As hard as it really is,
But somehow I got stuck in here,
Like I'm some kind of math whiz.

I attempt all the problems
Some make me want to wail.
Others are sort of easy.
I just hope I do not fail.

Abby Butler, Grade 10
Niangua High School, MO

Thought

Thought, 'tis but a word,
But what a mighty word it is,
One of few that evokes action,
Starts debates and breeds knowledge,
Settles arguments and starts them again,

To think is but to learn,
To learn is but to hear,

So listen, learn, hear and think,
But do not be afraid of what many fear.
Thought, 'tis but a word,
But what a mighty word it is.

Derek Llewellyn, Grade 12
Moorefield High School, WV

Don't Forget and Forgive

I Forgive You because you did not know how selfish your death was
Because you did not know you caused your son night terrors
Because you did not know you caused your wife to doubt everything
Because you did not know you made your daughter's heart hard
I Forgive You for your alcoholism and making it seem normal in children's eyes
Making it seem okay to drink your problems away
Making it seem as if you earned a hard drink at the end of the day
I Forgive You for disowning your own son
For shipping him to some school where his own family could not visit
For shipping away your daughter's brother and letting her forget who he was
For shipping away your wife's oldest, making her doubt herself as a mother
I Forgive You for pushing your wife away
Pushing her into household chores
Pushing her away from her friends
Pushing her freedom away
I Forgive You for putting too much pressure on your daughter to be perfect
Pressure to be a well-liked cheerleader
Pressure to be smart beyond her years
Pressure to be a little adult
I Forgive You for not knowing any better
I Forgive You because I know you were hurting in the end too

Jennifer Rademacher, Grade 11
Owasso High School, OK

Does Love Die?

They tell us love is perfect.
That it shall never die.
What they don't tell you
Is how many tears some have to cry.
What happens when the lover dies?
Doesn't the love die too?
Freak accidents happen. That's life.
But, how do lovers who have lost go on with that life?

Some people die before they can even find love!
How is that fair?
I wonder exactly how many hearts had to tear.
Just because the divine plan decides that the person doesn't get to have that chance.
But who said life is fair?
I guess no one did.
But maybe the person that said that
Possibly could have lived.

I guess I sound a little bitter.
But then again, who wouldn't after they lost a dear friend?
She was going to marry him.
He was going to love her.

I guess that love must have died.

Carrisa McKinney, Grade 11
Woodrow Wilson High School, WV

A Loving Lie

How does one know of true love?
When the words have never been spoken.
When the years pass and hard work can solve
But little if one does not. If heart broken,
Why does one feel bound to its sadness?
So much as to prove it without a doubt of shame.
One would rather feel hated than in happiness.
Yet this heart pounds at the sound of her pretty name.
And why do my eyes seem to draw away
From her beauty that is greater than any other.
I run away from her every single day
And why must I explain myself to her.
True love no it is but a fleeting illusion
That I have created in my mind.

Jesus Mendoza, Grade 12
Hollis High School, OK

Sonnet I

One hundred sonnets to thee have not I;
Immortalized thy never may yet be.
For beauty to remain unsanctified
Gravest error, my grievous sin of thee.
To supplicate myself, my one desire
Reveal to thee thy worship, goddess blest.
Secretly burned at altars of love's fire,
My heart 'til then shall find no earthly rest.
Still silent are the prayers within my heart,
My lips bemoan, unfit to sing your praise.
For cursèd am I never to impart
The ecstasy one glance from thee doth raise.
Yet past and evermore, I shall be thine
Though mortal soul shall never near divine.

Aubree Penney, Grade 11
St Mary's Episcopal School, TN

Tear Stains

If you searched my tears you would see my soul,
My heart beats,
And all the emotions I compose,
The pain I hold in,
The real devilish things within.
The real face under my makeup,
The real life from when I smile and fake up.
If you searched my tears you might really be scared,
Couldn't stay a moment in my skin if you dared.
But I dare you,
Double dog,
Triple dog dare you to try,
Try to avoid the pain within my eyes,
Try to holdup your head when the world beats you on it,
Try to fake like you have it all,
When ALL is what you never ever really wanted.
But you grin and bear it,
Because tears fall no longer,
At least from my eyes,
Because the tears I use to know no leave stains inside.

Ariel Linningham, Grade 11
Lincoln College Prep School, MO

The Principal's Shoes

When I was little, all I can remember is
Clip-clop-clip-clop.
I would straighten up,
Act right because the principal was going through the hallways.

As the footsteps got closer and louder,
I slowly lowered my head to get a glimpse;
Just one glimpse of the principal's Coach shoes.

The toe peeped.
The heel — thick, but classy.
(Sling-back, if I remember correctly.)
The color reminded me of hot chocolate after a cold day
Of playing in the snow.
The arch, curbed like a snake,
Nails into the ground perfectly timed—
Like a clock.

Her walkie-talkie interrupted my thoughts—
It talked with great importance.
She began to run,
The shoes gone from my view.

I couldn't wait until I heard another,
Clip-clop-clip-clop.

Amy Fenton, Grade 11
Germantown High School, TN

Eyes

Looking into those dark brown eyes,
Seeing her smile,
Hearing her laugh,
Holding her close
Sharing her thoughts,
Feeling her love
And knowing it's mine.
Our love seemed everlasting
I never thought it would end,
We were so happy, innocent, and free.
She was the beauty
I was the brains
She was the kind heart,
I was the brawn.
I loved her completely
She was the only one for me,
Always in my thoughts,
My heart, my soul.
But it all ended,
And what I wouldn't give to fall once more
Into those dark, brown eyes.

Robert Repp, Grade 11
Owasso High School, OK

The Clock on the Wall

It's the tick, tick, tick of the clock on the wall that uneases me and makes me feel so small.
The clock on the wall.

It continuously continues without any hesitation,
Keeping time in line for each and every generation.
The clock on the wall.

Oh how I wish it would just take a little break.
Is it oblivious to what's at stake?
I promise it would be for the best.
I just need a moment to close my eyes and get some rest.
The clock on the wall.

For some reason it refuses to listen,
The ticking continues and I grow restless.
I guess I'll just have to learn to cope and understand that there is no hope.
The clock on the wall.

Jessica Atteberry, Grade 11
Anderson County High School, TN

The Place That Calls Me

The moon shines so beautiful tonight, I could just grow wings and fly up and touch the stars. I wish I could fly as high and as far away so I could find that one place, the one place that calls to me. It calls to me in my dreams the place my heart calls home, if only I knew what home really was, a true home where you and your family are still a whole, a place where you can be yourself all the time with no regard to what lies around you, something is trying to call you into the darkness, trying to take your freedom away from you, trying to take that one part of you that makes you so special, if only more people thought like me then maybe just maybe the world may be spared, but that is just a thought I have when my dream place calls out to me.

Chelsea Jackson, Grade 10
South Intermediate High School, OK

Silent's Mountain

The air begins to clear as the dark, tangled, tree line breaks upon the open face.
He tumbles into crystalline sun and color, jubilant cries bursting from chapped lips.
The black, silent darkness below is no more, cast aside, he is now enveloped in light and life.
His reclusive cloak falls from straightening shoulders, a new smile breaking across his face.
He has climbed the mountain of quiet suffering to break free at its bright peak, ready to live.

Dancing, singing, the grace and passion that lay dormant wakes.
Spirited and heartfelt speech continues to bubble from a quick mind and loving heart.
Old friends are again his true, glad to see him return to the clouds, joining their fun.
They draw him in, welcoming with open arms and fond gestures, kind words and laughter.

Suddenly, he stumbles, feet flying out from under,
    limbs beginning to flail wildly, the edge of the mountain comes near.
He cries out once, but is silenced as he topples over the precipice.
The boulders do not stop his fall, only swell to break and bruise.
His fellows reach out, crying his name, trying to bring him back.

All is growing silent and still, save for the rushing wind crushing his chest.
His resistance to the encroaching darkness crumbles, realizing he can no longer cry for help.
Mountain's keep ready to reclaim him, the sinister forest ensnares, drawing him inward.
He cannot speak as he sinks once more to deepest despair, and begins slow ascent back to life.

This time, he vows, it will not take him again…

Kelly Shaner, Grade 12
Logan-Rogersville High School, MO

The Whisper of Shame

Defeat whispers in my ear,
But my eye refuses to shed a tear.
It comes like a thief in the night,
But I won't give up without a fight

Failure whispers in my ear,
But my eye refuses to shed a tear.
Deceit approaches swiftly burning cold,
I will not allow this scheme to unfold.

Disappointment whispers in my ear,
But my eye refuses to shed a tear.
Hope tantalizes the tip of my touch,
There is nothing but ambiguous anger to clutch.

Shame whispers in my ear,
My eye reluctantly sheds a tear.
My head goes down as my hands go up,
The shadow happily accepts my king's cup.

The risk is where the pulse will rise,
But it is too late before I realize.
The placebo effect affects the weak,
And higher praise protects the meek,
My window of opportunity is now oblique.

Ethan Gazaway, Grade 11
Owasso High School, OK

Tamale Day

With family bustling all about
The day's the craziest without a doubt
Frequent trips to the store,
But in the end we still need more!
Corn husks, masa, and chili powder
Now the laughter's getting louder
Once a year it's our tradition
We gather in that bright, warm kitchen
Now we put the music on
Listen to that happy song!
The little kids start to dance
Shy little boys even sneak a glance
Halfway through this dramatic day
The cooking's finally underway.
Worn out family takes a nap
In comes the cat looking for a friendly lap.
Finally the food is done!
Time to relax and have some fun!
For today is Tamale Day!
It's crazy and hectic in every way,
But we all know it's perfect anyway.

Hannah Doherty, Grade 10
Slater High School, MO

Indescribable

It's not just a feeling that comes and goes
And it's not a feeling that can be easily described.
It can be shown in many ways
And it's one that in one's heart is inscribed.
I see it in her eyes when she looks deep into mine.
I feel it when she strokes my hair.
When she holds me in her arms I feel it,
That deep emotion that's hard to tear.
It's a mixed emotion, Love.
But it's not just the physical attraction that's important.
The mingling of two's spirits is the truer love.
Love is an emotion that describing is something someone can't.
This is my first love and it's not like anything else.
Indescribable, incomparable, incomprehensible,
But love is not easily destroyed,
Indeed love is invincible.

Mark Lane, Grade 11
Germantown High School, TN

To Our Parents

Yeah we know,
You told us so.
You said we'd end up together,
We said, "Yeah and the moon's a feather."
I guess we were wrong,
We are where I think we belong.
We hope it's forever.
I don't know what we would do,
If it hadn't been for you.
If it wasn't for your thought,
We never would have have given it a shot.
Now I am here to say thank you,
I mean, where would we be without you?

Ashley Mohn, Grade 11
Glenpool High School, OK

Bad Breath

Is why I avoided what could have been
My first kiss that could have meant
Something more to mc besides just sealing
A deal with the devil for a week
Bad Breath
Is what got me sent to the office
For flinching at the knowledge
That was being carried to my nose
By my mint repellent teacher
Bad Breath
Is what you get when your throat
Becomes raw with the effort of
Voicing your opinions when you should
Be learning what Zen is all about
Bad Breath
Is how I deal with an unsuited suitor
When my affections have not
Even begun to be born
And he wants my breath

Kayla Cain, Grade 12
Oak Ridge High School, TN

Can I Forgive Her?

You said you were my friend,
but now I don't know
if that was a lie or the truth.
This summer I saw a side of you
that I have never seen before.

Sometimes I think you were just jealous,
but then again it could have been
the truth finding a way out.
I will never know.
You called me a lot of names
and then you wanted me to forgive and forget,
but to tell you the truth,
I can't forget.

I've spent a lot of time thinking about this,
maybe more than I should,
and at sometimes I feel like forgiving you,
but others I can't.
I can tell you that I have forgiven you
for some of the little things you said,
but for the other things
I still can't fully forgive.

Cassie Norris, Grade 11
Owasso High School, OK

Tired of Crying

Somebody asked me the other day,
If I don't talk about you
Because I don't love you anymore.
Well I didn't say anything,
But I realized
That I don't know what love is anymore.

Well you did your work well,
When you tried to rob me of my identity.
I don't even
Know now who I use to be.

But I'm tired of crying.
I'm tired of screaming in my head.
I'm tired of crawling in the dark
Looking for a light that isn't there.
I'm tired of trying
To forget the past and erase this emptiness.

But it's all I can do to hold onto my sanity.
And this vision of control
Is really just a mask for the void in me.
Still, I'm tired of crying.

Jennifer Novotny, Grade 10
Chickasha High School, OK

Faith in Your God

Where is your God when you need him the most?
He does not answer you when you call him.
Where is your God the holiest of hosts?
He does not answer your tiniest whim.

Where is your faith, do you still call him out?
You still prove me wrong, you still give him thanks.
You still call him out even when forced to shout.
You follow him to the ocean's last banks.

The strength that you show when you give him praise
Inspires the weak and cures all the sick.
He then answers you and clears you from haze.
This God is surely the right one to pick

You Christians have showed me the way to live.
You do not receive when you choose to give.

Michael Walsh, Grade 11
Covington Catholic High School, KY

Change

You promised to always be there
But where were you when I needed you to care
A few years passed and everything changed
How would life be if everything had stayed
Would we still be the best of friends
And have something that we thought never ends
Would everything still be ok
If we still saw each other every day
There is no way we can ever get it back
That which we lost we will now always lack
You had my entire trust
And you let it waste away like rust
I write all this just to say
That I will always miss those days
When we foolishly believed that things would never change

Justin Richardson, Grade 10
Chickasha High School, OK

McGehee Owls

We are so good in the light that beams
We play together all as a team
All the teams hate us
But who can take the blame
'Cause by December we will have the fame
We are so good it must be fate
By the end of the year we will take state
We can win and still play fair
And in the end the grudge they will be bear
Our colors are white and deep red
To show the glory and fearless blood shed
We have had three die over the years
And at the funerals everyone sheds tears
There are eight years of rings in sight
To show how hard our players can fight
It's not the end just the beginning
Of all the practices and the winning

Austin Henderson, Grade 11
McGehee High School, AR

Hurt

I know you saw me standing there,
And yet you kept on going.
I know you saw me waiting for you
When the wind and rain started blowing.
But you did not stop or pause or even look back,
My heart was shattering over the love that you lacked.

How did we end up like this?
Our happiness and joy now sorrow and pain?
I gave my all to you, heart and soul
I let you in and you pushed me away.
I said I loved you and you knew it was true,
But it's over now and the sorry one is you.

Leslie Cook, Grade 11
Woodrow Wilson High School, WV

Don't Judge Me

You can't judge me
by the way I
walk,
talk,
sing,
Or dance.
I am a black woman.
And black is beautiful.
African Americans today have come so far.
Please don't judge me for
what I am.
Take a look at yourself in the mirror for once.
See no one is perfect,
so don't judge me by the way
I think,
laugh,
or by even having friends.
This is the real world.
Deal with it.

Fantasia Kimbro, Grade 10
Rock Bridge Sr High School, MO

Adventures of the Night

Upon midnight little noises caused much fright,
As the cold young girls made their way back home,
They climbed into bed and found no sheets were in sight,
And the angry girls quickly picked up their phones.

They called the suspect to this horrid prank,
And to their dismay, he gave them a hint —
He built up the suspense and said to them "the lake!"
T'was obvious this news would be leaving a dent.

At once — the tired feet jumped from their bed,
And to the dock with air mattress' in hand,
Like the Holy One — top of water she fled
"Just like the sea," said she, "just without sand!"

This one brave girl was forever remembered
For stepping out of her comfort zone — like a true contender!

Jillian Smith, Grade 11
St Mary's Episcopal School, TN

Teardrops from Heaven

Out the window of my quarters, my eyes begin to drift.
Teardrops from Heaven, each feeling like a cold, moist kiss.
Slowly forming reservoirs as each one descends.
As it gracefully grazes and gathers on your skin.

Our adulation for Him withers, and fades with our actions.

Father is crying due to his children's rebelling.
They follow at the heels of others with their faith trailing.
My siblings search for answers, yet have no patience.
Does the One lament over us, or lament for his creation?

Our adulation for Him withers, and fades with our actions.

Living life in His name is a difficult task.
The pressure from our peers pushes us to crash.
He burdens Himself as the life giver and life taker.
Teardrops from Heaven fall, as does our love for our maker.

Ryan Bowen, Grade 10
Coffee County Central High School, TN

Life as a Principal's Daughter

M y house gets egged on Halloween. This happens when…
Y ou're the vice principal's daughter.

L aughter fills rooms when people discover who I am.
I get told mean things about my father.
F riends look for special treatment.
E veryone treats me differently.

Sarah Hawley, Grade 10
Capital High School, WV

Di Tchotchke

Tis a funny thing, memory,
to ring in each eyes
a sense of knowing.
To stay from an hour to a year,
never fading,
never paying rent,
never owing but a thought.

It is passive, it is dear, it is daunting.
It is so sharp, betimes it is cutting
to allow the flow of blood-like tears, Life,
like rain upon a window.
And once the storm has cleared,
still a voice you hear, and
her name is memory.

She sits near the mantle,
posed under a sheet of dust,
picking up a well-worn tchotchke
you indeed did not want touched.
She has no pity, nor sense of control.
She floods the room with a current of sentiments
known by the tenant and proprietor only.

Rebecca Wilken, Grade 11
Owasso High School, OK

Notebook

When the inked tip touches
The perfect lines of a
Single sheet of cut white paper
The imagination flows out
Its fantastic peaked tip
The pen is the wand
But the ink is the magic
Cascading to
A river of the deepest blue
All wonder waits until
Another page is opened
Another pool of ink
Another blinding white sheet
Beckoning the wand to
Graze the page
Drowning the blank
Vastness
Dreamers hold the
Fortress near
Protecting the limitless black
Magic

Lauren Buck, Grade 12
Beechwood High School, KY

Feeling of Love

I felt love
It was big but fragile
It moves slowly and softly
I saw its blue eyes and loving red lips
It speaks soft and tenderly
I felt…Love

Nathanial Simmerman, Grade 12
Madison C-3 High School, MO

Warmth

Bulbous bumps bloom on my arms.
Air conditioning has lost its charms.
Cool currents, bone-chilling blasts,
Arise in raring, determined drafts.

With numb digits like icy stones
And icicles stabbing at my bones,
Nothing more do I desire
Than in a balmy breeze retire.

I rush rampant through the halls
Clinging desperately to my shawls.
With excitement I reach the door,
And over me warmth does pour.

Once outside, my shawl's forgot,
I bask in what the sun hath brought.
As beams of gold touch my skin,
I feel warmth emanate from within.

Jenny Dabbs, Grade 11
Bearden High School, TN

People

People are good and people are bad,
People are happy and people are sad.
People are active or they can be lazy,
They change like the weather, sunny or hazy.

People are unique in a variety of ways,
Trying to go through a person's mind would be like going through a maze.
Some people are picky and some go with the flow,
Some like to go crazy and some are mellow.

People are different as you can tell,
Some may be quiet and some might yell.
This is what makes the world go 'round,
And also causes the universe to have a melodious sound.

Chelsea Butera, Grade 11
Woodrow Wilson High School, WV

Why?

I'm sittin' here in the dark corner with tears in my eyes. I'm alone,
Thinking about the horrifying words you said the other day on the phone.
Why does it have to be me when it could be someone else?
I'm in a trance of hate because that's how I felt.
When you said the horrifying words, they hurt me inside —
I find myself kneeling down and saying, "Papa, what did I do?
I'm just a little girl — only four years old. Whatever I did, Papa, I didn't mean to.
I tried to be a good girl. I tried to make you proud,
Papa, but instead I made you loud."
Well, I'm older now, Papa, and my life is coming out all right.
Maybe I wasn't the best little girl in the world, but Papa, I put up a hell of a fight.

Tiffany Peterson, Grade 11
Mount Vernon High School, MO

The Graduation March

Well, you're finally here —the day you've longed for, for so many years
It seems like just yesterday you started first grade
And today's the day you're taking the stage
You hug your parents to show them you're glad
For all the times they never got mad
The late nights, missed curfews, the sleeping in late
Just because they knew they were great.
You show up early to talk with your friends
Who have always had a shoulder to lend
You take pictures so you will remember this day
And shed a tear because it'll never be the same
You hear them call for your time to come
And can't help but think of all the things that you've done
The sports games, the cheering, the band playing loud
The homework, the good grades that made you so proud
The boyfriends, the breakups, and laughter and tears
Nothing will ever match these four years.
It's over, it's finished, an end has to come
An end to saying, "Our team, number one!"
So you hug all the people who've made this worth while
And you know that one day you'll look back and smile.

Bailey Bruner, Grade 12
Hollis High School, OK

Stories of War

Purging, my pen pauses to catch a breath.
Sighing. Heaving. The words spill onto the page.
My war story, a true war story.
It is of my country 'tis of thee.
From the Bouncing Betties
And the Vietnam dust, oh so red,
Let the freedom of truth ring!
As I agglomerate my story in chunks.
My war story, a true war story.

Teasing hallucinations tickle
And coax memories from hiding.
I used to suppress in order to impress
Diverging off topic from deferment.
Yet, in fact, I took a stand on a boat to Canada
And fell coward and went to war instead.
My war story, a true war story.

Intangible became tangible.
On the backs of all comrades
The weight of the world was carried.
What others could not bear, another picked up. We shared.
A true war story is never actually about war.

Mollie Robertson, Grade 12
Louisville Male High School, KY

Troubled

When I looked into her eyes,
Made sure it wasn't troubled,

In her eyes, pool of brown,
Lost looking in,
Looking in the window into her mind,
Falling into a wonder world of pain and love,
No more stars, more of a melancholy way of being,
Like a doll, with the curves like waves from the ocean,
What beauty she was!
She sat there letting me explore her mind,
Wrapping our eyes together,
Gently I held her in my arms,
Made sure she felt secure,
Gently touched her skin,
Our psyches meld together,

I said "Let your worries drip away,
Let's dream today girl, no point in worryin',"
As we fall in a trance of everlasting love,
"I'll show you how a man loves a woman,
Let's shoot for the stars,
No more regret, we can fly"

Manuel Guerrero, Grade 10
St John the Baptist High School, MO

Christmas Madness

Christmas time is coming near
Parents are running frantically in Fear
Trying to find the perfect gift
And doing their best to avoid a tiff
Hiding the presents all around the house
And keeping secrets better than a mouse
All the children's faces lit up with joy
In hope they'll get that one special toy
Wrapping and ribbons all over the place
Under the Christmas tree there's no more space
Hoping the madness will soon come to an end
With all the cards in the mail to send
The lights are lit with a glistening glow
The days and nights seem to be moving so slow
But come Christmas morning all that joy should be a sin
Although at the end of the day you know it was a big win.

Jessica Dawn Hager, Grade 10
Prue High School, OK

Kings Fall

The Kings of Europe claimed Divine Right.
The Reason for their Imperial Might.
All the kings fighting for that ever same feat.
To be crowned in Rome on the Vatican Seat.
Centuries of Kingdom Road, the End Came in Sight.
Murderers came on that dark and frozen night.
Republics proclaimed; Democracies in a new light.
"Don't Let The Kings Give Up Their Throne Without A Fight!"
Sadly alas, rebellions won over God.
One by one ancient dynasties fell from Grace.
Monarchs must now show their heavenly face.
Ever in flame their spiritual base.
Appealed to the Pope, but lost their case.
Hundreds of years reversed in a flash.
Nobility falls gracefully with a heart pounding smash!
Hapsburg, Romanov, and Hohenzollern cash,
Lost to misery when the God of War came!
Their revolutionary saviors now their hated bane!
Now trying to revive that withered family tree.
Who forgets that terrifying scene.
Of Lord and King, being led to the Guillotine.

Jesse Lobbs, Grade 10
Bauxite High School, AR

Mother Nature

The Earth — majestic.
She flows with grace and breathes life.
Tame her you cannot.

Intricate beauty.
Her light will brighten the dark.
Though most do not see.

Energy springs forth.
She strengthens those who believe
In nature's beauty.

Emily Isbell, Grade 11
Bearden High School, TN

Misjudged

My life is a mistake,
I have been misjudged by many,
My love is portrayed,
Without this I am nothing.
My heart is not to be destroyed,
But to be a keepsake among some.

Beauty is my weakness,
But not my only,
I'm strong in my own ways,
But misjudgment is torture.

Remember me as one who,
Will not misjudge someone.
My love is true from the heart,
Shall it be the last thing to be dead.
If not then cherish whatever is to be left.

Ross Wood, Grade 12
Watson Chapel High School, AR

Weary Soldier

O, my weary soldier,
you've traveled o, so far,
O, my weary soldier,
you have so many a scar.

O, my weary soldier,
you have fought a good fight,
O, my weary soldier,
you have fought with all you're might,

O, my weary soldier,
you've been marching for so long,
O, my weary soldier,
you're not nearly quite so strong.

O, my weary soldier,
don't let your heart be troubled,
O, my weary soldier,
you will find rest someday.

O, my weary soldier,
let not your faith grow thin,
O, my weary soldier,
you still have one last battle left to win.

Tasha Shubert, Grade 12
Rockwood High School, TN

Junior Year

Junior
Almost out
Laughing crying anticipating
Just one more year
Senior

Ryan Shoffner, Grade 11
Union County High School, TN

Standing Up for My Desires

Why thank you young Sir,
Thank you for noticing.
Yes, I am beautiful,
And yes I am desirable.
But oh, there is so much more.
It's all hidden under my surface.
Won't you take the time to dig deeper?
No, of course you won't.
You young Sirs never do.

Because there's only one thing on your minds,
And all because of my beauty.
And over the years,
I must admit.
I've become more willing to give in to your desires, ignoring my own,
All for a momentary taste of gratification.
That suddenly fades when I realize,
I have been used.

Why thank you young Sir,
Thank you for noticing.
Yes, I am beautiful,
But I desire so much more than to be used by you.

TaylorBeth Ellis, Grade 11
Owasso High School, OK

June 24, 2002*

Fluffy, flat, floating clouds covered the sky the day he died.
The sun shined while I swam in the pool,
And ordinary summer day without any school,
The sky grew dark and the rain began to fall once I heard my mother call.
She screamed at me like it was all wrong.
Telling me that my father was gone!
I didn't understand what was going on, I just listened and went along.
When we arrived at the house I could believe I started to cry then I hit my knees.
The man I thought could never die was laying there before my eyes.
Everyone seemed to disappear as I went to a place where the skies were clear,
I was confused for a long time, until I realized that he was actually gone.
When I finally got to see him he was not the same,
He looked sad and lonely and felt really funny.
As I placed a picture right beside him my tear fell on his body.
Up to this day I feel guilty for not saying goodbye,
But I couldn't help it, all I could do was cry.
He lies in a shaded area under a tree,
Where all of his family can come and see
I occasionally visit that shaded spot,
But I have begun to drift away from it a lot.
I hope one day I will be able to see him but then I'll always love him.

Cecilia Bernice Fleetwood, Grade 10
Slater High School, MO
**Dedicated to my father Vernon Fleetwood.*

Different

This year is different,
Time rustles by,
Moments aren't special — they just happen and pass,
Fun flies by and work consumes you like a dark, empty room.
I'm lost in it.
I used to know my way out, but I'm in too deep now.
There's a breeze pushing me around the darkness,
I'm only along for the ride.
It's a pitch black roller coaster with a destination
I have no control over.
No idea where it's going.
It's not just confusion,
It's much more than that,
Unknown.

Paige Harvey, Grade 12
Oak Ridge High School, TN

Beautiful Downpour

Swift rain pours down in sheets outside my window
To count the drops would last infinity
Upon such sight many would dwell in sorrow
Why cry for God's gift to humanity?
For those who sadden at the sound of thunder
Never do kiss the freedom blurred skies bring
Never do miss because they do not wonder
Of playfulness and LIFE they do not sing
As blissful showers tumble from night skies
Complaints are heard amidst the candlelight
Ignore their words, it's not the angels' cries
But dashes through God's sprinkler in delight
Drops hit one's lips and awaken the soul
Without acceptance one awakens not
But with, the rain washes away the old
And leaves one's youthful freedom blazing hot
So run like lightning towards the thunderous rain cloud
Be one with nature's tempest raging loud.

Claire Bailey, Grade 11
St Mary's Episcopal School, TN

tired

i'm tired.
i'm tired of hurting.
i'm tired of being in pain.
i'm tired of being in love with you.
i'm tired of crying over you.
i'm tired of thinking of you.
i'm tired of dreaming about you.
i'm tired of knowing you don't love me.
i'm tired of knowing i can't be with you.
i'm tired of my heart breaking over you.
i'm tired of my heart skipping a beat when i look at you.
i'm tired of waiting by the phone for you to call.
i'm tired of being depressed.
i'm over it.
i'm tired.
i'm sorry.

Kari Owens, Grade 10
Powell High School, TN

The Strike of Rain

Alone
I sit, linger, on soggy bitter grass and
I muse
On a hazy day
The drizzling of rain
And the laugh in my eyes
Make the only sound
The allusion of a smile plays around, on my divided lips
I muse
Free at last, liberated
Free at last

Shackled to the blinding light
Dishevelled
On almost any other day
But I can tell you today,
This bliss is here to stay
Genuine bliss is found
From the strike of lightning bolts,
They're more potent,
Than any ray of sunshine that
Ignorance brings to me.

Rachel Hamlin, Grade 10
Heritage Hall School, OK

Future Love

Have you ever thought of where you're going to get married
I have thought about it
imagine you're on the beach with your future love
Seeing the waves come in on the sand
Watching the water go back

Imagine you brother-in-law standing in front of you
Ready to say a long speech
You're standing there hand-in-hand with the man you love

You look out at all the people there
Watching you get married
Seeing your parents sitting there crying
Because their baby is getting married

Finally he is done with the speech
He gets to the vows
The man you love is putting the ring on your finger
Then you do the same

He says your name
Then you walk back down the aisle
Now walk past your mom and dad
Now you're married, you thought this day would never come.

Mackenzie Hibbs, Grade 10
Crowley's Ridge Academy, AR

Remote Control

You turn me on, then play me like a fool. You pause me and put me to the side of your interesting life, only to play me again, but this time you just mute me, making me pretend everything is fine, when really I'm hurting inside. Fast forward, maybe things are fine now. I open up and tell you I'm not ok. Instead of listening to me, you mute me again and then give me your input on things. You then contrast me to my dim days again, making me remember recorded past times of ongoing memory. You then try to rewind old memories and make it better. Instead you turn the master volume down and only hear what you want. You skip through all the horrifying memories, just so your feelings aren't hurt. I finally start to give out and quit working. Slowly, I fade, out of your new life; I'm gone. The whole 16 years of my life, a blur, full of memories of old past times, but I would give anything to get it back; but it's too late. You finally quit caring. You go to menu, then the setup. You pick DVD over your VHS and throw all of us away. The DVD is more important now. You finally did it; you've turned us off and away forever.

Brittany Barber, Grade 10
Valley View High School, AR

Ella Maude Taylor

While I was in the shower you were dying.
While you were dying I was riding to a convenient store.

I was at a convenient store when I should have been there,
when I wanted to be there. I remember that day so clearly.
Getting out of the shower, hearing the phone ring, and seeing the
expression on my grandmother's face. All of it, I remember all of it.

When I got there everyone was here and there with tears in their eyes.
A year has passed since July 13, 2006, yet it still feels like you are here.
Though, I know you are not when I go into your once bright loving home without you in it.

I will remember you! Your loving smile, warm-heart, and the smell
of you cooking bright and early in the mornings. Great Grandma Ella, I love you
and miss you so much. I am waiting the day we meet again!
R.I.P. Ella Maude Taylor

Jessica G. Stover, Grade 11
Woodrow Wilson High School, WV

The Waterfall

People swimming all around, clouds, misting down tropical trees
Beautiful birds, chirping, tweeting, Insects, buzzing peacefully.

Water drizzling down the concealing vines, sunrays sprinkling through watering skies
Swishing down the mountain side, unique sounds are all mine.

Water, blue as the sky on a warm spring day, plants, sparkling from the rain
Rocks, chipping off the mountain side, unique sounds, rushing, gushing on the plain.

Baby blue water creating beautiful gushes, heavenly sun, pouring down, nourishing
Springs of water, an avalanche, rushes, bees buzzing, flowers blooming, refreshing.

Short distance to the ocean, from the river above, can smell scents of tropical rain breezes,
Makes you feel as if you were in heaven, in love, lily pads moving around the creases.

Spring flowers have just bloomed, everyone, anyone, close enough, smells
Sight of moss, droplets of rain, mushroomed, water sprinkling on it, dwells.

The sound of water crashing down a hill, rocks, every size, glistening,
Near a waterfall, be still, be thankful for nature's blessings.

Caitlin Smith, Grade 12
Haworth High School, OK

Unspoken Mistake

Anger clinched between my teeth
My fists squeezed at my side
Words cannot save me now
She's already made up her mind
Communication is at fault
For here, there was none
How could I have known my wrong
Which now cannot be undone

Voices getting louder now
As painful words escape her mouth
Wishing I could walk away
I bite my tongue as I'm forced to stay
I hear them fighting and slamming doors
And I know it is my fault
I wish I would have known before
For this blanket of damage is a bore

I do not like this strident silence
That has been going on for days
But more painful than her silent cries
Is her refusal to look me in the eyes
All because of that minute, unspoken mistake

Ashley Prentice, Grade 11
Owasso High School, OK

On My Linen Sleeve

Subtle light-pink linen,
Pearl buttons up the sleeve.
Loose comfort and denim,
Remembering what had been.

Yesteryear, cowboy day,
Hug before beginning.
I flip, tip my hat,
Wild West parking lot:
Bliss, kiss the princess,
Slip, rip my heart.
Now put on face — own the place.

Secret bass and cello,
Remembered once alone.
Lovely voice, my Lovely.
Opened eyes to new lives,
Kept warm from the wind.

Forever a reminder
Underneath the bed —
As all was just beginning,
And long after the end.

Laura Eschbacher, Grade 12
St Francis Borgia Regional High School, MO

When I Pray

When I pray, I pray to God and thank Him
I thank Him for all He has done for me
He has helped me down from many high limbs
He always brings me back to sanity
I bow my head and close my eyes to pray
I clasp my hands and get down on my knees
I've a cross beside the bed where I lay
When I pray I often ask Jesus please
Please watch over my friends and family
Take care of them in all they choose to do
I know Jesus always walks beside me
He is there watching me and what I do
Jesus loves me tons this I know for sure
My love for Jesus is ever so pure

Barbara Henderson, Grade 10
Chickasha High School, OK

The Race

When the gate drops, I take off real fast.
Going in the first turn, I hope I'm not last.
The wheels, they spin. The engines they churn.
As I soar through the air, and rail through the turn.
I'm in second place. The leader goes wide.
I fly into the turn. I go inside.
We come out of the turn. We are side by side.
I pin it a second longer, holding on for the ride.
Now I'm in first. I'm so glad.
If I could win this race, it would be so rad.
Here comes the last lap, I'm starting to tire.
My best friend's behind me; the one I admire.
We go in the last turn, it's wire to wire.
He makes the pass and wins, only by a tire.
We come off the track with a smile on our face.
We plan to go at it again the next race.
I grab a drink and head to his camper.
Although, I was beat, I will not damper.
If I could do the race again, I wouldn't change it a bit.
Because, my best friend won, and he deserved it.

Tyler Nowlin, Grade 10
Coffee County Central High School, TN

Saved by an Ocean

So soft and sudden, you whispered passion
Into the air between our surreal dance.
A tear fell when time favoured regression
My hand in yours just a euphoric chance.
Once independent, alone we now cry,
You and my dreams until now intertwined.
My song leaves me with a destined goodbye.
An ocean brings change to our feelings inside.
A clock of reality before me,
The hands tick my ail to another place.
Without a chain I am now free to be,
I bask in my expanded breathing space.
I left in a shadow and found a light,
I opened my eyes to change and found it right.

Samantha Baumstark, Grade 11
St Mary's Episcopal School, TN

Both of You

I love you
But I love him too
I love you both equally
And I don't know what to do

I don't think it's a bad thing
But I know I have to choose
Or both of you I'll lose

I love all my friends equally
People think it's a crime to love two
But I don't care what people say
I still love both of you

So it's not impossible
I know it's true
And until I decide on one of you
I love both of you!

Kendra Jewell, Grade 10
White County High School, TN

The Typical Love

We hunger for the taste
Never knowing what will come
A blinding light shines down
It seems you've found the one

You spend every hour
Every second, every dime
The love you feel is real
But will it stay through time?

You hope and pray
You beg them to stay
Their love runs cold
Their souls went dry

You will never forget
How they made you feel
The love of your life
The love that was real

Sabrina Foster, Grade 11
Woodrow Wilson High School, WV

Together My Friend

We have grown together my friend,
We have grown wise together my friend,
We may be slow but we have
Grown together my friend,
I know you are growing weak my friend
But together we will be strong,
One may be gone in body but we are still
Together in mind, heart, soul, and spirit.
So together we'll be for the rest of
Eternity!

Casey Chasteen, Grade 12
Rock Bridge Sr High School, MO

The Reaper

Comes over you like nightfall.
Creeping up on you slowly like fog in the night slowly deadly, silently.
You sense his presence in your room.
Coming over you like a shadow in a dark alley.
Wearing his black cloak gliding towards like he's floating on air.
Through your bedroom window the light of the full moon reflects off of the dark
Creatures scythe blinding anything that stares.
He glides closer towards you like a glider shredding through the air.
His deep lonely face covered by a dark shadow.
Staring into the shadow was like staring into an endless black hole.
He calls your name like a fading echo in a dark cave.
He glides closer, and closer, and closer till.

You're Gone.

Lane Daniel, Grade 11
Hollis High School, OK

Dark Hole

Please don't leave me here in this dark hole I made
As I sit here and think to myself, you start to fade.
I thought of that person who was funny, smart and always there.
I sat and thought of you because you were the only one who cared
You can make me smile when I am angry or sad.
You can make me feel needed when I feel bad.
At times when I'm not you make me feel beautiful
And for making me feel that way, I am very thankful.
I thought I could either be your best friend or your girlfriend.
It doesn't matter to me because I'll stick with you till the end.
I love being with you because you are so gentle and kind
Like when you kiss me, my heart races and I lose my mind.
I come back to reality and the darkness is all I can see
I notice I'm still here in this dark hole where you left me.

Amber Crouch, Grade 12
Holcomb High School, MO

The Truth of the Fact That We Lie About

The undeniable fact is in the end we will face what we have denied
We will encounter all we evaded
We will be judged by the judged
All our sins will be there to join us in our sorrow
Maybe not today but surely tomorrow
We will find all we have lost or left behind
Remember all we forgot and what's hidden in our minds
Even with closed eyes we will be able to see our lies
Hanging on the tree that allowed us
To forget what we forgot and remember nothing
To wake up just to forget is what we breath and dream about
In the end we will find it all
In the end we will know it all
We will see it all
We will understand, how, why, and where
We will not share our knowledge and lie to the yearning faces
And leave them desolate
And leave them forgotten

Keith Tuggle, Grade 12
Cave City High School, AR

A Change

So much to do, so much to say,
How am I going to make a difference today?
Every move I make and every step I take
Will create a pathway, not a mistake.

I am going to step out and speak up,
With full confidence in who I am.
I know that wherever I go,
And whatever I do, I CAN.

When I have done all there is to do,
And said all there is to say,
I know I will have made a difference in some way.
The chosen path I will take and on it I will stay.

Mallonee Meritt, Grade 11
Woodrow Wilson High School, WV

The Name of the Beast

A great and terrible roaring beast
And all the world lays at his feet
The people sit and prepare to feast
And fail to see it is hearts they eat

They sit and tell beautiful lies
And the world is caught up in their disguise
The board of deception and deceivers
And caring not, consume the believers

The beast puts forth a terrible roar
And meek and mighty fall to their knees
The people cry for the golden shore
And find they drown in the hungry seas
For love is the name of the beast

Shasta Gibson, Grade 12
Buckhannon-Upshur High School, WV

Porcelain Tears*

A tear stained the porcelain face,
Of a doll on the shelf.
Dust gathers in her tight curly hair,
Her dress fading in color.
The twinkles in her eyes are gone,
No longer bright or deep.
She is no longer needed,
Not really wanted.
Her girl has grown up,
Left the doll behind,
To be nothing of need,
To be nothing of importance.
The doll remembers her little,
As she remains untouched on the abandoned shelf.
The girl may not need the doll,
But the doll needs the girl.
A tear stained the porcelain face,
Of a doll on the shelf.

Chrissy Pauley, Grade 10
Huntington High School, WV
**Dedicated to my sister*

Space for Comfort

where is it?
where did it go?
how to find it,
I don't know.
shuffle left,
then shuffle right.
no Space here,
none for me tonight.
phone rings,
hello, oh no.
why, I sigh.
I try, no you're NOT right,
at least not tonight.
on the way home,
garbage compiled in my life,
why must this world hold so much strife?!
why is this feeling of defeat so strong?
why is all I say wrong?!
I just need to find space, space from all.
how to find it, I don't know.
I guess, that's why, life is, such a ball.

Jonathan Biemesderfer, Grade 12
Northwest High School, TN

What We Have

These cloudy days of fall,
The trees sway limberly,
And the days are shorter but are feeling longer.
We step around our issues gingerly
While the cold keeps our thoughts inside.

It's been a long year.
It's easy to believe we'll make it through
But I can't remember the last time we talked with our hearts.
We've hid all we have behind our fear,
In used masks of uncertainty.

Maybe this year will be better than the last.
My mistakes were in missed opportunities,
You know what you've done
And that's all I can ask for.

It's one more day at a time in our mess,
Maybe we'll clear this up.
I wish we could.

Maybe when this cold leaves us be,
We'll gain a new sense of direction.
Maybe we'll realize what we can have.
Our lives are occasions; we have to rise to them.

Andrew Lynch, Grade 11
Owasso High School, OK

Don't Ask Why

Look into my eyes,
Notice the fear inside.
If you know the reason I cry,
Then why do you ask why?
Don't tell me hello,
Because hello always turns into goodbye.

Meagan Hunt, Grade 11
Madison High School, MO

My Hat

It is the colors of America
Red, white, and blue
It is just like a friend
Loyal and true

It covers up my shame
Just like a sheet
I even gave it a name
Without it I'm incomplete

It never leaves me
It's with me for the ride
Even when I take it off
It stays right by my side

And when it wears out
I will hang it on my wall
But I know without a doubt
It is the best friend of all

Ryan Hightower, Grade 10
Chickasha High School, OK

Lost and Alone

She gets pushed around,
Her heart lies on the ground.
She sits there alone,
Gathering the pieces
Of her broken heart.
She's the subject of humiliation,
Because they don't get her dedication
To be the best that she can be,
Even if that means
She puts herself last.
She sits there observing
Everyone around her,
Wondering why,
They treat her so badly.
But then one day,
A kind hand greets her,
Offering her a caring heart.
As she tells him her troubles,
He comforts her tears.
Ten years come later,
He's been there for years.

Megan Richmond, Grade 10
Shady Spring High School, WV

Final Wish

The old man sits on his rustic porch,
Overlooking the world with his overcast eyes.
With his pipe in hand,
He confronts a new day.
His prime years
Substituted for rocking chairs and bingo night.
His life far too long
In comparison with his wife's.
His skin,
Saturated with juxtaposed wrinkles,
Conceives a map of his past.
The dark secrets,
Hidden within,
Fabricate streams of salt and water that flood his palms each night.
With its lair revealed the doctors say,
"It's not benign."
"Surgery?"
He sits on his porch.
Fading away with the morning haze,
His final wish to lie in peace next to his wife
Granted.

Nathan Bond, Grade 11
Germantown High School, TN

Sunrise

I can see the lovely sunset,
Its cool colors dance in the sky;
But its beauty is of no compare,
To the morning sky, the sweet smelling air.

I can see the sunset, and yes, it is sweet
But after it's gone, the cold and dark sky.
It puts you asleep, the day turns to night.
Evil awakens, and light tries to hide.

What can overcome all of night's fears?
What is so powerful to calm, to bring light?
What kind of thing is an antidote for darkness?
Where is the sunrise, the fair and the bright?

You are my morning, the bright loving light.
Whey you are in view, no darkness is alive.
When you come in the morning, the birds start to sing.
Your warmth is a blanket. The dew it does bring.

I love you with my heart. Without you I can't live.
Without you there would be darkness, and a world without light.
The world would keep on spinning; the sun would never rise.
But now that you are with me, my life is very bright!

Darren Robinson, Grade 10
Trinity Christian Academy, MO

Change*

I was a nice and well behaved young man
I remember when I was a little kid
I heard people talking and laughing
I saw my mom and dad and the rest of my family
I worried when I first started school
I thought I would be little forever
But I changed

I am funny, caring, and most of the time, happy
I think the world is a harsh place
I need a well paying job
I try to do better
I feel lots of love mixed with some hate
I forgive most of the people who have done something to me
Now, I will change

I will have a loving family
I choose my actions carefully
I dream of growing old in a nice house with my wife
I hope I will have a good, happy life
I predict into the future
I know I have came a long way
No more change

Adam Holtsclaw, Grade 10
Capital High School, WV
**Based on "Freedom Writers"*

Dear Dad

I don't think anyone knows how having
A drunk for a dad is, it sucks. You never
Know when he is coming home or where
He is at.

I just wish that one day he would
See that it hurts me more than
Anything to see my dad this way.
Knowing that he could get hurt from
Doing this addiction.

Growing up I just wanted a best friend,
A hero, and a father figure there, but I never
Really had that because my dad was never
Really there when I needed him to be. I really
Hope he straightens up before it's too late.

Day to day I sit around hoping
That I will never get that call saying
Your dad is in jail or you need
To come identify a man who
We believe is your dad

Brittney Wilkins, Grade 10
White County High School, TN

Rage

Deep secrets lie within,
Hate, pain, and animosity never ends.
I search and search for the soul that's lost,
However, nothing surfaces but the serpent inside,
My life is treacherous.
The demon is immortal.
I wish there was another world beyond a portal.
Every step I take
Is another mistake I make,
Locked away,
Deep inside a cage,
Full of adrenaline and rage.
I wish life were just like a diary,
You can just turn to the other page.
As I age I just see another page,
Continued with rage.

Micah G., Grade 10
Audubon Youth Development Center, KY

Steel Overcoat

The acid stung her cheeks as it slowly slid down.
She vowed to never feel like this again.
The steel-colored overcoat blocked out the biting cold.
Just another barrier between her and the icy wind.

If she could just keep out the intruding pain,
Maybe she could make it through the day.
But she can't keep out something that is already there.
Like the memories that constantly seem to leave her bare…

She knows what she's missing, but it's too late to turn back.
They tell her she's fine, without seeing the painful gap.
So sarcasm will fill the void that's left within,
Left Defensive, bitter, strong and refusing to bend.

The overcoat slowly gave way to the seeping cold.
It wasn't the protection she believed to make her bold.
She let it wash over her, consume her, mold her.
She had no choice but to only give in.

Samantha Garrison, Grade 12
Hollis High School, OK

Snow in the Wind

You see it in the wind
It's cold and free
White, clear, blue
It's cold and icy

It's fun free and enjoying
People play in it
People jump in it
People throw it at each other

All in all
Snow is fun
Without it
Christmas wouldn't be the same

Ian Fowler, Grade 10
Jeffersontown High School Magnet Career Academy, KY

The Storm

I yank the covers over my head,
trying to disregard the deafening bellow
awakening all who slumber.
I toss restlessly in my muddled bed
as the overpowering clamors
pierce my ears indifferently.
I shut my eyes taut,
struggling not to see the flood of light
illuminating my room.
I flinch in my saturated clothes
as the world lights up
almost as if it was day again.
I pray to the angered gods
to cease the terrifying monster
raging in the clouds.
After some time
the torrential downpour lets up
and the thunder dies away.
Now, I can get some sleep.

Anna Tankersley, Grade 10
Germantown High School, TN

If I Could Only…

If I could only…
Go back in time,
So many unanswered questions,
A mountain I had to climb.
If I could only…
Ask why he couldn't have made it work,
For the family or friends
The thoughts of hatred that used to lurk.
If I could only…
Replace the memories that are bad.
Trying to be a man at eight,
When my mom and sister were sad.
If I could only…
Learn from mistakes
Which my dad made
There will not be as much heartache.

Jeremy Robinson, Grade 10
Hollis High School, OK

The Passion of an Untamed Mind

A transparent rose
In translucence blooming
Anchored in opaque thought
of the most blatant
Consistency

In it is coming
Perhaps to manifest
Vapid solidity
'til the fade into
Transparency

Ethan Lakey, Grade 12
Middleton High School, TN

My Poppy

M y Poppy is my favorite person in the world.
I n the worst of times he's always there.
C aring is not something he is always, but
H aving a very good sense of humor is.
E verybody knows him, but everybody doesn't like him.
A lways doing something for somebody, never asking for anything back,
L ives a life that anybody could be happy to live.

K eeps everything done when it needs to be done.
I s always playing around unless he needs to be serious.
L oves all of his kids and grandkids, no matter what they do.
B elieves in me even though I don't always believe in myself.
U sually cares deep down inside never showing it on the outside.
R eally just a good old man that works hard for his living,
N ever giving up no matter how hard it gets.

Randie Kilburn, Grade 10
Niangua High School, MO

These Three Words

When I first broke up with you, my blue skies were gone, but
I still muttered the words that only belong in old R&B songs.
The words I love you, with those three words you held on.
You held onto me like a child, and his kite.
The words I love you, were bound in our minds and our hearts
My heart did not want to let go, but yet my mind pulled with might.
The words I love you, pulled us together and broke us apart.
The words I love you were not vocalized from me once more.
The words I love you, is what you wanted to hear,
But the words never came near.
Once were the words of how we felt for one another.
Now it's just I love you friend.
The words I love you,
If these words mean any more,
To us it would be just as friends if you want it to be.
With these words…these words of love,
We could have climbed the largest mountains
Swam the longest sea, but
I messed it up

Nigel Benton, Grade 10
Fern Creek Traditional Magnet High School, KY

My Struggle for Perfection

I stare at my reflection, a modern day Narcissus.
My eyes make me look like a vagabond,
As if a child had vehemently drawn on me with a charcoal crayon.
Cowardly, I switch on the light.
For some reason Prometheus enjoys liberating his captive in my bathroom.
The fluorescent light immediately seeks out my flaws.
My amiable glow is now masked by the blemishes that appear,
My transient beauty has vanished.
I spit on my finger, and wipe away my raccoon eyes
Juxtaposed with my previous appearance,
The absence of my war paint reveals a dull, common person
Today, it will be a Sisyphusian struggle to create my illusion of perfection.

Madelon Crosson, Grade 11
Germantown High School, TN

The Road of Destruction

I choose to follow a road that many would not take.
This road leads straight to pain and into a world of fake.
I choose to take this road whenever I want to escape
from an unwanted reality and from my heartache.

This road forever leads me to the point of breaking down,
and it causes me to hurt everyone who is around.
Although this road causes me more pain that I do not need,
it's the medicine I desire, to heal me when I bleed.

This road has now become my closest friend,
for I know its twists and every dead end.
This heartless road I have chosen has left me numb
and I'll choose it 'til I leave...
...It's my lithium.

Deanna Marquart, Grade 11
St Francis Borgia Regional High School, MO

My Brother

I didn't really know my brother
I found out about him by my mother.
My brother died after he was born
My heart has been torn.

If he was alive today
I would watch him lay
I would want him to know
that he's not alone.

If he ever had a bad day
I would've told him that everything's gonna be ok.
I would've told him that he doesn't have to cry
Because I'll be by your side till the day I die.

Makayla Wilburn, Grade 10
Prue High School, OK

Tears of the Heart

Some people are afraid of change
Well I'm afraid of things staying the same
I fear that I would go on through the motions
Not living life to the fullest
I want to live without regret
To be able to cry
To cry with all my heart
I want to believe in something
So much my heart could burst
To live without fear
To be myself and not care
I want to stare the demon of life in the eye
And come out with my head still attached
I want to break the mold of human existence
to be a pioneer of the soul
I want to spread my wings
And not be afraid of how high I might fly
To be both genius and insane
I want to live as I never have before

Meghan Aul, Grade 12
Cor Jesu Academy, MO

Zoo

The single rose in fields of purple grass,
Crying out for more.
The smile of a lonely child,
Crying out for more.

The reflection of a lost love in dark sunglasses,
Crying out for more.
The tree's silent screaming,
Crying out for more.

The blurred faces that never stop,
Crying out for more.
The symbol for a lost ideal,
Crying out for more.

The death of an ice cream,
Crying out for more.
The broken glass of a turtle's back,
Crying out for more.

A dying planet,
That knows there is nothing more

Max Quick, Grade 10
Coffee County Central High School, TN

To Grandma

Who lived there, in that cramped house,
with her painful, arthritic knees.
Constantly refusing help with the yard, the roof, the cleaning,
unable to do it herself,
watching the neighborhood declining, her church dying.

Who blinded herself to the fact that she too, was declining
Who never admitted that she was "old."
in her 80's, driving all the "old" ladies to the doctor
for their checkups.
Who would not take herself to the doctor
unless practically forced to.

Who now sits there, in a nursing home.
struck down by a heart attack just before Christmas.
Whose brain is confused,
Whose body is a wreck,
Whose memory is missing decades.
Who now sits there, in a nursing home.
Whose cats found new homes.
Who is still loved by all of us
and who loves us too.

when she remembers.

Michael Horton, Grade 11
Germantown High School, TN

The Love

When I fall, when I fall, one look at you and I'm up again. Your beauty nullifies the strongest cold. The sun is frozen solid compared to you. My heart is longing for you to notice its love for you. If only you would see it and hear it calling for you. Every time it sees you with another it still hopes and prays it catches your eye. It beats for you and only you. If only you would give a chance. If only you would hear its cries for you.

Alex Schriner, Grade 10
South Intermediate High School, OK

My Cause, Without an Understanding

There she is again.
The confection of my eyesight.
Her sheer brilliance gleaming at me, I am afraid to look…
But nothing can stop the feeling she places in me…
A feeling that forces me to look at her…only wanting what I am scared to have…
At first the question "why" formed, why me…why her…why…us.
As I looked inside those eyes, my heart belonged to her. But my dreams of holding her crushed at my heart,
My idolized star in the sky, she shines so bright above the others, just too intense for me to embrace…
My questions of desire push me further away…when all I want is to be close.
Puzzled, I marvel at the unknown, confused as my own lust starts squeezing at my bitter heart from within.
My feelings, my passions turn against me, twisting around my heart.
My breath is once more taken away as she passes.
My very existence lies within her grasping will.
My dreams…My thoughts…My actions all lead to her and her shining smile…
As I view from afar, my heart beating faster as her footsteps come ever nearer.
I want her so close to me…I want to understand…to understand love…
If only she knew to help me…I look up at her, starting to cry on the inside…
My blood woven tears, wrapped and cradled in thoughts of her…Will she see me?
Will she notice how much control she has over me?
Will she ever know…the indescribable feeling she bestowed upon me?
Will I ever know…?

Harrison Gary, Grade 12
Jeffersontown High School Magnet Career Academy, KY

I Am From

I am from the rolling hills of clay and sand where a man has no limits to roam.
I am from a life of great sorrow, of lost daughters and murdered wives.
I am from a place where a man can be killed for the way he looks and the name of his people, the Apache.

I am from the great plains of rock and sand of great Arizona and Nevada, New Mexico.
I am from the Great Spirit, molded to be a warrior and a leader among my people.
I am from a band of warriors where the sound of a gun is what we hear at the time of our deaths.

I am from a place where a man's scalp is worth more than the air he breathes.
I am from a village where children play with dogs, and women work as hard as the men.
I am from the Great Spirit who holds my life, my being, in its hand.
It controls me, rivers, rock, the antelope: everything, even my death.

I am from the great mesas where a man can be hidden for days. Where the red rocks match the color of his skin.
I am from the land where I feel the earth, and I am the earth.
I am from where the power of one can ripple through time like a rock on a still lake.

I am from a place where the name of one man can arouse fear in the minds of Banditos
and at the same time, give courage to his brothers in war to fight till the very end.
I am Geronimo, a man from the great rolling mesas and hills made of rock, clay and sand, of Arizona, Nevada and New Mexico.
The place that will hold my death and where I was given life.

Isaac Chleborad, Grade 11
Central High School, MO

Eternity

I lie in bed at night and pray,
that you will think of me.
I cry until my eyelids close,
and dream eternity.

I wake to sunlight on my face,
for a moment I forget.
Then a cloud passes by,
and I realize this is it.

I carry on throughout the day,
feigning joy and feeling pain.
I long to gaze upon your face,
and share a smile, an embrace.

The day is drawing to an end,
and still I think of you.
I try to relax, but yet in my mind,
I wonder what to do.

So now I lay me down to sleep,
I pray the Lord my soul to keep.
And should you chance to think of me,
know that I love you — eternally.

Brittauny Clements, Grade 10
Mills University Studies High School, AR

The Way You Used to Be

I miss the way you used to be
The way you'd always smile at me
The things you used to do and say
Just to make me laugh all day
Do you realize that you're not the same
Do you notice that it's hard to blame
The things you do on coincidence
You know it's all on your expense
It's hard to look at who you've become
I try hard just to be numb
To the choices that you make
To the life you've chosen to take
It's hard to look you in the eyes
When you walk in drunk, stoned, or high
I pray that you'll straighten out
It's just a stage, I cannot doubt
That one day this will all pass by
No longer will I have to cry
And worry about you until I hear
The door open and know you're near
Brother please come back to me, be that boy you used to be

Kelsey Sailor, Grade 11
Owasso High School, OK

Tradition

I am from porcelain and tea,
And the land of opportunities,
The remnants of a culture buried
In the luxury of America
Unable to pull itself out.

I am a beloved dolphin confined at the zoo,
Afraid to penetrate the unfathomable sea,
Allured by its magnitude and mystery
A dandelion, stubborn and undaunted
Striving to overcome all adversity
A rainbow, shy and quiet
But vivid with possibilities all the same
A blank canvas, full of promises
Waiting for the artist's exquisite brush
To transform it into a masterpiece

I am the past, present, and future
Locked inside a box of life
Forever waiting to be released
I am me.

Amy Trang, Grade 12
Moore High School, OK

Gone

My dear I have something to say
Why do you have to be this way?
I told you I love you and told you I cared
And now you have my heart torn and scared.

Roses were your favorite flower
Now you would stand to see me for an hour,
I thought you were the one for me
Now you don't love me, how can that be?

When I look around what do I see
I see that you're not here with me,
Why can't you just hold on,
I look around and you are gone.

Chris Sodosky, Grade 11
Woodrow Wilson High School, WV

The Replacement

I know some question me, absurd to think,
The joy I find in my gas fireplace;
I do admit I first was on the brink,
The thought that this would never warm my face.
Growing up with one real in my reside,
Like the sun warms me on the brightest day,
Crackled as I slept by the fireside
Then I mourned as it was taken away.
The thought of a warming flame colored blue,
And no real wood lugged in from out of doors;
It was the heart of my day, oh so true,
And now this new one sat so still, a bore.
But then I saw that all hard work was gone,
Flick the match to turn this new delight on.

Jordan Reeve, Grade 11
St Mary's Episcopal School, TN

Memories

Love is a road,
Chosen by many.
The torn-up path
Lit by haunting ghosts of us.
My heart is broken and I'm just fine.
I'm looking up, hoping for the best,
All the mistakes, regrets, heartaches
Make it all worthwhile now.
Our time is gone,
But our memories are forever.

Holly Westmoreland, Grade 10
Hollis High School, OK

The Frustrated Day

I want to meet myself
Whom I lost one day
Looking shabby things
Deep inside of me

I'm talking to God
Whenever I feel like falling down
The world is changing in a
Shorter and shorter period

Some things never change,
Precious things that we are looking for
They are only waiting
Right in front of me

Whenever I'm in sorrow
I just want to cry out to God
I'm not really
Strong at all

"Are you still having a hard time?
With your way, with your belief?"
My answer is,
Not anymore.

Lucy Lee, Grade 10
Family of Faith Christian School, OK

A Missing Piece

As you can see my eyes are green —
represents fear and God to thee.
I may not be what you want me to be
but when you look back into my eyes,
there's something else inside me —
something special,
something bright,
something I can hold on tight,
something I'll never forget as me…
I will always be strong.
no matter what happens to me
but I'll never forget —
what you did to me…

Julianne Martinez, Grade 11
Hollis High School, OK

How?

How can a mother leave her child, never to return?
How can a father rape his daughter and the consequences never be learned?
How can brothers kill each other over something that happened years ago?
How can we fix these problems?
How can we make them better?
Is there anything we can do or is it going to be this way forever?

How can a child go into a classroom and blow the teachers and students away?
How can a man bomb a building, killing many people and children,
On an average work day?
How can a man hijack an airplane and think it's his debt to society?
How can we fix these problems?
How can we make them better?
Is there anything we can do or is it going to be this way forever?

How can a President lie to his people over a situation he created?
How can a President ban the rights of gays, which is heavily debated?
How can a President send soldiers to war and never let them come home?
How can we fix these problems?
How can we make them better?
Is there anything we can do or is it going to be this way forever?

We can make a difference, if we really try.
I'm not saying it's going to be easy because that would be a lie.

Katherine Barr, Grade 11
Owasso High School, OK

Our Hope in God

We will put our hope in God. We will praise Him forever.
In our sufferings we will praise Him.
Our God, our Comfort, our Savior.
In safety, we will lie and sleep in peace. For You, O Lord, are our dwelling place.
Your peace will rule in our hearts.
Our God, our Comfort, our Savior.

We will run and not grow weary. We will walk and not be faint.
For upon the Lord we will cast our worries and pain.
The righteous will not fall. Strength will be renewed.
Lord, when life is ebbing away, we will remember you.
We rejoice in the hope of glory. Through suffering we will persevere.
Pour Your love into our hearts, O Holy Spirit.
Outwardly we are wasting away. Inwardly we are being renewed day by day.
Therefore do not lose heart.

We have learned through this trial. We have learned through this pain.
The memories will never go away.
Yet.
When times are good be happy. When times are bad consider:
God has made the one. As well as the other.

Kayla Sanders, Grade 10
Hennessey High School, OK

The Difference Between Nightmare and Dream

I've been dreaming
Without seeing
What am I without you here?

My blood's grayish
My minds tainted
I can't seem to stand again
And, I don't need your pity

This dream has so quickly turned into a nightmare.
The difference between them doesn't seem fair.

Codee Rush, Grade 10
Columbus Unified High School, OK

The Sailing Cloud

The grass turns brown
As the trees fall down,
With little hope of salvation in sight.
The thermometer flashes its red glaze,
While the heat rises to form a kind of haze.

Off in the distance, like a sailboat flying high,
A dark puffy cloud appears against the blue sky.
And when it's directly overhead,
Tears stream down the tree's face.
Nothing compares to how sweet the taste.

But as ships sail on, so this cloud too;
Bring back the sky — so hot and deep blue.
And as for that moment of comfort?
Their memories will forever be,
As they hopefully await another cloud from the sky-blue sea.

Molly Arwood, Grade 11
Bearden High School, TN

Keep

Remember
His grip in the crush
And blow of the winter light
When his arm was once your arm
And your leg
His leg.
His hands were once your hands
And his neck once held your head
But eventually he tired of being the brace,
Instead deciding to be the weight
That dragged.
Yet your heart he never could
Steal because when it was his
It was still yours
To forever hold safe
And to delicately collect
From where he left it on your sleeve
Because your bones knew better
Than to let him
Hide his poison in their strength.

Anna Reddick, Grade 12
Oak Ridge High School, TN

My Love

My love for you is honest and true
As yours is for me, yet you say we're through.
I'm not sure what happened to the love we had
But somewhere along the road it was lost and sad.

I sit and wait and wonder when
You will come and profess your love again.
So come to me please today
And then everything will be okay.

I'm not quite sure where our love has gone
I know you love me, you have all along.
I miss all of our hugs and kisses
Will you come to me and grant me my wishes?

I remember one fine and glorious day
You asked me to be your wife and wished me to say
Yes, of course, I'll marry you
Which is what my intentions are to do.

I miss those days of our love
Come to me please, I pray to God above.
So please come to me today
Then maybe everything will be okay.

Jennifer Massengile, Grade 12
Union County High School, TN

Reborn

I don't know where I'm supposed to be
And I don't know if I can believe
When shadows fall and block my eyes
I was lost and I needed to find the way back
Till I flew through the Arctic Ocean to you, America

Wondering what's my purpose
Wondering how to make myself strong
I know I will falter; I know I will cry
I know you'll be standing by my side

Sometimes it feels no one understands
Why I do the things I do
When pride builds me up till I can't see my soul
Will you break down these walls and pull me through
Till I feel that I am worth the price

When Satan mocks and friends turn to foes
I feel like everything is out of my control
Till I find my home in you
You made me reborn

Nika Jiao, Grade 11
Family of Faith Christian School, OK

I Love the Way...

I love the way you look at me
I love the way you care
I love the way you laugh at me
instead of getting mad
I love the way you kiss me
and look into my eyes
I love the way you say my name
I love the way you smile
I love the way you get so mad
and give me that evil look
I love the way you hold me close
and never let me go
I love the way you make me laugh
I love the way you joke
I love the way you make me dinner
and laugh at how it tastes
I love how we can spend all night
just talking about our day.
I love the way you say I love you
I love the way you make me feel
you're all I ever wanted.

Brianna Mattern, Grade 11
Powell High School, TN

Stars

Tiny dots in the heavens above,
so mysterious, and far away.
What are they really?
And who truly knows,
for what they are, none can say.

But this one thing I do know
and now I tell it to you.
Stars are song,
the song that is life
played for an eternity through.

Stars are the story of heroes
we know not at all,
but these legends have trod
across the bright dome,
and their stories the stars recall.

The stars are like nothing
we know here on Earth.
Which is fitting, perhaps,
for they have been here
since the time of the world's birth.

Therese Spollen, Grade 11
Rock Bridge Sr High School, MO

This Emotion

Longing for a feeling
So many have discovered.
The floaty, fuzzy sensation,
To hard to be uncovered.
Like a secret,
Hidden deep within the soul.
Becoming deeper and thicker
like a quick sand hole.
Becoming numb, your body
seems to fade away.
All your cares and pains of hunger
Disappear from the day.
Searching for the word,
That defines this emotion
Like floating far away
On a deep blue ocean.
You wait for it to come
Like a cool winter breeze.
And it spells itself out
With patient simple ease.
LOVE

Leona Cooper, Grade 10
Haworth High School, OK

A Broken Guitar

A broken guitar
is a metaphor of life
we start out new
and then and the fight

Like the strings
we split and fray
when they finally snap
we go every which way

When our number is up
we take our final bow
the curtain is drawn
and a new guitar will spawn

We get used and worn
until we're torn
when there's no life left
and nothing to regret

Once we are broken
and truly done
people go out
and get a new one

Andrea Greenwalt, Grade 10
Festus Sr High School, MO

Throughout Our Lifetime

From the time we were young
To the age we are now
Many things have happened

Important dates in history have been set
We've gone to war
To fight for our continued freedom

Great presidents have came
And some have died
Along with many other great people

Scientist have found new cures
That have saved many lives
While also saying, "Pluto is not a planet"

Writers have written hit novels
Songs have become number one hits
And movies have set records

We will pass on
But even after we do
Great things will continue to happen

Hayle Clymer, Grade 10
Erick High School, OK

A Werewolf's Song

Night falls upon the land,
fur explodes from my skin,
nails lengthen in my hand,
teeth sharpen from within,
bones crack and break,
to take my true shape.

Skin by day, fur by night.
Running through the trees.
Letting your heart take flight,
so if you please,
leave me in peace,
while I run wild and free.

Singing to the moon,
and running with the wind.
Listening to our little wolf tune,
and then back to our human skin.
Now it's time to go home.

The night had been long,
and at least I had fun,
singing our beautiful song,
to welcome the morning sun.

Alyssa Nicole Samuels, Grade 10
Slater High School, MO

Quilts

I made you a quilt and you made one for me.
Detailed stitches, scraps, patchwork of our lives.
Conversations, arguments, information we exchanged,
It's been done and said repeatedly,
the same words rearranged.
How was your day? Fine. How was yours? Fine.
What's new? Nothing.
Nothing.
Always nothing.
I count the time that silence reigns.
It's a painful realization, when there's nothing left to say.
My ears are ringing from the silence in the room,
As the time slowly ticks away.
We've gotten every bit of use out of these security blankets,
They're old, worn and thin.
I've learned all there is to know about each patch,
and every flaw within.
These quilts have little left for you or me,
Nothing left to offer.
No matter how long I search there is nothing left to share.
So no longer will I bother.

Haley Noteboom, Grade 11
Owasso High School, OK

The Doomed

The moon glares down over the bare sea
The glorious sea that which I solemnly sail
To escape the cave of doom of my own self
To have the drab dream of finding my own self

My own self, what a pitiful prevaricate, truly
For the sea is only free of my own doom
My own doom, which a Raven destined for me
Or might have my father or mother destined for me?

In morning, the gloomy skies mirror my soul
For it is clouding out the sun that would give guidance
Guidance, Ha! Guidance which was given but not received
Thee taunts me with thoughts of lost guidance

I shun thoughts of my previous personality
A vivid personality, deceptively given to me
Surely, if not for the Raven, I could have happiness
But the past is past, as is my happiness

The other doomed dejectedly wander as I do
For I have seen I am not alone in my indestructible destiny
As such I am durably doomed,
It would be better to be a fleeting bloom than forever doomed.

Melissa McBride, Grade 11
Centralia High School, MO

Concert

I'm surrounded by people and movement
So loud I can only hear my heart beat
Ecstasy in the air, the thick scent
One hundred people moving, making heat

I've heard them, now I see the wonder
These anthems of my youth brought to sight
Sounds blasting through the crowd like thunder
My soul and mind have taken flight

Then I hear it, a symphony for today
I look to my left and get on the stage
I join in to dance in the crazed and frantic fray
I make eye contact with a musical sage

As I leave the hot red room I enter the cold night air
With the melodies running through my head like a prayer

Landan Hoffman, Grade 12
Covington Catholic High School, KY

On the Subject of Moose, and Their Beneficial Habits

Up in the north, near old Saskatchewan,
On a cold winter's morn with lot's of snow,
There sat a proud moose basking in the dawn.
This moose heard a cry; it called him to go.
The desperate cry that rolled in his ears
Was that of a victim, full of despair.
The moose knew his duty; he had no fears.
He donned his bright costume and flew through the air.
He lit on the street and saw the bank robber.
He used his antlers to stop the car cold,
The poor thief he proceeded to clobber.
He's the best hero is what I've been told.
Yes, the day has been saved many a time
By Super Moose Man, protector from crime.

Tom Flanagan, Grade 12
Covington Catholic High School, KY

Contradiction

You constantly remind me of the conflict at hand
I told you it was your choice, do whatever you can
I'll try to make this work, but maybe it won't
Neither of us is perfect, I think we both realize that now
We're not going to agree on everything, but we can try
We need to solve this problem, before it reaches the sky
I really want to talk to you
But you won't even try
It's starting to bother me, you won't even speak
You haven't looked at me, or made a peep
Do you want to solve this issue?
Or just leave things as they are
It doesn't matter to me
Do whatever you please
If it makes you happy
That's all right with me
But we need to solve this problem at hand
And we need to do it as fast as we can.

Elizabeth Crouch, Grade 10
Capital High School, WV

The Village by the Sea

As I walk along the shore,
The sky gets dark, the wind blows more.
A storm is coming swiftly now,
The trees all bend and bow,
To the mighty wind that rages on,
Down the beach and then is gone.
Gone to the town upon the hill,
Where there it seeks to do its will.

The town is quiet, calm, and still,
The little town upon the hill.
Not a spirit, not a soul,
Breathes as the storm takes its toll,
Upon that quiet, little town,
That sits and waits upon the crown,
Of the hill nearby the sea,
A treasure kept by lock and key.

The storm has gone, its gall abated,
Leaving behind the chaos it created.
The little people gather 'round,
To thank God they are safe and sound,
In the village by the sea.

Katherine Gale, Grade 10
Rock Bridge Sr High School, MO

Waterfall

Falling upon silk
Clear water spills from the sky
Of the waterfall

Kelsey Holley, Grade 10
Fort Towson Jr/Sr High School, OK

I Hear the Sea

I hear the sea it's calling to me,
Saying come, come and see.
I run to the shore what a sight to behold,
The sunset so beautiful, bright, and bold.
I hear the sea it's calling to me,
Saying come, come and see.

I hear the sea it's calling to me,
Saying come, come and see.
I watch as the waves crash and recede
A moment of peace so fleeting for me.
I hear the sea it's calling to me,
Saying come, come and see.

I hear the sea it's calling to me,
Saying come, come and see.
I look to the horizon and what do I see
But a dolphin so playful and carefree.
I hear the sea it's calling to me,
Saying come, come and see.

Megan Horn, Grade 12
Fort Towson Jr/Sr High School, OK

A Kiss in the Wind

I hear your voice, and turn my head,
Yet all I see, is the ground I tread.
Just because I don't see, doesn't mean it isn't there,
I can feel your presence; your warmth within the very air.
I can hear your laughter, your heart's steady beat,
Your voice is my safe harbor, a blissful, calm retreat.
I can feel the pressure of your so-smooth hands, grazing over my skin,
As you tug me back into your arms, I fool myself with pretend.
I feel every sensitive ridge on your flesh, each with a look at our past,
I laugh and I giggle; not knowing how long the wonderful lapse will last.
We roll to the ground, grass so green, and stare at every individual blade,
Yet I feel your body leave without me, your memory begins to fade.
As the leaves dance around us, I try to grasp your face,
You're leaving faster, turning into, once again, a plain and empty space.
The trees wave to you; the clouds wink down with love and care,
You look at me, smile, and run your smoky fingers once more through my hair.
A tear rolls down my cheek, I sigh; I'm missing you again,
As you leave your lips brush it away; a bitter kiss in the wind.

Kristen Kirchner, Grade 10
Capital High School, WV

I Am From

I am from the sounds of farm equipment
the many different sounds of wild animals
the sizzle of food as my me-me always cooked that great country food
and the ping of bats and fans yelling at the top of their lungs, "Go Will"
I am from those steaks that taste like heaven
that my granddad could cook just perfect
potatoes, chocolate cake, and chocolate chip cookies
and turkey for those gatherings at Christmas and Thanksgiving
I am from "Hey Tooter"
and "yall are just a bunch of goober smooches"
my granddad would say "awe he's all right, it ain't close to the heart, it won't hurt him
and how do you spell Record, R-E-C-O-R-D like a record player"
I am from a loving mother
who supports you, cries with you,
prays for you, and laughs with you
she'll do anything for you
and even though I don't like discipline, she disciplines
I won't understand until I have kids of my own
I'm from a regular country family of six people

Will Record, Grade 10
Gibson County High School, TN

Football

Football is just a game
Young men under the Friday night lights,
Feeling that great feeling on the hot summer nights.
Football is all fun and games
Until someone loses the game.
You feel like you wanna get sick,
But who's to blame?
You look at your opponent and ask how can we match their fame?
But always remember football is just a game.

Joshua Vaughan, Grade 10
Prue High School, OK

Slumber

I laid down and went to sleep for the night.
The dream I dreamt was peaceful and serene.
I was in a garden painted in red.
I saw the birds chirping in the distance.
The wind, it blew, singing a melody.
I saw the mountains, a brilliant purple.
The sky was clear, as in a summer's day.
The animals pranced and played all day long.
The crowd is gone and I am there alone.
"Why, God?" I ask. "Why is there no one here?"
Is this now my nightmare I am dreaming?
The birds flew away, the day turned to night.
The world was gone and I was the last one.
I woke to find the dream was not a lie.

Amanda Robinson, Grade 12
Glenpool High School, OK

Addiction

I am far too tired to go to sleep,
Wishing this weight would make me at last sink.
Wanting escape but I am in too deep.
Lost logic of this place it makes me think.
Does that deceptive haze create a smile,
When deafening silence says you're alone?
Do those hours make your bitter heart worthwhile?
You must feel great, another hollow clone.
This murderous habit never ceases,
Grasping those lies to help you disappear.
Are you aware my heart is in pieces?
Tormented, aching shards, they drown in fear.
Like a wicked shadow that ever looms,
This curse you've chosen shall haunt till your doom.

Caitlin Leggett, Grade 11
St Mary's Episcopal School, TN

A Fallen Angel with Broken Wings

An angel resides within my heart
But on the ground is where I start
How soon will I be in the sky
Free to go and always fly
The day draws near as I sit and wait
Embracing my known and one true fate
I take off quick into the wind
Where Heaven meets Earth and hold no end
I spread my arms and fly real fast
I close my eyes to remember my past
I hear the voice of my mother's call
I lose my balance and begin to fall
My wings tear up and feathers fly by
My heart soon breaks and I start to cry
I fall to Earth along with my tears
That fell like rain that'd been waiting for years
My body's all wet and I feel so dumb
I pull my knees to my chest and begin to hum
The words come out and the song I sing
Is "The Fallen Angel with Broken Wings"

Katherine Burns, Grade 11
Hickman Mills Sr High School, MO

Sacrifice

The thought and wonder racing through my head.
My life flashing before my very own eyes,
What would I do if this were to be true?
Could I still pursue my dreams and ambitions?
What would people think of me?
Will they look down on me?
Finding myself asking these questions,
And yet all the answers are not good enough.
Over time decisions were made,
But were they for the best?
Nobody knows for sure.
They say your senior years is your best,
But the people who claim this aren't in my situation.
I feel as if I am talked about, and looked down on,
But I am proud to say that I take responsibility for my mistakes.
This is a decision that will live with for the rest of my life,
And in good time this choice will fade into something good.
This trauma will have turned into a miracle.
That no one will every take away.
My miracle.
My miracle.

Geraldine Marie Narron, Grade 12
Slater High School, MO

Hidden Monsters

There's a monster hidden inside of us,
Each and every one.
Creating problems for us all,
Some are big, and some are small.
The monsters can be different,
Whether it be jealousy or hate.

They live off our emotions.
They make us see their way.
They never want to check out of the Haunted Person's day.
Some are most persuasive, and others are quite sly.
Their goal in life to make us see
The truths that we can hide.

Would our lives be better,
Without these monsters checking in?
Would we see the twisted things
That we always hide away?
Or would they come all out at once,
On an unsuspecting day?

The monsters are created by each of us inside,
Whether we choose to see them is what we must decide.
And each of us truly knows what feelings we can hide.

Amber Kirchman, Grade 11
Owasso High School, OK

Flowers

From this second-story window I have sat in silent solitude,
keeping my sorrow-starched eyes set on my small and simple garden.
Sleeping sprouts were summoned from safe soil; sacrificing their sacred slumber.
They stretched their stems toward the sun and saw the slinging sparrows soar across the summer sky.
They heard a symphony of ship's sails snapping in the wind,
and the voices of sailors setting off to solve the secrets of the sea.
They spotted several subjects sporting seasonal swimsuits and short-sleeved shirts
sprawled out on the soft and sandy shore, staring at the silky seascape.
Sedated by the serenity; steady and sure; solemn and secure.
They smelled the salty air, and tasted the sweet sap as it slid down their satin stalks like syrup.
They soaked up this setting without sunken spirit,
savoring every single second they were surrounded by this scenery, and they were satisfied.
Suddenly and all too soon, upon the hour of which I slept,
the shadow of Sin seeped into the system and stole the soul of my garden
searing her swollen skin with a sharpened silver scythe
leaving her severed and slain; scorched and scabbed, suffocated,
in the somber stillness of the night.
And so I stay up here in my seclusion searching for a solution
trying to make sense of this sad situation.
Someday I will sow a new seed. Today I will seek a new Savior.

Corey B., Grade 12
Audubon Youth Development Center, KY

Sugar

Your smiling face, your saving grace
Your way about life, from day to day
Your fabulous birthday, in May
Rain, sleet, or snow, you always told me to go
"Go out and play, oh and Pat have a good day,"
You ran, you jumped, you played, all, all for me, all so I could have one last day
A taste of this, a sip of that no matter bad nor good you always told me to give it a whack
You let me walk by your side, and when people came by, you held me high
You always referred to sugar, how sweet tasting it was, how sweet it was to be yours
Like anything sugar loses its taste and dies out
But no, no, not you Granny King, you'll never die out
While sugar is sweet to the mouth,
Your love is sweet to my heart, and that'll never die out
Granny King, you see you taught me one thing: It's called sugar
And that sugar is sweet for one last day with you

Patrick King, Grade 10
St Francis Borgia Regional High School, MO

Nature's Beauties

As I ponder upon all continuation of corporeal souls, I only see the memories from the purifying walls of a genuine society. What are behind these walls I question myself numerous times of every instant known to survival? I have found no answer, so I build castles in the air from my mentality of what I must envision. Ah, how the trees slightly tempt the sky to lower its clouds to a more civilized way of existing. How the many rivers of this globe flow so vigorously without restrictions and how the birds chant through so many aggressive storms. For I undergo at times the most breathtaking sensations when I view the outside ambiance of innocent ways; I observe nothing, but I feel the strong pull of all peace, ways and wonders for an accurate society. For I feel as though the flowers are God's personal signatures of love, the wind; a silent message to all mortal beings, but what is God's communication to us? Is it the hushed wind or the sunlight on zealous days telling us to only run free with authentic passion for upcoming occurrences? Ah, I quote it as nature's elegance and now I located myself in a feverish dream; never wake me up; for the brink of a sinless world is almost here; but only within my mind; what else can I speak?

Scarlett Amburgey, Grade 12
Menifee County High School, KY

Dear Sir, I Miss You

You were my everything.
Without any doubt.
You were the only one I ever thought about.
I never felt like this for anyone else.
But the day you walked out of my life
Was the day that it all came crashing down.

I would have done anything for you.
Anything in this world.
But I guess it was never good enough.
I would have given you the stars and the moon.
The sun in the sky.
I guess my love wasn't good enough.
I guess I wasn't good enough.

I will always love you.
Like no other girl ever could.
I hope that one day you will realize that.
Because if you only knew.
I love you.
I lost you.
I miss you.

Sydney Simmons, Grade 11
Woodrow Wilson High School, WV

The Forsaken Warrior

On a Nightmare he doth ride,
His heart apace with the fiery stride.
On blackened wings his Raven flies,
A messenger hid from prying eyes,
Against midnight clouds, on tearstained skies.

A warrior now for corpses dead,
Where gravestones rest a weary head.
His rotting flesh replaces skin.
Dead men have no friend nor kin.
For the living dead, death can only begin.

A hollow gaze across an empty field,
His sword in hand, more death to wield.
Forever doomed for all his years,
Hearing screams now heard that once were cheers.
For his eternal sins, in living death, he sheds no tears.

Swathed in shadows he walks the moor,
A demon of hell who guards death's door.
A battleground sowed in blood, this place,
By moonlight doth he bare his face,
A warrior living a sinner's death, his infinite disgrace.

Jessica Belvin, Grade 10
Comanche High School, OK

Life

I have big hopes and big dreams
The sky is the limit.
I will not be put into any crooked schemes,
I will just look up and live it.
Every day I hope and I pray
That I will always try my best.
That I won't just be the lifeless frays
On the ends of a ragged vest.
But what you might not know
Is that it's not as easy as it looks.
It takes self-discipline, love, and going with the flow.
By looking into your eyes
I know you secretly despise me
Because of how positive
I can be.
But if you look to the future
And never give up hope
You also will learn how to love
And how to cope.

Valerie Wade, Grade 11
Germantown High School, TN

Like a Grim Reaper

Old Father Time is never on my side,
For evil runs through his unforgiving hands.
He watches over me waiting to chide,
While it drops quickly the last grain of sand.

When Life plays its sweet melodies of glee,
Time flies by sneering victoriously,
But when Life deals a pair of twos to me,
He slows down his pace significantly.

Yet, I'm not the only soul that he bothers.
For, he turns our hair a color of gray,
and makes young boys turn into their fathers.
Like a reaper, he takes away our days.

He is the reason I'm constantly late,
But he holds the key to all of our fates.

Eliza Leatherman, Grade 11
St Mary's Episcopal School, TN

What Is Love…

What is love…
But what you would risk everything for,
Just to experience a moment you hope to never forget;
Trying to live a dream into a memory;
Wishing to never let it fade away,
Risking it all, for a single moment in forever.

But what you suffer from,
When your standing in the pouring rain,
Letting it disguise your tears in the darkness;
Alone with your shattered heart in your hands,
Broken into pieces that seem beyond repair.

Carolyn Evans, Grade 11
Bigelow High School, AR

Florida

The roar of the crowd
The shouts of orange and blue
The people who love success
And hate failure.
They come to "The Swamp"
Where the Gators call home
The town of Gainesville
In the state of Florida.
The team with one hundred men
Prowling for their next win
Led by Urban Meyer
With the greatest desire
To win at any price.
They give their bodies as sacrifice
The gunslinger on the offense
While the opponent's on the defense
And when it's all over
They will be counted as number one.
Beating the Bucks of Ohio
To make their season done.

George Buchert, Grade 10
Rock Bridge Sr High School, MO

Waiting

Waiting for a cure
We sit in the waiting room
I'm so scared and unsure
They say your heart is failing
All I can do is cry
The biggest part is understanding
I just scream why
Now our future is a mystery
Seems as if God needs you in a hurry.
Remember that I always love you
And please don't worry.

Delana Coffelt, Grade 12
Bixby High School, OK

A Dream I Love

If this be a dream,
May it never be broken,
As I treasure each moment,
Every word that is spoken.
If this be a dream,
May it replace all the others.
Leave me sleep all my days,
As we two as lovers.
If this be a dream,
Then send reality away,
Let this night last eternal,
And banish forever the day.
If this be a dream,
It is more than wondrous,
What could honestly be more perfect
Than a dream of the two of us.

Cheyenne Nixon, Grade 10
Chickasha High School, OK

Cowboy America (In Which Our Hero First Finds Himself Lost)

I don't wanna get an infectious disease
And I don't wanna be blown away
I don't wanna get down on my knees
And to a golden idol pray
And I don't want to speak a language foreign to my tongue
And I don't want to send an African child my love
Things are going fine for me in America

Why do the men keep crossing my river?
And plowing my fields of prosper
Why can't I get some sickness to end my fever?
And why is there an Indian accent on my doctor?
I don't want to eat only leafy greens
And I sure as hell don't want to see behind the scenes
Things are fine in my own little world

Did I ever get asked by my old Uncle Sam
If I wanted these things to be done?
Did they think I wouldn't notice the glam
Of a good old American hit-and-run
Thank God for the TV screens and computers
Or I fear I would just get lost in these waters

Maybe things really aren't what they seem?

Zach Kerns, Grade 11
Savannah High School, MO

Best Friends

Sparkly pink and bubbly met sparkly black and somber.
An instant friendship eight years and counting,
Two opposites to complete one another.
She's always available, for even a second.
I'm always there, even in spirit.
We share secrets and thoughts,
Memories and ideas.
She's the sister I never had.
I always know when she's too perky.
She always knows when I'm down.
I read her mind and she reads mine.
Homework and crushes have come and gone,
The friendship remains forever strong.
Soccer practice and cheerleading camp,
We've been apart, but always come back.
I smile when I think of the times she has been there,
Sometimes a hug and a cry,
Always a smile and a laugh.
I know I'm not alone in this world.
I have my best friend, my sister,
And it all started the day sparkly pink and bubbly me sparkly black and somber.

Sammi Smalley, Grade 12
Slater High School, MO

Mornings

Mornings lift my spirit.
This world becomes alive,
Prompting my soul to soar,
Drifting to wuthering heights.

Silver rises from the morning's mist.
Deer prance and squirrels shift.
On my face a smile subtly forms
As I peer upon my Maker's gift.

I make my assent to the top of the hill
And witness His power and see
His diamonds of beauty sprinkling the grass
And His gold on the tops of trees.

Mornings are sentimental reminiscences
Of God's love, faithfulness, and sacrifices He made.
To be witnessed, cherished, and fulfilled,
They promise the grace of a new day.

Erica Robinson, Grade 10
Coffee County Central High School, TN

In Your Eyes

In your eyes
My small friend
is the wisdom of the ages.
You have seen the Egyptians
building the seventh wonder of the world.
You have roamed the plains of Africa
and chased great herds of antelope.
We have changed and evolved
as you have sat by
silent, watchful, and unchanged.
You have shared our triumphs and defeats,
our joys and sorrows.
We have worshipped and persecuted you.
And yet you remain,
Always in the shadows.

Sarah Smith, Grade 10
Shady Spring High School, WV

Sonnet #1

I, as if a mountain, shall pierce the sky
And let warmth of the sun of my being
Heighten my perceptions, third eye seeing.
And it was your love, need not ponder why.
Why interlocking of our hearts shall tie
Like a crimson bow, with lesser needing
Faint, should produce a strength left leading
Through my life until the moment I die.

You, who had raised me to Zenith,
Could not understand nor could calculate
The feeling one has left in me to swell.
So, love me forever, and I'll love us both
For 'tis in the best interest of cold fate
That you lift me all to the tower bell.

Ethan Philbin, Grade 12
Niangua High School, MO

A New Beginning

Packing the boxes was a difficult task.
Looking in my room and remembering the past.
Talking to my best friend and looking in her eyes.
As tears welled up it was hard to say good-bye.
Getting in the car and driving off,
My dad pushes the pedal and I wish he would stop.
But there is no stopping now for it is time for a new beginning.
New friends, new teachers, and a new way of living.
I take a deep breath as we enter our home.
A fear passes over me and I feel so alone.
The days start out slow, but begin to grow.
I begin to meet new people and my heart starts to flow.
But I will always remember the times before.
Before I moved and shut that door.
For this is just a new start, a new chapter in my life.
I pray it goes well and turns out right.
But I won't forget those we left behind.
The pictures and memories are still vivid in my mind.
As far as it seems everything is okay.
This move has taught me a lot and given me strength,
And now I can live my life in a better way.

Athena Padgett, Grade 11
Owasso High School, OK

A Winter Day

It's too cold outside to play today
I wish, inside, I did not have to stay
The streets are slick, my trampoline full of ice
Cats run around like they're chasing invisible mice
Birds are squawking because of the chill
It makes them shiver all the way to their bill
The watery pond is now like a rink
Do I dare go out? I shall, I think!

I put on my coat, then goes on my hat
I step outside and the ground resembles a giant white mat
How I wish that I could do a cartwheel right now
But I know in the end, there would be no bow
It starts to snow and then to sleet
I go back inside to warm up my feet
It really is too cold to go out today
I think by the fire is where I shall stay

My toes are freezing, my hands are numb
I have no feeling left in my thumb
I believe that my body will never warm up
Until my mother brings in a steaming cup

Mmmm, Hot Chocolate!

Elyssa Kaufman, Grade 11
Owasso High School, OK

Only You

Hold your hand out into the sky.
Sing a sad song and ask me why.
Sometimes I hurt you so much,
I know not the reason we fight like this.
But one thing assuring is that you
are the person I can never not miss.
You smile, and I laugh.
You let go, and my smile
Turns to a tear.
Losing you is my greatest fear.
I love you and always will,
So hold your hand out into the sky.
Sing a sad song and ask me why
I cry so many tears at night.
I will reply with a smile
and say because I know that we can be together
until the day I die.

Colin Overby, Grade 11
Crocker High School, MO

Uncle C.B.

I wonder, wonder, and wonder why
I never had the chance to say
Good-bye?
Are you happy wherever you are?
Wherever that may be.
I wonder and wonder too,
Do you still think of me?
Life will never be the same without you here.
I constantly think of the things we used to do
Hunting and fishing you name it, we'd do.
All the memories I have when I think of you.
You were there for me
Through thick and thin.
I never had a chance to say good-bye
At the very end.

Shawn K., Grade 10
Audubon Youth Development Center, KY

The Understanding

Why do you run, why do you hide?
The truth you held deep inside
Would forever make me cry;
Standing alone on this road of mine,
Trying to understand true love takes time.
I thought love was forever
But for everything we had is sunken like treasure.
Deep beneath the earth's surface is
Where my heart will lie hopelessly
And still your picture is the one I hold closest to me.
I once loved with a passion so great
Not anyone or anything could get it to
Separate like chains together we said
Always and forever
Hard to accept you are gone, but for the memories
I hope they live on.

Sean Jones, Grade 12
Weems Academy, TN

Mama in Her Wedding Dress

They lowered Mama into the ground in her wedding dress,
The prettiest thing she owned,
The cleanest thing in her closet,
The only thing not stained with dirt.
She didn't ask for it.
She never mentioned her burial,
But I knew she'd be ashamed
If she were buried in anything else.
She loved that dress.
White, clean.
Untouched, unharmed.
Not bruised,
Like everything else in my mama's life.
She was proud.
That's why it had a plastic covering.
That's why she'd put it on once a year
On her birthday.
She'd sit on the couch and smile,
probably dreaming.
I wanted her to dream in that dress
Forever.

A.J. Heinz, Grade 10
Germantown High School, TN

Tomorrow's Yesterday

The day before last was the hardest yet.
The day when all the children cried
The day when my grandparents shed a tear in their eye
The only day that I can honestly say,
Could make me wish for tomorrow's yesterday.

Tomorrow's yesterday will never come
For it has passed into nothingness.
Nothingness is what I long for, and all I despise.
But nothing gives me hope that I won't have to die.
Tomorrow's yesterday is what I long for.

When I talked to my brother he told me what was true
When I looked for my parents they guided me through.
But when I looked for God He wasn't there
To hold my hand and show the way.
I was alone on tomorrow's yesterday.

When I went to the place I should feel warmth.
I felt a void while others rejoiced.
I thought I lost it all that day
They told me I was wrong, or so they say
I wish it was tomorrow's yesterday
Unfortunately, tomorrow's yesterday has gone away.

Ben Puzan, Grade 11
Owasso High School, OK

Doubt

I'm sorry that I promised to love you forever
I always thought that we would be together
But I never realized, we weren't meant for each other
I never realized how love is supposed to be
I'm sorry that I missed you every day
I'm sorry that I'm hopeless and lonely
I'm sorry that I lived for our memories
I'm sorry that I can't face the truth
Don't you know it hurts without you?
Don't you know what I wish every night?
That I could go back in time
Undo all the mistakes I made
Undo all the sadness in your eyes
And cheer you up every time you cry
I wish for you the best in life
A truly happy life that you deserve
I hope you will forgive me,
Forgiving all the time we've been through.
I hope you will move on,
Moving toward a new life without me.
And I hope we are not wrong about us.

Thao Nguyen, Grade 12
Greenwood High School, KY

Dawn to Dusk

As yellows collide with blues
The sun rises in my eyes
Waves tumble over one another
Causing the foam to glide to music heard by no other

The sun rises in my eyes
Wind bringing my hair to life
And causing the foam to glide to music heard by no other
Making me smile

Wind brings my hair to life
As the world goes to sleep
Making me smile
As I watch the tired sun

As the world goes to sleep
My eyelids begin to flutter
As I watch the tired sun
Say goodbye to the stars

My eyelids begin to flutter
While the stars crash into the sea
And say goodbye to the sun
As yellows collide with blues

Kristin Kopotic, Grade 12
Oak Ridge High School, TN

The Good Life

My good life is better than most,
Taking it for granted is the worst thing I've ever done.
There are some with diseases, some starving, and some dying,
I've finally realized after fifteen years that I have,
The good life.
My good life is better than most,
I got everything I wanted and so much more,
Cell phones, clothes, and place to live and a car.
I was so selfish now I know that I have,
The good life.
My good life is better than most,
I have a family that would do anything for me.
They love me, care about me, and want the best for me,
I guess a better life than what they had is,
The good life.
My good life is better than most,
I'm thankful now that I know it could be so much worse,
I could be pregnant, on drugs, or dead.
This is a thank you for giving me,
The good life.

Tammy Craig, Grade 10
Slater High School, MO

Torn

I am afraid of being alone
but I am more afraid of being loved
all this heartbreak has taught me the only way.

One says she loves me,
yet she is too afraid to be,
not knowing my love could set her free.

One says she loves me,
but we cannot be, for
she is involved with someone who is not me.

They do not realize my feelings;
I keep them locked away.
Because only their love should hear them
someday.

Chris Murphy, Grade 11
Mount View High School, WV

Writer's Block

W aiting for flashes of ideas,
R oaming the deep crevices of my mind as
I find the silence and space as cold as a vacuum.
T he silence is deafening
E re I finally find something
R eally good…until
S omething as heavy as a brick wall comes betwixt it and me.

B ack to searching the nothingness
L est I don't get extra credit to put me
O ver the top of the
C elestial stars. I wait,
K nowing something will come.
(Something…will come…)

Mark Webb, Grade 10
Mount Vernon High School, MO

I Am Water

I have never been a hidden man.
I walk within plain sight
and yet none dare approach me
to find out what's inside
and as it goes unfettered
my thoughts, my hopes, my dreams
I continue moving slowly
as lonely as a stream
and so I find a hidden stream
and join it in its path
and continue moving slowly,
to meet the ocean in its wrath;
The ocean represents the whole
my stream is only one,
and so ends my poem
but my story's just begun.

Ethan King, Grade 11
Northwest High School, MO

Contradiction

Weekend full of conflicts
Arguing and fighting
I'm miserable inside
Suffering and pain
I want to leave, but nowhere to go
I try to avoid this but the result is
Lonely and hopeless
I have to deal with this
Tiring and exhausting
No one to talk to
Crying myself to sleep
Waking up irritated
Angry and annoyed
Stressing myself over something
That can be solved
I'm confused inside
I bury myself in my worry
Try to think about happy thoughts
But my weekend is full of conflicts
Arguing and fighting

Brittany Davis, Grade 10
Capital High School, WV

I Am High for Jesus

Jesus is my savior,
He is the King of all Kings,
He is mighty fine,
He has me on high for Him,
Jesus can take me to Heaven,
He is at the top of the kingdom,
He makes the joy in me,
I will accept Jesus in my life,
Will you accept Him or not,
I am high for Jesus.

Bobby Young, Grade 10
Hilldale High School, OK

Swim

Pulled up by the net that trapped my life
Scarred from the motors that run our lives.
I am a scarred dolphin.
At first glance, you cannot see my wounds on my other side.
My outward beauty deceives until you see my other side.
Once you have seen my secret, my battle marks are all you will notice.
I am a scarred dolphin.
I long to swim free, not afraid of hurting and pain.
Especially when the storms come to capture me,
I swim that much stronger for my injuries cannot hold me back.
I swim to live, no matter what might be out "there."
If I stop swimming and allow myself to feel my hurt…I will drown.
For even when I sleep, I swim.
I rise above the waters I call home to finally breathe.
Then I go back under and swim to live.
Because if I stop and allow my scares to hurt me again
I will drown.
And be a dead, scarred dolphin.

Sarah Shaw, Grade 12
Valley View High School, AR

True Colors

Life's clock is not spared.
There tarnish blows,
Yet after its plague
The shade hesitantly fades.
And daylight dances up on the spring of life once again.

Fragments of thunder ruin this momentary harmony;
It's established, having in hand a spade defies the faith of a sincere heart.
Not of mine, your principles go amiss from my belief.

Should enemies be of us?
In the sense that we're all different makes us the same.
Must I conceal my true complexion?
In this I find blind death comes swiftly.

Jocelynn Ramiah, Grade 11
Germantown High School, TN

All I Can Think Of!

Setting up the tree and decking the halls.
I'm putting on my coat and gloves to go dashing through the snow.
I've been shopping at all the malls,
Buying presents for all the loved ones that I know.

It's wonderful to have family nearby,
I'm definitely not working on business that night.
I can't wait to have a slice of mom's chocolate pie,
While Santa is getting ready for his long winter flight.

As this magical time of year draws near,
I try to show others my love.
Being full of cookies, hot chocolate, and cheer,
Christmas time is all I can think of!

Rachelle Phillips, Grade 10
Chickasha High School, OK

If You Only Knew…

I love the way you look at me,
I love the way you smile.
I love the way you hold my hand through every darkened mile.
I love the days we spend together,
That's all I really want.
Is for you to be with me, for every coming month.
I love the way we never talk,
Especially on the phone.
Just knowing your there is all I need to make the dial tone.
I love you and that's all that matters, please stay with me.
I know I am not perfect, but who wants perfect anyway.
I love the way you understand the way life is supposed to be,
But you don't even have a clue of what you mean to me.
I love the way you take the time to drive so far away,
To see the one that's loved you since it seems the other day.
I love the way you brighten my day with just a simple call,
Just knowing that your there for me is everything and all.

Tiffany Zilkanich, Grade 12
Morgantown High School, WV

Feathered Preps

Deceitful preps with skin like chameleons
no longer interest me.
Nor do mermaids who secretly long
to drag a friend to the fatal depths.

Or those who shed their skins
only to reveal another false covering.

All these I could bribe, buy, or mold
into gilded statues as they loiter
in the garden:
scheming, critiquing, and condemning.

On cold nights you can see them
like snipers in camouflage with fogged breath
stalking their prey for a surprising kill.

I search instead for the victims.
Those who have real scars and stains;
maybe they were inflicted with peacock feathers.
We will never know them as victims.
They are now hushed.

Sarah Sax, Grade 12
Baylor School, TN

Secret

The eyes you see are not your own
but a gaze of hard steel and of cold stone.
The words you speak aren't the words you meant
but speech of evil and of threat.
Your ears seem to hear nothing, only the cruel night.
The terror of silence rages with continuous might.
"This is not me," cried I.
"Oh but it is;" the outer shell has gone.
You can no longer hide.
You, the real you was there all along waiting
in your secret, deep inside.

Joanna Sawyers, Grade 11
Neosho High School, MO

I Am From

I am from the clean apartment upstairs
Tree house clubs
Laundromat Dr. Pepper
And catching minnows.
I am from my dad's knowledge of war
To classical music ringing in my ear.
I am from German bread
To the photographs sitting in the closet.

I am from playing football with the boys
Fighting for the spot on top the swing set
When boys had cooties and my clothes didn't have to match
And cherry bombs, sparkles, and around the worlds.
I am from climbing Mr. Mofits tree
To being home when the street lights come on.
I am from fighting for the Pocahontas Barbie
To belly flops in Grandma's pool.

I am from the North, South, and West
Cold in the morning,
Hot in the afternoon
And a game of cards by night.

I am from tradition.

Emily Boswell, Grade 11
Owasso High School, OK

Shades of Green

I gaze into your eyes,
And what do I see?
Hope and my future
Staring back at me.
It's been so long,
And yet seems a day away
Since your hand first held mine,
And our hearts began to play.
Was it the wild curly brown?
Or the piercing shade of green?
Perhaps it was that amazing smile
That made me realize nothing could come between.
It was the music in your laugh,
The shape of your hands…
The things we talked about,
When we wrote our names in the sand.
I don't know if you realize,
But you've captured my heart.
I will love you forever,
Even if we're worlds apart.
Always and forever.

Taylor Warren, Grade 11
Owasso High School, OK

Sounds of War

The dawn of war rises as fluttering music cascades into a dying valley.
Music that held victory from each opposing side now clash into one another.
Though once — equal thoughts of victory tied them together.
Now only one sheds those thoughts, and bears the crimson color as the call of defeat drums over his land.
The other, not modest, blows out a victorious song boasting their win.
No songs are the same, the tune always different.
Back not turned they depart to tell the news of the valley to their own people.
Both play their songs; even though one holds dread and the other excitement, they are sounded loud — heard for miles.
Defeat or victory, conquered or triumph, these songs each ear knows.
Songs that hold similar sounds from our past.
These are the sounds of war.

Alyssa Jasper, Grade 12
St Francis Borgia Regional High School, MO

Eternal Tears

As life goes on, I am cut by the eyes of deceit.
Bond to a world full of lies and fears.
The people in this world don't care with their double-edged stares that cut you to the bone and
pride so high their noses touch the sky.
But to have too much pride in ones self is vanity.
No vanity you will ever find in me just insecurity.
The sacrifice is hiding in a lie.
If this is true, then I cannot move for I am chained to these shackles of sacrifice.
I replace my happiness with anger and that is a sacrifice.
You are not real a dancing memory whispers in my ear and a silent wind chilled my heart.
Keeping my mouth closed I try so hard to do because of the taste of sweet lies.
I try to dream but end up with nightmares. I see faces of the unforgiving.
But who can decide what they dream and I try anyway.
I feel the weight of negative pressure upon me and fall instead of trying to stand.
I try to remember myself because I often forget my name.
They say fear is the emotional state of the conscience and sub-conscience mind. I say fear is one's self.
Am I the only one who know every thing breaks including the hear and the people who
always smile and never frown eventually break down.
I guess I am because I am the experience and the consequence.
I am the result of broken memories.
A poison of melancholy set within me and with it the flooding impulses of eternal tears.

Jeremy D. Sanders, Grade 11
City University School of Liberal Arts, TN

The Last Day

The warm breeze blowing all around. The taste of apples in my mouth. The sun shining so bright, and birds chirping all around, and on the ground. The smell of wood in the air, and fresh cut grass. The feeling of joy over ran me. Just sitting there in his lap, hearing his laugh. I never knew it would be his last. Though the years have passed, and I have grown, I will never forget the lessons I learned. There's just one problem with this world, It's that there's so much to do, and so little time. So if I was to give you advice, I would say don't take for granted who, or what you have because you never know if it will be their last day on this Earth. So love and cherish, it's what I learned on his last day, on this Earth

Ian Frasier, Grade 10
White County High School, TN

Comrades

Comrades who have fallen, how I mourn you so. For the times we have lost, and the times we have known. Does it seem only yesteryear we met so young, to play in gardens and run in meadows? How I regret all my doubts of you, my friends who are gone. Shall I ever see you again, running through moonlit meadows? Will I ever be able to tell you how much you mean to me? That hope is shattered when I look upon your cold white face!

Mary Widener, Grade 11
Johnson County High School, TN

Winter Wind

I can feel the flakes falling on my soul
Bringing back the day I saw you go
Every fluff with its manipulative coercion
Caressing every inch of my person
Like winter wind
I see you as you pass me by
Without so much as a hello or goodbye
Tears run down inside my mind
So hard to stop, so easy to find
Like winter wind
Cold, icy gusts rap at my heart
The end of which will never start
Blowing through my veins so fast
Making the painful memories last
Like winter wind
Lightning strikes in my mind
Like a thunderstorm of a different kind
Furious white flakes encase my being
So quick to come, reluctantly fleeing
You pain my heart again and again
Like bare skin in Winter Wind

Kathryn Asher, Grade 11
Centralia High School, MO

Forgiving My Madre

I forgive you
For all the nights
We stayed up laughing.
For the long waits
In a house full of brownie smells.
I forgive you.

For the many things
We've done over the years.
For the amazing bond we share.
I forgive you.

For the selfless things
You've done for me.
For the many jokes
And crazy ideas.
I forgive you.

For making that day
When I know I must leave,
That day when I must step out on my own.
I forgive you, mother
For making that day
Almost unbearable to think of.

Kayla Capper, Grade 11
Owasso High School, OK

High School Memories

The fun adventures with friends are almost done.
The ones you look back on in days to come.
We all knew they wouldn't last.
The good ole days in the past.

So, hurry up and have your fun,
The hard part of life is about to come.
So go now and find some ways,
To make great memories of these days.

But hurry now the day is near,
To part our ways but do not fear.
The memories you make will last you long,
As we walk the aisle to our graduation song.

Lynn Chesney, Grade 12
Union County High School, TN

Checkmate

The man leans on the small concrete table,
His tanned arm propping up his weathered face
And a striped shirt draping over his shoulders.
Khaki pants rise above his shoes,
Exposing the high-rise socks.
His gray eyes gaze at the pieces,
Contemplating his master move.
Above his white-haired head,
Birds chirp in the trees,
Dislodging the morning dew from their feathers.
The man grins at the pieces in front of him
And moves his shining white steed onto a black square.
The game is over.
He leans back in his chair
And watches the birds above him.

Brian Worley, Grade 12
Germantown High School, TN

Love

I'm everywhere, I'm nowhere,
Your greatest joy, your deepest despair.
I cause more death than any knife,
Or be that which will save your life.
I'll lead you to bless, or take you to hell,
So it'd be wise to treat me well.

A timeless transcendence of boundary and rule,
Yet something you won't learn in school.
I find my place within just two,
Sought out by all, yet found by few.
Unless you look, I am not seen,
My beauty is clandestine.

Like arrow fire through blood machines,
I've killed many depressed teens.
Without me, you won't be whole.
You need the piece another holds.
To the naked eye, I am nothing.
To the heart, however, I'm everything.

Drew Zoellers, Grade 11
Centralia High School, MO

Influences

The way I talk and the way I walk,
The way I think and what I drink,
Who I am and where I stand,
I am forever influenced.

Those who teach,
And those who lead,
People of good manners,
And those of disgrace.

I choose to follow
And how to conform
When should I lead,
And rather transform?

Chris McBride, Grade 11
Woodrow Wilson High School, WV

My Secret Love

I wake up each morning
With you on my mind
I want to be with you
But I'm running out of time

I dream of you
Morning, noon, and night
I won't give up on you
Not without a fight

If everyone cared
It just wouldn't do
I don't want anyone to care
No one, except you

My secret love for you
Grows slowly over time
Maybe one day soon
You will be mine

Angela Risner, Grade 11
McGehee High School, AR

Yours Truly

You are my haven,
My security,
My underlying sanity…
Neither your denial
Nor your hatred,
Forever I will hold you
Nearest my heart.
I shall not chase you,
I will not obsess over you.
True love waits,
And
So
Will
I.

Stacy Fields, Grade 10
Glenpool High School, OK

16 and invincible

she's 16 and invincible
while wearing her boyfriend's jeans
and randomly dancing to the latest "it" band.

hiding behind her false-smile and her same worn out expression/excuse:
"i'm just a terrible girl and i can't change it."
when in all actuality, she just can't say no
when janice dickinson is twisting her arm, hissing in her ear,
"go ahead, no one really cares, so let's rip 'em a new one."

she's got a flare for the dramatics and has a way
of taking words to heart while waving goodbye
to the only person who ever truly wanted her
and the only person who ever really understood

because everything about her these days is taken out of context;
and everyone seems to be 'against her' — with her regular therapy visits
every other thursday and alternating friday, just to have the same old lies
spoon-fed into her conscience, her character, her person

so that the only real thing left is the skin on her bones,
but even her bones are cracking like the lines of her make-up;
the ten pounds of eyeliner she puts on every morning to keep up her image.
i'm 16 and invincible.

Andrea Pasillas, Grade 11
Bearden High School, TN

Dark to Light

Death, it torments us all
Regardless of race, gender, or age
None can escape its icy breath.
We have sympathy for those who feel its bitterness.
But we do not understand until its full terror chills our own marrow.
We do not know when it will come or who it will come to.
It is despair; it is great fear, and darkness.
But, there is hope again.
The darkness will melt away
To light and warmth of sun.
There is joy after sorrow.
Though there are sad memories,
Look past them, to the joy there was before
Live for that
For happiness
Do not despair, let the wounds heal
Let joy return
Do not forget, remember.
Honor those who are gone.
Do not brood in darkness.
Let light and joy return.

Kourtney Barnes, Grade 10
Ozark High School, MO

The Soaring Soul

With broad envisioment comes vast uncertainty.
Hope comes with ev'ry morn.
Each day brings a new curiosity.
Our joy has been reborn.

When I look at the glory around me,
And the majesty of the mountains so high;
God's creativity indeed surrounds me.
My soul desperately wants to fly!

If I descend to the valley below,
I find a trickling stream.
In the serenity my hope shall grow.
Then I open my eyes and find that it was all a dream.

Joy Newman, Grade 10
Family of Faith Christian School, OK

Look But Don't Touch

The door opens.
The room seems small to our party of five,
but holds the steel bed in the center.
It looks so tiny in the sparse, cold little place.
He looks asleep,
the blanket tucked up to his chin,
eyes closed, his face still that earth-child tan.
I want to say,
"Ha ha, good joke," or "C'mon, wake up so we can go home,"
but nothing is said.
Like an antique,
or something otherworldly,
the rule remains:
Look, see, cry, speak in whispers.
Do not touch.

Alexis McVey, Grade 10
Ozark High School, MO

Prowling Panda

I am a prowling panda.
Laying peacefully by the stream
drinking the cool refreshing water.
Getting up only to play and eat
helping younger pandas when they need it.
Searching for others with problems.
Laying up in a tree hanging on branches.
keeping calm while becoming agitated by annoying bugs.
Staying awake late at night
watching the stars in the sky.
Reflecting on the day's deeds
hoping that I've done some good.
Knowing that it's only gonna do a little good.
Accepting my faults
regretting that I didn't do enough
waiting for the passing day
hoping that it'll all work out.
Wishing for another pandas love
yet I'm almost certain I won't receive it.
I am a prowling panda.

Mitchell Grantham, Grade 10
Valley View High School, AR

How

How does it feel to know that you
Are my one and only
The one I call or run straight to
When I get scared or lonely

How does it feel to be the one
Whom when I'm with have so much fun
The one I think about all day long
The one who couldn't ever be wrong

How does it feel to be able to
Know exactly what to do
To make me laugh and make me smile
Even when I've been mad for a while

How does it feel to be so strong to be so smart
To have such a great big heart

To know that I need you
To know that I love you
To know that to you
I will forever be true

How does it feel to be you

Laci Durasso, Grade 10
Prue High School, OK

Big Voice

He was a big man with a big voice,
that sometimes sounded mean.
A big man with a big voice,
that would do anything.
The voice was deep,
but could also put any baby to sleep.
He made people listen,
almost like he had been sent on some type of mission.
One day the man got sick,
he became weak,
very very quick.
As he got smaller,
his voice got stronger.
It still touched many lives,
telling us all to thrive.
Then something went wrong,
but it made me very strong.
The man had died,
and although I cried,
I realized, that man with a big voice,
he had given everything I needed for my life.

Ashley Witt, Grade 10
Prue High School, OK

C the Way

Two people walking
down a lonely road.
Don't know where they're going
carrying a heavy load.

One is fat, the other slim
introducing each other,
to everyone they meet.
The lights are dim
barely light the street.

They come upon a house
that they can call their own.
It is such a lovely house
exception boring and old.

Now they have three children
two girls and a boy.
That road ain't so lonely
now with all that joy.

Cory Adams, Grade 10
Rock Bridge Sr High School, MO

Dive!

Take a leap
To the new beat
Do-it-afraid

Take a dive
Even times five
Until you do it right

Failure can only survive
As long as you *won't* dive
So be alert.
Be awake
Take initiative
Take flight!

Arianna Grondin, Grade 11
Woodrow Wilson High School, WV

College Jitters

My pathway there is unsure.
The Future looks to me hazy.
My methods and strategies pure,
Bystanders label me crazy.

I cannot seem to concentrate,
The letter comes today.
There's no need to hesitate.
I soon will find my way.

Opening oh so delicately,
Triumph marked upon my face.
Falling tears, releasing my fears.
Here it is true, this future's for you.

Megan Beeler, Grade 12
Union County High School, TN

Broken

We sit anxiously, most of us quite nervous.
Our palms begin to soak in sweat
As we grip our number 2 pencils cautiously.
We all know of the pressure that awaits us.

He places our paper carefully in front of us
As if it was made of a priceless glass.
But I know the actual fragile item.
My academic record will shatter into millions of worthless pieces,
Despite all the hard work through the years

I slowly write my name at the top of the paper
Dreading the questions that sit below.
I glance around me, everyone already at work.
The first question blackens me, as does the second and third.

Deep down I know that I am already broken.
I feel all my hard work just blow up in my face.
As if it never really mattered in the first place.

Tia Robinson, Grade 10
Jeffersontown High School Magnet Career Academy, KY

Be Home Soon

Right now you and I are alone, stuck spending some time apart.
No matter where I go you're the only one with the keys to my heart.
Sometimes we fall and don't feel like trying anymore,
we look back for comfort in the good times before.
Times get hard, trouble just falling asleep,
and I always get up because I'm yours to keep.
When you're home at night just looking up at the moon,
we're worlds apart, but I'm seeing it too.
I'll always love you and I'll be home soon.
Smile often, and keep your head up high.
These things always find us and we don't know why.
We'll make it through; I know it gets old but we have to try,
things get better on the other side.

Christian Pettry, Grade 10
Vicki Douglas School, WV

A Shield, Not Sword

Beware of those who use their religion as a sword,
A weapon against the world
These knights in shining armor come to rescue
But truly under the shining, shimmering steel lies
Hate
Malice
Covering their inner-selves with a fallacious image of gallant knighthood.

Instead look to those who use their religion as a shield,
A protection from the world
Harboring under their steadfast shelter
Love
Peace
Spreading light upon the earth with a glow from within.

Ian Little, Grade 11
Bearden High School, TN

Footprints

The snow is fresh and white
But footprints have been spread
As flakes fall from the trees
Landing on the temporary tread

The blanket of white is diminishing
While the rays shine down upon it
The tread is slowly melting away
We attempt not to forget

Ice from trees melt
And the water falls to the ground
Trying to wash the footprints from the lawn
So they will never be found

The grass is left wet
The final cloths of white are almost gone
Yet the footprints still exist
Imprinted deep in the lawn

The sun is high above
And the skies are blue again
Footprints are permanent
They never become thin

Jacob Welker, Grade 11
North Kansas City High School, MO

Life and Football

Love, hate, sweat, pain, family, enemies,
Not everyone can play this sport.
It's hard getting hit every play.
Is it ever easy to be this elite athlete?
My life is full of steps,
Each one has gotten me higher.
The one constant step is that
Deep breath before the game begins.
I collect my thoughts, gather my strength.
It's in this pause, this moment,
Where I am made or broken.
The mind must be in a crazy altered state.
The body must feel no pain, only heartbeat.
The eyes must see no fear,
But look forward to the next hit.
We play because we're a family.
If one is broken, we are all broken,
And we must rebuild as one.
I'm up off that first step now,
Pumped and ready to crack heads.
It's time to go pound the ball down their throat.

Daniel Leonard, Grade 10
Glenpool High School, OK

Words

What are these words?
That fill my head.
That dance delicately on the tip of my tongue.
What are these words?
The words that bring complete joy and utter sorrow.
That cut through lives, like daggers through flesh.
What are these words?
The words that fly through my head and careen out my mouth.
Words that bring smiles and tears.
How can I possibly understand these words?
These words that taste so sweet on my lips.
These words that spew like fire out of my mouth.
The words that fall, drip, and drool.
The words that prance, skip, and sing.
Words that seem like soothing rain,
And words that seem like nails in my skull.
What are these words?
They are the glory of heaven,
And the fury of hell.
These words that we speak,
Define who we are.

Matt Plodzien, Grade 12
Lutheran High School St Charles County, MO

Mud Fight

I sing of the delight of a good mud fight,
Of mud to my knees, squishy and dark,
Messy warmth and flailing arms.

Mud being flung everywhere,
Through the air into my friends' hair.
(Could this be happening under my mom's stare?)

I'm five and it's pure luck
That the landscaping has been left incomplete.
My friends are here, the mud is here, it's our time.

I even now think of the fun we had on that sunny spring day.
We threw, we dodged, and we got all dirty,
We hosed off, we laughed, and I'm tempted
To do it again.

Alex DuMontier, Grade 10
St Francis Borgia Regional High School, MO

Sit, and Wait, and Wonder How

I know that right now it makes no sense.
But maybe in the long run it'll all unfold
And fill the past that went untold.
It will all be worth it in the end
So until then my struggles I'll send.
Send to the stars and heavens above;
This prayer with wings just like a dove.
There is nothing that I can do now
But sit, and wait, and wonder how.
Would this ever work out?
Could this ever work out?
I guess I'll just sit, and wait, and wonder how.

John Moore, Grade 10
Hollis High School, OK

Beware of the Weeping Angels

The Guardians of the Garden
Angels with covered concrete faces
Who cannot look, nor see, nor move
While living eyes observe.

Then we look away. We close our eyes.
We blink.
When no eye with heartbeat looks,
In stone no longer bound.

Faster than imagination's sight
Angels behind us fly
Hands no longer covering,
No longer granite faces conceal.

Take heed of weeping Angels
Souls encased in marble.
Though seeking solitude in the Garden
You are not alone.

Josephine Edwards, Grade 11
Germantown High School, TN

Happiness

I saw happiness clearly.
She was tall and petite.
She turned and smiled and hugged me.
I saw her pink skin and blue eyes.
And heard her ask a question calmly.
And I felt happy.

Ashlee Martin, Grade 10
Madison Jr & Sr High School, MO

Magician's Dream

Occult spells,
And wishing wells,
With aerial flight,
The magician takes the light.

Going to far away times,
With quick little rhymes,
Creating havoc,
Whilst calling it magic.

The magician wakes,
Not knowing what it takes,
To fix his predicament,
That he had invented.

With a flick of the wrist,
And a slight twist,
He restores time,
By casting a restoring rhyme.

Matthew Wilkinson, Grade 11
Woodrow Wilson High School, WV

What Is Your Destiny?

You're looking for something better than this world,
Better than any drug or cigarette you've smoked.
So you knock on that door that stands in front of you.
That door contains a destiny, but no one answers so you knock once more
The door swings open with a sun-like glow bright enough to burn.
Yet the warmth of the light is like you're wrapped in love not burning a single soul.
So do you enter, would you enter?

A man who sacrificed his life reaches out his hand.
Will you take his hand and go with him?
Will you walk by his side and see what he has to show you?
Or will you walk away and leave it all behind?
Will you spend your whole life wondering what could have been behind that door?
What does your destiny hold?

I look for something more than this world holds.
So I knock on that door that stands in my way.
A man reaches out his hand. Will I enter?

A light shines in me; that bright golden light burns like flames.
I shine that light towards others. Will they follow?
Shall that light shine through them? I hold that man's hand
The nail scarred hand.
I'll get through life without a wonder.

Tesia Johnson, Grade 10
Niangua High School, MO

A Brush with Darkness

Always trapped until sundown,
Awaiting release from my wooden prison,
I crave the precious liquid that flows from the veins of my victims.
That night, I craved you.
Blending with the darkness,
I followed you,
Careful to stay hidden until the time was right,
But alert to your every heartbeat.
Young women should not walk alone.
And on that dark night, with the moon a waning crescent,
I could have drained the blood from your warm body,
But a curious feeling compelled me to abstain.
Your delicate skin shone brightly in the darkness — a beacon
Drawing me closer.
But I turned away, and stalked back into the night.
You'll never know how close to death you came,
I let you live for reasons still unknown to even me.
Maybe the small seed of humanity left in my shriveling soul
Prevented me from harming such a beautiful creature.
Or maybe it was something deeper, which I thought I was incapable of:
Maybe it was Love.

Lauren Hughes, Grade 11
Farragut High School, TN

Cruisin'

Aboard the boat I come at last
Across the sea we go full blast
To the Pacific we are coming near
Despite the sharks I have no fear
Toward the island, away from the noise
With the sea there are many joys
Underneath the deck we stay
I could live here almost every day
During the cruise some people will get sick
At the dolphins the cameras would click
Among the people, children were happy
Through the ocean the captain went snappy
Upon the location that we seek
Exiting the boat so to speak
On the land we stay for a week
Then back to the boat with our antiques
Onto the deck we would come to swim
Behind the clouds the sun was dim
According to the date our trip was about to end
Within my mind I have many stories to tell my friends.

Jordan McMasters, Grade 10
Comanche High School, OK

Ice

He moves so magically across the ice,
His chilly home where other creatures play.
But if you bother him he'll pick a fight,
That's why all other humans stay away.
To catch his food he plunges in the cold,
But has a coat of fur to keep him warm.
The best of all he's been since time of old,
His fortitude can weather any storm.
He braves the snow and blends with it as well,
A marshmallow, yet absent of the flame.
Is his home melting? Only time will tell.
He's captured me since to the Earth I came.
Although he's fierce he doesn't mean to scare:
Who is he? The majestic polar bear.

Bailey Bethell, Grade 11
St Mary's Episcopal School, TN

Undulations

A sea of strangers whispers in earnest,
Soon silenced by the extinguishing light.
Hums greet our souls with shivers in tempests;
As a lone voice rises, our hearts ignite.
Growing louder with the screaming replies,
The sound explodes from others he surrounds.
Thunder in our chests, we close our blind eyes,
Thankful for the life in our souls abounds.
Music is faith that feeds our emotions,
That hears the thoughts of inaudible cries,
Moves me to know these faces and notions,
To know if they feel as entranced as I.
I see them, not again will I know them;
Yet conjoined by sound, we will meet again.

Elise Lasko, Grade 11
St Mary's Episcopal School, TN

The Rain

Walking on empty streets, alone night,
Lifeless surrounds, no one in sight.
Sounds of footsteps, echo around,
Lightning flashing above, a roaring sound.
Raindrops slowly fall, the gray, black sky,
Teardrops fall down, my reddened eyes,
Masking no more, all my pain.

Crying in the rain, no one can see,
Heart ache and throbbing, becomes one with me,
My tears, from my aching heart,
Can I stand it anymore, us apart.
Living these years, my deepest regret,
Our love that grew, never forget,
The amazing memories, fresh in my mind.

Straying in the rain, wrinkled skin,
Letting wash away, pain within.
Tears that fall, swelled eyes,
Drifts the pain away, the pouring sky,
Rain slowly dissolves, finally stops.
Cheer wells my heart, worry dropped,
Thankful to the rain, a newfound hope.

Kayla Durham, Grade 10
Slater High School, MO

Convinced?

You leave me now?
When life is picking up
When we've got plans
And so close to the end
But I know why —
You are crazy if you think you can run.
You deny the truth
Tell me though, if it's not running what is it?
Is it moving on?
Coping with your loss?
No, you know as well as I — you run.

How can I convince you to stay?
I can't
I can see it in your eyes
You've made up your mind
There's nothing else to say
Is there something I can do?
In attempt to convince you
Oh what I would do —
You have no clue how much
I need you.

Rita Jones, Grade 11
Owasso High School, OK

The Night You Died

I thought I knew what it was to miss someone.
I did not really know until you were gone.
The night you died I felt the world stand still.
Your death was quite a shock to me.
But of course I should have known that you were not immortal.
Just last month I was able to kiss your face, but now all I do is stare at memories upon the wall.
Instead of hugging you, I have to clench a lock of your hair in my fist before I go to sleep.
Sometimes I'm unable to rest, and I just weep.
Imagine watching your wife die before your eyes.
The road was wet and the curve was too sharp.
I came as soon as I could.
As our tears fell, I remember you saying everything was all right.
I held you close and just gazed in your eyes.
They looked so afraid, almost as fearful as I.
My life came to an end, the night you died.

Jonny Wilson, Grade 12
White County High School, TN

The Doughnut Connoisseur

I am the world's most well-renowned doughnut connoisseur.
I am praised by censures and feared by bakers for my vehement reviews.
I tentatively perused my next victim's offerings, ready to expunge his hopes.
I grasped two of the olfactory pleasing pastries from the pusillanimous baker.
I juxtaposed the delicacies and the baker's eyes spread wide like Moses' parting of the Red Sea.
I slowly raised the doughnut to my mouth and allowed the glaze to transiently caress my lip.
I was utterly flabbergasted by the delightful sensation presiding in my mouth.
I was now able to savor the heavenly flavor of the gods' ambrosia.
I, for the first time in my career, was not forced to expectorate due to the taste of mediocrity.
I promptly purchased a dozen dozen of these glorious pastries and retired to my office.
I was forced to compose an amiable critique for this obsequious baker.
I wrote with such great honesty that George Washington would be in awe.

Stephen Zambetti, Grade 11
Germantown High School, TN

A Love of Jamaica and Shoes

Struggling with my algebra homework, I watch clouds glide swiftly across the sky.
I wish I was in Jamaica, listening to Bob Marley and living as one.
I miss the smell of the jerk chicken and counting to tree. I miss how they say my name: C-A-R-O-L-I-N-E.
I want to feel the tender touch of Alex, a friend from Ferry.

I enjoy walking my dogs with bare feet hitting the steaming pavement.
But, Ashton finds me crazy because I set foot outside without a pair
of glamorous wedges or a trendy Fendi pump. My shoes numb her mind.
Sometimes it's hard to be friends with a world class shoe designer.
Her dinner dates always include her best friend, Marc Jacobs. But it's fun to try on her funky flats.
Ashton's famous shoes do all the talking for you.
Be careful, her moccasins take the attention off your face.
But I want to show her the love I found in Jamaica. To journey there together on foot.
Someday, Ashton and I will walk to Jamaica.
She will wear her new spectator shoes, or possibly pumps, wedges, or boots, and we'll glide across the ocean.
This is certainly not a poem about hoping and dreaming. It is about knowing that one day we will journey across the world.
But today I'll finish my algebra homework with no more distractions by movements outside my window.
All it takes is a little bit of everything.

Caroline Mescon, Grade 12
Baylor School, TN

That's My Mom

That's my mom,
A woman willing to drop everything,
Just to make sure I am safe and well.
That's my mom,
So caring and compassionate,
She would put any doctor to shame.
That's my mom,
A role model for anyone, willing
To work hard to get what they want.
That's my mom,
Always putting others before herself,
No matter who you are.
That's my mom
A person who will do anything for me,
Even if that means losing a million dollars.
That's my mom,
Making sure I meet all my goals,
This might mean putting hers on hold for awhile.
That's my mom,
A mom who is continuously fun to have around,
Hanging out with her beats any amusement park.

Sarah Gerlt, Grade 12
Slater High School, MO

Overcoming

He could not, though try as he might,
Accomplish the task he'd been expected to do.
The idea was mind-boggling, couldn't be done.
On how to overcome it he hadn't a clue.

Everyone told him, "It's no big deal.
You can do this, you're the man."
When the day came, his friends will admit,
He started to look incredibly wan.

He stood alone, as time ticked on;
A woman approached him, and against his will
His hands began to shake, his brow started to sweat.
He immediately felt tremendously ill.

Then all of a sudden, surprising it may seem,
He felt around him an aura of calm.
His earlier doubts now had vanished;
He had in his mind not a qualm.

He summoned all of his courage and might,
To accomplish the task he'd been expected to do.
He lifted his head, looked into her eyes,
Opened his mouth and said, "I do."

Jonathon Duke, Grade 10
Coffee County Central High School, TN

The One

You are my first and my last,
my future and my past.
My now and forever,
whether we're apart or together.
My shoulder to lean on,
when things go wrong.
The holder of my heart,
that has been there from the start.
The one that wipes away my tears,
and chases away all of my fears.
The one who holds me at night,
and makes everything all right.
The one that says, "I love you,"
and I know that it is true.
The one that without I don't know what I would do.

Samantha King, Grade 12
Rockwood High School, TN

Amor

The world today,
a place of beautiful creations full of life
a place of mystery and unknown.
Love and hatred overflow in the lives of the living.
Wrath, despair, cruelty, and animosity overtake us all
I can make a difference
through the power of love to all creation.
To love someone,
to passionately express affection towards that person
to give your whole heart in return for possibly nothing
just as you have been loved.
To hate is to intensely detest,
but the strength of hatred is weak.
Amor omnia vincit
Love conquers all.
When love is broken,
it hurts far worse than the feeling of hatred.

Caitlin Hanisco, Grade 11
Germantown High School, TN

Never Letting Go

Yesterday shed my darkest tears.
Knowing all was lost and at least forgot.
The clouds darkened for death has just been here.
The unbearable pain controls my every thought.

A new day of battle has begun.
I hate the thoughts you control every day.
All will be lost and nothing won.
Why can't these painful tears all go away?

Today came with my shattered dreams.
Trying to erase the memory of you.
Knowing everything is not what it seems.
How could I bear the pain with nothing left to do?

And I did nothing and that is why you are gone.
The flashbacks of your life will always live on.

Kevin Ward, Grade 12
Covington Catholic High School, KY

There Was a Tree

There was a tree,
What a beautiful tree
Inside this tree, it was so bold
Outside this tree, how it was so cold.
Snow on the ground
Leaves not all around
How the winter days
Comes so fast.
The summer days
Never seem to last.

Brittany Bailey, Grade 11
Woodrow Wilson High School, WV

Moments

Wrong, enticing, and sinful
are just a few words that can describe
what I have just done
Deceitful and excruciating:
why were such things made
to make you feel the way I do?
And once it's done and
over there's no going back,
it takes over you like
a disease vastly spreading
The feeling stays with
you forever
never going away
and no matter how hard you
try the memory is always with you

Amanda Biere, Grade 12
Morgan County RII High School, MO

I Do Not See

I do not see
How sad I'd be
If all were gone
But you and me
I'd hear your tales
Of strength and woe
Without regrets or
Boredom to grow
I love you
And you love me
At least I think
Do you love me?
You say you do
But would you die
If all were gone
But you and I?
For then it'd be only me
And then I'd see
How sad I'd be
If all were gone
But you and me

Emalie Jacobs, Grade 11
Parkway South High School, MO

Just Yesterday

It seems like just yesterday that we were running around the neighborhood,
Leaving John behind to play in the dirt.
It seems like yesterday I was waking up to you watching Sesame Street,
Now I wake up and you are not there.
It seems like yesterday we were playing hide and seek, like brothers and sisters do,
Now I seek, but I don't find you.
It seems like yesterday I was asking mom when "my boy" will be home from school,
Mom's reassuring answer would always be "Soon, Sweetie!"
Now when I ask her when George will be home from college,
Her unsure reply is "Maybe in a few weeks."
We all come to realize in some part of our lives that we grow up too fast,
And all of our childhood times become nothing but wonderful memories
That will forever last.

Jessica Koch, Grade 10
St Francis Borgia Regional High School, MO

Fallen

Ever since I've been with you every day's sky seems ocean blue.
It's almost like I finally flew out of the cage that's held me,
And now I'm here with you.

I now see things in a light I could only dream about before,
And every day I smile when I see you walk in the door,
The look you have in your angelic eyes,
Captivates me and takes me by surprise.

How do you make me feel like perfection with just a smile or glance,
It's as though our eyes speak for us in a long and happy dance,
My knees go weak and I can't hold my stance
When I see you, all I want is your embrace,
Now all I can say is:
"I love you and please don't leave me or let me go,
for I have fallen for you."

Anne Kelly, Grade 11
Woodrow Wilson High School, WV

Rain

I hear the rain, it's falling down, it's tapping on the ground.
I fear the rain that's falling down, that's tapping on the ground.
That rain, that rain, that noisy rain, quit tapping on the ground.
That rain, that rain, it is the same, still tapping on the ground.
Rain, please, quit tapping on the ground.

Rain, the rain, I can feel a disaster as the rain goes faster, still tapping on the ground.
What is that noise? Is it the rain, or is it the sound of a distant train?
Yes, indeed it is a train. Get off the track! Where's your brain?
Oh my gosh, this is insane!
Rain, please, quit tapping on the ground!

Rain, the rain, it's falling down as they lay him in the ground.
With family near, they now all fear the rain that's tapping on the ground.
He's now in the ground, heaven bound, and the rain is still tapping on the ground.
That rain, that rain, that noisy rain, quit tapping on the ground.
Rain, please, quit tapping on the ground.

Tina Hutchison, Grade 11
Anderson County High School, TN

What Passed Between Jon Donne's Desperate Boy and Unimpressed Girl

That humble, lowly creature called the flea
That sits upon the hand that I do claim
Holds within, the blood of you; the blood of me
A union seen as pure; not sin nor shame.

Pray, do not persist. The flea shall die!
With it the cause for which you vainly strive
Its death is not murder nor suicide
For now the flea is dead but we alive.

Fell thief of life! Murderess of my conceit!
No more the chance that by your side I'll sleep.
You smile and turn, humoured with my defeat
Yet well I know that you in time shall weep.

When you are alone and then your folly see,
Remember, it was you that squished my flea!

Mary Lana Rice, Grade 11
St Mary's Episcopal School, TN

Cicada

We are under the ground for seven years.
Dark and damp, silent and soggy,
Just waiting for that moment of glory.

It's almost seven years,
The soil sucks up my tears.
The bright outer world is there,
Sun is shining and the air is clear.

Here I am! The world of free!
I cry out loud upon the tree.
Ladies, ladies, come around me!
I'm looking for the love that completes me!

I only have a week, I sound like a geek.
But I didn't wait for seven years,
Just for a chick.
I waited to find my tiny little love.

Yuya Kudo, Grade 11
Woodrow Wilson High School, WV

Contradiction

I love ketchup, yes I do
But I hate tomatoes, how 'bout you?
I tell people not to fight,
But I can get into an argument at any time of night.
I say, don't cuss, just don't it,
But I'm behind them throwing a fit.
Getting A's are a lot of fun,
But studying for them makes me feel dumb.
My best friends are the ones that keep me sane,
But we still always end up playing in the rain!
Contradictions are no fun,
I think I'd rather write a pun.

Andrea Perrow, Grade 10
Capital High School, WV

I Am

I am from preschool to high school
From tucking in at night to staying up past midnight
From apple juice to Jamba Juice
I am from Oshkosh to American Eagle
From Barbies to coach purses
From a little girl to a young women
From dress-up to make-up
I am from Little Mermaid to Aquamarine
From soccer to colorguard
From play phones to cell phones
From training wheels to a learner's permit
I am from You are my Sunshine to You're Beautiful
From Jesus Loves Me to My Savior My God
From rainbows to Xtreme
From not worrying about the future,
To wondering what I am going to do with my life
From a life that was carefree and fun,
To not having enough time do get stuff done
I start each day when I pray to God,
Help me each day with the decisions I make
And take care of me for the rest of my days.

Sarah Berry, Grade 11
Owasso High School, OK

The Crisis

ROAR! — the alarm clock startles me.
I smack the beast into submission.
Stop its howls.
The crisis looms close.

Homework mocks me,
Lying discarded on the floor.
The Calculus Creature will soon demand that bounty.
The crisis looms close.

The cover's sighs soothe me.
Fair nymphs, they clutch me and say,
"Brave knight, you need no adventure today."
The crisis looms close.

The howling banshee comes closer.
My mom peeks her head through the door.
I brace myself.
The crisis looms close.

"Why aren't you up yet?"
The worst five syllables ever invented.
I face the crisis head on.
I must get out of bed.

Andy Noelker, Grade 12
St Francis Borgia Regional High School, MO

She Calls Herself Love

Lust's alluring eyes seduce.
Her superficial beauty promises
what she cannot give.
She flirts with the unsuspecting,
wooing them into her trap.
Lust offers herself
to all who pass by,
but she is an
insufficient drug.
She deceives
and taints hearts with darkness.
She calls herself Love,
but do not be fooled.
Do not buy
Lust's lies
when
Love's truth
is given freely.

Shelby Weir, Grade 10
Nixa High School, MO

Love

In these past few months
I've fallen in love
I picture myself
In a dress as white as a dove

You're the one
I care about you
I say I love you
And you know it's true

When we're together
No one can pull us apart
You're everything to me
And now you have my heart

Kayla Masters, Grade 11
Portageville High School, MO

Wanderer

I am a wanderer:
I belong to no place,
my mind, it is ageless,
my blood without race;
the fallen St. Christopher
rises to guide me,
tho' his Catechisms
could never confine me;
I travel alone to
any place, when it calls,
but I grow no roots
and cannot be thrall'd.
The reigns of the world,
they worry me not:
for I am a wanderer,
soon to be forgot.

Lindsay Scaccia, Grade 12
Martinsburg Sr High School, WV

Can't Let You Go

I may not get to be with you as much as I like,
I may not get to hold your body all through the night,
But deep down in my heart I honestly know,
You are the one I love and I cannot let you go.

Roger Winneberger, Grade 10
Greene County Technical High School, AR

The Feeling of Defeat

I lie awake and wonder why,
after being defeated I want to cry.
I was the one who played the game,
but why do I always seem to come up lame?
All of our hard work should be paying off.
However I can't explain why we play so soft.
We're not soft girls, and by no means wimps.
We move up the court faster than the Goodyear Blimp.
Some come out flat and lost at times,
which leads the crowd to lose its chime.
Three out of five always on the same page,
making the coach unleash his rage.
Losing the first half, heads beginning to hang low,
but the second half is near, and time for "our" show.
Confirming plays in the locker room huddle.
We're ready to fight, there's no time to cuddle.
Back on the court, fire in our eyes,
playing together, our heart yearning for the prize.
Trying to dig ourselves out of this hole.
If we really want this game we must play from our soul.
Everyone knows they want to beat it...that's how I felt, going home defeated.

Rachel Gonzalez, Grade 11
Slater High School, MO

The Heart of Dancer

Do you know the feeling of a dancer?
As you slip on the costume and take a new identity
Feeling the red-hot adrenaline rush through your body
The butterflies and fireworks take over when you step into the curtain
The announcement of your name that makes you shiver
You walk into the bright lights with fear
Imagining the crowd in their underwear to lighten you up
You stand like a wax model until the music starts
Then you move your body to show them what you're made of
Losing that feeling, and becoming free
You start to build confidence and self-esteem
You flash a witty wink to the judge staring at you
Your solo is coming up, you stand there and pray
You begin to feel an outer body experience
You land your triple and flash a white smile
You kick it up a notch knowing it's the end
Your team becomes one dancer as you feel their vibe
Performing the last 5 seconds like it's your last
You strike your pose knowing you gave it your all
As you run off stage you tell yourself:
Dancing is the ability to showcase a talent like a picture in a museum

Paige Pregler, Grade 11
Owasso High School, OK

The Last Game

We go into this game with out a single win.
We could go on to the field and not try at all,
or we could end the season with a fight.
We want to win this game for the seniors
because for some of them this is their final game.
We are the first to get on the score board.
We know we can't let down
or they will answer right back.
We get the ball again because of their mistake.
Now it is time for us to score again.
Half the game went by in a flash.
We're still on top and can't let down.
The second half has just begun.
They answer with a score.
From here in out the game is almost even.
They get the ball and finally score.
And they take the lead from us.
There's not much time left on the clock.
None of us have a doubt in our mind.
We get the ball and then we score.
I looked at the clock and watched it hit 0.

Cody Skinner, Grade 10
Slater High School, MO

What Means the Most

Will you do
What means the most to you?
Or will you
Follow the ones in front too?

You walk past
What you care about most
Just to see
You're another host.

Will you see this too?
Is it all coming back to you?
Many are sucked into the trap,
Once in, there's no turning back.

Think about your decisions,
How you face the truth, don't end up in prison
Where the light is never again.
Keep your real friends.

Don't get sucked in, make the good decision.
To do what means the most to you
The decision flowing through your head.
Like the cool side of your pillow at home on your bed.

Jermie Pittman, Grade 10
Slater High School, MO

Nimbus

I leap from the roof
White wings folded now open
An angel in flight
Perhaps a dream or even a fairy tale
Gliding beneath this sacred realm of destiny
A powerful elegance
A ribbon of beauty
More gorgeous than anything
The mind has yet or ever will imagine
With an aerial view of an intricate kingdom
Transcending moments flow over the moon
A clear lifting passion in a silver-blue sky
A place set apart with smooth silky motions
Pale white feathers floating silently down
To the water's glassy surface
Breathless rapture
A dream that fled into the night

Cassidy Comerford, Grade 11
McMinn County High School, TN

Davy Jones' Locker

It is not like they described it.

There is no "Pearly Gate."
No golden streets,
No angels,
No one.

There is no "Flaming Pit."
No burning brimstone,
No demons,
No one.

There is nothing…

Nothing but the eternal grip of Davy Jones,
Clenching my soul with an everlasting grip.
I will forever roam this desolate wasteland,
Known as Davy Jones' Locker.

Tyler Berretta, Grade 11
Germantown High School, TN

Dangerous Shadows

Swift and sure, strong and steady
Danger lurks within the shadows
Stirring, resting, watching, waiting
Danger lurks within the shadows
Camouflaged cats hide in wait
Ready to spring to bring down prey
Silent as night and as bright as the sun
Hiding in wait for prey to come along
Beautiful Death is all it knows
For the last most see before they fade
Is the gleam of the golden eyes
Set in that fiery-stripped face
No longer living
Caught in the shadow's embrace

Ambriel Mickles, Grade 10
Mills University Studies High School, AR

You're Everything

You're the light in my soul,
the beating of my heart.
Though we're so far away,
may we never part.

You're the one that makes me
feel mighty and tall.
You're the angel that catches me
when I start to fall.

You're the song that I sing,
and the breath that I take.
You're the reason why I make
every move I make.

You're the morning sun
and the evening star.
Every night I dream
that I could be where you are.

So even though we may feel
too far gone,
I promise to love you forever
from now on.

Sarah Ward, Grade 12
Hollis High School, OK

My Big Brother

We yell and fight
We feud and we gripe
We laugh and we share
We go everywhere
You're always there for me
Whatever it may be
I'm always here for you
Whatever you need me to do
We joke around
We're both really loud
We play football in the house
You'll soon have a spouse
I want to hate you at times
But you're always by my side
I love you the next
That I'll never regret
We have each others' backs
On weekends we just relax
You can make me so mad
And I can make you feel bad
But I love you all the same

Alexsis Nicole Griffith, Grade 10
Slater High School, MO

The Future

Into my junior year,
I leave my old self behind.
My future is clear,
And so is my mind.
Toward college I will steer.

I fall to dismay,
For what shall I study?
As of now, I cannot say.
My future is muddy,
Yet I will not stray.

Just as a train
I will keep to my tracks.
My work will not be in vain
For I shall not slack,
And my goals, I will obtain.

Once college is complete
I have not a clue.
On my own two feet
The world will seem new.
My future is not so concrete.

Paul Bradley Slay, Grade 11
Bearden High School, TN

Connection

Ribbons tied to everything
Bad days
Ripples in the form of people
Stay still
Fraying ends
Undone
Worse days
Wet ribbons
Red used to be blue
Stains the people
The ripples
Rope burns
Lung burns
Stomach pains
Frayed ends
Tongues removed
Ears turned inward
Burdens to nature
Clear water
Ripples
Brown water
Rotting ribbons tangled in everything

Olivia Golden, Grade 11
McGehee High School, AR

Problems

On old comfortable bed
Sleeping silently sideways
Looking as though I'm dead.

Dreaming of the day
My dad left my mom
And I remember hearing him say
It's not your fault I'm leaving
It's my own in every way
He then said, "Seeing is believing."

I didn't quite understand
Until he turned around
And showed me what was in his hand.
It was a picture of his new wife.
She was horrendous in every way
He said he wanted to start a new life.

With her close by his side
I never will understand
But my mom has always cried
And now I finally realize
We never really needed him
And I will never apologize.

Khris Todd, Grade 11
Slater High School, MO

A Day to Come

Winds are blowing
Trees are waving
Leaves begin to fall

Hearts are pounding
Tears are falling
Things aren't set in stone

A question was asked
An answer is awaiting
While tears continue to fall

The question is answered
A day is set
When we'll walk down the aisle

Hearts start pounding
We start walking
To a new life of living just begun

It's all over now
Happy days begin
Future life now is in our hands.

Sarah Rose, Grade 12
Union County High School, TN

The Lake

As our car pulled up to the newly bought land,
There was no one around.
The only sound I heard,
Was the chirping of a flock of birds.

The area was surrounded by trees,
Like being engulfed by a pile of leaves.
The house would be set back,
Nothing much, just a simple shack.

But it would be our domain,
The place we would go for a weekend
Full of rain.
The untouched land was full of light,
Ready to be turned into a wonderful sight.

Patience, creativeness, and money were the keys,
These things would have to be perfected by my family and me.
It would bring our family together,
That's all I wanted, for us to be better.

Eric Pettyjohn, Grade 11
Woodrow Wilson High School, WV

Our Separate Ways

I'm so strung out now
I don't know what this is I am going through
I have a pain rooted deep in my heart
And no one put it there but you.
Tell me what I have done
To make you treat me this way
You break my heart and cheat on me
And you think I'm going to stay!?
Have you lost your mind?
Apparently so!
You can get on your knees and beg
But I'm still going to go.
Do you love me?
Do you even care?
Do you ever think of me?
Now that I am not there.
I still love you
But I just can't stay
I hope you have a wonderful life without me
Because we have to go our separate ways

Cianii Hansburg, Grade 11
McGehee High School, AR

Homework

The bell rings and you are out of there
The bus is what is keeping you from the weekend
finally you arrive at your house and jump on the couch
you hit the remote and your favorite show's on
but that teacher you hate gives you a book load
so you ask yourself what to do "yes or no to do or not to do"
you finally say
SCREW IT THIS IS MY WEEKEND I'LL DO IT TOMORROW

Benton Morris, Grade 10
Capital High School, WV

Chances

With all the chances we constantly earn
Why do we continue to let them burn?
Why don't we ever learn from our mistakes?
We only regret and our minds don't wake
Always thinking what we could've done
So many chances, we screw up every one.

Never learning
Always yearning
We're not earning
But we're burning
All the chances we ever get.

Of all the lessons we learn, just why
Do we always treat our mistakes like lies?
Why don't we every learn our lessons?
How come we have all of these confessions?
How come we never think of what to do?
Chances are rare, and we only get a few.

There's no lessons
Just confessions
We're not guessin' we're just messin'
We're just messing up the chances that we always get.

David Rosenblum, Grade 12
Concord Academy, TN

Confession

I have a confession, that I want you to know,
It's burning a hole, deep down in my soul.
It's like the blood that runs through the veins in my arms,
It's like the passionate bridge and the words of a song.
It consumes my thoughts ALL the time,
It's the prime feature that controls my mind.
I lay my body down to sleep,
And it filters my breath so, so deep.
I run outside to free my heart,
But this image and my brain will never part.
I try to cry and wash it out,
But all that comes out is a simple pout.
I reach out, as strong as I can,
My thoughts try to breeze like the air from a fan.
I try to go back to before this was now,
And come to the sad conclusion that there's no way how.
It's not me, It's the life I live,
And the world I am — my life's not willing to give.
I have control of nothing at this time
Yet what controls me is all of mine.
In the present I'm ok, and in the future…I guess I'll be fine.

Gabrielle Howell, Grade 12
Lincoln College Prep School, MO

Breathe in, Breathe Out

Higher senses
A complete understanding,
The wonderful feeling of
Fulfillment.
Things go slowly,
Everything suddenly beautiful.
I sit in silent contemplation.
Breathe in, Breathe out.

The sun shines,
The birds chirp.
Warm summer air caresses
My aged skin.
I never noticed the beauty,
Of such ordinary things.
My life was blessed,
I thank God every day.
Higher senses,
Complete understanding.
Breathe in, Breathe out.

Dominic McCarthy, Grade 12
Newcastle High School, OK

In the Darkness

In the dark we stand,
Waiting to be lead by hand.
Most just don't understand,
The reason behind this madness.
As we are soon to realize,
That we hear the others scream.
And where others have failed,
We are sure to succeed.

Ethan Thomas, Grade 10
Capital High School, WV

In the Woods

In the deep, silent woods
the only sounds I hear,
are those of the birds,
squirrel, and deer.

Their sounds are peaceful,
calm and warm,
as they stroll about
without alarm.

In this serene abode, I
would linger still,
but reality calls me back
against my will.

So I return reluctantly,
back into my world,
never to forget the moments
I stood in the deep, silent woods.

Timothy Plunkett, Grade 11
McGehee High School, AR

Breathless

The crowd only occupied the edges of their seats,
As they interpreted the performance, hearts skipping occasional beats,
The entertainer was vulnerable, yet her intent was clearly brave,
Her body was overtaken by a beautifully innocent wave,
The movements were all connected, like the journey of a fish,
Her ability to relate to the audience is an undisputed gift.

Caitie Moses, Grade 11
Newcastle High School, OK

We Can Change the World

We can change the world and create a new environment
Every day in the hood you hear nothing but sirens
We can change the world to a better place
Where the young children can roam and play
We can change the world by creating a vaccine to get rid of STDs
We can change the world by cleaning the air so we can have better breath
We can change the world by helping young people better understand the basics of life
Cause everything now is just not right
We can change the world for struggling and single mothers
We can change the world by understanding one another
We can change the world and pray to the one above
Everyone now needs to show more love
We can change the world by speaking on what we have to say
If you don't speak now, everything is going to be the same way
We can change the world by having a change of heart
Instead of tearing each other apart
We can change the world for the people over in Africa
What they are going through, you won't believe is happening
We can change the world and let the youth speak the truth
How the world is now, we children are the future

Lativia Jackson, Grade 12
Stratford Comp High School, TN

The Hardest Thing to Let Go Of

The hardest thing to let go of is my hatred.
From the inside,
It eats away at my heart.
At night, I stay awake
Crying because my hatred hurts me so,
But I can never let it go.
For if I were to let it go,
That would mean that I forgive him.
And if I forgive him,
Then that might mean that I actually love him.
But how can I love someone who was never there for me.
How can I pretend that everything's all right when he speaks to me.
For now,
I can only glare and curse at him
For the awful hatred he sowed in me.
I hate him!
I hate his laughter, because he laughs at me.
I hate his face, because they say we have the same.
I hate his blood, because it runs through my veins.
I hate that he is my father.

Lee Anne Williams, Grade 10
Powell High School, TN

Winter Morning

Once I step out,
the world greets me.
In the form of dried leaves crunching beneath my feet,
so my sneakers embrace the melody.
I wake to the world as the chill bites my cheeks,
reddening the sensitive skin there,
and the nipping wind embraces my form,
as an old friend, greeting after a separation.
There's things I'd rather not do today,
but that does not matter.
The air is cold, as it never is,
and I am happy because it reminds me of home.
Dew is frozen, as is the quiet earth.
And my hands are mine outdoors,
they are more agile,
feeling spreads throughout my fingers in the weather.
What is it?
Why do winter days kindle my spirit,
— teasing my extremities,
tingling my senses —
and excite my soul?

Ashley Hicks, Grade 11
Germantown High School, TN

There Is a Reality

Overprotected are we teens,
Still we fight to break free,
Supposed to believe what they tell us,
But all is not as it seems.

The adults see us as children,
We see ourselves as what we are,
Overprotected, over isolated,
And yet we know more.

We've seen more than you know,
We understand more than you'd guess,
More we are destroyed,
Through our feelings you suppress.

You cover our eyes to hide the real world,
But through your fingers, we can see,
All we see is the bad things you mention,
And we miss out on Earth's true beauty.

We know there is a reality,
More beyond these terrible things,
And no more will we turn to bad sources,
When, finally, you set us free.

Victoria Johnson, Grade 10
Cole County R-1 High School, MO

Let Loose

Today is not yesterday,
tomorrow never last forever
bringing up the past
make my life a competition.
You talk down on me because
you say I don't belong
in an environment where
dreams can be destroyed by
the chick standing beside you…
…smiling like a million dollars was inherited
Not worth the stress put into a jail cell
and bonds sky high, tears rolling down my mothers
face…so glad her only son wasn't killed by the
gunshots of some man…
of course his skin honey and darker.
relieved of pain just letting loose
like a clown dancers krumping,
just bananas when expressing what you feel
by flowing a free breeze of cries
Smiles and steam for the sunrise…
Never disappointing the thought…to let loose!

Deanne Applewhite, Grade 11
Little Rock Central High School, AR

Mom

She wakes me up early every morning,
She hugs me goodbye,
She will sometimes yell at me without any warning,
But she always comforts me when I cry,
She is my mother and my friend,
And I will love her until the day I die.

She tells me stories of how her childhood used to be,
And she paints my toes,
She teaches me about life so one day I will see,
How much a mother really knows,
My mom is a great friend, mother, and wife,
And her love for me truly shows.

Sarah Snelson, Grade 11
Anderson County High School, TN

Music Man

I'm so glad that you could be here with me,
To take the time to look at all the scenery,
I don't know in ten years where my life will be,
But I hope that yours could keep you right here with me.

I play in bars, and smoke cigars with friends I know,
Gotta sing just to pay the debts I owe,
I don't know where I will be tomorrow,
But I know I gotta make this guitar cry.

And when I'm old and I have taken to my bed,
I'll still have the guitar playing in my head,
And I hope that you don't think that I will dread,
The moment when my time has come and I'll be dead.

Kyle Berry, Grade 10
South Intermediate High School, OK

What a Friend We Have in Mildred

She was just lying there as if she were asleep.
Everything seemed at rest, and all the philanthropy was ultimately embodied.
Elderly friends and family assembled in the funeral house
In the town of Quitman, Mississippi to pay homage to a friend of everyone.
I heard my grandfather speak of times spent with Mildred, his wonderful sister.
To the right, memories poured out of an idle TV, and beautiful music played.
As the family was left alone to pray, I knew Aunt Mildred was watching us and that she could hear us praying.
Then the family slowly filed into the chapel which was already filled with mourners waiting for the service to begin.
A tall, slim figure broke through the veil of silence, and the slow, mellow sound of the organ began.
He sang "What a Friend We Have in Jesus."
After my Aunt Mari Ann had dispelled her tears, we all traversed to the cemetery.
Aunt Mildred was laid to rest under a plaque that said, "John Gay, Mildred Gay, married 63 years."

Rudy Saliba, Grade 11
Germantown High School, TN

Puddles

The bustling people pushed and passed each other,
Desperately staggering to save themselves from the hushed pitter-patter of rain.
Some shrink and shiver and even shriek from the surprise sting of the shower.
They cover their heads, duck under roofs, and hide under their hoods,
While others go about with their day as they would any other, unlike those who cower.
They quickly become chilly and drenched and even smelly from the rap of the rain.
The drenched grumble and mumble as they bustle, listening to the rumble of the stormy shower.
The dry cling to each other and watch and wait like rain drops cling to window panes,
As the storm passes under the safety of their covers,
The pitter-patter of rain fades while their final farewells are cast
To the ones left behind in the form of murky puddles,
Soon to be avoided and jumped in and even stepped in by
The bustling people who push and pass each other.

Julia Qualkinbush, Grade 10
Coffee County Central High School, TN

Cold October Night

A man, snow white hair, cut short to his scalp. His hands so smooth, but callused from work. His face wrinkled, soft warm cheeks stubbled with unshaved facial hair.

Grandpa! we called him. Though he was soft, sweet, and warm. Don't let that fool you. He was tougher than nails. Through hard times, painful and sorrow. He stood strong like a mountain, a stone. He was in the hospital almost every day, but somehow he always found a way to break through the pain.

Something in his chest, to keep his heart beating. But one cold October night, it was too much for him to handle. Something had made that mountain crumble.

My brother, a soldier, as is every man in my family. He got on a plane, coming here from Washington D.C.

One block away, we got a call. I love you Grandpa. We got there, I went to his bedside, held his hand, and kissed his cold cheek, still faintly warm to the touch.

I left him a note and left him in the hands of God. A tear rolled down my cheek as I walked away.

He lay there, cold still. All my life I never thought it would happen. Like an avalanche, very sudden and unexpected. The mountain was supposed to stand forever, but it was God's will to take him away and bring him home.

In no more pain. I know it's right, but I will never forget that Cold October Night.

Jessica Reather, Grade 10
South Intermediate High School, OK

Momentum

G oing, going, going
A gainst the obvious
I nterferences present in today's utopian society.
N egligence consuming the world,
I gnorance peeking; an all-time high.
N arcotic emotions blaring, yet he keeps on
G oing, going, going…

M omentum building, building, building
O paque walls built by
M illions of peers trying to tear him down,
E xcept he is shielded by the momentum
N ow building, mounting, blossoming.
T he destination of a mature crowd seems —
U nfortunately for them, he is still going strong;
M omentum building, building, building…

Andrew Bowling, Grade 11
Bearden High School, TN

Love

Love is something that will never go away.
It will still be here, day by day.
Young or old, no matter what the age
There will always be that love for a person
that will never fade away.

It all started in Pre-school one day,
I said to him, "Hey what is your name?"
And he acknowledged me with just a wave.
I felt so special, nothing to me was ever the same.

There are many years that have gone by so fast,
But all I can think about is my blast from the past.
As I said before, love will never go away
It will always be in your heart to stay.

Katie Wilkerson, Grade 11
McGehee High School, AR

Coming into the Real World

Coming into the real world,
I feel alone.
Scared because it's going to be,
a long time before I go home.

Coming into the real world,
I could never imagine.
Would I be home or locked up,
with inmates watching Christmas pass by me.

Coming into the real world is unfair.
Sometimes you lose all your friends,
and go broke with no one to care.

Coming into the real world,
I will succeed, no matter what happens.
God and my family will love and take care of me.

Demekus T., Grade 11
Audubon Youth Development Center, KY

Change*

I was a bad and evil person
I remember stealing from corner stores
I heard the sirens behind me
I saw the cops telling to me to halt
I worried I was never going to see my mom again
I thought I was going to be in jail forever
But, I want to change
I am a new man
I think I can influence other people
I need to be a role model
I try so hard to be looked up to
I feel people won't forgive me for my past
I forgive myself and that's what matters
Now I can change
I will be a positive image
I choose not to be negative
I dream of a perfectly normal life
I hope people will change with me
I predict that they will and move on
I know that I'm a better person
I have changed

DeQuan Smith, Grade 10
Capital High School, WV
**Based on "Freedom Writers"*

Light Against Dark

He takes a stand, sword in hand,
And marches to the field.

The darkness rises, in all shapes and sizes,
But to that he'll never yield.

As he nears, the darkness sneers,
The battle shall soon begin.

Justice and kindness, chaos and madness,
Who knows just who will win?

Days and weeks go by, months and years fly,
Neither brought down to their knees.

He stands and is shocked, their weapons still locked,
And now he finally sees.

He follows his morals, but against darkness immortal,
No one will ever win.

But he will stay, not run away,
For he shall never give in.

Nathan White, Grade 10
South Intermediate High School, OK

Superman

He is the superman
Because I know he can,
And if you need some help
He will lend a hand.

When you need out
And you can't find a way,
Just shout his name,
And he'll save the day.

He died on the cross
To pay the cost,
So the souls of man
would not be lost.

He is the superman —
The saviour of man
Cause he's the son of God
And the son of man.

To get that help,
Here's some advice.
His real name is
Jesus Christ.

Wade Hampton Myles, Grade 10
Hamburg High School, AR

The Gray Hatter

If Good was Bad,
And bad was good,
Would the world be
All as it should?

Would thieves be Kings,
And killers are Ace?
With this corruption
Towards the end would we race?

Would mercy exist
In a lone man's heart?
To spare a woman
And from her depart.

That man would die,
For a cause so true.
To break a law,
Doing good to you.

The world is gray,
Some good, some bad.
The world is gray,
And we're all just mad.

Spencer J. Barrett, Grade 11
Grove High School, OK

Taking Flight

Oh, how I long to be an Eagle soaring high above the clouds,
To beat with gentle rhythm the songs of my wings,
To glide with such grace across the sky,
To break free from this world,
To spread my wings and fly.

Elizabeth Wolf, Grade 12
Sevier County High School, TN

Last Thoughts on Jack Kerouac

I think of Jack Keroauc on such nights
When I feel the need to pack up and leave
When I certainly feel the weight of the world beneath my burdened skin

When I wake up lonely — missing the American night
And all of its devious creatures

Of course I think of Dean Morarity out ON THE ROAD
And all of your burdens,
Wash them away in a bottle of scotch

I think of hitch hiking on a cold night,
Recounting the Buddhist way
High on some desolate peak

If you were here Jack Kerouac,
I wonder where you'd be?
You see I can't dig 47,
I wanna be 83
But I've got this funny feeling that you're somewhere here with me.

Molly Haines, Grade 12
Franklin County High School, KY

That Day

I had a feeling all day,
That something bad was going to happen.
You were as happy as you could be that day
I figured something was wrong because I never saw you that happy
Later on that day, laying in your bed
You called our names for help
You said it was hard for you to breathe
We asked if you wanted us to call for help
You said "no I'd be okay"
Then seconds after that
You weren't with us anymore
Tears started to fall from my eyes
You were just in my arms, not moving, not breathing
I didn't know what to do
We didn't get to say goodbye or I love you
We watched them take you away in the car
With tears falling down our faces
Blaming ourselves about what happened
Not knowing about how things were going to be
My whole life changed that day,
That day I lost my grandma.

Kamika Jo Allen, Grade 10
Slater High School, MO

Life

Some things can scare you and bring you to tears
Others can cheer you and make you forget all your fears
All my thoughts the good and the bad,
Disappear for moment a small space in time
A second, a blink and the moment's past
Back to reality, it happened so fast
I look behind and can't ever forget —
The mistakes the regrets
It seems like a dream
A nightmare at that
Created and dreamt on a movie screen
Flashing in front of my eyes minutes at a time
To create the one movie the biggest of all
No fast forward, no rewind
It can't be rewritten replayed or retaped
It's the one reality no one can argue
What happens is fact and there's no changing that
Its title is known to living and dead
Some love it, others hate it
It begins with an L and ends with an E
and the big unknown IF is in between.

Megan Tucker, Grade 11
Owasso High School, OK

Mad Mama Cows

New life entering the world,
A miracle in itself —
Taking its first breath as a delicate calf.
Mama cow guards bravely
Her creation — her calf.

We stare from a distance, checking for problems.
We mean no harm.
She wants us gone.
Snorts bellow from her nostrils,
Intent fills her angry eyes —
We are in serious trouble.

Dashing to the four wheeler,
Adrenaline pumping, heart racing,
Safety is no where to be found.
Gunning the gas across the open field,
She is right behind us.

Relentless charging suddenly halts.
She casually returns to her calf.
We make it to the gate,
Staring in disbelief.
Running of the bulls has nothing on mad mama cows.

Nicole Cribfield, Grade 12
Germantown High School, TN

Lonely

Lonely is the color black
It sounds like dead silence
It tastes like bittersweet lemons
And smells like dirt
Lonely looks like tears streaming down cheeks
It makes you feel useless

Tiffany Legrand, Grade 10
Madison High School, MO

Mom

"How are you?"
How are you feeling today?
Would you like a massage, Mom?
Ok, where would you like it?
Here? There?
Should I massage your back,
or should I massage your life?
Let me knead away this knot in your tendon
and that knot in your troubled mind.
Can I pound my fists into your shoulder blades,
then into your fears also?
Would you like me to karate chop your spine,
or your cancer for you?
Perhaps if I loosened your tensed muscles
I'd then loosen your constrained anguish.
I wish that I could poke or pinch or peel
these worries from your thoughts,
as a masseur would rid you of your physical pains.
May I save you from this endless pain?
Just relax, Mom.
I will save you from this endless pain.

Sankalp Bhatnagar, Grade 11
Germantown High School, TN

Forgotten Youth

I am a child of only thirteen,
Finding a place in darkness to escape,
Letting them in when I am so young,
Without a care I fell deep,
Feeling like I am mature,
Longing for the touch,
I am a child of only fourteen,
Foreign I am to even me,
Lending myself to any for the heat,
Wilted is my soul, my life, my childhood,
Forgotten is my family and friends,
Lying to all, not excluding myself,
I am the one to blame,
For a light starts to shine,
Lucky I thought for a little while,
When the light left, so did I,
Forward with the emptiness, I march on,
Light shines down in the form of a disease,
I realize how close to drowning I have gotten,
For I am a woman of only fifteen,
Learning how to love myself first.

Jamee Little, Grade 10
Morris High School, OK

A Ballard About a Mallard

The mallard floats peacefully in a pond
Paddling away in the water
He quacks loudly in search of his duckling
"Oh where are you my duckling daughter?"

"Here I am, father
I see your green head!"
"O thank God you found me
I thought you were dead"

Off in the distance two men approach
The pond in search of duck
They have their rifles loaded and ready for action
The mallard could be out of luck

The men see the mallard in plain sight
They aim their guns toward the pond
As the mallard comes into view
They fire at the mallard like James Bond

The mallard is bleeding badly
He struggles to flap his wings
Death is approaching the mallard
As he takes his last breath and sings

Jeff Dyas, Grade 12
Covington Catholic High School, KY

Best Friend

I reach high into the sky my fingers stretching for the sun;
Fingers brushing smooth white wings, maybe I can fly!
When I dream, there you are.
Up the stairs I falter and I slip;
The darkness closing in, I yell out for help.
When I stumble, there you are.
A smile flows across my face, excitement bubbling over;
A laugh escapes from my lips as I share my joy.
When I'm happy, there you are.
My eyes are glistening, tears are threatening;
I can't suppress them, they overflow onto my cheeks.
When I'm sad, there you are.
But when I reach and when I fall,
And when I smile and when I cry,
You're not just there, you are with me.
I see your hand reaching, reaching out with mine;
I see you kneeling, kneeling by my fallen form;
I see you laughing, laughing by my side;
I see you worried, worried as I cry.
You are there, always there beside me,
Sharing every moment. Thank you.

Bethany Bozzay, Grade 12
Parkway South High School, MO

Stars of Life

The stars in the sky, so bright, so bold,
They seem so new, yet they are so very old.
Light-years away, they burn up space,
Some shoot away like some sort of race.
Some think of stars as spirits above,
Shining their light for all to love.
They say each time a life is lost,
A new star appears like the first winter's frost.
Wish upon a star and your dream will come true,
The star may be a loved one watching over you.
Each time you see the stars in the sky,
Watch for angels, they may just fly by.

Andrew Simpson, Grade 12
Gateway Christian Schools, TN

Change

I gave myself to a person I thought loved me.
Now my heart's filled with pain.
It's hard for me to be with any boy or trust anyone.
Then over the summer, he told me he loved me the same.
Now I'm four months pregnant with his baby boy.
And still he treats me like I'm some kind of toy.
Sometimes, I wish we could switch places.
Something telling me in my mind,
He wouldn't be able to escape it.
I want to hate him but I can't.
My love for him is too strong.
But it seems that he has moved on —
And left me all alone.
Now all we do is argue about our past and our baby.
He says we are friends
But it doesn't feel that way.
I think it's time we go our separate ways.

Lelia Richards, Grade 10
Capital High School, WV

Tradition

The sport I play is one of real pain.
This sport has a name, football.
It is never to be taken as a joke.
One hundred yards is what you try to gain.
The team is hoping that you do not choke.

The crashing of my pads is extremely loud.
Like the full-force collision of two, raging locomotives.
My victims roll around in pain and agony, knocked out.
Their state of being makes me very proud.
They know who is better. There is no doubt.

Electrolytes are needed for such a game.
We waste sweat and tears for our true love.
Sometimes water is just not enough.
The teams we play experience great shame,
Because it turns out they could not hang tough.

Tough enough to stop a mighty Maggie win.
Afterwards we say our prayer, amen.

Brett Bell, Grade 11
McGehee High School, AR

A Sonnet for Spinach

Notoriously feared by children are you
Whether you're cutleaf, chopped, raw, or creamed.
But I do not believe this to be true,
To me you are more than all I have dreamed
If only I had the strength of Popeye
My hope rests assured in your iron rich leaf
Without you I'm a bird who cannot fly
Weak and incomplete I am filled with grief
Separated by evil E-coli,
You were taken from me for a long time
Without your sweet taste I thought I might die,
But finally we were saved from this crime
Thy wonderful taste to thee none compare
My love for you I pray others will share.

Catherine Vaughn, Grade 11
St Mary's Episcopal School, TN

Night

Another cool, breezy autumn night,
The dark room's illuminated by the soft moonlight.
I listlessly lie in bed, hearing the wind blow,
You were supposed to call an hour ago.
I hope that you're thinking of me
Wherever you are in Tennessee.
As I drift off thinking of that mischievous smile,
Your name flashes on my phone in its usual style.
My evening was awful and late,
Dust swirls in my head and I can't think straight.
But at the sound of your voice,
My problems fade without a choice.
Being with you fills me with delight,
You can make me laugh even after midnight.
The first time we met, I never knew something would hatch.
But now I look up and find I'm attached.
I know it's too late to break the ties now,
I'm stuck, something I never thought I'd allow.

Shelby McGaha, Grade 11
McGehee High School, AR

Sports

I love sports to death
basketball is the only one to take my breath.
All the hard work and effort put in a game
My team will put your team to shame.
Even though our team is the best
We still never have time to rest.
I love winning for a reason
Oh look it's baseball season.
I throw another strike
Against the team I didn't like.
For a team to be great you have to believe
As you can tell I will never leave.
This day will come again once and for all
I will still love my best friend "the basketball."
I'm young I can still see
I can see Lebron James has nothing on me.

Chance Cavin, Grade 12
Prue High School, OK

School

We come to learn.
Not only bringing our books,
But spirit, and open minds too.
With fifty minute classes, and twenty minute lunches.
All full of drama, and laughter too.
Learning and listening like never before.
The teachers are speaking,
Only a few are listening,
And all others are giggling.
Some choose to prepare properly for their future.
While all others silently sleep.
But the restrooms!
Are simply smelly, stinky, and always sticky.
Along with homework, with its entire headache.
All this learning!
All the activities and sports
On that shiny gym floor
Brings all school spirit.
But leaves the work, and learning in your dark locker.
School is stressful
But is the road to my future!

Jeremy Wilson, Grade 11
Slater High School, MO

All in White

She comes out smiling all in white
And lets the people think what they will.
All stare in amazement at the sight.

Everyone knows it isn't right.
It doesn't bother her still.
She comes out smiling all in white.

What was she thinking that night?
The silk drapes to cover her chills,
All stare in amazement at the sight.

Her father steps and sighs in spite,
Of letting his daughter think she was run-of-the-mill.
She comes out smiling all in white.

The new man in her life waits ahead in the light.
Her face turns pale and she begins to feel ill.
All stare in amazement at the sight.

She starts to think this idea wasn't so bright.
Her insides send to her brain a screaming shrill.
She comes out smiling all in white.
All stare in amazement at the sight.

Kara Williams, Grade 12
Oak Ridge High School, TN

Number 37

Many a kernel
Could stand to be learned
Of a love eternal
And of cities burned
If we could listen
When it came our turn

Many a conflict
Could be subsided
If we let things tick
And if we provided
Everything needed
Wise things would be decided

If we heard the echoing voices
We could learn
How to make our choices
So our great cities won't burn
Let's just hope that we can listen
Because now, it's our turn

Krystina Long, Grade 11
Anderson County High School, TN

Our Flag

It waves in the morning light
above the glorious fight.
It stands for liberation
our newly created nation.

Men and women stand for its justice
they're everyday people just like us.
They make the ultimate sacrifice
as they lay down their very life for us.

It stands red, white, blue
it gave freedom to me and you.

Jonathan Kidd, Grade 10
South Intermediate High School, OK

The Game

The roar of the crowd
The announcer's shouts

The glare of the lights
The wall of people

The hotdogs grilling
The buttered popcorn

The ice-cold colas
The fresh greasy fries

The heart pounding suspense
The rush of victory

Gregory Kenney, Grade 10
Holy Angels Academy, KY

The Power of Money

Money is the building block for construction
It fuels desire and greed, and is the cause for destruction
It is the upcoming and downfall of the people
It is the source of some good, and the root of most evil
Money pays for food, water, and even light
It pays for a sound foundation to sleep on at night
Money Pays
Money pays for warmth on winter nights and a continual breeze on summer days
For some, money is the reason for life, death, and everything in between
And for others it is just paper that happens to be green
Money stirs confusion
And cloud thoughts for delusion
But for me, money is just an illusion

Krystofer Turner, Grade 11
Mills University Studies High School, AR

The Test of Time

Like any other kind of love, friendship can be a blessing from above.
Friendship can pick us up off our feet,
And help us out when it feels as if the world has us beat.
When you left I was mad at God you know,
I was not ready to let you go.
I miss you and everything you meant to me,
Maybe when I am older, I can accept that it was meant to be.

I expected to forget you but it seems,
That almost every night I see you in my dreams.
It's been two years and at times I still can't hold it together.
Am I going to feel like this forever?
You couldn't be there for me the day you left,
I remember the feeling I had and how hard I wept.
The nosey nurse kept telling me, "You'll be okay one day."
But I knew in my heart that was just something she was told to say.

Thirty years from now, I will look back on it all,
Remembering all the goofy times, we had such a ball.
Our friendship stood the test of time; we made it through it all.

Morgan Jobe, Grade 11
Anderson County High School, TN

You Can!

You want to be something that is hard to become
Everyone says you can't do it
They're wrong, because if you believe in yourself
And believe you can succeed,
YOU CAN!
If someone tries to put you down or say that you can't do it
Well, it doesn't matter what they say, because if you think you can,
YOU CAN!
Whatever someone says to you
It doesn't really matter,
What matters is that you believe in yourself.
Believe in yourself and,
YOU CAN!

Brittne Rucker, Grade 10
Capital High School, WV

The Stall Tactic

Give me time to work this out
She's breaking out of her shell that's what it's all about
And as we search for some things to say
We wonder where this conversation went astray
This is the stall tactic in my mind
I've never had to search for something I couldn't find
Give me something
And I'll be fine
This is the poem you couldn't write
Wasted in your dreams last night
I will wait for you
This is the life you've never had
But I still want to make it last
Forget those thoughts in your dreams
Nothing really is as it seems
And as we grace upon this sacred hour
The poems we write hold a mighty power
This is the stall tactic in my mind
I've never had to search for something I couldn't find
Give me something
And I'll be fine

James Borders, Grade 10
Bishop McGuinness Catholic High School, OK

Fairytale Dream

From where I sit looking on the lake,
I drift off in a dream of Venice.
My feet engulfed by the sand.
The water shimmers in the sunlight.
Oh, how I wish I were in Venice as gondolas float by
and the homes above fit like a puzzle.

As the coast line disappears and day turns to night.
Aladdin, my ego-boasting friend,
soars by on his magic carpet,
carrying a smirk
and swaggering as if he were the real prince of Agraba.
Soaring by once more the carpet winks at me,
as I am taken aboard, to smell the lush air,
then dropped like Icarus into the sea.

Oh how I wish I were in Venice,
under the sea as a mermaid,
swimming with Poseidon, Flounder, and
Sebastian, my tasty-red friend, to my castle beneath,
to dine on bonbons and drink champagne.

This is not a poem of grim reality
it is a poem about dreaming big.

Samantha Craig, Grade 12
Baylor School, TN

Missing You

Since you have been gone
I'm stuck here wishing you were home
You were like my backbone
Supporting me with a shoulder to lean on
If only you could be here with me right now
I would sit and show you how loving you were never so wrong
Missing you I feel all alone
Being together I acted very shy
But now I can't sleep at night I just want to cry
Having a friend so dearly as you
You were the reason the sky was always blue
Circles of laughter turned into sorrow
Not knowing I wouldn't see you tomorrow
If only you felt my pains and aches
You would soon find out leaving was a big mistake
Just know that I love you so much
I'll be happy just to feel your touch
Hearing your voice will be okay
Please hurry and make it happen today
Me being the best person I've grown to be
Just don't forget about good friends like you and me

Whitney Watkins, Grade 11
McGehee High School, AR

That Face of His

Burns even the skin of Persephone,
The Queen of the Underworld.
Even repels Poseidon's winds.
Not even Circe would want to lure him with her magic.

The intimidating scar above his right eyebrow,
Is a physical burden,
Embedded from an after-school fight.

Oedpidus' strength glows,
Glows in those blue, sunken eyes.
His flesh tones are models of Penelope's woven quilts,
Teeming with character.

Never showing his supercilious alter ego.
Serene, reclusive…yet diabolical.

The avarice is only noticeable,
In that face of his.

DR Itayem, Grade 10
Germantown High School, TN

Who Are You

Who are you to tell me I can and can't talk to girls,
who are you to tell me who I can and cannot see,
who are you to tell me that I can't go no where,
who are you to buy to come control my life
when you just worry about your own,
this is my life so you cannot run me; so that means,
you can't spit in my face, turn around and
tell me you love me without hurting me.

David Scott, Grade 11
Mills University Studies High School, AR

I Miss You

Even though you are gone
the warmth of your heart lingers on.
The thought of you in my mind
remembers you being ever so kind.
I only wish you could see
the person I have become to be.
I miss your strong and loving arms
that protected me from all harm.
Someday we will meet again.
I miss you my friend.

Ashli Moerke, Grade 10
Shady Spring High School, WV

Acid

The rain remarks
While sighs the tree bark,
Screams the sky
Shouts the birds away they fly,
Constant battle are the sun and moon
The winner of outcome we'll know soon,
The sleet, the snow
Roundabout they go,
Fro and to and to and fro
The winter is done and will soon melt,
The bumblebee forgets what it felt
And Mother, she pines
While all the trees dine,
On leftovers and light
As the white rabbit takes flight,
And all the metaphors in the world
Are dreamt up by little girls.

SaraAnn Keller, Grade 11
Pulaski County High School, KY

The Loving Mother

Her eyes shine bright
When babies are near
And through the night
She hopes to hear
Her children dreaming
Of stars and moon
Of when they'll be seeming
To grow up too soon
She works all day
And into the night
Get out of her way
She puts up a fight
She hopes and sees
Her children grow
Know that they'll be
There to show
That if you see
Sister and brother
Close behind will be
The loving mother

Melina Long, Grade 11
McGehee High School, AR

Mud

Stopping, thinking, looking back, it is a hot summer day.
I am sitting on a cold concrete porch. I am mixing, smearing,
Smashing, stacking, slopping, smushing, squashing, spreading,
Chunking, playing in dark, cool, mushy mud.
Oops! Mamma sees me.
Now I am rubbing, scrubbing, rinsing, and cleaning.

Erin McDonald, Grade 11
Family of Faith Christian School, OK

Always Miss

I forever dodge the calm raindrops but get swept up in the flood.
See through the flocks as beauty flies away
But catch the bitter winter in my glove.
We forever see the shadow but miss the child cast it at sunset.
Loiter on lost hopes of what could have been
Yet let today's choices grind right by.
Can't recall the day I learned to trust but still feel when it's broken.
One rarely sees what they have until it's stolen
When the moments prove to never live again.

I lost the days years ago
When my parents could adore
They dreamt of an everlasting home
Often shared a sincere hug.
When I was young, so small, little
I always missed the shine in our eyes
But after I grow a little older
Forget that everything has changed
Forgive the storms slicing through our river
Still I always miss unrecalled love.

Katharine Williams, Grade 11
Edmond North High School, OK

Long, Narrow Road

Life is a long journey through rough roads.
Life is full of heartbreaks and sadness, love and happiness
I thought he was the one
He was perfect, he was my everything
Time went on, we came and went
Oh I loved him so, through this journey on this long and narrow road
My heart was broke
He took my emotions, shattered them
He stole my heart away, ripped it to pieces
On that dark winter day, oh how I am cold
The thought of him with her, just melts my soul
Oh but I loved him so
Those many years, have now grown old
I still remember the day on that long narrow road
But now I am here to say, even though he left me for her
I will always carry around my shattered, broken soul
For the guy I loved is now controlled
I still walk down that dark winter road
But I look forward with the hopes so I say;
I loved you but only for a day

Emily Riggs, Grade 10
Gibson County High School, TN

Fourteen Months

Beating, cringing, earth shattering presence,
I feel the separation from the world.
The wretched sense of constant resonance
Makes my life be forever, always, swirled.

In a state of waiting for redemption,
Much like longing for the end of the war.
Days come, days go, can I find exemption?
Will this ever change, wait one moment more.

Please no beaming light, not a blasting sound,
Paralyzed by pain I lie hopelessly.
Searching high and low, no cure can be found;
Loved ones, doctors, God above, find the key.

Learning to live despite the constant pain.

Sasha Joyce, Grade 11
St Mary's Episcopal School, TN

Emily

As I look into the sunset, I see your face.
I think about the times
that my mind has not erased.

It becomes clear to me that you are still with me.
A sense of peace falls over me,
as I look to you for guidance.

I feel so lost without you,
but you reassure me that everything will be okay.

A sudden rush of cheer fills me,
and I begin to feel that I shall see you.

I feel the weight being lifted
and you begin to fill my heart with warmth.

Soon my days get shorter
and my nights seem to be brighter.

I cannot escape this wonderful feeling.

Sarah Keith, Grade 10
Centralia High School, MO

Cries from the Sky

In a cloudy, gray blur,
Rain falls in droplets from the sky,
Blurring the world's sights,
Like tears from a weeping eye.
The sun is covered and hidden,
Not to be seen and out of view,
Unable to shine its golden light,
On the world, me, or you.
With icy, cold breath blowing,
The wind does ferociously howl,
Who would have ever thought,
That our spacious skies could be so foul?

Jannah Williams, Grade 10
Hillcrest High School, TN

Veritas

Congruo:
To conform, coincide, or agree.
Fitting in was the most important thing to me.
Scelus Sceleris:
A crime, a sin, or an evil deed.
I was offered that drink, and I didn't take heed.
Timeo:
To fear, be afraid, or to dread.
If they found out, they would have my head.
Culpa:
Having fault, guilt, or to blame.
My fear diminished, and was replaced by shame.
Veritas:
Meaning truth or confession.
I laid it all out and told of my transgression.
Venia:
Pardon, forgiveness, or grace.
They gave me this gift instead of pounding my face.
Resurrectio:
An awakening, renewal, or rebirth.
Veritas has finally restored my self-worth.

Jennifer Gray, Grade 11
Owasso High School, OK

Under Cover

The world is under cover.
Media says everything is fine.
That daughter wasn't hit by her mother.
That teacher didn't cross the line.

There's no such thing as homeless.
Earth isn't in danger of a subzero degree.
The wealthy give to the penniless.
Minors don't have access to pornography.

The people will investigate.
Unabomber's will come out of hiding.
Reality of abuse will be too late.
That student will always be crying.

That girl plays and lives in the meadow.
God cannot prevent the next ice age.
Bill Gates' generosity is at an all-time low.
That minor's addiction is in a sheltered cage.

The world is under cover.
And it's an inconvenient truth.
How will we discover
what is left aloof.

Jordan Cease, Grade 11
Elizabethtown High School, KY

November Feast

Gather around the table — this time comes but once each year,
A time to feast on stuffing, turkey, and the stories of family amassed into a blur.
Each one holds a plate and a curious ear to discover something sweet,
A morsel, a tidbit, or a crumb of what they will savor for the next year.
I look around to see the faces and catch a wink and twinkle in each eye,
I see merriment, fulfillment, and hope for everyone's betterment,
I finally see what I am looking for, the last of the cornbread before it can disappear.
This time is a wormhole from which nothing escapes — no matter how light,
Not a blink or twitch, a clap or whistle, a candy apple or an aunt's fruitcake.
From the moment one enters one seems to see the end,
A tunnel so bright that at the end is not day but the conclusion of light.
I hear sounds that twang and the clap of feet as champagne takes its full effect,
I listen to the country music and I can't help but be caught by the rhythm,
I hear that not everyone can keep up the beat.
This particular day is no every day — it will set the tone,
A mood to carry through the holidays and to the New Year.
This picture will last a lifetime,
In it the warm feeling of the oven baking the fuzzy skin left in the peach pie whispers its tone.
I feel each sound, smell each taste, and touch each sight,
I know that soon the turkey will have me dreaming of feasts past,
I take in a breath and feel the warmth of nostalgia and the crisp of a new winter.

Evan Halton, Grade 11
Owasso High School, OK

Just Me and Me Alone

Up high in a tree, just me and me alone, breeze of a cold, swam a chill in my bone. Just me and me alone, surrounded by darkness, that ignites my fears, a brisk of a cold, can't quite bring tears, wishing to myself to come forth of what ever that leers.

Up high in a tree, just me and me alone, blended with the forest, winds of might came though as if a chorus. My heart pumps, body jumps, soul and veins collide with great thumps. My defense is my bow, my weapon is my bow, joy in life itself is my bow, the pride that lies with in my heart is my bow. Nothing will pass before my eyes with out the fear of my bow.

Up high in a tree, just me and me alone, a shatter of a clatter that erupts my soul. I dare to care, squint and stare, for my eyes to share, the dark of light hardly fair, behind the shadow of a tree my prize awaits me there. My target is waiting, a feeling of a hating, its only quest for the day is the thought of mating, is this real or to myself am I only faking, my prize is mine for the taking.

Seth Smith, Grade 11
Anderson County High School, TN

Finally, the Truth Be Known

When you wake up in the morning, what do you think?
When you look in the mirror, who do you see?
When you take a peek into your heart, is there anything there?
I can tell you what I see.
When I wake, I think, "Damn. I woke up."
When I look in the mirror, I don't see me, but a drained young man staring back at me, with his dreams shattered and gone.
When I peek inside my heart, I see a Black Hole, sucking in whole essence until I am a literal shell.
My song has been sung, and now there is silence.
My light switch is fried and I live in Darkness.
My cable went out, and all there is is Static, white noise, creeping into my soul.
Can the World imagine?
Can the World see?
No.
All it does is torture me.

Spencer Graves, Grade 10
Chickasha High School, OK

I Am Sorry Dad

When I close my eyes, I see your face
But this is the only time I see you
In my heart, you are losing your place
Something came between us
A wife, a family, a love so new
Where was I to go?
I was so lost to you
Our love has slowly faded
It fading to nothing Dad
Do you even care?
Waiting for you has driven me mad
It was because of you that we are apart
I sit by the phone or stare out the window
I have realized how much of an inconvenience I am
Knowing you won't come back consumes me with sorrow
I used to look up to you
Now I can't even look at you
The man you are today, I never knew
I am giving up
I am ME
And if you can't accept that, I am sorry.

Brandi Kidwell, Grade 11
Owasso High School, OK

Detention

Teacher please, can I have your attention?
I'm only asking for a little comprehension
This is nothing more than a misunderstanding
And I'm pretty sure that you're just pretending

Today I've done wrong, but I ask your forgiveness
I didn't mean to do it; I only want you to listen
So as I speak, here in your wake
I want you to know I've seen my mistake

They all dared me, and said I was scared
That's why I painted your desk and chair
I had to prove them wrong, I couldn't slack
I just had to do it, to get my dignity back

The sentence you've dealt me is quite unfair
It was me, my friends were there
Yes they were innocent, but in the same place
Guilty by association, is this a lying face?

I know that you're right in doing what you must
No matter how much I hate this, I do want your trust
But teacher please can I have your attention?
I still don't think I deserve this detention.

Joshua Onstott, Grade 12
Fort Towson Jr/Sr High School, OK

Divine Percussion

The cadence of equestrian surge,
Anon sedates the masses manifolds;
With sweet hum of beating hearts shall it merge,
To echo a pulse Existence beholds.

Amidst the Hippodrome's nuclear aisle
Antiquity's Golden Chariots stir.
One pulsates with radiance soleil
As bodies to it gravitate and defer.

Yet misjudge this not for a spectacle;
For it is a movement, living, breathing,
Progress synchronized by drumming, focal;
Like ripples extending each realm's sheathing.

Alas! The race commenced, and angels sang,
With the strike of divine percussion: BANG!

Lavanya Mittal, Grade 11
St Mary's Episcopal School, TN

My Oh My

Well I just found out today that life is very hard
There are cuts, bruises and even broken hearts
The world isn't as bright as the traditional fairy tales
Cinderella doesn't always get her prince
It all seems unfair

So what is a girl suppose to do when living in despair?

Find the light you say, but where can it be found?
Beyond the world of darkness or in the frozen ground
Where are all the fireflies that shimmer in the night?
The candles that shine the castle halls
The stars that glow so bright

So, how long will this shadow linger
Please not be too long
I need to feel the sun again
There has to be another, much happier song

Deirdre Mason, Grade 10
Chickasha High School, OK

Petal Support

When painful tears do fall from my blue eyes,
There are but Two whom I wish to dry them.
The Two who cannot stand to hear my cries,
I am just the flower, They are my stem.
My troubles to Them I daily confess;
With Them, certainly, life is better than
Without Them; life: a painful, dreary mess.
Upon my meeting Them my life began.
Without its stem this blossom would perish,
No comforting shoulder, no concerned glance.
These simple things I deeply do cherish,
The meaning of my life they do enhance.
This changing weather that I endure here,
Is better with my stem, and that is clear.

Lindsey Driver, Grade 11
St Mary's Episcopal School, TN

The End

As he holds me tightly,
and tells me not to fear.
I tell him my feelings,
what I know he needs to hear.
I try to tell him,
but I don't know where to start.
I'm in love with someone else,
but how can I tell him?
He'll say he hates me,
and my lights will go dim.
Am I doing the right thing,
by breaking his heart?
Will I be happy,
when we are apart?
I don't know what to do,
what to say.
But I have to end it now,
before my heart has to pay.

Kaitlyn Brantley, Grade 12
Union County High School, TN

From the Eyes of a Broken Heart

I'm begging you.
I'm down on my knees.
Please help me, please oh please.
I'm down here because of you.
You gave up on me,
when I needed you.
How can you be so evil and mean?
How can you let me lay here —
suffering from this pain —
when you know deep down —
that you're to blame.
How can you stand to see me cry?
How can you, can you tell me why?
Do you enjoy it?
Knowing its tearing me apart.
Can you believe all this pain
is just the pain
of a broken heart.

Kelsey Bare, Grade 10
Sullivan East High School, TN

Life's Storms

The unsteady realm.
That is my mind.

The toss and turn of my life's waves.
Rocks the boat of my soul off course.

Riding out the storms.
Enduring till it ends.

The sea subsides.
Into its gentle motions again.

Mary Patton, Grade 11
Newcastle High School, OK

daddy dearest

though you're not my father, I'll love you just the same.
though you're not in my blood, daddy will be your name.
you've been there for me even when my own has not,
you've given me a place to rest from all the fights I've fought,
though I don't have your name, I'm almost just like you.
though my heart knows another man as father, it sees daddy as you.
a daddy is someone who shows you the love you need and shows they actually care.
a father is someone you're stuck with sharing nothing but DNA and hair.
you've done a lot for me and Aaron through the years.
stepfather from this day forward you're my daddy dearest.

Christle Mercedes Goodwin, Grade 10
Booneville High School, AR

With Greatness Comes Doubt

Like the Father of Modern Science,
Like the one who brought about the starting point of modern astronomy,
Like Christ,
Great thinkers are never understood
Until their ideas are viewed throughout the world.
Like a flower living in winter,
Like one living longer than the two weeks the doctor told him he had left,
Like David beating Goliath,
Great triumphs are never understood
Until they happen to someone else.
The changes in life occur without understanding,
And everyone has to come to accept
That life is not perfect,
That changes happen for a reason,
That Galileo, Copernicus, and Jesus were only helping the world.
But people's opinions will never change,
Because they are afraid,
Afraid of everything that is not considered "normal."

Brian Vinson, Grade 11
Germantown High School, TN

Two Fourteen

Bolting down the path, she pushed herself to get farther away
Calmly creeping, it followed the trail of fear she had left behind
She turned a sharp corner into a damp and hollow alleyway
Her eyes widened and she backed away slowly
It came nearer without leniency, but with awful desire
The harsh hammering of her heart grew at a faster pace
Hairs stood on end as her whole body began to quiver with fear
Horrific thoughts raced through her head as the figure crept closer
Opening her mouth, not one bit of sound came out
Straining herself to scream only gave her more pain
Tears rolled down her soft pale cheeks
She knew the true meaning of being frightened
Closing her eyes shut to keep away brought her back to reality
Sitting upright in her bed, beads of sweat dropped from her temple
Glancing at the clock, it was two fourteen in the morning
Her heavy breathing slowed as she sighed and laid back down
It was all just a nightmare she thought reassured
As she closed her eyes and silently crept back into the world of dreams

Siobhan Drury, Grade 11
Germantown High School, TN

Home Again

I never thought I would make it home
That I would always be alone
I would tell myself it would be all right
But continued to pray real hard at night
I didn't know who I was or where to go
Time just seemed to go so slow
Each house was entirely entrancing, some good some bad
But I was never myself and always sad
My friends from each town helped me get through rocky times
Also in my right mind and out of crimes
Then one day it happened, I'll never forget
Just when I thought you would never commit
You came and got me, it happened so fast
You said lets go home we'll have a blast
I followed you like a child
You took care of me
You made my life good again
And filled it with glee
I don't know what to say but will say this
"I can be happy now till the end
And thank you God for getting me home again."

Rebecca Nicole Williams, Grade 11
Slater High School, MO

Awe

The breeze flowing through your hair
A sigh of relief
Knowing that stress has left and peace is there
Twirling through life
Crafting memories at each scene
Yearning for a pause, but craving fast forward
A tingle throughout your senses
Life is good
Down through the valleys, up on top of the mountain
Taste the sweet aroma
Mmmmmmmmm
Relish the moments, no slices left over
Believe…

Sarah Bowman, Grade 12
Springfield Catholic High School, MO

Death Behind Door

The rapping the tapping the bump and the thump,
The constant banging on the door.
Everything in the house just made me jump,
So I am lying on the floor.
Thinking, wondering "What should I do?"
The question is "Should I open that door?" for I am stumped.

I tremble I freeze,
I say softly "go away."
I get on my knees and I say "sir, please"
It is not my turn today.
But death came a knocking,
And I sat there in the cold icy breeze,
And prayed.

Kortni Nay, Grade 11
Anderson County High School, TN

Love Lost

I cried myself to sleep last night, hoping that you'd call
As much as I willed the phone to ring, it didn't ring at all
You acted like you liked me and I got in too deep
You hold my heart in your hands, it wasn't yours to keep

How can you act like nothing happened
I thought what we had was real
I suppose you don't mind me hurting
And don't care how you make me feel

One day I might feel better
If you were nowhere near me
Sadly, that is unlikely
Since I can't erase my memory

I hope your dreams are haunted
With what we could have been
I know mine will be
I've lost my trust of men

I know we are over
You made that clear last night
My pain is so great right now
Soon, I should be all right.

Taryn Manners, Grade 12
Durant High School, OK

If I Had a Daughter

If I had a daughter a daddy I would be
She will be the end of the rainbow in the sky, my pot of gold
She'll be a reflection of her mom my bright and shining star.
She'll be the spirit of Christmas, my star on the top of the tree.
She'll be the Easter Bunny to her mommy and me.
I wouldn't trade her for anything
She'll smell as good as a rose
And she'll be as beautiful as a garden
When she gets scared at night
I'll be there to hold her tight
And when she cries I'll hold her tighter
I'll wipe every drop of her tears
And when she smiles
She'll be the perfect star in space
Her first words will be daddy
And on that rare occasions I'll cry
On her first day of school
She'll be the smartest girl in school
Whether she's a baby a child or a woman
She'll always be my little baby girl
She sugar, she spice, she everything nice, her daddy's little girl.

D'André Payne, Grade 10
Rock Bridge Sr High School, MO

I Am Different!

I am different!
Not because I have to be,
But because I want to be.
People like me for who I am.
I no longer change to fit in.

I am courteous.
I know, to get respect
You have to give respect.
I accept others for who they are,
I do not try to change them.

I am proud of who I am,
No matter what others think.
I have my confidence,
I DEFY their negativity.
I won't change myself.

I am original,
No others are just like me.
I am the one, the only,
I am me, and
I am different!
And that is all I have to be.

Ryan Dunkerson, Grade 11
Owasso High School, OK

Seasons

Hopeless summer
Endless drought
Fall is here
Without a doubt

Warm weather
Gone away
Freezing weather
Here to stay

Leaves slowly change color
Then they fall
Sleeping trees
Standing tall

Winter sneaks up
Way too fast
Soon this fall
Will be past

When that happens
I'll be okay
Because I'll be
Ready to move on anyway

Samantha Murphy, Grade 10
Coffee County Central High School, TN

Friendship

You fell in love and our friendship went away.
I knew you would have a closer friend someday.
And I thought that the closer friend would be me.
But things have changed, as you can see.
You will fall in love again someday.
And once again our friendship will go away.

Vanessa Nguyen, Grade 10
South Intermediate High School, OK

What Is a True Friend

A true friend is someone you can talk to when you're feeling down.
A true friend is someone you can tell your secrets to.
A true friend is someone you can chill with when you're bored.
A true friend is someone you can ride with.
A true friend is someone you can hang with when you're at a party.
A true friend is someone you can rap with.
A true friend is someone you can walk with at school.
A true friend is someone you can go shopping with.
A true friend is someone you can eat with.
A true friend is someone you can move in a house with.
A true friend is someone you can go out of town with.
A true friend is someone you can go skating with.
A true friend is someone you can make money with.
A true friend is someone you can spend the night with.
A true friend is someone you can wrestle with.
A true friend is someone you can read a book with.
A true friend is someone you can work with.
A true friend is someone you can be cool with.
A true friend is someone you can go swimming with.
A true friend is someone you can get girls with.
What is a true friend to you?

Dorian Hill, Grade 10
Rock Bridge Sr High School, MO

Different Place

Teens today are growing up in a very different place.
People never change only their face.
It is hard growing up in this time.
I want just a little peace that I can call mine.

Older people never seem to care.
They never seem to have time to spare.
They say there is nothing new under the sun.
But the race they ran was easy compared to the one I run.

Don't get me wrong my life is not all hell.
But sometimes I do feel like I'm in a prison cell.
Because I'm female they tell me a lady I should act.
I wish everyone would give me some slack.

If only people could look at my generation and see our true face.
Instead of looking at what we've done, our family, or race.
So here I have laid out my case.
Now look at us and help us in this different place.

Diane Wilson, Grade 11
White Station High School, TN

The Race

The race begins, not a soul in sight.
It's only me, and my will to fight.
Pushing and striving until the end,
The place at which I will ascend.
To the Savior who has donated the prize,
He who gave it as a sacrifice.
I will do my best not to stray,
But stay the path and win the day.
Though my enemies lurk behind every turn,
I will seek the finish line for which I yearn.
Although I will encounter splits in the road,
I will keep to that of which I have been told.
Though I will be tempted by those born of the fire,
I will focus on my one and only desire.
At times I will stumble and fall to the ground,
But I will get up and continue toward what I have found.
And as my race is reaching its last,
I will look back and celebrate its past.
For I know when I finish the race,
I will be engulfed by His warm embrace.
So, the race ends, every finisher of the race in sight.

Trevor Conner, Grade 11
Owasso High School, OK

Evil

It's coated over in denial,
A self-inflicted trickery, targeting millions,
But the bullets aren't starving,
And the numbers don't lie,
So why, like ignorant mammals,
Do we turn a blind eye?

Horror — blood — tragedy,
Hollow the eyes of the youth,
No less deserving of a warm embrace,
Just because of where they're living.
So why instead of selfishness,
Don't we devote our hearts to giving?

Who made us into these uncaring creatures?
Was it,
  a wheel spun,
  a roll of die?
Or the fanatic ultimatum of some blank deity?
I believe we are closer to this demon,
Though I'm not sure what you would call —
The bloodthirsty, tortured monstrosity —

The evil within us all…

Sarah Naomi VanDyck, Grade 12
Blackwell High School, OK

Pursuing the Clouds

I gaze with awe into the light blue sky
Nothing else could be so massive, so vast;
I follow a cloud with attentive eyes
And view the transformations drifting past.

Opportunities change as time goes on
Like clouds moving out of sight, out of grasp.
Many will slip from view, forever gone,
While others I manage to save, to clasp.

Which opportunities am I to take?
So many choices and so little time;
Not a moment to spare, time has no breaks,
Life is the poem, a choice is the rhyme.

By pursuing the clouds, I find my way
In this life, self constructed, day by day.

Carrie Wohlschlegel, Grade 11
North Bullitt High School, KY

Medieval Battle

You shall laud the Lord
To make propitiation for your sins.
You shall gird yourself with armour;
For the men we condemned
Come to buffet our defenses,
But we shall impede the invasion with our forces
And adapt our fighting methods to defeat them.
They shall not be able to use a subterfuge to escape.
Our army shall shove morsels of food into their mouths,
And send them into paroxysms of absurdity.

Hunter Pettie, Grade 10
Germantown High School, TN

Gamer's Delight

Super Smash Brother's Melee, a button smasher's dream,
Where destroying the other players is the ultimate theme.
One, two punch attack, damaging the sly Fox,
And morbidly slamming Bowser with a box.
Destruction to an enemy with the death ball,
Sending another character to a fatal fall.
Cheering the slashing of Donkey Kong,
And the extinction of Yoshi, not long.
Missiles, bombs, it is hammer time.
Hearing the enemies die, a beautiful chime.
A test of luck and thumb's speed.
Playing the game until your thumbs bleed
And your eyes begin to forever cross,
For the sole purpose to be the supreme boss.
To defeat the invincible video game
Will obtain the advent of player's fame.
A sweet addiction for hours to keep
Till your muscles and back unwillingly weep.
Playing the game with demonic delight.
With destruction of the players, a beautiful sight.
Super Smash Brother's Melee, a button smasher's delight.

Scotty Chaney, Grade 11
Spring Valley High School, WV

I Need You

I have never needed anyone.
But you my love I need,
I need you like the flowers need the sun

I need you to survive
You are like the air I breathe
But since you have been gone I have
Suffocated in my own depression.

People have said there's plenty more
Where you came from, but I don't
Want anyone else.

I only have eyes for you
You are my obsession,
You are the one I need.

Michael Burton, Grade 11
Woodrow Wilson High School, WV

A Moonlit Walk

It was another sleepless night,
And I woke up to the moonlight.
I stared at the moon infatuated,
And got out of bed activated.
It was a cool evening.
I noticed my toes were freezing
As I kept on treading down the sidewalk
With the moon shining on my blue frock.
The cold was too much to endure;
I had to go back home for sure.
I climbed into my bed
With the moonlight shining on my head.
I laid in bed dazed by the light.
It was another sleepless night.

Patrick Call, Grade 10
Coffee County Central High School, TN

We Are Connected

I reach out through the
darkness
To find the ones
I need
I send my spirit
with a message
To find their spirits
where they reside
We are connected
by time
We are connected
by fate
We are connected
by life
We are connected
by death

Courtney Mattox, Grade 10
Waynoka High School, OK

The Sight of Beauty

The sound of thunder echoes in the hills,
With the hope of rain,
The clouds turn dark and start rolling towards the forest,
With the spring showers, summer is almost here again...
Drip, Drop is the sound that comes from the tree branch,
Just moistened with rain, the sign of life is yet again renewed,
Followed by the morning dew sparkling in the sun...
The bright colors red, orange, yellow, green, blue, indigo, and violet,
Are appearing in the sky above me, the smell of lilac is in the air...
The sky has turned blue again with fluffy white clouds,
The sign of rain is gone,
For now the life of the world has been refreshed in one single rainstorm,
It has made a beautiful sight for life to witness,
For just a brief moment of time,
For when it rains again the most beautiful thing will come out,
And life will bathe in its beauty, and we will soon call it a rainbow...

Stephanie Strebler, Grade 10
St Francis Borgia Regional High School, MO

My Savior

Who will be there for me when all is lost, when my money well is dry?
My family.
When I'm in need of help, when I have nowhere to go realize I will look for my family.
Who blessed me with this family?
My Savior.
So whose name will I praise when I wake?
To whom will I give thanks because my family is so great?
My Savior, Jesus Christ.

Quinten Blackshire, Grade 12
Carl Albert High School, OK

The People Who Know Me

The people who know me are my friends
They have been with me through thick and thin
They let me know that they care
They let me know that they love me
I would be nothing without them
They keep me company when I'm down
My friends are like my sisters
They are my life
They tell me the truth when I need to hear it
We laugh about almost everything
They tell me great advice
My friends are my everything
I look to them for help
I help them with their problems
They look up to me as I do to them
They are trustworthy
They are loyal
We love to watch funny movies
We act like crazy little kids, but that's what makes them great
We are goofy when we all hang out
My friends are the people who know the true me and I will always love them

Molly Nicole Brumit, Grade 10
Slater High School, MO

Our Loving Savior

You have always stood by through thick and thin.
You suffered on a cross at Calvary,
Just asking for us to believe again.
You only did it to set us all free.
Every day I take the time to just pray —
The Father, the Son, the Holy Ghost —
To know You will be with me every day.
You are the one man who truly cared the most.
There You stand with a face so full of love,
And when it becomes the day I will go,
Your light will shine brighter while You're above.
Your pure blood will wash me white as fresh snow.
Jesus Christ I will give You all my heart.
I know that You and I will never part.

Emily Matthews, Grade 10
Grove High School, OK

The Curse of Religion

This religion is one of corruption
Creating rules for our society,
Driving society to destruction,
Claiming to work for the All-Mighty.

Its preachers of trust cannot be trusted.
They teach about God's power and will,
But young children many have lusted.
Even in the past people would, for God, kill.

The opposite of God's teachings they were near;
Supporting slavery and sometimes worse.
Luckily it has improved in its years,
Hopefully it will learn from the bible verse.

The power of the church should not be everywhere,
But in our heart and spirit, it should be there

Zachary Tewes, Grade 12
Covington Catholic High School, KY

Memories...

Laughing till you cry
Reminiscing about last night
Of the times that'll never die
Tearing down back roads only seems right

Singing as loud as we can
And playing a solo on the air guitar
We're always making a plan
To escape this town and go somewhere far

Our dreams are so large
That we'll never forget
Those days when "We" were in charge
They're not close to being over yet

Our memories will never fade
Cause they're the best ones we have ever made

Lauren Burge, Grade 12
Hollis High School, OK

Last Man on Earth

August heat wore on and on
September fruit trees stood barren
October wind was forlorn and icy
An empty season bearing down

Fallen leaves in empty streets
A school bell ringing in vain
The rising sun greets no one,
Except a last witness

The onlooker's steps resound in silence
Disturbing curious vultures
Stuffed on fetid society,
They pay the man no mind

In darkest night
He sits abandoned
The last man on Earth,
Raps a finger to fracture maddening calm
"I'm forsaken, so alone."
The last man on Earth's,
Floorboards creaking, "Alone, alone."
The last man on Earth,
Hears a knock on his door

Corben Rosenthal, Grade 12
Memorial High School, OK

Picture Perfect

Looking through the viewfinder
Trying to find a perfect picture to arrest
Adjusting the light or position
Deciding whether to be goofy or sincere
Photography is a form of art
The scenery is delightful
Colors flow together as a river
Try to capture the moment through a photo
This picture will last forever
It will behold many memories
Be sure this photo is neither blurry nor off-centered
The photograph will express a point of view
Or it will interpret feelings and emotions
But the most important point is the subject
With the swift click of a button
Snap, the picture has been taken
The flash has brightened your face
Do you remember the second you took that photo?
The memory is all in that priceless picture
It's one of a kind
Not another picture just like it.

Hayley Archer, Grade 11
Owasso High School, OK

Destined for Me

At the bottom of the aqua green sea, where the flirting fishes float among the weeds,
a kingdom of mystical merpeople hosted a tragic tale, about that beautiful bashful boy, who was destined to always love me.

I was his princess and he was my peasant, as we played in that aqua green sea and fell so deeply, drowning in that love,
the powers of the sea could see, that fate had met its match, for he was destined to always love me.

That king father of mine could not abide my beautiful bashful boy,
whose blazingly brown eyes, consumed, controlling me, royalty was not to rove with a pauper.
So a luminous shell cached a lifetime of devotion in that aqua green sea.

The day the tides turned thrashing that green sea, time had come for him to leave —
for war was calling, claiming his name, I gulped and grasped for him to stay,
while the churning, yearning waves swirled and hurled the sand, which were calling, calling his name.

That last sight of the boy as he caught my eye and whispered goodbye, I knew that the ignorant, infidelity of a father,
plotting and planning a wager of war for assassination; putting an end to the boy, who was destined to always love me.

Years and years past, I am still with him, hearing his voice singing through the shell,
from that tragically thrashing day, where they took my life away.
In that aqua green sea, he is still destined to always love me.

Brooke Thibodaux, Grade 11
Lafayette Sr High School, MO

No Longer

In the future I will no longer be a teenager in her mom's house waking up to the sound of her voice saying "it's time to get up." Instead I'll be waking up to the sound of a noisy alarm clock wishing it was my mom instead. No longer will she be there to fix me dinner after a long day at school. Instead I'll be putting mac n' cheese in the microwave for a fast dinner. No longer will I be in high school. Instead I'll be on my way to making a career path of my own. Making decisions on my own. Doing the things that were once done for me, on my own. Then I'll finally appreciate all the things she's done for me in the past. In the future I'll be a woman on my own.

Rheana Auvil, Grade 10
Capital High School, WV

The Girl I See

Her face so soft it makes you believe that she has had nothing wrong in her life
Her eyes full of confusion and sadness
Her past so rundown and full of let downs
But yet she is strong which confuses a lot of people that know of her past and still
The light of hope shines throughout her life in her hard times
Now the New Year has come and she has found another bad thing to put in to her hard past
But from what I hear from her voice each time I talk to her she is starting to trust one guy
Just enough that he might have a chance to be in her life
He knows of her rough past and life
That he has seen and heard from standing beside her since the day he met her
She had gone through one relationship that really left a mark
He hopes that with his love and care he can fix her heart as good as new
This guy knows that his chances at her are really quit slim
But he just wants her to be happy
Is what I hear and I hope that she sees that and lets him in to her life
Knowing that it might be a risk but risks come and they go you have to take them
Or the ones you see that are fighting for and from what this guy has told me
She is a risk worth fighting for and when he has it protect it at all costs
He says that she is like gold that has had a hard and brutal life
But still shines like it were just found

Christopher Flowers, Grade 10
Gibson County High School, TN

Sacrifice

On this day in '82
Some were standing
But only a few

There is a memorial in the big Washington D.C.
For everyone in the world to see

It all started in '59 in Vietnam
Because no one there gave a damn

We went in and took them out
We knew we could without a doubt

Now it is one big memory
Cause, that's what it takes to be free

But there is one thing lastly I have to add
That makes a part of everyone feel so sad

All gave some
But, some gave all

Brandon Decker, Grade 12
Richland High School, MO

Drowning Without Water

Strength was never my companion
nor with my spirit deep inside,
So I cowered in the corner falling
as my heart dropped beneath the floor.

The one to whom I had given all
abandoned our delay,
to break the saddened silence
shielding us from further pain.

Swallowed by destruction's wave,
my breath burning through my chest
too meek to push the fear away,
too broken to fight back.

The ever-looming danger
had arrived before its time.
Sand slipped through the foggy glass —
to mark the deadlines ever past.

My soul forgotten, my body failed
lying shattered in this place
I should have pushed a little harder
to avoid this crushing fate.

Hannah Elise Schuckmann, Grade 11
St Francis Borgia Regional High School, MO

Cheese Cake

Oh how I love to eat a fresh cheesecake
I marvel in its cheesy, rich delights
A taste unlike any other it will make
As it enters my mouth I get the frights
All this thinking has made me hungry
I must have a nice big cheesy slice
I think that I will get a nice piece of brie
It will have just the right amount of spice
But wait what's this, the cake box is spent
Alas the point of my existence is gone
Hope! Into my nose has come a cheesy scent
Where is it from, the hunt for a slice is on
I follow it and find an empty plate
Alas it's gone, the world had dealt me a cruel fate

Patrick Fagel, Grade 12
Covington Catholic High School, KY

Handful of Choices

Life is full of choices
many which you make,
whether they're right or wrong it's for your own sake.
The decision is not up to others, but up to you,
being loyal and dedicated always stay true.
Every day you wake up live life and never let go,
morals should stay high and never low.
Most people have dreams so shoot for the sky,
don't give up always try.
Sometimes when life is down and in the rough,
just remember that life isn't easy it's tough.
Always show respect and expect it in return,
from your mistakes you should learn.
Not wealthy or live a rich lifestyle,
don't ever be someone you're not or in denial.
Learn lessons early and then don't regret,
if your mind is right then your life should be set.

Harrison Haugland, Grade 12
Bixby High School, OK

The Presence of Pain

Remember the day love fell upon them —
And how at on time they had been at peace?
She never expressed her likeness for him...
But he knew because she had been so at ease.

For only a minute they'd talk by phone...
Cause the next they'd be standing side by side.
They never thought the other would be gone,
But then one day their love began to die.

She pretended everything was just fine,
But deep inside her she can't help but cry.
She won't put her feelings out on the line,
So she sits in her room and simply sighs.

She knows she will find someone of her own,
And that she never wants to be alone...

Elizabeth Hopkins, Grade 12
Sparkman High School, AR

Memories

I miss the time
When my grandfather hugged me

I miss the time
When my mother taught me how to write

I miss the time
When I first made friends

I miss the time
When I fought with my sister

I miss the time
When I first graduated

I miss the time
When I first met you

Oh…I miss
Those times

Sung-won Mun, Grade 10
Family of Faith Christian School, OK

Rain

Watch the water fall
As it falls fast from the sky
In the cool morning.

Bionka James, Grade 10
Fort Towson Jr/Sr High School, OK

Safe at Last

I don't know her mother
And I don't know her dad
But when I see her at school
She always seems so sad
She hardly ever smiles
Or even says a word
But from the bruises I see
Her pain is still heard
She escapes this world
To a far away place
Where she feels happy, and loved,
And protected by God's grace
Her name written in stone
With an angel nearby
With her wings outstretched
And her face toward the sky
She is now with God
The pain is gone away
For her world of hurt has faded away
She is now with him
To forever stay

Raven Knowles, Grade 10
White County High School, TN

Here I Sit

Here I sit all broken hearted,
I feel so lonely, yet so in love.
I met this girl whom I really like.
I would ask her out but here I sit.
So I can sum up all my feelings in one sentence.
Here I sit so broken hearted, yet so in love.

Corey Steed, Grade 10
Bradford High School, AR

I Am*

I am shy.
I remember moving from Charlotte.
I heard my friend talking about me.
I saw nothing.
I worried about my cousin when she was in an abusive relationship.
I think my life is going to be good.
I am adventurous.
I think the world is good and bad.
I want to graduate from high school.
I try to do better in school.
I feel great.
I am sweet.
I love my friends, family, and my boyfriend, Eric.
I dream to be famous one day.
I hope to still be a good daughter and girlfriend.
I predict I'll be the same person I am now.
I know I will be the same person I am now.
I am me.

Sara Paxton, Grade 10
Capital High School, WV
**Based on "Freedom Writers"*

Stand and Believe

I, America, am beginning to shatter
But my people make the dreadful suggestion, "Does it really matter?"
Yes, it should matter; this is the land of the free
And then I ask myself, "How could that be?"
In a time, we can't even live without fear
All because of one frightful day that wasn't so mere
Two planes crashed into the World Trade Center
And from then on everything went cold like the winter
These days in '07 it's so hard to make a living
And very few people are out there still giving
In '05 Miss Katrina ruined a day
And people "up there" didn't even pay
Pay for the damage that shouldn't have been done
And now you walk away thinking you've won
There's times when you need to realize
That most people are hidden; in disguise
Just like you said on the news
That is the way I choose
I want you to remind yourself day after day
All these words and what I'm about to say
I'm neither a pessimist not an optimist; I am a realist.

Alex Chow, Grade 10
Gibson County High School, TN

A Baby Angel*

I once held this little precious baby girl,
A beauty that you can only dream of.
All I wished was to watch her dance and twirl,
But now she is in the heaven above.
This precious girl, Angel her given name,
The only life she knew was in the womb.
Without her things will never be the same,
Since all we can do is visit her tomb.
Life here on Earth is so precious you see,
Please don't take it for granted.
I can explain, only if you ask me,
Life is not something just to be planted.
Always remember to hold those so dear,
Close to your beating heart and have no fear.

Angela Grizzle, Grade 10
Tuckerman High School, AR
**In loving memory, Angel Lorene Grizzle 1-31-05*

The Last Ride

We moved quickly, our anticipation growing,
we watched the other riders spinning, the music loudly flowing.
We edged up excitedly to the front of the line,
with an even bigger line growing behind.
Finally it was our turn, and we searched for a seat,
an interesting song came on, but I can't remember the beat.
He sat on the inside, and I to his right,
we were ready to strap in, and our ride to take flight.
Slowly the ride began to go.
Quickly it sped up to begin the show.
The lights flashed, and the music blared,
and there was a lot of laughter he and I shared.
I remember our complaining that night,
as the ride stopped it's flight.
Down the steps though, we happily stumbled.
To our family, about our adventure, we rumbled.
The moon found us an hour later,
our happiness could not be greater.
Curled up in the back seat, fighting sleep,
we thought about our day, a memory we'd keep.
Side by side, we soon fell asleep.

Holleigh Hatcher-Mullins, Grade 10
Shady Spring High School, WV

Hair

My hair likes to talk to me
Some days my hair is tired, and it falls flat on my head
Other days it's perky and excited, full of volume and life
Many days I find myself cursing at my hair
It's just so uncooperative, and I get frustrated
Other days I give up, and don't even care
But when neat hair is needed
I attack with a full of arsenal of brushes and products
A gel for curls
An iron for straightening
My messy hair screams to me in pain and defeat
But I curse back saying HA! I have tamed the beast!

Elizabeth Stagich, Grade 10
Germantown High School, TN

Illusion

there's so much tension inside
that my thoughts are pushed aside
wondering who I once was
wondering who I am because…
I am lost; I am found
now I'm safe; now I'm sound
this just makes my head go round
as I tumble to the ground
it's ok, I am here
but you are nowhere near
this is just as I might fear;
to the right path I attempt to veer
I search everywhere to find
that something in my mind
to provide assurance of escape from the bind
that keeps me entangled and left behind
but you are here; you are near…
are you going to chase away my fear?
I thought you were a friend to hold dear…
now this has ruined the rest of my year…
did I find you? or did you disappear?

Amanda Devine, Grade 11
Washington County High School, KY

In His Arms

In his arms my problems go away
In his arms my world stands still
In his arms I could stay for a day
In his arms nothing seems real

When he holds me I'm always breathless
When he holds me it's like no one's there
When he holds me I'm never restless
When he holds me I don't have a care

But in his eyes I see nothing but pain
In his eyes I know confusion's there
In his heart his hurt has left a stain
In his heart he wants someone to care

In my mind I want him to know I do
In my mind his name's always there
In my mind there is confusion too
In my mind I want him to care

But I cannot let my feelings show
I cannot fall for his charms
I'll just stay here knowing what I know
While I'm safe here in his arms

Brittany Shannon, Grade 11
Spring Valley High School, WV

Did I Let You Know?

Hold my hand.
Don't go away.
I love you more than anything.
Why did you have to go so early?
Tell me why.
Tell me why you had to go so early.
I saw you lying on the floor.
I didn't know what to do.
Tell me why.
Tell me why I didn't know what to do.
Did I let you know I love you?
Did I let you know you were the best?
Did I let you know you were my hero?
Did I let you know?

Anna Hyatt, Grade 11
McGehee High School, AR

Among the Sun*

Among the sun
and sky
I saw the letter "W"
in red
on a black and orange
racquet
moving
swiftly
unheeded
to aces
racquet swings
and clapping hands
through the air.

Megan Williams, Grade 11
Union County High School, TN
**Parody of "The Great Figure"*

For You, Son

Bitterness inside
Joy showing out
Sorrow in the eyes
Smile from the mouth

Fear in the heart
Courage on the face
Skeptic on the inside
Trusting to the face

Laughter during day
Crying in the night
Weak in the dark
Strong in the light

Wanting to give up
Staying for the light
A single drop of hope
The love of one small life

Kimberly Fouty, Grade 10
Capital High School, WV

Eternal Fire

My life is an everlasting fire,
that no one could possibly put out.
My soul being the indestructible wood
that keeps the fire about.
My spirit being the eternal flames
that keeps my contentment abundant.
My heart being the water
that keeps the fire stable and fluent.
The fire will still be burning
the very moment I close my eyes.
This beautiful, eternal fire
is my life in disguise.

Delene Gonzalez, Grade 11
Hollis High School, OK

Purifying Water

Thy water is purifying thy soul,
As thy glimpse goes to a stare.
It flows like blood in thy veins,
It may cleanse thy soul with purity.

Purify thy heart,
So hatred wouldn't be a burden.
Cleanse thy heart,
For what has been darkened,
May banish forever.
Thy soul and thy heart,
Be purified.

Pamela Bixman, Grade 11
Parkersburg South High School, WV

Uhhhh…

Have you ever wondered,
what if we're the real reflections,
on the other side of the mirror?
what if our reflections,
are the real ones?
What if they, wonder the same thing?
Have you ever wondered
why is that person so crazy?
Do you think they ever wonder,
why we are so crazy?
Maybe the things they see and hear,
are what is true.
Maybe we are the crazy ones.
Have you ever wondered,
which way is up?
Which you is the real you?
How many mistakes you have to make,
before life is the way you want it,
and all your questions,
disappear?

Christina DeChaine, Grade 11
Powell High School, TN

Losing Someone

Losing someone dear,
Having an empty feeling.
All of the sudden fear,
Almost as your lips are sealing.
All that we have gone through,
Wasting all our time.
Paying off your dues,
Listening to all those lies.
Getting over the thoughts,
Believing everything you said.
Staring at the dots,
That was such a dread.
Fighting when we would talk,
Yelling over nothing.
Needing to take a walk,
Now listening to the screaming.
Realizing real regret,
Look at all the clues.
Now it's time to set,
Finally getting over you.
Losing someone dear.

Elizabeth Hager, Grade 11
Slater High School, MO

The Storm

The lightning struck
The thunder cracked
The barn split in half
From the massive impact

The tornado touched down
A mile away
She began to wonder
If she would see another day

The air got quite thick
The rain turned to hail
She opened her eyes
As the wind seemed to exhale

The power came on
As quickly as it had gone out
She didn't know
What all of this was about

For she was just ten
And oh so alone
She continued to wait forever
For her parents to come home

Gemma Hardy, Grade 10
Coffee County Central High School, TN

Confusion and Sadness

I sit here
by the window while the fall sun sinks low.
I wait until the wind comes near,
and that is when I'll know.

I know your absence is here,
but I know not how.
With it running through my mind comes a tear,
and I have to go now.

But where shall I go?
Somewhere away from home.
But then again I do not know.
Then I remind myself, I am still alone.

The thought of you gives me chills,
like the slight touch of a feather,
the feeling of time standing still.
And then I feel like stormy weather.

I don't know where we went.
I guess we've had our share of good times.
Those were memories well spent,
like the earlier readings of small children's rhymes.

Chelsey Smith, Grade 12
Union County High School, TN

Awaken

the wet dewy grass lay silent in search of a new day
i feel the mustard sun blaze with passion
as it seeps through my naked soul
it battles with the fragile breeze refreshing my bones
the flag hangs lifeless as the whispering wind
pauses to catch a breath
a falling leaf streaked with butter
as autumn's rebirth peaks through the towering trees
a withered body and wrinkled smile
almond, fading gray
stands rigid, strangled by the serpent
gasps for air as it reaches up
up to a cloudless sky
close to god
but one day i'll be closer
now only the presence of a lost love
lingers over the ground
i see the stones lie subdued
screaming, yet no one hears
a question of second life
arises.

Christina Dilley, Grade 11
North Bullitt High School, KY

I Have No Words

I could say you were perfect
But that wouldn't be you
No words can explain
You're great beyond compare

I could say you are amazing
But you're much more
I can't even describe you
Way sweeter than a flower and a rainy day

I could say you were handsome
But your gentleness extreme
Can't even put two words together
You wipe my tears away

I have to say you were…

Lacey Marie Heather, Grade 10
Slater High School, MO

Come Together

Because they hate they hear only noise.
With minds closed and ears blocked, differences scare.
Colors, ideas, shapes beautiful, hate grinds and destroys,
And with each loss our Earth becomes more bare.

Some of us sparkle and exude our light.
We could spend our lifetime waiting for change.
Let your light blind those hearts that live in night;
Force tolerance to reach a higher range.

We are pieces in the mighty puzzle.
When we come together a mosaic made.
Silence breaks us so take off your muzzle,
Properly united, more precious than Jade.

So let us melt and abandon all fears;
All humanity hand in hand, retire tears.

Alexandra Baker, Grade 11
St Mary's Episcopal School, TN

Making a Difference

I can make a difference by giving
time, knowledge, or means.
I can make a difference in the world
affecting one person or many.
There are many ways a difference can be made
many ways to change the world for the better.
A difference is made by changing a life,
man or child.
A difference is made by lifting one up,
be he broken in need of repair.
A difference is made by educating the world
be it about a religion or a crisis
A difference is made by one person
These are all paths to making a difference;
all paths of how I can make a difference.

Asad Ali Sajwani, Grade 11
Germantown High School, TN

Nightmare

It was just one of those days
When no matter what you do or try
Everything goes wrong in every way
And you cannot imagine why
Hoping you're sleeping, you look around
And find that you are wide awake
For a safe place you bound
As you feel your hands starting to shake
Your boyfriend's sad
Your mom is calling
Your best friend's mad
And you feel like bawling
It's the worst thing to feel
To have a nightmare when you're awake
You wish it wasn't real
As your whole world starts to shake
Tears are falling
Your world starts to quake
Everyone is calling
It's a nightmare while you're awake

Crystal Solomon, Grade 10
Comanche High School, OK

Life or Death

Where we go when we die
Is determined by our lives.
And if you believe, through faith, you will
Find yourself better off still,
Some do choose to end their life
Without the love of Jesus Christ.
If you turn your life to God,
He will lift you from the fog.
And take you to Heaven where you shall
Never rot in the halls of Hell.

Cory Jenkins, Grade 11
Woodrow Wilson High School, WV

Faces

Faces, all around me
laughing at my sight.
People, saying it will
never be all right.
What have I done
to deserve this?
Just for once
I want bliss.
Why do they laugh
as I am crying?
Do they not know
that inside I am dying?
They must not think that
my life should be spared.
They don't, now I know
that no one ever cared.

Josh Ingram, Grade 10
South Intermediate High School, OK

The Window of Life

I peer into life, a stranger watching through the window.
Feeling misunderstood, out of place, asking myself, "Why am I so different?"
The answer is simple, I am me and no one new
I smile to myself, and keep living.
Only realizing that we are all different,
Special and talented in our own way,
I peer again into this window.
Watching, listening, learning,
I find myself wondering, "What is the outcome of this so called life."
Again the answer comes to me,
The outcome is what you want it to be.
A phrase used by many others comes to mind,
Live, learn, love,
Three simple words with much depth and meaning,
The time has come for me to take my place in life.
I will no longer peer through the window,
For it has prepared me for what is to come.

Blanca Martinez, Grade 12
Commerce High School, OK

His Word

Have you ever felt sad, hopeless, or depressed?
Have you ever wondered if there's more to life than you could have ever guessed?
Jesus Christ came into this world to tell us that there is,
so if you don't believe my words then just accept his.

He is the Alpha, the Omega, the true King of Kings,
the one who gave all of heaven's angels their wings.
His father, our Lord, created us all.
He will always be there to help us when we stumble or fall.

So, if ever in a dilemma, go to him and pray.
He is available for discussion every second of every day.
You may think this sounds crazy, but don't knock it 'till you've tried it.
Once you're filled with God's grace and joy there's no way you can hide it.

Alexis Williams, Grade 10
Coffee County Central High School, TN

Inner Self

The rage teems through my system
My head aches in remonstrance to insane thoughts
Hate, like that of Antigone,
Will eventually be my downfall
Diabolical thoughts race through my head
Crushing any compassion
Avarice quickly follows
Poseidon's storms cannot match my fury
I clench my fists in a futile effort not to explode
My family, those who are supposed to love me, do incite my rage
There is no Athena to guide my actions
My fit of rage culminates with a resounding scream
Then flows away
Leaving me to deal with the consequences

Margaret Durnett, Grade 10
Germantown High School, TN

My Grandmother

My heart is aching with a loss;
She was my strength, my supporter.
A wonderful lady who loved to cook;
An empty place in my stomach remains.

I remember all the card games we used to play;
All the fun we had together.

Without her, my life is less;
She meant so much to me.
Now she is in heaven with all her love;
she watches over me all the time.

Benton Stott, Grade 11
Bearden High School, TN

From Rhyme to Reason

Don't bother them with complexities
They've heard them all before,
Just give them the facts and nothing but —
They have no need for lies.
Where is simplicity?
They've grown too sick of mystery,
To care much for the abstract things,
Those things in life that mean so much.
And they used to be poets!
They say to themselves,
Men and women and restless hearts,
Who beat for them both rhythm and rhyme.
But somewhere along the line,
They lost what they possessed.
Searching for words in a logical world,
That had long ago abandoned them.
And so they traded in their rhymes with unfeeling reason,
Desperate souls for unflinching science.

Michael Norris, Grade 11
Russellville High School, AR

Wake Up! Take Your Cross!

I hear him calling, calling my name
When will I answer? Why would I stay?
His vision is better, His will is deeper.
He is the Glory risen, my life to Him is given.
I hear Him now, "Take up your cross and go.
Why would you stay? When will you go?"
He's shown me their faces, shown their lost souls.
I hear their cries; they're dying inside.
I am a mobile soldier of the Lord Most High.
He's chosen me, sent me for them.
Their daily terror is coming to an end.
Time doesn't stop; eternity won't wait.
I want to meet the lost, give them more than fate.
He chose me for this task, to intercede for the battle at hand.
So intercede I must to save their souls and then
Will His victory and Glory be complete in the end.
So here I am taking up my cross,
Only then can we save the lost.

Devin Pringle, Grade 10
Family of Faith Christian School, OK

The Most Wonderful Time of the Year

Oh, I love this time of year!
The weather is changing,
The leaves falling, guided to the ground by the frigid wind.
Everyone listening to carols,
Singing "Fa la la" and "Joy to the World,"
And going shopping for loved ones.
Even the father, grumbling as he puts lights on the house
Finds time to be jolly and festive.
The kids peek into the store windows
Dreaming about what surprises their parents are planning,
The anticipation building and building,
Until the children think they'll burst with excitement!
Then, finally, Christmas Eve arrives and
The kids go to bed early so Santa can come down the chimney.
Even before the sun rises in the morning,
The children pounce on the sleeping parents
Screaming "He came! He came!"
After the presents have been opened,
And the mess cleared away,
It starts all over again,
A never-ending cycle.

Emily Neldon, Grade 11
Owasso High School, OK

Expected Report

"I'll be expecting you report next class"
What?! I haven't even started yet!
Anxiety, pressure, fear consuming me
I arrive home and sit at my desk
Cluttered and out of order like my mind at the moment

I start
Nothing comes out
Still thinking
Still nothing
Distractions everywhere

What's on TV?
How many tiles are in the ceiling?
I wonder what my friends are doing
Focus! I start...finally
Words come out
Maybe not the best but words none the less

A late night behind me I walk into class
After hours of anxiety and pain
The first words of the school's day
"Assignment moved to next week"
I sink.

Kyle Boland, Grade 10
St Francis Borgia Regional High School, MO

Then and Only Then

Then and only then when you smiled did heaven become thrust down upon the earth, and you ascended above it to become the embodiment of perfection.

And when our lips meet, it is as if the two souls that used to be ours ceased to be separate, and became one, and I would turn down heaven again and again to continue to thrive in the personal utopia that we created for each other, were no impurities could ever befoul it.

And how I envy the wind, the wind that gently brushes against your face, hence its very purpose of its existence, and should the wind ever become enraged, your presence could cease its anger and it would remember why it was put on this earth.

And should eternity ever cease to be, I would not fear it, for I have known what perfection is, and our souls became one, and that could never be faded out in nothingness.

Matthew Lear, Grade 12
Centralia High School, MO

Unanswered Questions?

Why does it hurt so bad to love someone? Does it hurt because you know that life is not going to be the same without that person? Does it hurt because you loved them so much until you forgot how to love yourself? How come I never saw that one day you would leave me? Why did I only see a bright future for you and me? I never saw that you wouldn't be by my side. Why did you say that you would always be with me and that you would never leave me? Does the pain have to hurt so bad that when you cry you give yourself a headache? What do you do when you love someone and you cannot tell if they love you back because their actions say otherwise? How do you get pass the pain and the hurt; will it ever go away or will it stay with you forever? Will I ever find someone as sweet and special as you were; will that time be better than the last? Why does it seem like the people whom you love the most hurt you the worse? Where does the pain come from, has it always been there just waiting to break through and turn you into this evil deceitful person, someone you do not want to be? Will I ever be able to love like that again or will I find a way to forgive and forget and allow them back into my life? Will you hurt me again? Grandma I love you so why did you have to go? Will their ever be answers to my questions, or is the answer live and as you live you will learn that's just how life is? Does the answer live in me who knows that's all part of unanswered questions?

Leslie Stewart, Grade 12
Middle College High School at Southwest Tennessee Community College, TN

Searching the World for My Missing Puzzle Piece

Growing up, it was clear to me that something was missing; there was a missing piece to my puzzle of life.
My missing puzzle piece was almost within reach; you were it.
The puzzle was nearly complete,
Then, your mom took you away and Dad never mentioned your name.
I was left in a state of utter confusion, my puzzle still incomplete.
Eight years later, I picked up my phone and heard your voice on the other end.
Could it really be you?
My missing piece was getting closer once again.
My head asked, "Will the outcome be the same as before?"
While my heart said, "Give it a shot, what could it hurt?"
So, I gave it another try.
We met up at that lonely old gas station,
Then, almost suddenly,
You disappeared again and I was lost, confused again.
As I sit here with my world in disarray,
My heart broken,
My mind completely puzzled,
My puzzle piece lost yet again,
I wonder where you are; where could you possibly be?
You're my older sister; I don't understand why you always disappear.

Amanda Brown, Grade 11
Owasso High School, OK

Shattered Pieces

It's not enough
For one to go on in a household like this
To feel the pressures of everyday life
To feel left out by one of your family.
Fourteen years have passed
Since he decided to finally notice me
We spent endless weekends together
It felt like he really loved me.
But then it happened
He left me again
Shattering my world into tiny pieces
And I fell apart…again.
You see, once you've been broken
It's hard to come back from it
You pick up all of the pieces
And try and put them back together.
Trying to fit these pieces together
You find that some are missing
Because they are lost to you
But I will never forget those memories
So maybe I can have the hope of reawakening them again.

Kaitlin Stacy, Grade 10
Capital High School, WV

I Don't Understand

I don't understand,
How could this happen to you
I don't understand,
But I know that you'll get through
It's such a mystery.

I don't understand,
You were always the one that cared for me.
I don't understand,
Couldn't you just be forgiven?
I don't understand,
Why no one can know
I need someone to understand me.

I understand,
That you're worried that I wouldn't care.
I understand,
The friends that would be hurt.

I don't understand,
The future and what it may bring.
We are both scared of that thought and the pain.
Please, just let me tell you one more thing:
I will never fail, I will always be there.

Kenna Sudweeks, Grade 11
Owasso High School, OK

Surface

"Resurface"
In a violent gale of teenage paroxysm,
A sliver of scorn and despondency upon my face,
I hurl a door closed
In a technological world of many connections,
Of USBs and flash drives, of resolutions and mega-pixels,
I am detached

I stride, bobbing in black still water,
Asphalt, chill in the first glimpse of fall's pale somber visage,
Moves beneath my pale pink-shaded toes

I inhale the fragrance of the afternoon,
No longer incased in the cavern of self pity,
No longer within the pit of teenage dejection
The sun bathes my face, and I smile

Jennifer Dobbins, Grade 11
Bearden High School, TN

My Love Tragedy

The tragedy of love within my life
Takes a hold of me and strangles my soul.
It's very strong grip on me takes a toll,
Tears through my heart like a razor sharp knife.
It steals my soul like the Grim Reaper's scythe.
It turns my once clean heart as black as coal.
Though I try to fill the deep, deep hole,
I can't get over this horrible strife.

But there still is hope for my horrid fate.
For hope has been restored through his blue eyes.
His loving voice brings me a hint of joy.
Once again life I can appreciate.
When he talks to me, tears of joy I cry
Because I know with my heart, he won't toy.

Brittany Ryser, Grade 12
Niangua High School, MO

Wondering

the leaves of autumn
the short days of our life
roll on as summer turns to fall
and us, as the leaves change
we are full of color and life
beautiful highs and lows
our souls blow in the cool autumn breeze
as I watch us age waiting…
wondering…just what's going to happen
trying to separate what's real from fiction
wondering if I'll see the brightest of my days
and now it is time
too much time wasted wondering and waiting
and with the swift cold wind
of winter, all is gone and now
all I can say is what if and why now
I shouldn't have wasted so much time wondering

Zachary Wiseman, Grade 12
Rockwood High School, TN

I Am Done

You said you'd be here,
When I needed you,
You filled my head,
Full of words, thoughts,
You made my heart,
Smile like the sun shining,
I thought you,
Were the one,
But not the one for me,
You turned around,
You broke my heart,
Wasn't there for me,
When I needed,
You the most,
You were not
Sorry,
But now you,
Want me back,
But I can't,
Take that chance,
To get hurt again.

Allyson Chaney, Grade 11
Slater High School, MO

Pain

Love, Hurt, Damage, Tears
All these feelings are feared
Crying in the night
Struggling with the fight
Being pulled from each and every side
Never smiling, continuously
praying to be saved
For it seems like nobody dares
To come this way
Wondering when the time
Will come when everything ends
Hearing a voice saying that it's only began
Scared to death to see the rest
Heart beat slowly fading away
veins are popping day after day
Until there is no longer anything left,
But yet nobody knows
that he who struggled
is now dead.

J'Meia Molina, Grade 10
Mills University Studies High School, AR

Love Stays

Hours fly,
Flowers die,
New days,
New ways,
Pass by,
Love stays.

Cody Smith, Grade 10
Crocker High School, MO

Mom

Having to cry at the thought of you.
Undoing the way I feel, isn't an option.
Rewinding in my mind the lies you've led,
To understand why you pushed me aside.
Inconsiderate thoughts that are poison.
Neglect that was overdone.
Grant me the peace, you'll never feel.

Stacy Sorrell, Grade 11
Colbert High School, OK

looking back

looking back i know how much she was there
looking back i know how much she cared
looking back i don't know how she gave me this life
looking back i can't imagine the hurt she suffered
looking back i cannot comprehend the drive she must have felt
looking back i know her love is unconditional
looking back i wish she would have received the amount she gave
looking back i can't believe i almost lost her
looking back i am so glad she took me to church
looking back i am proud of the qualities she instilled
looking back i realize the person she set me up to be
looking back i know she was the one i always strived to please
looking back i don't know what i would've done without her
looking back i know she is the one i feared to disappoint
looking back i cherish all the fun times we've had
looking back i know she could have chosen other things
looking back i feel privileged to have been put above all
looking back i know she thinks she should've done things different
looking back i know she did everything as planned
looking back i wouldn't change any moment for the world
looking back i love being able to call her momma

Jenna Fuller, Grade 11
Owasso High School, OK

Lazy Mornings

Extremely early.
Twilight zone.
Airy feelings say "We quit."
What do I want?
Thinking about trying not to think.
Fidgeting with a pencil, rolling smoothly between my knuckles.
Flash of a rickety, old room, an art studio with hours of paintings.
Monday mustiness of Jahan's shoe store on Main Street,
Aroma of newly shipped, rubber-soled shoes.
Odd sensation of just waking up again.
Wind blowing through tattered, milky blinds.
Moth holes in everything.
Idle couches in the corner.
The sun blanketed by lavender clouds.
I am dizzy.
Thinking about trying not to think.
Thinking about trying not to think.
The bed, my black-hole, pulls me back.

Rasheeq Jahan, Grade 12
Batesville High School, AR

Friends

Like thine own self set apart
Lost in a world tasteless and tart
Subordinate to most grown-up people
Clinging to God's word under the steeple
Praying for each other to get by
Under a roof with stars in the sky
Although sometimes acting possessed
Losing sight on how much they've been blessed
Picking each other up when one falls
Acting like it was nothing at all
Backing them up for moral satisfaction
Not worrying about the consequences of their actions
Prepared to endure blows in a fight
No matter the time of day or night
Laughing together when they catch a break
Knowing how much each one can take
Sharing what they want to do with their life
No matter the trials, tribulations, or strife
Changing as much as each new clothing trend
Promising to always be close to the end

Trevor Kinkead, Grade 11
Centralia High School, MO

What We Feel

We're going on what we feel.
We're going on what we think is right.
If this is the way it's supposed to happen,
Then why would we try and fight.
What our hearts are telling us:
This is how it's meant to be.
Our hearts and minds are saying the same.
For once, they finally agree.
Being with you, I won't regret.
The words you say, I'll never forget.
The way you look into my eyes
Is how I know I've found the right guy.
Taking the risk and chancing the fall,
We're putting it all on the line;
But since you gave me your heart,
I finally decided to give you mine.
Though I don't know where it'll take me,
I'm ready for this adventure.
It doesn't matter where we end up,
As long as we end up together.

Brianna Romero, Grade 10
Grove High School, OK

My Broken Name

Something has happened to my name.
It has been battered, bruised, and beaten
By those who do not share it.
Actions of others caused this abhorrence
Of my autonym.
I do not understand why my name
Has to suffer sequestration for the crimes
Of evil men.

Paolo Viguali, Grade 11
Germantown High School, TN

Butterflies

Floating through the sky.
Feeling as though I'll never die.
I am a butterfly with pretty wings.
Two eyes on each side, and peaceful I sing.
I flutter around and feel no pain.
Oh no, HELP ME, it's starting to rain.
I float to a bush, shielded by a leaf.
I think about times as they used to be.
I remember when I was in a cocoon so small.
And when I was a worm, who could only crawl.
So green, and fat, eating leaves like the one I'm under.
HELP ME, I'm scared, it's starting to thunder.
Back to memories of when I couldn't fly.
All I wanted to do was roll over and die.
In the end I got my wings.
But until the rain stops listen to me sing.
I sing songs of love, peace, and happy stuff.
Even about times when they are tough.
I hate the rain and miss the sunshine.
Wishing that it was all, and only mine.
I hope you made sense of my life as a butterfly.

Danae Eddy, Grade 10
Slater High School, MO

Deeper in She Falls

From upside down to right side up
I see true beauty in your eyes
All tears fall, but not for bad
Just for good she cries.

She's always looking down
Too scared to believe in the true beauty
She's falling in love, but scared she lies
"To me, things like this don't happen."

She asks herself a million questions
Like, "Why this do I deserve?"
In the blink of an eye, life can't go from bad to good
She cries, "Dear Lord, I must be dreaming!"

The goose bumps overwhelm her
As she trembles at his touch
As she craves for one more kiss
As she falls and can't get up.

Everything else matters
But he matters more than all
She's scared of love and what it does
But deeper in she falls.

Brittany Turpin, Grade 10

Boy of My Fantasy

Oh boy of my fantasy
Is that really you waving at me
Is that you finally noticing me
And realizing who I am

Oh my boy of fantasy
I have waited so long
I have waited for the planets to come in alignment
I have waited for them to play my song

Too long have we been just friends
Too long have I been just there
Now is the time you notice me
Now is my time to shine

I dream every day of what we could be
And all the things that we could share
All the journeys that we would embark
And you would be by my side

And as I am pulled back from my fantasies
I realize a heartbreaking thing
I realize that you're not waving at me
You're waving at the girl at my side

Rachel Weatherby, Grade 10
Campbell County High School, KY

Rock

I floated free as a rock
All the world seemed to mock
Me and my sunken state
A comedy act, first rate
I ran and I skipped and soared
All the way to the sea floor
There I rolled and tumbled fast
'Til the bottom I rolled past
Above me in the ink black sea
Are fish built abnormally
In the dark some don't have eyes
Others create light, their hunger it belies
They'll eat up the weak who fall for their light lies
Fish are not concerned with me
I sit and stare and all I see
The world only goes up from here
What else is there to fear?
Evil looks I mock
You can't intimidate a rock
Of the sea I am king
I am not rolled or moved by anything

Randall Kania, Grade 11
Powell High School, TN

A Crisp Twenty

Walking down aisle 16, she holds her
Prada in one hand and Sidekick in the other.
Her perfectly French manicured hand
brushes back her sun-bleached hair
off her bronze Greek goddess-like skin.
She texts on her phone like there is no tomorrow.
Not paying attention to the world around her,
she nearly runs over a scraggy little girl and boy.
"They must be hungry," she thinks.
"The little girl looks five,
and the little boy looks barely two."
Their baggy clothes are torn and dirty.
The words her snobby parents say fly through her mind.
"Filthy, beggars, trash, dirt, not worthy of life..."
Looking at them, she feels terrible.
She hands over a crisp twenty-dollar bill
and walks away before they can thank her.
She looks back just in time to see
the smile on their mom's face.
The mom just received more money
than she had made all week.

Audrey Loyd, Grade 11
Germantown High School, TN

Change of Hate

How easy it is to be happy and free,
Then join in with hate, the result will be me.
The day starts out happy, bright as can be.
It shows in my smile, my voice full of glee.
When you think life is great and you can't be pulled down,
Your love has been stolen, a car crash downtown.
What do you do when life gives you hate?
You ignore it and move on without debate.
What do you do if that hate starts to follow?
You spring wings of hope and fly off, past the hollow.
What do you do when the hate holds on tight?
You shake it right off, though it could take all night.
When that hate turns to friendship, oh when that time comes,
That is when you welcome it into your home.
What do you do if it reverts back?
You could try to blind it with a nice empty sack.
When the hate turns to rage, what would you say?
I would say "Sorry, I had a bad day."

Kenneth Odiorne, Grade 10
South Intermediate High School, OK

Teenage Girl

What do you see
When you look at me?
Nice, sweet girl
Or do you look deeper within?
Do you see my longing for acceptance
Which I portray well, by joking around?
But I found a way to be me
Through Jesus Christ who strengthens me
To be me

Kree Lester, Grade 11
Family of Faith Christian School, OK

His Dwelling Place

When all roads lead to darkness
And I'm blinded by my tears
I can't even feel God's presence
For I'm engulfed by all my fears.

I shut my eyes so tightly
For you see, inside there is a light
It is my Savior calling
"Come and rest awhile tonight."

In here the pain cannot find me
In fact, the world has gone away
When I'm awash in His presence
There are no minutes, hours, or day.

Pure love surrounds me
It is so real, it knows my touch
I start hysterically weeping
My heart cannot hold this much.

I've just told you the most wonderful secret
But do you grasp it, it's really true
It is hidden like a treasure
Go seek it, inside of you.

Steffi Danford, Grade 10
Chickasha High School, OK

The Thrill of a Lifetime

There is nothing like it.
For the two and a half minutes on the mat
Your adrenaline is rushing;
Your heart is pounding;
You have the biggest smile on your face.
The coaches have taken their place by the stereo.
The crowd's cheering goes silent.
Twenty teammates walk out on the mat together.
All the stress and drama forgotten
The music starts and you experience the thrill of a lifetime.
A couple stunts may fall but you don't care,
As long as you gave it your whole heart
That's all that matters.
You hear the last beat to the music
And hit the ending motion, the sharpest a motion can be.
All the sweat and tears pay off.
Your teammates are your best friends at that moment,
No matter past history.
At awards all the teams gather to hear who is the best.
You pray to take that national title.
And the national champion is…

Erica Graham, Grade 11
Owasso High School, OK

Ode to a Diet Coke

A vast journey forth I made to taste gold,
Where my precious carbonation drink rests,
That so keeps me as it waits to be sold,
There is no telling it is but the best,
All other quenchers cannot wrongly boast:
I imbibe you after every day's end;
I can even drink you with my burned toast,
The fear of your absence too great to send,
Sounding a noise to tell of your entry,
You replenish the soul and have no shame,
For I believe tea disgusts the gentry,
And even you remain silent in blame;
My Diet Coke, how shall I cope without?
The answer too great yet so full of doubt.

Sarah Donaldson, Grade 11
St Mary's Episcopal School, TN

Why

Why does life have to be so hard
Why does it have to be so mean
Why are people so unfair
Why can everyone go unseen

Why can we not live our lives to the fullest
Why do we not make the best decision at times
Why do we not give all we have
Why do we feel so different

Why do we give our hearts to people we hardly even know
Why do we not let our true love show
Why do we not allow our whole heart to be known
Why will there never be a day it is shown

Kinnsey Appleberry, Grade 11
McGehee High School, AR

High School Football

It's the lights and the dew,
The tears and the blood,
Where weak men are few,
And dirt becomes mud.
It's the clenching of jaws
And the pounding of hearts,
As the coach makes the call
And the play is about to start.
It's Friday night fever
And it's definitely real,
Everyone isn't a believer
But I know how it feels.
When my feet hit the field
I am ready to play
Because it's football, it's real,
And that's what any true player would say.
It's my dream and my life
And someday will make a great story,
But as for Friday night
It's about pride, power, and glory.

Taylor Morphis, Grade 11
McGehee High School, AR

Release

Anger.
It boils inside you,
Waiting to be released.
But how?
Fist fight, maybe?
Hurtful words?
Screaming, yelling?
Or maybe through the pen to paper?
So many ways,
So many people who let it out differently.
How will you choose to let it out?

Bianca Soto, Grade 11
Montgomery Central High School, TN

Turn

You are nothing.
You are everything.
Without you time stops,
no one can breath
and in long absences
the world dies without your presence
then is reborn of your breath
like millions of phoenix
we are your ever lasting pets.
Pushing away from the master
running our temporary world
into the burning ground
killing ourselves a little at a time.
Slowly you disappear
cruelly tossed around
by your own people.
Why wouldn't you destroy us?
You turn to near myth
and we…
we become everything,
we are nothing.

Sarah McCall, Grade 12
Sullivan East High School, TN

Adults

Why must every step be watched
By a judge with but one setting?
They only glance, when by chance
Your craft you are forgetting

So many flawless moves are made
When you are in the moment
You hear a cheer, and lose your fear
But wait…for your opponent?

So working hard and striving high
They sometimes overlook
Now you must learn, to wait your turn
And take an inner look

Kelsey Gold, Grade 11
Bearden High School, TN

911!

A calm, quiet, uneventful evening —
in a large southern house,
with a wrap around porch.
A pecan grove in the front;
a big lake completing the back,
and no neighbors for miles.
Dad working endless hours,
and two teens with better things to do than stay at home with mom,
Who is left alone in her enormous brown leather recliner,
watching a Do-It-Yourself marathon.
When suddenly a knock is heard,
from the unused front door
creating concern for her.
She answers the door with a bewildered expression,
to the man who quickly exclaims,
Your chimney is on fire!

Tara Lewis, Grade 12
Germantown High School, TN

The Stone

A stone cold statue huddles around a feeding trough,
Like a recluse shading his hideous face from public view.
An elegant marble block is modeled after a man,
Who Circe turned into a grumbling swine.
Walking to the left, through the icy corridor,
I see David dueling a monstrosity of a painted giant,
Marching across the rough canvas.
The diabolical Sirens incite me towards them,
With silent but assumed beautiful voices.
The halls are teeming with life, that of which Poseidon brought,
Marble horses and white quartz Cyclops with humongous clubs fill the room.
The cupidity of Athena,
The woman in gold,
Culminates my trip through the museum as I walk into the warm sunlight.

Robert Sheehan, Grade 10
Germantown High School, TN

Elections

Why must the elections split the people so?
Why can we not agree to disagree?
Why can't we say that we have differences?
There is more than one way to the right solution.
Why can't we just say "I agree with this person?"
And then move on?
Why must we all be wholly on one person's side?
We are all individuals, we all are different.
So why does the public force people to conform to one man's or woman's ideals?
Why must we be so conventional?
The elections should not be about slander.
It should not be about crushing one another to win by default.
It should be about unity.
Saying something to speak your mind.
For the better of the whole country.

Alex Petersen, Grade 12
Rock Bridge Sr High School, MO

Memories

Memories of mine past and present,
Memories of mine to keep,
Memories of mine to regret and resent,
Memories of mine to release.
Memories of mine,
Of me and my friends,
Memories of mine,
Memories that never end.
Memories of mine,
Of times that I have been sad,
Memories of mine and others,
Of the fun times we have had.
Memories of mine past and present,
Memories of mine to keep,
Memories of mine to regret and resent,
Memories of mine to release.
Memories of mine,
That happened in my life,
Precious memories of mine,
Memories that through my time and life,
Will stay and forever be mine.

LeAndra Grant, Grade 11
Mills University Studies High School, AR

Momma Don't Cry

Momma don't cry,
Wipe your tears, and dry your eyes.
It is a struggle we all go through,
at some point in time.

You grew up without your father,
And so did I.
However, if we prayed to God,
then maybe hope will fly by.

Momma don't cry,
It will not be like this forever,
We will get through as long as we stay together…

Momma don't cry,
The struggle is over.
I told you we would make it,
Even if the world's on our shoulders.

Airrice C., Grade 10
Audubon Youth Development Center, KY

Choices

They say the choices we make
Will determine the future we have
Choices can bring pain or joy
They can bring life or death
You only have one chance
So you better choose right
So when the choice comes up
Be ready to make that hard decision
You never know when a choice will change your life

Arkadiy Lenchik, Grade 10
Germantown High School, TN

I Can't Believe

Sitting, staring at the screen.
I can't, no, I *won't* believe what I'm seeing.
Those Twin Towers fell, just like that,
I can't believe they came down so easily.

I can feel it building up inside me,
I can feel my anger seething,
I can feel my shock neutralizing,
I can feel my heart freezing.

My peers are all around me,
Staring just as I,
Thinking the same thing,
"No. This can't be happening."

Oh, but it is.
It is all too real.
Those two towers are no more,
They didn't just disappear.

Here comes the fear,
I can feel it sweeping the nation.
Where will they strike next?
Who will be the next to die?

Rai Feltmann, Grade 11
St Francis Borgia Regional High School, MO

Her Broken Heart

Her heart thirsts for love,
But yet he seems not to care.
Trying too hard to forget every memory
Of him or ever wanting him back.
She remember every tear she shed
From the time he broke her heart.
Not knowing what to di with
All of the bad thoughts of him.
She needs some help,
Some kind of hope.
While she is trying to find herself
And get back to the way she was,
he comes back into her life,
Wanting just one more chance.
She takes him back
With a few concerns.
She wonders why women want
The happiness that is almost impossible to find.
However she knows that
It won't be long
Before her heart is broken again.

Jennifer Rader, Grade 12
Slater High School, MO

No More

I can't stand you anymore so
Why do you have to look at me
with that flirty smile
lead me on, hold my hand
but for just awhile

I hate how you look so good
even when you sweat
but this becoming anything
I wouldn't take a bet
When you talk to me
you look me in the eye
but when your head is turned
you make me want to cry

I just can't get away from you
cause your always there
but sometimes I have to wonder
if you really care
I'm trying to forget you
and have another start
but your name will always be
locked inside my heart

Paige Colpitt, Grade 11
Owasso High School, OK

When It's Gone

What do we have
when it's gone?
Why do we hold in
our deepest thoughts for so long?
We take advantage
of what we have.
But when it's gone
that is just too bad.
Now with only memories
of the past.
They are slowly fading,
but why so fast.
What do we have
when it's gone?
Why do we hold in
our deepest thoughts for so long?

Emily Beanland, Grade 11
Hollis High School, OK

More Than Just Daisies

My life is buried treasure
hidden deep beneath the earth
waiting to be discovered
and give wealth to everyone.
Until then I will stay buried,
covered by the world...
Pushin' up daisies.

Charity Penington, Grade 11
Hollis High School, OK

Anticipate

Anticipation is...the color orange.
It sounds like...a timer ticking.
It tastes like...sugarcoated candy.
And smell like...cookies baking.
Anticipation looks like...a cat ready to pounce.
It makes you feel...impatient.

Sara Brown, Grade 10
Madison High School, MO

Time

It happens every year.
Like the leaves that fall from a tree.
Or the flowers that spring from the ground.
It follows the same routine with new meaning.
The children have it marked.
Adults have to ration what they have to brace for its wintery assault.
Elderly look back at the time with great affection.
They follow the same routine with new meaning
The stores bring in support.
Cars packed full of surprises that will make anyone smile.
Closets full of stowaways until the time is made right.
The same routine is followed with new meaning.
The sky gathers in preparation.
The eve of Christmas comes and moisture builds.
The temperature begins dropping in cooperation.
They work in harmony to follow the same routine with new meaning
The sun peaks over the horizon.
The snow begins to sparkle as the light hits the little ice crystals.
The surprises have suddenly appeared in their places.
The children, adults, and elderly all enjoy what they have been given.
The routine has been followed with new meaning for everything.

Will Layne, Grade 10
Coffee County Central High School, TN

The First Moment

I walked through the brightly lit arch to find darkness
Suddenly the sound of music and smell of perfume blew me away
As my heels came off the carpet I heard them hit hardwood
We crossed the floor to get punch and small snacks
Then he pulled me on the dance floor, during a slow song
I felt his hand on my waist and his other closed on mine
As we stood close and danced he pulled me ever closer
I could smell my perfume and his cologne become one
And his boutonniere and my corsage's aroma stood out
His tux and my dress became so close the fabrics looked entwined
I could feel it coming, because the timing was so right
I knew it would be the night
Suddenly I could feel his soft, warm lips against mine
And I could taste my strawberry lip gloss
It was the perfect timing with the perfect guy
And from that first moment I felt that spark
I knew it was love.

Jonissa Stewart, Grade 10
White County High School, TN

Call for Alteration

From the darkness of the depths arises deception
Caressed by the black-hearted fools who react to creation
With a vengeful smirk as the plot of desecration
Strikes its fierce blow upon the weak-hearted conception.

For what purpose does one devastate
And wreck the beauty of what another creates?
What reasonable explanation could appropriate
Relief from the damaging pains one delegates?

Action should be appropriated to devise
A plan to bring about a reason to revise
This irreproachable demise
Of the familial household that should be given to rise.

No call can bring about a reason
To recreate the original season
Of treason
Upon the right of man to create reason.

Philip Shapiro, Grade 11
Germantown High School, TN

Under Grandma's Trees

So many memories under those trees
All the good the bad and the make believe
All the scrapes and scratches all over our knees
Those were the childhood gifts that we did receive

All the generations those trees have seen
It started with my mom and down to me
An old stove sits and has started to lean
From baking dirt cakes to boiling mud tea

Under the trees spoon dug rivers have lain
Rivers filled with water from granny's crock
Some people might have thought we were insane
They'll never know what those trees had in stock

New generations have began to play
The old trees and new memories can stay

Brittany Sales, Grade 10
Chickasha High School, OK

Rest in Peace

It's been almost three years since I've seen you last,
Remembering all those memories, but now it's just the past.
Wondering how you could do such a thing,
I never knew how much sadness it could bring.
I know you had a really horrible life
And how it involved so much pain and strife,
But that doesn't give you a reason to
End your life; you should have started new.
Sometimes I just go and lay on my bed
And that is where all my tears were shed.
Some day I might find the strength to forgive.
For now I just see the life that you lived.

Alyssa Parnell, Grade 10
Glenpool High School, OK

How Did It Come to This?

What has this world come to?
We live in a world
Where there is nothing but anger, hostility, and fear.
All of those mixed together
Lead to the destruction of the things
We love and also hold dear.

What has this world come to?
We worry about how much money
We're going to make.
When we really could be helping
Someone live another day.

But assure them that everything will be okay.
Isn't that the golden rule?
Treat others the way you want to be treated
And you will be blessed by being treated the same.

David C., Grade 10
Audubon Youth Development Center, KY

The Surprise Visit!

The sun was bright but different that day,
I'll never forget the way the wind swayed.
I was coming from recess when I heard the teachers cries,
The day many people said their final goodbyes.
We turned the button on the television screen,
To be absolutely blown away by what we seen.
Terrorists jacked airplanes in the U.S.,
To hit the World Trade to put people to rest.
It was real, although it felt fake,
Knowing our freedom was at stake.
So, soldiers laced their boots and put on their gear,
Showing a lot of hate but hating their fears.
We went to war known to be the best,
Although red, whites, and blues still took their last breaths.
So, now we pray to God about these tragedies,
Hoping He will bring our troops back to their families.
So don't take for granted the things we have today,
Because you never know when it can be taken away!

Robert Taylor, Grade 11
Holcomb High School, MO

Control

I try to throw this feeling away
But you and your thoughts are everywhere
And I detest knowing that you are nowhere.
With you went my friend, my muse
You had everything to lose, yet
It seems like you lost nothing.
And how can it be, you seem to still have the key
To everything that is no longer here.
You told me once what it all meant to you
You still mean what you meant to me
This couldn't be meant to be
But it stays how it stands
And it stands how it stood.

Allison Warren, Grade 11
Prue High School, OK

Into Her Eyes

As I look into her eyes she looks back at me I wonder what she's thinking or if anyone can see
Those eyes look so familiar where have I saw them before? Tears streaming down her face as she hits the floor
As I look into her eyes eyes so very red yes, life can be horrid but at least she's not dead
It's hard not to stare, at a girl who seems so crushed and I know this for a fact no one cares too much
As I look into her eyes color blurred from tears I question myself, if anyone can hear
I have a funny feeling as I look into those eyes I know this from experience she sits at home and cries
As I look into her eyes I pray to the Lord because I know of her life in this hypocritical world
Thus I saw a sparkling crystal on her trembling lip did fall as she waits on the couch for someone who will never call
As I looked into her eyes memories began to dart and I realized only impostors found refuge in her heart
And I know it's reality because feelings don't lie they're something that you're stuck with something you can't deny
I am able to blink, my vision is much clearer with tears streaming down my face as she looks back through the mirror.

Kelsi Henline, Grade 10
Webster County High School, WV

Friends

Friends are like trees,
When you need someone to lean on they're the sturdiest of them all.
Their arms are like the branches that catch your every fall.
Friends are the listeners, listening to your problems.
They're the people who don't mind to kick you in the butt when you've made a bad mistake.

Friends are the shield that protects you in battle,
And the sword that helps you fight.
Friends make you laugh, when you feel like you'll never laugh again.
They make your world brighter when everything around you is dark.

Friends are always there,
To help you along the way of this journey we call life.
They help take away all your pains and strifes.

Emily Shirkey, Grade 11
Woodrow Wilson High School, WV

Shiftless Sands

A citrus sun embarks on another day,
Dribbling juice across the desert's grain —
An eye watching above the angular tips,
Mounted gold, a spinning helix.
Structures so old, yet resolute
The sun slants over their shadows in hasty salute.
Shiftless sands beckon on, and a strained silence follows,
Within the crypt there will be no sunlight to greet the morrow.
Embalmed with spices and dignity, an ancient funeral pyre in the center of a dream.
Rubies, emeralds, precious gems — ephemeral beauty, incapable of grasping infinity.
Gilded plates and costly treasures, wealth beyond all mortal measures.
Thus he sleeps in jealous unease, even death a worthless victory.
Cross the lake of shapeless silver, beads of dancing mercury, poison bought to ward off thieves,
A man with a thirst to live forever, a lust to finish a life incomplete.
And what has been left but a monument? To whose glory and greatness and why?
Honoring a figure who did little to be remembered in life.
No government or foreign exploits to distinguish a name.
No recollection of deserved fame.
And the sun rises yet higher, a fledgling dropped from a blue nest in the sky.
For things don't change as quickly as dreamed,
In the sleepless hollows of the Valley of the Kings.

Laura E. Matera, Grade 11
Rock Bridge Sr High School, MO

My Favorite Place

An angel sent from above,
He has all my love.
When I feel let down,
I don't walk with a frown.
I bow down and pray
By the casket where he lays.
It's almost like heaven,
It will be a year in 2007.
It's my favorite place,
I decorate it with lace.
I try not to cry,
But it was so hard to say goodbye.
It fills me with memories
And gives me time to think and relax with ease.
It's a special place to me,
I just sit there on one knee.
It makes me feel so real,
I can't explain how I feel.
It's beautiful to me
And it's where I love to be.

Jordan Wilson, Grade 11
Glenpool High School, OK

Solidarity

A gentle flitter in the breeze
The trees dancing simultaneously to a rhythmic tune
The lonely caterpillar inches toward victory
A leaf awaiting his belly
His pace steadily increasing
It is not far from sight
Alas, the caterpillar hits a great brick wall
This is no leaf at all

Robby Schranze, Grade 10
Germantown High School, TN

How to Make Tennessee

First you get a lot of farmland,
that is oh so grand.
then you get a lot of animals
for your land
Then make sure all the people you get
are kin folks as well.
Then mix this combination together,
oh so swell.
Then add the hay and crops
for all of the animals and people.
Then add the church
and its Massive steeple.
Make sure that all of your people
are hillbillies and rednecks.
then supply them with entertainment.
such as banjos and cardecks.
mix this together oh so well.
mix this together oh so swell.
then when you're done your mixture will definitely be:
GOOD OL' COUNTRY TENNESSEE.

Haley Melton, Grade 12
Powell High School, TN

Jumpshot

At this moment in time, all eyes are on you.
There's movement, there's talk, and the squeak of your shoe.
The ball's passed at you, directly at your chest.
You catch it, turn, look and hope for the best.

There's cheerleaders cheering, and fans yelling
As you put the ball to the floor.
Quick like a cat you pull up fast,
Your body squared to the goal.
The ball rolls off your fingertips
And soars right toward the hole.

You land on your feet, watching, praying,
And hoping the ball doesn't get caught.
The crowd goes wild in amazement,
You have just drained a jumpshot.

Jay Miller, Grade 10
Niangua High School, MO

Rise Again

She walked alone, a child unknown,
Mottled black and blue, falling only to
Get up again
    Fire to ash, fire to ash
    And rise again
He sighs heavily, how to feed his family
Turning his skeletal face to another work place
To try again
    Fire to ash, fire to ash
    And rise again
Her son went to war, now she wonders what for,
His empty chair — though life's not fair
Smile again
    Fire to ash, fire to ash
    And rise again
The phoenix bird cries unheard
It smolders and burns, and thus it learns
To rise again
    Fire to ash, fire to ash
    And rise again

Sarah Adams, Grade 11
Bearden High School, TN

One

One white rose lying on my bed.
One late night call so I can listen as you breathe.
One more kiss that blows me away.
One look that sends a chill down my spine.
One song that melts my fears away.
One more day with you by my side.
One little bear that I hold dear.
One letter that says, "I'll always be there."
One more memory of us laughing in the rain.
One moonlight stroll all alone with you.
One guy who loves me no matter what.
One moment with you and I was in love.

Jamie Russell, Grade 12
Metcalfe County High School, KY

How to Be Human

Be born one day
Grown up the next
Make your life worth living
From start to end
Nobody's perfect
So Make Mistakes
Learn from your errors
Grow stronger with pain
If you love someone, tell them
Apologize when you should
Don't let failures discourage you
If you did all that you could
To Be human
You never take more than you give
Accept the fact you have faults
Let it go
And just live

Emily Rittenberry, Grade 10
Northwest High School, TN

Running Cross Country

Muscles burning,
Muscles tightening,
Legs and arms getting sore.
Making sure you check,
Fresh and clean,
The uniform that you wore.
Stretch out and get loose,
Settle your mind
And get ready to set.
Start at the line,
With your team
And cheer on the others that you've met.
Prepare yourself,
In beginning position,
And listen for the sound of the gun.
You shoot down the straight-a-way
Passing others,
Across the country as you run.

Jzanese A. Weekes, Grade 11
Woodrow Wilson High School, WV

Climb

She climbs to the top of the mountain
in her little blue dress
wishing to be alone.
She gives this life everything she has
but what she has to give isn't enough.
She has fought so hard
yet nobody has paid attention.
Tears stream down her face
but are covered up by the pouring rain.
As she stands alone on the mountain,
she realizes what's real.

Carly Blasingame, Grade 10
Chickasha High School, OK

Two Minds on One Truth

A man walks in and out of sleep,
Drifting from life? Or drifting from love?
His mind wanders as his body fails him.
He might ask, "Why?" He may not. Isn't that my choice?
I control this man, the man driving my mind.
I test on him; he's my science mouse.
He is my toy, my rag, my thoughts,
But he is not entirely meaningless, and he has a point in life.
What is it? Well, I'm unsure right now, because I haven't written it.
I am in control, the creator; he is nothing but mist,
The sort of mist that bites at your face
On a cold, dreadful night under that full moon.
I force him to walk along a desert road.
Nothing, but the sun and the sand.
His mouth dry, out of words to speak.
I'm testing him; how long will he last?
Will he snap?
Will I snap?
Maybe I need him to run my mind.
His time grows shorter, as mine grows longer.

Samantha Sanders, Grade 10
Glenpool High School, OK

All Good Gone

Seize me from this pit of shame
I've grown tired of swimming in it
With all these dirty organisms.
Snatch these worthless words from my gullet
I'm done with speaking them
To those I care nothing about
And who care nothing about me in return.
Pinch the blackness off my eyes, and powder off my skin
There's not enough to coat my transgressions
Several of which I don't regret.
Scour the dirt beneath my nails and see how old it is
And what the new dirt looks like in comparison
That French manicure can't save me now.
Scrub my mind until it shines bright
And blood pops up like pimples
The coils of its appearance aren't the only things twisted up there.
How did such filth accumulate?
I know it wasn't all that secondhand smoke
Or broken hearts over empty reasons
Or starving faces on the television that I ignore
It must have been my jealousy. Yes. I am now convinced. It ate me inside out.

Mary Means, Grade 11
Germantown High School, TN

untitled

from the first time i saw you i knew you was the one
your eyes were the light and your teeth was the sun.
i hope we would be together cause this can't last any longer.
everyone knows we should be together cause everyone knows you are the one.

Alex Wade, Grade 10
Gibson County High School, TN

Finding Strength Through Loss

It was the end of her hurt and the beginning of his;
She lives with peace and him with regret.
Her smile and laughter, he will long miss,
And his heart will remain upset.

To him, she was most faithful;
She is not just a pretty face,
Lovely, pure, true, and admirable,
That was always her place.

She misses her best friend,
But her life will go on;
Her heart will soon mend,
And his will stay lone.

There is no love like hers;
And he will come to find,
That her touches were his cures,
And she will forever cross his mind.

Krystal Warden, Grade 11
McMinn County High School, TN

The Woe of Winter

A speck of snowflake falls from the sky,
a minuscule crystal from heaven.
That wondrous geometric formation of frozen water,
that bringer of joy to schoolchildren,
that captivator of serenity and peace.

The thought alone shocks the spine with cold.
Winter is approaching!
The cold, the wind, the ice and all the other terrible gifts
the season brings with it
forecast the months to come.

Yet sitting by a warm fire awaits
as does curling under warm bed sheets.
Feelings of relief only the cold can bring.
Oh the beautiful Snow!
Curse my living in the South during winter!

Nathan Tempco, Grade 11
Germantown High School, TN

Mrs. Everingham

You were like a star to me.
You are now in heaven.
Mrs. Everingham, every morning I was
In your class you called me "kiddo!"
I will always remember that.
I thank you Mrs. E.
For what you taught me.
You were such a good teacher.
You taught me many things.
I just want to tell you,
Thank you Mrs. E.
For what you did for me.

Michael H., Grade 12
Audubon Youth Development Center, KY

Where Did You Go?*

Where did you go?
We miss you a lot,
Why did you have to go?
We need you on the spot,
We miss you Grandma so very much,
We think and dream about your very soft touch,
I'm so used to seeing you right by my side,
it was the worst day ever, when I found out you died,
I was in school with my friends,
When my cousin came up in a very slow touch,
I knew something was wrong by the expression on her face,
she said, "Tiffani I have some very bad news"
then I realized today had been the day,
I'm not happy that your gone,
but I'm sure your in a better place,
and until this day,
all I can ask your picture is "Grandma, where did you go?"

Tiffani Waterman, Grade 10
South Nodaway High School, MO
**RIP Grandma we love and miss you*

What I See

I'm a 16-year-old with a lot of stress
I'm going to make the best,
Until I rest.
All I want is peace
My mother and brother are deceased.
I'm all alone,
I'm not at home,
My family is gone,
I want my mother back.
I want my brother back.
If they were still alive
I probably would not have sold the crack.
Just let me be,
I don't want to see.
Sometimes I think
WHY ME?

Reggie G., Grade 10
Audubon Youth Development Center, KY

Sonnet 88

Is there such a thing called love at first sight?
I knew when I saw her that's what I liked
That beautiful color so glossy and shiny
To your shoes that aren't so tiny
Your body style is a work of art
You should know that you're on my top five chart
The music you play calms me down
Because the bass feels like a massage all around
When we're together you're so quick and clean
Don't try to catch up to us because you'll get creamed
We make everyone jealous because we're the perfect match
This isn't a lie, I'm just giving you the facts
I have to thank my dad and mom
Because you see my new ride is a 2006 Tiburon

Niko Aguilar, Grade 12
Hollis High School, OK

Still Here

As twilight settles
in our reflective eyes
I begin to wonder why
We have yet to compromise

It's all so clear now
But so hazy back then
I wonder when and how
this stalemate will end.

Minutes tick by
like days of the week
Every minute of silence
encompasses the bleak

But the sun has gone down
yet we are still here
Wondering how
we'll get over this fear.

Chelsea Sparkes, Grade 11
Bearden High School, TN

A Lesson Learned?

I am so angry
I wish you were mine
You broke my heart
You crossed the line
Red roses you bought me
Your love was so fine
You know you don't own me
Why do I wish you were still mine?

Kristi Reyes, Grade 11
Hollis High School, OK

Hoping for the Worst

Dying to forget your face —
Throwing all of you away.
Wishing you'd care for only a moment
But knowing it will never happen.
I wonder how you became so cruel.
Perfection is never enough —
Somehow it can always be better.
One day you'll see me.
Grown up — not 3 anymore
Beautiful — not fat anymore
Strong — not scared anymore
Dying to forget your words.
Round and round
You go in my head.
Haunting my very being
Every inch of my body
Crawling with your evil sentiments.
How could you blame me?
They hated you —
But I know it was all my fault.
I'm dying — dying because of you.

Shawna Standiford, Grade 11
Owasso High School, OK

The Scary Hippie

I saw joy clearly.
He was a longed haired, skinny hippie.
He turned and tried to give me a hug.
I saw his blond hair, white smile and tan skin.
And heard him sing with happiness in his voice.
And I felt very uncomfortable.

Travis Koncor, Grade 12
Madison Jr & Sr High School, MO

Arkansas Outlaw

He's a country music singer in a rock-n-roll band
He plays those honky Tonk bars every night he can
He rides a Harley, got a four-by-four and a muscle car
He's an Arkansas Outlaw trying to be a country star
Well, he learned to play that old guitar
Sitting on his daddy's knee
He said, "Son, three simple cords
And a little bit of rhythm is all you need."
If you really want to take your dream that far
You better pick up the tune and start playing that guitar
Cause your an Arkansas Outlaw trying to be a country star
His momma said, "Son, don't take all your money and throw it away,
Just get out on that stage and let them hear you sing."
Cause your an Arkansas Outlaw trying to be a country star
You play those honky Tonk bars every night you can
You ride a Harley, got a four-by-four and a muscle car
Your an Arkansas Outlaw trying to be a country star

Jacob Lindsey, Grade 10
Harrisburg High School, AR

Brain Lapse

Dancing, twirling, spinning, brain lapse, are they asking too much?
Little girls are show dancers at age 7,
Performing at top level to show their perfection,
Crazed mothers with daughters 8 going on 40,
Hairspray at the crazy hands catching careful hairs,
Before we go on, tiny tappers turn toes to tie tennis,
We get wished lots of luck then whisked away to the stage,
Signs are everywhere for everything, but can we read?
Should silly small signs sit in circles?
When you finally go on you are too nervous to think,
No one ever messes up,
You don't even know what the weather is outside,
But everyone expects you to be the next Marilyn Monroe,
Do you even remember the dance?
Halfway through the song
and suddenly everything goes blank.
What do you do? Run away and cry, or turn and laugh,
Minutes later you remember and fly across the stage, with your heart coming out of your mouth
Did you mess everything up for everyone?
Dancing, twirling, spinning, brain lapse, are they asking too much?

Megan Soetaert, Grade 11
Owasso High School, OK

Introspection of the Lonely Heart's Transformation

I've never been aware,
This weird percussion, always there.
It takes control, moving me.
Someone save me, set me free,
Save me from the center stage.
Inanimate prisoner, and I am the cage.
Thump-thump.
My heartbeat brings me back,
Keeps me sane, keeps me on track.
My fears are high, stress is plenty.
Can't recharge batteries that aren't empty.
I need to be alone, need to weep,
Go for days without sleep.
Thump-thump.
I've lived my life like a trend,
Think of the lies I haven't spinned,
All the days I could borrow or lend,
Children for themselves to fend,
And my iron will, finally bend,
My heart, my love, is at an end.

Forrest Cheadle, Grade 12
Glenpool High School, OK

Unorthodox

Her imperial majesty
Donned in luxurious attire
Cloaking rivers down her aged tomb
And the solid earth beneath
By which her fluffy minions gather.
Her giant structure
Greatly contrasts the pigmy cluckers below.
A mortal Gaia,
She holds a burnished black pail
In one hand.
The other fingered appendage,
Extends a tipped ladle.
Feed overflows, falling from
Its long-armed prison
To nourish the bickering man chickens and hens.
Proudly, they shake their tail feathers.

Ezinwanne Rosemary Emelue, Grade 11
Germantown High School, TN

Inner Thoughts

Somewhere in the darkness you hear a scream
But then you wake up
And you know it was just a dream
But your mind tells you otherwise
You wonder what it could mean
You get up and walk around
Take in the whole scene
You open the door and walk out into the hallway
It appears that nothing's wrong, it had to be a dream
You go back into your room, but something's not right
The shock numbs your mind as
You find your body lying in the floor as dead as the night

Josh Stephens, Grade 12
McCreary Central High School, KY

Tired of You

Tired of everything you do.
All the promises that didn't come true.
Tired of running back to you.
Forgetting all the songs that remind me of you.

Tired of remembering what we used to do.
And all the places you took me to.
Tired of you and the things you put me through.
I just wish the best for you.

Tired of saying I'll always be here.
When all you do is turn your back.
And you said you would never do that.
Just looking at the past makes it hard to laugh.

Tired of knowing I still love you.
But never saying it to you.
And not being true, because I'm not all that
Tired of you.

McKenzie Williams, Grade 10
Hollis High School, OK

New Life

Two wet foot prints are left behind on the wooden porch
Symbolizing everything she is leaving behind.
As she crosses the threshold of her new home
In a new city, a different world

As one life ends, like the leaves falling from their branches
A new identity is assumed.
Looking back is hard enough
But knowing everything she had is over is even harder

Starting over the next day
In a new school, a new town, a new life.
A new leaf is turned in the breeze of her surroundings
Her old life left behind in the dust

The lawn is consumed with flame colored leaves
Like the fire that took everything
She begins to realize that even in her new home
Her old life will always exist

Laura Hudgens, Grade 10
Coffee County Central High School, TN

Turned Backwards

Life declines, in the monsters eyes
Emotions can hide inside its host,
Love once held, none no more.
Inside should be a graveyard —
It calls, the heart it desires.
The darkness calling, waiting to consume
After eternity, it comes with the calling
Giving up life; outside turns inside;
The reverse goes back. Life falls —
As existence is time, turned backwards.

Angel Rohan, Grade 12
Edmond North High School, OK

Feelings (Emo Kids)

Our anger leads to sadness.
Our tears lead to depression.
Our anger doesn't show.
People call us outcasts
When depression sets in,
We hide within the shadows.

Aaron Greene, Grade 10
Canadian High School, OK

World Images

A desolate beauty
That covers the land;
Anciently recent
But not made by hand;
Brilliantly stupid
As are the sea's waves,
As they hit the earth's shore
And they decay;
Whispers of yells
Heard on the wind
That blows so fiercely,
Yet calmly within;
Spacious yet crowded
At the same time,
Quiet as the loudest
Sound of a chime;
Derived from transgressions
And auguries alike,
Surviving the day
To become once more
What might become Night.

Danielle Cowart, Grade 11
Owasso High School, OK

Key of Irony

A darkened room
Large barred door
Complete silence
Raised alarm

Tapped and lost
With a known location
Sort through life
New destination

A ray of light
The softest sound
The lock, a key
Turned it around

Silhouette stands
Blocks my path
Now I feel
Irony's wrath

Creeanna Ertl, Grade 10
Bourbon High School, MO

Who Are You

Do you love me or do you not know,
Do you care about me or do you care about you.
Do you mean I love you or does this not mean a thing.
It seems to me that you care about you than me,
No one sees what I see, I see a boy who's scared to say what he feels,
I see a girl who cares about you,
But she needs to know does this boy care about her.
She's in love, but is he.
Who knows only the boy inside the man knows.
You say you do love her, are you saying this
Because she's in love, or are you.
Is there a boy who loves me, or is it that he is afraid to let go,
Because he will hurt me,
Tell me how you feel, I just need to know.
This girl is afraid to lose you because we do everything together
We have favorite songs, movies and places we go,
You were my first, my first real boyfriend,
I could not bear to see you with anyone else,
This hurts, but this is me telling you that I love you, care, and think about you,
Do you do the same, tell me, who you are.

Sierra Sellers, Grade 11
Neosho High School, MO

Home?

Alone I sit; alone in my room. Freaking out a little bit.
Hearing what I know is hate. Hiding, hiding from my fate.
Doors slam then re-open. Banging. Clanging. Breaking. Broken.

I do not dare peek out, for if I do, I seriously doubt,
My life would return normal; pretending to be, oh so, formal.
Blinking away my tears. Fighting away my fears.

This cannot be real; it is numb I feel.
An illusion. They are just a delusion.
A fake, a phony, fraud. The choice to leave; a mirage.

My family, the people I love, used to fit like hand-in-glove.
But now we are distant. Now nothing is consistent.
Only smiling when we leave to go and do whatever we please.

My heart is breaking. My head, my soul, my body, achy.
Where is laughter? Fun? Love? Now we act like a loaded gun.
Whatever chance we get, ready to fight. Souls, souls of blight.

Inside I am torn up; broken. Outside I am poised; focused.
Who I am people do not see. For if they did they would definitely flee.
Hiding behind a mask, I assure you, is no easy task.

What if they found the truth? Would they stick around anymore?
Would they laugh at me? Or would they turn for the door?

Kelsay Reichert, Grade 11
Centralia High School, MO

The Demon

A sad ballad at the end of gruesome destruction
The buildings that once stood tall
Now tumble and bow to merciless power

If ever there was a way to have stopped this colossal terror
And put out the fires it creates
There would be one more reason to rejoice
But now there is only reason to extract revenge

Millions gone, soon to be forgotten
For this monster has infiltrated our minds
Few remember
And these people set out to rectify its wrongs

But nothing can stop it
For it fuels from the rage of man
And consumes all that man has worked for
Even death has no say in it
Because war is an immortal demon

Justin M. Johnson, Grade 10
Greenwood High School, AR

The Difference

I'm terribly lonely and I know why
It's not that I'm an outcast or that I'm a lie
It's not that people don't listen or that they don't care
It's not that I'm unstable or that they're never there

It's the difference in the minds that separates our hearts
It's the frame I'm built into that makes me an abstract art
It's the soul behind the eyes that hides behind the shell
It's the way I see things differently that puts me in this hell

I have a reality of my own that the world will never see
I have it because the world has exiled me
Not on purpose of course for I escaped myself
But the reason is the same I'll put it on the shelf

It's the difference in the worlds that makes mine a better place
The world repeats over and over but with a different face
Mine never repeats but there is no face to find
For my world isn't your world it is only mine

Laurie Luckritz, Grade 10
Richland High School, MO

Right from Wrong

You always tell me when I'm wrong
Never that I'm right
I do a good deed
And hardly get appreciated
I try hard to make you happy
But it's never hard enough
The things I do wrong
The way I talk
Even when I'm right
I'm always wrong

Phillip Weaver, Grade 10
Jeffersontown High School Magnet Career Academy, KY

Lady Too

I looked in her eyes and I saw something familiar,
Something that none of the other horses had,
A need to be loved by someone,
Someone who had been through the same things as her,
A little girl, Me.

She had been ridiculed by an adult,
So had I,
She had been afraid to live, afraid to be herself,
So had I,
Then, I found her and she found me,
Together we became each other's family,
Each others best friend, each other's hero,
Two once hurt souls became each other's everything.

From then on, no one saw us as the "ugly ducklings"
They saw us as an example.
An example that everyone can make it,
No matter how big nor how small,
They just have to believe.

Cassandra Jennings, Grade 10
Bourbon High School, MO

Identity Crisis

Small questioner, know that I feel your ache!
The ceaseless throb of wondering who you are.
This world's too vast and seldom sense does make
To bean-sized eyes that yet cannot see far.
What hushed clamour storms within your ears
As each day you swim through such murky water.
What bolts of doubt must strike upon your fears
And in your self-uncertainty find fodder.
Your blood is hot; your heart can also burn.
Your true nature in these traits may reside.
Yet oft your identity takes a turn;
You birth deeds both frigid and calcified.
But pause your quest, 'lest worries take their toll
They are too grave for a platypus' soul.

Natalie Jacewicz, Grade 11
St Mary's Episcopal School, TN

Victorious

I have emerged victorious and great
From trials and perilous long days.
I have emerged victorious and great
Because Christ Jesus is with me always.
I have come through glorious tough trials
For greatness, honor, strength, and victory,
I have come through glorious tough trials.
I have not lost the battle for glory.
The battle for holiness shall remain.
I have won because He is love and light.
The battle for holiness shall remain.
The meaning of life is like a great fight.
Christ, the Lord, has conquered the sting of death.
This I know until my final last breath.

Benjamin Smith, Grade 10
Capital High School, WV

He Loves Me, I Love Him Not

It's a crying shame that I have built up hate for the one that I love
The vibration of speed and the blurring feed of my music have me speechless
He's my weakness and I just can't take this
Forgive I can do, but a lie is that I can forget
He's pushing close to my book of childish regret
He's just a bad habit that I had in my life of sin
Now here comes my hatred for him screaming back into my head again
How is it that one can take you and break you for all that you have ever had
Well I'm indecisive on every one of my decisions and I've got it bad
These days a touch just feels like pity
I would know this because from him I've had so many
And now I'm praying for a change just to forget him
Yep I said it, but now look what I've got myself wrapped up in
It's a crying shame that I have hate for the one that loves me

Tegan Hillix, Grade 12
Hollis High School, OK

A Coal Miner's Prayer

The air is cold, the light is gone as I enter in through this hole
My light is on, my mind is clear I'm ready to load some coal. Lord, I'm ready to load some coal

I say this sweet prayer as I put on my hat and begin the long night's work
Dear Lord, please keep me safe while I'm down here under the dirt, while I'm working down under the dirt

The sweat starts to pour, my eyes start to close and my back begins to ache
Lord, I'm aware of the danger I'm in and the decisions that I must make. Lord, help me with the choices I make

The night is half gone, my work is half done as the lunch horn starts to blow
I eat up my food and continue my prayer Lord, please help me get some more loads. Oh! Please just a few more loads

I hear a loud crash, something is wrong as the sirens begin to sound. Lord, give me courage in this dark time of need
While I'm trapped down here in the ground. Oh Lord! I'm trapped down here in the ground

I think of my family, oh how they worry about me and my dangerous task
Lord, please keep me safe so I'll see them again if it's not too much to ask. Oh Lord! That's all I ask

I don't want to die here all alone while I'm way down here in this hole
I yearn to be home, with those that I love but if You call, I'll surely go. If You call me Lord, I'll go

I'll pass from this world with my mining light on and my skin all dirty and cold
But with Your help and patience, Lord I'll have gotten my final load. Oh Bless that final load

Katlin Bishop, Grade 10
Westside High School, WV

Bipolar

Depression comes as a dark wave crushing hopes and dreams leaving a wide terrible path the swings or our moods crash in and drown our happiness hurting friends and family

Rain comes as a soothing touch caressing our cheek embracing us in boundless ways it envelops us in a blanket and pushes the sorrow anguish fear and hatred away the mania leaves quickly all that is left is calm

Calm and peace come it penetrates our skin and warms our heart we feel better now no more depression no more mania or hatred just pure simple calm with the moon and the stars peeking from the clouds dripping rain all enveloping us making us feel safe and warm. Loved

Caitlyn Little, Grade 11
Bearden High School, TN

Inside and Out

I look in your eyes and I can see your soul
It's like a window to your after world
Just staring in I get so cold.
Shivers down my spine goose bumps on the outside.
The window is starting to frost.
We all have to say
What we can and cannot do today.
Listen to the words of those who care
Because that's all that we have to share.
The world is so very unkind
But don't pay any mind.
Don't lock yourself in a hole
Because you'll find yourself to be very alone.
Trust another and you'll get through.
Don't forget — I'm here for you.

Samantha Yellen, Grade 11
Anderson County High School, TN

16mm Film

Memory is a tenuous thing,
flickering glimpses of the past then present,
like ancient decomposing 16mm film.
Feelings escape me there in that parlor
where fancy words are traded for things like gossip

growing and sprouting more plants which hug trellises
with a loving embrace, they sit admiring.
Faces are vague,
the line between fantasy and reality blurring dangerously,
past becomes present becomes future
which is lost in a vast ocean of blue

Yesterday seems to come packaged
in ribbons of beautiful pain and regret
but tomorrow is yet to come.
Perhaps there is hope in the curiosity of tomorrow?
Without it, I'd be sitting on a window sill,
a frosty pane my company

Elizabeth Windle, Grade 11
Welch Jr/Sr High School, OK

The Terror That Will Soon Begin

When I look to what I know should be,
I find that this is what I see,
A world that sings with the song of birds,
Smells that are so sweet it cannot be put to words,
This world in which I can see what is right,
I find the dew on a rose petal shining in the morning light,
Soft clouds in the sky,
With daffodils waving as the wind's breath blows by,
I hold these joys in my heart,
Knowing soon we will have to part,
For I know one day,
As that last sweet scent blows my way,
This world I see hidden from a city,
Will soon become a world of pity.

Kit Godfrey, Grade 10
Rock Bridge Sr High School, MO

In Response to "To the Virgins to Make Much of Time"

Gather ye rosebuds when you wish
Do not beg for a kiss
I may be old but I am wise
Do not fall for those lies

If he forces you to marry
Do nothing but tarry
There may be a ring
But that doesn't mean one thing

If he loves you he will wait
Until you find that perfect mate
You are young so be strong
That way you will never go wrong

Hold fast and never give in
He doesn't want to be your friend
So just listen to what I say
If he wants to marry, push him away.

Amy Ray, Grade 12
Union County High School, TN

Under the Canopy

Stars gleaming above the tin canopy
Looking deep into the blue depths I want to swim
Like a mirror, the blue stares back
With emotion

I long and plead to touch the blue of the soul
Deep in me I feel a numbness escaping me
Seeping out, touching the world, immobilizing
The world halts

Happiness and love burst and overflow
Making everything in the darkness glow with love
I breathe for a moment, staring back
The world again awakens

How long will it be until I see this again?
Months will pass before I ask for another such as this
All I can do for this disease is wait
I will be cured

Chloe Joslin, Grade 10
Crowley's Ridge Academy, AR

Love

Love is an overwhelming feeling from the heart
A feeling of happiness just from the start
Thinking about them every night and day
Him crossing your mind as you go to sleep and pray
Enjoying every minute we spend together
But also thinking nothing last forever

Wondering how love could be as great as this
Baby you changed my life with just one kiss
Our love is a dream come true
I close my eyes as I thank God for meeting you

Hailey Moss, Grade 11
McGehee High School, AR

Invisible

Being invisible
Just to fit in
Why can't I speak my mind
Give myself a chance,
To impact the world
Is there another way to let it out
Whatever "it" is
Inside of us,
Growing and swelling
Until emotion is
Let out into
The world looking
Upon them.
To find out who we are
In the world around us
To find ourselves
In us.
For our voice
Is important to
Grow as a person.

Sarai Stone, Grade 11
Mills University Studies High School, AR

Persevere

Do not give up.
You can succeed.
Sometimes it is easy,
other times you may bleed.

It is the hardest thing to do,
not to just get up and go.
When the going gets tough,
the tough just take it slow.

To reach all goals,
you must stick it through.
But when you make it,
you will realize what you can do.

Lanny Meadows, Grade 11
Woodrow Wilson High School, WV

gone but not forgotten

when i was in my deep sleep
people said you were gone
oh why take you instead of me
what's my destiny
i was two seconds to death
without a breath
it was so quick for you
what purpose did you serve
on this earth
i'll never know
but i'll never let you go
in my heart
our love will never be torn apart

Miranda Lee, Grade 11
Thorn Hill Learning Center, KY

Follow Your Dreams

Let the light shine through your soul
Your dreams will then fly through the open window
At this moment they seem so far away
Just hold your head high and don't listen to what others say
Someday all that you've ever hoped for will come true
You'll stumble along the road of life full of obstacles
Integrity and persistence will help you make it through
In the whirlwind of life we lose sight of the important things
But it's simple and easy to stay true to yourself always

Brook Wright, Grade 10
Coffee County Central High School, TN

Rain Drops Falling

Splish, splash
You hear the rain drops falling,
You feel each cool, wet droplet on your warm skin.
The drops continue to fall upon you soaking you as time goes by.
You feel a childish emotion come over you at once,
You then take a huge leap into a muddy puddle.
You feel the mud squish and ooze in between your toes.
You run on jumping into each passing puddle,
The mud splashing all over.
Giggling and dancing joyfully,
Having no cares.
The rain begins to cease.
Your childish emotion starts to fade away,
You realize your foolish actions.
You look at yourself in disgust,
Soaked with mud and rain.
You walk away from the puddles,
You realize that this fun can only last for so long.

Blaire Williams, Grade 11
Woodrow Wilson High School, WV

My Love of Me

As I look out the old foggy window today,
I pick up your picture then hear you say,
In the sweet simple way you say my name,
That the only thing love is to you is a fun game,

You took my heart and made it shatter,
I fell so hard it made my clothes tatter,
But now I have come to tell you about something new,
It replaces my heartache and all the thoughts of you,

It is a love that I cannot explain,
But I am not telling you all of this in vain,
I forgive you is my reason for writing this letter,
I hope your life is like mine and turned out for the better,

I see now that what you did changed my life,
It used to be the dull end of a sharp knife,
You made me jump back in and I found something that I never thought could be,
Because the love I had found was my love of me.

Hannah Fox, Grade 11
Woodrow Wilson High School, WV

Hands

They rest there, over on the table,
holding the ginormas cereal
bowl that was bought as a gag gift,
just because they are so big.
They are rough and weary from every day's work,
trees and chain saws really take their toll.
The scars that are proportionally as large as they are,
the ones that he was too stubborn to get sewn up,
accent the pair like jewels.
The palms are callused from years of swinging a wooden bat
and from hitting me grounders over and over.
It is they that held me when I was young,
that threw me in the air and do the same with my sister now.
It is they, these large, strong, sturdy hands
That gently hold our small dog
that he can't help loving so much.
These hands are the hands of my hero,
my coach, my dad, my everything.

Samantha Everett, Grade 12
Baylor School, TN

A Contradicting Life

Life is so busy, that I have no time,
But I'm on the computer almost every night.
I will randomly sing at the drop of a dime,
But getting me to practice is always a fight.
I eat ketchup like a fiend,
But tomatoes and I don't get along.
It makes me feel better when my room is cleaned,
But I haven't seen my carpet in so long.
Getting A's on tests is always good,
But studying is no fun.
I always try to do what I should,
But I end up acting dumb!
My mom and I are the best of friends,
But watch out when one of us gets mad.
I'm not one to follow trends,
But sometimes they're not that bad.
All my friends are important to me,
But sometimes I just want to hit them!
People think I'm normal, but soon they see,
Normal is not how I am condemned!

Erin O'Neil, Grade 10
Capital High School, WV

Together

For one it is the end of the day
And for the other it is just the beginning
Both connected by the sun, moon, and stars
But separated by miles of land and sea
They feel as if they are by each other's sides
Neither can stand being apart
Slowly fading,
Until —
No more.

Tyler Woodling, Grade 11
Germantown High School, TN

Hatred

The blood in my veins is cold,
With the darkness,
Creeping in through the holes in my heart.
It gets darker and darker,
As I get hurt more and more.

Though you hurt me so much,
It will never be the same.
The hate grows stronger with the ever growing pain.

The bruises will always fade,
But the scars will never go away.
Day after day, I, myself start to fade.
With the hope of being loved,
Not hated.
But I guess,
That day will never come.

So as I take my last breath…
All the hate will finally go away.

Kim Ledbetter, Grade 10
Grove High School, OK

A Place

As we raced across the battlefield
Our eyes blurred with sweat
Our bodies battered and bruised and tired
Each of us wondering about the other one
Knowing that we all won't make it back.
As we raced back to a place, one we all hated and feared at first
But now loved and wanted so much —
The place comes into sight.
That place is our base.
Looking around myself I see hatred and love:
Hatred for our enemies;
Love for our brothers.
All of us carrying each other in our own way.
As we are making it back to our base and we close the gates,
I listen for cheers and sounds of happiness from my comrades.
And then I notice I was the only one left —
And now I sit in the place that seems so cold and strange
A place I now love even more than before
A place…now my home.

Scott Crowley, Grade 11
East Carter High School, MO

Missing You

I'm sitting here on the edge on my bed
looking at pictures of our wedding day
the pictures have begun to fade and I
want you to know there's not a day that
goes by I don't think of you
I can remember the days and I feel the tears
and they feel like a rushing waterfall
and I try to stop but the more I do
the more I miss you.

Billy Howard, Grade 10
Van-Cove High School, AR

Our Soldier

In spite of your fears
As they live in you,
Like a worried soul.
Without thought and understanding.
Up against all odds,
Through the trenches,
Past the doubt,
Because of your strength
Because you never quit
Because you are you.

Jason Singleton, Grade 12
Timberland High School, MO

Unknown Things

This silence is overwhelming
This feeling is sinking deep
I'm sick of independence
Making promises I can't keep
And I'm scared of the morning
And what it will bring
Knowing soon there's a chance
That I could lose everything
Tired of depending on independence
Sick of losing all my wars
Can't seem to shake this endless slump
That I've fought so long before
So now I've got to leave
But I can't get going
And I'm running out of time
Cause it's hard not knowing
Which direction I should take
And which promises to break
I can't believe I'm in between
Those things I want and things I need

Karla Wallis, Grade 12
Bixby High School, OK

Fade

You look —
and your faces
blank with terror.
A scream —
terrible noise;
peace comes only
with the loveliness
of my voice.
I see the world
black and white;
absolutes will remain.
You catch a glimpse
of my shadow —
real, but vague;
but you'll never know
who I am before
I fade.

Alyssa Earp, Grade 10
Moore High School, OK

To Everybody Who…

To everybody who
Has constant cuts from a knife
To everybody who
Cannot understand the meaning of life
To everybody who
Hides in a closet to escape their abuser
To everybody who
Is always alone and only name is Loser
To everybody who
Is burned and beaten for their faults
To everybody who
Lives day by day on insults
To everybody who
Has to fight for their next breath
To everybody who
Is in constant fear of death
To everybody who
Always feels so low
To everybody who
Just doesn't seem to know
…It gets easier

Alexandrea Tyron, Grade 11
Northwest High School, TN

The Evil Thing

Evil things are evil,
Evil things are mean,
Evil things are things,
Sometimes things unseen.

My evil thing is unseen,
But my evil thing is still mean,
It causes me nothing but pain,
And puts a wear on the brain.

Everyone seeks this evil thing,
Even though it causes nothing but pain,
But I don't trust this evil thing,
Does that make me insane?

It hasn't always been like this,
I used to trust the evil thing,
Just to get dissed,
Over and over but it still stings.

Have you guessed what I do not trust,
With only the text that is above,
No the thing is not lust,
The evil thing is love.

Steve Ware, Grade 10
North Bullitt High School, KY

Wonderful

Let this day be wonderful,
The best we've had this year,
Make this day be wonderful,
And bring my love back here.

Make the snow fall gently,
Exactly as it should,
And make the wind blow calmly,
Just like I hoped it would.

Let the sun rise slowly,
Don't let it rise too fast,
For if it rises quickly,
The snow surely will not last.

If the snow should disappear,
I can tell you it'd be wrong,
Because my love could not be here,
And couldn't sing his song.

So please let this day be wonderful,
And let the snow fall free,
So that my love could come back here,
And sing his song to me.

Emily Keener, Grade 11
Morgantown High School, WV

Unwanted Memories

Unwanted memories
forgotten tragedies
forever are kept inside,
drifting on the surface
of the lake of time.
A touch, a ripple
and days, weeks, years
memories long forgotten
bring back the tears.
We try to drown them
and make them disappear
but alas, we all have the fear.
Although losing someone
is a burden, a curse
to forget would be a fate
far, far worse.
Unwanted memories
forgotten tragedies
forever are kept inside,
drifting on the surface
of the lake of time.

Billie Jennings, Grade 11
Johnson County High School, TN

The Magic of the Season

The magic of the season begins with snow
And slowly the awaited day comes
Anticipation grows as the night seems so long.
Children's stockings are hung
Neatly by the fire and with care
And as each hour ticks along
Thoughts are full in each child's head
Visions of the impending goodies and treats
And gifts cloud nighttime dreams.
Fresh milk and cookies are left
Because a jolly guy is coming
Sleepy eyes try to stay bright and merry
But Santa is coming and the children must go
Off to bed now so turn out the light
Dream sweet dreams of sugarplums and whatnot
The magic of tomorrow may be full of surprises for everyone

Emily Gray, Grade 11
Germantown High School, TN

What Is Always Is

As I look into the horizon, mountain tops are all I see
Surrounded by a blanket of haze as blue as can be
Reminding me of all that once was and all that will be
Thoughts enter and exit as fast as they arrive
The ones that tell of all the world's problems
Then the ones that describe only mine
They're like dreams replayed over and over
Never letting me forget all the damage that was done
Making me feel like I'm the only one
Lost in life like a cloud floating by
When mixed with others it's must part of the sky
How can a simple blue haze bring so much despair
Is the question that remains in the air

Christain Stowe, Grade 11
McGehee High School, AR

Me and You

From the first time I saw you, I knew you were the one
I got so scared all I could do is run
Run from you and run from love
But just like me, you knew I was the one
I can't believe I left without even knowing you
Now I see my life as if you left me, I don't know what I'd do
You said you would always be there for me
I still remember you going down on one knee
Now I'm here and I don't even hear your voice
I still can't believe I made that poor choice
Do you forgive me?
Of course you told me you love me
I will never forget the day I said goodbye
Or how I said I'll be by your side until the day I die
I feel like I'm in a race to you
It's looking at your picture that gets me through
I can't wait for the day to see your sweet face
But until then I'll be dreaming of you here
In this place

Briana Billiot, Grade 10
Cookson Hills Christian School, OK

The Greatest War Revealed*

Are my eyes obscured with worldly gloom,
Or are they vivid and clear?
When you peer into a looking glass,
For what is it that you search?
Perhaps when you find yourself in a trance,
Separated from all else,
You will find the answer that you do not desire.
When engrossed by a mirror,
All things shatter,
Including destiny.
Now as I remove this posy of violets,
You will fight a "great war."
But when you look through the looking glass,
Crafted by your creator,
You will gaze into the most complex mirror of all,
A mirror of the soul.
A mirror that opens all that you know,
All that you are,
And every pain you have ever felt.
Now all is exposed,
All is vulnerable.

Wilson Gabbard, Grade 12
Rowan County Sr High School, KY
**Inspired by: "The Great War" Rene Magritte*

I Fold My Hands

I fold my hands,
and start to pray,
For hope of living
a better way.
My life's been with drugs,
My life's been with crimes,
My life's been with death,
My life's been with time.
I've spent my share of time,
behind a wall.
Not listening to God when
He tried to call.
Now I have folded my hands,
In order to pray.
He is taking my life,
The other way.

John M., Grade 10
Audubon Youth Development Center, KY

My Son

My son cannot understand,
why his dad is not at home.
My son cannot understand,
why when we talk, it's over the phone.
My son cannot understand,
because he's only two.
My son cannot understand
why stuff like this is going on.
One thing he does understand,
is that I love him and I will soon be home.

Jamar D., Grade 12
Audubon Youth Development Center, KY

Fat

If you don't know his name:
He's the guy who moans
And breathes hard
Who talks about
Who eats a lot
The one who cares about
The one who drinks
The one who smells
Who likes to say
Who prefers to wear
The one who connects food with
Who has trouble with
The one whose girlfriend disappeared
We know him,
No need to make fun of
or threaten
or exclude him.
He is often seen
but still invisible, unreachable.

Stephan Jaeger, Grade 12
Baylor School, TN

White Hot Flame

I ventured out to see
If what I had heard was true
This white hot flame
Of my love for you
Cannot burn your image away
Could we have but known
That your life would burn so swiftly
Would we all not then have but sat
With such little show of emotion
As your face seemed to turn to ash
Right in front of me
Leaving us to wonder
What more could we have done
But now this no longer the question
In this white hot flame of my love
The question is now
What do we have to see
When this flame goes out

Brandy Samples, Grade 10
Pleasure Ridge Park High School, KY

That Boy

He hides beneath his hair,
Lazily slouched in his assigned station,
Staying still and silent,
Obviously deep in thought.
His aura dark and mysterious,
The only thing holy was his denim.
Along with his personality,
His sneakers were black.
I wonder if his heart is the same.

Taylor Gorton, Grade 10
Glenpool High School, OK

100 Years from Now

100 years from now, life expectancy will be prolonged to 110,
diseases will be cured, cars will run on water.
But war will still be in the world.

100 years from now, there will be lavish houses,
extraordinary buildings, and flashy cars.
But war will still be in the world.

100 years from now, there will be microscopic computer chips,
technology filled labs, and intelligence beyond imagination.
But war will still be in the world.

100 years from now, there will be children crying,
people going hungry, and third world countries.
But war will still be in the world.

100 years from now, there will be different ways of killing,
extreme hate everywhere, will it ever stop?
And war will still be in the world.

No matter how many years shall pass, people's lives changed,
and increasing amounts of cash, war will always survive each decade,
and hold its grip on the world.

Rachel Holtmeier, Grade 11
St Francis Borgia Regional High School, MO

Don't Flow Down River

Fight back! Fight back!
I told myself as I could feel the strong and over taking wave's crash on top of me.
I had no strength to push the heavy weight that lay upon me.
Gasping for air when I had the chance,
I noticed that the white raging waves of the river lay ahead.
My head got pushed back under; I saw only the black darkness
that spreads across the bottom of the river

FIGHT BACK! FIGHT BACK!

It got more difficult fighting for air
for my muscles were no longer of any use.
I could feel the water
take me farther down under each time.
Then out of nowhere, just only for an instant it went black.
I could feel the force of the water
pressure in my lungs building up,
at that moment I felt a warm touch against my hand.
It was as if an angel had come from above and pulled me to safety.
Opening my eyes I saw that it was just a non-existing image of what my life felt like.
Realizing that it doesn't matter how far
Or what you are in,
rely on your friends to pull you to safety.

Quinn Gray, Grade 10
Shady Spring High School, WV

My Love

The warm embrace of your arms
Tells my soul that I'll suffer no harm
The green radiance of your eyes
Seem never tainted by stabbing lies

Your heart reaches out to me
Limitless, like the wide open sea
Never beside you do I feel alone
When I am with you, I am home

When my today is ruined with sorrow
Your soft voice soothes the day
And betters my tomorrow

Take all of me, for I charge no fee
Forever in your arms I wish to be
I am yours now and forever
Your love has changed my life for the *better*

Tiffany Gosnell, Grade 12
Jeffersontown High School Magnet Career Academy, KY

Christmas

Some would say it's the best holiday of the year.
Snowmen being made outside your window,
Kisses under the mistletoe.
Stockings being hung over a warm fireplace
Children eagerly anticipating the arrival of Santa Claus!
Ornaments and bows of every size, shape, and color
Hanging from a tall bushy green tree.
Snow angels.
Sledding.
Reindeer.
Snowball fights.
Eggnog.
Hot cocoa.
All seasonal favorites
December 24th
The big day is almost here
Everyone rushing to get a last minute present
Or fixing up the holiday delicacies
Christmas…
The best holiday of the year.

Tara Vogel, Grade 11
Slater High School, MO

God's Words to My Mother

Your heart is like gold,
Let God into your soul.
He will tell you,
His Son is always with you.
No matter where He is
Or where He goes.
He is always in your soul.
He loves you very much,
No matter what.

John F., Grade 10
Audubon Youth Development Center, KY

Torn for You

It's really hard to say this
But I'm falling in love with you.
My heart can't decide
What I should do.
It's so hard for me
Every time you say "I love you"
I want to cry
When I can't hear your voice.
I think about you when I shouldn't.
How can I love you
When I'm spoken for?
What is it about you that makes me crazy?
That makes me feel
Like I shouldn't do it, but I should?
It doesn't make sense.
You say all the things
I wish he'd say.
You do all the things
I wish he'd do.
I love you too much and it's killing me.
I'm spoken for, please understand.

Erin Spencer, Grade 10
Piedmont High School, OK

A Damp Fall Evening

A figure standing solitarily
Silence seemingly envelops me
Like a blanket over a cold child
Sitting at home aside a crackling fire
Fire…like leaves of ever-changing hue
And leaves like flames which shoot from oaken branch
One and the same, at least in my aged mind
So strange, that one my age could feel so old
That blazing heat of day could feel so cold
While God observes, with mercy, not in wrath
Silent cartographer of this world's path
The ground under my feet, not snow, but rain
The thought of green winter does cause me pain
And pondering another tepid fall
My vision fades to black, and that is all

Andrew Pliagas, Grade 11
Bearden High School, TN

Something's There!

Ever walked to your car, and heard your name
Then you turn around, and everything's the same
Ever sat in your room, but then heard a noise
Got up, looked around, and said it was my toys
You swear something moves, and you stop to see
Thinking to yourself, what could it be
Walking by yourself, but then turn back around
Walking faster now, cause you still hear that sound
Home by yourself, and you're on the phone
Heard some creeping, and turn ALL the lights on
You're thinking in your head, and swear you don't care
But it's in back of your mind, something…is…there.

Jay Adams, Grade 12
Lincoln County High School, TN

Enough

She wakes up to the sound of screams and shouts.
Coming from the door down the hall, with a hole punched out.
Eating breakfast at that old rusted table all alone.
She sees the birthday cake she bought for herself, with one piece gone.
Walking out the door with her head faced down.
With a frown on her face only to be seen from the ground.
On the way to school she thinks to herself.
I wonder if I'll ever be good enough for them, or for that matter anyone else.
She sits in the corner with all the answers, too scared to speak out loud.
The teacher hands her another A on a paper with a smile showing she is proud.
The girl with no friends sits alone at lunch, counting the hours till she must return home.
The teachers and faculty talk about her bruises and when asked about she just says no.
While she is walking home the salty tears begin to fall down her face.
She knows she has got to get out of that place.
So she quietly and quickly packs up her things.
Heads down to the park and sits on the swings.
She prays to God to help her get through this hard time.
Walks down the street and gets on bus nine.
Looks out the window into her past place.
Thinks to herself I did it, with a huge smile across her face.
Thanks God every day, for helping her say enough and helping her get away.

Shelby Roller, Grade 10
Chickasha High School, OK

I Hear America Crying

I hear America crying, the desolate voices of the innocent I hear.
Those of the homeless, each one crying for shelter and tenderness of another's love.
The runaways crying their story to be heard and understood.
The families of DUI victims, cry out for justice over the loss of a loved one.
Farmers crying upon the Lord to provide nourishment to the open mouth of the land.
The heroic firemen crying as one of their "brothers or sisters" fall saving one of our own.
The soldiers cry for our American pride and return safely home to their beloved.
The cries of those heard 'round' linger on as the first star peeps through the haze
And the early, morning chill brings dawn as the world keeps moving on.

Samantha Sharp, Grade 11
Union County High School, TN

I Am From

I am from sleeping, and stretching out in the warmth of the sun on hot summer days,
From sitting outside and writing stories though my stories aren't that good.
I am from my warm cozy house that I hate but love where it's located because when you feel alone all you have to do is go outside and there is always someone to talk to.
I am from the sleepy streets on the east, not the west
and from the big LOUD football field around the corner.
I am from sitting in front of the TV, watching Barbie with my mom and eating popcorn though I'm starting to get too old.
I am from my Mommy, Jackquline, and my Daddy, Jeff.
I am from arguments and heartbreak
I am from being told to keep my head up and my mom saying:
"Smile Doolittle you can do it!"
Though I sometimes doubt what she says because I don't know if I am strong enough to do the things that I am expected to do.
I am from Charleston, West Virginia
From Fried Chicken and my Auntie Shirley's homemade macaroni and cheese.
I am from Rugby Street, where I stay with mom and not my dad
I am from Rugby Street, the street where all my friends are around me.

Gabrielle Hill, Grade 10
Capital High School, WV

The Crash from Below

Asleep on couch pillows, aside my soft bed
I dream of damnation from doubts of my dread
Dare I awake to that crash I've just heard?
Or is it this dreaming that's left me more stirred?

My vision is coming as eyes open wide
This window lay open and blood at my side
"What's happened? My Lord!" I stumble with shock
A hand to my head: "How unfriendly a knock!"

It's sore to the touch and I hardly reclaim
My sight till I settle on he who's to blame
"Who are you?" I speak with a fearful old head
"A bad dream," He speaks and I go back to bed.

Nathaniel Calvert, Grade 11
St Francis Borgia Regional High School, MO

Minnie and Freckle

We've had lots of animals in our family,
And I'm not talking about, Matthew or me.

I am referring, to the four legged kind,
Be they joeys or turtles, or even canine.

For some reason, we always get them in pairs,
Like Evan Almighty, if anybody cares.

We have two cats, which we've had for some time.
They are from China, but know English just fine.

We used to have Mickey, he was a cat,
He fell from the balcony, and "yuck," he went splat.

The thing that they say, about cats landing neat,
Isn't quiet true, from 200 feet.

But Minnie, his sister, and we have her still,
So we got freckle just so they could chill.

Daniel Urban, Grade 10
University Heights Academy, KY

Things Have Changed in Mythologyville

Circe's diabolical plan had to end.
Her island was teeming with animals.
This situation culminated into
A fine from the Humane Society.
Cyclops has become a recluse in his cave.
He is embarrassed he has only one eye.
His self-esteem isn't what it used to be.
Poseidon's arthritis put him in abeyance.
He's confined to his room at the nursing home.
Cyclops, his son, doesn't visit anymore.
Athena, once the smartest of them all,
Now has Alzheimers and thinks she's Britany Spears.
She constantly sings, "Oops I did it again,"
And Hera and Aphrodite goad her on.

Rachel Goar, Grade 10
Germantown High School, TN

Sussicran

What mortal man can compare with thee
in your strength or beauty?
God's image perfected, every being can see
Your visage's superiority.
Eyes, blue as Poseidon's dwelling,
reflect the soul within.
A starry sonata in the din of Life.
Each lady's cheek becomes sanguine with infatuation,
Each gent's green when you pass
What human with sight cannot fill with admiration,
O Knight errant,
For you are loved by every lass.
Could Paris, admired by Venus,
have a countenance so winning?
If there were but a contest
as to who could keep Helen grinning the longest.
A warrior poet, brave and tender,
girls melting at your physique and imagery.
You're sight to behold, O Mirror, Mirror.
More's the pity, there's only two of us.

Robin Lee, Grade 12
Boyd-Buchanan School, TN

Snowglobe

A world within covered in glass
No one can penetrate without destruction
Some people gaze from afar while they pass
Others stop to admire close their function
These fragile creatures can, will be shaken
These disruptions shake their world and cause dismay
Their perfection can never be taken
For no one dare break their beauty away
Turning different views but never part
The world inside is envied
All details intricate taken to heart
Place of wonder amazing and fancied
Without change what are we — human not so
I choose the real world pain and all — let's go

Gracie Gelfand, Grade 11
St Mary's Episcopal School, TN

Friday Nights

Friday nights are very fun
you laugh and play around
although you are not in the sun
football players are out on the ground
excitement is in the air
cheering and clapping is the only sound

Cheerleaders are cheering and dancing
football players are tackling the other team
the band is on the field prancing
the lights on the field beam
there is no other night like friday night
it makes me want to scream

Paul Longmire, Grade 11
Anderson County High School, TN

Grandpa

Just to get this started
All I want to say
Is that I miss you all
In every other way

I cry every day knowing
That you are all gone
Can't come home any more
To say "Grandpa I'm home"

It's hard without you all
I can't do this anymore
Because I go crazy
When I can't see you all anymore

You all are gone but not forgotten
In the big blue sky
Wishing I could see you passing by
Man, it's so hard to say goodbye

To what was special to me
But you all will always be in my heart
Forever you'll be...

De'Angelis Bullard, Grade 11
McGehee High School, AR

The Heart That Breaks

Oh the shadows that haunt me
Falling with the cloak of night
Stalking, screaming, and lurking
Filling me with thoughts of fright

Talking, whispering, calling my name
Wanting me to come
I shall ignore for they know my shame
Hidden just under my flesh

How I long for the love of another
Not to be cast away
For I am not invisible
Nor under any cover

See the pain beneath the smile
Feel and hear my heart
Calling for the beat of another
Needing the touch of a lover

No longer shall I hide behind the lies
I shall wear my heart on my sleeve
For what is love to us
Love is the heart that breaks.

Michael Alvarez, Grade 10
Prue High School, OK

A Brother's Love

When I see him I know he's there for me
I know he has my back he's there for me
I'm glad he's here he helps me out with all my problems
and when I'm in trouble
he's like a brother who helps me
when I'm down or need help
I'm glad he's here
without him I'd just be a lonely person with no one to talk to
I'm glad he's in my life
and I'm also glad he's my brother

Casey Camp, Grade 10
Capital High School, WV

Forever Friend

I met you with fear and doubt in my heart,
And now I can't imagine us being apart,
When we go a week without talking at all,
It makes my heart begin to fall,
I don't like when we scream and shout,
Or when you make me feel down and out,
But soon you come back to me,
With your heart open freely,
We've been through the pain, hurt, and love,
But no matter what happens our hearts will always go above,
Above the mess and silly lies,
And reach each other when we look into one another's eyes.

Rachel Gilliam, Grade 11
Family of Faith Christian School, OK

Blossom

Painted smile on a painted face,
Classic beauty paired with an angelic grace.
A lifetime lived, in a moment spent,
A day of years forever kept.
Rain washes away the sins of the past,
Yet shadowy memories are made to last.
Words are lost, meanings uselessly,
Failing to describe your hold on me.
We are forever glancing back, eyes telling each other we pray it won't last.
Each of us is leaning away from what we used to be,
To a future which could possibly
Mean everything to me and thee.
It could be the end of Blissful Innocence,
And for my final penitence,
I've written you one last list of the grievances we never spoke,
And tried our best to overlook
Into the flame our list will be, never again, anything between thee and me.
Let flowers grow from those ashes, so when we look back we can see,
Beauty
Where hate would be.

Theresa Nienaber, Grade 11
Cor Jesu Academy, MO

The Plunge

Looking at the water,
Wondering if you can swim.
Taking the leap to go farther,
Excited, but scared of splashing in.

You knew it was sink or swim,
Still you took the chance,
Proving you fell for him,
As you begin life's dance.

You see how great it feels
Just to be held by someone
But then a little time reveals
How relationships sometimes run.

You get through the rough
Because you know you're like hand and glove
So you have to stay tough
That's when you know you're in love.

Jenny Horton, Grade 10
Prue High School, OK

Backflashes (This Game)

She always says to me,
'Don't be stupid, don't be stupid, don't be stupid.'
But I didn't know I was being stupid.
I was just being myself.
Does that mean I'm stupid? Probably.

I may never master
This fine art of human relation.
I will persistently try,
And persistently fail,
To create an immaculate connection of communication
Between myself and this woman.

With her there is no real system of trial and error.
Only trial, trial, trial
And loss, breakdown.
After years without a victory
Or a single inch of gain
I've decided —
I'm just no good at this game.

Krayton Rodgers, Grade 10
Chickasha High School, OK

The True Meaning of Christmas

Trees covered in red and green
under it neatly wrapped presents gleam
but this is not what Christmas means
the meaning goes back before you and me
there was no sound in town
born was a king with no crown
angels came down in the night
as shepherds shuddered in fright
they sang of the one Jesus Christ
On one starry, starry night

Austin Basansky, Grade 10
South Intermediate High School, OK

Raindrops

Raindrops are the tears of fallen souls
Who cry from the heavens
When families are torn apart
Angels sing of sadness
Sorrow is all around
Love is falling to the Earth
Raindrops are the tears of fallen souls
Be drenched in it
The sky is slowly darkening in the light
Huge clouds are forming
Only broken images of the past
Raindrops are the tears of fallen souls
The rain is a collection that slowly grows bigger
And when its full it bursts
Raindrops are the tears of fallen souls
You are slowly getting soaked
Memories flow to the mind
The thirst is quenched
Raindrops are the tears of fallen souls
Another rainstorm is brewing
The souls will cry once again

Heather Lile, Grade 10
Barren County High School, KY

Spring

They enter the arena.
Confidence exudes them.
They know they're the best,
These goliaths of the game,
But this is no day to change the scriptures.

"We know we're the underdog,
But we like it that way.
We play better like this.
Besides America roots for the underdog,
That's where we'd rather be."

These warriors of the modern day,
We're not world beaters at all.
The scriptures held true this day.

"We knew we had it in us.
We didn't know we were this good!"
As the scoreboard reads 12-0.

Adam Boone, Grade 12
Germantown High School, TN

Heart of Sand

I know your body as if it were my own land,
But when I reach for your heart I reach in the dark.
When I try to hold it in the palm of my hand,
It slips through my fingers like grains of sand.
I can't get to your heart because you've built a wall,
To protect you from hurt and so in love you don't fall.
You've built it well, so strong and tall,
But lucky for us, I've got a new plan.
I'll tear down your wall down, in you heart I'll stand.

Ethan Milligan, Grade 12
Concord Academy, TN

Cotton Field's Story

It's just another day,
I'd rather be a horse eating hay,
A slave just pickin' cotton,
If I try to run I'll be shottin',

Have a name but dem whities call me Nigga,
White youngins three foot tall seem so much bigga,
Singin' spirituals pass the hour,
Twenty-nine 'n' rain has been my only shower,

I was bred like a horse for my masta,
Do what he says cause I hasta,
Waitin' for Moses to set me free,
My sista's inside serving tea,

Got a son who was sold from me,
They took him to pick in Montgomery,
It's just another day of strife,
Just another day in a slave's life.

Trey Millard, Grade 10
Rock Bridge Sr High School, MO

Boy and Girl

My life changed ever since that night.
Until then, nothing seemed right.
Staying up talking about the past,
Never thinking this thing would ever last.
Every time I'm with him, it's so much fun.
It's amazing to see what he's done.
I never knew how happy I could be
Until the moment he kissed me.
Wishing for that night to never end,
As he slowly became more than a friend.
I'm glad that I met someone I could be myself around,
And even happier that it's him I found.
I don't have to wear make-up and he wouldn't care,
He's just happy that I'm there.
I'm glad we won't ever part
And happy that he stole my heart.

Lyndzey Goff, Grade 10
Glenpool High School, OK

Alone

You think I don't notice, but oh, I notice.
The eyes of your desire
covertly scan me,
hastily
trying to find
the words to say.
Your heart stops, the hair on your neck rises,
and you attempt
to catch your breath, but you can't.
It's lost.
Your chance is gone,
and you go back to your life, alone.
You think I don't notice.

Kelly Barker, Grade 12
Baylor School, TN

Miss You

I miss you so much,
Can't hardly wait to see you again,
Hearing your voice over the phone,
Makes me smile,
Slowly all my stress from the day blows away,
The sweet smell of your cologne still tingling in my nose,
Softness of your lips pressed gently against mine,
The coziness of you holding me tight slowly slipping away,
Staring in to your beautiful brown eyes,
Warmth covering me like a security blanket,
Feeling so safe laying next to you,
Kissing you between every word,
When we finally meet again,
I'm going to rush in to your arms,
Holding on tight hoping that you never let me go,
The feeling of you finally covering me once again,
I know I will have to leave you soon,
It makes it hard,
Just to say,
Good-bye.

Lacy Caspers, Grade 12
Asher High School, OK

Fallen Angel

Inches from my reach is deliverance
Hate cruelly dangles
I just can't seem to accept
That my fate is eternity as a fallen angel

In my soul
I can hear the heaven's sing
While I've been condemned to this burden
That I still carry upon these broken wings

I reach for his hand to save me
For I have fallen from grace
As the hurt of betrayal consumes me
Tears stream down my face

I've been left unable to fly
Broken hearted and in pain
From innocence I've been departed
And a fallen angel I remain

Korie Shepherd, Grade 12
Fort Towson Jr/Sr High School, OK

I Love You

I love you, not for the way you look or for what you wear.
Not for your beautiful eyes, or the loveliness of your hair.
No matter what you look like it doesn't matter to me.
I love you for you even though you don't love me.
I used to hope for love, and how I'd love to hope,
but now I possess neither though I long for both.
Without you here I'll stay, to dream my lonesome dreams.
This place deep in my heart, in this domain you're queen.
You forever rule my love, you control my fate,
for my love for you is eternal and forever I will wait.

C.J. Bray, Grade 12
Buckhannon-Upshur High School, WV

What Do You See?*

What do you see when you look in a mirror?
I couldn't see things more clearer.
I see who I am.
And who I'm going to be.
It all makes perfect sense to me.
No matter what it all begins with school.
If you don't stay, you're simply a fool.
Show up and make good grades.
That's all, and you've got it made.
Your job's not hard when you like your work.
It's actually a perk.
One day, when you have a kid and wife.
You will look back at your life.
Sit and think about the things you've done.
And think "I'm one of the lucky ones."
Wonder about the life you would have had.
If you would have chosen the road named "bad."
Digging and shoveling out in the heat.
Coming in every day smelly and beat.
I would simply sit and stare.
And be very thankful I'm not there.

Nathan Miller, Grade 10
Grove High School, OK
**Inspired by my mom the plumber*

Christmas

Outside the window the snow is falling
In the middle of the night bells will chime
"Happy holidays" most will be calling
For now here come the days of Christmastime

"'Twas the night before Christmas" red and green
Children can't sleep for all the excitement
Santa is coming to lick the plates clean
And to give toys bringing enlightenment

Yet light of the world He was born to save
The dawn of a season all about giving
The baby Jesus our roads He would pave
But for only presents are people living

Though about others once upon a time,
These days all people say is "mine, mine, mine!"

Elizabeth Ansbro, Grade 11
St Mary's Episcopal School, TN

God Doesn't

God doesn't leave you when you're in despair.
Even though it may seem that no one is there.
He doesn't speak "Peace be still,"
To make the waters rise.
God doesn't cease to amaze us.
Even when we think we're wise
So when you feel the devils' pound,
Just keep in mind that…
God doesn't save to lose and
He doesn't carry to let down.

Sarah Lawler, Grade 12
Cotter Jr/Sr High School, AR

A Lover's Sorrow

There is a lady I know so well.
On her my mind constantly dwells.
In my heart, there is a place that secretly waits,
for the chance to take her on a date.
Oh, she has such prominence and pose.
How she is so beautiful, only heaven knows.
How I am tortured when she sits so close to me there.
My shyness forces me my love for her to bear.
I come close to insanity when she's not near,
but become sane when her voice I do hear.
The voice of a choir of angels singing,
happiness and calm her voice to me bringing.
She is so wonderful, she could only be made by immortal hand.
Compared to her, every other female is bland.
Sad tidings come forever closer my way,
when she leaves me like a boat leaves a bay.
Gracefully floating off onto the sunlit sea,
leaving dark empty waters rippling inside me.
For the unknown love inside me is doomed,
when she disappears all that's left is gloom.

Thomas Wells, Grade 10
Ouachita High School, AR

Like a Snapping Turtle

…I'm always scared to come out of my shell
I never think you'll wanna hear what I have to tell
…And every time I try to inch my way out
it only leaves me with that much more doubt
…I worry that if I did let you in
you'd be the one that left in the end
…I'm sorry if I've pushed you away
I hate the way this makes me feel today
…Underneath my shell that's weathered and worn
you have no idea how much I am torn.

Brylee Courkamp, Grade 11
Tyrone High School, OK

An Ode to Jack

Good boy good boy, you are my love and joy
You make me smile and, too, make me laugh
And you stand proud like brave Hector of Troy
You are the best, you are my other half;

I love to see you and your big brown eyes
So soft and warm like a summer night's air
And to hear your deep voice, what a surprise:
The two of us create quite a nice pair;

The way that you greet with a wink and smile,
My days would darken with out all of that
Your thousands of kisses, very worthwhile
And it is humorous to believe that…

This love comes from my dog, this girl's best friend,
I on you and you too on I depend.

Austin Nichols, Grade 11
St Mary's Episcopal School, TN

She's Like Mercury

She's like mercury,
As seductive in her element
As she is toxic to the touch.
She holds your gaze,
Gray eyes, near metallic shine,
Both aware of your immediate lust.
Crumpling her innocence,
Demanding your every desire satisfied,
You hold her too close, and break her binds.
She slips into your hands,
And falls, into you, as beads of quicksilver;
Leaving her fear and virtue behind.
Her presence consumes you,
Insanity seeps in, you wait for her lethal kiss,
To come and find your lips.
You'll never be the same again,
As you sense, a chemical change,
Your every atom,
Melting, twisting, turning,
And forming to hers.
And she's like mercury.

Sarah Taylor, Grade 10
Hillsboro High School, MO

Confessions

Life is full of confessions,
And denial,
Dismay and distrust.
Confession is a way to relieve stress
It can be hard or easy.
Life is short, never too long
Confessions are important,
To express your emotions.
Life is hard never too easy.
When times get hard,
Remember your confession.

Tyler R., Grade 10
Audubon Youth Development Center, KY

The Power of Imagination

Your agility,
Your natural ability…
Productivity from the highest grade facility
All becomes worthless to you
when boredom begins to accrue.
With nothing to do,
maybe trying something new
will stop your inner voice
from telling you that suicide's the only choice.
Still no games to play?
There's still a way —
Just close each eye.
Let out a sigh.
Make all the old feelings go
and let you imagination flow.

Khalid Rosli, Grade 12
White Station High School, TN

Untitled

Everything is starting to change
supposedly healing all the pain
for better or worse, nobody knows
is that what scares you the most;
not knowing what awaits you?
looks like all the things trapped inside
of you are starting to rise to the surface
are you ready for all to know your darkest
secrets and lies, even worse your truth?
now you catch yourself constantly looking
over you shoulder
you're hearing your name in every little whisper
fearing what lies around the corner…
listening to the rain fall, day by day
cannot defend what you cannot understand
all these thoughts and feelings
they're right there, but you still deny them
yet they're dull and fading out quick,
they still remain
so what is there left to fear now?

Jessica Nash, Grade 10
White County High School, TN

For You

Two people are getting married today
I know they are right for each other in every way.
From the moment, I saw them
I knew they were meant to be
And that I can plainly see
I know they will be happy together
And their love will last forever
There are bound to be little fights
But in the end, each of you will say the other is right
This is my wedding present for you
And I hope all your dreams together will come true.

Michelle St. John, Grade 10
Coffee County Central High School, TN

Lost in Abyss

Out from the soil a life has sprung
a twig for the time, a lowly one too.
The nurturing soils and sun make it strong
and through care, its boughs reach up to the ethereal blue.
This tree, this modest contributor of life
rests nobly amongst the evils of the earth.
Kindly providing for us as a gentle mother
we are her garden, and she our rebirth.
Strayed from her path though
some lost the simplicity.
Drones of technology, of things complex
they complicated, the earth devoid of innocent felicity.
The tree disappeared like a whisper in the wind
a secret remnant of the past.
In our rapidly paced world
the good things never last.

Jaclyn Melcher, Grade 10
Assumption High School, KY

Sisters by Love!

The days of tears and laughter
We found a time to share.
The years have formed a friendship
That's beautiful and rare.
Our hearts were made to coincide.
God planned our role on Earth.
He created us as sisters,
By love, not through our birth.

Miesha Chrisman, Grade 10
Grandview Alternative School, MO

Lucid Unconsciousness

Falling backwards without warning
Descending into a realm of wonder,
Warmth and emotions surround the mind,
A sanctuary to escape from reality.

A person, familiar to strange events,
Obscure or realistic,
Bliss, nostalgia, anger, or terror,
Each encounter brings diversity.

Is it fantasy, an illusion?
Or secret dreams and aspirations?
An experience only you will feel,
The meaning remains unsolved.

A noise awakens the mind
From its intense hours of hibernation.
The images and sounds evaporate.
The sun breaks, it was only a dream.

Elizabeth Miller, Grade 11
Bearden High School, TN

The Soul

This ravaged soul sits calmly and quietly waiting…waiting;
For a chance to strike;
Tired of being made fun of;
This ravaged soul holds it all in, so it won't try to fight;
It takes all its might;
This ravaged soul tries to fit in…into the crowds it shouldn't;
It tries and tries;
But mostly to no avail;
This ravaged soul sits by himself; independent of all the rest;
Little did it know, this was all just a test;
Alone in a dark room, oh, but a familiar place;
'Nothing left to hold onto' cries from its face;
This ravaged soul wants to live without fears;
It finds itself on its hands and knees;
Pleading…Crying out from its tears;
From the corner comes a great light;
And delivers it from its plight;
This ravaged soul was existent no more;
Its life would go on Forevermore.

Buddy Moad, Grade 12
Central High School, OK

Winter Has Arrived

Snowflakes softly fall.
A chilling, biting wind blows.
Winter has arrived.

Lukas Meadows, Grade 10
Shady Spring High School, WV

The Art of Painting

On my canvas, you're my growing wish.
Day by day, tiny strokes become your melodies.
Yet, the colorful tunes start to fade.
You become dry, weak and with nothing to show.
My mind is gripping at something to paint.
You pay no mind to what is at stake.
Your friend's canvas is a cheap work of art.
Still, you look at me with an open heart.
I sit there with small marks and dots.
While you try to cover up what has already been bought.
Your bristles are tired and worn from such work.
Yet, still looking at me thinking what might have been.
Well, my friend, it is much too late now.
Seeing my pallet is full of white, stop asking how.
Clean again, just like the beginning.
I open my eyes to a million dipped brushes before me.
All different shades and sizes.
One brush lies in the artist's palm.
Its strokes and strides are quick and calm.
It is a flawless masterpiece in every which way.
Oh, how I shine. Starlight Starbright.

Kali Laird, Grade 11
Owasso High School, OK

Forever Wait to Marry*

Gather ye rosebuds while ye may,
Young time is still away
and this same flower will smile every day,
Tomorrow will be blooming.

The glorious lamp of beauty, like flowers
The more he awaits
The more he will cherish you
And nearer he will be.

The age of beauty live long
Even when you're young and old
But being young is fun, but old is loved
Times still succeed and come around.

Young ladies use your time wisely
And while ye may not marry
For having fun is not a crime
You may forever wait to marry.

Ashley Garrett, Grade 12
Union County High School, TN
**An answer to "To the Virgins"*

A Light

When you see a light
You will know that it's Heaven
You are with God now!

Cassie Jones, Grade 10
Fort Towson Jr/Sr High School, OK

Nature Around Us

I'm walking through the trees
Looking around I may be able to see everything
But there is no sound

Every day I go through those trees
Ha! I remember when
I got chased by those bees
During lunchtime I sit by the pond
Watching a squirrel come up to me
Wanting to bond

Looking at the water sparkle in the sun
Having a great time and having lots of fun
As it gets dark I'm lying on a hill watching
The stars pass as I'm staying still
I'm trying to find a picture in the dark blue night
As I'm looking I listen to these two birds fight

I had a swell day today
And now I'm through
Maybe someday we can
Go together just me and you.

Raymond M. Rousseau, Grade 11
Grove High School, OK

Sun Seasons (Behold the Sun)

At the rise She
Paints the pale pastels of spring
And increases to full bright bloom
 the time in which all rise to wake
 or fall to sleep
At the zenith She
Blinds the world with bright summer
And warms our aching bones with day
 for most who have lived strong the morn
 ache much indeed
At the fall She
Splashes the sky in autumn
Then fades so all might see again
 to stroll home in preparation
 for next season
At the end She
Darkens the world with winter
So all might sleep in dreaming peace
 a long and heady restful dream
 of rise and spring
Behold the Artist, behold the Mother, behold the Sun

Raeh Burns, Grade 11
Union County High School, TN

We Grow Further Apart…

I thought he was different,
I thought he understood.
I thought we connected,
I guess I misunderstood.

We were friends from the start,
But now might be the end.
My words came from the heart,
But with every rule I bend,

We grow further apart…

Brandy Williams, Grade 10
Huntingdon High School, TN

So Wait

The fire burns
But hot is not.
It's cold to the touch
Your spirit envelops me
It saves me.
Forever yours.
Your love surrounds me
This is not goodbye
I will see you again
It will just take time
So Wait.
Wait for me at the gates
The gates to our kingdom
A kingdom of blue sky's
And fields of flowers that go on and on for miles
We will fly high on the wings of angels
Sit on clouds made of cotton candy
And sleep on the rings of Saturn
We will never part again
So Wait.

Amanda N. Roberts, Grade 10
White County High School, TN

Winter Snow

Dashing through the snow so fast,
people forget of Christmas past.

The joys of fun and laughter,
no longer sought after.

Work and business the center life,
causes many holiday strifes.

But when it's time to snow,
the people they all slow.

Everything made just so right,
with snow falling with all its might.

So enjoy and smile,
and stay home for a while

Hunter Southwell, Grade 10
Chickasha High School, OK

Young Poets Grades 7-8-9

Note: The Top Ten poems were finalized through an online voting system. Creative Communication's judges first picked out the top poems. These poems were then posted online. The final step involved thousands of students and teachers who registered as online judges and voted for the Top Ten poems. We hope you enjoy these selections.

Top Poem Grades 7-8-9

Creation: What I See

Blue skies glistening like a sapphire
Forests of trees, deep green leaves, bright yellow sun
As bright as New York City
Meadows, as endless as an open sea
Assorted flowers as different as you and me

Birds chirping, frogs croaking, crickets cricking
Each giving their own attempt to praise God
Wind howling like a lonely animal

Fresh air like a new beginning
The first bite into a juicy red apple
Like a teaspoon of sugar has hit your lips
The first slice of a sumptuous steak, an unmatchable taste

Fresh cut grass as the first big whiff comes up your nose
Daisies, roses are just a few flowers from God's flower shop
Flowering trees, the beach's amazing smell marches up my nose like an army of small little soldiers

Sun's warmth, happiness, freshly fallen snow
Each grain of sand against my feet, joy, smooth rocks
Rain refreshing my dry thirsty lips
Take a moment each day to acknowledge creation
Be like God, say all is good

Jonathan Bartolone, Grade 7
Our Lady Catholic School, MO

Top Poem Grades 7-8-9

Midnight's Mysteries

Sleeping World is silent for now
Bright, pale moon hovering over shimmering ocean waves
Where does soothing moon hide,
When light returns to brighten dark skies?
Pitch black sky, filled with golden white stars glistening away
How many stars span black night skies?

Howling wolves calling to pack
Asking for guidance across empty prairies
Snakes slithering slowly across silently sanded deserts
Trees casting ghoulish shadows upon dark, dusty, dirty forested trails,
Like ghosts cast shadows upon gravel roads
Owls cooing above swaying tree branches,
While their head turns to watch for deliciously good midnight snacks
Why do they stay up so late?
Sleeping world is silent for now

It's calming, peaceful, soothing
Grasses swaying on deserted beaches,
Listening to wind's voice singing them to sleep
Ocean waves crashing into sandy shores,
Like cheetahs capturing their prey
Sleeping world is silent for now

Meredith Bratcher, Grade 8
Barret Traditional Middle School, KY

Top Poem Grades 7-8-9

Match the Sky

At first the rain falls softly,
As the sky weeps silent tears of sorrow.
My mood then drops to match the sky's,
And my own tears slide slowly down my cheeks.

The sorrowful drops fall faster now,
And my heart now drums to match the thunder,
With each strike of lightning my mood darkens still,
And my own tears streak faster to match the emotions.

My heart and tears slow as the rain lets up,
And my ashen face mimics the color of the clouds.
Just as my heart slows to normal,
I see a sliver of sunlight over the glistening treetops.

After the emotions of despair I've been feeling,
This slight sliver of hope blooms in my heart.
My heart gives way to hopeful anticipation,
As I scan the mist filled sky.

When I find the rainbow in the sky,
My tear stained cheeks split in a smile.
I gaze out at that colorful aerial beauty,
And find my heart matches the happiness of the sky.

Julia (MaLee) Crouch, Grade 8
Hallsville Middle School, MO

Top Poem Grades 7-8-9

Confidence's Sunrise

Ghosting through life as a shadow in the background,
Noticed only when I wish the opposite,
I sit outside watching the sun go down,

The moon rises and my mind is lost,
Huddled against the darkness and fear I dare not open my eyes,
No one really wants to know what is out there.
My shadow is dancing across the landscape,
A weak, pale thing barely surviving,
The shadow of a shadow,
What a pitiful thing.

My heart is heavy, my pulse fast,
I reflect on the day with joy and fear,
Fear of the future I must face tomorrow.
Light breaks over the crest and an idea enlightens my mind,
Slowly I lift my head, liking what I find.

Each day the sun rises anew,
A new day,
Just waiting for me.
Dew sparkling on the grass, color spreading across the sky,
Just like optimism in my mind,
With a lightened heart I face the sun.

Cara Duprey, Grade 9
Elmwood Jr High School, AR

Top Poem Grades 7-8-9

This Is Life

"Love," she says with warmth in her eyes.
"Fear," he whispered, ready to cry.
"Hope," screamed the girl with her dad at her side.
"Death," mutters the demon with the blood red eyes.
This is Life.

"Compassion," said she to the heavens above.
"Hate," from the man receiving no love.
"Joy," yelled the girl whose spirit flew like a dove.
"Sadness," cried the baby being shoved.
This is Life.

All these emotions of Life consists
Without all these feelings, we couldn't exist
If you're feeling sad, you must persist
All these feelings, I made a list
This is Life.

Taylor Felton, Grade 8
Belle Isle Enterprise Middle School, OK

Top Poem Grades 7-8-9

Fall Wind

When the tawny grass does rustle in the cold and frosty wind,
Like a leaf on this breeze, my journey will begin.
I'll ride on the wings of eagles, the saddle of a horse,
And although I seem to wander, I follow a destined course.
As that frosty wind blows again, frozen needles striking me,
I must not stop, I must not falter, as I travel land and sea.
The sunset, orange and red, burning on the horizon,
Twilight descends upon us with the sinking of the sun.
With no light to show their colors, brown and orange leaves turn to grey,
And with the birth of this cold night comes the death of that cold day.
So when the frosty wind had blown, so it began,
And so it shall begin — again.

Haven Hogan, Grade 7
Nettleton Jr High School, AR

Top Poem Grades 7-8-9

Ode to the Monster

I fearfully walked onto the stage and gazed into its eyes.
It captured me like a photo; I was prepared to meet my demise.
Its ivory teeth were shining.
Its ebony coat was blinding.

My fingers were frozen like ice.
My feet wanted to move like mice.
I could feel my face start to burn.
I was at the point of no return.

I sat on my perch an arm's reach of his teeth,
And rested my foot on his feet beneath.
I tickled the ivory and a sound came out.
A song of sadness began to sprout.

Like a plant, it grew and grew.
And suddenly came something new.
A flower of beauty and grace,
That brought a smile to the audience's face.

I breathed a sigh of relief,
As I looked with disbelief.
My dreaded nemesis had become my friend.
A gentle warmness entered my body and my soul began to mend.

Mikiko Joiner, Grade 9
Hamburg Jr High School, AR

Top Poem Grades 7-8-9

Listen Not to Words

The world is shades of gray,
But mine is black and no white.
No matter where I turn,
I cannot find the light.
Things change before my eyes,
And I think I'm losing me
Behind the layered mask I wear
With no way to get free.
I walk among these smiling people
But my grin is forced.
This laughing, happy girl you see
Is just an act, well rehearsed.
Inside is fear and sorrow and pain
And the tears fall when I'm alone.
I take refuge on a sheet of paper,
For these words are my only home.
All I ask is that you listen
But not to my false words.
Know that what I don't say,
Is often what needs to be heard.

Mary Ruth Robinson, Grade 7
Grassland Middle School, TN

Top Poem Grades 7-8-9

Our Freedom Preserved

America, the land we love,
Home of the brave and free.
Eagles soaring high above;
It fills our hearts with glee.

With thankfulness for those who fought,
The ones whose lives they gave;
Our freedom with great cost they bought.
Flags fly upon their graves.

So honor the flag with a warm salute,
And thank the ones who have served.
Democracy was their main pursuit;
Our freedom they preserved.

Amanda Vincent, Grade 7
Home School, OK

Top Poem Grades 7-8-9

Smiles from Heaven*

Never a harsh word spoken
Or a promise made that was broken
Her grand kids: forever the apple of her eye.
She loved baking delicious chocolate cake and sweet pecan pie.
Cows to tend and crops to harvest each and every one,
Farming: all day long never a chore undone.
The years began to show in her shiny white hair,
Each wrinkle caused by laughter and tender care.

My Great-Grandpa the only love of her life;
Over 50 years she was his caring wife.
Children, husband, family and friends:
Thinking of others to the very end.
Mending skinned knees and a broken heart,
Forever with us; how soon she did part.
Armful of hugs given with love,
We now must think of her with God above.

Smiles and laughter gently calming every fright:
Now her smiles help to light the night.
Look up and you will see,
Two beautiful stars in Heaven,
Shining brightly as they smile just for me.

Kaitlinn Wright, Grade 8
McLish Middle School, OK
**Dedicated to the memory of my great-grandmothers.*

The Game

Song is the passion
Rap is my fashion
Whether it's present or the past
It never seems to last

Going from one place to another
Seeing every different color.
No one sees the same,
But I am going to stay in the game.

People hating and degrading.
O well, I will still be debating.

James Dustin Keller, Grade 9
Izard County High School, AR

A Perfect Christmas

1. Begin with a bag of snow.
2. A pinch of warmness.
3. A packet of presents.
4. Put in a dash of lights.
5. Stir in a pound of snowman.
6. Mix in hot chocolate.
7. Add cookies and milk.
8. Stir in peace.
9. Pour in Christmas trees.
10. Serve with Santa Claus.

Christina Miller, Grade 7
Meredith-Dunn School, KY

My Mom

My mom
Cares and loves me
The way I like her to.
She wants me to succeed in school
"Mamma"

Kyla Hoover, Grade 8
Belle Isle Enterprise Middle School, OK

Apples

Apples are
green and red.
They are
tasty and sour.

I love apples
and grapes.
when they are frozen
they are better.

I just want
to tell you that
you need to try
frozen grapes
and apples.

Jessica Worrell, Grade 7
Dyer Elementary & Jr High School, TN

The Outcast

the girl in the back of the room
is as quest as can be
people laugh and stare at her
I don't see the point
no one knows the silent battle she might be fighting
but they don't care
they just see her as the freak
the outcast

maybe if they knew how she felt inside
or what she has to deal with they wouldn't be so harsh
it's weird that she could go a whole week and not say a word to anyone
and still get more criticism from people than anyone in the whole school
she sits alone
dares not speak a word

maybe someday someone will reach out to her and give her a chance
a bit of hope to hold on to
that things will be ok
show her that not everyone is filled with hate
maybe someday

Melissa Mathis, Grade 9
Fern Creek Traditional Magnet High School, KY

Basketball

Basketball, basketball I love basketball
I love the feeling of the ball in my hands
I love stuffing the opponents' shot from the air right back in their face
I love the sound of sneakers skipping on the hardwood
I love the sound of the fans yelling at me on the free-throw line
But most of all
I love the sound of the nets singing my favorite song "swish"

Kelton Hall, Grade 7
Independence Charter Middle School, OK

Mornings

Up in the morning before the birds fly,
My alarm clock goes off, then I barely open one eye.
I twist and I turn just trying to get up.
She kicks and then screams in my ear
Then threatens to ground me for a year.
I get up, then dress with my eyes still closed.
Then my mom blows.
She goes off about something that I don't want to hear.
"Guess what, Mom?" I say. "I think the bus is near."
Go out the door to the lane, waiting for the bus to come.
It appears finally from the mist, the doors open, and finally a smiling face.
My bus driver is one of my favorite people from the human race.
I fall asleep on the bus seat again,
Then SLAM, the bus door crashes into the wall.
That means it's time to get off.
Walk in the school and grab my stuff for the day,
Then I lay my head on my hand on the desk
And drift away.

Chris Smith, Grade 8
Musselman Middle School, WV

My Favorite Place

In your arms
By your side
In your heart
In your dreams
With you forever
My hand in your hand
Saying "I love you" with meaning
Laughing and talking with you on the phone
Hearts with our names in them
In this sometimes, tragic, beautiful place called LOVE.

Kandyce Lewis, Grade 8
Heritage Middle School, TN

Hidden Faces

We looked into the photograph
And saw the smiling faces
The pictures got us wonderin'
What happened in these places
We looked it up, we saw the truth
We saw the hidden faces
The one we fight for,
The ones we give for
The ones that come knocking at our door
We saw what happened in those places
So many lost yet so many gained
Battles fought, battles lost, came at the biggest cost
Are people lost worth freedom for others?
We seem to think so
We agree and told ourselves
To give up ours for theirs
We saw the bloody places
We saw the destroyed races
We saw the truth behind their disguises
We saw the mixed sorrow and joy in their eyes
We saw the hidden faces.

Megan Beamer, Grade 8
Belle Isle Enterprise Middle School, OK

Mighty Rushing Waters

Bright blue water shining gloriously
Wind creating soft peaks like mountains
Rushing waves slamming crystal shores
Bright orange sun cooking sand-like ovens
Blazing sugar-like beaches
Soft like baby powder
White as snow
Crabs as bright as tomatoes
Crawling and digging deep holes
White soaring seagulls screeching,
Swooping,
Flying,
Calling
Completely natural
Amazingly superb

Cory Elmes, Grade 8
Barret Traditional Middle School, KY

Absorbing Sunlight

Jade green stalks of layered joy
Shadowy haven for scrawny mice
Seeking refuge from sizzling waves of heat
Frightening, eerie hiss of endless layers of aged skin
Stretching to lie on patches of earthen, plowed ground
Delicate sepal supporting dependent seeds
Ready to leap out of their cushions to start a new life
Supportive company of growing buds
Glamorous beauty of endless petals
Aging tips tender with ancient years gone by
Sweet whisper of wind knocking on your roof
Everlasting petals reaching for each other
Intertwining their stretched fingers together
Each body forms together into clusters
All one pack and family dependent upon one another
Staying huddled together, packs seeking warmth
Your radiance strikes my soul like speeding sharks
Blinding strength is enough to warm anyone's soul
My everlasting sunflower

Dan Cannon, Grade 7
Barret Traditional Middle School, KY

Fall

The leaves are red as fire
The grass a light yellow
Outside is warm, peaceful and mellow
Kids are outside enjoying the weather
Riding bikes and having fun with each other
Until nighttime when they all go to bed
Anticipating the new fall day ahead.

Ciara Hill, Grade 8
Wilson Middle School, OK

Friday*

Friday — Last day of school for the week
Friday — No homework...Yes!
Friday — Tests are all complete
Friday — Who wants to go to the football game?

Friday — Picked up early by Mom
Friday — Rush to the vet's office for a cat emergency
Friday — Petting my long-haired beautiful cat
Friday — Start to cry as they take her back

Friday — She fights the sleeping shot
Friday — They take her back once more
Friday — The doctor comes out with a box
Friday — We bury the box — inside a beloved cat

Friday — Try not to cry as I think about never seeing her
Friday — She was the best cat who's ever lived
Friday — I remember every detail as it was yesterday
Friday — Sadly, it was yesterday

Hannah C. Williams, Grade 7
Musselman Middle School, WV
**In honor and memory of Whiskers*

The Light Left My Eyes

You can't speak
It feels like the world is
Spinning faster than light.

I swung my head outward
Then I was on the floor.

I bumped my head on something
Was it a shoe, a chair, or
My imagination.

I woke up with a
Teacher and a nurse
At my side.

I thought I was
Alright, but then I
Found out I
Passed out.

Shelby Keiser, Grade 8
Winfield Middle School, MO

Dreams

Dreams may come
And dreams may go
But with each dream
Is an open window
Where it may lead
Or where it may go
Shhhhh!!!
Quiet, or I may never know

Alesia Gilbert, Grade 9
Alpena High School, AR

Love

Anybody can love
Everyone is loved
In love everybody
Is a somebody
You might have nothing
But in love
You have everything
Anything can happen with love
Many believe in love
And few don't
But either way I know it's there
Love is in the air

Courtney Dye, Grade 8
Pigeon Forge Middle School, TN

Obey Your Parents

The boy lay around.
The cow was not fed or milked.
His father was mad.

Daniel Sumler, Grade 8
Rocky Comfort Elementary School, MO

Change

People will change…
Some will live in the light and others will live in the darkness.
Life will change…
Depending on the decisions that you make life will become better or worse.
Attitudes will change…
Some will become positive and others negative.
Families will change…
Some will grow closer while others will grow farther apart.
Friendships will change…
Some will last a lifetime while others come and go.
But God's word will never change.

Matt Kammer, Grade 8
St Gerard Majella School, MO

Looking for the Answer

Forget violence and drugs.
Need to help one another.
Look around your neighborhood most people are brothers.
Not trying to be racist but mostly black on black crimes.
How are we supposed to help each other and we decrease multiplying.
It's like a subtracting problem.
So what is the answer.
Dice games on the corner kill people quicker than cancer.
There is no cure for cancer.
But there's one for selling drugs and shooting dice.
If you want money get a JOB for once in your life.

Kevin G., Grade 9
Audubon Youth Development Center, KY

Basketball

Basketball is like life. It's more than just a sport,
It's the way you feel when you first step on the court.
You're full of nerves, but you hope the feeling never stops.

Running down the court, you look, pass, and score.
You glance at coach, who is up from the bench,
He's smiling happily as if it was a synch.

Basketball is more than just a sport,
It's the way you feel at half time, when you're back on the court.
You're down by one to the zero,
So you call the give and go;
But your shot's off, and you can't block the opponent's throw.

Play number four works though, again and again,
So you're winning, but then you foul, and they make a free throw.

Basketball is more than just a sport,
It's the way you feel when you have to step off the court.
You're tied this game,
So your head's down and you feel really lame.
But then you look up, and the crowd screams,
And somehow you still feel like the number one team.
Basketball is like life, you'll always have overtime.

Cassandra Green, Grade 9
Alpena High School, AR

Ceaseless

As one sees an endless road
And problems and worries seem to unfold
Don't step back or have fear
The end of it is soon to be near
Take some time and figure it out
Times of struggle shouldn't wear you out

Sierra Jensen, Grade 9
Bearden High School, TN

Batting a Thousand

Bottom of the ninth, two outs, bases loaded, tied game.
Muscles tense.
Sweat drips.
The coach announces who is at bat, on deck and in the hole.
The pitcher stands, glove over his mouth.
Waiting to throw the perfect pitch,
he runs his hands over the ball seams.
I step up to the plate.
The swish of the bat moving through the air,
followed by the ding of solid contact.
Deep in center field there is a look of determination.
The outfielder runs as fast as he can toward the ball
hoping to throw the runner out.
The third base coach waves his arms like a windmill
signaling the runner to score.
He slides in safely
just beating the throw to home.
Shaking hands, back slapping.
Congratulating the losing team on a game well played.

Michael Herrin, Grade 7
Baylor School, TN

Graveyard

Walking through the dark graveyard,
the crowd of headstones in front,
the moonlight shines on every grave,
with fog rolling over each one,
their watch dog standing over them,
the nice cold dirt covering them
the wind playing their favorite song
the sweet sound of the noise beneath your feet.

Kassandra L. Salcido, Grade 8
Southern Reynolds County R-II School, MO

Basketball

Basketball is my favorite sport,
How we dribble up and down the court.
Maroon and white
We fight, fight, fight.
We're number one because,
Two is not a winner
Three no one remembers.
We're the Alpena Lady Leopards
And we're coming at you like a hot chili pepper!

DJ Daniels, Grade 9
Alpena High School, AR

Christmas

White snow falling, falling from the sky,
On Christmas morning we say our hello's,
And then our good-byes.
Presents clustered around the tree,
The ones on the left for my sister,
On the right, for me!
Family together again, after Thanksgiving Day,
We ate a lot, then went away.
The exchanging of presents, all around,
The children running in to open them with a bound!
After the day is over, again do us part,
And again next year, filling with presents,
The CART!

Tyler Holland, Grade 7
Perry County Middle School, MO

Love, Hate, and Deceit

Sweet pure twilight kiss.
Innocent cuddle of night
True love's delight!

Morning dew, your kiss so sweet.
As my knees grow weak,
I think of you,
my heart begins to break,
My love for you will still be strong,
but
you broke my heart!
Shattered, like glass!

I give up, you win.
'Cause in the end, you're in love
with her and not me.
I dream and dream,
But dream as I do,
I'll never be,
With You.

But remember this,
And only this,
I'll be waiting for you to come and love me.

Sam Strange, Grade 8
Owasso 8th Grade Center, OK

The Turtle

The turtle, so cute, so strong
He runs as fast as molasses
His tough shell is as a warrior's armor
The turtle is black and yellow
He lives on water and land
Leafy green vegetables are his favorite treat
His house is his body
The turtle lives on, and on shall he live
The turtle is my favorite animal and that he shall stay

Ethan Gulley, Grade 8
Highland Rim School, TN

A New Beginning
In the darkness of night,
When the moon is bright,
The blood red tears fall to the ground,
The loneliness of the night left no sound,
As the clouds filled the sky
A light flashed by.
Even the things were taking a slope
The light was a new hope
A new beginning.
Caleb Moorehead, Grade 8
Highland Rim School, TN

Hero
Do you see the way she looks at you?
The way she sits and stares?
I see the way she looks at you.
I see the way she cares.
The love in her eyes,
Shines through her tears.
The strength of her heart,
Shines through her fears.
It shows in her actions,
That you have a special place,
Right in her heart,
No one could erase.
Her admiration for you,
Will never run out.
You're her hero —
There is no doubt.
Kathryn Brown, Grade 8
Wainwright Elementary School, OK

The Sad Life of Tires
Round, Round, Round
Round is all I know
Round I am round I go
Round and round to and fro
I go fast I go slow
Come here and you will know

Shrinking thinner this is clear
The end of my days is very near
Sharp objects that I fear
Pins needles and screws I veer
Yes indeed my end is near
Trever Carreon, Grade 8
Ketchum Jr High School, OK

Riding Horses
Climbing up in the stirrup.
Swinging my leg over.
Gripping the reins.
Bouncing in the saddle.
Riding horses is my life.
Katie Vantrease, Grade 8
Rocky Comfort Elementary School, MO

Avisto in Grade School
In grade school each day was another boring day.
Gym was the only thing that kept me coming back.
I enjoyed getting my knees all puffed up and sore with bruises.
I did everything to prevent the dodge ball from hitting me.
There were teachers who called your parents if you pushed someone.
I feared two things at school: the librarian and the cafeteria food.
I could never finish my reading goal or pass reading quizzes on books
I'd read but never understood.

My parents always got calls from teachers.
I couldn't go a day without a teacher chewing me out about something.
I was sent to the principles office.
I had saved a seat for someone.
Everyone thought I was in big trouble.
There was always a little devil watching
Even now
That devil watches me and tells teachers my every move.
They know that Avisto threw the pen.
The teachers knew who went to school each day just to play dodge ball.
That it was Avisto who was first out of the school building.
They knew it was me ready to go home and play video games.
Every day I had to suffer until three o' clock then I was free.
Harrison Avisto, Grade 8
Baylor School, TN

Football
F ootball coming at your face faster than you have ever seen
O utside it is cold but you can't feel is because you are pumped up
O ff sides on the defense five yards up for the offense
T all line backer wrestling you to the ground at the two-yard line
B last through the hole for a ten-yard run up the middle
A t the one-yard line your gut sinks to your feet
L ast play for the wind I score a touchdown the crowd goes wild
L ongest game in my life I was cold but I was on fire
Jake W. Freeman, Grade 8
Greenfield Jr/Sr High School, MO

My Grandpa's Hands
He calls them his mitts
His palms wide and full, his fingers thick as a wide tip marker
My grandpa's hands are perfect

He uses his hands to pat my head, to catch a baseball, to take a fish off my pole
A fish too slimy and wiggly for me to touch

My grandpa's hands are different from mine
My nails uneven and weak
His smooth and strong
The skin on my hands fair
His freckled and tanned

My grandpa's hands remind me of his Spirit
Big, strong, and brave
Yet at the same time soft, kind, and gentle

Morgan Jones, Grade 8
West Jr High School, MO

Undeserving Love

Why would He love me so much?
I don't deserve it.
I've made too many mistakes.
Why would He die for me?
I don't deserve it.
Why would He want me to be with Him?
He is so mighty, so powerful!
I am so undeserving of this love God has given me!
But He loves me so much,
And even though I fail every now and then,
He's wild about this undeserving teenager!

Austyn Moore, Grade 7
Niangua High School, MO

Love

Love is a very powerful word
What does it mean to you
To me it means trust, care, and friendship
A love between a mother and a daughter
is a caring relationship
A love between a father and son
is something you can cherish forever
the love that give you butterflies
From a first kiss
Or from the first time
you held that lucky guy's hand
that's making a memory
Although the word gets misused
It means so much
True love grows with every waking moment
And with the increasing of age
Just like an older couple
That acts like they're engaged.

Hannah Huston, Grade 8
Chelsea Jr High School, OK

Wonders of Earth

The roar of a tiger so powerful and giving you a warning to stay back. The chirps of a bird so calming and beautiful giving a bright morning song. The howl of a wolf at the wonderful full moon giving a beautiful night sound. The howl of a monkey cool and smart giving a sound of power. The sound of a bat in the night that tells where they are giving us knowledge of how smart they are. The screech of a wombat strong and terrifying giving us a fright. The smell of a skunk stinky and nasty giving us a warning to not come near him. The annoying crickets giving us a midnight tone. The whoo of an owl gives us a scare in the middle of the night, but is so beautiful.

The world is
covered with
so many beautiful
animals, why destroy them
by tearing down their homes?

Christina Whisenant, Grade 8
Stuart Middle School, KY

Snowman!!

Black silky hat rests on the gentle
but tough snow flaky head.
Orange crunchy carrot digs into the head
like a groundhog looking for a place to live.
Green M&M's form a circle to make
the most breath taking eyes of a snowman.
Cheerios line up like a class ready to go outside,
but with a little curve.
Plaid scarf wraps around the snowflake head
to offer comfort to the snowman.
Then it lightly falls in front
to design a lonely old man.
Silver buttons to add a sense of style
and to say there is always room to fix things!!!

Kelsey Volle, Grade 7
Southern Boone Middle School, MO

Renamed

Everyone cares as of now
I wish I could explain how
I really feel inside
I'm as happy as a bride
I now know that they care
So I don't have to tear
My feelings anymore
Because there are people galore
This is where I want to be
I'm no longer lost at sea

Frances Price, Grade 7
Southern Reynolds County R-II School, MO

If I Could Be Mickey Mouse

I wish I could be Mickey Mouse,
So then Disney World would be my house.
I could hang out with Pluto and all my friends.
The joy of being famous never ends.

Rachel Bax, Grade 8
St Joseph School, MO

Fire

Fire runs through the trees
Smoke blows by in the breeze.
People look for someone to blame
Sad faces near the flames.

The heat is unbearable
The destruction is horrible.
Into the towns and the cities showing its wrath
Destroying all in its path

The destruction is horrible
It leaves everything deplorable.
But the destruction stays
And so do the memories of the blaze.

Grant Martin, Grade 8
West Jr High School, MO

A Friend Is Like a Diary

A friend is like a diary,
You can tell it everything.
You can trust a diary,
You can trust a friend.
You can tell a friend everything
Like something exciting
Or something involved with your mom
Like fighting.
A friend is like a diary because
You can tell them everything
That had happened that day and ask,
Them not to tell
A friend stores it in their head
And they promise not to say a thing
About what you've just said.
A diary is special to me
Just like a friend is special too.
I find a diary is a treasure box
With happy feelings or even
Sad feelings and great memories
Just like a friend.

Shelby Feldkamp, Grade 7
Meredith-Dunn School, KY

Soccer

Soccer
Fun and beautiful
Juking, curving, laughing
Joga, Bonito, play, beautiful
Futbol

Luis Anguiano, Grade 8
Belle Isle Enterprise Middle School, OK

Magen Albritton

I am a girl who loves soccer.
I wonder what I will do in the future.
I hear the crowd cheering.
I see a huge field.
I want to play this dream.
I am a girl who loves soccer.

I pretend to be a famous soccer player.
I feel I'm on top when I play soccer.
I touch the game ball.
I worry I will not be good enough.
I cry that I will fail to do this.
I am a girl who loves soccer.

I understand that this takes time.
I say anything is possible.
I dream I will be the greatest player.
I try to do my best and stay positive.
I hope to play pro soccer one day.
I am a girl who loves soccer.

Magen Albritton, Grade 8
Elkton School, TN

These Are the Ways I Love You

I love the way you sweet talk me
I love the way when I'm mad at you make me not stand it
I love the way you look at me
I love the way you talk to me and make me feel so special
I love the way you hold me and make me feel safe in your arms
I love the way you kiss me so tender and soft
I love the way you say you love and mean it
I love the way you say I'm beautiful and I don't believe a word
I love the way you make me feel like the luckiest girl in the world
I love the way your soul and heart connects to mine
I love the way you love me for me
I love the way your eyes look into mine
I love the way you smile when you look at me
I love the way you complete me and believe me
I love the way we're meant to be
I love the way you will never change who you are
I love the way unconditionally you are there for me
Basically what I'm saying is I love everything about you
These are the ways I love you

Jessica LeeAnn Wright, Grade 7
Hebron Middle School, KY

Dandelion Battlefield

I am five. I crawl through the high wet grass in the field behind our house.
I spot the enemy thirty yards away, taking cover from oncoming fire.
Rifle raised, sweat on my brow, I pull the trigger.
The fake rifle sound blows out the side of the toy M16,
like white seeds flying through the air in strong March wind.
My brother falls over clutching his chest, crying for the pretend pain to stop.
I wonder what God thinks when soldiers shoot each other?
My brother's death scene ends as quickly as wind scatters the seeds.
He hops up, clothes grass-stained, leaves in his hair, ready to play again.
While he is climbing up the steep hill,
I take cover behind a tree. Where are my reinforcements?
I feel like a lone green stem in the grass.
My brother loses his footing and almost falls.
No rolling down the hill or you might fall in the lake or break a leg.
I wonder why he is so clumsy? Guess he was born that way.
Mama says not to make fun of him
because he is as sensitive as the first flowers in Spring.
That hill is as steep as the escalator at the Atlanta airport anyway.
At the top he stops, bends over, and plucks a dandelion
and with one swift blow, he sends a million white seeds drifting.
Now I have a clear shot.

Chase Beard, Grade 8
Baylor School, TN

My Friends

My friends are a lot of things,
They're like a hot fudge sundae, warm, sweet, and really good.
They are like the wool in a sweater, so close
to make you feel warm and comfortable.
They are like a note, funny and sometimes random and unpredictable.
But they are great friends overall.

Caroline Nelson, Grade 7
Meredith-Dunn School, KY

Deer Hunting

Deer hunting is a great sport
you dream day in and day out
about the monster buck.
You get up early and wait in your tree stand
until your deer comes out
and once you get the shot
it's the best feeling.

Dakota Kent, Grade 8
Highland Rim School, TN

Tiger of Sky

As slate-colored clouds
Chase afternoon sun away,
I am forewarned by smell,
Humid feel of air around me,
Of rain, of thunder, of storm.

As violent as angry tiger
And strong as golden lion,
You're sure to take cover
When you hear its thunder rumble,
Crescendo 'till it gets to great big BOOM!

Rain pounding dusty ground,
Making little puffs of smoke.
Drops reflecting light like little seas,
Shimmering like so many stars.
They end their lives on hard-packed earth.

Though many fear it,
For me it's different,
A steel-hued sky is my favorite kind.
It instills feelings of fear, anticipation,
Of rain, of thunder, of storm.

Zachary Jones, Grade 7
Barret Traditional Middle School, KY

Haseo's Heart

I'm trapped in my mind
Hoping to get out in time
Waiting for my love at world's end
Heartless things surround me in darkness
Words are said of pain as I try to fend it off
My hope will last till the end
So every minute of every hour
I sit and hope my love is safe
As the voices talk about her suffering
I scream and yell,
"SHUT UP It's not true
she is safe and sound hoping I will return for her"
But one fateful day a little light is seen from a distance
I get up and run straight for the light
as I get closer it gets bigger
I see the thing that is setting me free is my beloved Shino.

Mikey Cox, Grade 8
Chelsea Jr High School, OK

One, Two, Three, and Maybe Four

It happened again tonight
The old one two maybe three four too
I cried until I couldn't cry no more
I don't know what happened this time
Maybe I didn't have dinner cooked in time
Or I didn't turn the TV on right when he wanted it on
He has just gone off the edge this time
Throwing things at the kids and me
Ohh how I wish my mama was here
This kind of stuff never would have happened to me
I remember when we were in love
Now we live on different planets
They tell me to leave him
But I just cannot do that
For I am scared he will come after me
So I lie alone at night praying he won't come home
But God never answers my prayers
So I better get ready
'Cause here it comes

Erica Beck, Grade 8
Mayflower Middle School, AR

Autumn Leaves

Autumn leaves as colorful as crayons,
falling like rain on a stormy day.
Raking, shriveling and the animals are ready.
It's the beginning of a cold and white winter.
Summer's gone, not very much daylight,
School is starting and the fun is almost over.

Jacob Yerton, Grade 7
Wilson Middle School, OK

My Granny Means a Lot to Me

My granny meant a lot to me,
She knew all sorrow would have laughter
My granny meant a lot to me,
We would take pictures the best moments we would capture
My granny meant a lot to me,
She would sit next to me when I was sad
My granny meant a lot to me,
Her voice would cheer me up so I was glad
My granny meant a lot to me,
I first got the news; she was gone
My granny meant a lot to me,
I wished I could have said "so long"
My granny meant a lot to me,
My papa was never the same
My granny meant a lot to me,
There was no one I could blame
My granny meant a lot to me,
I remember like it was yesterday
My granny meant a lot to me,
Our love for her will never fade away
My granny MEANS a lot to me

Alexis Tillman, Grade 7
Seven Holy Founders School, MO

Empire of Life

Pass round the bowl of life.
Take a sip, enjoy it.
The cold wind blows,
From grave stone to grave stone.
Warm it up with love.
Warm it up with life.
Make this empire erupt with joy.
The joy of life.

Andrew Carroll, Grade 8
Musselman Middle School, WV

On Your Way

You may sigh
you may cry
you may be just plain sad
life goes on
day by day
week by week

It's not so bad
you'll be okay
don't you pout
you'll get through it
month by month
year by year

There you go
on your way
did you know
you could say
life goes on
day by day
week by week
month by month
year by year

Tara Adcock, Grade 8
Lewisburg Middle School, TN

Ode to Cheese

Cheese, you are so true.
Even though you stink sometimes;
you are still my friend.
When I eat you,
you are delicious, but after a while
you hurt me.
Why?
You are still my friend though.
Cheese, when you're gone
It's so sad!
It makes me want to cry,
but I know you will be back
when my mom buys you
from that Food-Rite store.
Ode to Cheese.

Katie Barton, Grade 7
Dyer Elementary & Jr High School, TN

Since Then

Before I was three
Upon a banyan tree
Outside I lay alone,
For I thought sadly
About my hurting so badly.
Around four o'clock
Beneath me a dog and a boat dock.

Savannah Ownby, Grade 8
Pigeon Forge Middle School, TN

After School

What to do after school.
Lots of times I don't know,
Go to the pool?
Play in the snow?

Today, I consider a special day,
Because I know what to do,
Actually I know what to play,
Let's play chess, me and you.

I would drive,
But I can't,
If I did I might not be alive,
So I guess I won't.

Maybe I won't do anything,
Maybe it will be nice,
To do something or maybe nothing,
I might just roll some dice.

Ben Menke, Grade 9
Fulton Sr High School, MO

Friends Forever

F orever we are together
R ight to the end
I n and out of problems
E very other day of the week
N ever backstabbing one another
D rama does not separate us
S o nothing will ever come between us

Chelsey Martin, Grade 8
Greenfield Jr/Sr High School, MO

Greenland

G laciers
R ocky coastal fringe
E skimos
E nglish explorers
N ear the ocean
L and
A ir
N eighborly
D ependable

Brandon Bowman, Grade 7
Clarksburg School, TN

Friends

Friends who stand by you
And then run away —
Well, they're not real friends.
It's just those who stay.

Friends who praise you now,
But next week they blame —
Well, they're not real friends at all.
It's those who are the same.

It's when you've lost most things
And troubled days begin —
Well, that's one way to find
Just who are your true friends.

Marah Powell, Grade 8
Wilson Middle School, OK

What Is the Opposite of Anger?

What is the opposite of Anger?
little kids singing,
people dancing,
laughter of little kids,
a baby looking at you for the first time,
a child's first smile,
child's first step,
roses in a field.

Jade Stamps, Grade 7
Cheyenne Middle School, OK

Knowledge

Where are you when I need you?
Where are you in a test?
Where are you when I'm in trouble?
You'd be the best.

You are always with me,
No matter where I am.
For you are my top choice,
When my thoughts are crammed.

I am young,
So I might not use you,
But you will always be there,
For me to get a clue.

Politics don't always use you,
For they think conscience is the best.
But I know
You'd surely ace the test.

So stick with me now,
And stick with me when I'm old.
For I will surely use you,
When I need to be smart and bold.

Ashlyn Benfield, Grade 8
Rhea Central Elementary School, TN

Finish Line

You're almost to the finish line
Keep going for the gold
Senior year of high school
You're really almost done

College is running ahead of you
Middle school behind
Elementary school was long ago
Man that was a long time

The gold is at the end brother,
You just have to find it
Scold yourself and get there
You'll sure be excited

Keep going for the gold
How proud we'll be of you
Don't let yourself down brother
run faster than the other few

Take the right path
You'll be at the end fast
The gold is at the end brother
I swear you want to win

Kaylin Kraft, Grade 9
Fern Creek Traditional Magnet High School, KY

Fall

as red leaves are torn on the ground
all the other colors flow around
it's fun to rake leaves and then fall down
fall has many beautiful colors like a box of crayons
most of the leaves to me are pretty and brown

Angelica Medrano, Grade 7
Wilson Middle School, OK

Madness

I'm in a world full of crime,
Where thousands are dying,
From hunger and sadness,
Why all this madness?
Could we not love one another?
As sister and brother,
Through anger and hate,
We stand by each other
United in freedom.
From the land of great Eden,
Where Earth was on perfect,
And in the end,
He shall rebirth it,
A world without hurt and shame,
Not a drop of pain.
No hunger or sadness
A world without Madness.

Quinton D., Grade 9
Audubon Youth Development Center, KY

Courtney

Courtney
Who is a fun-loving, crazy, loves to party type person.
Who is sister of Chris Dodson.
Who loves her mom, her friends, and Jesus.
Who feels good inside, rowdy, talkative, and full of energy.
Who gives advice to many friends, and lots of love.
Who fears walking slowly in the shadows of the darkness.
Who would like to see pigs fly.
Who shares secrets with her friends.
Who is very fun to be around.
Who lives in Clarksville.
Dodson

Courtney Dodson, Grade 8
Montgomery Central Middle School, TN

I Don't Want to Miss You

I am not envious of anyone.
To love anyone, I have no desire.
My soul feels so empty with no passion.
The only thing I crave is your feelings.
I only feel hate, nothing more or less.
It seems so hard for you to look at me.
I question how your feelings have just changed.
I only hunger, you holding me close.
When you kissed me upon my lips, time stopped.
As you looked in my eyes, happiness came.
Butterflies were always in my stomach.
You left one day, no good-bye, just one mind.
I want you to seek me in every thought,
To let you know how I felt every day.

Audrey Brixey, Grade 9
Glenpool High School, OK

Eggos

Eggos, yes Eggos
So delightful, not spiteful, but sweet
The thought of a waffle with eggs is amazing
White, blueberry or wheat
Two waffles per serving
Two servings per meal
If Eggos were locked in a bank, I would steal
I can barely wake without a sigh
If I don't eat them, I feel like a jerk
And my taste buds just plain out die
This may seem a bit drastic
A wee bit far fetched
But I get a bit spastic
When my Eggos are gone
Oh, when my Eggos are gone, or when they expire
What do I do when I starve that desire?
I eat some good oatmeal or a fruity parfait
But they never do feed me like Eggos, per se
No one understands me, they laugh and they scoff
But never will Eggos start turning me off

Charlie Davis, Grade 8
West Jr High School, MO

Love

When you love someone,
you love with your heart.
You love with your soul.
Love is a part of life.
Love is something you can't explain.
Young or old
Stranger or friend
Love is all around.

Amberley Carter, Grade 8
Elkton School, TN

Hunting Is About Having Fun

Hunting is always a challenge
It's all about the sport
It's always about having fun
When you see a monster buck
Your heart starts to beat
You're always on the run
When you see a deer you point your gun
Hunting is not about killing
It's about sport and having fun

Dakotah Harmon, Grade 8
Highland Rim School, TN

You Will Never Know

You will never know
How I feel about you.
But one day I hope you will.
For you fill my heart with glee
Whenever you're near me.

Michael Blatzer, Grade 8
Musselman Middle School, WV

Freak Out

Face red
All hair on ends
Bare feet
Wind pounding
Head spinning
Eyes closed
FREAK OUT
Higher and higher
Up up away
spinned twist move
Scream
FREAK OUT
Open eyes
Shut
Open eyes
Scream
Kick
FREAK OUT
I freaked out
On the "FREAK OUT"

Bethany Roberson, Grade 7
Dyer Elementary & Jr High School, TN

The Wind

A cool breeze gently touches your face lifting your morale on a sweltering school day,
Bringing the prospect of chilly weather to come…
Yet, when autumn actually arrives we shun the very same wind that brought us relief.
And as December approaches we launch complaints about the freezing air.
With summer we start the whole cycle afresh.
Why is it that there is always a bad point to a good concept?
Or is that only the way we view everything?

Mythili Ramachandran, Grade 9
West Jr High School, MO

My Sleeping Slumber

As class drones on,
The scorching heat possesses me,
I slip into a deep slumber,
Anything to escape the dreadful heat

Bundled up in layers of coats
Shivering down to my bones,
I am standing on a huge, snow-white hill,
Children are cheering and bright red toboggans are aglow.

Suddenly I plunge over the edge of the gigantic hill,
Immediately the electric blue sled accumulates speed, racing to the bottom,
At the end I advance into a heap of snow,
My mouth numbs as a huge clump of freezing snow finds its way in.

I wake abruptly
Only to discover I have ventured back into class
I have goose bumps from my slumber
They quickly fade due to the unbearable heat.

Addison Reed, Grade 9
West Jr High School, MO

Theory

If all you ever did was concentrate
on H
A
T
E
You wouldn't get anywhere at all.
If there were no religion or races
No different F
A
C
E
S
Not a person would ever fall.
If war wasn't constant and politics didn't E
X
I
S
T
There wouldn't ever be a need to resist.
If you take all of this to heart and cling to every word — start.

Hannah Hodge, Grade 8
Greenfield Jr/Sr High School, MO

Permit Me to Tell You About Sailing

Permit me to tell you about sailing.
The boring dullness of a large margin blow out,
The excitement of a down-to-the-wire race,
The sticky feeling of a hot, no wind day,
A chilly 15 knot wind.
But the race I'll never forget
Left me surprised and confused by a type of race I thought
Was only possible in a movie,
Discovering again that no race is won
Until somebody crosses the finish line.
We great racers,
Amazed at our great victory.

Bobby Lacker, Grade 8
All Saints School, MO

Destinies

Our destinies will intertwine,
Someday.
When that day comes,
I'll be waiting.
You will be different though,
As will I.
We will look different and act different;
In all, be different.
You will definitely be a forensic scientist;
As for me.
I will be working,
Towards my dream.
Someday I will be waiting,
Because I miss you so much.

Kimberly Armstrong, Grade 8
Owasso 8th Grade Center, OK

Friendship

F riendship is a powerful bonding
R especting of everything in your life
I mpenetrable power when together
E ncouragement for success
N ever giving up on each other
D readful events to overcome
S upporting when down and hurting
H aving memorable events
I ndestructible bonds when put to the test
P rotective if ever you need help

Mark Khadoo, Grade 8
Owasso 8th Grade Center, OK

The Ice Skater

Twinkling like a star under the vast spotlight,
Moving like an angel gracefully to the music,
Gliding on the smooth ice like a fall leaf in the autumn wind,
Jumping like a frog on his lily pad,
Spinning like a child's top,
The ice skater performs.

Alyssa Gresham, Grade 9
St Charles Homeschool Learning Center, MO

Friends

Things in life are tough
and rough,
but with friends by your side
there is nothing to hide.
They make you laugh, they make you cry,
but they will always help you get by.
Years pass by and you get older, everything changes,
but the memory of your friends are still stored in the pages.

Kendall Hudson, Grade 8
White Station Middle School, TN

Secrets of Jacob Loescher

Jacob
Artistic, creative, shy, punk
Brother of Maggie Loescher
Lover of music, art, and TV
Who feels angry, confused, and yet happy about life
Who gives sarcasm, happiness, and homework to teachers
Who fears losing music, friends, and family
Who would like to see war, lying, and cheating end
Who lives in Tennessee
Loescher

Jacob Loescher, Grade 8
Montgomery Central Middle School, TN

New Life

I must be close to genius by now
If I've learned from every mistake,
I've found the only way to change my life
Is by changing the choices I make.
How come the past can repeat itself?
If I can't repeat my past?
It seems unfair I can't go back
Those years were gone so fast.
I wouldn't undo the mistakes I've made or
Take away the pain inside.
Because I learned it always finds me
No matter where I hide.
I'm not yet comfortable with having feelings
Moods that rise and fall
But it's better than being numb to the world
Pretending to have none at all.
I know I don't need new yesterdays
For a better today and tomorrow.
I've gained the strength and courage now
To face any grief and sorrow.

Jesse Jenkins, Grade 8
Clark Middle School, MO

Something Never Forgotten

Fall is like a season that is never forgotten.
Fall is something for all to enjoy,
play in the leaves and throw 'em on your friends.
The lovely colors they are!

Jasmine Watson, Grade 8
Wilson Middle School, OK

My Missing Uncle

When I was nine years old,
My uncle and I were the best of friends.
Then he went off to South Carolina.
I anxiously waited for him to come back,
But when I sat on the carport,
My family told me he'd left us
To live in the next world above us.
It really hurt to hear those words.
So now he's gone
I can do nothing.
I can't see him,
But he is watching.

Kyle Cirasa, Grade 8
Musselman Middle School, WV

My Love

My Love for you
Is like a rose garden
that will never run out
Just as I will
Never forget you
You will always
Remain in my heart
My Love

Kendra Saunstaire, Grade 9
Van-Cove High School, AR

Butterfly

The fat caterpillar crawls along,
Singing his silly, old song,
Watch as he goes,
And amazes those,
As he turns into a butterfly,
I sit and sigh,
As he climbs the tree,
It amazes me to see,
He spins a cocoon,
And he takes till noon,
Soon he appears ever so bright,
He gets ready to take his first flight,
As the wings unfold,
See all the beautiful colors to behold.

Holly Blackburn, Grade 7
Sikeston 7th & 8th Grade Center, MO

Derby Cars

Derby cars
Derby cars
That's all I ever work on.
I like to build them.
I like to tear'm apart.
I put bars in them to keep me safe.
I'm going to run in the derby.
And I'm going to burn some rubber.

Jacob McGill, Grade 8
Elkton School, TN

God's Creation to Me

God created everything. He surrounded us with beauty.
Stars like night lights in the sky.
Flowers, beautiful pictures in the day.
Thank you God for all the things we see.

God surrounds us with heavenly sounds.
Crickets chirping us to sleep at night.
Birds calm us with their songs during the day.
Thank you God for all the things we hear.

God surrounds us with a variety of smells.
Sweet smell of pine during the holidays,
And the aroma of burning, crackling wood.
Thank you God for all the things we feel.

God has given us many different tastes.
Hot, spicy jalapeno peppers stinging my tongue like a bee stinging my skin.
Sweet taste of ice cream reminding me of all the fun I had last summer.
God, thank you for all the wonderful things we taste.

Dylan Elbl, Grade 7
Our Lady Catholic School, MO

Midnight Magic

Till the dark comes pressing deep,
I lay solely waiting, whenever pondering…Fully in anxious sleep,
They always said that I was strange,
Twilight shimmers far overhead,
As I raise from my creaking, bungle of a bed,
My body feeling what my hands could not,
And seeing beyond my eyes that sought, standing, heading to the sea-lined border,
They always said that I was strange.
Strolling through to the dampened edge,
Rocks severed, aged and gray,
Life and time's result as it slowly wears away,
Water splashes, arching frosty waves of white roughcast
With each wave as zealous as the last,
They always said that I was strange,
Be with stillness, hush, it will happen soon,
Not by harsh streaming sunlight, but it's flowing fine contrary, the moon
Floating in the open water as far as could be,
This is when it happens, this is when I'm strange
They always said I was what I was to keep me from the reality
It is I who is sane, that makes them all stupid and deranged
Just for the unnatural actuality, my magical fin of the otherworldly.

Jameelah Wright, Grade 8
Pleasant View School, TN

Kittens

The kittens meow for their cat mother.
The kittens are colorful one gray, one white, and two black.
Drinking milk from their mother.
Climbing on walls and wooden posts.
The kittens are scratching, meowing, and getting on your last nerve
But that's what they do.

Shernell Payne, Grade 7
Highland Rim School, TN

The Sun

The sun is shining in the sky.
It is bringing warmth to the Earth.
As it is in the sky the flowers bloom.
And as it sets gracefully in the sky,
the light slowly dims down and it becomes evening.

Walt Duckett, Grade 8
Highland Rim School, TN

God's Creations

God made the crisp rivers cutting through the landscape
With Earth's beauty soaking into my eyes
The amazing animals always living everywhere I look
I see the lush gardens of God's own hand

God made the beautiful songs of birds, cleverly written
I hear the crisp hum of a rushing river, flowing constantly
God made the wind, howling like a singing ghost
I love the rustling leaves, crunching and snapping

God made winter mornings with much fresh air to breathe
I smell the sweet pollen of fresh spring flowers
God created the smell of fresh bread, ready to eat
He made many wonderful smells, pleasing to his people

God made feeling of cool grass on bare feet
I love the wind, blowing around my face
God made the perfectly smooth water, flowing around me
I feel the calm Earth, full of life all around me

God made the crisp fruit, juicy and wonderful
I taste cool water flowing down my parched throat
I like the soft crunch of a salad being consumed
God made all the wonderful tastes in the world

Joseph Richmeyer, Grade 7
Our Lady Catholic School, MO

Obesity

How come people are too lazy to cook?
They complain about being overweight.
They think the food at McDonalds is great.
Are they too scared to open a cook book?

It seems like they can't take the time to look.
But they get so overwhelmed they can't wait
To take a look at what they just ate.
Their minds don't know what their bellies just took.

Did you notice your clothes started to grow?
Why can't you cook yourself a healthy meal?
Do people notice they're getting big?

Now what you ate is beginning to show.
Do you think that the scars will ever heal?
Will you become slim? Or large as a pig?

Jacey Luther, Grade 9
University Heights Academy, KY

You Are What You Eat

I tried to tell him not to eat it,
for it's bad for the body
and there could be harsh consequences.
But I was ignored and after one bite
he transformed into cotton candy.

At first he couldn't believe it.
After all, his head was now fluffy and filled with air.
He laughed and said,
"Not to worry. This is just a dream.
Just a dream."
But after I pinched off a few handfuls
he understood and started to cry.

I told him, "Crying will only make things worse."
But he couldn't hear
for there was only fluff between his ears.
My dearest friend dissolved
in his own tears
into a sticky blue-pink goo on the table,
"Wait, no, Don't eat that!"

Brittany Davidoff, Grade 8
Baylor School, TN

Sounds of the Night

Things I hear at night
then rain hitting my roof,
the wind whistling through the trees,
the cars driving by,
these are the sounds I hear as I drift to sleep.

Dalton Wright, Grade 8
Leeton Middle and High School, MO

I Am

I am an athletic girl that loves softball.
I wonder how long things will last.
I hear the snapping of softball players playing catch.
I see the sky raining bubbles.
I want to become a famous softball player.
I am an athletic girl who loves softball.

I pretend I am a professional softball player.
I feel strong about girl power.
I touch the clouds and the stars.
I worry about when the world is going to end.
I cry for the poverty and death in the world.
I am an athletic girl who loves softball.

I understand that everything happens for a reason.
I say that anything boys can do girls can do better.
I dream that there will one day be world peace.
I try to do my best at everything I do.
I hope that one day everyone will get along.
I am an athletic girl who loves softball.

Emily Christine Eiberger, Grade 7
King City High School, MO

Funny Ferrets

Ferrets
Social animals
Mischievous by heart
Playful, funny, and loving
Polecats

Spencer Daniel, Grade 8
Belle Isle Enterprise Middle School, OK

Fog

Wet,
Soothing,
Calming,
Charming.

Soft,
Moist,
Relaxing,
Scarce.

Gray,
White,
Disappearing
Headlights.

Anna Garcia, Grade 7
Benton County School of the Arts, AR

Colors Come and Go

Fall is like a wood-stained rainbow,
The leaves are red, brown, and orange.

As they all turn colors,
They fall off the trees.

Then winter comes,
They're all covered up.

Spring arrives,
The leaves are green again.

Sydney Flynn, Grade 8
Wilson Middle School, OK

Rodeo

I am Hercules the huge white bull
The strongest, meanest bull
I'm told
I go to rodeos each week
I go to Smithville rodeo
In my big red horse trailer
I am in the bucking shoot
They let me out
I buck him off
Before the buzzer sounds
I am Hercules
The Huge White Bull

Tod Provence, Grade 7
Van-Cove High School, AR

Katie Lynn Collin

Katie Lynn
Who is tall with blonde hair, ugly with blue eyes
Who is a sister of Charles Parker, Daniel and Rebecca Hutchison
Who loves her friends, family, cute boys, and animals
Who feels sad, happy and all right
Who needs to spend time with family, hang with friends, and have a good time
Who gives money, love and help
Who fears dangerous snakes, bears, and spiders
Who would love to see Rock City, the Rocky Mountains, and the Great Wall of China
Who lives in a trailer, in the woods, in a crowed house
Collin

Katie Lynn Collin, Grade 8
Montgomery Central Middle School, TN

Dear Loneliness

Next time you tell me music controls me
I'll tell you it fits me to a T
It helps me ignore you to a high degree
It helps me to know that someone feels the same as me
Someone feels their life isn't what it should be
Someone feels as though they are not who they are
Someone feels as though everyone looks at them as though they are peculiar
Someone feels like everyone else's life is perfect
Someone gives authority as much neglect
Someone feels like they have to hide behind a fake smile
Someone wants their life to be a party all around the sundial
Someone can't write their life lyric style
Someone knows that music doesn't control me it just helps me ignore you

Kasey Schemel, Grade 7
West Jr High School, OK

Concealed by Words

High in the tallest oak tree a poem hides,
waiting to be jotted down.
In the stone cold silence of an abandoned barn
a poem sleeps beneath the hay.
In the remembrance of World War I, a poem lingers.
In the pile of fallen leaves a poem is concealed
from all eyes,
except yours.
A poem lies in the distant aroma of my grandmother;
she has the sweet fragrance of green apples before they are picked.

To all those searching for a poem:
you are about to inherit the secret.
Look for them deep in your deepest thoughts.
Look in your past, present, and future.
Always, everywhere you look, there is a poem,
but it is hidden.
Writing a poem is like a game of hide and seek with simple words.
These words form a poem.

A poem is where you look and, if you listen to me,
you will see them clear as day

Jake Standefer, Grade 8
Baylor School, TN

Wish

I wish I had your love,
I wish I had a day where you didn't see me as just a friend
I wish I had to see your beautiful smile,
I wish I had a world where no one gets hurt.
I wish I had a heart of steel.
I wish I had you to hold me.
I wish I had to spend my days with only you.
I wish I had a magic wand
To make all my wishes come true.

Makayla O'Brien, Grade 7
Newcastle Middle School, OK

The Fight

Nice cool, dewy morning
Water dancing from activity
Fish exploding on water like bombs
Catching them is fun and thrilling
Hoping and scoping for that monster
Waiting for him to come
He is exploding the top of the water
Pulling like a bulldozer
This is a fight for his freedom
This fish is a hog full of muscles
Finally his freedom is mine
Shimmering green, white, and black
As I look at him trying to breathe, wanting water
Our eyes connect
I can see he wants to be free
Gently laying him in the water
He disappears with a thrust of speed
Back he goes into the dark cool depths

Dustin Walker, Grade 9
Hamburg Jr High School, AR

Stage Lights

Heading to the show, with the lights and cars
I jog to catch my group but halt to gaze at the wondrous sight.
Folding out in front of me is a whole new world
A show that would change my life.
It seems like home, so far away
As the bright stage lights glisten
The show waits for nobody, but is always there
Enthralling all latecomers ready to join
The hustle and bustle is a different story
Though still part of the fun.
The cast always changes
But the set remains,
As the backdrop of a play in a fabulous theatre
The tall buildings, bright signs, and the hasty pedestrians
Help this masterpiece to become special,
But the real reason that I call Broadway 'home'
Is that it is like a stage
Calling me back
To act; to be known

Karen Schaeffer, Grade 7
White Station Middle School, TN

Heaven

Despite what people think and say
Within my heart I know it's there
Above the skies
Beyond the clouds
In my soul I believe it is real
Within the Bible I read of its wonders
Among the angels
Through the pearly gates
On streets of gold
With loving arms Jesus welcomes you into heaven

Nikki Brewer, Grade 8
Heritage Middle School, TN

The Best Pest

My puppy, what a great addition to the family,
she came as a Christmas present, and how happy I was!

As a puppy, she ripped up things and ran all over the house,
but how could you scold her when she cowered like a mouse?

As you opened the door she ran right out,
which make you chase after her and shout.

As you sit right down in a chair, she'll jump up on your lap,
which puts you in a sitting trap.

As you take her on a car ride,
she'll poke her head out the window with pride.

As my dog is being very lazy,
I'll want to play with her, but she'll sit there and drive me crazy.

What can I say? She's better than the best,
I'm so glad I have her, that little pest.

Thomas Place, Grade 8
Annunciation Elementary School, MO

Sidney

This girl has a twin.
They are not at all the same.
She has smooth, velvety hair
And her hair balls jangle
Like the giggle from her little sister.
I feel an intelligent mind
Beyond her oily scalp.
Her laugh is like a hyena's voice.
She swims like a soaring mermaid,
And her mellow heart soothes
The bitter feel in my mind.
She's tough in spirit,
But soft in heart.
I've learned to appreciate her.
I'll never forget when I see a twin,
There are never two minds alike.

Bryttney Dixon, Grade 8
Lee A Tolbert Community Academy, MO

Trees

The loud snap of the bark,
That almost stopped my heart.
The soft color of the leaves,
That sway in the breeze.
So soothing in spring,
Makes the bluebirds sing.
With the sun, oh so hot,
I roast in one spot.
My complexion will change,
My shades have range.
Secluded in winter,
No need to be bitter.
I rock in the wind.
My branches, they bend.
It's hard to miss me,
Some things you don't see.
Always changing from season to season,
If you ask me, that's my reason.

Jordan See, Grade 8
West Jr High School, MO

Werewolves

Vampires
Dark, mysterious
Biting, flying, hiding
Cross, stake-silver, scary
Snarling, chasing, snapping
Tall, hairy
Werewolves

Parker Pearce, Grade 7
Greenfield Jr/Sr High School, MO

Destruction

Crackle, Crackle
Sizzle, Sizzle
The sign of fire's
Deadly approach
It cackles maliciously as
It engulfs and destroys
Everything in its
Vicious sight
The trees cower
As they sense their
Gloomy death and
The clouds grow dark
As smoke hurls their way
A destructive vortex
Sweeps debris
Into its immense
Ravenous mouth
The malignant fire recedes,
Leaving nothing but
Charred remains and
Broken hearts.

Braxston Jamal Miller, Grade 7
White Station Middle School, TN

Seasons'll Change

As the days go by, the seasons change.
Sometimes it can be really quite strange.
First comes winter at the beginning of the year.
Christmas is over, but you still have that holiday cheer.
Spring is next, and we watch as the flowers bloom,
But brace yourself for spring cleaning, so grab your mop and broom.
Next comes summer when school is out.
We're so happy, all we can do is scream and shout.
Last we have fall when all the leaves drop
While the farmers are out in the field harvesting their crop.
So there it is, all the four seasons.
We love them so dearly for all different reasons

Kristina Glassl, Grade 8
St Gerard Majella School, MO

Hectic Home

This is what I call "home"
Laughing, screaming, crying
It's all the same here…chaos

We run around like maniacs
This chaos never ends
Phone rings off the hook
Cars come and go

Soccer mom, daddy, chef, maid, taxi driver
It's all the same to us
They are like some kind of superhuman freaks
These are the people we call parents

Playmates, opponents, just another one of *them*
Our feeling for each other change often
These are the people we call siblings

The only place I feel the least bit sane is in my room
All alone…as close to quiet as I'm going to get
My room is my tank in this battlefield
It's the only thing in this chaotic house I can call *mine*

The only thing that remains in this hectic house is FAITH, LOVE, AND HOPE

Abbie Paloucek, Grade 7
Annunciation Elementary School, MO

Permit Me to Tell You About Childhood Memories

Permit me to tell you about childhood memories.
  Moving away just as you get acquainted,
  Seeing new places, and being able to call them home,
  Hunting Easter eggs in Vermont, the snow still falling,
  The rush of jumping in to a pile of hay from the level above.
But the memory I remember the most
  Is giggling under the covers with my sister on a warm night spent at the Fay farm,
  Running barefoot through the grassy fields and having a real taste of freedom,
  Playing Legos with Jon while my parents were away,
  And having the best place in the entire world to just be a kid.

Amelia Martin, Grade 8
All Saints School, MO

Music

The blaring radio is up way too loud.
The walls are shaking and they might break down.
My mom is pounding on my bedroom door.
As I sprawl across the cold bedroom floor.
I lie there and think of what might have been.
If only I could turn back time again.

Jennifer Webb, Grade 9
Bearden High School, TN

I Am From...*

A family
From Asia and America
I am from the small home
It feels great being home with fresh air
I am from the cucumbers
The backyard with plants
Whose long gone limbs I remember as if they were my own

I'm from rice and speaking Vietnamese
From Sandy and D.J. (aka Jason Doung)
I'm from dancing and singing and from drawing

I'm from a gifted family and I'm smart
And happy birthday
I'm from a family that speaks Vietnamese and English
I'm from St. Louis and Ho Chi Minh city
Fried rice and fish

From my grandma, grandpa, and uncle
They had all died in tragic accidents
Loving each other until the end of time
In my heart is where they live
They are a part of who I am.

Kaven Bui, Grade 7
St Cecilia Academy, MO
**Patterned after "Where I'm From" by George Ella Lyons*

Fall

Leaves are all around.
Floating to the ground.
Black cats sneak about out of sight.
Like something that goes bump in the night
Many people will be giving thanks
While others play pranks.
In the morning frost is on the ground.
Dew is nowhere to be found
Boys get ready for football season.
While fans put on face paint for no reason.
A time for pumpkin pie.
And many new things to try.
Summer has just died down
But winter has not yet come to town.
I tell you all of the things I see.
Fall is all around me.

Emily Medley, Grade 7
Nettleton Jr High School, AR

Down with Big Brother

How would you feel, if the government was watching you?
Paying attention, to every single thing you do.
Hearing every single thing that you say,
Knowing what you do throughout all your day.
I do not like it,
In no way is it legit.
I'm telling you now, that it must quit.

Tanner Smith, Grade 8
West Jr High School, MO

Fall Leaves

The changing fall leaves
And small children asking for trick-or-treats
Leaves the color of brown
Only just falling on the ground
The changing fall leaves
And small children asking for trick-or-treats
Children disguised as witches and ghouls
Parents look like you-know-who's
Candy now haunts my dreams
My sisters are dressed as monsters
In the changing fall leaves
And small children asking for trick-or-treats
When I get hungry for a midnight snack
I sneak a piece from my candy stack
Yellow and red leaves
Brown is the color I see when leaves drift from trees
The trees are now bare
In this cold, chilly air
The changing fall leaves
And small children asking for trick-or-treats

Cassie Harder-Neely, Grade 7
Nettleton Jr High School, AR

Fall to Winter

The fall is so crisp and inviting,
bringing chill into the air,
as red, yellow, and orange leaves fly from trees,
and scatter on the ground,
from the blustery fall wind.

The creek glistens from the early morning frost,
with winter arriving soon you see smoke,
puffing from chimneys,
and families sip on hot cocoa,
by the red glowing fire,
that warm the houses,
So cozy and warming.

The stores are bustling with holiday shoppers,
I myself love the fall and winter,
and I myself will wake up every morning,
and wait for the first flake of snow to fall,
to know that winter is finally here.

Rylee Loving, Grade 8
Owasso 8th Grade Center, OK

Winter in North Dakota

in the open
among the snow
beyond the fences
of my grandfather's farm
like a teddy bear all bundled up
with my cup of cocoa
under a lonely tree
beside the horses roam
as the snow clouds roll by
despite all the snow
and during the darkest night
joy is all around
just look around and you'll see

Rebekah MacFadden, Grade 8
Heritage Middle School, TN

Christmas Morning

I get up early.
I can't sleep.
I can't wait for Christmas morning.
For my presents.
I seem to fade away
For I get the stuff I want,
On Christmas morning
When I get done
I try out my stuff
To find out they're terrific.
That is why I like
Christmas morning.

Jon Allen, Grade 8
Chelsea Jr High School, OK

My Dad

Wearing suits is kind of his thing
My dad's a businessman you see.
He comes home early
And works through the night
When he has no work
We play the PlayStation.
It's always football,
Which I enjoy.
He tends to win,
But who's counting.
Oh right, he is.
He doesn't like dogs,
He prefers cats and fish.
My dad's into trees and shrubbery.
If he could he'd buy every tree
Under the sun,
And plant them in our backyard.
He swears we'll have a forest one day.
I want to be like my dad someday.
With his smarts and his talents.
My dad's a cool guy, you see.

Jordan McDonald, Grade 8
Musselman Middle School, WV

The Ode to Earrings

Oh earrings
I love you so much
Polka-dots, stars, and hearts.
Oh earrings
All the colors of the rainbow.
Oh earrings,
You can be anything you want.
Stripes, skulls, hoops, animals,
Letters, words,
Big or small,
I LOVE THEM ALL!!!

Anna Lovell, Grade 7
Dyer Elementary & Jr High School, TN

Highway Halls

The bell rings
and here we go
down the halls
and through the flow
of kids and pack and pencils and so…

Weaving and waiting,
on our way to each class.
Waving and calling to all
when we pass.

Picking up books
and dropping some others,
we race through the halls like
sisters and brothers.

We cruise and talk,
laugh and play,
as we all make it through
to the end of the day.

Nathan Fox, Grade 8
Annunciation Elementary School, MO

Out in Front

Behind the curtain I wait
Nervous, excited and scared
I go over my dance once more
The chasse turns, the arabesque, the jete
And now it's time
I run gracefully
Out in front of the crowd
In my white tutu I stand
Then a chasse and a leap
Until I feel that I am above everyone
Then pirouette and land
I arabesque and go into an attitude
And I spin off
I can't believe it,
I am finished.

Acadia Kimball, Grade 7
Benton County School of the Arts, AR

Why'd You Have to Go?

Why can't I forget you?
Why aren't you out of my head?
Why can't I stop crying?
Why do I feel so dead?
When we were together
I knew I was alive,
But now I'm not even sure
If I can survive.
I guess you've moved on,
Because we haven't talked in a while,
I won't let you see me cry
So I'll just fake a smile.
Please just answer me this,
I really need to know.
You said you would always love me,
So why'd you have to go?

Audrey Cashon, Grade 7
Gray Elementary School, TN

Death

Loving life,
not wanting death.

Piercing pain,
only crying is left.

Friends will come,
but also go.

You'll be left,
all alone.

Death will come,
and you'll be free.

Next in death,
will probably be me.

Some will burn,
others will fly.

Either way,
we'll all die.

Miriah R. Bennefield, Grade 8
Hollis Middle School, OK

Sensations of Autumn

Autumn
Orange, brown
Rigged, crackling, carved
Eating, soccer, plants, animals
Swimming, hiking, boating
Flowers, warm
Spring

Jordan Schultz, Grade 7
Musselman Middle School, WV

Pure Abhorrence

A shy pale girl enters the class, Away from her hurtful family at last.
In the corner of the room she sits, Praying no one see the scars on her wrists.

She stares remembering what happened last night, Encouraging herself to forget that big fight.
"It's all my fault mom and dad always yell," "I'm the cause of their marriage from hell."

She thinks to herself remembering why, She hates her life and frequently cries.
And out of the blue her name is called, Because the teacher is waiting for the problem to be solved.

A soft spoken word comes out of her mouth, But nobody hears anything come out.
At the end of the period the teacher wants to know, If anything is bothering her at school are at home.

She replies with a no and walks out the door, While the bruise on her thigh is still very sore.
By the end of the day the small bruises have healed, And now she's just wondering which cuts will stay sealed.

Just a word for all the forgotten, Sooner or later your life won't be rotten.
As long as you remember someone cares, You'll find the answer to all of your prayers.

Saja Abdallah, Grade 8
West Jr High School, MO

A Much Needed Friend

There are so many things a friend is needed for in life. How different would our lives be if we had no one to laugh with, talk to, or share secrets with? No one to help us out during the hard times, walk in when the rest of the world walks out, and catch our tears, or be there for us when no one else can be. A friend can be like a sister in some ways. I think to myself quietly, and I wonder if friends are here for when we need more than just family. And as I sit here thinking of how much I need my friends, I gratefully thank God for putting them here for me, and pray that I can be as good a friend in return.

Kelsey Armes, Grade 7
St Mary of the Woods School, KY

We Are His Creation

Beautiful is God's creation, for without his love for us
This place would be a fiery, dark, evil place only the devil could dwell on.
He made the flowers of rose, with its bright but peaceful state of beauty.
He made the mountains, as if they were as big as the moon or stars that dwell in the sky.

He made the fruit of life, the juicy filling of a pineapple,
With us salivating when we bite.
The natural sugar he made for us to enjoy, a taste of heaven.

The creation of sound is His greatest creation.
To hear the choirs of angels,
The xylophone's sweet soft music,
Even a lullaby puts us to sleep.
When God speaks, you are amazed.

Incense is the presence of holy, smoky, but sweet it is.
Sweet apple pie in the window sill.
Fumes created by us, the smell of heaven is as good as any smell on Earth.
To feel we will never lose, when we touch the soft smooth skin of a baby,
To feel the wind, not just on land but on sea, the fresh air we breathe.

God we thank thee for all thy creations.
We cannot express our joyous feelings that you made this.
The world is yours, heaven is yours, we are yours.

Corey Schmidt, Grade 7
Our Lady Catholic School, MO

Hunting

I love to turkey hunt early in the morning
When I am turkey hunting it is not too cold or not too hot the weather is just right
While I am sitting in my blind it is fun to watch the monster gobblers fly down from the roost.
When they fly down it will pump up your adrenaline that now becomes your time to start calling them in.
Many times when you start calling them in they will start strutting and running to your decoys.
If you have a gobbler decoy he will sometimes come and start attacking it.

Wesley Bevels, Grade 8
Highland Rim School, TN

You and Me

I fell in love, in love with you, you didn't like the way, the way I played the game, you broke my heart and I told you I would change, change for you, you just told me you didn't care, caring for me was hard, hard for you, but it was fun, fun for you, you tell me you want to be single, single for a bit but there's no promise, promising you to be with me I have to move on, moving on is the best way, the best way for me so, from now on I will see you in the hall, seeing you in the hall will be hard, hard for me, I don't know if it will be hard, hard for you, I hope you can move on, moving on will be the best way for both of us.

Jessica Perkins, Grade 9
Sherwood High School, MO

Seth

Seth
Silly, fun, smart, funny
A brother of Shane Givens
A lover of the Internet for myspace, my dirt bike, my four-wheeler
Who feels sad when I watch sad movies, happy when I get stuff, mad when things get stolen
Who gives people a good time, a fun day, free stuff
Who needs an Xbox 360, a new TV, gas for my dirt bike
Who fears heights on a roller coaster, going air born on a four-wheeler
Who would like to see outer space, Mount Everest, Japan
Who lives in Clarksville, Tennessee
Givens

Seth Givens, Grade 8
Montgomery Central Middle School, TN

Cycle of the Clock

The clock points to seven,
And night begins.

Stomachs bulge from the dinners recently gobbled down,
Water patters against the grimy dishes as they're rinsed.
The smell of peppered chicken and buttery potatoes continues to waft around the room,
And some begin to consider going back for dessert.

Homework is hastily being finished,
With wooden pencils flying across the pages.
TVs and computers start to whir into motion,
As favorite shows begin and instant messages bleep onto the monitor.

For some night owls, the fun is just starting,
Concert and party doors are thrust open,
People rush in like herds of elephants,
While earsplitting music blares and booms.

The clock creeps on,
And the night continues.

Allison Good, Grade 9
West Jr High School, MO

Civil War

C onfederates fought the Union.
I n the years between 1861-1865.
V ictory went to the North.
I n the Union 110,000 were killed in action.
L incoln, Grant, Davis, and Lee led the way.

W hen the war was over slavery was abolished.
A ntislavery gained control.
R ights were established, but in war it comes with great cost.

Logan Hampton, Grade 8
Clarksburg School, TN

A Broken Heart

I've thought of you since the day we broke up,
Over a little silver necklace I made such a fuss.

It was a mistake on my part, very dumb
You will always have a spot in my heart filled with love.

I write this today with love and compassion
And believe me, I've learned my lesson.

Everyone thinks we make a perfect pair
So do I, yes I swear.

I hope we can be more than just friends
If not my heart may never mend.

Matt Alderman, Grade 8
Marlinton Middle School, WV

Nurse

A very special person,
Who cares and loves for those who are sick.
They make you feel better,
With their knowledge,
And their tools.
They can help you when your rich,
They can help you when your poor.
but overall they are always there for you.

Danielle Robertson, Grade 8
Hartville Jr/Sr High School, MO

Out Where the Cotton Grows

Down in the fields where the cotton grows,
Where the irrigational system flows.
In a town no bigger than my own,
Out where the cotton grows.
Plants the size of the palm of my hand.
Tanned workers farming the land.
Out where the cotton grows.
200 pounds of cotton by hand a day,
Great-granddaddy Smithee picking away,
Out in the sun his seven kids to play.
Out where the cotton grows.

Bailey Arnold, Grade 7
Alpena High School, AR

A Wondrous Achievement

"The sun shall never set on so glorious a human achievement"
That's what Mandela said
when his country was finally free
from all the segregation and inhumanity.

Through perseverance,
unswerving belief,
and nonviolent resistance,
his followers were able to accomplish such a feat.

But resistance comes at a price
as he was sent to jail
for disobeying those unrighteous laws against blacks
that he knew would someday fail.

So when Mandela was demanded to be set free,
he seized that opportunity
to require a change in society
so that black South Africans could have rights
equal to the dominant whites.

Mandela ran for president once those changes were made,
and he was not afraid
because he knew that justice always won,
and justice was the reason why he decided to run.

William Lee, Grade 9
West Jr High School, MO

Generations

Please take my hand as our journey begins.
Tales to learn about the times long ago,
Our stories passed down from parent to child.
The family traditions year after year,
From beginning of time until the end,
We leave behind to our family and friends,
The knowledge we have gained from now and then.

Katie Banks, Grade 9
Bearden High School, TN

Football

The thought fires me up
As I walk onto the field
For the greatest butt-kicking fiesta ever
The thought of tackling is running in my mind
The ref flips the coin we win the toss
We choose to kick
The first play is a bootleg option
They say down, set, hut
I see him drop back
I push my guy off
He never sees me coming
He is down
A loss of 20 yards
At the end we win 34 to 6

Josh Ridgaway, Grade 7
Highland Rim School, TN

Wooden Hearts

Trees swaying in the breeze
Swaying left, swaying right
Whispering words unto the night
Don't cut us down, we beg you please!
Come daylight you hear them say
At least we have another day
To live in rain, or sleet, or snow
But when we're cut, we do not know.
Once cut, we're carved and turned
Into hearts that always burn
With strong passion and love
But also with the grace of a dove.

Shelby Gillespie, Grade 7
Tyner Middle Academy, TN

Invisible

I'm invisible.
People look right past,
Just like they're looking through glass.
It's like I am not even there.

Maybe if I dye my hair
People might stare.
People still won't see me.
They will just see nothing.

Maybe it is better to not
Be seen than be seen for
Who I am not
I'm still invisible.

Eulalia Johnson, Grade 9
Niangua High School, MO

The Rain Forest

As cool as the breeze
Beautiful as a flower
As gentle as song

Amanda Schmelzle, Grade 8
St Gerard Majella School, MO

Fall

Fall colors
Red, yellow, orange
Autumn winds
Changing leaves
Scarecrows and pumpkins
Fall recipes
Fall friends
The fun will never end.
The autumn harvest
Corn, wheat, and beans
Can fall be put to the test?
But the biggest, greatest thing of all,
is all the joy that is in fall.

Ittalo Clark, Grade 7
Elkton School, TN

A Day in Thanking God

The moon, a bright light when it's dark.
When the stars are able to run a marathon,
anything is possible.
God made all of these, praise him and thank him.

Wind howling like a wolf famished for food.
Wondering how you'll ever fall asleep,
But soon you wake up to the birds chirping on an early Saturday morning.
God made all of these, praise him and thank him.

For breakfast, fresh fruit that's cold as ice
And crisp like the air on a fall day.
God made all of these, praise him and thank him.

In the afternoon smelling freshly cut grass, as sweet as honey.
The humid air before rainfall.
God made all of these, praise him and thank him.

In the evening, the sun winking its wonderful warmth through its rays.
Wind in your face, feeling free, and untouchable.
Grains of smooth, blisteringly blazing sand.
God made all of these, praise him and thank him.

Kathryn Chamberlain, Grade 7
Our Lady Catholic School, MO

Grid Iron Pride

My black and white size eleven Nike's are my home away from home,
as I beat running backs on Haywood Stadium.
I am a Roman gladiator with my shoulder pads as armour.
My helmet is like a Roman's, and my weapons
are my strength, speed, and my never-quit will to survive.
This turf has seen many battles.
The smell of hot dogs linger.
The crowd makes a first class earthquake of noise.
Some destinies have been born, and some have been terminated.
Heywood is a give-it-all-you-got type of home.
It is the Alamo, and I must defend.
Its soil has been fed with blood, sweat, and pride.
Wearing a red jersey gives me that sense of home.
The red binds with your blood and the two Baylor School paw prints control you.
Winning is everything.
You need heart.
You need self esteem.
You need determination.
Pride determines which people lead and who is led.

Spencer Craig, Grade 8
Baylor School, TN

Snow

Snow may mean different things.
To some it may mean no school or extended weekend!
Some people may like to think of snow as a wonderful and delightful thing.
Many others may think of it as fresh white powder waiting to be shred.
It doesn't matter what some may call it as long as they can all enjoy it.

Michael Johnson, Grade 7
Maury Middle School, TN

Beautiful Blue

Sun shining brightly making waters so blue,
Huge waves going CRASH against lumpy gray rocks,
Raging waters cool like a winter breeze,
At first so shallow, later on so deep,
The ocean is home to many things.

Bright colorful fish look like rainbows in the water,
Dolphins jumping so high above the water,
Hungry sharks looking for fish for dinner,
Slow large turtles swimming close to the ground,
Seaweed wrapping around my ankles.

Beautiful sandcastles lining the beach,
Sand is blowing in my face,
Sand so soft and warm like a blanket,
Why is the sand so soft?
Why is the ocean so pretty?

Kaitlyn Drummond, Grade 7
Barret Traditional Middle School, KY

Alone

I waited, in the dark, in the cold
for you to come back.
But no one did.
Not a sound stirred.
Nothing rose from the dead
of that unnatural night, but silence.

The dead did not stir
in their graves of ash
and blood and soot.
The ground, and those entombed beneath it,
all quiet.

I stared, blankly, at that world
of deserted cities, shelled out and burnt like corpses.
I stared, at the fog,
gray and gritty, waiting for you to walk from it.
But you never did.

The sun is lost to us
and the seas scarred by us.
I am alone.
The end has come and gone.
And you went with it.

Zach Gaines, Grade 9
University Heights Academy, KY

Andante

Rather depth than length
Rather quality than quantity
Even if it's a little slow,
I want to live as much as allowed, depth to me
I tell myself, andante…andante

Ji-Yoon Ha, Grade 9
Family of Faith Christian School, OK

Help!

My tears fall, my internal wall breaks.
That's all it can take,
So many things come at once,
No one to love me, no one to save me.
Walking alone through this cold, dark world,
My life is hurled against the wall, breaking it all up.
Afraid to love afraid to trust.
You say you won't hurt me but is it true?
My heart can't handle the truth.
I look in the mirror and break it with my fist.
How can someone feel like this?
I cry quietly with no one to hear —
No one to protect me from my fears.
I will wait for the day when I'm not falling.
Still there's no one to catch me, no one to care.
The air is cold, crisp, but still harsh.
My tears still fall,
My hope's still shattered,
But take my heart as a token.
It's broken, bruised, and extremely confused.
Why didn't you help me?

Devon Fore, Grade 8
Musselman Middle School, WV

Little Debbie

Little Debbie
Gentle, loving, loud, lazy
Sibling of LJ and Twinkie
Lover of the cool barn
Who feels loved by Cherokee
Who needs food 24-7
Who gives me responsibility
Who fears being sold
Who would like to see wide open green grass fields
Resident of the pasture
Early

Mallory Early, Grade 7
Leeton Middle and High School, MO

That One Guy

I want that one guy
Who I used to have.
We used to be in love but
Now I've got it bad.
Should I change my ways
Or just keep crying, nights and days.
I'll wait for you for as a long as I have to.
I need you and I want you to love me.
You're the only one for me
You complete my life and you make it all right.
Why did we even start this stupid fight?
When I hear you talk about her it,
Reminds me that I love you
Always and forever.

Skylar Raymond, Grade 8
Wilson Middle School, OK

Barracuda

See how he darts
from caves with a zoom!
See how he lingers
by the coral,
in the reef.
He races past flounder
and angels alike.
Quickly he swims
through his rainbow of color.
With a chomp of his teeth
and a whip of his head,
another poor soul is on its death bed.

Kristen Vredeveld, Grade 7
Baylor School, TN

Pigs

Pigs
Fat, delicious
Slow, smelly, loud
Tasty when cooked
Balls of fat

Edward Halter, Grade 8
Avenue City Elementary School, MO

Boys

Boys, sometimes they're nice.
They're like a spice
They can be hot
Or, they can be not
They're unpredictable like dice.

Destiny Mason, Grade 8
Pigeon Forge Middle School, TN

The Graveyard

In the graveyard
Behind the mausoleum
Beside the headstone
Of one long gone
Far from the church
With holy protection
In front of the gargoyle
Inside the rickety shack
Lives the groundskeeper

Patrick Taylor, Grade 8
Pigeon Forge Middle School, TN

Without a Monkey

Without a monkey
throughout the world
under the ground
above the sky
beyond the universe
towards Pluto
is without a monkey

Aaron Price, Grade 8
Pigeon Forge Middle School, TN

Tyra

Tyra
Intelligent, humorous, courageous, and dorky
Older of two; calls younger Collin Hunter "brat"
Loves computers, rock music, goofy guys, and humor that isn't at someone's expense
Turns giddy and wild when talking to loved ones
Has no chance of survival without Internet, music, and the Codex Alera
Provides her mother much reason for frustration and pride alike
Fears nothing known but karaoke
Would someday see most of Europe and if possible
Shares secrets, feelings, hopes, and daily life with her mother and "penguin"
Is an apt pupil, computer guru of sorts, trustworthy friend, and honest person
Content — for the moment — resident of Palmyra
Fairchild

Tyra Fairchild, Grade 8
Montgomery Central Middle School, TN

Wildly Free

They run free and fast.
For they are horses running without any worries.
They graze as if they are starving.
For they are horses eating without despair.
They stand still as a statue.
For they are horses sleeping and dreaming.
They are as strong as an ox.
For they are horses with mustang blood.
They are beautiful.
For they are Mustangs with a flourishing appearance!!
When They gallop the ground shakes as if there is an earthquake.
For they are horses and mustangs running wild and free without looking back.

Richelle McCarty, Grade 7
Green Bank Elementary-Middle School, WV

Happy

We go through life being told to be happy, which makes us choose to be mad
Not on purpose of course, it's just nature I guess.
We begin to lose friends, one after another.
They just can't stand us anymore.
So, we sit back and think.
We dig deeply, deeply into a part of us that we didn't even know existed.
After days, months, maybe even years of thinking,
we find something, something special, someone special,
Something that makes us happy, someone that makes us happy.
And that one person, the one you hurt so long ago,
The one that never moved on, never forgot,
Takes that something, or someone, away. Not because they want it,
No, that's not it at all.
But because you did, and they wanted you mad.
Maybe mad is not the word to use, upset? No. Depressed? No. Dead? Almost.
Gone.
They wanted you gone, from their heart, mind, and soul.
So, you were gone, just like that. And they wanted you back.
They realized what they had done, and they wanted you back.
So, now it's their turn, to find that something or someone,
And be happy.

Cameron Vulgamott, Grade 9
Savannah High School, MO

Building Things*

I wanted to be a builder of things, from furniture to buildings.
I wanted to build anything.
"Saw, saw." The wood was cut.
"Hammer, hammer." The sides stood.
"Measure, measure." The shelves fit in place.
After building one bookcase with my grandfather,
I knew that building furniture was not for me.
I wanted to design and build rockets.
"Saw, saw." The wood was cut.
"Hammer, hammer." The sides stood.
"Measure, measure." The shelves fit in place.
Pump, pump, pump. Whoosh!
Air rockets soar.
How far can the rocket fly with three pumps?
I will see.

Kyle Cantrell, Grade 8
Baylor School, TN
**Patterned after "Paul Zimmer"*

Father

My leaf is green,
So are your eyes.
Your heart is red,
Like the fire that burns inside me.
My eyes are brown like the dirt you walk on.
Just like the way you walk all over me.
You said you loved me and you lied.
My heart is dark,
Because of the way you make me feel.
I want to cry,
And let it all out.
But my emotions are lost,
They just walked out,
Like you walked out on me,
You've ruined my life,
Now I'm all alone,
And empty inside.

Ciara DeClue, Grade 8
Northwest Valley 7th & 8th Grade Center, MO

Trona

With a warm personality,
Her hair is angel-soft,
Her heart shines like lip gloss.
Gentle eyes, feathery eyebrows,
Sunshine smile,
And a smooth, laid-back style.
Quiet as a lion stalking its prey,
Her intelligence bursts out of her mouth
As her breath goes away.
Shyness is present,
She has fun in front of friends
And stays true to herself
Until the end.

Tanesha Hill, Grade 8
Lee A Tolbert Community Academy, MO

The Woods

I go to the woods looking to get away.
Hoping to see a few woodland creatures
such as deer and turkeys.
But strangely as night was creeping behind the afternoon
and I was leaving to return home.
I saw these big eyes staring down at me, from a tree.
It was an owl, something you can't normally spot
in the woods easily due to the owl's camouflage.
Well anyway, as I noticed the owl's big eyes I was startled
and started to hurry home.
You know, the longer I thought about
how I was startled by the owl.
And when I returned home I felt safe and calm.
I think home is anywhere you can go away
or hide in and feel safe.

Brian Richards, Grade 8
Southern Reynolds County R-II School, MO

I Want Someone

I want someone who lets me be me,
Someone to let me be free,
To come to my rescue and save me.
I want someone who will hold me at night,
I will feel protected, he is my light.
When things go bad, he'll tell me it's all right.
I want someone to be by my side.
On the dance floor, he will guide.
Someone I can count on until I die.
I want someone to wipe away my tears,
Someone to destroy my fears,
Someone who is sincere.
I want someone who says I will go far,
That tells me to reach for the stars,
Who whispers my limits are farther than Mars.
I want someone to feel my pain,
Someone who will love me even when it rains,
His love and respect I would gain.
I want someone who is patient,
Who can hold a conversation,
And who loves this nation.

Jacquinta Hammons, Grade 8
Lee A Tolbert Community Academy, MO

Hockey

On the frozen surface, they give their all,
Only to be laughed at if one were to fall.
Harsh hitting goes on near the boards,
Some of the players are shaped like gourds.
Tripping and roughing are some penalties,
Power play and penalty kill are the specialties.
Sticks clashing, pucks dancing,
Fans cheering, skates prancing,
Anyone who plays will have fun
As the tradition of hockey continues on.

Taylor Wagner, Grade 8
St Gerard Majella School, MO

Fall

Leaves are changing
And blowing away,
As the wind blows
You can hear them fly away.

Birds are chirping
and flying away,
Like hunting season
is coming their way

Thanksgiving is near
Family gathers together
Chit chatting away
Closer and closer

In the end,
winter is here
The birds are now gone
And here comes a new year.

Katie Weyer, Grade 7
Nettleton Jr High School, AR

Cobra

I see a cobra
Every detailed scale
I see a cobra
With its beautiful tail

I touch a cobra
Half slimy, half rough
I touch a cobra
It gives me goose bumps

I hear a cobra
A high pitched hiss
I hear a cobra
The sound of death

Evan Tillman, Grade 7
Benton County School of the Arts, AR

Rodeo

R oping the runaway horse
O n the back of the bucking bull
D ust and mud, bulls and blood
E veryone cheering you on
O ff the horse to tie up the calf

Amy Friend, Grade 8
Greenfield Jr/Sr High School, MO

Pumped

Blood is pumping.
Seat is dripping.
My heart is racing,
As the game is still going.

Samantha Orr, Grade 8
Rocky Comfort Elementary School, MO

When It's Over and Done With

When it's over and done with
I think about what used to be.
I think about how we made each other feel.
I think about how we were there for each other when we needed it.
When it's over and done with
all I think about is how happy we used to be
When it's over and done with
all I think about is why it ended so soon,
you said you'll never hurt me,
you said you'll never leave me
you said you'll never make me cry.
Now look at us now
We are such a mess
We thought we were meant to be
But now it's over and done with
There's not one thing we can change
about what happened between us
When it's over and done with
all there is to say is goodbye!

Brandy N. Mooney, Grade 9
Delta C 7 High School, MO

Christmas at Grandpa's

Frosty windowpanes and
snow covered ground,
it must be Christmas at Grandpa's.
From the stockings on the mantel
to the warm burning fire,
it must be Christmas at Grandpa's.
Relatives I see once a year,
especially my favorite cousins,
it must be Christmas at Grandpa's.
Aunt Maxine's gravy, warm and thick,
the smell of roast turkey rising from the oven,
it must be Christmas at Grandpa's.
Hearing the jingle of reindeer bells
brings a surprise visit from Santa and Mrs. Claus,
it must be Christmas at Grandpa's.
Shiny presents with blue bows and red ribbons,
make up the "Present Train,"
it must be Christmas at Grandpa's.
I go to bed dreaming of tomorrow's broom ball game on the ice.
It was a great Christmas at Grandpa's.

Ryan Taylor, Grade 9
West Jr High School, MO

Friends

They are something very special.
Most people have them.
They have their doubts and their fights.
When you are in trouble they help you out.
They come in handy during breakups and are great study partners.
They all have special talents that no one else has.
This person I am speaking of is called a friend.

Lindsey Warren, Grade 8
Highland Rim School, TN

Friends

Such a meaning and descriptive word
friends tell you everything, fulfillment of the
best thing that has ever happened to you
calling someone your friend is like the
transition from a flower bud to a beautiful rose
having a friend is such a wonderful thing,
that if you lose it, it could follow you the rest of your life,
haunting you like a terrible dream
my friends mean the most to me,
everyone should have the same

Brenna Tarver, Grade 9
Lexington High School, OK

My Shadow

In the pitch of darkness, my shadow is gone
But In the light, it walks along
Even when no one else is around
I'll always have my shadow safe on the ground
Standing beside me through rain or snow
It follows me wherever I go
But it always leaves, when twilight replaces the sun
Till tomorrow, alone I run

Aquil Muhammad, Grade 8
Pleasant View School, TN

Summer Days

Waking up late,
Staying out until dawn,
Going on weekday night dates,
Or jumping in the sprinklers on the lawn.

Free from all the homework,
Free from the mess.
Full of all the perks,
Full of no stress.

Oh! The summer days,
Oh! The wonderful times,
Oh! All of the craze,
Oh! I miss summer sometimes.

Cheryl Dale, Grade 9
Bearden High School, TN

Autumn Is Near

A time that is bound with the months
That comes between fall and winter
That when the leaves fall and the weather is chill

It leaves behind summer and brings the winter thrills.
It brings Halloween nights and ghost brings a fright.

Then Thanksgiving comes with a bountiful banquet.
This time is autumn and it comes once a year,
But don't forget it comes only once a year!

Carly Carter, Grade 7
Hebron Middle School, KY

Misery Behind the Eyes

We walk through life,
As if it were nothing,
Walking past fear,
Walking past love,
We only have one life,
Every breath you waste,
Every second of every day,
You're hurting yourself,
It's not because you meant too,
It's because you ignored the one life you could have changed,
Instead you walk through life,
With no emotion,
As you look at me with your blue eyes,
It starts to rain,
As you breathe your last breath,
I realize the rain is crying for all those people,
That stand alone,
Cry alone,
Walk alone,
And most of all live
Their one life they have alone.

Abbey Mock, Grade 8
Summit Lakes Middle School, MO

Another Dream

As I walk, his voice calls out my name
a vision of him floats and drifts in the distant light.
He said he didn't love me, but yet, he came,
he takes my hand, and holds me tight,
we begin to dance, slow and long,
he gazes in my eyes, his face so full of love,
nothing I feel could ever go wrong.
I feel free like a bird, hopeful, like a dove.
The song has slowed and is fading out.
So in the sand we sit and watch the sun,
as it sets behind the gently rolling waves.
A tolling sound begins to chime,
the land is going black, soon enclosed by darkness.
His voice is hazy and his smile vanishes.
He begins to fade, like dust in the wind.
I open my eyes, and stare down the hall,
the light of the porch is mocking me.
I lay my head upon my pillow once more,
my eyes close, my mind drifts,
to a world entirely my own
one more night another dream.

Leilani Allen, Grade 9
Indianola High School, OK

Winter

I watch the snow fall and hear the wind blowing.
The trees are bare and not a single green blade of grass is seen.
It is all covered by an icy sheet of white snow.
This is the season I favor most.

Grace Clayton, Grade 8
Highland Rim School, TN

Water

Water
Pure, powerful
Rushing, flowing, racing
Fast, quick, cold, calm
Freezing, chilling, fishing
Layback, relaxed
Creek

Samantha Jaggars, Grade 8
Wickliffe Elementary School, OK

Yes, No, I Don't Know

You say you're not ready,
You need more time.
I'm trying to understand,
Is it meant to be?
There is so much at demand.
Should it have happened already?

Brandon Crow, Grade 8
Malvern Jr High School, AR

Where's Peace

Across the street
Along the walk
Beyond the city
Out in the country
With peace

Hunter Bonner, Grade 8
Pigeon Forge Middle School, TN

Fall Scene

All of the maple leaves,
In orange, yellow and red;
Fall down to the ground,
Along with acorns, nuts, and pine cones.

Little chipmunks scurry,
Like little racing cars;
The trees start to lose their leaves,
And grass starts turning yellow.

Little animals look for food,
And store it in their nests;
Hopefully they will find some,
Before the winter starts.

Birds migrate south for winter,
And bears start to hibernate.
It reminds me of people,
Right after the Thanksgiving feast.

There are many things about fall,
That people like to see;
But for me, that's simple.
I like everything!

Tyler Rasmussen, Grade 7
Nettleton Jr High School, AR

Proscella Dedalea

Below the peerless blue mirror
Into the depths of ghostly waters,
The echo of the oceans lament,
Stirs.
Above fair moonlight casts its eerie glow,
Like pale lovers, the sea and land share a parting kiss
Waves that move in an eternal dance
In the distance a siren sings its tempting song
Calm air poisoned with the impending of the doomed,
Thunder quakes, as lightning flashes like the conflict of opposing swords
Beyond a battle rages in the heavens,
The clash of the Titans.
An armada of waves charge toward the feeble land,
Wailing a hoarse battle cry
The wind weeps, the tempest howling in rage and grief
I turn my ashen face to the sea, once serene and calm now crazed
With sorrow
In they own heart, that has known true sorrow,
Strength pulses
I rise to meet the terror of the tempest.

Hayley Pierpont, Grade 8
Heritage Middle School, TN

A Victim of Divorce

A child in my perspective is a victim of divorce,
Life seems to be headed for the worse,
There is a lot of feeling of sadness, madness, and even happiness,
It doesn't seems to get any better if you don't talk to family, or even friends about it,
It's not easy going parent to parent house every other week or weekend,
It's hard to fit everything into 12 hours of daylight homework, time with friends
and family, sports, school, and free time by yourself,
Life seems to fly by, and days end quickly,
You always wish your parents marriage never ended,
But today just another day as a victim of divorce,
It will always be that way even if your parents marry someone else,
Because it will never be the same,
You'll always be a victim of divorce,
Just trust me because I'm a victim of divorce

Melissa Hagan, Grade 8
St Mary of the Woods School, KY

Casey Smith

Casey
Quiet a lot of the time, patient, creative, and eccentric
Sister of little brother Johnathan
Lover of Skittles, all types of music, and the movies
Who feels shy, annoyed by her brother, and cravings for chocolate
Who needs music every day, a maid to clean her room, and her braces off
Who gives marvelous sleepovers, advice to friends, and her brother a hard time
Who fears any type of snake, mice, and rats
Who would like to see a sunset over a Hawaiian beach
Who is a resident of Cunningham, TN
Smith

Casey Smith, Grade 8
Montgomery Central Middle School, TN

Christmas

Christmas here we come
Christmas is so lovely
It is fun to play in the snow

Santa Claus here he comes
Watching you more than your parents
Santa Claus is magic

Grandparents here they come
Joining us on that special day
Lots of present under the tree

Children make more magic for Santa Claus.

Adam Brodack, Grade 7
St Joseph Institute for the Deaf, MO

Up, Up and Away

Riding along on my best friend's boat,
I felt so relaxed and peaceful.
I closed my eyes
and felt like I was flying
up, up into the air,
to a height only the birds had been.
I soared up and down through the clouds.
I felt freer than ever before.
I felt as though I had wings
that could take me anywhere I wanted to go.
I couldn't see any other creature in sight
except for the beautiful eagle God had created.
I was happier than ever
as I flew through the sky.
Then all of a sudden
I heard my name being called.
I opened my eyes, and there I was,
Sitting right beside my best friend on her boat
and remembering what it was like to fly
and wishing I could do it all over again.

Allison Harris, Grade 8
Baylor School, TN

The Roof

Above the ground without any sound
Below the sun really is quite fun
Under the stars until the twilight
Within the world without a doubt
Through the window into the air
Not a sound in the world with no despair
Beyond the planets, inside the earth
Among the foundation, but far away
If you go there you'll have no display
Between the houses from a year
That is distant to the ear
Into the window with a new remembrance
So that I can reminisce

Andrew McDonald, Grade 8
Heritage Middle School, TN

I Am

I am a witty girl who loves to have fun.
I wonder what I'll be like when I'm older.
I hear dozens of people laughing.
I see people playing games.
I want everyone to have fun.
I am a witty girl who loves to have fun.

I pretend that some things are funny.
I feel the happiness in the room.
I touch the clouds as I fly high.
I worry that people expect too much from others.
I cry when I get very frustrated.
I am a witty girl who loves to have fun.

I understand that everything isn't fun.
I say it will all turn out for the better.
I dream that everybody is happy.
I try to be the best person I can be.
I hope for everyone to get along.
I am a witty girl who loves to have fun.

Cheyanne Stoll, Grade 8
King City High School, MO

Halloween

H aunted houses
A fter curfews
L aughs
L ightning skies
O wls
ho **W** ls
E vil
hayrid **E** s
N ight rides

Hannah Johnson, Grade 8
Southern Reynolds County R-II School, MO

Trick or Treat

Inside a haunted house,
Scarecrows pop, ghosts jump, and zombies scream;
Candy corns, caramel apples, trick or treat.
The pumpkin is yellow
Boo! yell vampires.
Hearts race,
Frankenstein hides around midnight.
Black bats run through haunted neighborhoods.

Penelope Parker, Grade 7
Heritage Hall School, OK

Perfect Score

Today I managed something that I've never done before.
I turned in this week's spelling quiz and got a perfect score.

Although my score was perfect it appears I'm not to bright.
I got a perfect zero not a single answer right.

Shelby Mullins, Grade 8
Clarksburg School, TN

The Hunting Shark

He hunts for his prey.
He doesn't find fish for night,
But success will come.

Timothy Neumann, Grade 7
Rocky Comfort Elementary School, MO

Rain, Rain, Rain

Rain, rain, rain,
A rainy day,
If only it would go away.
It's raining here,
It's raining there.
Rain, rain, rain,
Everywhere.

Brittney Jackson, Grade 7
Big Sandy School, TN

Plymouth Rock

P ilgrims landed here first
L oving the land
Y es, they decided to stay
M ountains all around
O n the ground lay snow
U nder the safety of the tent from
T hc cold
H ere is Plymouth Rock

R eturning to the boat
O n the way to tell others to say
C ongratulations you are the first
K ind people to stay

Amanda Gross, Grade 7
Rocky Comfort Elementary School, MO

Love Is It

Trust with my life,
loving even when I die,
being alone will make me cry,
even if I can't see love with my eyes.
I know it's mine,
Yeah, quote somebody,
romantic ones are hotties,
even if it was a tiny lie,
my trust it can't buy,
bein' sad ain't the only way.
I live my life
Pray for another day.
To it I say this all today
Does my way have to be the same?
Its way is my light
that love is tight,
it's the one I like,
it bein' mine.
Is that all right?

Breana Jordan, Grade 8
Summit Lakes Middle School, MO

Autumn

Autumn,
Glides gracefully in after the hot summer months,
Slowly showing everyone, "Autumn has come."
It colors the world with cozy relaxing tones,
By elegantly changing the color of the leaves, from
Fiery reds, to glowing oranges and yellows,
It hits everything at different times, the trees, the
Leaves, the grass, the climate, the people.
The climate is chilled,
The people relax and become festive,
The millions of leaves and miles of grass become
Blankets of wonderful colors which bring about comforting emotions.
No one completely understands this subtle but extravagant change,
We all enjoy it while we can, then
The season slowly fades,
And moves out like a sly fox…

Amy Niehaus, Grade 9
Nerinx Hall High School, MO

That One

That one makes me feel.
As she sits there I can't help but gaze.
Beauty like that of a sunset gently fading away over an ocean front.
Hair like a river softly flowing through a set of mountains.
Smile that could brighten even the most darkest of days.
Personality that attracts many to her.
Kindness that I wish I had.
When I am near her my legs get weak.
That one makes me feel.

Miles Ward, Grade 8
Belle Isle Enterprise Middle School, OK

Best Friends

True friends see the hurt in our eyes, while others are fooled by our smiles
When it is a miserable day, seeing our best friend makes it all worthwhile.

We weep and cry on each other's shoulders
We tell each other everything because we're the best secret holders.

We laugh while we sing into hairbrushes and do silly dances.
Best friends do funny dares and take crazy chances.

We hang out on weekends at each other's houses.
And during the week do our homework together after school,
While in the summer, we stay all day at the neighborhood pool.

I remember when I met you in Pre-K
You stuck up for me when I was teased all day.

I would take your snack while you took mine,
We were rebels back then; we stayed up during nap time.

We've got each other's backs, and do everything together,
What can I say; we'll be best buds forever and ever.

Laura Milles, Grade 7
Seven Holy Founders School, MO

In My Pocket

In my pocket
I have a stone that says
Faith
Have Faith in God
for He will make your paths straight.
Like a bird has faith in its mom to bring
back food for it.

In my pocket
I have a stone that says
Dream
Dream up a story of a lifetime.
Dream to be great.

In my pocket
I have a key
I have Faith in this key
to open the right door.
What lays beyond the door is a Dream
until I open the door with the key.
This key will unlock the door to my future.
The world beyond it is a mystery
up to me to solve.

Rachel Janka, Grade 8
Belle Isle Enterprise Middle School, OK

Those Towers

Why did they do that?
I really don't understand...why?
Why did they destroy those beautiful towers?
Where they once stood is now...nothing
I was in first grade when it happened
It was a horrible day for our country.
All those people will never see their loved ones again
I remember watching replays on TV
Those towers were filled with smoke
Ambulances were everywhere
Our nation was shocked
But...why did they do it why?
Why did they put us through that torture?

Spencer Schaetzel, Grade 7
Seven Holy Founders School, MO

Plane Ride

Nervous, stomach twisting
I look down out of the little circular window
The ground even before takeoff seems far away
The engines start
The plane starts moving
Faster and faster
It makes me want to laugh
And then I'm in the air
Earth gets farther away
I feel free

Katie Blessing, Grade 8
Alpena High School, AR

Memories

It's sad when you lose someone
especially someone that you were close to,
that you loved very much,
losing someone is very sad, you could cry and cry,
but it was their time, their time to go,
crying is a good thing so don't feel bad just let it out,
I once got told that someday it will be your turn to go,
they say it's better than suffering to death,
just think about the past, present, and future,
you just never know what could go wrong.

Brittany Hart, Grade 8
Southern Reynolds County R-II School, MO

Choices

The grave awaits the youth,
With a wide open mouth.
When danger's in their face
They seem to see it well.
Their loved ones always told 'em.
There's a place called heaven,
And a place called hell,
A place called prison,
And a place called jail.
They chose not to listen.
Five years later, they found the truth.
Listen to those who love you,
Or have your face on the news.

Antoine R., Grade 9
Audubon Youth Development Center, KY

Free Like That Bird

I saw a bird one day.
He was flying in the sky.

I don't remember what I was doing that day.
Time seemed to just pass me by.

He looked so free, so uncontained.
His wings were all spread out.

I wish I could feel that way.
I wish I had no problems to worry about.

To feel like that bird, to feel surreal,
Then happiness I could finally feel.

I wish I was free like that bird.

To feel free to be myself,
I would be exposed.
Escape from my enclosed shell.
Fear I would not show.

I wish I was free like that bird.

Kiersten Lacey, Grade 8
Licking Jr High School, MO

Hairless Dog

I'm smart.
I'm cold.
I'm bald.
I bite when I'm scared.
I haven't a care.
I whine in despair.
I sleep in a chair.
I hate the sweaters I wear.
The furniture will not repair.
Try if you dare
To take my treat.

Bethany Buckner, Grade 7
Greenfield Jr/Sr High School, MO

Homework

H ate it
O ffensive
M akes me mad
E veryone has to do it
W ork yeah right
O h my am I done yet
R ats!!!
K now it has to be done

Samantha Smyser, Grade 7
North Nodaway Jr/Sr High School, MO

Hurt

H urt is an
U nusual and very
R eal
T hing that happens every day!

Reagean Ellingson, Grade 8
Hartville Jr/Sr High School, MO

Thanksgiving Dinner

The turkey is heaven to me.
There is no fee to be with family.
The squash, corn, and pumpkin seeds
is what decorates the beads.

The apple juice falls — Splash!
The corn on the cob rolls — Ping!
It hits the cranberries — Splat!
Oh, What a mess!

Have no worries,
I caught the berries.
The plate is okay
because I saved the day.

Now we say blessing.
An angel is the dressing.
The pie is what I've been craving
with the coconut shavings.

Jessica Bishop, Grade 7
Nettleton Jr High School, AR

A Dangerous Message

A hero is sent a message from his foe,
Stating a challenge, a dare!
"Riggedy, riggedy, white,
Come and spend the night.
We'll play some games,
Some wild, some tame.
'Cause if you will, you might."

Christopher Forbus, Grade 9
Family of Faith Christian School, OK

The Angel's Path to Heaven

Hurry, hurry
He's waiting
Look, look
Can't you see it?
Run, run
It isn't far
Come on, come on
We're almost there
See, see
The gate is open
There, there
Now you're home

Lyndsey McKinley, Grade 7
St Mary of the Woods School, KY

Fear

It haunts the vivid wars of the soul.
It devours our golden dreams.
Fear rings with soft silence
and avoids the splendors of sunset.
Fear reflects in dark blue oceans
and connects with fog and rain.
It thunders over prayers.
Fear is a large mountain
with no way off
unless you face your fears
and explore.

Allison Young, Grade 8
Baylor School, TN

Morning

The sun rises,
    Birds chirping,
Chipmunks playing
    Dogs barking
Wind blowing
    Leaves rustling
Kids playing
    Dad mowing the lawn
Mom weed-eating
    Bubby playing video games
It is morning

Chelsi Mustain, Grade 8
Rocky Comfort Elementary School, MO

My Friend

J oyful
E xotic
S hy
S illy
E ccentric
C rafty
A ffectionate

Ashley Nichols, Grade 7
Kiowa Jr/Sr High School, OK

Unsure

I'm alone with no one here
Sitting in front of a mirror
Who is that girl looking back at me?
I know it isn't really who I am
With all the lies upon myself.
All the lies I have told them
Is hurting me inside
And now the pain is hurting me
Like a hundred stabbing knives.
Will I go to heaven when I die
Or will I go to hell
And burn in flames?
How will death feel
When I am so plain?
Will I be okay
With the way my life ends?
But I know that I have been happy
Sharing it with my friends.

Macie Cryer, Grade 9
East Newton High School, MO

My Sister

Caring, passionate, forgiving, loving
Mean, annoying, selfish
My sister is a lot of things
I still love her with all my heart
We do things for each other
And have our fights once in a while
But I'll always remember
She's my baby sister.

Hannah Coomes, Grade 7
St Mary of the Woods School, KY

December

D ifferent changes in your life.
E ach person gets to ride on a sled.
C hallenge yourself to go down a big hill.
E xcitement is your life.
M ake different changes in your life.
B est day of your life.
E ventually you will want to do it again.
R emake things you break.

Courtney Davis, Grade 7
Hartville Jr/Sr High School, MO

Jacquinta

Her round, pulpy cheeks
With her circle brown eyes
Are like a beautiful
Red-orange horizon.
She's intelligent,
Especially when she speaks.
She laughs and giggles
When she screams.
Sometimes looking serious,
I can hear her thoughts.
Just by looking in her mind,
I see what she has brought.

Dorien Banks, Grade 7
Lee A Tolbert Community Academy, MO

Turkey Hunting

Turkey hunting rocks
they strut spit drum and gobble
shoot them in the head
and they won't wobble.

Chad Richards, Grade 8
Southern Reynolds County R-II School, MO

Chess

The stress on the mind is on the edge
The thought of foresight would make it too easy
Strategy is the weapon and the power
The fuel is the desire for the king
The queen has the pick of her space
The rook walks a straight line
The bishop has a crooked eye
The knight has a stagger
The pawn is the first off the line but the slowest to move
The board is confusing with so many colors
It's like a maze with so many colors
The spaces blank and tell you nothing
Chess is a challenge for the board.

Dylan Head, Grade 7
King City High School, MO

Butterflies

I look out the window and see yellow butterflies.
They have little spots.
They remind me of butter as they fluttered in the garden.

Paige Dunham, Grade 7
Ketchum Jr High School, OK

Family

Your family is people who are related to you and love you.
Family is there when you need them the most.
Mother, father, sister, brother,
grandparents, aunts, uncles, and cousins are all family.
Some have large families, and some have small families.
But some don't have any family at all.

Baileigh Kimbrough, Grade 8
Highland Rim School, TN

Dying Lovelies

How do you describe a rose, a flower?
Varying from white, to red, to yellow
Looking perfect a vision of power
Soaking up the sun's cheerful rays, mellow

Surrounded by a sea of impostors
Loved by all that are good and prosperous
Hated only by evil and monsters
Deemed foolish, such thoughts are preposterous

Winter turns the proud from strong to weak, bleak
Chilly weather makes flowers run scared
A dying flower started off so meek
However a flower is set, prepared

The flower will return next spring prepared
For everyone to know that is was spared

Tykeara Mims, Grade 9
Bearden High School, TN

A Dream

I hear the sound of the ball going through the hoop.
The sound of my new shoes sliding on the slick floor.
I hear the sound of people cheering,
Then I hear the buzzer and see the ball
Sailing through the hoop.
I hear my alarm clock,
To see it all was just a dream.

Hannah Payne, Grade 8
St Mary of the Woods School, KY

Frog*

See how he bounds from stone to stone,
across the glimmering creek.
Webbed feet pushing and soaring,
from each dark, damp rock.
Gliding past minnows and leaves,
butterflies, bees, grass and trees.
Flinging himself into the air,
trying to find some food.
The rushing current beneath him,
an ocean of wildflowers all around.
On he frolics,
a goal set in his mind.
See how he soars over the rushing water,
to grab himself a fly.
Before you can shout before you can scream,
a fly drifts into his mouth.
Caught by his rope of tongue.
Then again he floats across the rushing stream.
Plunging himself into a cave of soft water.
Then all wet and dripping he surfaces slowly,
then lets out a satisfied "ribbit!"

Jacqueline Adams, Grade 7
Baylor School, TN
**Inspired by William Jay Smith's "Seal"*

Fall

The wind is blowing,
the leaves are falling
like a thousand birds
landing on the ground.
There is a lot to do,
mowing grass and raking leaves.
It is getting cold and
we are winter bound.
I look up in the sky
and see the birds so high.
Oh, don't I wish I could fly
along with them.
The fall, the fall
my favorite season of all.
The fall, the fall,
don't we all love the fall?

Kirby Banks, Grade 7
Nettleton Jr High School, AR

The Ring

Stop, listen, can you hear it?
It's the ring,
The ring of spring!
Rabbits scurry across the lawn;
The radiant birds are no longer gone.
All the leaves are coming back,
Not giving winter any slack,
So listen to the ring of spring.

Adam Oester, Grade 8
Musselman Middle School, WV

Ducky

Ducky ducky
Swimming through a
Pond, having your
Little ones is so
Much fun, round and
Round their mom they go
And make their mother
Proud

Lindsey Backward, Grade 8
Wickliffe Elementary School, OK

The Amazing Basketball Game

As the buzzer buzzes loudly
for the game to start,
they battled until the fourth quarter.
They were tied.
As home took the ball out,
visitors stole it — they shot for a three,
but it was blocked.
Home got the ball for the countdown.
they shot from half court — it sunk in.
the visitors walk away in shame.

JaVarian Moore, Grade 7
Elkton School, TN

Dreams

Sometimes I cry and I scream, and there are days when I
just don't understand about the pain I have felt for so long
has never melted nor even faded away.
I go day after day putting on a happy face playing the role of life.
But when night falls and darkness hits the Earth and I lay
my heavy head down to rest, it all comes rushing by in a whirl of winds.
I think cautiously to myself about the situation I portray.
I think whether thy love thy pain or even thy agony I hold
inside shall never scar my heart truly, and when I wake up
when the light shines again my light almost weightless
head seems to float off my pillow…for thy can dream.

Raven L. Houghton, Grade 8
West Jr High School, MO

Farming

I see the cows grazing, the horses resting after a long ride
along the farm, I see the vegetables growing day after day.

I hear the tractor starting, the rooster crowing, the goats
as they chew their cuds, the birds as they sing a sweet song high in the sky.

I smell the sweet smell of molasses, the smell of
flowers, the smell of dusty hay, the smell of sweat, after his work day is done.

I taste the ripe tomatoes, the taste of fresh night air, the
taste of sweet tea while sitting on the porch watching the sun set.

I feel the heat of summer days as I work in the garden.
I feel the heartache of losing farmland and the family farmer.

Charles Edward Stivers III, Grade 7
Hebron Middle School, KY

I Thought of You

I saw a red rose this morning. It looked so grand.
I thought of you.
I saw a yellow daffodil this morning. It looked so sweet.
I thought of you.
I saw a purple violet this morning. It looked so dear.
I thought of you.
I saw a white lily this morning. It looked so sacred.
I thought of you.
I saw a pink tulip this morning. It looked so angelic.
I thought of you.
I saw a white daisy this morning. It looked so gay.
I thought of you.
I saw the sky this morning. It looked so clear.
I thought of you.
I saw a mother and her child this morning. They looked so loving.
I thought of you.
I saw the sunset all orange, pink, and yellow. It looked so peaceful.
I turned to you and said, "I thought of you all day today, Mother."
I thought of what I wanted to say.
"I Love You."

Jimi Wilson, Grade 7
Wakita High School, OK

I Am

I am a thankful teenager
I wonder why I sometimes don't show it
I hear my friends and family laughing
I see the happiness all around
I want to prove that I am thankful
I am a thankful teenager

I pretend like I don't care
I feel the love in my heart
I touch the sad faces of the ones who have nothing
I worry that they will never be okay
I cry when I see them smile even through the hard times
I am a thankful teenager

I understand that I should be more thankful
I say that I am
I dream that I always will be
I try to make that dream come true
I hope someday I will
I am a thankful teenager

Hannah Watson, Grade 7
Newcastle Middle School, OK

The Wedding

There I am in my purple dress
I look cute of course
My pearls are shining
They glisten in the light

The tree is so tall
I am so short
In a park a wedding
Many cars arrive so early

My hair is done all pretty
I have a group of flowers to hold
You can see my tan line
But it is okay because I had a great time.

Courtney Ness, Grade 7
King City High School, MO

World of Warcraft Is Awesome

World of Warcraft is a great game to play.
I love to play it every day.
From questing to getting new gear,
I love to play it, that's crystal clear.
Running instances and dungeons is really fun
That's because I'm number one.
Getting epic gear is my goal
I give it all my heart and soul.
I take control of the battlegrounds,
And even though I have my ups and downs,
Owning noobs is what I do.
I am officially a World of Warcraft guru.

Bridget Brinkman, Grade 8
St Gerard Majella School, MO

Hidden Behind Closed Doors

Anger, fear, and hate was all she knew.
And even without it,
she doesn't know what to do.
Behind closed doors she hides away,
waiting slowly for that one fateful day,
when she is released from suffering her sorrows.
But, she stays behind closed doors,
and no one will ever know.
The truth she hides inside locked away from the world.
Her secrets are kept inside her lonely mind,
locked away so no one may ever find.
The secrets she keeps and the truth she hides.

Julia George, Grade 7
Madison Middle School, WV

War and Peace

W hen peace stops and bombs fall
A fter the bombs fell and the devastation is left
R etaliation of the enemy

A cts to help the country survive
N o more violence
D emocracy

P roblems resolved
E nvironmental protection
A cts of righteousness
C entral fair government
E ntire peace not war

Colton Moore, Grade 7
Clarksburg School, TN

The Flower of Fall

When the searing summer is over,
And autumn is starting once more,
We watch them ripen over time.
Their colors shine like a beautiful full moon.
The colors appear whimsical,
As flowers do in the summer
Bringing life to everything around them
Like they do every other year,
Connected like a mother and her child
Bonded by their long green stems until ready to part.
When orange and brown, once again,
They are ready to be withdrawn from the solid ground.
We create new images with them.
Faces, names, and pictures we carve
When carved, almost shriveled in the inside,
We illuminate them with a tiny candle
The candle brings new life to them
Glowing like lightning bugs on a scorching summer's day.
They continue to flicker during the night
Glowing on and on, without end
Continuously glowing, until it is time for fall to end…

Elmaz Bendinelli, Grade 9
Hamburg Jr High School, AR

Too Loud

Too loud to know.
Too loud to grow.
Too loud to flourish and thrive.
Impossible to learn.
Impossible to yearn.
Impossible to flourish and thrive.
It will be possible to learn someday.
Kenneth Hendee, Grade 9
Bigelow High School, AR

The Losing War*

Every day is a battle
A cerebral battle we fight with ourselves
We can choose to give up
Or we can choose to keep fighting
It's the way we decide to fight
Even with the knowledge
That one day, ultimately, we will lose
Never to rise again
That makes us who are are
We are fighting a losing war
Clashing with an unbeatable enemy
It is impossible for us to win
But the bravest of beings
Relish the challenge
Fight with all their might and strength
Outwit the devil
Win another day
And prepare for
The next battle tomorrow
Daniel Teitz Zuo, Grade 7
White Station Middle School, TN
**Dedicated to my grandfather*

My Sister

My sister she is there
When I need her she's there
When I don't need her
She still loves me

When I am mad
She still loves me
When I get on her nerves
She still loves me

All the time and forever
She still loves me
We have so many memories

Together and not together
She knows that I love her
Very Very Very much
She's my little sister
And always will be
Danielle Durham, Grade 9
Van-Cove High School, AR

A Recipe for a Perfect Little Sister Named Amy

1. Start with a cup of kindness
2. Then put a bag full of love
3. Next add an ounce of respect
4. Now put a packet of obeying
5. Then put a dash of calmness
6. Next stir in a pound of fun
7. Now put a tablespoon of non violence
8. Then add a dash of hyper
9. Now put a batch of humor
10. Next put a jug of smiles
11. Now put 3/4 of play
12. Then put a gallon of good spirits
13. Next put a dozen of unselfishness
14. Now preheat the oven to 120 degrees
15. Serve this on a hot pink and lime green plate and eat it for a week at lunchtime

You will start seeing your sister Amy act different in no time.
Allison Epps, Grade 7
Meredith-Dunn School, KY

Seasons Created by God

Snow, like little cotton balls, dropping from the sky.
Seeing white powder, covering the trees and shrubs,
until Spring comes.
God, thank you for this time of cold until Spring comes

Spring, birds chirping. Deer running through the leaves
like a graceful dance. Leave, that crunch beneath their feet.
Rustling in the grass of little creatures.
God, thank you for this time of life. God thank you for this time.

Summer, the sun, like the juicy peach in my mouth.
Juicy watermelon tasty in my mouth, honey sticky.
God, thank you for this time of vacation. God thank you for this time.

Fall, the feeling of leaves. Acorns falling from trees
and the huge, scratchy trees losing leaves.
The color of leaves, the color of fall like a rainbow of colors.
Picking apples and getting ready for Winter.
The smell of fresh apples, leaves and rain everywhere.
Smelling fresh rain coming for Winter.
God, we praise you for all these seasons.
Thomas Stoll, Grade 7
Our Lady Catholic School, MO

The Sea

A relaxing breeze sweeps across the calm flat surface of the sea.
Reflecting deep, blue, the waves, stirred and tumbled.
Crash, crash, crash, waves smash against high rocky cliffs.
The sky darkens, huge, gray gathers above the sea.
Wind roars, thunder cracks, and water crashes down like waterfalls above the sea.
Schools of small fish panic, fear grips. (As they're being tossed.)
But soon, clouds part, the sun shines down, heaven's rays glisten on the surface.
Tranquility is restored, and gulls squawk happily near the sea.
Rhythmic patterns of tides, a vast expanse of blue water throughout the sea.
Simon Strickland, Grade 7
White Station Middle School, TN

Christmas Morning

As I roll over,
I grasp the covers closer
to my chilled body.
When my brain begins
to process my thoughts,
I am reminded it is Christmas morning.

I look at my alarm clock.
5:00 a.m., the harsh green numbers stare back.
"Go back to bed," my head screams,
but anticipation steals my attention.
I quickly scamper into the living room,
no longer able to hold back my excitement.
I adjust to the bright lights surrounding the
tangy smell of the pine tree.

As I look at the presents covering the carpet
and the stray sprinkles from brightly decorated sugar cookies,
I hastily glance at the clock on the solid oak mantel.
6:00. Good, I can finally justify a reason to wake the household
and alert them of this glorious Christmas morning.

Katelyn Foley, Grade 9
West Jr High School, MO

Noise/Silence

Noise
Loud, rowdy
Shouting, annoying, disrupting
Chaos, confusion — peacefulness, calmness
Relaxing, sleeping, thinking
Tranquil, hushed
Silence

Amanda Weber, Grade 8
All Saints School, MO

Snow

Wow! Look at all that snow!
It seems like a winter wonderland.
In my hair, on my face it will blow.

More! More! I demand!
On to the fun, make the snowmen.
The snow, it looks like a harmonized band.

In the snow have you been?
Or down the hill on the sled?
After you go in, you can hardly bend.

The snow I want to be my bed.
I always love to throw snowballs.
You're addicted, my mom said.

In to dinner my mom calls.
No go to sleep with your dolls.

Jessica Schanuth, Grade 7
Center Place Restoration School, MO

My Mom

My mom is really fun and cool,
we talk every day after school.
Shopping, talking, laughing makes it fun.
She picks me up when I'm down,
because she knows just what to say.
Thinking of her makes me have a great day.

Katie Swinford, Grade 7
Highland Rim School, TN

A Dark Room

I was hiding in a gloomy room,
A room of death and fear.
Its presence overtook me
I could feel it coming near.
I leaned to the left, then to the right,
And there it was a glistening light.
I hoped to escape this dark, gloomy room,
But disappointment overtook me
I could feel it coming near.
Disappointment had a face
And it was a mirror.
I saw my face
And the face of many others,
The disappointed and the disappointers.
Which one am I?
Which one are you?
I'll give you a hint,
I'll give you a clue
Are you the one in the dark, gloomy room?

Kalah Pendleton, Grade 9
Family of Faith Christian School, OK

Love

You never knew it was coming.
Until one day you met this one person.
They really caught your eye.
So you start talking and flirting.
When you're with this person you feel like
Nothing could ever hurt you.
And you don't want this day to end.
Even if you were with your best friend,
You'd rather be with him/her!
You think you have found your one and only!
But the only problem is your parents.
They don't like the person the way you do.
They don't understand the way you feel
When you're with that person.
If only they would trust you,
Believe in you, or
Just trust you and believe what is right for you
Ok so you might think I'm writing this
Just for fun, but I know just how it feels.
I have gone through it all.
and always will.

Crystal Collins, Grade 7
Dayton City School, TN

School

School is like an open field,
it has a wide range of things.
It has math, reading, social studies,
and other things.
It's also like a tree
it has many branches too.
it has many fun things to do.
My favorite thing is recess
you can run, jump, and play.
but I can do that anyway.
Basically school is a lot of things
or any kind of way, now let's go play!

Dan Johnson, Grade 7
Wilson Middle School, OK

Fall

F alling leaves.
A ll around.
L oving the smell of pies.
L ots of family together on Thanksgiving.

Makala Stephens, Grade 7
Rocky Comfort Elementary School, MO

Fall

In the fall it is peaceful,
Like an open field of flowers,
Except for the leaves
which crunch under my feet.

The trees are yellow, red, and brown,
Swaying in the wind,
All the pumpkins are in the field,
either big or small.

The sky is dark and grey,
With clouds everywhere,
I am carving a pumpkin,
With a crooked mouth,
And large eyes.

I love the fall,
very much.

Dalton Hodges, Grade 7
Nettleton Jr High School, AR

My Heart

Take my heart and run with it,
but be careful what you do,
because if you run to far or fast,
you might end up breaking it,
and then I would not know what to do.
So hold my heart and cherish it,
until the day our time here on
earth is done and we go home.

Kayla Knox, Grade 8
Navajo High School, OK

My Inspiration

Everyone has an inspiration, and mine is my mom.
She always says, "You can do it," even when I don't think I can.
When I am sad, she makes it better, and when I am happy, she is too.
If I need help or have a problem, she is the first one I go to.
I know I can always count on my mom to be there when no one else is around.
With her short, brown hair and her big, blue eyes
I am glad to call her
my best friend and
my inspiration!

Cara Levi, Grade 7
White Station Middle School, TN

The Call

I picked up the phone and talked to my aunt.
The call which gave me the sad news,
that stunned me.
Why would God turn his faithful head away from my family?
I knew that my Uncle Paul now laid his ill head in silence on the pillow of peace.
I remember his positive attitude,
his bright, optimistic smile,
how he and I were so close,
how he was always a leader for the rest of our family and watched out for us always,
how he always told me to stay up when I was down,
always great advice I think about daily.
I hung up in tears.
Despair, Sadness, and Worriment raced wild in my busy head,
with Hope, Love, and Compassion wishing he was still there,
He has truly passed away.

Hannah Leigh Marsh, Grade 7
White Station Middle School, TN

Night Flight

Stillness encases me,
its arms enclosing me in warmth like my blanket soothing my ever weary soul.
I lie alone on my rickety mattress,
my eyelids drooping from the heavy weights upon them.
My mind wanders beyond the edges of the universe.
Tranquility and silence accompany me
as if the hands of the ticking clock have ceased
and the world has been frozen in ice.
I draw out my soul from my body,
severing the chains that connect my soul's pure edges
to my drained physical form.
I allow my spirit to reflect, to look into the window of the past,
evoking moments of fiery, burning triumph
and regretting those of icy, biting sorrow.
But the stillness gradually fades like a mist clearing over a vacant field.
My spirit begins to sink to earth,
having the burning desire to hold once again that intangible serenity.
My soul's feet lightly touch the ground,
returning to my body with great distress.
The heavenly calm that surrounds me
is shattered by the cacophony of beeps from my alarm clock.

Sarah Catanzaro, Grade 8
Baylor School, TN

Love

Love will never end. Love will never fade. Love will never go away. When I leave this dreadful world I hope that all my love extends to all the people like a dove soaring above the clouds. I wish for robbing, homicide, and abortion to disappear in the starry night sky which will soon have harmful gasses floating around in the air. I pray for all the people to love, and never forget the person above. I hope, wish, and pray.

Chelsea Howard, Grade 7
St Mary of the Woods School, KY

Can't Believe

I can't believe you don't like my dog just because he woke you up last night barking at the cat.
I can't believe you don't like my cat just because he claws you and sheds a lot.
I can't believe you don't like my horse because it's the second time this week you've hit the dirt.
I can't believe you don't like anything.

Stephony Webb, Grade 8
Rocky Comfort Elementary School, MO

Stage Fright

Life is like a stage.
Everyone is dancing for different purposes.
Many different songs are being played, and sometimes they all run together.
Just like performing on a stage, in life one can move left, right, up, down, and various other directions.
During this dance, both friends and enemies are made.
Sometimes people forget their lines, and then others have to cover for them.
Journeying through life is just like dancing on a stage.

Rachael Harmony, Grade 9
Bearden High School, TN

Morning

Morning is life
because God let you get up and live another day.
Morning is a Saturday soccer game
with my bottles of Gatorade used to quench thirst.
Morning is an awakening
when an alarm buzzes in an attempt to wake you with its annoying persistence.
Morning is fast food
for those whom McDonalds is a source of life.
Morning is a flower's opportunity to shine,
when it spreads its beautiful petals and glows in the sun.
Morning is a smell of freshness,
when all things are washed clean by the sparkling dew.
Morning is a cartoons golden age,
when kids wake up and immediately turn the TV on and the arguments over the control begin.
Morning is a cup of coffee and caffeine drinks,
which will eventually stunt your growth but you still drink it any way, cause you say it give you your energy.
Morning is death
For those who die and will either go to Heaven, or to Hell.

Montel Chan, Grade 8
Science Hill High School, TN

True Friends

When you lose a loved you, everyone feels sorry for you, a true friend prays for you. They will stay with you, no matter how long it takes, until you find the things you need. True friends will always be there to talk to when nothing is going the right way. True friends will hang on through the ups and down, because they have someone to believe in. When you cry enough to make a river of tears, they will make it so that a bridge is there. They do not do this because they can; they simply do it because they are my true friends.

Elizabeth Howard, Grade 7
St Mary of the Woods School, KY

Neverland

Above our snowy roof tops,
Within another dimension
About the hopes of many children
Beyond the second star to the right
Until forever we'll be children
For we are in Neverland
Up, up we go
Through the clouds
Past reality
Between hopes and dreams
During our childhood
Until forever
Along, sailing in the sea
Against fairy dust and Tinkerbell's wings
At the most wonderful time in my life
As I am now
Except I am never growing up
In my imagination

Eva Adams, Grade 8
Heritage Middle School, TN

Catch Me

I'm on top of the world,
I'm flying high now.
You say you are with me,
At least that's your vow.

But will you still be there
If I happen to fail?
Will you be by my side
When I'm tired and frail?

If things turn out wrong,
And good times turn bad,
Would you leave me behind
Like yesterday's fad?

For now, I still soar,
For now, I stand tall.
But will you catch me
On the day when I fall?

Meg Buckley, Grade 8
St Gerard Majella School, MO

Eyes of the Lord

The birds are singing
The children are playin'
All is good in the world.
A baby cries,
A man lies
All is good in the world.
No matter what happens each day,
All is still good in the eyes of the
Lord.

Hallie Moore, Grade 8
Perryville High School, AR

Carnival

The curvy and loopy roller coasters
Catch your eye as you walk in.
High pitched screams and rickety roller coasters fill your ears.
The sweet smell of cotton candy and melting nachos
Over power the nasty smell of vomit.
When you take a bite of a tasty cheeseburger,
or of those salty fries
Your taste buds go to heaven.
When you launch down that great big hill
on that great big roller coaster,
Don't worry, that hot protective padding will keep you safe.
And just remember the whole place is on a sandy beach in California.

Jesse McGee, Grade 7
Southern Boone Middle School, MO

The Flow

As water flows gracefully through the dark and discomfited forest
It brings to light scenery that was thought to have lost all hope
As it leaves the forest, it stretches to far ends of purple mountains
With water mimicking everything it sees
Fantastic fragrances fuming, making gloomy air more clear
Lively colors shining vividly
Making raging sun look like barely any light
While in full motion, streams break off
Causing birds to chirp and other animals to squeak
Flowers race to bloom first, just to see a beautiful stream
Now radiant sun is turning over and mystical moon is shining so brightly
Starlight gaze makes everything seem all right
Moon trying to compete with its mystical light
Only hoping to bring more to this astonishing sensation
And as water flows gracefully
It makes purple mountains, chirping birds, with other animals squeaking
A beautiful stream has more than enough reason
To be one definition of unbelievable
And as it flows into the dark and discomfited forest, it sheds light to all faces

Kameron Bottoms, Grade 8
Barret Traditional Middle School, KY

The Sense We Don't Have

You never know what's gonna happen next.
Something good could come,
or something bad could come —
You just never know!!
So it is true when they say life is full of taking chances —
You have to take a chance to get an outcome.

I think that's what we are all afraid of —
the sense of not knowing.
That will make us think harder than anything in the whole world!!
That's why we worry —
That's why we cry —
That's why we're scared —
It's because we don't have the sense to know.
It's scary I know, but it's the sense we don't have!

Ember Caruthers, Grade 8
Horace Mann Middle School, WV

Siege of Lightning

Rolling thunder in the clouds,
See the lightning flashing proud,
It streaks the sky with scratches long,
And shows the picture it has drawn,
Life stands by with frightened hearts,
And then the song birds sing like larks,
Because the siege of lightning now is gone,
It won't come again until next dawn.

AnnaMarie Morrison, Grade 8
Shepherdstown Middle School, WV

The Perfect Day

The leaves are rustling
And no one is a' bustling
It's a peaceful day in May
The flowers are swaying
And the trees seem to be saying,
"It's a perfect day."
Geese are squawking
The peacefulness is shocking
The sun is shining bright
The wind is fresh and cool
The sunset's like a jewel
Today everything seems right
The grass is soft and green
Bunnies are everywhere to be seen
The cliff overlooks the bay
The sea isn't stirring
Everything seems so luring — What can I say?
It's a perfect day!

Laura Clart, Grade 8
West Jr High School, MO

Boyfriend

I walked along a road today,
With thoughts of you on my mind.
My memories are a thousand miles away,
Thinking of what I must find.
My heart has a stinging glow,
The time to see you is getting near,
Love comes out in an overflow,
When I see you my dear.
I think about these things,
All the offers that it carries,
And all the joy it brings,
With the thought of getting married.
You arrive for our date out,
We question our whereabouts for the night,
Let's decide without a doubt,
We'll go walking under the moonlight.
I love you with all my heart,
We'll walk along hand in hand,
Through the years, we'll never part,
you will always be my man.

Rebecca Chick, Grade 8
Highland Rim School, TN

The Tall Tall Tree

Branches reaching,
The tall, tall tree towering over me,
Making a dark cold shadow on the dried, yellow grass.
Its leaves covering the ground
Making it golden brown.

Branches reaching,
The tall, tall tree towering over me,
Standing like a house on the neighborhood street.
Its long branches reach out
Sheltering me from rain and snow.

Branches reaching,
The tall, tall tree towering over me,
Marching tall and straight on the open field.
Like a soldier to a general
Saluting with its leaves.

Tessa Vellek, Grade 8
West Jr High School, MO

Heather

There once was a girl named Heather,
Who weighed as light as a feather.
She liked making jokes
To see if someone choked.
The thing that weighed her down was leather.

Rachel Calvert, Grade 7
Rocky Comfort Elementary School, MO

Calvin Lemley

We didn't know each other
Never saw each other's face
I saw him when he said bye to his mother
We just happened to be in the right place

We didn't talk much then
But boy do we now
Every time I hear his voice I grin
I don't want to like him, but I don't know how

I don't know if it would work out
Between him and I
But when we don't talk we both sit and pout
And when I think about life without him I start to cry

Hopefully one day we will meet again
We'll hug and kiss
Because we're more than friends
He's the one that I love and miss

Until that day comes
We will have to stick to talking friendly
But one day I'll get off my bum
And I'll say I love you Calvin Lemley

Hannah Fulmer, Grade 8
Mayflower Middle School, AR

Prepare for the Feast

It's that time of year when leaves start to change colors.
Grandma is running to her children one after another.

"Dear child, can you buy me a turkey that is plump like a roast?"
"But buy it at the cheapest price of all that is certainly affordable at the most."

"Oh my goodness, it's almost time for the feast, oh Tia, can you help me?"
"You need to make the salad, sweet potatoes, and sock-it-to-me, at least that's what I see."

So we're running around like maniacs trying to get everything done.
We've been up from eleven o'clock cooking and decorating until the morning sun.

Oh goodness, I need a rest.
Tonight is like a mad house, I know that at best.

It has been a long time since I tasted Grandma's famous cooking.
I'm going to have a bite of that cake, I hope no one's looking.

Lytia Lee, Grade 7
Nettleton Jr High School, AR

House on Steed Avenue

It lies there, the third house on the right coming off of Georgetown Road,
the house on Steed Avenue.
Mahogany bricks stand proud on the once chartreuse lawn, browned by the deprivations of water,
where shrubs and small trees lurk around the perimeter.
My love for the house never came easily.
I had once feared it, feared the idea of leaving what had once been my home,
the one we had previously inhabited and the first one I had ever lived in.
To this day, I occasionally coax my mother to drive by the house in Everhart.
The house remains the same, its pale green shudders appear dark in contrast to the white house.
The back yard fences where Hershey and Cara used to play remains.
I was six when we moved to the house on Steed Avenue.
I remember getting lost on the way to what was supposedly my room.
The house on Steed Avenue was not my home, not at heart.
The room that had been carefully selected by the process of elimination,
in other words my sister had the right as the first-born to pick her room before me, was not mine.
It took me years to finally claim the house on Steed Avenue as my own.
Now I have come to realize how much I appreciate it,
but it does not matter where the physical location of where one lives,
for home is where the heart is.

Laura Johnson, Grade 8
Baylor School, TN

You and Me

Sing the songs of sailboat sails and share all
of the wonderful tales of when we were small,
with our little hands in the air wishing we could be near those beautiful seas,
share the thoughts of all our nightmares and dreams.
Though we are twins we always win compared to you and me. The day you left me I could hardly see the light of day.
Though some people say that you are still with me, you are gone until the day I go away.
So wait for me among the stars,
for all of those moments are still mine and yours.
While you are in heaven and I am on earth,
I know that your life cannot get any worse.

Allison Rushing, Grade 8
Mayflower Middle School, AR

I Am

I am a girl who loves to draw.
I wonder if I will get better at it.
I hear the pictures flow.
I want to go to an art school.
I am a girl who loves to draw.

I pretend to be the greatest drawer.
I feel the wind blow against my face.
I touch the puffy white clouds.
I worry that I won't get better at drawing.
I cry when I mess up horribly.
I am a girl who loves to draw.

I understand how the pencil moves across the paper.
I say everyone can draw.
I dream of being a professional artist.
I try to draw lighter with my pencil.
I hope that I keep on drawing as I get older.
I am a girl who loves to draw.

Crystal Olney, Grade 8
King City High School, MO

A Love of Music

As I feel the rhythm pulse through my fingers,
I can sense a certain presence that lingers
A feeling of freedom and a notion of pride
A sensation of excitement bubbling inside.

High notes and low notes float through my mind,
All is forgotten as I relax and unwind.
Filled with the joy that music can bring,
So wondrous and blissful that some start to sing.

Teeming with a fantastic aura of peace,
I want it to last another hour at least.
Packed with pitches and notes, my head starts reeling,
But where else can I experience such a marvelous feeling?

Sadness hits while playing the last part of the tune,
For I know the song will be ending soon.
I do not know where and I do not know when,
But I cannot wait to play my music again!

Maria Orr, Grade 8
St Gerard Majella School, MO

Is It True?

Right now I'm pretty upset.
How can somebody do that?
They say love's very important to them.
They still cheat on you with someone else.
They say they love you but do they really mean it.
They say that you're all they ever wanted but is that true.
Basically don't believe everything
they tell you because they lie.

Kaylynn Summers, Grade 8
Southern Reynolds County R-II School, MO

My Home

Where I feel at home is a lush green football field
smelling freshly cut grass
and looking around at all the fans.
I feel at home when I put on
my red Baylor uniform, it's my battle armor
My home can also be in the locker room before the game.
I feel at home when I step onto a field that everyone has,
given all they had for the team
when I play under the lights,
at Heywood stadium
when I know we are going to beat
the rival before the game starts,
when I sack the quarter back,
or recover a football at the 10 yard line
Feeling the hard leather of the football
Getting pumped up before the game
Seeing the big red tiger paw,
or the big B painted out on the fifty yard line
That's when I feel at home

Barrett Gouger, Grade 8
Baylor School, TN

Her Eyes Saw

She dreamed of a world without prejudice,
one without anguish.
She knew one day she'd help the needy,
change the world.
Her heart was in her head, her head in her heart —
and she saw the end.

Tears flowed down her cheeks —
glowing with a light so radiant.
Tears grew life, harmony would remain.

Though young, life grew rapidly —
Her arms were waves, bringing
drowning ones to shore.
That day, blood spilled
but flowers sprang from it —
another Hyacinth.

Many never knew her but know her name.
They took her dream and
brought it alive.
Her eyes still watch,
but they had seen today before.

Elizabeth Albuquerque, Grade 9
Morgantown High School, WV

Bow Hunting

Bow hunting is hard
I'm not an Indian you know
I stick to the 270
Cause that's how I roll

Garrett Prince, Grade 8
Southern Reynolds County R-II School, MO

The Worst Day Ever

Woke up late
Missed the bus
Late for school
Failed a test
Tripped and fell
Lunch was cold
Got sent to the office
Stayed after for detention
Missed my favorite show
Got grounded
Worst day ever!

Samantha Moore, Grade 7
Rocky Comfort Elementary School, MO

Flying Bird

I dreamed
I was a bird
in the sky
getting shot at
constantly

Dennis Bendabout, Grade 8
Wickliffe Elementary School, OK

You and Me

When I saw you in the sixth grade
All I though about was you
I was so disappointed
Because you wouldn't let me through

You had a brick wall up
It was thicker than thick
I tried so hard to get you
But you played hard to get

You used to make fun of me
You used to laugh at me
But now I see…
It's all because you liked me

I was afraid to tell you how I felt
Because I was afraid of what you'd do
But today I've realized…
All I want is you

Alyssa Williams, Grade 9
St John the Baptist High School, MO

Falling Autumn

Fall leaves scattered on the ground,
turning just a little browned.
Running, hopping, skipping, playing,
someone else is also singing.
Fall leaves falling in the distance,
never need any assistance.

Ryan Warren, Grade 8
Wilson Middle School, OK

San Tran

San Tran
Short, Asian, Dude
Really likes Cajun food
I especially like the wings
Spicy!!!

San Tran, Grade 8
Belle Isle Enterprise Middle School, OK

Diddle-Dum-Fuss

Diddle-Dum-Fuss
Lives in a bus
Eats plenty of trash
No need for cash
"Boing-Boing" he does that
Pulls rabbits out of his hat
And that is that

Jake Blevins, Grade 7
Benton County School of the Arts, AR

A Different Point of View

My eyes are yellow
Yours are blue
But if I see no difference
Then why do you?
I have four paws
And a long tail
And you are quite fur less
And your skin is pale,
But we're not so different
Me and you
I only wish
You could see that too.
But I don't understand
Why you call me a beast
You could call me a creature
At the very least,
But we're not so different
Me and you
Just remember I,
Have a different point of view

Abby Kinghorn, Grade 7
Seven Holy Founders School, MO

Que Es Amor?

What is love?
Romance
Feelings
Being there for one another
Heart touching
Heartfelt emotions
Communication
Happiness
That is love.

Lucy Andrade, Grade 7
Newcastle Middle School, OK

The United States

The United States
is a free country
The United States
has laws that we
are supposed to
follow and rules
that we sometimes break.
The United States
is a free country.

The United States
is an honorable country
The United States
has helped the poor
and fought in war
but it is still standing
The United States
is an honorable country

The United States
is a wonderful
country the colors
red, white and blue,

Sabrina Murillo, Grade 7
Clarksburg School, TN

Where Is School Pride

Why do I feel the shame
When I take someone else's blame
What does it say about school,
When you gotta be bad to be cool
I can't go to the dance
I can't take the chance
When a kid's got a gun
It's just not any fun
I'd like to take pride
But I'd just rather hide
Kids with babies
Couldn't they say no instead of maybe
The principal seems sincere
But where's the kid's fear
There's endless drugs
But where's the pride in hugs.

Jessica Wilcox, Grade 9
Alpena High School, AR

Summer Time Is Gone

Summer time is gone,
oh what a bummer!
It was fun,
but sometimes it was boring
well maybe next year,
it won't be storming.

Audrey Battiest, Grade 7
Wilson Middle School, OK

Christmas Time

Christmas is here.
Presents under Christmas trees,
Talking and giggling make happy people,
Snow falling.
The sun gleaming on fresh fallen snow.
Children playing snowball fights.
Kids with newly opened presents.
Candles lit,
People sit,
Dinners here,
Let's bring in the new year!

Courtney Boles, Grade 8
Rocky Comfort Elementary School, MO

I Am

I am a sports loving and active person.
I wonder if I will go to KU for a sport.
I hear fans cheering as loud as they can.
I see my teammates by my side.
I want to go to KU.
I am a sports loving and active person.
I pretend to be the best when I'm around people.
I feel bumps on the basketballs and footballs.
I touch the footballs and basketballs.
I worry that I will get injured.
I cry when I get shut out really really bad.
I am a sports loving and active person.
I understand that I won't always win.
I say I'm pretty good.
I dream I will go to KU.
I try to get better at sports.
I hope I go to KU.
I am a sports loving and active person.

Preston Scott Vannaman, Grade 7
King City High School, MO

Christmas Time

The year is gone
It's time again for
Shopping and fun
Gatherings and parties
All around to spread the joy
Of Christmas

People are decorating
Going nuts over what to get
No matter who wants it
People searching all around
For that one thing for that one special someone

The time has come to get together
For the fun but
Most of all the reason for the season
So merry Christmas

Ashley Brown, Grade 8
Houston Middle School, TN

Chain Reaction

Somebody smiles
so everything, everybody, everyone smiles
but if anybody, anyone, or everything frowns
and somebody, someone, something frowns
so always smile
never frown
and everyone around the world
will be happy
whoo-who!

Hailey Ownby, Grade 8
Pigeon Forge Middle School, TN

Envy

Envy is dark and gloomy
It tastes like something unknown
It smells like rotten milk
It reminds me of death and sin
It sounds like threatening voices in your head
Envy makes me feel nonexistent

Abbie Branch, Grade 7
Benton County School of the Arts, AR

My Brother's Room

To cross my brother's room,
You must get past the upstairs hall,
But the stench of his room nearing
Makes your insides crawl.
Holding your breath, you grasp the doorknob
And open the creaky door.
At one glance, you shiver.
Now you may have nightmares forevermore.
You slowly take a step forward
And cautiously look around.
Scattered video games, and tossed cards,
and sweaty socks all lie on the ground.
On the shelves are broken trophies and clothes, dirty and clean.
Near the corner are torn stuffed animals,
And beware of a week old sandwich
or an open cup of Danimals.
Make sure to dodge the Bionicles
as you walk past his guitar.
You may trip or stumble over many obstacles.
Some of his things may seem a bit bizarre.
Now you have survived and crossed my brother's room.

Abby Stewart, Grade 8
St Gerard Majella School, MO

My Chemical Romance

Bob starts off, banging on drums,
Ray and Frank follow with their screeching guitar strums.
Mikey's bass playing slowly comes in,
Leading up to a thrill that's about to begin.
The singing and screaming of Gerard Way's voice
Is what makes My Chemical Romance my musical choice.

Madeline Menius, Grade 8
St Gerard Majella School, MO

Moms

They can be loving and caring,
Or they can be mean and hateful,
But no matter what,
They will always love you.

They are always there,
Be it homework or sports,
Family or life,
They are always there.

Tyler Logan, Grade 8
All Saints' Episcopal School, TN

Baseball

Whether the crack of the bat
Or the colored hats
Or the sound of the ball
Going over the wall
In the rain or the snow
The players make the show

Some may say to cheat is the way
But in baseball that's not how we play
You only get three strikes, and you're out
But if you stay and play like a pro
You'll blow the ball out
And put on a show

The fans in the stands
Cheer for their team
And clap their hands
In the rain or the snow
I'll be there
Yelling go team go

Tyler Offutt, Grade 8
Shepherdstown Middle School, WV

Creations of My Imagination

From my mind it flows
Through my hand like so.
From there to my brush
And the bristles just go.
From bristles to page
Page to eyes
The artwork resides now
In both you and I.

Rachel Ghazarian, Grade 8
St Gerard Majella School, MO

Lilly

Lilly
Chubby, cute
Fast, playful, loving
The best
A dog

Elizabeth Barsch, Grade 8
Avenue City Elementary School, MO

Pain

Everyone goes through pain.
Some physical, some emotional, some spiritual, and some a mix of the three.
Sometimes we go through so much emotional pain we experience physical pain.
Sometimes we need to let it all out through sobs in the pillow.
Sometimes we need to run or go outside and scream.
Sometimes it hurts so bad we can do all these and more but it won't leave.
Sometimes your heart hurts from it all.
Sometimes we refuse to cry.
Pain, Pain, go away and leave me with joy.

Raelynn Bennett, Grade 8
Avenue City Elementary School, MO

Him

He means the world to me. He is all I wanna see.
He means everything to me, just to hold him and sit on his knee.
I wanna hold him close, wanna hold him the most.

Wanna hear his voice, when I hold him and hear him, I will rejoice.
I wanna hear his beautiful voice near me. To be close to him is my final plea.
I wanna hold him close, wanna hold him the most.

Wanna hear a story told in his beautiful singing. The sound is in my head lingering.
Hold on to the sound tight, I have to fight.
I wanna hold him close, wanna hold him the most.

I have to fight to stay alive, once he left me alone and deprived.
He is back. I hear his voice and feel his embrace I have lacked.
I wanna hold him close, wanna hold him the most.

Amanda Ogle, Grade 9
Bearden High School, TN

My Playground

As I walk out the doors to go to the playground.
The first thing I see are some boys trying to play ball of some kind.
I take a few more steps to see the wannabes,
All dress up as someone they're not.
Then I see the jocks.
On the basketball court,
Out on the field are the football players.
As I move more into the playground.
I see the heavy metal boys,
All in black, all around their table.
As I go to…
I turn right into some girlie girls,
A.K.A. preps!
I take a few steps backward then they started to laugh and giggle.
I turn around and shake my head and started walking again.
I get to the end of the playground where I hang with mine,
Friends, family, homies.
I turn around to look at all of us out here.
I stop to thank how we all are,
Lost, alone, afraid, scared.
Then it hits me, all of us are alike.

Savanna L. Swift, Grade 8
Chouteau Mazie Middle School, OK

Fall

Being back at school is like being hypnotized by learning,
Fall leaves scatter on the ground like ants,
They crunch like a burnt patty,
They look like a bad sunburn,
But that's okay,
Because it's fall!

Karena Casares, Grade 8
Wilson Middle School, OK

Aim High, Make Your Move

There's more to life than just dreaming
Yes, that's only the beginning
A spark starting in the heart
Aiming high thoughts soaring to the sky
You have to do it get out and try
The obstacles may be tall, you may fall
Get up with might, undaunted by the sight
Keep going
Falling, you have not failed, you fail when you don't try
Aim high
When there's a will, there is a way
If you want it to be, it needs to be
You must see, needing to believe
That you can
With the strength of a man or feebleness of a woman
Make your move
Take a stand
When you succeed accomplishing your need
The dream fulfilled feeling thrilled
You are strong like singing a sweet song
Just the same you overcame

Kalli Ann Wilkens, Grade 7
Jellico SDA School, TN

The Guitar Man

The stage is set,
Left hand on the fifth fret,
Now I regret that fourth cigarette.

The time is near,
That is blatantly clear.
I have no fear of the people here.

I'm about to perform.
The crowd is a storm.
That is hardly the norm, I am gladly informed.

With a pick in my hand,
I'm at destiny's stand.
My fingers look like sand, coarse and tanned.

I pluck the first string,
There is no equivalent thing.
The chords now spring as I begin to sing.

Tom Blood, Grade 8
St Gerard Majella School, MO

The Special Holiday

Waking up from a deep sleep,
I walk into the den finding a mountain of toys.
I scream. I shout. I dance!
Almost waking up everybody in the world,
I dive into the pile of toys as if it was a swimming pool,
Finding just what I wanted.
Did Mom and Dad go to the North Pole and talk to Santa?
Lying there in a plethora of toys, I destroy the wrappings,
And glancing upward, I located my sister
Wearing the look of a shocked deer.
She and I open all of the presents.
When the gifts are decimated,
We dash to wake up our parents.
Unnn, stoppppp! Go to sleeeep!
In bed like sacks of potatoes,
We get them up, finally,
To share in our celebration.

Jared Moses, Grade 7
White Station Middle School, TN

Have You Ever Sat and Thought?

Have you ever sat and thought,
About why the world goes round?
Have you ever sat and thought,
About those animals in the pound?
Have you ever sat and thought,
About why a windmill blows?
Have you ever sat and thought,
About how the grass grows?
Well if you haven't sat and thought,
About any of those things,
You should get up and start to spread your wings.
Fly high, like the birds in the sky.

Julee Lee Sheng Tin, Grade 7
Blessed Teresa of Calcutta School, MO

Cardinals 2006 Playoff Run

It's in October and the playoffs are at its peak,
And the St. Louis Cardinals are on a hot streak.

Playing the Mets in the NLDS was tough,
But the Cardinals won game seven by just enough.

The sound of cheers and cries of joy
Another playoff win, oh boy, oh boy.

The sight of the World Series straight ahead
Their hopes and dreams never to dread.

When they arrived they came to play,
Showcasing their grit and talent each day.

And in the end the Cardinals had won
Beating the Tigers, the unexpected was done.

John Grigone, Grade 8
St Gerard Majella School, MO

Nervous

Talents crumbled
By a

Booing voice

Hearts flail and shudder
Tears gather

A strained voice

Cheers
Happiness
Talents rebuilt

Anika Johnson, Grade 8
Belle Isle Enterprise Middle School, OK

My Escape Route

To slip between
their covers is
the sweetest bliss
to lose myself
in another's
problems of life.
I forget all
my own life's doubt.
But worth nothing
to one but me
these treasures bring
no gold, but lie
on humble shelves,
my favorite books.

Katelyn Mercer, Grade 8
Center Place Restoration School, MO

The Wisest Gift

They are blue and green
Oh boy! They are fast
swift as the wind
powerful as a tiger
slick as grease
Man oh! Oh man! Are they fast!

They rise so high
covering the right parts.
They are irresistible
as if sirens,
It's not their song though.

They are the wisest gift,
as if of the Magi.
Gold nor silver can buy these.
Classic as if they belong in a museum.

They are my sneakers!

Brandi Jackson, Grade 9
Prue High School, OK

Stunning Stream

I see slick, shiny, shimmering, smooth water,
I stroll down intriguing rocky beaches,
I see trees playing tag,
They sway back and forth hitting each other,
Crystal water is like a snake, I watch it slither down vivid mountains,
Thrilling waterfalls gushing down water,
Complaining as it never stops moaning,
Kids doing somersaults as they jump off large rocks,
Incredible mountains, like waves as they roll over glamorous land.
Heaven shining down beams of light, seeing them hitting mysterious water,
Astonishing water, crystal clear,
Clean enough to drink.
Sensational wind howls, gliding across the jagged mountains,
Birds fluttering around singing sweetly with howling wind,
I look and I ask, Water, where do you go?
It's beauty to my eyes, this wonderful mountain stream,
It's almost as though I am in a dream,
Trains chugging up mountains,
Fish swimming in coves.
I will always remember this stream,
It's a wonderful place.

Jason Campbell, Grade 7
Barret Traditional Middle School, KY

I Am Thankful For…

I am thankful for friends and family
There are some people with no family or friends
to talk about problems in the world
I am thankful for sports
Some people aren't able to play sports due to injuries
they might have been born with
I am thankful for food
People in other countries may not have money
to put food on the table so they starve
I am thankful for love
There are people in the world that are not loved
so they take it out on innocent people
I am thankful for God
Unlucky people in other places may be forced not to believe in God
And most of all I am thankful for computers
Without them I would not have been able to type this beautiful poem

Ryan Janni, Grade 8
Avenue City Elementary School, MO

Just Don't Matter

I may live in the ghetto.
And look like a gang banger that has the wrong attitude,
But I know deep down inside that I don't tell messed up lies.
Plus don't hang with teens that ain't pretty inside.
I go to school and tell kids not to listen to rap video rhymes,
They may not listen but I try and try.
People tell me every day that living in the ghetto won't get you no place,
But to me it just don't matter.
Along as I get my education to help me along the way.

Karessa Burnham, Grade 8
Academy of Kansas City, MO

Hunting

H unting for things that move
U sually you'd see something
N ever gets boring seeing what God created
T hinking about wildlife (and looking for)
I nteresting sights
N ever getting tired of nature
G etting the animals to come out

Kody Payne, Grade 7
Hartville Jr/Sr High School, MO

Bryttney Dixon

I met this girl with a
Silky, sandy, warm
Wouldn't-let-go-of-touch
From the dazzling blue sea.
She smells like a sweet-scented
Fragrance from the heavens.
I see a tempting, mellow scream
From beyond the eyes,
Piercing for attention.
A young lady, a little girl,
Who is introduced with
A thunder of voices
From beyond the mountains
And a rage of light
From the creeping sunrise.

Sidney Matthews, Grade 7
Lee A Tolbert Community Academy, MO

Imagine

Imagine a world where the wind blows so soft.
And laughter and joy is heard frequent and oft.
Where you know if you're sad there are places to go.
A soft shoulder to cry on as you let your pain go.

Now imagine that world on a bright summer's day.
As you stand there and watch it all get torn away.
After three months of mourning you're in a new school.
When you're the youngest and the dumbest, you feel like a fool.

For the warmth that you loved has blown off on the breeze,
Now you're shivering and cold always ill at ease.
You flee from the lunchroom and dash for the stairs.
Knowing no one will find you because nobody cares.

And as tears streak your face at noon every day.
You wonder if ever, you won't feel this way.
Imagine a world of deception and fear,
Of lies, drinks, and drugs that don't belong here.

And imagine just what you do,
If this new scary life came upon you?
I need you right now so please stay with me friend,
Through this nightmare of change until we reach the end.

Cassie Jackson, Grade 7
Wainwright Elementary School, OK

Grief Is My Master

On the night of Thanksgiving
I received the news
That no one is thankful for
My friend is dying from a disease with no cure
My tears are all gone
From the sleepless nights I spent crying
She tries to fix it
She tries to comfort me
I look at her and say I'm all right
But my heart aches and an old scar is opened
I think of the time we spent together
And I cry some more
My grief is my master
I obey its whim
Because that old wound is open with the loss of a friend
My tears are all gone
I try to smile
But inside I cry
She is happy for the last few months
When her time is up
Begins my year of sleepless nights with tears.

Jorhdon Hardcastle, Grade 8
Benton County School of the Arts, AR

Between the Pages

On top of a bed,
Under a tree,
Laying on a couch,
Close to the sea.
Inside a plane,
Near a stream,
Outside your house,
Before you dream.
Between the pages of a book.
Inside your head, your imagination is running wild.

Evan Nelson, Grade 8
Heritage Middle School, TN

Cracked Orange Wing

The not so optimistic butterfly swoops down
as she lies on tall pink and white flowers.
Falling every time it flaps,
the butterfly adjusts to the wind.
With its cracked orange wing
it has a unique pattern
unlike no other.
Of beauty,
the little girl dreams,
outside her cracked, tsunami childhood.
She lifts her feet off the ground,
like a wave lifting off a film of seaweed.
She spreads her wings and her wounds heal.
She soars through the air without worry,
then crashes onto the earth's pink and white flowers.

Kelly Pannell, Grade 8
Baylor School, TN

Ocean Magic

Soothing sounds on the oceans waves.
The sound's calm,
the thoughts of those listening.
They listen quietly,
like a mouse.
Remembering the
memories lost.
Running through the forest
in our minds.

As the ocean sings its melody.
People have fun in the
warm sand, the cold water.
While the bad memories
are hurting them,
dissolved by those
that make them loved.

Michelle Nguyen, Grade 9
St John the Baptist High School, MO

Let Him In

Jesus
came in
light shows all around
and darkness became deceased
joy is everywhere
love flies high
people happy
laughing and singing
believe to see
spread love
— AWAKEN —
love spread
see to believe
singing and laughing
happy people
high flies love
everywhere is joy
deceased became darkness and
around all shows light
in came
Jesus

Stephanie Parker, Grade 8
Benton County School of the Arts, AR

Music

Music can be soft
Music can be loud
Music can be sad
And music can be proud
Music can be made with instruments
And even with hands
Music can be made with drums
And music can be made with pans

Haiden Katt, Grade 7
Benton County School of the Arts, AR

The Girl in the Mirror

When I look in the mirror, I don't see myself.
I see a girl who really needs help.
All her life has been a struggle
When all she wanted was to be hugged and snuggled.
She never realized her talking would come back
And she would have to make up for what she lacks
Because she missed it all while talking and now
She's walking a lonely path toward a dark place
Oh, how she wishes she would've applied herself
Because, for this, is not where she needs to be
She's smart and talented she's just being challenged
And so far she's losing, all of her pain is oozing out in her tears
She has so many fears. Will she stay a part of the class of 2012?
Well, she really doesn't know. Will all this hard work and effort show
Will it come to her rescue when she needs it the most
Or will this all just turn out to be one great big hoax
Oh, if it is, it really isn't funny anymore. I could just die and lie flat on the floor.
But I have a life to live and a lot to give!
For I'm me, myself and I shall overcome. With God on my side I will overcome!
There's nothing I can't do because the girl in the mirror,
Is true to herself and can do anything and so can you.

Kendra Townsend, Grade 8
White Station Middle School, TN

Permit Me to Tell You About Swimming

Permit me to tell you about swimming
The endless hours at the pool,
The four main strokes: backstroke, breaststroke, butterfly, and freestyle,
The early morning meets,
The trips to the many different pools.
But the swim meet I remember the most
Left me excited and wanting to swim some more,
Knowing that I had improved my times in each of my events,
Having so much fun cheering my friends on,
And swimming my hardest until my legs felt like Jell-O.

Katie DeAvilla, Grade 8
All Saints School, MO

The Perfect DS Game

1. First start with a sack full of game chips.
2. Then add a batch of megabytes.
3. Meanwhile mix in a saving card.
4. Now mix it all together while adding fantastic graphics.
5. Then pour it into a big pot to let it sit.
6. Then test the new game and get rid of the bugs and glitches.
7. Add some mini games for something to do when you're bored.
8. Then let it cook in the oven for 12 minutes at 70 degrees F.
9. Now let it cool for 20 seconds.
10. Now put a teaspoon of color and stir well.
11. Now add characters and stir it twice.
12. Next reheat oven to 60 degrees C.
13. Next take it out carefully and pour it into its case and let it cool for an hour.
14. Take it out of its case, name it and enjoy!!

Alex Schulz, Grade 7
Meredith-Dunn School, KY

School

Today as school
flew by like a breeze
I looked outside
and saw leaves falling off of trees
they were on the ground,
laying around
no homework today for me!

Shyann Henderson, Grade 8
Southern Reynolds County R-II School, MO

Fat Is Beautiful Too

So what, I'm overweight.
Does that make me less important, less of a person than you?
Fat is beautiful too.
So what, I can't run as fast as you.
Do I have to prove myself to you? No.
Fat is beautiful too.
So what, I eat more than the normal person.
Does that mean I shouldn't be treated like a person? No.
Fat is beautiful too.
So what, I can't fit a size small.
Does that mean I should starve myself so I can? No.
Fat is beautiful too.
So what, I don't fit your description of beautiful.
Do I care? No.
Fat is beautiful too.
So what, you don't like me for who I am.
Does that mean I have to change for you? No
Fat is beautiful too.
So what, I get made fun of.
Am I ashamed? No.
Fat is beautiful too.

Sheena Riley, Grade 9
Niangua High School, MO

Tarryn

I was sitting there just watching people pass by
When a girl with brown hair came in the room
She was kind and pretty without a care,
But deep in her eyes you could see the pain,
The despair that held her imprisoned for so many years.
The pain from losing who she was,
The suffering that came from her leg.
She could not stop it and she never would,
But she did not need to run, jump, and swing
Because all that she wanted to do was sing.
So she went and she left my sight
To go tell the story of her life.
She sang it at the top of her lungs
And let nothing stop her.
She had reclaimed who she was,
A confident, beautiful, wonderful person
And that is the girl I am proud to call my sister.

McKenna Hamman, Grade 7
Greenfield Jr/Sr High School, MO

Chocolate Kiss

I look at my desk and what do I see?
A small teepee wrapped in foil in front of me

It looks like a small mountain in the sun
It feels like a smooth rock with a lot of fun

It smells like heaven with a cocoa mill
It sounds like paper lying very still

It tastes like chocolate and heaven too
I'm eating a Hershey Kiss let me chew

Trent Osceola, Grade 7
Heritage Hall School, OK

Why?

Why do we do the things we do
Why do we say what we say.
Why do we ask why
Have you ever wondered why
Is it a thought, is it a feeling.
Why should we care. You say why
And I say it too
Maybe you know why
Would you tell me
Have you ever hurt someone and made them cry
I bet the first thing that came to mind was why
I hate how you can go a day
Without hearing why
So I will end this now by just saying why!

Robert Oliphant, Grade 9
Grandview Alternative School, MO

Staying Inside the Lines

Staying inside the lines was a lot easier
When I was six.
The smooth crayon glided across the page,
Making rich colorful marks.
The lines clearly drawn; black and bold, easy to see.
Staying inside the lines has a whole new meaning
Now that I'm fourteen.
It seems that every comment
Crosses someone's line.
Instead of a smooth, clean picture,
Smears and jagged lines stick out from the pages of life.
The lines are not defined.
Every person has a different picture;
Some people's pictures have bold lines,
They stand out.
Some people's lines are hidden from sight.
Instead of crayons,
Permanent markers are used.
There's no erasing if the marker strays.
I wish I could stay inside the line.
It was a lot easier when I was six.

Jessica Vaughn, Grade 9
West Jr High School, MO

About Angel

A ngel
N ice and funny
G ood at talking on the phone
E nergetic
L oveable

B ubbly
O ver happy
W alking to see my friends
E very day exciting
R eady to win
S assy

Angel Bowers, Grade 7
Ketchum Jr High School, OK

Shooting Star

Standing in the light,
Wishing for a star,
Hoping things would get better.
Crickets creep, and mice weep,
Not making anything better.

I stare in the night,
Looking for a shooting star
And thinking life would soon be better.
I cry in the light, not seeing a star,
And know I will be miserable for life.

I turn around, seeing a star,
And wished life would get better.
I opened my eyes,
Screaming and crying.
My wish had finally come true.

Susan McMahon, Grade 8
Musselman Middle School, WV

Family

You might fight.
You might yell.
You might laugh.
You might cry.
Through all of this,
you know that you will
love each other
'til the end of time.
Together you are strong.
Apart you are weak.
Your love is stronger
than fear and hate.
Your family will always be
there for you
when the long road
through life
gets rough.

Tara Carter, Grade 7
Elkton School, TN

Fall

Going back to school is like waiting for a catastrophe to happen, anxious...
Fall leaves strewn about like dancing swirls of red hot fire.
A warning that old man winter is well on his way...
AND SANTA! YAY PRESENTS! WOOO!

Dakota Roses, Grade 8
Wilson Middle School, OK

Snowberry

I am five.
The outdoors is my playground.
I walk outside and see with joy what God gave.
The ground is laden with snow.
Winter has taken its toll on my yard.
The flowers have long been shriveled, and the trees are still bare.
Mama says, "Go have fun. But no goin' near the road."
We scurry to piles of snow that smile back at us.
We take up our positions for war.
I am the general. My brother is a soldier.
My opponent shares my blood. I am five.
After I shamefully raise the white flag,
I begin to wonder what victory tastes like?
Afterwards, we promptly begin building
the tallest snowman ever built.
Our snowman is Honest Abe.
He sees the plant life around him as tiny shacks.
I wonder why he grows so tall, and why I can't copy him.
I pull out my blue, round sled we use to surf down the hill.
After many hours of exhaustion,
the sun creeps past the horizon.

Tyler Blackmon, Grade 8
Baylor School, TN

Blink

You always think that when they say it is just for the best
You imagine that they are just
Giving excuses, making up lies
But they really just want closer family ties
They know what they are talking about
When you storm off and go pout
When you go in your room, scream into your pillow
And just wish your parents were a little more mellow
Next time this happens, just stop and think
That they, like everybody else, could be gone in a little blink
It could all be gone, your house, family, even your life
When your parents ask you to do something and you just sigh
Remember, it could be gone in the blink of an eye
When you are mad because you have to mow the lawn
Remember, with a blink, it could all be gone
If you want to go outside and play, but instead you're out back rakin'
Remember with a blink it could all be taken
When you open your mouth to start lying, just stop speaking
Remember, with a blink it could all be seeping
Out of reach, out of control, out of mind, with all of your sneaking
Wouldn't life be better without all of the blinking?

Taylor Doubek, Grade 8
Clever Middle School, MO

Appreciation of Nature

The resonance of cheerful birds,
and the rushing of air past leaves.
The warm welcoming of the sun awaits,
with just the opening of a door.

Moist cushions of green grass surround,
and trees protect with their height.
Changing colors of leaves,
And the chirping of afternoon crickets.
The lingering aromas of strawberries remain,
even after being picked long ago.
The brilliant red shine of the sunset,
And the crisp sunrise glisten.

A release of all emotions,
and a never ending relaxation.

Selma Padilla, Grade 7
White Station Middle School, TN

Skateboarding

Skateboarding's cool, skateboarding's fun,
I love to do it in the sun.
You might wipe out, you might get hurt,
you might even eat some dirt.
But don't get mad, don't get sad,
and especially don't take it out on your dad,
I think you know,
you can't skate in snow,
I think it's best if you go.

Aaron Jones, Grade 8
Highland Rim School, TN

Swim Practice

Imagine a pool with ice cubes floating around
This place is called 'Mizzou'
After we work our abs
After we run a bunch
Then you start to ache all over
Oh the horror of Meagan
Walking in the boys bathroom
The water is freezing
So I wear a cap
This keeps me from turning into an ice cube
I get in and swim
I feel like I am dying
Because I just did a whole fifty meters
With only two breaths
As I am gasping
Turn around and do twelve more
Finally after swimming the Arctic Ocean
It is kind of cold
So go take a shower!
Eat, homework, sleep
This day is over

Luke Ragsdell, Grade 8
West Jr High School, MO

Our Heroes

A soldier is an honorable man,
A hero left unknown.
Everything they give for us,
Is everything they own

When people think of soldiers,
They think of guns and bombs,
When I think of soldiers,
I think of ordinary dads and moms.

I think of our country's heroes,
Risking everything they've ever gotten.
And because they give the ultimate sacrifice,
May they never be forgotten.

I feel we should highly respect these people,
Their actions keep us free.
They keep this country safe and secure
For people like you and me

Connor Bennett, Grade 7
Seven Holy Founders School, MO

Happiness

If happiness was a color,
it would be green
As calm as a field and still summer.
If happiness was a feeling,
it would be as warm as the summer sun.
If happiness was a smell,
it would be birthday cake as a delighting scent.
If happiness was a sound,
it would be kids' laughter
as a game was being played.

Shelby Flood, Grade 7
Newcastle Middle School, OK

The Reason

Why be sitting on your toosh,
When you could be making a swoosh.
Why be shopping at the mall,
When you could be playing basketball.
Why be taking pills,
When you could be doing basketball drills.
Why be getting in fights,
When you could see a wonderful basketball sight.
Why be a cheerleader rooting,
When you could be a basketball player shooting.
Why be sitting on the ground,
When you could be getting a rebound.
Why be talking to your sibling,
When you could be in the gym dribbling.
Don't' be sleepy and lazy,
Because if you don't play basketball, you are Crazy!

Destany Wooten, Grade 8
Chelsea Jr High School, OK

Football

Tons of complete passes
Yard breaking runs
A lot of sacks
Recovering fumbles
Bone crushing hits
Tons of flags
Wives think you're at work.
Bosses think you're sick.
Football is here!

Travis Meador, Grade 7
Rocky Comfort Elementary School, MO

Margie the Evil Twisted Baby Sitter

Margie the evil twisted baby sitter
Ran up and down the streets
Looking for a baby sitting job

When parents went out
Margie turned into
An evil twisted baby sitter

When the parents came back
Margie turned into a little sweetheart
And the kids never fought again

Margie Sandlin, Grade 7
Van-Cove High School, AR

My World

Out the door
Through the grass
Across the rocks
Along the trail
Past the trees
Toward the hills
Beyond the bridge
Between the fence
During the spring
Among the sunlight
The little place of peace

Halie Reefer, Grade 8
Heritage Middle School, TN

The New Fallen Snow

Children playing in the new fallen snow,
Happiness and joy wherever you go.
The sound of carolers fills the air,
It is so cold, but no one seems to care.
Kids having snowball fights,
People putting up Christmas lights.
When it gets dark, we put up the tree,
Next to the window so that all can see.
Happiness and joy wherever you go,
Children playing in the new fallen snow.

Ashlee Armon, Grade 8
Owasso 8th Grade Center, OK

Autumn Senses

Gooey pumpkin pie
Crunchy, dead leaves, raked in piles
Cider after walks.

William Slonaker, Grade 7
Musselman Middle School, WV

The Ocean

The ocean
Is a very big, deep, blue place
Where life flourishes
An endless place full of salty water
And fish of all sizes
Scary to most, beautiful to others
Ships of love, treasure, and war
Have fallen to their death
Forever on the bottom of the sea
A reflection of the misty sky
Makes the water a wonderful place

Kayla Burlette, Grade 9
Grandview Alternative School, MO

Winter

Winter is really
Nice and cold,
The second snow
Is always bold,
Winter makes
Everything white,
But it's still
Black at night,
Making snowmen
And riding the sleigh,
Drinking hot cocoa
All day,
Watching TV
In your pajamas,
Wishing you were
In the Bahamas.

Levi Pitts, Grade 7
Benton County School of the Arts, AR

Softball

Cold dewy nights;
Big glaring lights.

The wind in your face;
As you run past second base.

The sand in your hair;
Dive, your glove and the ball, a pair

Your hands leading the bat, "Ting;"
I will forever remember "that ring."

Johnica Hanke, Grade 8
Rocky Comfort Elementary School, MO

Money

Money very nice to have.
Yet have we stopped to think
it's just a piece of paper.
It tells us whether we're rich or poor.
Tells us whether we sleep outdoors
or in a warm house.
Tells us whether we eat or starve.
Tells us if we walk or drive a car.
Tells us if we get clothes or not.
It tells us all these things
and yet it's just a piece of paper.

Zack Boehmann, Grade 7
St Mary of the Woods School, KY

Christmas Carolers

Christmas carolers singing,
going form door to door,
their bells and voices ringing,
everyone wanting more.

Christmas carolers leaving,
everyone shouting NO!
Then they just keep on singing
'till it starts to snow.

Christmas carolers dancing,
singing "Jingle Bell Rock."
They just keep on singing
'till they have to stop.

Kealsie Hale, Grade 7
Center Place Restoration School, MO

Rainy Weather

Trudging through the water
Wishing it was hotter

Snuggled in my coat
That's keeping me afloat

Raining all day
Wishing it will go away

Creeks overflowing
Man how I wish it was going

Will it ever stop
Mom yells Johnny get the mop

Houses are leaking
Mothers are freaking

When it clears
Everyone cheers

Jonathan Darnell, Grade 7
Meredith-Dunn School, KY

Tragic Love

Have you ever experienced tragic love?
The kind of love that is unheard of.
It cannot be found in a fairy tale.
It can't be cast in a love spell.
It is the kind of love that drives you insane.
This type of love will cause you misery and pain.
This type of love will cause you to cry.
It will make you look to the God above and ask why.
This kind of love is when you love someone.
And then that someone decides that you are no fun.
It doesn't sound bad if you haven't experienced it.
But if you have you know what Tragic Love is
You know it will cause you to quit.

Dillon Green, Grade 8
Mayflower Middle School, AR

Kechell

As she sits in class
I can tell she is not outspoken
But screams with talk at home
With her friends.
Her eyes are as deep
As the Grand Canyon with thoughts,
Her heart is as tender as a humming bird
Singing in a tree.
It looks like she could be as wild
As a heated rhinoceros,
And here I sit like a lost penguin
In an Arctic Blizzard.

Desmond Banks, Grade 7
Lee A Tolbert Community Academy, MO

The Race for Life or Death

Jumping onto the back of my awaiting stead
Who at the slightest touch
bolts and weaves through the trees
I bend low over his muscular neck
his mane teases my face as it whips in the wind
Our movements and breathing are one
as are the beats of his hooves
and the beats of my heart
With evil in quick pursuit
we define speed racing for that life giving place
where evil dare not go near
As we dart around the bend
I can see the light up ahead
I hear evil gaining ground
I dare not look behind into evil's eyes
I urge my trusted stead on toward the light
and I pray with all my might
In an instant we were surrounded by the light
we made it to the place of life
where evil dare not go near

Shawnie Marvin, Grade 8
Chelsea Jr High School, OK

Souls Betrayed

A dark cloud looms ominously overhead
It brings a violent storm of rage with it
A cursed cloud of disappointment and sorrow
Lightning races down bringing pain to those it strikes
A cloud of regret brings a storm of fury
In due time the vengeful storm will pass
Long after the soothing rains cleanse the mind and soul
The cloud will forever remain
Not in one, but in the cheated few
A few brought down by the spite of one
Their souls are laden with agony
They feel betrayal like Joseph and his coat
Their souls will be forever tormented
The despair will remain, buried deep inside their hearts

Johnathan Pounds, Grade 9
Hamburg Jr High School, AR

Mamaw

Rushing in the hospital
Celtic stage, dialysis, life support
Family crying, hugging, screaming.
While asking ourselves why her?
As her days pass she gets weaker and weaker.
Until she just couldn't take it anymore.
The shell we saw was not her, just the way we knew her.
Now at the gate of heaven she is waiting for us, her family.

Hailey Roby, Grade 7
St Mary of the Woods School, KY

Africa

Far away, it's a different world.
Rural, exotic and overwhelming;
The animals, the people, the place,
There, you are an outsider.

Diversity. Language and culture.
Dutch, English and Afrikaans fills your ears.
It is slow paced and quiet.
You are not on a tight schedule.

Earthy colors surround you,
Burnt orange dirt blankets the dirt roads,
Shades of browns are spread across the land,
You are not on a tight schedule.

The terrain: rocky,
The mountains; towering,
The sights: expansive
Unbelievable and never ending.

It's strange to see a giraffe on the side of the road
As we see deer, it is no big deal to the locals,
It's wild and amazing,
Totally different for our lives.

Allie Rost, Grade 9
West Jr High School, MO

A Dog Named Spanky

There once was a dog named Spanky
Who liked to sleep with his blanky
He hated baths
Ran and crashed
Now he's really cranky

Evan King, Grade 7
Newcastle Middle School, OK

The Mountain

Always watching and protecting
Ever standing never failing
A natural made barrier
To keep man out and to keep it safe
Providing shelter for the animals
A place of harmony a place of peace

With lush green vegetation
Crystal clear streams running down
To feed a magnificent lake
From where the animals drink
A place of harmony a place of peace

Always watching and protecting
Ever standing never failing
Keeping this place
A place of harmony a place of peace

Cameron Perkins, Grade 8
Owasso 8th Grade Center, OK

My Favorite Place Is the Woods

In the woods
Under the tree
Among the animals
Near a stream
Between the fog
Over the hills
On the stand
Toward the deer
Past the river
Without any worries

Robert Hutsell, Grade 8
Heritage Middle School, TN

Love

A kiss is just a kiss
Until it's with the one you love
A hug is just a hug
Until it's with the one you're thinking of
A dream is just a dream
Until you make it come true
Love is just a word
Until it's proven to you
Winter is all about this
Cause a kiss is just a kiss

Ruby Wallen, Grade 7
Maury Middle School, TN

Storms and Rainbows

Sometimes I am the color black like the stormy sky —
Angry and loud
Ferocious and infuriated,
Like someone who has held their frustration in for years at a time
But other times I am a multitude of colors —
Exciting and happy
Delighting and comforting,
Like a rainbow shining bright after a storm.
These are the colors of me.

Rachel Phillips, Grade 8
Leeton Middle and High School, MO

Boy to Man

Ah! Look, there is a baby born on this average night.
Now he is a toddler. Watch out! He can bite!
The years pack on, and soon he's ready for his high school decision.
He makes up his mind, and now he faces his first pick's inquisition.

He zooms through freshman year, sophomore, junior, senior.
He knows his Alma Mater and has exceptional demeanor.
The fine fellow jumps into college, a great medical school.
As the stress builds up, he can hardly keep his cool.

Alas, his graduation day rapidly nears.
Along with it comes satisfaction and cheers.
He gets a job far away, as a pediatrician,
But the draft beckons him. He has no volition.

He fights all night and day, his desires back with friends.
His heart and soul are in his letters he so frequently sends.
The war soon ends, and he gratefully returns to home soil.
He still has his mind set on a career he hopes did not spoil.

His experience in the armed forces helped the common good.
His fellow pediatricians welcome him, not misunderstood.
Well into his life, he has a family of his own.
A pediatrician and a soldier, wow, this man has grown.

Joe Mungenast, Grade 8
St Gerard Majella School, MO

Open Up

A tower falls,
An army is rallied,
Protesters prepare,
Two crowds one on each side,
One crowd yells oil and sabotage,
Others yell freedom and engagement,
As the sonorous of dreams continue the White House shuts its doors,
With a cacophony coming from the mouths of the crowd's one thing cannot be done,
Listen.

Shut your mouth
Open your mind

Mike Richardson, Grade 8
West Jr High School, MO

Indefinite

No one really appears to be just anybody,
cause everyone has to be somebody.
Some people want to be someone they're not,
but others are who they appear to be.
Some people are what they are not,
and several others are not what they are.
Everyone has someone in the inside.
for everyone else to see.
Many many see it, few will not,
but it matters whether or not, they let it show.

Lynsey Ramsey, Grade 8
Pigeon Forge Middle School, TN

Forever

Steady beats carve the pavement
Two souls merge to one, a love that lasts until the end
Forever seems to fly
While the colors blend,
As the scenery passes by
I grip tightly to his mangled mane
Something catches my sight
We drop to the ground, I look to the sky
A plane
We wait...and once again take flight.

Ashtin George, Grade 8
Walton Elementary/Middle School, WV

I Just Can't Seem to Let You Go

The one I love.
My one and my only.
The one for me.
Mine and mine only!
There are many guys and many girls.
but none of them are for real.

My love for you is so strongly true.
That if you leave me, I'll be very confused.
I'll be so devastated.
Because...
I'm madly in love with you.
For that I believe with all my heart and all
my soul
Because...
I just can't seem to let you go

Brittany Cunningham, Grade 8
Chelsea Jr High School, OK

Soccer

S occer is fun to play and is athletic.
O utrageously awesome and ready to play.
C an be a good player and play your best.
C an make a goal and win the game.
E very day practice to keep you going.
R unning all the time to do your best.

Kevin Dean Prock, Grade 7
Hartville Jr/Sr High School, MO

Growing Up

Here we are growing and learning
Facing all the challenges among us
Going to school for a wonderful education
Although we're just counting the days to summer
Here we are growing up

Shane McCoy, Grade 8
Highland Rim School, TN

Scare Mare

I go and get on the bus.
I'm getting extremely excited
as my adrenaline begins to rush.
When I step off the bus,
the cold air jolts across my bare face.
I buy my ticket and stand in line.
As I stand there I hear a slight stir behind me
and suddenly a man with a chain saw
comes at my friends and I.
All I can do is brace myself
and think about what is yet to come.

Hannah Kimbrough, Grade 8
Highland Rim School, TN

Christmas

Christmas is my favorite holiday.
I love the smell of Christmas dinner.
I like to go outside and play.
While having snow ball fights all day.

I don't like winter because
I can't play basketball or ride my dirt bike.
But that is okay, it is Jesus' birthday!

Snow boarding is one of my favorite sports
I love to be in the snow
I like to go down hills real fast while
hitting lots of jumps.
Now I know why they call Christmas
the best time of the year.

Dylan Bowen, Grade 7
Maury Middle School, TN

Heaven

Heaven, way up in the air
Where we walk on streets of gold
In heaven the deaf will hear
In heaven the blind will see
In heaven the birds fly high
In heaven you be what you are, not what you be
In heaven you have no enemies, you have no fears
Up there you have no worries, just happy tears
So when I think about heaven I just can't wait
To walk through the streets when I open that gate

Jesse Hackworth, Grade 8
Heritage Middle School, TN

Eagle

E arning respect
A lways keep trying
G rateful
L earning from mistakes
E ager to help others

Kyndra Robertson, Grade 7
Hartville Jr/Sr High School, MO

God's Great Gifts

God's most wonderful creation
Was making us
And the beautiful world we live in
The birds chirping like
A choir of angels we love them so much
For they give us hope

Mountains in the distance
Standing as tall as giants
They make us appreciate the world
A cool breeze cools us
On a hot summer day
We thank you so much Lord

The minty smell of pine trees
Give us a sense of
Peace and belonging
Wild berries that fill our mouths
Are satisfying rivers of taste
God thank you for everything

For you made us
And the world we live in
And for that we are forever grateful

Crystal Beffa, Grade 7
Our Lady Catholic School, MO

Leaves

Leaves
colorful, crispy
falling, sweeping, flying
maple, oak, dogwood, poplar
gliding, stopping, tumbling
big, small
Fall

Shauntae Wood, Grade 8
Wickliffe Elementary School, OK

Faith

Faith is blood red.
It tastes like wine
It smells like fresh homemade bread.
And reminds me of a cross.
It sounds like a hymn.
It makes me feel like smiling.

Fisher Smith, Grade 7
Benton County School of the Arts, AR

The Stone in My Pocket

I carry a stone in my pocket that says love.
Love is like calculus for a first grader.
Hard and confusing, twisting your brain.
I carry a stone in my pocket that says friendship.
Friendship is the center of a teenager's or anyone's life.
The heartbeat that changes but never fails.
I carry a stone in my pocket that says family.
Family is the backbone of life, holding you up when you're weak.
I carry a stone in my pocket that says respect.
Respect is the key to opportunities.
Opening doors, even in small ways.
I carry a stone in my pocket that says moody.
Moody is anyone and everyone just in different proportions.
I have many stones, with many words.
Which stone?
It depends on the day, sometimes even minute to minute.
Some stones are always with me, call them my morals.
Others are situational stones, call them opportunities.
What stones do you carry?

Jessi Setliff, Grade 8
Belle Isle Enterprise Middle School, OK

Facts of My Life

My life started out very plain,
Now it's everything but the same,
Easy homework, lots of true friends
More outside time and only concerned about holding hands.
What once was dolls and toys,
Soon turned into make-up and boys.
Now it's pre-algebra, and back stabbing friends
Working out in the gym, and let's just say no more holding hands
What happened to this simple life you ask?
I truly don't know but it's lost in the past.

Amber Leigh Medlen, Grade 8
Highland Rim School, TN

Love Broken

I grieve in silence the loss of my love
Hoping he can't hear me from heaven above
My tears so heavy, my mind so light
Praying he won't remember that horrible fight

And through the pain of a love lost forever
I discovered the truth of him and his secret lover
She came out and told me a story so fair
But all I wanted to do was rip out her hair

It angered me to know he had been untrue
So my anger blossomed and flowed through and through
I took one step toward the door of the women

Who caused so much pain and whose words were so cruel spoken,
As I asked for the answers of questions unspoken,
She told me of her love and the soul that lie broken.

Andrea Terry, Grade 7
Crocker High School, MO

Attaining Happiness

"Now and then it's good to pause in our pursuit of happiness and just be happy." — Guillaume Apollinaire
Happiness is curling into a ball on a breezy winter night,
Stars and moon gleam down on my face, like
a soft soothing blanket wrapped around my body
except for my little piece of head poking out.
It is lounging on that velvety couch
propped up against a pillow, eyes reflecting
the fire's hypnotic dance. The feeling of comfort,
the smell of light smoke permeates the house,
my eyes are fighting a losing battle. Then without warning, I lose.

Happiness is devouring the burnt marshmallow:
black, crusty, and swollen from fire.
It is barley attached to the long dirty stick;
marshmallow is glued everywhere on my face.
Happiness is gamboling through a pile of leaves
across the sidewalk on a sunny Autumn afternoon.
It is the family trip to Wyoming riding horses like John Wayne,
along trails filled with yellow daffodils.
I wake up at three in the morning to dress in five layers of fleece and long underwear.
I gaze at shooting stars while lying comfortably in a goose-down sleeping bag
4,000 feet up with no lights around for thousands of miles.

Zach Watson, Grade 8
Baylor School, TN

Fall

Summer, Winter, Spring, Fall. Fall is my favorite season of all. Whistling in the wind, laughter in the air. Falling leaves, naked trees, raking and jumping in piles of leaves. Climbing trees, having fun, leaves are falling and birds are calling. Time goes by quickly as the days fly by. Everyone watches nightfall come by. School is out, friends are having fun, that's what fall is all about.

Billie Lanners, Grade 7
Maury Middle School, TN

Left in the Past

Forgotten friendships submerged in the past.
She walked away, and as her voice fades everything slips away.
Everything we promised and everything that passed
Has become an experience of the past.
If I try to talk to you will an inconspicuous scar from the past
Emerge from behind all the fake smiles,
or the "hi, I'm so glad to see yous."
Which have no meaning behind them.
And all the tears shed from the loss of the
Most trustworthy, most dependable, loving person I ever had.
I'm left in the midst of what our friendship captivated.
I wish I still had the most valuable
Most compatible most reinforcing person by my side through my journey in life.
All I have now are those photos that engage the most precious memories of the past.
As I hold them in my hand I can remember these moments as if they were just yesterday.
The memories that were captured in photographs
and the other that's aren't touchable, but even more important.
The scent of that watermelon, long lasting, great fragrance
Or those hot pink boas on my 12th birthday,
and even those burning fireworks on the Fourth of July.
Was that the end of our friendship, or the beginning of an edited past?

Ashley Tesreau, Grade 8
St Katharine Drexel School, MO

Lisa Tanner Flies and Lies

Lisa Tanner can really fly,
But she likes to make lies.
She likes to lie through the window
Claiming that Jill likes Psycho.

Lisa Tanner has a "D,"
But she says she has a "B."
Lisa Tanner makes lies to Clark
Saying that James is afraid of the dark.

She says her mom's cooking is great
But her cooking is what she hates.
Do you know what too is a lie?
Lisa Tanner can't really fly.

Darius Wolfe, Grade 7
Dunbar Middle School, AR

Soldiers

Bang! Bang!
that's about
all the
United States

Army, Marines, Navy, Air Force
hear in
Iraq and Afghanistan.
We hear

about it
every day on
television and radio
even though

it's a long
ways away
we still
care for them.

Lonnie Tharp, Grade 8
Chelsea Jr High School, OK

You Don't Know Me

You used to know what I thought
And when I was upset
I used to know when you were angry
And when you needed to be alone
We used to be close
We used to be able to lean on each other
Then you changed to be with them
Fights were fought
And scars were made on our hearts
Our friendship went up in flames.

You used to know me
But you don't anymore.

Michaella Hogan, Grade 8
Benton County School of the Arts, AR

Rare Azalea

Oh, rare azalea, orange with yellow-red.
Do your hues match any other?
Your star-like flowers stand out among the leaves.
You are the finest flower that I have ever seen.
Your beauty is fair and fragile as if it were a rose.
Unlike your uncommon rival, you can't grow too far from your native soil.

Oh, rare azalea, orange with yellow-red.
Your hues shan't match another's.
You surely are the very best of all the wild flowers.
'Tis a shame, my star-shaped friend, that your range of growth is limited.

Oh, beautiful azalea, orange with yellow-red.
How long will you choose to stay?
How did you become endangered?
Will you go extinct or be spread around the globe?
Grace us with your beauty, the best of any plant.
For just as long as you exist.

Christian Dennis, Grade 8
Barret Traditional Middle School, KY

I Am From

I am from candy from sour and sweet.
I am from the loving home
Where it smells like cookies
I am from the trees
The blossoms that spring up with life

I'm from Kwanzaa and speed
From Rebecca and Darreon
I'm from biting nails and sports
And from buying pets

I'm from "don't run in the house" and "take part in your culture"
And "what doesn't kill you makes you stronger."
I'm from Jamaica.
I'm from South Carolina and Africa.
I'm from cheeseburgers and pizza.
From grandma built a statue
Out of clay
Gold, ruby, sapphire, jade elephants
Grandma's house.

James Cocroft, Grade 7
St Cecilia Academy, MO

Reflection

You weren't sculpted to have joy last inside you,
A dying flame, craving for someone to come and give it life again,
You weren't made for this,
To soak in their scrutiny like a sponge, only to turn into collateral damage,
Your vision is spotted in black and white, obscuring your sights on the hopeful,
Some people are afraid of the dark, others of heights,
You're afraid of that blaring reflection.

Shannon Perry, Grade 8
Ceredo-Kenova Middle School, WV

Home

It's been six years today,
Since the Twin Towers fell.
Today people will cry,
and others will dwell.
Wishing for their loved ones to come back,
but they are gone, and that's that.

If only it didn't happen,
and all of those people didn't die,
maybe, just maybe, they would still be alive.

It's hard to believe I know
but there was a reason, God wanted them to go.
He wanted them home, home where they belong.
Home, where the angels would sing them a song.

A song of happiness, a song of life.
Home is a place where we will never die.

Austin Blevins, Grade 7
Newman Middle School, OK

Praising Our God

Thank you God,
for making the mountains form like needles in the sky.

The eagles cry, the sound I love,
was a whistle, and I thank you God for it.

Thank you God,
for the cattle, whose meat is as tough as leather,
who roam at the base of the mountains.

Which are surrounded by flowers and their fragrance,
which smells as sweet as honey,
this I also thank God for.

I also want to thank God for the water side of Earth,
all the oceans, lakes, rivers, streams, and ponds,
whose waves are a rippled chip.

Montana Kempfer, Grade 7
Our Lady Catholic School, MO

Peace

Is lying in the sand watching the sunset.
It's seeing the ocean glisten in moonlight.
Peace is the defenseless hush
of distant, crashing waves.
The shine in our eyes,
like stars in the night brings a calmness.
The secrets of the shells,
and the close of the day have a happy feeling.
Those bring peace and
peace brings joy to the world.

Palmer Avisto, Grade 8
Baylor School, TN

What Is Beyond Our Planet?

What is beyond our planet Earth?
If it exists, it must have worth.

They say man can live on Mars.
But I am content to gaze at stars.

What is the meaning of the constellations?
The government spends tons of money on explorations.

I am thankful for the stars.
But never plan to visit Mars.

Scott Poligone, Grade 9
Bearden High School, TN

Christmas Day

C arolers everywhere on the street.
H aving fun with friends and family.
R unning around with joy.
I ncredible day for all.
S creaming with excitement while opening presents.
T errific gifts for everybody
M erry Christmas to everybody
A ll night parties.
S ounds of great laughter at parties.

D ancing on the dance floor.
A great day to everybody around you.
Y awning kids and grown ups, the Christmas Day is over.

Chimeng Vang, Grade 7
Rocky Comfort Elementary School, MO

Teaser

I will always remember
His coat and mane so soft and smooth,
With his glimmering eyes
One brown, one blue.
Four white stockings on his feet
His demeanor oh, so sweet and kind.
He did not even mind
If I walked under him while he was eating.
Now his memory follows me wherever I go.

Bryanna Fischer, Grade 8
Musselman Middle School, WV

Spring

The sun is shining.
Birds are singing in the trees,
And flowers are blooming beautifully.
As caterpillars change to butterflies,
The kites are flying freely in the sky.
Bees are buzzing busily,
And children are playing happily
As soft breezes and puffy clouds blow through the skies.
Ah, Spring!

Masha White, Grade 7
St Joseph Institute for the Deaf, MO

Fall

Fall is the time of cold weather.
The leaves fall and turn brown as if
they were spoiled apples.

Fall is a time for children to play
in the leaves when they are stacked
as high as a building.

Crunch, crunch, crunch,
goes the leaves under your feet.

Fall is a time where you get to
enjoy the time where your toes
turn to popsicles.

But after it is over, you will be
relaxed from your nose to your toes!

Fall is a time where children dress up
and scare people on the hunt for candy!

Trick or treat!
Boo! goes the children.

Lauren Roberts, Grade 7
Nettleton Jr High School, AR

The Pitch

Gripping the stitches,
Holding ball in leather glove,
Fingers release. Crack!

Jack E. Mimlitz, Grade 8
St Gerard Majella School, MO

At the Creek

By the creek, I am sitting.
Among all stress and noise
Without a care in the world,
Beneath the shady trees.
As fish are nibbling at my toes.
Inside and out I am still and quiet.
On the other side a peaceful forest.
Except for my side, a noisy town
Beside the creek I wish to stay.
For the peaceful feeling it brings
Within.

Kendra Chapman, Grade 8
Heritage Middle School, TN

The Tree

Two trees standing tall
Branches that look like big claws
Wave in the summer breezes
Making shadows on the ground
Shade us from the sun

Matthue Sparks, Grade 7
Leeton Middle and High School, MO

Smile

Sometimes I am scared to open my eyes,
Because I'm scared of what my future might lie,
A believer is what I'm trying to be,
But Like so many times the rug will get pulled from under me,
I am a soldier, drafted in a war called life,
And my tears are like bullets and they cut like a knife,
At night I cry for my mama, cuz one day she might be missing her baby,
I'm waking up to live a nightmare and it's driving a crazy,
People tell me to hold on but I don't know how long I can do that,
Trying to live an easy life, but still watching out for my back,
I know this life can seem kind of rough,
But the only thing I ask from you is to smile,
Just smile for me one time,
It might lighten up my dark mind,
I am like a picture painted by an unknown artist,
Never to put their name down though it took their hardest,
You'll never know the artist and why they made it,
Here's a message to the baby soldier yet to breathe,
Listen to your mind or you'll became like me,
Most importantly don't forget to smile,
Believe me it might last you awhile, smile.

Jaquita Stewart, Grade 9
TN

Brittany

Brittany
Funny, smart, honest, loving
Daughter of Kendra and Dwight Byard
Lover of dogs, cats, pizza
Who feels love, caring, helpful
Who gives help, a good attitude, and knowledge
Who needs friends to talk, a family to depend on
Who fears spiders, snakes, and death
Who would like to see Rascal Flatts, Miranda Lambert, Disney World
Who lives with a caring family
Byard

Brittany Byard, Grade 8
Montgomery Central Middle School, TN

Thanksgiving

Eating the delicious food is fun,
Laughing with your family is too
But when the party ends cleaning up
Is always so horrible
Though I can't wait until next year
When maybe I can stuff a little more food in my stomach
And still have room for dessert
Hopefully my stomach won't hurt
From all the tasty food
Such as turkey, the rolls which are so good you can't just have one
The mashed potatoes, corn, and all the foods you have to have seconds with
The dessert is always the best, the cake, the pies, and all the other wonderful desserts
You won't need to eat all week after my family's Thanksgiving dinner
Yay for Thanksgiving!

Rebecca Lynn Evans, Grade 8
Alpena High School, AR

The Night

Tonight is the night
I will finally see the light
But without a fight
It wouldn't be right
Tonight's my last night
In the moonlit night
So I won't be a-fright
To go see the light.

Jennifer Lanham, Grade 8
Southern Reynolds County R-II School, MO

Curiosity

The fluffy, golden retriever puppy
Sits curiously on the shaggy, beige carpet,
Thinking about chewing on the
Smooth, citrus orange and gum pink high heels.
The blue, black, and white tie lay
Thrown on the unmade, coffee comforter.
Cotton candy blue walls sit
Behind the wheat-colored puppy.
Freshly painted walls surround the glass window.
Green spearmint gum floats
In the clean, pure air.
The air conditioner blows ferociously,
Causing the coffee comforter to rustle.
The puppy whines in anticipation.
The colorful high heels hit the musty carpet.
The adorable puppy pounces excitedly
On the delicious shoes, chewing them to pieces!

Kara Pauley, Grade 7
Southern Boone Middle School, MO

Indian Boundary Campground

Up the mountain they walk.
Near the pier they talk.
Beneath the sun they lay.
In the water they swim.
Across the lake a family sits.
Before the family came here, they fought.
Now sitting beside the lake,
Despite their differences,
They no longer fight across the dinner table.
At night they sleep great.

Cody Wagner, Grade 8
Heritage Middle School, TN

Brother

My brother is my friend.
He is nice and loving.
SOMETIMES!!!!
He is an athlete.
He plays basketball, football, and baseball
I love him very much!!!!
His name is Joseph Jay Meeker.

Julia Dry, Grade 7
Ketchum Jr High School, OK

Hope? Or End of World?

World is darkened,
light fades away and we are covered in swarms of shadows.
No hope for a new,
no hope at all.
People's masks shatter and their true form emerges.
Color in the world turns to gray,
happiness becomes engulfed by the ever so cold
feeling of loneliness.
Shall anyone come to brighten our days,
will we be saved,
or will we be left in the cold, dark world we call home.
More evils slowly emerge from the shadows,
lies, deceit, war, depression, sickness, murder.
All of the world's evils cover us in a blanket of pain,
will the Lord our God help us?
These questions no mortal human could answer,
only a thing we know as fate,
will decide for us.

Chris Turner, Grade 8
Villa Madonna School, KY

The Girl No One Can See

She sits there, in her room
As lonely as can be.
She cries her heart out all the night,
But still no one can see.

The pain she feels, both night and day
Is heavier than strongest man can take.
No one notices her tear stained face
Or that the smile she's put on is fake.

Not one person could understand
Why she feels this way.
She's lost, confused, never to find her way,
And no one notices the feelings that she's put at bay.

Kelsey Kernan, Grade 8
Musselman Middle School, WV

My Baby

Your beautiful brown eyes
Your wonderful warm smile
Your sensational sweet kiss
When we are not together
It is you that I miss
I want to hear your voice
And feel your hand on my waist
I want you to love me
Same as I love you
I can't wait to see you
Hopefully it will be tonight
I can't wait to ask my mom
I'm sure she'll say it's all right

Kasea Marquardt, Grade 8
Mountain View Elementary and Middle School, WV

Peace

Peace, what is peace?
Is it an expectation seen in many eyes but never reached?
Is it a goal looked for but never found?
Or is it a prize waiting to be won?
We've never reached peace, and I don't know that we ever will.
But we have given an effort and tried many times.
From Martin Luther King Jr. in 1963 to our soldiers in Iraq that are there to this day.
But this is a mission that has never fully been accomplished.
Which is why some choose to believe it's simply a myth, impossible, and will never exist.
But will it, can it?
If so how will we find it, how will we know it's arrived, how long will this wait last?
I can't imagine how it would feel in a world where peace and happiness walk the earth.
All I know is that it will be a long and hard struggle of many wars, battles, and fights ending with the reality that it may or may not ever come true.

Myles Cheadle, Grade 8
Summit Lakes Middle School, MO

All of God's Creation

A tree towering over the ants and insects, like a skyscraper over a bustling city,
The moon is like a half eaten cookie floating in the sky, the stars surrounding it twinkling,
On and off like flashers on a car in the rain,
Thank you God, for all that we see.

In the evening the cicadas making sound like a rain stick, going up and down,
A stream gurgling as it beats on the rocks sticking out,
The rain beating on my roof, almost as if it's trying to let itself in,
Thank you God, for all that we hear.

I think about cattle and pigs that were used, every time I bite into steak or bacon,
Juice of fruit trickling down my chin,
The water running down my throat like water falling down a hill,
Thank you God, for all that we taste.

Walking by a rose bush the sweet tang of delicate flowers fill my nose,
On a spring morning I can almost smell fresh dew shining on the grass,
I walk in my backyard and immediately smell pine trees,
Thank you God, for all that we smell.

The warmth of the sun sinking in my skin, the rain showering on me, soaking my clothes,
As different seasons change, so does the weather,
The grass beneath my feet is soft and sticky,
Thank you God, for all that we feel.

JoEllen Grohs, Grade 7
Our Lady Catholic School, MO

Towers

The crystal white stars flash back and forth.
Violet takes over our sky
the towers stand tall and proud,
towers like someone staring you down when something happens because of all the windows.
The moon sleeps with his white and blue striped pajamas.
Shiny dew, green grass and sparkling baby blue water surrounds the enormous black coal towers,
with the lovely night background.
The perfect setting for a portrait, how lovely.

Amanda Guevara, Grade 7
Southern Boone Middle School, MO

School

School, there are many things going on there,
Like fights, games, rumors, and plays.
The fights are mainly girls, sometimes guys,
The games can be basketball,
Or even a game on the playground.

The rumors, they are terrible,
They come from people who tell lies about you,
Those lies get spread around the school,
Then home, then the town.

The plays are fun, you can try out for parts,
Sometimes you make it sometimes you don't.

All this you see is very complicated,
For all of this you may make or lose some friends.
This could be good or bad, for some of us.

Andrea Wilson, Grade 7
Wainwright Elementary School, OK

Halloween

I like Halloween how about you?
Witches scarecrows goblins too.

Vampires sneaking through the streets.
Lurking for some kids and treats

Pumpkins and ghost saying Boo
Better be careful they'll get you.

Trick or treating oh so fun
Get ready, get set, run.

Almost over so so soon
Look at the werewolf howling at the moon.

Zane Wagoner, Grade 7
Small World Academy, WV

Red

Two true loves diverged on opposite paths
One west, the other opposite of that
They stood with many, but they stood alone
Neither loved with their everything, or could.
Their humanity isolated them,
Their outward fronts could finally dim.
They both seek solace in each other's eyes.
She kissed his footprints; he sees her and sighs.
No longer alone, but now side by side.
Under their masks, they no longer hide.
They leave the darkness and step into the light.
Their happy ending is finally in sight.
Now they are together, and angels do sing.
They continue walking 'til church bells ring.

Mackenzie Cover, Grade 9
Bearden High School, TN

Autumn Night

The white wind howls with a wolf at the moon,
The great house moans like a person in pain,
The young hound bays as she chases her coon,
All say goodbye on a dark autumn night.

The bushytail fox yips at her pup,
The snow owl hoots as she scouts her prey,
The dark water moves as a great carp jumps up,
All say goodbye on a dark autumn night.

The brand new mom lays her child down for bed,
The first time dad adds logs to the fire,
The newborn baby gently lays down her head,
All say goodbye on a dark autumn night.

The twittering birds greet the new day,
The grand old rooster struts through the yard,
The bullfrog croaks as if to say,
All say goodbye to a dark autumn night.

Kristen DeArmond, Grade 7
Nettleton Jr High School, AR

It's Your Time

Your window is closed, but your mind is open.
It races with wonderless dreams!

Go after what you want the most,
you know what it takes!

You can't just wait for the sun to shine on you.
You choose your fate!

The leaves fall slowly, but before you know it,
your window will stand wide open!

Then, it will be your time to shine!

Kelsey Brown, Grade 8
Gresham Middle School, TN

First Time Love

When I saw you that day, I had nothing to say.
I was speechless.
I was in love.
You made me feel like I was important.
You were my light,
When I was in the dark.
You made me smile, when I wanted to frown.
You introduced me to love.
It was the first time we've met.
It felt wonderful, and I wanted it to stay.
When I needed you most,
You were by my side.
This is how I feel.
Love is on the inside.

Kasey Miller, Grade 8
Boones Creek Middle School, TN

Gentle Crawler

Gentle butterfly,
Calm and peaceful creature
Sweet as lime
But never sour as lemon
As it comes out in beautiful days
Its wings shine like rainbows
Only enough to put glares in my eyes
Small enough to barely be seen.
And when seen
Could not be unwatchable
Vacant sounds are empty
But full of silence all around
Nature's forest is flowing
With mesquite throughout the air
But still a tenuous gentle,
Calm, peaceful creature
Glides throughout
The ground level breeze
Like a leaf off a tree

Macey Klosterman, Grade 7
Barret Traditional Middle School, KY

This One's for You

Have you ever stopped for a minute,
And watched the world fly by?
But who's to say their time is worth?
Untold, it all, but why?
When we could be saving lives,
For the poor kids young and old,
Who sit all day starving,
Not to mention, bitter cold.
But why do they all have to starve?
Nothing at all left to bare.
Some no mom, dad gone too
Why all this isn't fair.
They live their lives all day to day
In a shack made out of goo.
Not fair, but who's to say?
Now this one's just for you.
We all should take a minute
And pray for those too poor.
Little cherished, sad, depressed,
Scared forever more.

Amanda Schad, Grade 7
Annunciation Elementary School, MO

Football

making money
hands dirty
exhausted muscles
throwing a touchdown
getting hurt
football is here.

David Bragg, Grade 7
Rocky Comfort Elementary School, MO

Rethinking

As I flip through the air,
Falling down to earth.
I have some second thoughts,
About how I lived my life.

I wish I could take back,
All the things I had done.

As I start to regret,
I began to repent.
So the Lord gave me a second chance.

Philip Quick, Grade 9
University Heights Academy, KY

Heaven

Up in the sky
Beyond this world
Through the pearly gates
In heaven
Over the streets of gold
In my new body
With my siblings
Standing beside the Savior
Throughout eternity
In my future

Jordan Elliott, Grade 8
Heritage Middle School, TN

What Is a Good Book?

What is a good book?
A chance to be someone else
An invitation to dream
A new life
New ideas
Completely understood
A choice to make
Life-changing experience
That is a good book.

Ashley Ray, Grade 7
Newcastle Middle School, OK

This Life

My name I shall not say,
Life shall waste away.
I never made a team
Or won a single thing,
But I don't mind,
I'm doing great.
I don't care what everyone will say.
For in this life,
Kindness drifts away.
And it's your friends and family
That have the final say.

Kyle Parker, Grade 8
Musselman Middle School, WV

Eagle's Flight

I dreamed
I was an eagle
Flying in the sky
Looking for others
Peacefully

Tristan Budds, Grade 8
Wickliffe Elementary School, OK

Distance

He's far away along the beach,
Too far away for me to reach,
He is my only dad,
So cool and rad,
Oh how I love him dear,
I only wish he could be near.
Why did he move so far away,
And leave me here to stay?
He left me all alone and sad,
Extremely angry and extremely mad,
So now I'm here all sad and lonely,
If only he could be here, if only, if only.

Taylor Poling, Grade 8
Musselman Middle School, WV

What's Done Is Done!

They stare, they look.
the heartache shook.
They shout, they laugh.
About things long past.
They live, they learn.
Begin to yearn.
To take it back.
Back time to turn.
But yet they know.
As sure as snow.
When rise the sun
What's done is done!

Savannah Stevenson, Grade 7
Elkton School, TN

Whirl Wind

It spills and twirls
A whirl wind of debris
The sound of a freight
Train passing by.
A destructive cyclone
A funnel-shaped
Twister.
It twists
And turns
As the violent
Winds destroy.
A Tornado!

Curtis Reinkemeyer, Grade 8
St Joseph School, MO

Peace

Sunlight glides through the window,
dappled with the shadows of a thousand leaves.
It hovers on the sill,
dances on the couch,
jumps to the floor,
to rest on the small black cat on the rug
asleep
and warm.

Mary Biggs, Grade 9
Bearden High School, TN

The Ferryman

Charon is a Ferryman; he rides the river Styx
His paddle is a reaping scythe; his boat is black as pitch.

You do not pay in silver; you do not pay in gold.
Charon asks for nothing to cart away your soul.

By your deathbed side he'll wait,
Scythe in hand and scales to weigh —
Your actions and your deeds in life.

Whether you were rich, or whether you were poor,
To stone cold Charon it matters not as you stand upon his door.

Death makes us all equals.

John Hagele, Grade 8
St Gerard Majella School, MO

The Long Road Back

Someone who was very dear
Went away sometime this year
When he didn't return, I cried and cried,
For suddenly I knew that he had died.

At first it cut me like a knife,
For I knew that he had fulfilled his life.
He was in a far better place, this I know,
But I wish that he had not had to go.

He was a very special man, this you can see,
And that is why he is so dear to you and me.
As time goes on, my wounds will heal,
But my love for him is so real.

He always told me to keep my head up
And when I started to fall, he picked me back up.
Now he is gone and I don't know what to do
But to keep on counting from one to two.

I am older now and he is no longer here
For he has captured my very worst fear.
I'll meet him in heaven and then you will hear
All the church bells ringing loud and clear!

Arianna Tharp, Grade 9
East Newton High School, MO

Difficulty

I'm losing my control,
Letting everything unfold,
Never found a happy ending,
Everyone began to crush me.
I'm going into something I know I'll fail,
Never found that small detail,
I wasn't good enough, not what you wanted,
Never going to be what you needed.
Why can't this hurt be through,
I miss the old days, where have they gone,
It was when you had not one single clue,
Now, I'll just be invisible, from now on.
You never knew I was agliophobic,
I fear all of this pain,
I'd never be pluviophobic,
I would have loved to dance with you in the rain.
I'm the worst off person in the world,
But I know one thing, I'll,
Cry and reach for more than the world,
I cry, but I wear the biggest smile.

Erica Harper, Grade 7
Caverna Middle School, KY

Christmas Time

C hoosing trees
H anging little ornaments
R inging bells on the sleigh
I nside the house
S itting by the fire
T elling Santa what you want
M unching on candy
A fter you empty your stocking
S itting opening presents

T earing away paper
I nside what you asked for
M any people said "Thank you" to Santa
E veryone talks about what they got for their friends

Josh Clevenger, Grade 7
Maury Middle School, TN

Pretend

She didn't know why;
She asked a million times.
But every night she would sit down and cry.
They were all happy and they would all talk
While she just faked a smile and tried to walk.
She couldn't bear the pain of losing her best friend.
What went wrong?
Will the pain ever end?
Pretend to be happy, just try.
Wipe those tears,
Try not to cry.

Heather Nelson, Grade 8
Musselman Middle School, WV

Melting

Drippings of Rocky Road ice cream
Down hands from the scorching sun,
The cone quickly melting
Until the tasty treat vanishes:
Of no more use,
Like the days of youth
With time quickly ticking away,
Take advantage while it is here,
For it will never return.

Mallory Uekman, Grade 9
Bearden High School, TN

Fall Is Here

Fall is here
Listen to the kids cheer
Because fall is here

Winter is next
Kids love it the best
Because the snow comes down
And the schools let out
All the kids scream and shout

Now it's spring
All the kids laugh and sing.
They can go outside
And slide down their slides
Now that it's spring

Finally it's summer
It's definitely not a bummer
Now that it's summer

Fall is here
Listen to the kids cheer
Because once again fall is here!

Dana Miller, Grade 8
Shepherdstown Middle School, WV

Rebekah

R eady for anything
E xtremely outgoing
B utterfly is my BEST stroke
E xtremely good at swimming
K ind
A good Jew
H appy person

Rebekah Durham, Grade 8
White Station Middle School, TN

Annoying Brother

Annoying brother,
It is practically my job,
But I don't get paid

Taylor Williams, Grade 8
Owasso 8th Grade Center, OK

Wilkins in School

School was so boring
that imagination reigned.
Evil blossomed in me.
I lived in the trenches of the classroom,
and fought battles on the playground.
I built whole forts out of sticks and mud.
The stench of sand from the crushed rocks from our rock pulverizing.

The slide jams,
the stick fights,
and the acorn race tracks.
The adrenaline flowed.

The red card ruled me.
I never went a week without getting one.
Pulling out peoples hair, giving them bloody noses,
The game between the teachers and I never ceased.
I was the king of liars.
The master of history.
The annoying kid that never stopped talking.

Connor Wilkins, Grade 8
Baylor School, TN

A True Friend

A friend will always be there. They will never let you down.
A friend is a person who cares, loves, and will never forget you.
They will always be at your side to help you when you are down.
A friend is someone you can talk to when you are hurt.
A friend is someone you can look to for anything.

Katey Mattingly, Grade 7
St Mary of the Woods School, KY

The Coral Reef Life

Where water is blue-green and salty,
That sparkles under the sun,
Far from here where oceans sway,
dolphins come to play, sharks on the prowl,
with might and power, their hunger never ceases.
Fish and shrimp linger at a coral reef,
where eels hide and crabs sleep, they are all safe at this sanctuary.
Below on the sand where manta rays glide,
scallops clap and prance like in a Mexican dance.
The octopus creepily crawl on rocks,
like a spider, waiting for prey to hop.
Barracudas wait beyond the reef,
like a cat, pouncing on the fish that swims nearby.
Comes now a jewfish that slowly crawls along,
like a tortoise climbing up a hill.
And if you carefully listen,
you can hear the cries of the whales,
just passing by.
The fish start to go home from their playful yet busy day,
because when the sun sets, the fish need their rest.

Anna Gibson, Grade 8
Cedar Bluff Middle School, TN

Deer

Deer are gentle caring animals
The does take care of the young.
The bucks protect the territory and the doe and its young.
The bucks fight and spar.
The does blow and throw a white tail up and run.

Timmy Shelton, Grade 7
Highland Rim School, TN

I Miss Her So

I guess some pain I have regressed,
Cause sometimes I feel depressed,
Sometimes I feel so alone,
As if I were out on my own.

At times I feel as if I might cry,
Yet I still am not sure why,
My sister says that my room is like a memorial,
Because I have so many pictures of this girl.

It is not my fault that I cannot let go,
Because I still miss her so,
I wish that she was still here,
Because I'm tired of all the tears.

It is not her that is to blame,
It is the guy that turned into that lane,
The guy that hit her with his car,
When he did he broke my heart.

Mikayla Mohon, Grade 8
Hebron Middle School, KY

Goodbye for Now

I wish I knew what to say
About how I think of you every day
Though my heart aches for you
I know my dream will never come true
what I like about you I do not know
everything I do reminds me of you
Doesn't matter whether there's rain or snow
When I'm with you the sun is shining bright
My heart is broken and can't be repaired
Now I realize you never cared
So now I know I don't need you
me and you are really through
My life is so much better
Now that your gone
I can't believe it took me so long
to realize how much better off I am
Maybe I'll see you again someday
until then I'll remember you and
all the things we've been through
farewell my lover and friend
can't wait to see you again

Allexa Bonner, Grade 8
Lewisburg Middle School, TN

Fridays

The alarm clock goes bring bring,
I mumble and grumble trying to stay asleep.
The school bell rings and it's time to sing
We all get to go home for the weekend.

Andrew Simms, Grade 7
Highland Rim School, TN

Mystery Woman

As the wind blows across her face,
She walks to her car and starts to drive,
She doesn't know where she's going,
But she knows where she is heading,
Out of town out of sight.

She is a lonely woman,
And wants to make a dream come true,
She is going to that house where the sun shines through,
It belongs to that person that makes her stomach get all tingly,
He knows she exists but is too shy to talk or be mingly,
So he doesn't open the door,
And she goes on a long walk.

It gets dark and starts to get cold,
She better drive home like she has been told,
The man decides to open his door,
And he starts to walk and to try to find her,
The mystery woman that knocked upon his door,
He knows what she looks like,
But can't remember her face,
So he leaves and forgets her without a last trace.

Kaitlyn Golab, Grade 7
Hebron Middle School, KY

Secrets

Secrets hurt,
Secrets kill,
Secrets can't be what is real.
Why hide something, why hurt the one's you love
over someone who has secrets.
Why care for such a person
if you have no belief for the one in your eyes?
Everyone has secrets but most are in disguise!
You can't spend your life trying to figure someone out,
you must move on with no doubt!
You cannot hurt
You must stay strong
You must keep on believing
If you want to move on
Secrets hurt,
Secrets kill,
Secrets can't be what's real
Secrets can make you sick
Don't hurt someone you love
You might regret it!

Ashley Sams, Grade 9
Iroquois High School, KY

Ode to My Sunglasses
Ode to my sunglasses
Oh sunglasses,
The best in the world.
Oh sunglasses,
You are brown and pretty.
You are cool and stylish.
You are my favorite, of course.
You are special to me.
Oh sunglasses,
I love you so.
Faith Abbott, Grade 7
Dyer Elementary & Jr High School, TN

The Best Gift of All
I am light,
an open flame,
I see myself in the future,
I look like I do today.
I do my own thing,
I go at it alone,
but when people come to help me,
I let my true colors show.
When I have no one,
no family,
no friends,
I know I'll get through it,
I'll be strong till the end.
When they come stand beside me,
I feel my heart lift,
they give me warmth and joy,
they're all I ever want as a gift.
I'm a free bird,
a star filled night,
when people threaten who I am,
I put up a fight.
Emily Hawkins, Grade 8
Lewisburg Middle School, TN

Aqua Blue
Ocean waving aqua blue
Calming, soothing, and happy too
Like icy glaciers floating by
Aqua blue like the summer sky
Destiny Rehagen, Grade 8
St Joseph School, MO

Nuisances
Mom
Grateful, delicate
Working, concentrating, good-looking
Teacher, educator — farmer, trucker
Laughing, working, driving
Funny, crazy
Dad
Emily Daniel, Grade 8
Greenfield Jr/Sr High School, MO

My Heart
Day and night as I wait for you, to hear your voice
But…I wait and wait…day after day
You were unseen. I wish, I get to hear you say
"I Love You" once again

Minute by minute, you were no where insight
You make a crack in my heart, day after day
And my heart began to pull apart
Tear of my heart, drip drop down slowly…crying over my sadness

Then…a stranger appear in front my face
Glowing like a star, shining my broken heart
Pulling from piece to piece, gluing my unknown
To a whole new perfect shape
And the shining of star, drying my wet continuous tear
Sweep away my sadness and pain by the kindness of star
Bring me to a whole new world of love and care.

And now your turning back to me, asking for another chance looking for romance,
sorry, but I have to say
"We're absolutely over, I can't love you anymore"
Now my heart are giving, to someone new
They belong, to a different person
And not as it used to be…belonging to you.
Ha Nguyen, Grade 7
Bowling Green Jr High School, KY

Jones Guilty of Wonder
I'm six years old in the first grade.
Five days a week and eight hours a day,
her cold aura enters into the cramped room.
Hostile and relentless, she insists on drilling things into our minds,
commanding our class like a battalion of marines.
I now look upon those years and wonder
what it would have been like
to have the teacher just across the hall,
the one with freshly picked daisies on her desk.
She knew exactly how to treat six year olds.
Longer recesses, an occasional smile here and there from her.
But most of all someone who truly cared,
about a wondering first grader.

Alex Jones, Grade 8
Baylor School, TN

My Daydream
Into my daydream,
As you will soon see,
On the rainbows are gummy bears,
In so many colors that you can't believe,
Under the rainbow I see me and my boyfriend snuggling by a tree,
Beside us the most beautiful flowers blowing in the breeze,
Among our hair we feel the wind bring it up,
Without a doubt our love grows freely,
Through the warm joyful autumn night.
Jennifer Loudin, Grade 8
Heritage Middle School, TN

Sisters

Sisters are wonderful
Sometimes sisters are the only opportunity you get
Sometimes they can be nice
But sometimes they can be hurtful
Sometimes sisters are the only ones
They are always there for you no matter what
When you need someone to confide in
That's your first choice
When you and your sister have a fight
Doesn't mean they don't care about you anymore
But you also have to know they are strong and brave
But your sisters always love you

Keri Brown, Grade 8
Highland Rim School, TN

Nightingale

You do not have to sing
a melancholy tune
to say that you are in love.
You do not have to weep
the tears of bitter life
to say that you are heartbroken.

Tell me about your life,
Tell me about your loves,
Tell me about your fears and woes,
Tell me about your pain.

Meanwhile life goes on.
Time speeds past,
roses bloom and wither;
the tides come in and out,
rain pelts the ground.
One leaf falls.

The world calls to you
in the gentle hum of the whispering winds,
again and again murmuring in your ear
Heartbreak is not the end.

Mary Hughes, Grade 8
Baylor School, TN

Friends

Let's be friends forever
You and me
We will share great moments together.

Living and laughing
Every second of the day

No matter where life leads us
Always remember this
Today, tomorrow, forever
We will always be best friends.

Joshua Johnson, Grade 8
Southern Reynolds County R-II School, MO

My Father

In the new year of '94
I lost someone whom I've never met.
Although I fret and get upset,
I will never forget.
Even though its been many years,
I still have those fears and tears.
It's not the same without him;
it feels very grim and dim.
I'll never know how it would have felt
to have you here for Father's Day brunches
or lunches.
I'll never know how you would have:
Held me, kissed me, hugged me, smiled at me,
or been proud of me.
Although I never got to do any of those things with you,
it's like your right here beside me,
watching, so carefree
protecting me from everything.
And now that this poem has come to an end,
it's time for me to befriend a man
named God who so lovingly understands!

BreAnda Conley, Grade 8
Science Hill High School – 8-9 Campus, TN

Out Here

"Out here there are no complications,
There are only two sides,
Conflict and struggle victory and defeat."
A loser, and a winner.

Out here nothing else matters.
Out here there is a rhythm like no other.
Out here you are freed from you life and trapped in the game.

Out here there are two goals,
Two sidelines, two end lines,
A box with life all its own.

Out here a new type of energy courses through my
blood, filling my whole being.
Out here I am in control.
Out here I am stronger, faster, better.

Out here is lacrosse.

Mark Weber, Grade 8
Annunciation Elementary School, MO

Leaves Like Chocolate!!!!

Fall is like a hurricane of leaves
They fall quicker than you can say fleece
The leaves are as brown as chocolate
It's so fantastic to jump in a pile of leaves
When you are done all you have is a pile of trash bags

Mayela Estrada, Grade 7
Wilson Middle School, OK

Cars

Cars
Move quickly
Motors running and working
Expensive, needy, and costly
Needed gasoline —
Red, and blue, is paint
Well made
Mirrors, windshield
— Reflect—
Windshield, mirrors
Made well
Paint is, blue and, red
Gasoline needed —
Costly, and needy, expensive
Working and running motors
Quickly moving
Cars

Caleb McDaniel, Grade 8
Benton County School of the Arts, AR

That Magic

It's that little bit of moon
In the darkening sky.
Those tiny, golden eyes that
Float right on by.
It's that friend you find
And always plan to keep.
That breathless feeling you get
In the ocean deep.
It's that feeling you get
When you're high in the sky
It's those feelings
You'll keep until you die.
It's that starry night
And everything's perfect
It's that day you've been hoping for
And you find it's totally worth it.
These moments don't come often
Only every once in a bit
It's magic you find
And you'll never forget.
It's that magic…

Mary-Margaret Iles, Grade 8
West Jr High School, MO

Fever

I have heard
there is a disease going around
but I hunt day after day
and hope not to catch it
then one morning
when sitting in my tree stand
a giant steps out and I go to draw
and I catch buck fever.

Jeremy Brown, Grade 8
Highland Rim School, TN

God Is in Everything

See God in everything. See Him in tall, towering trees.
See Him in small, fragile flowers.
See His strength and love in everything.
Hear God in everything. Hear Him in thunder rumbling like a drum.
Hear Him in trickling streams.
Hear His anger and happiness in everything.
Taste God in everything. Taste Him in sweet watermelon.
Taste Him in crisp apples.
Taste His sweetness and goodness in everything.
Smell God in everything. Smell Him in fresh air.
Smell Him in the salty ocean waves.
Smell His joy and giving in everything.
Feel God in everything. Feel Him in the soft wind.
Feel Him in rocks, sharp as knives.
Feel His gentleness and pain in everything.
See God in Everything. Hear God in everything.
Taste God in everything. Smell God in everything.
Feel God in everything. God is everything.

Molly Olten, Grade 7
Our Lady Catholic School, MO

Fighter

You think I am mad at you.
But that made me that much stronger.
You can't take me, I'm free.
You made a fighter out of me.
A fighter is what I've become.
A fighter.
I look through these fighting eyes.
You hurt my heart, but you made me stronger.
How can you go on in life knowing you made a fighter?
That's who I am now, a fighter.
Fighter.
That is who I am.
Let the fighter out of this torn soul, who can't defeat itself any longer.
The fighter is who I am now.
Fighter.
How can this be who I am?
Because it was you who caused it.
For me to get stronger to become a fighter.
The world has become colder.
Fighter.

Rosanna Hawkins, Grade 9
North Shelby High School, MO

The Peacefulness of God's Creation

God makes all creation, peace can be found in most of God's creation.
Like when you see the snow covered hilltop as white as the clouds on a cloudy day.
You can hear the sounds of the birds chirping, singing a wonderful song to God.
You can taste the berries that are as sweet as candy corn on Halloween.
You smell the wonderful flowers and see the bed of different colored flowers.
You can feel the soothing bristles of the fresh cut grass as you see all of God's creation.
You see all the wondrous things God has made, yet he cares for you all the more.

Kenneth Ervin, Grade 7
Our Lady Catholic School, MO

Football

All summer the coaches wait
Until that wonderful time of year.
Preparing and waiting until August first.

Shoulder pads are strapped on,
Helmets are snapped on,
Preparing for the ultimate challenge.

All week long they practice long,
Surviving the heat and pain.
No need for a pep talk when Thursday rolls around,

For the men can smell victory.
They give it their all and leave everything on the field.
They have no fear nor tears.

After the last buzzer,
Their souls keep playing,
Because that is what the men left behind.

The men strive for excellence,
And a district championship.
Each year they come up short of their goal.

Bodhi Swan, Grade 9
Hamburg Jr High School, AR

After the Storm

After the storm I ran outside
To see what I could find
I found dirt and mud and bugs of every kind
Worms were wiggling,
Crickets were chirping,
And birds were singing
The world seemed clear and at peace
When after the storm I ran outside

Paul Glenn, Grade 7
St Charles Homeschool Learning Center, MO

Although Everything Is Lost

She lives alone,
Her heart broken,
She doesn't know what choice to make,
In shame, confused,
Loving the only thing she has left,
Sadness gleams on her face,
She prays for a miracle each day,
Helpless, in need of guidance,
Stands strong with courage,
For what she has left cannot live without her,
Loving with the remaining pieces of her heart,
She has to stay bold and strong,
She lives for the last thing she still has,
Her children.

Stephanie Lingenfelter, Grade 8
Willard Middle School, MO

Colors

When your world is black and white
All you need is a dab of color
Red, orange, yellow, pink, purple or green
Whatever states your mood
Or makes you feel good
What looks cute
Or what looks right

A little here
And a spot there
It's sure to brighten your day

Color her hair red
And her shirt yellow,

The sky blue
The clouds white
Don't forget to erase that dark rain cloud

What a perfect picture.
It's amazing what just a little color can do.

Natalie Kroninger, Grade 8
West Jr High School, MO

Unsuspected Ravages of War

The cool crisp air brushed across her fair face,
as the two young lovers enjoyed the day.
Peering at the sea in a loving embrace,
emotions grew and seemed to never fray.

Their love flourished as they said their I do's,
and in two simple words, their lives were one.
How happy both were to start life anew,
both wanting a marriage jam packed with fun.

The sad day when her husband deployed came,
their five-year-old son sat crying alone.
Her husband came back but was not the same,
he refused to talk, if she asked he'd moan.

The commitment they had made years before,
helped the couple get through the senseless war.

Hannah Diener, Grade 9
Bearden High School, TN

Pearl Harbor

Pearl Harbor was the start of a war
People were bombed at the harbor
The battle ships sank during that war
United States entered the war after Pearl Harbor
The battle ships were bombed
Soldiers died
When then tried
Now the ships are under the water beneath the sky

Ariana Jelson, Grade 7
Clarksburg School, TN

The Mountains
Beneath the sunrise
Beyond the valley
Within the breeze
Among the smell of nature
Under this tree I am sitting
Instead of inside
For now I can think
Around nothing but calming sounds
Beside this small rushing creek
At nothing but peace
Megan Whaley, Grade 8
Heritage Middle School, TN

The Forest
Among the trees, a flower grows
Between the ferns, a river flows
Above a hill, the sunlight shines
Beside the hedge are swift, tall pines
Below the sun, a clearing sparks
Inside there is no creature of the dark
Outside of stones, so cold and dim
Within a view of the mountain rim
Without a stop or kind of break
Inside the forest, half awake
Taylor Ford, Grade 8
Heritage Middle School, TN

Helen Georgia*
I always loved vacation best
You can eat fresh veggies
From Betty's
And chips
And doughnuts
And chocolate,
And you can grill steaks
And chicken too;
At the cabin
And listen to the
Trees rustle in the wind
And the squirrels
And the crickets
Late at night
With my sister
And stay out late
Talking, Laughing
And love.
Brittany White, Grade 9
Gallatin High School, TN
**Inspired by Nikki Giovanni*

Symmetrical Flowers
Budding in the spring
Pretty symmetrical sign
Lovely like a song
Emma Kliethermes, Grade 8
St Joseph School, MO

My Kitten
Slinking soundlessly through the hall.
Stalking a fly that flies from wall to wall.
She is now crouched and ready to pounce.
She jumps. But it flew right out of the door like a pixie.
Then something caught her eyes, a tiny thing crawling on the floor.
In the corner of her eye there was a spider on the floor.
She chased it from here to there.
But in a flash it was gone with a gulp.
She had swallowed it yum yum.
That's my Tinkerbell.
My cute little Siamese cat but like a tiger at heart.
Alyssa Leuschke, Grade 9
St John the Baptist High School, MO

Cecilia
I'm sorry I didn't get you a card,
like all the others you've read.
But I want to give you something from the heart,
so I'll write a poem instead.

Firstly, I want to say I love you like a sister,
and even though things are bad.
Know that God loves you too.
Never give up, and never be sad.

You may feel like giving up at times,
but never doubt the love I have for you.
Best friends till the end.
Know that that's always true.

No matter what happens,
always stand tall and be strong.
Because the storm will always go away,
before too long.

Also a little wisdom from a sister.
When you look forward and back, and there's no one there at all.
Look right beside you and your friends will be there,
ready to catch you, when you fall.
Jocelyn Couch, Grade 8
Chouteau Mazie Middle School, OK

That Place in Your Life
That place in your life that is beautiful.
That place in your life where you go to find peace in life.
That place in your life where life is the most interesting item.
That place in your life where you can go to ease the stress of life.
That place in your life that is vacant until you arrive.
That place in your life where you go to escape the sound of the city,
and to hear the wildlife in harmony with the environment.
That place in your life that is secluded and untouched
by all the forces that harm nature.
So my friends, if you can think of a place like that,
That is where you truly belong.
Osiel Sanchez, Grade 8
Belle Isle Enterprise Middle School, OK

Blue Eyes

Do they represent the water in the springs?
Or the happiness felt when a blue jay sings?

Are you supposed to feel small when you look into them?
Just like you do when you stand by the ocean.

Are they sweet like true love's first kiss?
Or bitter like sour apple crisp?

Do they represent a happy life?
Exactly what is behind blue eyes?

Alecia Turner, Grade 9
Alpena High School, AR

What Matters Most!

It's not the thrill,
It's not the thrive,
It's all about what you've got inside,
If you believe that you can do it,
The only think left is putting your mind to it,
If you agree to the terms and conditions,
The next thing you know you're on a mission,
It's not about getting a homerun,
It's not about scoring a touchdown,
It's not about being the first to succeed,
It's all about being all you can be!

Danielle Hutt, Grade 8
Chelsea Jr High School, OK

Memories

Memories come to you
and refuse to leave
then when you finally need them
they seem to fade away
you try to catch them before they're completely gone
but they just keep fading away
but thoughts can be saved
by sharing, saving and securing
keep your memories safe
for they may help you in the future

Michael Scroggie, Grade 8
Alpena High School, AR

The Beaten Path

The path is beaten and worn out,
The path is in bad shape no doubt.
Some have taken it to far places,
Others have tripped and fell on their faces.
But I plan to make it all the way
And maybe I'll be great someday
If you believe that you can too,
Don't let anybody doubt you.
If you strive and work hard,
You could end up on a business card.

Joshua Gaylor, Grade 7
Canadian Elementary School, OK

Fly High

In the darkness there's a light
It may be dim it may be bright

Through the lies and deceit
We shall rise and defeat

In the light we will soar
Going up and up with galore

We shall stay up and not be held down
We shall fly high and wear the gold crown

We will leave this hatred and go afar
We shall shine among the stars

Connor Moore, Grade 8
West Jr High School, MO

My Fantasy World

Over hills and valleys so wide,
across rivers and streams so deep,
through the tallest of trees,
inside the castle sits a young princess,
through her eyes she sees a world so different,
along the road ride the beautiful unicorns,
beneath their hooves the ground so soft,
under the stars covered by wings,
among the stars fly dragons so big,
this is my fantasy world.

Kaley Martinez, Grade 8
Heritage Middle School, TN

Your Eyes

I remember how you looked at me
That night not long ago
Your eyes told me everything
Now they're cold as stone
Your hand once was warm
Sending heat up my arm
Now your touch is like ice,
I can tell you want to let go
Your smile, once a candle
Lighting up my days
Now it's just a blinking beam
From a light that's fading away.
Your arms were my blanket
You kept me warm and dry
I wish I could say
I love you
But why even try?
It's hard to say I love you
When there is no one to say it to
It's hard to say I love you
To anyone but you

Emily Walls, Grade 9
Fern Creek Traditional Magnet High School, KY

One Drink

You approach the light
Glowing red, yelling at you to stop
But do you stop?
No
Your foot is on the pedal
And your hand is on the bottle
Cold and smooth
Or is it really rough and boiling hot?
Breaking glass
And smashing lives
Uprooting family trees
That took years to grow
Killing
Killing the innocent
As well as their families
Devastated and heartbroken
Everything gone
All from
One person
One hit
One drink too many

Allison Luecke, Grade 8
St Katharine Drexel School, MO

My Favorite Food

Picadello
Always simmering
Pops in mouth
My ultimate favorite food
Ground beef

Lizette Aparicio, Grade 8
Pigeon Forge Middle School, TN

Sunshine

My cat Sunshine loves the sun
Whenever she's cold she lies in it
She's a goofy cat who rolls in the mud
When you rub her she's warm as toast

Jade Knisley, Grade 7
Highland Rim School, TN

First Day of Summer

Open the door
On a sunny afternoon,
Rushing in over my skin
Warm, but not burning, heat
It envelopes my exposed skin.
My cheeks flush a rosy pink
The hair on my arms rises
And sends chills up my back.
I take in a deep breath,
It's the beginning of summer,
The beginning of new memories.

Emily Bruner, Grade 8
Benton County School of the Arts, AR

Jake Awad

Jake
Short, young, awesome and brown eyed
Brother of Sara and Aiyah Awad
Lover of cars, traveling, and comedy
Who feels bored, tired, and hungry
Who gives respect, honesty and gifts
Who fears God, Dr Ellis, and Dr. P
Who would like to see Carlos Mencia
Who lives in a big world
Awad

Jacob Awad, Grade 8
Montgomery Central Middle School, TN

Snow White/Maleficent

Snow White
Sweet, beautiful
Red-lipped, singing, waking
Cottage, dwarfs — poison, apples
Horrifying, killing, defeated
Mean, ugly
Maleficent

Bailey Beeson, Grade 7
Greenfield Jr/Sr High School, MO

In the Woods

in the woods
between two cities
near the ocean
beyond the mountains
on the ground
among the animals
beneath the stars
by the river
down the path
upon a bed of leaves
in front of a waterfall
at the entrance of a cave
on an island far away
in solitude
without witnesses
until the end of time
against a tree
in the woods
is a huge snake

Samantha Lamon, Grade 8
Pigeon Forge Middle School, TN

Storm

Storm
Violent clouds
Dark skies above
Lightning, thunder, rain, hail
Storm

Ian Curley, Grade 8
Belle Isle Enterprise Middle School, OK

Easter

People dressed up
Barbecue aroma all around
Crazy cousins laughing and having fun
Boiled eggs and chocolate of all types
The hay from baskets all around
Easter

Samantha Telep, Grade 7
Newcastle Middle School, OK

Time

Different cities, different states
All the same goal in mind
The gun shot fires, I take my first step
And so begins the time

The strive for beating the clock
The enthusiastic calls from the side
My wings fly along the asphalt
Pacing all my strides

I can hear my heart pounding in my ears
Like a hammer hits a nail
My arms pump as my feet move faster
I know I cannot fail

The ribbon is in sight
I accelerate with all my might
It gently splits across my chest
Giving me a thrill of success

Kayla McElroy, Grade 9
Hamburg Jr High School, AR

My Brothers

Brothers
Best friends
Make me smile
Can be extremely annoying
Family

Athena Nguyen, Grade 8
Belle Isle Enterprise Middle School, OK

Our Soldiers

Soldiers are soldiers
Great to see come
Home, but it's sad
To see them leave
'Cause you can hear
Those soldier boys
Shout, and guns and
Gun powder every
Where, just hoping
To see them come
Home soon.

Domonique Davis, Grade 7
Clarksburg School, TN

Ahmad Beleaguered

At school I ask myself why I am the one
to let everyone take advantage of me
and push me into the indigo box
like a broken toy.
Never to be seen as a friend with anybody
unless they wanted an A in order to pass a test.
I am Ahmad.
I cannot hide anything.
If I say something unforgivable
they always tell an adult.
They always beat me if I make a mistake.
I live in the darkness.
Even now,
as I grow up,
and make new friends
they know that I am Ahmad,
the one pushed in the indigo box
like a broken toy.

Mekaal Ahmad, Grade 8
Baylor School, TN

Win

Victory, happiness
Running, screaming, shooting
Triumphs, accomplishments, hopelessness, downfall
Suffering, hurting, tearing
Lost, farewell
Lose

Ali Syler, Grade 7
Leeton Middle and High School, MO

For the Broken and Bruised

Seeing the world through a tear-filled eye,
Unable to let out a single cry.
The wounds on His back,
The lashes, the cracks
His scars made Him beautiful.
Falling down, lift Him up.
Painful cries, glory to God.
His heart dies, giving life to the broken.
His scars made Him beautiful.
Seeing the world through a tear-filled eye,
Unable to let out a single cry.
The bruises on her body
Her body so thin.
She needed something beautiful.
Falling down, does anyone love me?
Painful cries, should I be alive?
Her heart is dying, but Someone gives her life.
She found something beautiful.
For Him she cried.
For her He died.
His scars made her beautiful.

Mercee Nelson, Grade 9
Family of Faith Christian School, OK

The Blank Piece of Paper

The blank piece of paper
Just laying there
Filled with wonders and dreams
The blank piece of paper
It's blank it seems
But its not
From your imagination
It starts to fill up
With a wonderful story
About a blank piece of paper
That has a word or two
It's about your imagination
Running wild
With your dreams or beliefs
You pick up your pencil
And start writing
So let your mind free
And write a good story

Terry Wofford, Grade 7
Hazelwood Northwest Middle School, MO

The Gray Man

There was a man whose life was gray,
He would not leave his house during the day.
But during the night he would visit the bay.
When he arrived at the bay he looked up at the moon,
Thinking that someday things would be better, someday soon.
At least he hoped the day would be soon.
He gazed at the moon and the stars every night.
Begging them to relieve him of his plight,
For a day with color to come in sight
The gray man wanted color in his gray life
Something to get him out of his strife
He needed color in his gray life
Nobody knew him so would anyone care
If this gray man threw himself into the air?
But the gray man thought not and down he flew.
Down to the water, to an ice cold blue.
But one person would care as the gray man flew through the air
And saved the gray man from his strife
And at last color entered the once gray man's life

Jack Schoelz, Grade 8
West Jr High School, MO

Mad Turkey Mom

In the early morning the gobble wakes me from my sleep.
The turkey's call telling me to come eat.
She struts and pecks all around the house,
Tail spreading, feathers flinging.
Gobble! Gobble! Gobble!
Scolded for an unclean room.
She draws me close, folded in her wings.
A peck on the cheek
Everything is okay.

Lauren DeLay, Grade 8
St Charles Homeschool Learning Center, MO

Years

2007,
a long year,
but a fast one,
just another year,
but a different year,
than all the others,
a good summer,
not much school,
but harder school work,
a year to be left behind,
but not forgotten.

Jesse Spencer, Grade 8
Benton County School of the Arts, AR

The Characteristics of Fall

The leaves turn their different colors
red, orange, yellow, brown
They peacefully start to weaken
and fall to the ground

The nights become colder
There's a chill in the air
In the morn' there is a surprise
frost within our stare

I hear the birds a'chirpin'
as they nest high in the tree
then I see a furry squirrel
attentive but carefree

The sounds and looks of fall
make me want to smile
although the truth is
it will only last a while

Jennifer Hacker, Grade 7
Nettleton Jr High School, AR

My Window

I look outside on a sunny day
All of my dark feelings blown away
I wonder what will come in near time
I will just wait to see what may

The sun brightens my distant past
However no shadows have been cast
Things are better now
Now that the sun has brightened my past

Nicholas Kiser, Grade 8
Gresham Middle School, TN

White Paradise

Praying for no school,
Falling down like a feather,
Hot chocolate time!

Aleesa Breese, Grade 8
St Joseph School, MO

Brackett Guilty of Perseverance

"Get up, Brackett! Get back up! Get up, Brackett!" I scream in my mind,
but instead I shove my face further into the neck of my jersey,
holding back tears and hiding myself from onlookers.
My hands smear my bruised thighs.
I slide my hands down my calf and unlace my cleats.
I rip off my jersey, the number fifteen beams as I sling it over my shoulder,
and I hoist myself upon my feet, holding my stomach like Napoleon.
I stumble to a corner where the sharp, silver fence whispers "Failure,"
and I listen to boys giggle, capturing videos and snapping pictures.
"This is my game, not yours. How dare you show up and make fun of me."
Do they have no life? I sob in disgust.
And cough what feels like jagged glass, slitting the insides of my swollen throat.
I'm huddled over: throwing-up.
Through my blurry vision, I see the field freckled with red and blue
and my heart is bruised purple, I lie on my back in the dirt
Even now, I can't live down the rumors.
I will never forget the words that were thrown at me, like, "Faker."
but I am Brackett, the girl who took too much energy gel and got food poisoning,
the one who listens to them cackle, the star of a 'hilarious' video.
But more importantly, the one who will persevere.

Chloe Brackett, Grade 8
Baylor School, TN

Life

My heart like bark, tearing from the core of my soul.
Should you care, I might dare.
But you don't, so I won't.

Life is like an hourglass.
Each day a grain of sand falling, falling, falling,
Never again can it fall.

Disease is like a tap to the top of the glass.
Death like a hammer smashing it all into bits and pieces,
That combined add up to life,
But individually are nothing more than grains of sand and broken glass.

But love, love is when gravity stops pulling upon the grain of sand and it stops,
If only for a moment, the moment you admit to yourself,
You have fallen for your love,
Your one true love.

Laura Figueroa, Grade 8
Owasso 8th Grade Center, OK

Never Forgotten

Left only with memories, never forgotten.
My head in my hands, thinking of the times we had.
I want to feel deja vu in remembrance of those happy times, never sad.
reminiscing of our love for each other
your my best friend and I'd have it no other way
there aren't words in the dictionary that could ever explain
our bond and trust towards ourselves
and onwards to the future.

Mariam Salem, Grade 8
Pleasant View School, TN

Permit Me to Tell You About Love

Permit me to tell you about love.
The hurt and terror of rejection when you deeply care for one person,
The joy of having someone's arms wrapped around you when you need comfort,
The affection given every day because you know you will stay together forever,
The feeling that's unexplainable when you know you have found the right one.
But the love given to me that I remember most
Lifted my spirit and brought me to understand every kind and loving soul around me,
Fixed my heart no matter how broken it might be,
Held my head when I poured my trust and tears into all their hearts,
Made me laugh when I desperately needed to because my heart was breaking in two,
And yet, my heart is patched by their love, soul full of trust,
And head full of knowledge of who I can really love.

Taylor Tumminello, Grade 8
All Saints School, MO

The Perfect Night

I sit waiting quietly on my little brown couch.
I'm dressed and made-up like a Barbie Doll.
Hoping that he'll soon arrive so our wonderful night may begin.
With a break in the silence the door bell beckons, and my heart jumps in my chest with fear.
Do I look good? Will he be impressed?
I gather my courage and answer the door.
In the door way is the silhouette of a boy.
He's my knight in shining armor.

Kelsey Morgan Murphy, Grade 8
Alpena High School, AR

My Life Story

I have my ups and downs. One of my ups is that I had gotten adopted in 3rd grade. It was the best day of my life. My downs is that I get myself in a lot of trouble. Well, I guess you can't blame my parents. This is my life. I am proud of it too. My ups is better than it would be with my birth mother. I'm glad I had gotten adopted because I wouldn't know my friends that I have right now. God is the reason for my life story.

Charles Sanders, Grade 7
Highland Rim School, TN

Discovery

Glittering dust layers the clearing.
Moonlight caresses the blanket of newly fallen snow.
As Midnight swathes her cloak about the forest glen, silence reigns supreme.
The silence seems to hover for a moment before shattering into oblivion as a yawn echoes around the glad.
Two endless pools of jade light crack open lazily.
A rustling of dried leaves and a breath of air inside the cozy warm den sends shivers down the creature's spine.
Something just wasn't right.
An onyx-tipped snout swiftly appeared, twitching as frigid air greeted it with an icy embrace.
Disappearing suddenly, the maw and its owner appear again with vengeance in a shower of leaves.
The owner of the muzzle, a young vixen, yelps in surprise as she lands face-first in a pile of snow.
Her fiery white tipped brush flicks back and forth in dismay.
This powder was cold!
The fox's emerald green eyes then sparkle in laughter.
Snow!
Frozen water that one walks in.
Giving a sharp bark, the vixen pounces into a pile of snow.
Frozen water that one cavorts in.
Certainly this was an odd discovery.

Amy M. Schattel, Grade 8
Shepherdstown Middle School, WV

The World

The world is like a top
It keeps spinning and spinning
But no one will know when it stops

The world was once all ice
Like a big frozen ice cube
Where mammoths and mammals collide

Some say the world will end in fire
Some say in ice
But God will decide on the fate
Of our lives
Because we are all God's children.

Jacob Wiesler, Grade 9
St John the Baptist High School, MO

Fishin'

The grass is green.
The sky is blue.
I'm going fishin'.
How about you?

Gonna cast a rod
While sittin' on the grass.
Tryin' hard
To catch me a bass.

When the sun comes up
What you gonna do?
I'll be catchin' fish.
How 'bout you?

Dillon Holt, Grade 7
Elkton School, TN

Magic the Gathering

M ade for playing
A t any place
G ame with cards
I ntellect required
C an be played by anyone

T eams are a possibility
H elp can be given
E verybody has a color

G reen, blue, white, red and black
A mazing and fun
T here are combos
H umans are a type of creature
E ven snakes and merfolk
R arity doesn't matter
I nferiosity is not prohibited
N ever give up
G ame with all types of creatures

Adam Shifflet, Grade 7
Hartville Jr/Sr High School, MO

Inequality

Sad as you are, because you compare,
You feel worthless.
Though you never count your blessings,
And of everything you have.

You look at people, with the bottom corner of your eyes,
for you think you are so good.
You walk with your back straight,
And now, you cannot learn, for the blindness of the pride has killed you.

The world is not perfect, and everything inside it.
What a fool you are, if you are arrogant,
and a Wise man if you are humble.

Learn from your experiences, for that is the valuable thing to do.
Your life is yours, and your future is in your hand.
Yesterday holds the past, and tomorrow holds your hope, don't look at others,
for God is very fair.

Anna He, Grade 8
West Jr High School, MO

Joshua

Joshua
Caring, funny, smart, athletic
Brother of Amanda Gail
Lover of Dr. Pepper, pizza, and video games
Who feels loved at home, cared about, and good when having fun
Who gives love, compassion, and friendship to others
Who needs sports, video games, and food
Who fears Mrs. Murphy, my dad, and God
Who would like to see the Red Sox, the Yankees, and the Braves
Newsom

Joshua Newsom, Grade 8
Montgomery Central Middle School, TN

Is It Over Yet?

Ba-boom, Ba-boom
My heart is pounding as I stroll into place.
Anticipating,
"Can we just get this over with," I think to myself.
The room goes dead silent while the music begins.
My cue is coming.
I can feel my stomach fall 1,000,000 miles down.
"This is it!" I think to myself.
My leg lifts as if I were a gazelle prancing across the grassy meadow.
I twirl, jump, and wave my arms,
Here the finale is.
I spin around staying as balanced as possible.
The song is over now,
Yet for a few more seconds I hold this awkward position.
My leg is bent at an angle placed against my left leg like a flamingo.
I look over to the corner, and my instructor gives us the signal to put our legs down.
We form our line to take our bow as the crowd applauds joyfully.
I smile as I gasp for air.

Margo J. Parks, Grade 7
White Station Middle School, TN

An Autumn Day Prayer

She walked very slowly, her head held high,
Gazing with awe at the infinite blue sky.
Her feet faltered as they dragged gently through,
Rustling leaves of crimson, bronze and amber hue.
The limbs of the trees were bare and the grass grey,
Yet glorious beauty surrounded the forest, that day.
The wind whistled through the trees so very soft,
Where merry little birds in the boughs were aloft.
Though flowers of fairness were quite scarce and few,
Peaceful, timid deer graced the forest, she knew.
Her heart seemed to sing as she looked all about;
"Surely, surely, the Lord is creator!" she longed to shout.
"Though man can create, nothing compares in the least
To all that God has made in love without cease.
His hand is shown in all that I see this marvelous day;
May His name be exalted forevermore, I pray!"

Rebekah Parish, Grade 7
Coram Deo Home School Academy, MO

Macey Hodges

Macey Noel
Silly, fun, short, caring, smart
Daughter of Patty and Ronald Hodges
Lover of basketball, 4-wheelers, talking on the Internet
Who feels fun with friends, dancing, eating food
Who gives friends many laughs, good times, bad times
Who needs Mountain Dew, Internet, pizza
Who fears bad grades, black widow spiders, and the dark
Who would like to see Australia, Canada, Cuba
Who lives in Clarksville, TN
Hodges

Macey Noel Hodges, Grade 8
Montgomery Central Middle School, TN

My Mission for Eternal Love!

When I look into your eyes, I see the sun.
When I look into my heart, I know you are the one.
If you believe in me, I'll believe in you.
Then I know we'll see our love through.

If you could be my eternal love,
our love will stretch to the stars above.
When God put you here just for me,
I knew our mission was to spread love for our destiny.

My heart used to be filled with nothing but hate,
but when I met you, I knew you were my soul mate.
I know we've been through bumpy roads,
but still I wonder where our love will go.
Always through thick and thin, I have to pick up the pieces
of where our love will begin

As long as I have you, I know we will see our mission through.
Always we're together, our love will last forever.

Jarrett Long, Grade 9
Grandview Alternative School, MO

Air to Compare

The whipping winds slash across my cheeks
As we get deeper into the weeks

The melancholy clouds make me blind
Making me vacant in the mind

The whipping wind wraps around my body
Making me embrace the thin air
Because it is autumn
And there's no other season to compare

Samantha Coates, Grade 8
Houston Middle School, TN

Take Me as I Am

I love me for me.
I love life for what it is!
But, why judge when it's already hard to be you.
So many people lie, just to be lying.
I say, why lie, and the truth is as easy as a pie.
I live for tomorrow, hopefully not dying today
Meaning you should really cherish each day.
I try so hard to be real
Because fakeness fades away all day.
So, as I was saying, don't Judge me today.

Porsha Dockery, Grade 9
Hillcrest High School, TN

Life

Guys and girls always go for whirls.
here and there sometimes anywhere.
But when you're left all alone,
you feel so bad you don't even want to talk on the telephone.
Crying sobbing, weeping if you must,
at some point in our lives it has happened to us.
If not yet it will later on.
And you may be bawling from dusk to dawn.
But you need not to hurt anyone.
For you all should know it is not fun.

Haley Thompson, Grade 7
Highland Rim School, TN

About Me

Austin
Athletic, intelligent, sometimes understanding, able to cooperate
Son of my loving mother Judith Amber Wills
I love my mom and she loves me
Who feels that everyone has a chance
Who needs to have friends that are there for me
Who gives it 110% on and off the baseball field
Who fears to fail something
I would like to see a world series baseball game
I am a resident of my loving mom
Wills

Austin Wills, Grade 8
Montgomery Central Middle School, TN

The Clock

Life all squirms and starts to form
On the day you come to form
You hear the voice inside your head
As you lie within your bed
"For you doors will soon unlock
It is time to start the clock"
You blink your eyes and you're at school
You go to class and find your stool
"Tick by tick and tock by tock
Ten years have gone 'round the clock"
You turn around and your in your dorm
Studying for a test at morn
you think of future roads to take
The possibilities that you could make
"Your future is within your grasp,
Twenty years have come and passed"
You in your bed back at square one
The journey's over and you are done
Lying there white as chalk
Thus the voice begins to talk
"It is time to stop the clock"

Joseph Wolfe, Grade 8
Maple Park Middle School, MO

Christmas Cheer

Christmas time is finally here
People spreading Christmas cheer
Seeing smiles on all the faces
Christmas cheer is in all places

Kelsey Collins, Grade 8
Hartville Jr/Sr High School, MO

Guide Me

Wrong has blinded
Me
Grief and pain have weakened
Me
The cruel world has pushed
Me
Bondage has kept
Me
But I need someone to guide
Me
There is no light for
Me
The ground is hard and mean to
Me
It isn't soft and comforting for
Me
To fall onto
But God, I need someone to guide
Me
Will you guide
Me?

Brianna Sitz, Grade 7
Johnson Traditional Middle School, KY

Tiffany Tuerck

Tiffany
Smart, caring, intelligent, nice
Sister to Cody, Chris, and Adam
Lover of family, pets, and, money
Who feels shy, wonderful, and annoyed by my brother
Who gives toys, donations, and presents to the poor
Who needs a family, friends, and my cell phone
Who fears snakes, spiders, and haunted house
Who would like to see a sunset in Hawaii, a famous actor, and Disney Land
Who lives in Tennessee
Tuerck

Tiffany Tuerck, Grade 8
Montgomery Central Middle School, TN

Brittany Mutters

Brittany
Crazy, fun, energetic, intelligent
Sister of Destiny, Nicole, and Allen
Lover of skating, Myspace, and the phone
Who feels sad when someone is mad at her
Who gives love, laughs, and fun
Who needs love, sugar, and socialization
Who fears spiders, frogs, and bugs
Who would like to see Hawaii, the Bahamas, and Cute Is What We Aim For live
Who lives in country filled Clarksville, Tennessee
Mutters

Brittany Mutters, Grade 8
Montgomery Central Middle School, TN

Thank God

For my playful dog, and my smiling family.
The grass in my yard, vibrant and beautiful.
For the trees that give us oxygen, and in the fall,
The leaves that plummet softly to the ground in their bright colors,
Like the sparks of a bonfire.
Thank God for sight.

For birds chirping, and dogs barking.
Like cannons breaking the sound barrier
And cicada that you can find a tune.
Thank God for sound.

For juice, liquid gold on my tongue.
For bread, warm and soft bread that melts in your mouth.
Thank God for taste.

For roses, fresh-cut grass, and fruit.
The citrus and natural scent of fruits.
Thank God for smell.

For smooth pebbles to chuck across the water.
And cold refreshing water in summer.
Thank God for touch.

Nathan Fischer, Grade 7
Our Lady Catholic School, MO

Never Another Night

That night I lie upon the hill,
Face open to the cool night air,
Watching my every warm breath turn misty,
And quickly disappear into the sky.
My eyes staring up into the countless stars,
My thoughts start to settle in my head,
I can't remember a time when I've ever felt safer,
As the sacred night falls around us,
My best friends and I.
Knowing that camp will never truly end,
We slowly drift to sleep as the stars fall.

Matt Lickenbrock, Grade 8
Annunciation Elementary School, MO

Thankful

I am thankful for video games
For there are those who can't afford to buy them
or never experience them

I am thankful for God
For the things He brought in and out of this world

I am thankful for chocolate
For those who can't enjoy the taste of this
wonderful sensation

I am thankful for sports
For those who can't experience this because
they have had an accident that had ended their career

I am thankful for music
For the people who could never hear, because
they are missing out on a lot of beautiful sounds

I am thankful for friends
For those who can't get along with anyone or are
very lonely because no one likes them

Damien Fangman, Grade 8
Avenue City Elementary School, MO

Above the Crowd

The wind blows softly across her face
She stares into open space
Her mind races to grasp what happened in moments past
And she never wants to turn back

Rewinding the moment to keep the feeling
Thanking everyone for helping with her healing
The scars have left her face
The memories will soon be erased
Absolutely loving her current place
She runs to make her parents proud
That she finally lives above the crowd.

Briana Phillips, Grade 9
West Jr High School, MO

Spring Storm

All afternoon we stay indoors
Safe from the driving rain.
As it pounds and persistently pours
Into the gutter and down the drain.
Swirling masses deep and dark
Swarm over the yellow moor
Over cemeteries, grim and stark;
The sleeping hear thunder's roar.
Hopeful buds on the branches of trees
Toss and billow with each sapphire drop
And with every jewel, comes a breeze
As we wait for the storm to stop.
But then a yellow ray of light
Pierces the angry clouds
And with an awfully colossal might
Touches the forest shrouds.
So now born from the terrible storm
Is a shining rainbow of every shade,
Its beauty shines on everything, and makes the world warm.

Laura Magerkurth, Grade 8
Bernard C Campbell Middle School, MO

Fall

The scarecrow hanging in the field
Quietly watching fall build.
The leaves are falling on the ground
Different colors are all around.
Farmers harvest their crop
Like dirt being picked up with a mop.
There is a chill in the air
Coming from who knows where.
A feast for many we prepare
At Thanksgiving we will share.
We have been waiting a whole year
Now we can go shoot some deer.
In the fog you don't know where you are at
You are blind as a bat.
And now that it is fall
You can hear the swish of a basketball.
At the end of the day
I hope fall won't ever fade away.

Nicole Duty, Grade 7
Nettleton Jr High School, AR

The Journey

Take a journey through life's curved path
But be sure to stop and smell the trees
And be sure to feel the warmth of a summer breeze
That all the Earth may have

Always stop to watch a sunrise
And keep on going until you can't give anymore
Instead of closing, always open the door
And notice the welcoming growing in your eyes

Zach Moyers, Grade 8
Highland Rim School, TN

Winter

Winter.
Cold mornings.
Frost sprinkled lawns.
Snowy days, flakes falling.
Christmas.

Alexia Gonzalez, Grade 8
Belle Isle Enterprise Middle School, OK

Rain

Rain fall is like the sky crying
The rain is tears falling from a face
It longs for something it lost or someone
The rain falls because It's sad
The rain falls for someone it lost
The rain falls on a gloomy day
It makes people sad like it is

April Boothe, Grade 7
Greenfield Jr/Sr High School, MO

Possessed

Hypnotized more every hour,
As it grows in its power,
Controlling me with my mind.
As my eyes grow weary and tire,
If I stop the results will be dire.
Why am I here being so lame?
Possessed in my room by a video game.

Eli Smith, Grade 7
Greenfield Jr/Sr High School, MO

Fall Is in the Air

Oh, no
Time is going back
Whispering breeze
Colorful leaves
Coldness in the air,
More warm clothes to wear
It is Fall
Fall is a fun time to cheer
It's the best!
It's even a time to rest
Live, laugh, love
It's all in the air above

Ashley Walker, Grade 7
Edgemont Elementary School, TN

Snowflake

Flake
bright, cold
flying, falling, freezing
stiff, shape, white, fluffy
melting, shaping, shifting
colorful, soft
Snow

Laura Budder, Grade 8
Wickliffe Elementary School, OK

Do You Remember?

I remember when the world was not so worried
I remember when those planes hit the tall buildings
I remember how the world was so afraid
I remember almost exactly what happened on that very tragic day.

Chelsea Bax, Grade 8
St Joseph School, MO

When Creation Stands Out

Leaves falling from the trees doing loopty loops like a rollercoaster,
Clovers all in a bunch like sardines, the grassy mildew making it sweat,
Dark clouds covering the sky like glazing your ice cream with chocolate syrup.

Dogs barking, crickets sounding like a fire alarm, fly's buzzing,
Crows calling their flock, cars driving by like the sound of the ocean,
Trees and leaves whooshing together like the sound of rain.

Cattle grazing tasting those juicy spices, strawberries,
Watermelon, corn, and the sweet taste of honeysuckle.

Roses wafting through the air like my mom's perfume,
The fresh smell of rain, humid, smoky air,
Breathe in and out with God's great gift,
Thank you God for the precious air.

Sand rushing through my toes; grass flossing my feet,
Water crackling on my ankles.
The sun a big flashlight beating down on me with great heat.

In this world is God's great creation,
Air and ground, we might not stop to admire,
But don't let your love for God ever expire,
So thank you God for I praise you.

Kristen Gaylord, Grade 7
Our Lady Catholic School, MO

Missing You

I know this might sound crazy, I know that I'm too late
But I wish that you would listen, I wish that you would wait
I know that we are over but I wish it wasn't so
I wish I was still with you and those times didn't have to go
I miss everything about us, I miss the little things
Like the way my heart would soar whenever the phone would ring
I miss the way you smiled when I'd see you in the hall
I miss the way you'd pick me up whenever I would fall
I miss the twinkle in your eyes and the laughter in your voice
I miss knowing that I had the best because you aren't like any other boy
I am sorry for the things I said and I'm sorry that I lied
Believe me missing you makes me lonely inside
I know that I'm the reason that sometimes we would fight
And now it gives me pain in the middle of the night
So I know that this sounds crazy, I don't mean to bring you pain
I know I'm stirring up the past and now there's not much this can gain
I don't expect you to forgive me though I desperately wish you will
Just know that my next man will have hard shoes to fill

Dovie White, Grade 8
Branson Jr High School, MO

The Lullaby

She sings to me a lullaby
Every night after the sun leaves the sky.
Her voice so mournful and serene
Like the lake in which her pale face reflects,
She sings to me of all the things she has seen.
In the life she has lived so very long,
Her voice so full of sorrow

She sings of how lonely it is to be so beautiful
So far away with only the stars to keep her company.

She tells me stories of forest spirits.
They dance and sing in perfectly peaceful harmony.

Forever alone she watches over us,
By her light she watches as the world blooms,
Most never even give a second glance.

Mercedes Simpson, Grade 9
Morgantown High School, WV

Monkey

See how he swings,
from tree to tree.
See how he eats bananas,
in the forest.
On top of the trees,
on the safest branch,
where only very faint sounds of other monkeys talking comes.
The taste of the bananas,
so fresh and sweet.
See how he lives up on the tallest tree.

Alyssa Chaudhari, Grade 7
Baylor School, TN

I Am

I am strong and courageous.
I wonder how things happen so fast.
I see memories from the past.
I want to live in the now.
I am strong and courageous.

I pretend to be strong when I am hurt.
I feel love all around me.
I touch people around me.
I worry when I really should not.
I cry when I feel sad.
I am strong and courageous.

I understand why things happen.
I saw what I feel.
I dream about the future.
I try to do my best at everything I attempt.
I hope to be the best.
I am strong and courageous.

Dakota Schildknecht, Grade 8
King City High School, MO

What America Means to Me

America means pride
I am proud of the men and women who defend our country
America means religion
I am thankful for God
America means freedom
I am free to be what I want to be
America means education
I am thankful for my teachers
America means sports
I am thankful for baseball
America means belonging to a community
I collect cans for the canned food drive
America means history
I learn about our country's past
America means standing up for what is right
I stand up to bullies
America means justice
I obey the law
America means preparing for the future
I am the future.

Cody Ressel, Grade 9
Comanche High School, OK

Confused

He says my name, what do I do
He tells me he loves me, but I love you
I see his face, but see your smile
He walks away, I think awhile
He stares right at me, but I see your eyes
He broke my heart, but it's for you that I cry
He holds me tight, yet it's for you that I burn
He leaves me alone, yet I pray for your return
He says my name a second time
And I hope that you are saying mine

Ashlie Green, Grade 8
Chelsea Jr High School, OK

These People

I get to the door,
I'm so excited.

This day is going to be a blast!
I walk to my seat
and see all these people.
They are dancing, singing, and praising.
They lift their hands up high,
these people seemed so happy.
I now have been there for an hour,
I'm so used to these people in
just that amount of time.

I join them, I sing, I dance,
I am praising the Lord.

Courtney Gore, Grade 8
Southern Reynolds County R-II School, MO

Storm Day

I watch a storm approaching from my porch step I see the dark gray cloud against the light blowing winds, with a roll of thunder, and a strike of lightning, I feel a drop of rain against my face, raindrops began to fall harder with every passing minute leaving raindrops dotted on my clothes, with lightning striking against the sky, I found myself dreaming of days gone by.

Kimberlynn Young, Grade 8
Highland Rim School, TN

Multihued, Magical Rotation

Passionately, come bountiful expressions of love and jovial, foolish pranks,
Springing forward into the regular old time, losing sleep,
Heavens shed tears of joyfulness that produce our true magical wish.
Rainbow honeydew stamens and petals are replete with venturesome, whizzing butterflies.
Rustling wings of birds fly back to home.

A blazing, luminous star stoops and scalds my head.
Hot as magma, bare feet scamper off of sidewalk stoves like eggs frying in a pan.
Traveling around like newborn shouting spiders whisking,
whichever way the talk of the wheezing wind blows.
Amusement parks and tasteful, culinary venues vacuum our frail, paper gold.

Plants wrinkle and shrivel from being wise and old;
like everything else they go away like a cold.
Sniffles and allergies caused by frigid temperatures,
Turkey and sweet cinnamon accompanied by yellow, red, and brown leaves.
Harsh winds blow the resting leaves into a clockwise, necklace swirl.

Spirit of Jolly shivers and sings for Christmas with the ardor it brings,
Millions cheer spirit except few with a melancholy focus.
Cooking s'mores over a furious warm red and orange light,
Windows ice and bells ring to give in the season of giving and support those less fortunate.
Crystalline, shimmering snowflakes sprinkle the dewed ground with a taciturn atmosphere.
Building a Jack Frost that melts as the Sun's rays peek out yet again, once more.

Ramona Durham, Grade 7
White Station Middle School, TN

The Universe

The universe is a peaceful celestial cosmos,
Filled with millions of sparkling stars and luminous planets.
Around and around the planets proceed and orbit,
Circling the bright and burning star.
Lifeless and never changing do the planets revolve.
Tranquilly they rotate, never ending; circle within circle.
Slowly they spin in an orbital trance through space each day.
Days turn into months; months into years; years into centuries.
And among this never-ending rotation, is a shining blue marble,
Filled with glorious life and energy.
Beautiful seas and roaming lands embody the globe,
Making it truly unique.
Lives constantly begin, end, and start again.
Souls are transformed from the most horrifying ugliness, to the most remarkable beauty.
Humans are lost and found again.
Tiny fantasies are imagined, spectacular lifestyles become realities.
The galaxy within the universe and the planets within the galaxy,
Make up the great and powerful solar system.
Truly remarkable are the planets that revolve around the sun.

Lindsey Morphis, Grade 9
Hamburg Jr High School, AR

Anne Marie

Anne Marie was born in Memphis, Tennessee,
A really funny gal who,
Is always telling jokes,
Refuses to grow up.

Warm hearted and loving.
She has a lot of imaginary friends,
Who always makes me laugh.
When she talks about them all the time.
It is as if they are a part of her family.

Her visits are very special
Because she lives far away.
My eyes get all teary
When I know she will leave for New York City.
Because she is my favorite aunt.

Daniel Barrach, Grade 7
White Station Middle School, TN

Love

I love the rough feeling of the ocean's waves
crashing on me as I swim along the sandbar.
I love watching the stars
as they sparkle through the clear night sky
onto the dark face of the once luminous Earth.
I love seeing the sun shine
on the morning dew drops,
each one glistening with the light.
I love finding a new blessing in my life,
and the blissful feelings that rush through my mind,
as I examine the flawlessness of each blessing…
The blessing of life
as it breathes in my soul,
and breathes its pureness
in the souls of others.
The blessing of laughter
as it projects from my heart,
and expresses the joyful feelings that lie within.
The blessing of love as it surrounds me every day,
and cradles me with patient, perfect, loving arms.
And the greatest blessing of these is love.

Sarah Hencke, Grade 8
Baylor School, TN

Alone

To have sorrow, to have grief,
to wake up every day with no relief.
No brothers, no sisters, and sometimes no friends.
It feels like life has come to an end.
And no one could ever feel this way,
only me, all alone every day.
The years will pass and it will still be me,
but maybe one day I'll finally be free.

Helen Beach, Grade 7
St Cecilia Academy, MO

The St. Louis Rams

These Rams, these Rams,
They're playing like little, little, lambs.
They are 0 and 8 and this city has no love, just hate.
Next week they are going to be 0 and 9.
The Rams might as well start to whine.
They play a team with not many wins,
But they are still going to get beat by the Dolphins.
Can our St. Louis Lambs turn into Rams again?

Caleb Stroop, Grade 7
Hazelwood Northwest Middle School, MO

The Beat Goes On…

For every door there is a key
If you unlock it they will be set free
But if the key doesn't fit, tough
You just ran straight out of luck
In every home there is a desperate cry
The beat of their wings cry out to the sky
With their wings pointed towards the sky
They close their eyes and wish to begin to fly
But the sky is locked out of their sight
They crash into walls when they try to take flight
No way to leave, no way to escape
And without the key there's no way out to break out
Release them from the locked door
Release them and watch them soar
Find the key and plan their escape
A simple key is all it will take
Unlock it and watch them fly out
And there it is their simple escape route
With the key through the door and them gone
It's finally done, wherever they are, wherever they've gone
When they're soaring, the beat goes on

Arika Wilson, Grade 7
Hazelwood Southeast Middle School, MO

A Story of a Cat

Once upon a time, a story would start,
Whether it will be sweet, or whether it will be tart,
My story is about a cat
This cat is mine in fact
If you are sensitive then stop if you would
But if you are not then read on, you should
This cat was fat and lovable
He was sweet and adorable
However this cat you could say
Was too sweet in a way
Because one day he ran away
Or just was kind enough to come to somebody else
I still hope he is okay
But sometimes I doubt myself
I still miss him but I have moved on
Found another cat but I still miss him
O very, very much

Ethan Baxter, Grade 8
Greenfield Jr/Sr High School, MO

Penguin*

She how she plunges
toward the deep blue sea.
She how she submerges
so gracefully.
Swimming through, under and
around the shark homes she
searches for a fellow penguin
to play with.
Before giving up all hope
the penguin finds her new friend.
They swim and slide all day
and into the night
until they fall asleep exhausted
waiting for day light.

Paige Partrick, Grade 7
Baylor School, TN
**Patterned after "Seal"*
by William Jay Smith

Storms

The house rattled and jarred,
As the storm approached quite hard.
The winds swirled like a blender,
By now the sky was scarred,
The rain felt like ice cubes,
So frightening and so frozen
Loud thunder down from under,
With bright lightning quiet as a mouse.

Madison Gallagher, Grade 7
Highland Rim School, TN

obviously only important to me

walking through the park
on a sad day for me
my family, my friends, everyone
has forgotten something important
apparently only important to me
the feeling of being forgotten
makes me cry in pain
the day important to me
was my birthday
obviously only important to me

Will Fisher, Grade 8
White Station Middle School, TN

Poetry

Poetry is not just writing
It is about what is inside
It comes from the heart
Poetry is a feeling
It is an expression
It can be about anything
Poetry is you

Skylar Brian Mefford, Grade 8
Highland Rim School, TN

Life Is

Life is a never-ending journey
with no definite purpose.
Life is like a pool of water
gleaming at the surface.

Life is only temporary
so live it to the fullest.
Do what makes you happy
even though it's not the coolest.

Life is made of emotions
depending on how you look at it.
Life is like a candle
whose wick has just been lit.

Life is a secluded path
that has many twists and turns.
Life is what you make it
and that's what you shall learn.

A.J. Collins, Grade 9
St John the Baptist High School, MO

Love and Butterflies

Love…
might as well be a butterfly.

Hard to catch,
yet precious when found;

Difficult to hold onto,
yet worth every moment;

Needs to be kept close,
yet desires the freedom;

Unusual and different,
yet absolutely breathtaking.

Yes.
Love might as well be a butterfly.

Shivani Goyal, Grade 9
Bearden High School, TN

Deer Stand

The leaves are red and yellow
The grass is damp.
Walking to my stand I'm unheard
I get to the stand and wait a bit.

BOOM!
The silence is over and
There lies a deer
That will never run again.

Johnathan Horn, Grade 7
Kiowa Jr/Sr High School, OK

Our House

Our house is cluttered,
As well as dusty.
In it, mice have muttered;
Its metal is rusty.
It is home to many creatures —
Possibly even a gnome.
It lacks extravagant features,
But nevertheless, we call it home.

Bronson Pennington, Grade 9
Bearden High School, TN

Thanksgiving

T hanks to all friends and family
H olidays
A rmy troops that fight for us
N ot greedy
K indness and the love on this day
S ay grace and send love to your family
G rateful
I nvite your family and friends
V isit your family
I ce cream cakes
N ovember
G iving and caring

Kassandra Zebell, Grade 7
Niangua High School, MO

Dirt Bikes

Dirt bikes are awesome to ride.
Outside in the warm sun.
Riding in the soft, green grass.
It almost looks like you're floating.
Going so fast you look like a blur.
Dirt bikes are fun to ride.

Riley Malone, Grade 7
Highland Rim School, TN

To Love

Trust
An indescribable emotion
Keep no score
One step closer to perfect

Love
Cherish the moment
Cling to the instant you find it
Never let it slip away

Restore your ability
Renew your capacity
Never forget how

To love

Sammi Davenport, Grade 8
West Middle School, TN

Ocean

Beautiful I may be,
But carefully my children swim.
Foe evil creatures lurk,
Willing my children uncareful adventures,
Some have a destiny that's quite grim.
For I am unforgiving,
To those who steal from me!
Some escape from my wrath; others not.
But soon I shall be calm,
As calm as sister sea.

Stephonie Dailing, Grade 8
Bueker Middle School, MO

Friends

Friends are always there for each other.
Loving to everyone they see.
Nice and laughing together.
They love each other.
Kind and nice helping people when needed.
Friends are awesome people.
They're very sassy, but loving.
No matter what type of friends they still love you a lot.
They're caring and loving and just great.
They always talk to you, and sometimes talk about you
But you still love them.
I love having a true friend.
Friends are great!

Becca Tanner, Grade 8
Highland Rim School, TN

Watching a Snowflake

I watch, as a snowflake lands on my window sill,
It is there for a moment
Then, as quickly as it came
It is nothing more, than
A small cold drop on my window sill.

Another snowflake comes
It is larger than the last
It sits on the sill
In the short time it is there
I notice the pattern.

It has eight points,
that are jointed in the center
So simple
So lovely
The beauty of nature.

But like all snowflakes
It is there for a moment
Then, as quickly as it came
It is nothing more, than
A small cold drop on my window sill.

Megan Sheehan, Grade 8
Annunciation Elementary School, MO

Friends

A friend is like a family member,
So loyal and trusting.
They keep your secrets,
They keep you in their thoughts
But most of all they keep you in their hearts.

Sarah Brawley, Grade 8
Southern Reynolds County R-II School, MO

The Rose That Arose in the Concrete

You are the Rose!
The one that FOUGHT!
You penetrated your boundaries!
You are; self-sufficient, self-taught,
and gloriously light!
You are beauty,
merciful to all,
Which is lovely to life.
You are the one who never gives in!
Never gives up! You came from the rough dirt!
BOTTOM!
You are The Rose That Arose in the Concrete.

P.S. This is to all those who never give up,
and keep their head up through all weathers.
You are a leader, and give to others what you have.

Zebulon Peterson, Grade 9
Webster High School, OK

Fighting Change

Today, tomorrow, and every other day
I feel like my life is slipping away
From all I have and all I am
And all the times I said, "I can."
I'm fighting the change that's taking place.
I don't want to be like you, and quit the race.
I have your eyes, your ears, and nose,
I even have your same dang toes.
Can't you see I strive to be
Like the One who created me?
So why am I changing? I have no clue;
I just know I'm fighting change to not be like you!

Aubrey Hatton, Grade 9
Cookson Hills Christian School, OK

This Is Why

This is why I want to stop the world and get off.
This is why I want to get away.
This is why I want to escape.
This is why I always cry a silent tear.
This is why I always cry a hidden tear.
This is why I always run away and hide.
This is why I want to disappear.
This is why.

Carmita O'Bryant, Grade 7
Asher Middle/High School, OK

Love

Love is green and always growing
love tastes like hot cocoa
it smells like freshly mowed grass
It reminds me of my dad
it sounds like a bird flying
it feels like a feather

Andrea Mays, Grade 7
Benton County School of the Arts, AR

Lola

Your fur so shiny.
You're as tough as a brick.
You never back down from a fight.
You will never quit.
I love you Lola.

Kaylie Stroud, Grade 8
Avenue City Elementary School, MO

Recipe for the Perfect Snow Day

1. Begin with a pinch of hot chocolate
2. A dash of laziness
3. A tablespoon of throwing snowballs
4. A batch of having fun
5. Add a pound of laughter
6. Mix in with snow sledding
7. Pour in with rounding down snow hill
8. 3/4 cup of watching TV
9. Half a bowl of chocolate pudding
10. Add a jug of warm milk!

Alexis Hines, Grade 7
Meredith-Dunn School, KY

Sudden Melancholy

Dark and dreary
in the doom of day,
the phone screams
a warning call.
I detect my mother's urgent voice.
I know
something
must be wrong.
Trying desperately to hold back tears,
she tells me
Grandma just had
a heart attack.
I feel an evil force
constricting me deep within,
wrapping and choking me
beyond endurance.
I finally let it out.
Waterfalls stream.
Wars rage.
And I hear Grandma's last whisper,
"I love you."

Ellen Chai, Grade 7
White Station Middle School, TN

Don't Cry on the Rainbow

When you're feeling low,
And don't got anywhere to go,
So just say sorry for your lies
And don't cry on the rainbow.

'Cause crying's for the clouds
And weeping's for the willow trees.
Because, baby don't you know that this was meant to be?

Picking daisies by the waterfall.
Don't cry
'Cause I'll be there, waiting for you after all that we've been through.

Kayla McKenzie, Grade 8
Greenfield Jr/Sr High School, MO

You Make Me Smile

You make me smile. Smile like I never did before I met you.
You make me smile like I never do, unless I see you.
I love to see your perfect face,
it's like a picture you could not trace.
I'm not sure if I'm in love. Sounds like it, but I'm still a little young.
You always catch me when I fall
and smile when I'm seen in the hall.
The little annoying things I do, don't even bother you.
You make me smile. Smile like I never did before I met you.
You make me smile like I never do, unless I see you.
You and I were meant to be.
Is this even reality?
I always laugh at your dumb jokes. You make me think that there is always hope.
You slump over your desk just to look at my feet,
but it makes me feel at rest and I love your eyes when you look at me.
You make me smile. Smile like I never did before I met you.
you make me smile like I never do, unless I see you.
You have a funny rhythm and a funny walk.
But I love when you stop by my locker just so we can talk.
You make my world go round I'm so glad that you've been found.
You seem so laid back and cool that's why I'm in love with you.

Sara Senseman, Grade 9
West Jr High School, MO

Camping

The crisp mountain air nips at my nose as I climb out of my tent,
The smell of the fires all around must be heaven sent.
I grab a cup of cocoa to warm my frozen hands,
As I sit down with my cousins to make the day's plans.
We love to go exploring and wading in the creek,
My brother likes to climb big trees and reach their highest peak.
After the night has settled we gather around the fire,
Placing on more logs, we watch the flame grow higher.
We get our sticks and marshmallows and toast them nice and brown,
We listen to old stories that never make us frown.
The embers of the fire glow bright and red,
As I climb into my tent and snuggle in my bed.

Allison Migun, Grade 9
Bearden High School, TN

Hand in Hand

Every day I give her my love,
I feel like it will never be enough,
Day after day week after week,
Even year after year,
As I give her my love,
And she starts to give it back,
And as we walk down this path,
Hand in hand, gazing deeply in her eyes
I whisper 3 simple words "I love you"
And as she whispers them back
I know we're together at last.

Jared Curd, Grade 8
Southern Reynolds County R-II School, MO

My Friend Jessie

No one saw it coming,
She was only eight years old.
Her brown eyes sparkled like sunshine
And her bright smile was very bold.
She left us in a car crash
That I won't forget.
I'll always remember the way she laughed
And the time that we first met.
We used to play together,
Outside and after school.
She looked up to me like a sister
And thought I was really cool.
This young girl did not deserve
This result of her mistake.
She wasn't wearing her seat belt,
And now many linger in her wake.
This happening made me think and question,
Why'd she have to go?
This is the true, but perilous story
Of my friend Jessie Dou.

Amelia Ramsey, Grade 7
White Station Middle School, TN

Why Not?

What a shame we all became
The lies, the hate
Those who discriminate,
Why can't we love?
Why can't we see?
The way we are living,
Wasn't meant to be.
Filled with pain,
Filled with sadness,
When it should be filled with pure happiness.
If we could stop and take a breath,
We might be able to see
The way we are living
Is one big mess.

Kelsey Skidmore, Grade 8
Owasso 8th Grade Center, OK

In Such a World

In such a world, there are roses for the living, and past gone.
In such a world, the sun, moon, and stars will shine above.
In such a world, the children laugh and play.
In such a world, girls and boys find their true calling here.
In such a world, parents watch the children grow and learn.
In such a world, flowers bloom, and birds take flight.
In such a world, we live and die.
In such a world, we learn to strive for love and trust.
In such a world, elders smile as the children give them kisses.
In such a world, the hearts of the caring will always shine.

Amanda Prock, Grade 8
Hartville Jr/Sr High School, MO

I Miss You

I lay in my bed
Trying to sleep
I can't help my self I have to weep
You left me and this world
Not so long ago
I can't help myself I can't let go
I think about you every night
And remember when you use to be in my sight
Your hugs were so warm
They made me feel safe
And when you left I wasn't myself
My life just changed and I couldn't fix it
Come back and fix it all
Please
I really miss you

Merisa Dedovic, Grade 8
Pleasant View School, TN

Christmas Tree

We are putting up our Christmas tree
the lights shimmering in our eyes
the marvelous garland wrapped around the tree
and we hang our ornaments on the green branches
until we couldn't hang any more.
Then we put the star on the very top.
Then we wait until Christmas morning
to find that Santa has come.

Devin McGovern, Grade 8
Highland Rim School, TN

Skateboarder

Steve skateboards to school
Because he thinks he is cool.
They call him pirate and
I know why because you can only see one eye
He rides his skateboard around town
Until he hits a rock and falls to the ground
His mom takes him to Claremore,
so he can skate some more
sometimes he skates the pools after school.

Hayden DeLozier, Grade 8
Chelsea Jr High School, OK

Among the Leaves

Here we are among the leaves
around the trees so green.
The festivals around town and out
all smiling faces to be seen.

Pumpkin, wheat, and stalks of corn
all around the street.
People wearing coats and a hat
many kind folks to meet.

Cocoa mugs and roasted marshmallows
fill our town with joy.
Let's go play some tag football
with this little boy.

Let's turn our clock an hour back
so we can get more sleep.
I'm a bear and ready to dream
don't you make a peep.

Have a campfire in the moonlight
with all your family and friends.
Celebrate our love and laughter
we don't want the fun to end.

Mckenzie Catt, Grade 7
Nettleton Jr High School, AR

What's Fun About Autumn

I love to play in the
Leaves and the hay

Going down the slide in a line
Playing in the flowers yelling
Louder and louder.

As we play during the day
And sleep at night dreaming
Of tomorrow's daylight

Brailan Brown, Grade 7
Maury Middle School, TN

Football

Footballs made of hits and tackles,
safeties, fumbles, and even injuries,
but the best feeling is a touchdown
made just by you for your fans.

Joshua Davis, Grade 7
Highland Rim School, TN

Heaven

Acorns and leaves
falling to the ground.
Open your windows
to the nice smells and sounds.

Austin Rowland, Grade 7
Spring Mills Middle School, WV

Temptations

Sliding down the face were beads of sweat.
Tiring in class, praying for clock hands to budge.
Distant voices, rarely absorbed into thought.
The heat of summer, steadily rolling in.

Urges too appealing to avoid,
As the boy dropped into a cool doze.
Of the cold he desired, pleasures unveiled in dreams.
The boy was absolute that this desirable idea was untrue.

A land where no disturbances were abundant.
A land containing a crisp, light breeze along a swift, flowing river.
This could not be a land with any summers, rather two springs.
Never did the boy wish to return to reality.

Realization appeared a fragment too soon, as the boy rose.
Settings returned, with a loud smack of hand upon table.
The instructor had no reason to blame, though.
The boy's dream, ever so tempting.

Jared Swope, Grade 9
West Jr High School, MO

I Am

I am a helpful person
I wonder why people think they don't need help
I hear people crying out for help every day
I see my friends hurting
I want to encourage and support them

I pretend like I'm ok so I can be strong for someone else
I feel like I could fall apart anytime now but I touch the lives of those I know
I worry that the people close to me don't truly know how much they mean to me
I cry because I need to be loved…but you don't love me
I am a helpful person

I understand that God is alive and well, working in my life
I say that all the time
I dream of being with Him, and laying in His arms
I try again, and again to be strong so I can be strong,
  not for me, but for those around me
I hope that they know how hard I try to be someone they can lean on,
  how much I hurt when they hurt
I am a helpful person

Rachel Ann Talley, Grade 7
Newcastle Middle School, OK

Friends

My friends are always there for me no matter what happens
They always pick me up when I am down
I will always remember our ups and downs, our good and bad times
But isn't that what friends are for
Remembering our ups and downs, good and bad times
And helping us try to get through them
Truly that is what friends are for

Erica Hill, Grade 7
Highland Rim School, TN

Thanksgiving

The Thanksgiving turkey sits on the table,
While Uncle Tony tells a fable.
The fresh air blows through the trees
As we hear buzzing bees.
Momma's in the kitchen cookin' away.
And the children are down by the bay
Everyone's mouth waters from the smell of food
And they're all in a great mood!
The men are watchin' NASCAR,
And Grandma yells to the kids, "Don't go far!"
Finally, all the cooking's done,
And the children have to come in from their fun.
The house is filled with sweet smells
And everyone's glad the pumpkin cake didn't fail
Pa Andy leads us in prayer, thankin' God, before we eat
Then we dig into the turkey that's full of heat!

Hannah Griffin, Grade 7
Nettleton Jr High School, AR

To Fly

To fly,
and feel the gentle breeze,
and to taste the salt of seas,
to hear the roar of the cities,
to see the glorious splendor of a setting sun,
framed forever on a red-gold canvas,
to smell the oh-so-sweet scent of freshly bloomed lavender,
waving gently in its own breeze,
that is truly what it means to fly.

Elizabeth Hurd, Grade 8
Belle Isle Enterprise Middle School, OK

Falling Snow

Looking out my widow seeing the snow
Slowly falling as my eyes follow
Putting my cheeks beside the window
Letting it cool off for a while
Listen to the snow melting on the glassy window
As I count the falling snowflakes one by one
There were too many so I let it go
Watching the full moon and stars
Shining over the snow
As I turned off my lights and watch it
Glow

Arika Lee, Grade 8
Chelsea Jr High School, OK

Nature

As I walk through the path
The peacefulness and tranquility compels me
The breeze wisps through the trees
I hear the woodland creatures scurry across the leaves
I hear the stream trickling over the rocks
Everything is at peace

Callie Clendenon, Grade 8
Highland Rim School, TN

Here I Lay

Here I lay,
In this dreamy world,
World of happiness,
World of kindness,
The world I describe,
Is a wonderful land.
No hatred, or bullies,
No fighting, or teasing,
Nothing negative should enter,
Only happiness should stay.
Here I lay,
As happy as the Sun,
So happy and delightful,
There is nothing painful here.
Here I lay,
I think I will,
Go to sleep now,
I hope to see you,
In this wonderful world.

Colton Wilcox, Grade 8
New Martinsville Elementary School, WV

A Poem Is…

A poem is emotion,
put into words…
…such as the love or fear of anything.

A poem is a loss of control
for the better…
…so the fury won't be used on more delicate things.

A poem is an artistic form
made for the enjoyment of the artist…
…and where a pen turns into a paintbrush.

A poem is a rebellion of conscience,
a rebellion that needed to happen
sooner or later.

A poem is an inside voice
finally set free…
…and we give it that freedom.

Daniel Graves, Grade 8
West Middle School, TN

He Has Forgotten

he has forgotten he loves that dove
he is very sad to let it go
crying so the dove will come back
holding his hands low he releases it
fly high little bird fly high
don't forget who saved you when you had a broken wing
I will never forget you the dove replies

Jane Alsup, Grade 8
Belle Isle Enterprise Middle School, OK

Chase Melton

Chase
Responsible, mature, determined, and good looking
Who is an awesome brother of Nicole Melton
Who love his parents, wonderful life because of friends and family, and amazing Jesus
Who feels special, cared for, and 100% healthy
Who needs friends that are trustworthy, lots of baseball, and lots of money
Who gives kindness, a warm heart, and laughs
Who fears my giant woods in my backyard at night
Who would like to see my two idols of baseball Albert Pujols and Derek Jeter
Who is a resident of wonderful Clarksville, TN
Melton

Chase Melton, Grade 8
Montgomery Central Middle School, TN

What Am I Becoming?

Oh my gosh, I love my life
But am I becoming something I am not?
I'm becoming something I never wanted to be
I'm becoming this girl that likes to flirt with everyone

I'm also becoming the girl who thinks she's the coolest
I'm becoming the girl who thinks she gets everything she wants
I'm becoming the girl who likes all the guys
I'm also becoming the girl who likes to order people around like a queen or princess

I'm becoming the girl who thinks she should go out with everyone
I'm also becoming the girl who thinks she's smarter than everyone
I'm also becoming the girl who I DIDN'T want to be
I am becoming the girl who loses all her friends over BOYS

I used to be the girl who was shy, nice, and polite
She was the girl to hang out with
But I'm not her anymore
What am I becoming?

Devan Benz, Grade 7
Hebron Middle School, KY

To Alex

If it weren't for you,
I'd never have experienced what it is like to laugh your hardest.
If it weren't for you,
I'd never have experienced a ride on the ambulance.
If it weren't for you,
I'd never have known how to play soccer at the age of three.
If it weren't for you,
I'd never have had a friend or family member to talk to.
If it weren't for you,
I'd never have known what it is like to sled down a hill full of snow with a dog in control.
If it weren't for you,
I'd have missed out on a cousin to swim against on the swim team.
If it weren't for you,
I'd have missed out on a whole lot of my life that I have now.
If it weren't for you,
I'd have missed out on having a true friend.

Jess Speak, Grade 8
All Saints School, MO

Track Star

I'm a track star,
I love to run afar,
But when I get tired,
I run to a car at times I don't feel up to par,
Sometimes I fall getting a scar,
Forcing me to use medicine from a jar,
But I will always love being a track star.

Morgan Haff, Grade 8
Ketchum Jr High School, OK

Ode to the Fabulous Ponytail Holder

Oh, ponytail holder,
I love you so.
Your colorful stretchy body
that wraps up my hair
when my neck gets hot and sweaty
makes me feel fabulous.
Your beautiful variety of colors
amazes me.
Small and big,
for all different kinds of hair.
You fit perfectly every time,
for all those bad hair days
when I just don't know what to do.
I can always find you right away.
You're always right where I left you.
I could never leave
the house without you.
Oh, ponytail holder,
I love you so!

Mallarie Riffe, Grade 7
Dyer Elementary & Jr High School, TN

Lord Created It All

Trees tower above our heads and a sea of vegetation below us
The sunset shines as we say goodbye to day

Birds sing a sweet melody as day passes by
Coyotes howl to the darkness of night
Crickets chirp and play their midnight song

Sweetness of fresh fruit in my mouth
Reddest of apples waiting to be eaten
Bright yellow bananas dangle from a tree above

Soft green grass like a pillow below me
Warm sand between my toes
A nice breeze cools the air

The sweet aroma of vanilla calms me
And fills me with joy

Lord created it all

Caroline Basler, Grade 7
Our Lady Catholic School, MO

My Fragile, Fluffy Friends

Clouds are symphonies of white and gray,
They are our guardians in the sky,
Their different shapes make us stare,
They inch across clear blue skies like snails,
My fragile, fluffy friends.

Greenish-gray, grumpy rain clouds,
What they are on rainy days,
Sun brightening gray, thin, wispy clouds,
Why do you let shining rays of sunshine see through you?
My fragile, fluffy friends.

Your booming thunder makes me shiver,
Your hail, snow, and rain beating down on innocent ground,
Do you get smaller when you let weather out?
You awaken all of my senses,
My fragile, fluffy friends.

Graham Koch, Grade 7
Barret Traditional Middle School, KY

The Holiday Dash

Hurry! Hurry! Scurry! Scurry!
Families buzz around with worry
As they bet the holiday rush,
Giving presents with wrapping so lush.
Darting and flying through the stores,
They search for the special gift that is yours.
The Christmas tree so beautiful dyed
In red, silver, and gold, it's anything but dull.
The ornaments arranged delicately on the tree
Resembles everybody's joy for Christmas Eve,
Slowly the clock is ticking away,
As people impatiently wait for the next day.
Children, full of anticipation,
Await this day of celebration
They place treats that are deliciously sweet,
Beneath the tree for old St. Nick to eat
So as the event is finished and forgotten
Like week old trash, that concludes our
Holiday Dash!

Ana Beatriz Maclin, Grade 7
White Station Middle School, TN

Pie

Pie my favorite of all treats
Of all candies, chocolates, cakes, and sweets
Chocolate, cherry, pumpkin, and chess
Pecan, blueberry, and all the rest
Pie is very succulent food
It puts me in an everlasting good mood
Whenever that savory treasure touches my lips
I start dancing and shaking my hips
Without pie things just wouldn't be the same
It easily puts all other desserts to shame

Eric Smith, Grade 8
Highland Rim School, TN

Friday

The school bell goes ring-ring.
Students rush to homeroom.
Eagerly shoving books into lockers.
Teachers squeal with delight
at the thought of Saturday.
What wonders the weekend holds.

Erin Moyers, Grade 7
Highland Rim School, TN

Sports

The NBA is run by Kobe Bryant.
All you fans know I'm not lyin'.
I wanna be just like Dewayne Wade
'Cause you know he be gettin' paid.
No one can catch like Randy Moss.
All wide receivers know he's the boss.
Woo Pig Sooee, number 5 Darren!
He be snackin' on that Red Baron.
I wish I could hit like A. Rod
On commercials about Bod,
Hit it like Derek Jeter,
Maybe hit farther than a kilometer,
Skate like Tony Hawk,
Walk the walk and talk the talk.
I wanna be like them.
Just me. Bam!

Curtis Reeves, Grade 7
Dunbar Middle School, AR

Daydream

In a place of happiness,
Where I'm alone
I travel to
A place unknown.

My world of happiness,
Where all is untouched
Where there are perfect rules:
Not too few, not too much.

All is perfect,
All is peace.
Time flies so fast
You can barely speak!

Staring into the
Empty space
I get lost in
The beauty's embrace.

I'm lost in this feeling,
It can't be what it seems!
Then suddenly I wake
From my peaceful daydream.

Mary K. Geraghty, Grade 7
Annunciation Elementary School, MO

Faith

There once was a man who was fifty-two,
He was diagnosed with cancer, which made him blue.
He learned that he would die in just a few days,
So the man went to Mass and he knelt and he prayed.

And in that same town another man could be seen,
Who was falsely accused and to be put to death on the scene.
For the mayor's brother was to blame but the mayor would never say,
So the man sat in his cell and began to pray.

Now that man had a nephew, who lived in that town,
And when he heard about his uncle, all he could do was frown.
He sat by the old tree and cried all day,
And with tears in his eyes he looked up and he prayed.

Now as they all prayed, a thunderstorm came through town.
Striking the man with cancer who fell to the ground.
And to the doctors surprise on that stormy dawn,
The fifty-two year old's cancer was completely gone!

And the thunder stopped the prison's electric chair,
As the mayor's guilty brother called and confessed then and there.
And so the accused man went to his nephew, who lived by the bay,
And their family was thankful and the family prayed.

Jacob C. Hoog, Grade 8
St Gerard Majella School, MO

Sinterklaas

As Christmas time rolls around each year
Thirty-two *Clothique* Santa Clauses
March out of their secret boxes
One by one they come
Each Jolly old elf,
Unique in his own little way.

Papa Noel stands holding the mistletoe
Waiting for his missus to come and kiss
On his bed, Santa Claus reads a wish list until falling asleep
Not able to reach an anxious moose, Sinterklaas stands on a green stool
And decorates the moose with colorful Christmas lights

With a modern look,
He holds a briefcase under his arm,
And a cell phone in his hand
Santa is ready for work
With a stopwatch in his pocket,
And a whistle in his mouth
Santa Claus is ready to start the day

Riding his sleigh
Across the white sea of snow
He leaves for a year to come

Vera Gardner, Grade 7
White Station Middle School, TN

The Beach!

Crashing waves on the shore.
Beautiful, orangy sunsets and creamy sand.
Golden-bronze tans and flip-flops.

Brittany Smith, Grade 8
Pigeon Forge Middle School, TN

Autumn Days

Every year leaves turn colors.
The temperature drops,
and so do the leaves.
The changing temperature makes me sneeze.

Red, orange, and gold leaves cover the ground,
and crunch as I walk around.
The air is crisp and clean
and reminds me of bare trees.

I have to go inside earlier than I usually do.
Not only the time changes,
It gets darker, too.

Samantha Doyle, Grade 7
Maury Middle School, TN

I Thought You Did

I thought you loved me
I thought we hit it off.
Lately, you've been acting like someone else.
Around your friends, you act like I'm not there;
It's like you never cared.
I care about you, but maybe that's not enough
I can't make you care or treat me right
So I guess I'll end the fight.
You'll act heartbroken
But we both know you won't be.
Maybe the next girl that comes along
You won't treat like you treated me.

Anna Barr, Grade 8
Hartville Jr/Sr High School, MO

Christmas

I can't wait
I stay up late
The stockings are up
I lay out cookies and pour milk in a cup
Santa and his reindeer land on the roof
On Dancer, Prancer, and Blitzen too
That's what he'll say when he's on his way
High High High up in the air
Red and white that's what he wears
Putting up the Christmas tree with
friends who come around
It's so much fun when Christmas comes to town
The best time of the year when everyone comes home
With all this Christmas cheer it's hard to be alone

Demetrial Allen, Grade 7
Maury Middle School, TN

A New Year

I look up to the winter sky.
Boy, have these twelve months flown by!
I stare into a sky so clear
And think about my eventful year.

The frosted hills roll on for miles
As I recall the laughs and smiles.
In my eye I feel a soft tear.
I will miss this wondrous year.

I look out at the frosty view.
I feel as if I've become someone new.
I feel more courage and less fear
As I approach this upcoming year.

I have new wants and higher goals.
I plan to fill up last year's holes.
The grass is now iced over here.
What a beautiful sight to start off the year!

Robin Graves, Grade 8
West Middle School, TN

School

It's the middle of seventh hour.
Listen, write, answer
Please, not homework again
Hand cramps
Boredom
Ring. Ring. Ring.
The cacophony in the hallways is music to my ears.
The bus is in sight.
Home, at last!

Christian Ackmann, Grade 8
West Jr High School, MO

Here

I am invisible
No one knows I'm here
I just wander around aimlessly
People don't even turn when I pass
Do they even know that I exist?

I am lonely
My friends act like they love me
Until I turn my back
Then I just go back to loneliness
Are there any true friends in this world?

I am here
In this world all alone
They think I have no feelings
I am just an imperfection in a world of perfection
Why am I here?

Jessica Branstetter, Grade 9
Perkins-Tryon High School, OK

Somebody

Everybody seems all quiet.
No one seems to be quite normal.
Many people seem happy,
and some seem sad!
Something's not right
Someone needs to break this silence.
Anything would work, it doesn't
have to be much.
Each person seems tense.
Everything needs to be brighter,
because everything seems dull.
Sara Thomas, Grade 8
Pigeon Forge Middle School, TN

Too Fast

I am standing
With people all around me
Scurrying and hurrying about
Everything is moving so fast

I can't keep up
I am falling back
Trying to keep up
Everything is moving too fast

Help!
Someone please help me
Why won't you help?
Everything is moving too fast
Help me
Please!
Susan Duffield, Grade 7
Family of Faith Christian School, OK

Choices

Make the choice
Or the choice will make you.
Choose carefully,
You might regret it later.
But try to make the best of it,
It might be better than you thought.
Eleanore Boyd, Grade 8
Belle Isle Enterprise Middle School, OK

Latrisha

L oving and caring
A ngel who
T ouches lives
R emembered by her
I nspiration for life
S o sweet and
H appy
A s she suffers
Ricky Roberts, Grade 9
Van-Cove High School, AR

Thanksgiving Time

It's Thanksgiving time in Tennessee!
We always go hunting
My brother and me.
We go through the woods
In his pickup truck
Hoping to see that eight point buck.
So when the day is done
I feel like a winner
And we both go to Grandma's house
For Thanksgiving dinner.
Jake Watts, Grade 7
Maury Middle School, TN

The Great Lakes

Near the water
on the sand
past the horizon
under the stars
beyond all worries
along the shoreline
into the water
despite the cold
below the surface
as time stood still
Jordan Ownby, Grade 8
Heritage Middle School, TN

The Setting Sun

The sun sets
With creaking of hinges.
The day's door
Slowly closes.
Shutting out light,
Leaving the world in darkness.
Mary-Mc Alexander, Grade 9
Bearden High School, TN

The Apple

Red as the blood in your veins
sweet as a lovers kiss
hard as the ice that covers your heart
as white as the purest snow
as clean as a virgin's love
sour like a lovers scorn
bitter as an old maid
beautiful with poisons touch
a merciful death it awaits on the ground
wrinkled as grandmother's hands
smooth as a polished pearl
tempting as a perfect rose
delicate as a mother's love
easy to destroy if held too hard
and seeds to carry on another generation
Amber Moore, Grade 9
Hart County High School, KY

Geography

G eography the world around us
E arth where we live and breathe
O ur home where we eat and sleep
G enerals, Soldiers
R angers
A rmy, Navy, Marines
P eople who fought for our
H ome and freedom for
Y esterday, tomorrow and the future
Kyle Denning, Grade 7
Clarksburg School, TN

Fire vs Ice

Fire,
Hot, red,
Burning, exciting, exploding,
Flame, sticks, snow board, ice skates,
Freezing, storming, falling,
Cold, blue,
Ice
Christian Brune, Grade 8
St Joseph School, MO

Teachers

T alented individuals
E xpecting the unexpected
A lways pushing you to do your best
C orrecting your mistakes
H elping you understand
E nforcing rules
R efusing to give up
S upportive of your decisions
Catherina Khadoo, Grade 8
Owasso 8th Grade Center, OK

Grammy

I know that I have to move on
And not dwell on the past for too long
You're still with me,
Though I can't see,
But in my heart you live on.

You may have passed away,
Leaving us this day,
And we know,
It was your time to go,
But in our hearts you'll stay.

And there's one thing I hope you knew,
Because words to say are so few,
But deep down,
Even when we'd frown,
We always loved you.
Amanda Francis, Grade 8
Bueker Middle School, MO

Zach Nicholson

Zach
Creative, lazy, weird, and funny
Brother of Haley Nicholson
Lover of my dog, my family, and my horse
Who feels happiness when I finish home work, sadness when I don't, and anger when I get hurt
Who gives laughter, charity, and food
Who needs money, video games, and a new saddle
Who fears spiders, sickness, and death
Who would like to see the Appalachian Mts., Mickey Mouse, and a Liger
Who lives on a horse farm
Nicholson

Zach Nicholson, Grade 8
Montgomery Central Middle School, TN

All I Need…

If all I was to have in this world were you, then my life would be great; actually my life would be more than great. My life would be perfect! Because all I need in my life is you!

So, if you have the same feelings for me as I do you then you will show me by loving me more than you love anything else in the world. Because that's how I feel about you!

So just to let you know, I love you more than I will love anything else and I will always be there for you no matter what. So, tell me the truth, do you love me as much as I love you?

Pollie Jones, Grade 8
Boones Creek Middle School, TN

Creeks

Creeks are wonderful as they flow freely downstream
You can hear them and feel them as they swiftly move along
The sound of a creek brings so many thoughts to my mind
A creek gives me a feel of freedom like no other
They can be gentle and fun or rambunctious and dangerous
Joy will come to you when you play in a creek
A creek can bring new plants and animals to your attention you have never noticed before
Creeks are as beautiful as they are fun
The water of a creek will glisten in the sun as it passes ever so slowly
Creeks are one of God's amazing creations that I love the most
I would love to run freely through hills, valleys, and meadows like a creek does
There is no telling what lands the waters that creeks carry have seen.

Austin Honey, Grade 8
Highland Rim School, TN

Him

His eyes are like a gray-green ocean, so warm so safe. When he smiles they glisten like ice on a lake. His smile so broad but yet so hidden, like a mouse hiding from a kitten.

His hair like chocolate covered almonds, so rich so sweet. But inside he's still the kind of guy you want to meet. The hugs he gives are full of power. I wish he wasn't breaking my heart right here under the stars.

His life is full of happiness and humor, he makes me smile under any circumstances. Loads and loads of friends that still can't take him. He has more power than a heavy weight champion.

In my eyes I see greatness, if only you could see what I see in him. His beauty and smile always break me down. If I had one moment with him I would make it last a lifetime.

Jennifer Harrold, Grade 8
Gresham Middle School, TN

Charleston, South Carolina

In Charleston, South Carolina
Among the people,
Towards the ocean,
Under the sun,
Through the sand,
Out of state,
Beyond the mountains,
In the warm weather,
Around the coast,
Without any worries.

Mickaela Vaughan, Grade 8
Heritage Middle School, TN

The Color Black

Infinite beyond reason.
Losing yourself in it.
Like a black hole.
Not even the tiniest sign of light.
Therefore, there's nothing to escape.
Sadness makes it overwhelming.
Hate.
Frustration.
No kindness.
No happiness.
You can't see because there's no light.
Black isn't even really a color.
It's a nothing.
Black is infinite.

Kayla Shiflette, Grade 7
Dyer Elementary & Jr High School, TN

Four Wheelers

F un for everyone
O ur way to speed away
U tility
R iding on a summer day

W ay to get away
H ill jumps
E veryone can hopefully ride it
E very dad's money well spent
L aying black lines on the road
E verywhere you see them
R acing around the gravel roads
S port

Austin Potter, Grade 8
Avenue City Elementary School, MO

300

They fought for their freedom
Yet they died to a powerful kingdom
Many others followed their steps
And finally put the Xerxes to rest
The mighty 300 were known as greats

Tyler Plezia, Grade 8
Mayflower Middle School, AR

Courtney

Courtney
Energetic, funny, nice, and smart
A sister of Ashley and Michael Loveless
Who loves skateboarding, school, and sleeping
Who feels happy, anxious, and sad
Who gives love, friendship, and hate
Who needs chocolate, friends, and family
Who fears spiders, heights, and Freddy Cougar
Who would like to see Mount Everest, Ryan Shekler, and Bam Margera
Who lives in Clarksville, Tennessee
Loveless

Courtney Loveless, Grade 8
Montgomery Central Middle School, TN

Mother Nature

Night sky — like lyrics of a broken heart
Morning day — like lyrics of a new start
Nothing compares to sunset light
The rainbow glow giving me sight

The grass is greener on the other side
Trees, a place for squirrels to hide
Wake up and smell the roses
The sweet scent filling up our noses

Thirst is quenched with zesty apple juice falling from trees here and there
It's always relaxing to stop and stare
Fresh tomatoes, waiting to be picked
Fingers after eating one, waiting to be licked

Feel the wind on my face
Memories you can't replace
Flower petals as white as the clouds above
Just another thing on Earth we all love

Birds chirping from the trees
Singing a song for you and me
See the beauty God created
Nothing in nature should be hated

Hannah Osman, Grade 7
Our Lady Catholic School, MO

Life

Life is so unfair
when you are unaware of the possibilities
you get so confused, and lost in yourself
you feel confined like a bird trapped in a cage
it is like a mystery, and you are the detective
life is like a field of roses you never know if you are going to get a rose or thorn
sometimes life is hard you don't know where to turn but you always have a choice
you think you are so far away from your goal but it is right in front of you
so when life gives you hurdles jump them but never give up
life is a maze and there's only one way out
your way, the right way

Faith Flynt, Grade 8
Highland Rim School, TN

Fall

Fall is here, let's celebrate!
This time of year is really great!
The leaves are green and orange and gold.
Some days it's hot, some days it's cold.
The wind is chilly as it blows
As it gets closer to the time it snows.
The days get shorter and darkness comes fast
Before you know it, the time has past.
On certain days, the rain falls down
And there's no sunlight to be found.
But other days bring beautiful weather
If only it could last forever!
Some people may sit back and ask
Why summer had to leave so fast,
While others sit and wonder why
There isn't snow falling from a winter sky.
But there are few who choose to say
That fall is here, so we should play!

Andrea Trierweiler, Grade 9
West Jr High School, MO

The Storm

The wind whistles its arrival to me.
Thunder explodes in the nimbostratus.
Busting through doors to go downstairs to see.

As it arrives all the power turns off.
Wind blowing hard makes all the trees bend back.
Trying to find somewhere to hid, am lost.
Seeing all my horses run in a pack.

Hearing the roar of the storm, and a tone.
Debris hitting and shaking against the house.
Storm comes closer and I heart its loud moan.
I was really scared like a little mouse.

The furor of the storm raging outside.
Makes me feel so small and just want to hide.

Jalin Ladd, Grade 9
University Heights Academy, KY

Fall Comes

The rustling leaves in the crisp grass.
The singing birds singing like a Greek choir.
Zoom! As the fall animals run by.
The gobble of the eager turkeys.
The smell of awesome apple pie your mom makes.
The beat of your heart pounds like a bat hitting a ball.
The fall spirit calls to you like a falling star.
As the wish comes true.
The sound of schools starting.
The pumpkins growing!
Fall calls!

Brenton Hicks, Grade 7
Nettleton Jr High School, AR

The Shining

Hiding behind majestic clouds,
And fighting to show yourself in the sky against clouds,
with rays of your yellow supernova,
like a giant explosion of light
in your blue blanket of sky,
trying to escape.
Yet your rays are blinding
to my naked eye.
Stinging of sunburns.
Your head is like a
flame thrower on my back.
Sounds of kids
playing in your pool of heat.
Will you keep me warm forever?
Will your brightness keep me joyful?
You do so much
for our world.
But it saddens me
when you go down,
when black takes over
and Earth is cool.

Colin Evans, Grade 7
Barret Traditional Middle School, KY

Frog's Philosophy

A frog says, "Thou that can't sit on a lily pad shall not learn."
"Step away from my lily pad, because I bite."
"Fly you better fly away, because I am hungry."
"Lunchtime flies and bugs mmmmmmmmmmmm tasty."

Bobby Long, Grade 7
Ketchum Jr High School, OK

Winning Isn't Everything

My heart pounds,
As does my opponent's.
Tick, tock, tick, tock,
Says the clock.
My adversary questions himself,
"Will he make a mistake?
Will he mess up?"
I make my move,
And trade a piece.
Now in the endgame, we are.
A crowd has developed,
And eyes are staring.
Who will win?
Only time can tell.
Finally, the game looks even,
But not for long,
For my opponent sees the mating move,
Checkmate, says he.
Alas, I have lost, but a lesson I uncovered,
Although it is great to win,
It is greater to learn.

Jason Gupta, Grade 7
White Station Middle School, TN

A Winter Wonderland

As you walk outside in the snow
all you see is white
as far as you walk
we look for a lush green tree
in a forest of piney evergreens
swaying in the chilled breeze
sending a rush of excitement
the one we see
is large and tall
smells like pine
and snow
we chop it
down with care
snow flies all around
making snowmen
playing in a sled
we're a mesh of color
on the ground
all around us
lay white fluffy chilling snow.

Tiffany Ramanowski, Grade 7
Maury Middle School, TN

Lee's Bare Feet Hitting the Mulch

I'm the champion of the swings,
soaring so high birds weep with envy,
air whipping through my bare toes.
Below, a fifth grader prowls
waiting for the chance to strike.
I plummet back down
through whipped cream clouds
preparing for the return trip.
Suddenly I'm back in the sky
minus my guide line to earth,
the ground eager to meet me.
My feet are like pincushions
full of malevolent wood needles.
I weep as I crawl
and curse that fifth grader's
long ugly nose.

Sam Lee, Grade 8
Baylor School, TN

Dad's House

At my dad's house,
under the sky,
through the front door,
in the living room,
through the hall,
in my room,
on my bed,
under the covers,
beneath my eyelids,
thinking of sleeping.

Erin Lovegrove, Grade 8
Heritage Middle School, TN

Say Goodbye

Should I say goodbye?
Or believe your every little lie?
Should I let go?
Or let my family say I told you so?

I'm afraid of what might happen if I say goodbye.
I might regret it and wonder why I ever even tried.
I might find myself in everlasting happiness,
or maybe reaching out for just one last kiss.

I fight so hard to try to say goodbye,
but the thought only makes me cry.
It's too late!
I've already realized you not only cheated but you lied too,
Like it was simply nothing.
But don't start to feel any shame,
you're not the only guy that has tried to play these immature games.

When I see you, I know what I must do,
so sorry I'm putting up a fight for you.
As I'm strong enough to say goodbye and walk away,
I will always remember the time you had me thrown away.

Lacey Purma, Grade 9
Logan-Rogersville High School, MO

The Beach

Across the board walk
Beyond the glistening sand
Lies against the expanding horizon
Despite the darkness the waves crash into the night.
During the day the children play in its presence.
Runs beneath the pier
Underneath the surface lives beautiful sea life.
Above the surface natives play in its flowing splendor
Along with many other people I listen to the sounds of the ocean.
Instead of walking on the boardwalk I stroll along the shoreline.
As far as I can tell I always feel carefree at the beach.

Laura Frahme, Grade 8
Heritage Middle School, TN

Joshua Hannah

Josh
Intelligent, responsible, trustworthy, and caring
Brother of Carrie and Jacob Hannah
Lover of listening to music, playing Runescape, and his dog
Who gives food to the dog in mornings, love to family, joy to brother
Who needs to hang out with friends, sleep, and get on the computer
Who feels joy with friends, playing basketball, and camping
Who fears some heights, bad grades on report card, and snakes
Who would like see the Grand Canyon, his grandparents, and relatives
Who is a resident of Cunningham, Tennessee
Hannah

Joshua Hannah, Grade 8
Montgomery Central Middle School, TN

Ode to My First Pointe Shoes

Tattered and torn
A dream come true,
Broken and worn.

Now it's time for new shoes
Years of practice and dedication
In you my dancing grew.

Dancing is a form of celebration,
Expression without compromise.
Admiring your pink ribbons fills me with elation.

You were a wonderful birthday surprise.
Looking at you through my tear filled eyes.

Stephanie Wilson, Grade 8
Benton County School of the Arts, AR

Skating

Every single day I always love to skate.
It is one thing that I could not hate.
Ollieing three decks or ollieing a six set,
Or just landing a trick that is hard to get.
I skate around town and skate with my friends.
I skate all day until the day ends.
I go around town and find the best spots.
Then I kickflip board slide the ledge at the parking lot.

Nick Rotruck, Grade 8
Musselman Middle School, WV

Broken

I just don't want to live anymore.
My heart is just far too sore.
You took my love as if only to borrow,
Then left me in the wake of 'morrow.

All that time I wasted with tears.
All those stupid, pathetic years.
You teased me and cruelly taunted,
And in the end left me haunted.

There is no peace from the pain inside.
It seems I cannot redeem my pride.
My heart is badly broken.
You act as if you were only jokin'.

I lie here slowly dying.
I won't even think of crying.
You were nothing but wasted time.
I allowed you to commit the crime.

So, it seems I'm completely broken,
And you said you were only jokin'.
Lookin' at you I laugh at your lie
Because now I'm walking away waving goodbye…

Madison Ross, Grade 9
Winston High School, MO

The Volcano

The volcano, resting peacefully,
amongst the beautiful scenes
of the natural world,
are all part of this wonderful Earth:
from the ant crawling on the ground,
to the eagle, soaring high above in the sky.

Suddenly the birds aren't chirping,
the bugs aren't roaming,
what is possibly the matter?

An ear-splitting,
glass-shattering boom
fills the air
as the volcano erupts
in a violent frenzy!

The once beautiful landscape
has turned into smoke and ash!
The odors are so putrid
That one cannot breathe properly.

Look over there!
A new island has begun to buzz with excitement
as life begins.

Kevin Wang, Grade 7
White Station Middle School, TN

Is It You

Are you the one for me
My dream come true
Are you meant to be my everything
Are you meant to be my boo

I have no clue
How far we could go
If we could last forever
The answer I don't know

Are we supposed to be
For eternity
Is this love supposed to last long
Is the feeling I have been having for you all along

Are you the reason why
I can't sleep at night
Are you the one
I want to hold me tight

Are you the one
That I should give my heart to
Are you the one
Is it you

Genell Loyd, Grade 9
Lindbergh High School, MO

Autumn

Leaves
Colorful, flaky
Falling, rustling, blowing
Joined, captive, screaming, dying
Sitting, swaying, shaking
Strong, coarse
Tree

Kayla Dillon, Grade 8
Musselman Middle School, WV

Evil Word

We wish
Every day for beauty
Eternal beauty
We look around
To people we admire
Not knowing our desire
'Till we look into a mirror
We see only our flaws
And not our beauty within
We have a low self-esteem
Like many others.
Like many others,
We wish for beauty
For skin, face, hair
But beauty is an adjective;
An opinion
An opinion it,
That makes us feel
Sad, angry, anxious, lonely, ugly
"Beauty" is an evil word

Crystal Smith, Grade 8
Choctaw Jr High School, OK

On the Edge

I'm on the edge,
no one can save me now —
even if they could,
they wouldn't know how.

I'm tired of it all
I refuse to deal with this
Into no arms will I fall —
Instead, a cold-bitterness

With my final steps occurring
before I reach that place
no one can see me during —
the tears run down my face.

My heart is racing wildly
I know just what to do.
I'll be falling off the edge…
If you really want me to.

Natalie Waddell, Grade 8
Willard Middle School, MO

After the Rain

After the rain, nature becomes still as the puddles that remain.
After the rain, the trees become still
and the leaves become little squirt guns, dropping drips on unlucky beings.
After the rain, the wind becomes a fog that lingers amongst the trees.
After the rain, the world is in a peace trance,
that is haunting and mysterious, and also relaxing at the same time.

Savannah Frame, Grade 7
Northwest Valley 7th & 8th Grade Center, MO

I Love You*

Some days it's too hard
Too hard to look at your face on the wall, to know you're not there
And that I can't see you any more
You're the greatest person I knew, I know you're in a better place
But I feel left dark by myself; I was so close to you
It's so hard for me to think about you without crying
Because…you were my world, you were my life
you taught me to love and how to care
Now all I know how to do is cry
I pretend to be brave for the people around me
Who loved you too, sometimes I hurt them
BUT I'm hurt inside, without
Because…you were my world, you were my life
You taught me to love and how to care
Now all I know how to do is cry
There is so much I wanted to tell you
And didn't get the chance, there's a hole in my chest
Where my heart used to be, it's determined to stay
It won't go away, I miss you so much
I just wanted to tell you
That I love you.

Lexie Dickes, Grade 9
West Jr High School, MO
**Dedicated to Grandpa Joe*

Might, Great, Invincible

Your waves, journeying throughout ebbs and flows
Your children, taking off, learning how to survive on their own
Sun rays, giving you light to see all your possessions down below
You are might, you are great, you can face anything
Instigating fights with outside worlds, you never give up
Who will save you?
Who will protect you from invasions and wars?
Don't worry, you are might, you are great, you can face anything
Seaweed skipping through your body
Your sandy, squishy, sinking floor provides homes for many
Creative colors of coral dancing in your presence
Whales crashing against your canopy, like a tree falling to the ground
Crash! Boom! Bang!
You are might, you are great, you can face anything
Your midnight layer mysteries scare all
Glowing fish hover your floor in deepest, darkest areas
Your friend, moon, shimmers on your top
You are might, you are great, you can face anything

Morgan Mattingly, Grade 8
Barret Traditional Middle School, KY

Rain, Rain, Blow Away

I hear drip, drip, drip
Outside my window
I hear sip, sip, sip
From my mom drinking her tea
All through the night
As cold as can be

I hear swish, swish, swish
The sound of the wind blowing at the leaves
I hear tic, tic as time goes by
Will this storm every leave

Finally it stops to rain
I don't hear drip, drip, drip
Or sip, sip, sip
I don't hear swish or tic either

I put on my coat and head outside
Brrrrrrrrrrrrrrr!
It's freezing from the night's cold air

Kylie Noltemeyer, Grade 7
Meredith-Dunn School, KY

Life

It may get hard
But go ahead and open up
Let the light in
You just want to be left alone
Don't run out on your life
Sometimes that mountain you've been climbing
Is just a grain of sand
Your whole life is in your hands
When you finally figure out love is all you need
Everything else shrinks down
And seems so small
Try not to get lost inside
Like a river deep and wide
You just get so lost inside
Don't worry about the things you can't change
You can't get time back
It's moving so fast
Make your life count
You won't get it back.

Kourtney Brockman, Grade 8
Bueker Middle School, MO

September 11th, 2001

September 11th 2001.
I was sitting in Ms. Davis's 2nd grade class
all of a sudden I hear a voice on the intercom
telling the teachers to turn on the TV.
I was so scared the day that the towers had been struck.
That day was September 11th, 2001.

Taylor Morris, Grade 8
Southern Reynolds County R-II School, MO

A Lifetime Dream

Once in a lifetime
somebody dreams of becoming an astronaut.

The rockets are big,
loud, and can carry an aircraft.

They produce a lot of pollution
but they help mankind.

If somebody has a dream
to become an astronaut,

Just believe you can
and you will become one.

Christian Taylor, Grade 8
Ketchum Jr High School, OK

The Old Pine Tree

The old pine tree so huge like a castle.

I go there when I want to be alone
so I can think about life.

I climb up it see the bright birds
flapping their wings.

I hear cars going by, in my back yard.
kids playing screaming, yelling.

I smell the bark surrounding me
like a cozy woodsy blanket.

I can taste the honey
drip
drop.

I touch the needles,
pointy like a porcupine's back.

And when I'm ready to leave, leave, leave,
the old pine tree.

Joseph Green, Grade 7
Hebron Middle School, KY

Lightning Dances

Lightning dances in the night
Telling everyone a storm is on the way
Lighting up the dark sky with colorful sparks
Gracefully stepping from its bed of clouds
And racing down to earth
Dancing to the music of the thunder
With its steady beat strong
So if you ever get the chance,
Look outside and watch the lightning dance

Melody Dixon, Grade 7
St Charles Homeschool Learning Center, MO

He Tripped Over a Tree

He tripped on a tree.
Got stung by a bee.
But found a seed.
That grew a gigantic tree.

Jeremy Morrison, Grade 7
Ketchum Jr High School, OK

Baseball

I like baseball.
It is a fun sport.
My friends and I
like to play
baseball all the time.

When I first joined baseball
I played for Alfords Tire
and it was fun. I loved it,
and I got to spend time
with my friend A.J.

One day A.J., me, and my brother
were in the backyard playing baseball.
All three of us got hit in
the head with a baseball
every time we stepped at the plate.

One day A.J. hit the ball so hard
he made a homerun.
It was so awesome.
I love baseball it is my favorite sport.
Baseball is the best.

Brandon Halford, Grade 7
Dyer Elementary & Jr High School, TN

A Special Place

I place the seeds in the soil
As the sun beats on my back,
How long until the fruit is ready
For patience I do lack

I pull the brim of my sun hat
Over my face for shade,
The blossoms peak out of the ground
And flowers they have made

They wind blows the soil
Straight into my face,
Slowly, I begin to sneeze
As I work at a steady pace

Today I have a garden
As pleasant as can be,
And now I'm glad all this hard work
Made a special place for me

Kay Fischer, Grade 8
West Jr High School, MO

Missing Homework's Song

The bell rings, the students rush out, the teachers slowly leave
I poke my head from a nook (or cranny), and remember all the students that grieve.

'Cause when they can't find me, the missing homework, they moan and groan
And it's all their fault, you see, because they really should have known.

That homework likes to move; float on the breeze, dance a little, escape!
And when we're gone we laugh a little laugh, when we see your incredulous gape.

We realize you can't quite believe, that your homework just stood up and walked away
But it's entirely true, we abandon you, and rejoice in your apparent dismay.

We scuttle under beds, slip out of backpacks, and jump from desktops galore
It we didn't cause you a zero, then our life would be an absolute bore.

The only time you'll find us, is when your time runs out
When you can't turn us in anymore, we show up and watch you pout.

Being homework is so blah; we have to jazz it up somehow
So don't get mad, when we go poof and leave without even a "Ciao!"
Because being homework isn't fun, unless we leave you, that I vow.

Kira Lubahn, Grade 8
West Jr High School, MO

Under My Umbrella!

Under my umbrella, I watch the rainfall. I
hear the thunder and the lightning bawl.
Then as it dies down I see a rainbow, big
bright so close but yet so far away.
I reach out to touch it but I FAIL, so then I
remember, I can't touch the sky.

Haley E. Black, Grade 7
Ketchum Jr High School, OK

Sorrow

Sorrow is a tasty tangerine waiting for hands to pluck it.
It is the music of Rainbow Fish gliding through the ripples of the pond,
you only have to listen.
It is the murmur of lilacs,
secrets are guarded in their silences.
Sorrow is the waving of grasses
their cries are unheard and stifled.
It is the rumble of the Oaks as they tumble like rain.
The weeping moon frowns and ponders,
"Why destroy something so one-of-a-kind?"
Sorrow is the emerald forest vanishing.
It is the surprise of a Raven without a home.
It is the smell of murky smog seeping into the green sea of moss.
Sorrow is the ivory polar bear sliding away into the unknown.
Listen to the hummingbird's sorrow song.
They hope. They dream. They wait.
Within sorrow lies the seed of hope.

Kiki Rogers, Grade 8
Baylor School, TN

This Day

We knew this day had to come someday,
but it's hard to believe it's actually here.

Sadness, filling throughout my body,
giving me a sudden loss of words

The thought of you, not being here with me,
sends a tear rolling down my cheek.

You have always been there to walk beside me
now, I am left alone, to walk with my shadow.

We say our good-byes as we share a hug,
then you slowly walk away

We knew this day had to come someday,
the day my best friend moved away.

Michelle Deves, Grade 7
Seven Holy Founders School, MO

Fourth of July

I love the Fourth of July
Eating cheeseburgers and hotdogs until midnight
The smell of horses, food, and the smoke of the fireworks
Seeing the beautiful colors red, white, and blue
Cars and hotrods rumbling on the street
Celebrating our country's birthday
Seeing different people, friends, and fireworks
That's why I love the Fourth of July.

Jordon Miller, Grade 8
Greenfield Jr/Sr High School, MO

Season's Beauty

Walking with crunches underneath you,
Red and orange leaves fall from the tallest trees,
Rocking as they fall,
Robins soar overhead to endless south,
Seasons come and seasons pass,
Bare trees the only thing you see,
Except the lights of the angels,
Gleaming as beautiful as a lit snowflake,
The first fluffy snow drifts,
Stacking like presents under a Christmas tree,
Seasons come and seasons pass,
Ice turns to droplets,
Falling from the blooming beauties,
As a light drizzle pounds on the leaves like drums,
Animals feed off the freshly sprouted buds,
Seasons come and seasons pass,
Big red glowing from a position in the west,
Nights under the stars of heaven,
Riding into scorching heat,
Diving into a cooling sensation, splashing against your face,
Seasons end while others begin.

Daniel McClure, Grade 9
Fulton Sr High School, MO

The Swimming Pool

Clear water lies inside of the Hershey chocolate border.
Kids play and splash water
Onto the downy smelling towel.
While sitting in the lemon floaty.
Chlorine lingers in the fresh air and onto the wet plants.
I sit on the marshmallow chair
And turn pages in my mystery book,
While my brother sits and laughs
On the wet, white chocolate steps.
I had cherry shorts, a black olive shirt, and a brand new book
As my snack bag sat on the vanilla tile floor.
The eye-burning water made the pole slick and squeaky,
A kid climbs onto the tiled walls
And into the poofy intertube.
I smell the air of happiness while I read
In my dark chocolate sunglasses

Alivia Forck, Grade 7
Southern Boone Middle School, MO

Christmas

C hurch
H aving people over
R ipping presents
I nsightful
S ensational
T errific
M emories
A pple pie
S haring

Patsy Dawn Atkinson, Grade 8
Southern Reynolds County R-II School, MO

Kangaroo

Look at her go, around the bush
She passes by fast, she leaps with a "swoosh!"
Through shrub, over hill, forward she launches
Exercising her hip-hopping haunches
But she's oh-so careful, a joey's inside!
Bouncing along on this up and down ride.
Swooping and swerving, she's quick to react
Using her tail like a balancing act.
Through trees and shrubs, her monstrous feet
Land on the ground to a steady beat.
Ears standing upright and eyes open wide
She bounds to her friends with their scent as her guide.
Bounding and springing, padded feet thumping
She never gets tired of high and low jumping.
A muscular build, feet pounding the earth
An adorable face, a miraculous birth.
She does not get fatigued when using her muscle
Hurrying, rushing, a big, busy bustle.
So next time you visit Australia or zoo,
Be sure to look for our friend kangaroo!

Madeline Rose, Grade 7
Baylor School, TN

Cody Miracle

Cody

Creative, funny, artistic, and fun.
Brother of Kenya and Michael.
Lover of drawing, playing football, basketball, and dirt bike riding.
Who feels happy and joyful around friends.
Who gives great respect if given to him, along with his love towards family, and the world we live in.
Who fears of losing friends, family, and his grateful life.
Who would like to see the Cleveland Indians go to the World Series, Montgomery Central High become undefeated,
Along with Montgomery Central Middle.
Who lives in the quiet country of Clarksville, Tennessee.
Who needs great friends, loving family, and a football scholarship to go to college.

Miracle!

Cody Miracle, Grade 8
Montgomery Central Middle School, TN

Permit Me to Tell You About Snow

Permit me to tell you about snow.
The excitement of watching the snow flakes on the ground pile up one by one,
The arousing feeling that you get when your mom finally says you can go outside and play,
The moment of truth when you get to make the snow angel you have been waiting for,
The disappointment when you have to go back inside,
The secret in the back of your mind knowing that if you beg, tomorrow you will do it all over again.
But the snow I remember the most
Left me amazed at how much fun I thought I never would have had,
So cold I could not feel my fingers,
Speechless,
With great memories.

Kristen Schramm, Grade 8
All Saints School, MO

Ashley Dabbs

Ashley
Who is loud, talkative, and fun to be around
Who is the lovely daughter of Debbie and Denny Dabbs
Who loves talking to her friends on the computer and family including her pet, and God
Who feels excited about skating and the game this weekend, and about high school
Who needs her flat iron for her hair, phone to talk on, and a jacket to be warm
Who gives love to her family and a headache to her mom from talking so much
Who fears scary slimy snakes, big furry spiders, and deep drowning water
Who would like to see her best friend Khroy, Starbucks, and Justin Timberlake
Who lives in a white house in Clarksville, Tennessee
Dabbs

Ashley Dabbs, Grade 8
Montgomery Central Middle School, TN

Winter

As the snow falls each unique crystal, its own world. It shines in the light making a rainbow in maybe the smallest form. Catching them on your tongue then as it melts away you want to catch more. It's putting its blanket in a vast area of dreams. Children are out of school, laughing and playing. With snowballs a flying with the sliding down the hills. Cheers of joy as the miracle of nature has its coldest season. Winter romance holding hands, hugging and the ice skating. The dreaming and wishes with snow covered kisses. The thoughts of a new year are ringing in your ear. With Christmas joy and cheer. This is what winter brings every year.

Danielle Biddle, Grade 9
West Jr High School, MO

Moon Journey

Shimmering, shining, sparkling shadow
Rising from your darkened grave
A pearly white face shines eerily in the dark
Angelic aura commands dominance
Over kingdoms and seas alike
Haunting many a soul in their beds
Watching my every move
Your gleaming, glinting, glistening surface
Attracts the eye of late night wanderers
While howling wolves cry their midnight song, "how-w-w"
Entrancing features hypnotize me
Like a swaying pendulum
Peachy skylights are appearing
Life is stirring down below
You slowly sink back into oblivion

Hannah Botts, Grade 7
Barret Traditional Middle School, KY

Your Choice

Each day you fall a little more from grace.
Do you ever wonder if you will see Jesus face to face?
With everything in life you choose,
You determine whether you win or lose.
God is waiting for you to invite Him in.
He loves you so much, He forgives all your sin.
That first step is yours to take.
Heaven or Hell is your decision to make.
You set examples for your children
More than you will ever know.
I pray you make the right decision,
So you and your children know which way to go.
You never know how long you will be here,
But if you choose God, you have nothing to fear.
So with the choice of Heaven or Hell,
I pray you make your decision well.
God loves and cares dearly for you.
So please choose Him first in everything you do.
Just open your heart and let Him in,
And never again will Satan win.

Grant Douglas, Grade 8
Perryville High School, AR

Mamaw's Pool

My favorite place is at my mamaw's pool.
Swimming in it for hours.
Jumping off the diving board.
Swimming to the bottom.
Getting on a float.
Being without lotion.
About to get out.
Seeing how many floats we could jump over.
Going under forever.
Swimming with people brings much happiness.

Randy Reeves, Grade 8
Heritage Middle School, TN

Hide n' Seek

As the seeker counts from 1-10
We all go running into the den
We look around for a place to hide
I can't find any so I run outside
And then I walk past the slide
I stop by the swing for a little ride
Then I realize that I'm wasting time
I run to the front past the wind chimes
I ran to the bush a perfect place for me
Then I hear the seeker counting "93"
But I am not worried seeing that I'm done
Just in time because the seeker says "ready or not here I come"

Reem Khdier, Grade 7
Pleasant View School, TN

Dreamers

Summer days, midnight skies,
Swimming pools, and hot guys.

Hanging with friends, dreaming all night.
Waking up, I just might.

Looking at clouds in the sky,
Thinking how lucky we'd be if we could fly.

For all the things we cannot do,
Why we dream, is to make them come true.

Josiphene Weaver, Grade 8
Wilson Middle School, OK

It's Just Life

Life is like someone you love.
Once you lose them they never come back.
Life is like the heavens above
It will never slack.

Life is like me and you
It will never stay the same.
Life is like a line of things.
Life is nothing to blame.

Khalia Jade Milton, Grade 7
Duncan Middle School, OK

Love

There's one little word,
As little as may be,
Can confuse all of us,
As much as to we can't see,
We use this word,
To parents, brothers, and friends,
This one word should never, never end,
This one little word,
As powerful as all,
It is the word that makes us big, strong, and tall.

Stuart Martin, Grade 8
Owasso 8th Grade Center, OK

Born for the Stage

On a big stage,
One person
Catches your eye
Holds your concentration,
The whole performance long,
Her spirit never dies on stage,
Not even with a falter.
With a smile on her face and a
Presence high with passion,
Neither you nor I could ever deny
That one person that God made
Who was born for the stage.
As you watch her, you just don't
Want to turn the page.
Why?
That person was born for the stage.

Mary Beth Prince, Grade 8
West Middle School, TN

Dream

F
a
l
l
i
n
g fast,
Into another world.
Not knowing when,
Or why,
Or how.

Meeting purple creatures,
With polka dots and fur.
And seeing flying saucers,
With flashing lights.
Or hiding from a monster,
That talks to you in French.

Then comes the realization,
Of blankets and a pillow,
The smell of pancakes,
And the shouts of your sister.

Megan McGarel, Grade 8
All Saints' Episcopal School, TN

Caring

C aring for other people.
A ppreciate other people's property.
R espect others.
I n return they should help.
N ever bully anyone.
G ain respect by giving respect.

Tannis Moomaw, Grade 7
Greenfield Jr/Sr High School, MO

Two Tones

Some days I feel green
Like freshly cut lawn
People walk all over me.
Or I feel greedy
And I am the only one in the world.

Other days I feel like a peach
Normal and well behaved on the outside,
But juicy and hyper on the inside
Like a fresh peach.

Gage Reynolds, Grade 8
Leeton Middle and High School, MO

Thanksgiving

The leaves are falling
the birds are calling
and everything is quiet like a mouse
That holiday is near
when thanks are very dear
and everyone is humble
I understand
that man hand-in-hand
can make the world go 'round
The turkey and the hams
that we buy at Sam's
are better than ever before
We hear the story over-and-over
while we sit shoulder-to-shoulder
listening to how our country began

Morgan Petersen, Grade 7
Nettleton Jr High School, AR

My Love, My Dearest

Do you remember
The first time we touched,
The feeling you had
That you loved so much?
Do you remember
When I held your hand,
That day on the beach
As we walked through the sand?
Do you remember
Our first kiss,
The feeling you had,
The feeling you miss?
Do you remember
The feeling we shared
As we sat on the swing,
The wind in your hair?
Do you remember
The day you died,
The day I held you
And couldn't help but cry?

Connor Tracy, Grade 9
Glenpool High School, OK

What Do You Do?

What do you do when nobody cares?
When they shut their eyes
When they should be watching,
What do you do?
When they walk away?
When you ask for help?
Do you scream?
Do you cry?
Do you fight back at all?
Do you laugh?
Or do you die?
And your empty old heart
Does it start to heal?
Can you pull it together
When it all falls apart?
When does it end?
When did it start?
What do you do?

Justice Murchison, Grade 9
Niangua High School, MO

The Sorrow of the Holocaust

She was in the Ghetto for so many years.
So many people have died…
Having her mom getting killed there,
In a shed that no one could find…
Knowing only hatred and fear…
When taken out of the Ghetto,
And put in that bloody death camp.
Seeing death and people's corpses.
Wishing she was not there…
Feeling the sorrow she could not bare…

Sam Day, Grade 8
White Station Middle School, TN

Snow

Snow
Crystal, glimmering
Streaming cold flakes
Cold, frosty, flaky, marshmallows
Flurries

Snow
Shiny, gorgeous
Run and play
Wet, soft, icy, frozen
Flurries

Snow
Radiant, sparkly
Bitter and harsh
Chilly, wintry, arctic, glisten
Flurries

Stephanie Brammer, Grade 8
Summit Lakes Middle School, MO

Hockey, Here's to You

Hockey, here's to you.
With your licks and your skates
And your sticks and your saves,
And of course, don't forget the disputes.
Hockey, here's to your boldness,
With your goalies and players
And layers and layers of rock hard coldness.
Hockey, here's to your physical play,
Your players go at it, hit the puck,
Or bat it all livelong day.
So hockey, here's to you.
'Cause to me and many others,
You're more than just something to do.

Matt Davis, Grade 8
Owasso 8th Grade Center, OK

No Reply

Why is everybody gone in a time of need
Why is it when you need another
Someone has took their leave
Everyone is missing anyone has left
Anything and everything is gone to my regret
Several seats are empty many spots are bare
It seems somebody left without a care
Both either and neither has disappeared
And where a few other are just isn't clear
Each day no matter how much I try
Nobody is the one that gives a reply

Amanda Burns, Grade 8
Pigeon Forge Middle School, TN

Ever Love

Call my name and tell me you love me
through your eyes I can see
Through your arms I will be
Your perfect love casting out there for me

I was made to adore you and be cared for
There is no one that can change the way I feel
Maybe our love will catch like fire and burn right through us
The dream is over as I steer out the door
Can't bear it when I'm gone
Can teach me when I'm here
Anything I own I would give it away for you
I'm not just a girl lost in this world
but in a sea of faces

You are the waves I feel when I'm sinking
The day is brighter here with you
The night is darker here without you
Steering into space
Trying to find my place
You are my star that shines in the night
You are on fire like the hot burning sun

Tiffany Harper, Grade 8
Chelsea Jr High School, OK

Marti Smarty

Marti Smarty was very small
Marti Smarty had trouble climbing a brick wall.
One day Marti Smarty grew two feet tall
Marti Smarty still had trouble climbing the brick wall.

Marti Smarty didn't care if she couldn't climb a brick wall
She was happy that she grew two feet taller,
And Marti Smarty stayed
Four feet tall!

Brittany Sheets, Grade 7
Kiowa Jr/Sr High School, OK

Nyah

A fluffy thing jumping ecstatically
hopping up and down left and right
as I enter the doorway

Constantly running and playing
in the yard

As she runs and jumps I watch
in awe as if this magnificent creature is
Anything more that I could imagine

To so many just a simple dog,
But to many a loved animal

Kristopher Blanton, Grade 7
Hazelwood Northwest Middle School, MO

Football Player

The courage of the football player on the field
Would build a bigger and better football team.

Then they will strive to win the game
They might cry if they lose the game

If they work enough they might win state championship
And they will be known in history as the best team.

Mike Addison, Grade 8
Ketchum Jr High School, OK

Summer

The warm sun shining above me,
The green grass cushioning you when you fall,
Hanging out with your friends and a soccer ball,
Waiting for that inviting call,
This is summer time.

Running through the grass with glee,
Drinking cool lemonade with a friend,
Writing a postcard to send,
Hoping this time will never end,
This is summer time.

Tyler Mitchell, Grade 8
Owasso 8th Grade Center, OK

Stars

The stars twinkle
when I'm praying,
twinkle when
I'm singing,
twinkle when
I'm sleeping,
twinkle when
I'm awake,
twinkle when
I'm laughing,
twinkle when
I'm crying,
twinkle when
I'm being still,
and twinkle when
I'm moving.
The stars will twinkle,
when I'm here and when I'm not.
Keep twinkling,
my little stars,
ever, oh, so far and clear.

Alyson Ewigman, Grade 8
Father McCartan Memorial School, MO

A Recipe for a Perfect Day

First start with no school
Then add in no homework
Pinch in a cool sunny day
Add a dash of excitement
Stir in a pound of fun
Mix in some stay up all night
A cup of good weather
A teaspoon of movie rentals
Served with a holiday

Dylan Thomas, Grade 7
Meredith-Dunn School, KY

Cocoa

Warm, delicious cocoa,
sitting on the stove,
with tiny, little marshmallows,
swimming in the mug.

A cup of it,
down my throat,
warming my cold insides.
Around me a fuzzy, warm blanket
keeping the warmth inside.

And as I look out,
I see snowflakes falling from above.
Then I wonder and say
"how nice it is to be inside,
with a cup of nice warm cocoa!"

Rose Livingston, Grade 7
Annunciation Elementary School, MO

For I Cannot

You're a phone call away but I still miss you,
For I cannot disturb your restless sleep.
You have been gone for hours but your kiss still lays on my lips,
For I cannot think of anything else.
You have been off the phone for an hour but your voice still lingers in my ears,
For I cannot make your words leave.
My hand has been alone for the day but I still feel the warmth of yours,
For I cannot move without the thought.
My chest is light from the lack of your head but I still feel you breathing,
For I cannot sleep without it.
My dreams are filled with your smile,
For I cannot dream of needing another.
My life is now complete,
For I cannot believe in life without you.

Creg Cash, Grade 9
Senath Hornersville Sr High School, MO

Geometry Miracles

I plop myself at the granite countertop reading my Geometry book.
I ponder the answer,
and tap my number two pencil on my head which click, click, clicks.
I imagine being outside playing tackle football.
The freshly cut grass calling to me.
No, no, no I advise myself, I have to finish my work.
My face is as red as a cherry with frustration.
Suddenly, I hear a tender whisper.
The whisper so supple I could hear a needle hit the tile floor.
There it is once more now a little louder,
I bellow for my mom but no answer.
I start to undergo a cold chill running down my spine.
X=17 the voice whispers.
Wow! That is the answer.
I must be going crazy because I look
down and the problems are solving themselves in the book.
So, this must be how Einstein did it!
Problems 1, 2, and 3 are completed before I could blink.
Then, when I blink, 4 through 30 are all solved.
I flip the purple, Geometry book closed,
and I wonder if I will be so lucky next time.

Nic Bullard, Grade 8
Baylor School, TN

Permit Me to Tell You About Crushes

Permit me to tell you about crushes.
The butterflies in your stomach when he walks by,
The embarrassment when you look like a fool in front of him.
The hours on end you spend talking to your friends about him,
The doodles all throughout your notebook with his name and a heart around it.
But the crush I remember most
Stuck in my head for weeks,
Only to be a figure in my memories,
Sweet as can be,
Handsome and hot,
Made my heart skip a beat.

Mary Bindbeutel, Grade 8
All Saints School, MO

Fall

Oh, what a spectacular day it is —
To see the sun shining down, down on me.
Every bird is singing a calm tune.
The fresh air is soothing to the body.
A mild breeze keeps me quite cool and content.
Leaves are turning into a golden sea.

Tayler Moon, Grade 9
Bearden High School, TN

Behind Closed Doors

You never know what goes on
Behind closed doors.
Could couples be fighting?
Could children be sleeping?
A door is like an ocean,
Keeping its secrets from the world.

Unlocking its secrets can bring
Devastation or inspiration to the world.
Could nightmares be happening?
Could a soul be searching for freedom?
Behind the door, someone could be dancing
In an opulent ballroom full of shimmering chandeliers.

Seeing the shadows on the floor,
Wondering what is happening behind the door.
Could it be someone simply
Reading a book on their bed?
What happens behind closed doors,
Is a mystery to me.

Weston Clark, Grade 9
Hamburg Jr High School, AR

The Dream

I am on a swing,
swinging.
I close my eyes.
I feel like I'm flying,
like a bird.
I jump off and to my surprise,
I am a bird.
I fly away and venture beyond
what my eyes have ever seen.
I see beautiful mountains, trees, and oceans.
These are only things I see in books,
through my mind.
But it's not a book,
It's real.
Suddenly I feel a jolt.
I fall…
I open my eyes and see my mother is standing over me.
This is when I realized,
It was only a dream.

Savannah Ruiz, Grade 7
Independence Charter Middle School, OK

Sometimes I Wonder

Sometimes I wonder
why He put bad people on the earth
people that do bad things
Sometimes I wonder
why they make fun
of other people
and be mean to us
Sometimes I wonder
why they do what they do just for me
Sometimes I wonder
why He died just for us
and did the things He did for us
Sometimes I wonder
why you don't look my way ever
Sometimes I wonder
why He took Mrs. Darmody from us
Sometimes I wonder
about things I know you wonder
about too and think about like I do
Sometimes I just wonder
WHY?? Why people do the things they do!

Amanda Koebbe, Grade 7
St Katharine Drexel School, MO

The Whistling Leaves

Golden Brown leaves as soft as a cat.
Being back at school is like a winters day.
The leaves are falling like crazy,
Some people are getting lazy.
Christmas time is almost here,
Soon it will be the new year!

Thomas Bissland, Grade 8
Wilson Middle School, OK

If I Were in Charge of the World*

If I were in charge of the world
I'd get rid of spiders
Make world peace
Make school one day a week

If I were in charge of the world
There'd be nicer people
No sicknesses
And no vaccine shots

If I were in charge of the world
You wouldn't die young
You wouldn't have drugs to make you sick
You wouldn't have nightmares
And I'd be a famous guitar player

If I were in charge of the world.

Shayla Fryrear, Grade 7
Newcastle Middle School, OK
**Patterned after "If I Were in Charge of the World"*
by Judith Viorst

Unknown

Happy, yet sad.
Almost positive of being unsure,
which makes me mad.
People ask, but I hide.
Hoping they will swallow their pride.
Tired of old,
dreaming of change.
Maybe I'm being a bit too bold.
But, my thoughts have stuck,
just like glue.
So here I sit…
not knowing what to do.

Christina Gagner, Grade 8
Owasso 8th Grade Center, OK

Savior from Pale Blue

Running to an edge
Preparing to jump
Like a panther
Pounding
"kerplump"
Sliding from smooth surface
Sinking at one thousand miles an hour
Into pale blue I go
Blur of bubbles
Darkness beckons
Light pulling me closer
As bright as golden sun
Into oblivion
Then it happens
Like eagles snatching their prey
I'm being pulled up thanking
My Savior from pale blue

Hunter Schanz, Grade 7
Barret Traditional Middle School, KY

That Day

My heart was breaking,
When you said good-bye.
You drove away,
And never looked back,
Never gave a second thought,
That you broke someone's heart.
Someone who loved you,
Cared about you,
Risked everything to be with you.
I always wanted you by my side.
I couldn't stand being apart.
Then you just…left.
I still cry when I think about that day.
But the funny thing is,
As much as I needed you,
The farther away you went,
The less it seemed to hurt.

Kelsey Steed, Grade 8
Mammoth Spring High School, AR

It's the Way…

The way you kiss my forehead, the way you stroke my hair
The way you give me goosebumps and feelings I almost can't bear.

The way you make me smile so big, my grin as wide as the moon
The way you bring me so much joy, your voice, it makes me swoon.

The way I can't resist you, the way you softly caress my skin
The way your face is shaped so handsome: your eyes, your lips, your chin.

The way you wear your rocker clothes, the way your hair flips out
The way you get a little jealous, in a caring way, no doubt.

The way you get competitive, the way I can feel your fast beating heart
The way you stand and hold me close, the tickle fights you always start.

The way you like me for who I am, the way you brighten my day
The way you always make me feel better, my feelings for you won't go away.

The way I'm really falling for you, falling for you fast
I know that you're the boy of my dreams, and I know that we will last.

Sarah Hanshew, Grade 9
Hedgesville High School, WV

I Am Thankful

I am thankful for my family,
Some people do not know any of their family members.
I am thankful for my home
Some people don't have a home to live in.
I am thankful for my friends
Some people don't have great friends that love them.
I am thankful for food
If we didn't have food we'd die and some people do not get food.
I am thankful for my clothes
For some people do not have more than 1 pair of clothes to wear.
I am thankful for sound
For some people are born without being able to hear music and the sound of nature.
I am thankful for my pets
Some people don't have pets to tell secrets to that you can't tell others.

Brett Gay, Grade 8
Avenue City Elementary School, MO

The Sea

The great sea lord Neptune continuously pounds his great hand on the rocks,
As if he has just had an argument with someone that he loves.
And in come the seagulls, the lowly sea thugs,
Searching for their breakfast of dead fish and slugs.
The sound of their morning squabbles reaches my ears.
I can hear their squealing and their squawking,
Their pecking and their gawking.
Then comes the wind with gargantuan gusts
And sends the pesky maritime creatures
Into an oceanside bluff.

Thomas Dale Miller, Grade 7
White Station Middle School, TN

Friends

I have many
They're all lots of fun
One is Alyssa
Another is Jessica
So different, but alike
They're both the same

Kali Smith, Grade 8
Southern Reynolds County R-II School, MO

The Last Points

Both my opponent and I have
fought tough all three periods,
for five minutes,
but now it all comes down
to who wants it most.
The score is tied eight to eight.

My heart leaps in and out of my chest.
The room spins, my head
throbs like somebody hit it
with a sledge hammer.
My body feels like the Japanese felt after the
bomb was dropped on Hiroshima

I want it the most.
I take a shot, it feels like the
shot that takes two seconds
is an hour long.
He falls straight on his back.
The whistle blows, the referee raises
my hand. I win.

Matt Bodine, Grade 8
Baylor School, TN

Deception

Dancing the tango
Playfully caressing the smoldering logs
A rhythmic chanting
Lifts from restless graves
Setting the beat for the dance of fire

Smoke rises in a graceful twirl
Circling like a gypsy dancer
Beating her drum

The entrancing beauty of this ritual is transcendent
Hearing a voice calling, "Come closer, closer"

Light glittering upon your face
Growing envy taking over your mind
Closing your eyes, holding your breath
You plunge into the fiery abyss
Flames consuming your soul
As your body turns into ashes

Olivia Ensley, Grade 7
White Station Middle School, TN

A Harmful Word

You crave it; you want it,
The spotlight, you own it,
You will destroy all who get in your way,
Before you give it up,
The spotlight, it's yours,
You ignored me, and left me aside,
I, feeling rejected, started to fight you,
Rejection, such a harmful word,
It killed me.
I, being so naive, fed your desire,
You hurt me.

Caitlin Zaretz, Grade 8
Family of Faith Christian School, OK

A Day in the Woods

Here I am sitting in the woods quiet as can be.
I hear some squirrels barking at the birds up in their tree.
But I am sitting here with my bow.
I would like to see a monster buck or a big doe.
As I am sitting here patiently.
I hear something stepping through the leaves.
A nice buck steps out of the brush
And gets broad side just for me.
So I draw my bow back without a peep,
Get him in my sights, and shoot.
I hit the monster buck right in the heart.

Terry Horner, Grade 8
Musselman Middle School, WV

The World of God

Thank you God…
For the fluffy clouds floating
Up to you in the heavens.

Thank you God…
For the sound of an owl
Hooting, echoing through the air.

Thank you God…
For the delicious apple I am eating,
Crisp as a winter's day.

Thank you God…
For the flowers smelling like
Perfume in the humid summer air.

Thank you God…
For the sand rubbing the bottom of my feet
And trickling through my toes.

Thank you God…
For making the world
A beautiful place.

Holly Magre, Grade 7
Our Lady Catholic School, MO

Home

Atop this tree I lay
blanketed in shadows
gazing out at the setting sun
taking me to the past.
Of other times I sat there
in that same tree.
Watching the fireworks show
fade into the dark moonlit sky.
The birds and the bees wake me.
From my flashback reverie.
My heart felt like it was close to tears.
I was swept away. I finally realized
after all this time
and all these sunset days,
that here and now up in this tree,
my heart truly feels at home.

Matthew Vallot, Grade 7
Lewis and Clark Middle School, MO

Love for Freedom

Today we are free,
But tomorrow we may not be.
A war is going on,
And out troops have sworn.
To protect work from the greatest,
And defeat the most hated.
To save us from sorrow,
So we may live for tomorrow.
When you bow your head to pray,
Ask for their protection every day.
As you send your love,
Send it through the Lord above.
So when they get the call,
They'll do everything but fall.

Rebecca Miller, Grade 9
Moorefield High School, WV

Ocean

O pen, inviting waters
C alming and relaxing
E xciting new adventures
just awaiting to happen
A nxious to come; hate to leave
N ever ending waters

Whitney Haddox, Grade 8
Owasso 8th Grade Center, OK

Travel Is Life's Adventures

Travel is like life.
Never knowing what to expect,
Or how the day will turn out.
Adventurous and breathtaking,
Leading to a new destination every day.
Travel is like life.

Kim Hodges, Grade 9
Bearden High School, TN

Sun Rise, Sun Sets as We Follow the Pattern

These dark streets only seem to bring my defeat
As the willowing and falling of the changing leaves
Breeze by and are swept away with the wind —
Fall is escaping and winter is returning from the long abyss of summer
It's time to face what has come between my realizations and the truth;
We only bury ourselves inside the changing of the seasons
And the deep, concealing snow of our emotions
We are bright and refining throughout the scenes of summer
But during the winter, we put on our perpetually constant masks
They act as our efficient weapons, with which we hide ourselves from the world,
For we are afraid of change
We are afraid of ourselves
We are afraid of what we might do to others and/or ourselves
So this is the best way I can describe it
As I also bring out my mask to arm myself from the brisk of winter
We have all forged this in our minds
We have all become accustomed to the routine
As the sun rises, and the sun sets
We plaster our masks across our faces, then discard them at the end of the day
And at the end of it all, all we have learned
Is that it's all basically the same.

Paige Warren, Grade 9
Norman High School North, OK

Why Me

Why am I the only one that gets blamed for what someone else did
Why am I the only one that tries and then gets smacked in the face
Why am I the only one that gets caught doing what I'm not supposed to do
Why…why…why…
Why me
Why does it always come back to me
Why am I the only one that goes through bad days and hurting times
Why do I always feel like someone is there making me feel this way
Why am I going through some of the things that others would hate to go through
Why…why…why…
Why me

Daylin Heman, Grade 8
Sherwood Middle School, MO

A Part of Your Life

He might be stupid,
He might be nasty,
He might be funny,
and he might be fantastic,
He probably does not get straight A's,
He probably says weird things,
He probably will make you laugh,
and he may be perfect,
You know he is not perfect,
but you still believe it,
and he doesn't want anyone because he doesn't want to get hurt,
but you can't explain to him you would never hurt him
even in a million years
because you have to admit he is a part of your life.

Samantha Moody-Walker, Grade 7
Lewis and Clark Middle School, MO

All About Me!!!!!

Lindsey
Funny, loving, blonde, nice
Daughter of Mike and Brenda
Lover of my dog, best friends, and family
Who feels happy, loved, excited
Who gives advice, hugs, kisses
Who fears scary movies, roller coasters, and dying
Who would like to see my grandfather, and Paris Hilton
Who lives in a big white house
Underwood

Lindsey Underwood, Grade 8
Montgomery Central Middle School, TN

Baby Dragon Guarder

See how he flies
from the top of the tower,
with a flimsy flutter of dragon power.
See how his wings rapidly flap
down to the bridge
to join his mother.
As he soars slowly to meet the edge
a look of the eyes
finds Prince Charming at the other side.
As eyes meet at that very moment
a smell of fear reeks in the air.
See how he blows a ball of fire
leaving a petrified Prince Charming
to fall to the ground.
Inside the tower awaits a priceless princess
hoping for her Prince Charming
to go beyond the deserts
to go beyond the Baby Dragon Guarder
just to come and take her away.
Leaving the Baby Dragon Guarder
in peace on that very day.

Anna Chennault, Grade 7
Baylor School, TN

A Night in the Snow

It was really just mother and me as we walked
through the snow on just our bare feet.
I had told her that for this was like *standing on ice cubes.*

She had told me that was true,
only for her it was *like being in Antarctica nude.*
I told her oh mom stop, you're just overreacting.

Then she said no I'm not and pointed to a catfish.
The catfish was making an eerie sound,
like the scratching fingers on a blackboard.

It hurt my ears, but I slipped the pain away
thinking to myself we might get out of here someday.

Kayla Ulsas, Grade 9
St John the Baptist High School, MO

How

How could you go and just leave me that way?
Without a tear, you left me standing here,
it's been a while, but yes I'm ok.

You don't feel any shame for my dismay.
You knew just want you were doing my dear.
How could you go and just leave me that way?

I first thought I could live through the day,
but now I see I shed too many a tear.
It's been a while, but yes I'm ok.

One of these days, you will have to pay
for what you did, for giving me this fear.
How could you go and just leave me that way?

All I can do is sit and not look away,
and stare at the face that looks back in the mirror.
It's been a while, but yes I'm ok.

It seems my downfall I couldn't delay,
I'll have to wait for the pain to disappear.
How could you go and just leave me that way?
It's been a while, but yes I'm ok.

Meghan King, Grade 9
University Heights Academy, KY

My One True Friend

When I first met you,
I knew you were here to stay.
We laughed and cried together.
We had a feeling that we would be friends forever.
We have been through the good and the bad.
We have been happy and sad.
We have been through messy situations
To joyous birthday celebrations.
We have had many problems.
But we get through them.
We have been through it all
From fights with our parents to midnight phone calls.
You will be with me til the end,
I know I can never forget my one true friend.

Mady Parisot, Grade 8
St Gerard Majella School, MO

The Light Is No More

The clock is ticking, my time will soon end.
I'm not ready to go, but I have no choice.
The lightning strikes upon the tree of life,
Ending pieces of my life with every branch that falls.
I'm full of holes from wood peckers of depression and loss.
The light that feeds me has gone.
My time has come, the clock ticks no more,
My time is up…goodbye.

Drew Tharp, Grade 8
Newman Middle School, OK

Skiing

Skiing, flying on snow
Gliding down the mountain far from slow

Like riding on clouds, face with a smile
Big mountain, goes on for miles

Bright sun reflecting of green and white
Skiing, a snowy delight

Trent Saunders, Grade 7
Heritage Hall School, OK

The Donut

I walked in the door,
To pick out what I wanted
I spotted it on the shelf,
Saying 'take me away!'
It was a donut covered in chocolate
I paid, and left the store
A grandma hit me and I dropped it
I ran and ran and could not catch it
Then we came to a crosswalk,
It was in the street and I was on the side,
SMASH!!!!!
SPLAT!!!!!!
It was gone, gone forever.

Trey Scott Grisham, Grade 8
Alpena High School, AR

Thanksgiving

Sarah sat still in the chair
While playing with her hair,
She dared not say a word
For she might not be heard,

It was Thanksgiving Day
There was no time to play,
We knew not what to do
For all this was so true
The door bell rang
Pots fell with a clang.

Sarah sprang to the floor,
Walked to the door,
In came her mom
With crazy Uncle Tom.

They had their favorite food
And Sarah's brother Jude
They ate till eight; were fine by nine

They said good-bye
The baby did cry
But everyone could say
Thank God for Thanksgiving Day!

A'Shauna Brown, Grade 7
Nettleton Jr High School, AR

The Lord's Creation

Looking out what do I see? I see the world's sea of flowers
The world's blanket of grass The world's carpet of meadows.
Do you see them Lord of course you do
Thank you Lord for all that I see
Chirp, chirp, ribbit, ribbit, woo, woo Animals sound in my ears,
The world's music set was before me.
Do you hear them Lord of course you do
Thank you, Lord for all that I hear.
Berries, apples, watermelon, peaches on the trees
The sweet river of taste on my tongue, That taste, that wonderful taste
Do you taste them Lord of course you do
Thank you Lord for all that I taste.
Pine trees, flowers, cut grass in the afternoon sun,
Smelling so good, so wonderful, so great, so fresh.
Do you smell them Lord of course you do
Thank you Lord for all that I smell.
Rock, tree bark, fish scales all so bumpy, all so rough
Animal skin soft as velvet in the touch of my hand,
Wet silky rain falling, dripping down my face
Do you feel them Lord of course you do
Thank you, Lord for all that I touch.

Victoria Surdyke, Grade 7
Our Lady Catholic School, MO

A Man in the Army

A man in the army is serving his country by the means of war,
When he is suddenly hurled back.
He spots a little girl.
He picks her up and brings her to safety.
She looks him in the eyes and says, "Hope you make it back safely."
Back on the fields with his squad of friends,
He shoots at the enemy through tears and thinks of his wife and daughters.
He wipes his tears and sighs while one of his buddies dies.
He prays to God that he will make it home to his wife and two kids.
But he lifts his chin, remembers his country, and fights for the flag.

Adam Brinkley, Grade 9
Jamestown High School, MO

Alaska, from the Ground Up

Across the Great Plains and the Northwest
Over five thousand miles
To the land of the Midnight Sun
Above the Pacific Ocean
In a valley surrounded by mountains
On a coast laden with snow
After the snow has had its time, green grass begins to show
Along with green comes the rest of his fellow colors purple, red, and gold
Beyond this field of color
Upon the mountains, lies a perpetual white that is slowly withdrawing
Past this, farther north is the majestic Mount McKinley
Up here among the clouds is where the Last Frontier begins…
From the sky-down.

Isaac Goodson, Grade 8
Heritage Middle School, TN

Fall

The fall is finally here, like a cautious young deer.
Now it is time for orange leaves, and the loud crunch under your feet.
Summer has gone like an adventurous crow, migrating way down below.
The orange turns to brown, mammals burrow deep into the ground.
As the autumn finally comes, leaves are swept away in the crisp noon breeze.
Dew arrives at night, Halloween gives everyone a fright!
Suddenly, the huge trees lose their leaves, as the leaves fall they are stolen by thieves (rakes).
It begins to feel lonely, as life all seems to run away.
Yes, it is very lonely, the cold soon comes to stay.
There is one thing that stays; the hidden life that will begin in spring.
Soon winter will be here, and it will be the joyful part of year.

Morgan Miller, Grade 7
Nettleton Jr High School, AR

The Mask

I am hiding behind a mask, a mask of pain.
My world is falling apart, I cry even when it rains.
I am hiding behind a mask, a mask of fear.
My life has no direction, it is not yet sincere.
I am hiding behind a mask, a mask that hides the eyes.
It hides it from tears, sweet hello's, and sad goodbye's. My eyes — do they lie?
Or are they truthful?
Most of the time, that is when I'm not crying.
I am hiding behind a mask, a mask the world cannot yet see; I am too busy just trying to be me.
For as long as I could remember I have lived in a world of emotion,
pain, and deceit, heartaches, dedication, and devotion; not yet all as one are flowing through me.
But could it be that I am scared, scared to get out and see what the world has in store?
It's all fun and games right now, but one day it will all be a bore.
I will settle down somewhere and play my broken tambourine.
The song will be so sweet and it will be just for me.
I am hiding behind a mask, a mask of harmony.
While you're laughing and playing, my heart will be crying.
It will be crying tears of joy, tears of pain, tears of love, tears of heartache, and tears from the sky above.
It will be singing a song with an unfamiliar tune.
A song just for me, you, and my mask, too.

Tania Marr, Grade 9
Hillcrest High School, TN

Changing Skies

The clouds blanched in the royal blue sky, and other days different hues.
The grass is emerald green, wet as morning dew.

The sky is covered in royal blue and pearly white.
The sun shines so bright its glowing like a light.

When it rains the royal blue is gone it is all bright with grey. No animals in sight.
The storm is coming down with all its might.
The iron grey is holding the sun so very tight
There's so very little light
When it's pitch black the sky is lit up by the stars
And the headlights of cars
The sun is gone and the moon is shining, the moon's light shines through the midnight blue
Now it is time goodnight.

Timothy Smith, Grade 7
Knight Middle School, KY

Gossip

Gossip, gossip, gossip
We all love to hear.
Who did what?
Who went where?
Who did dare?
Gossip, gossip, gossip
Music to our ears.
Psst! I got some gossip.
Do you want to hear?
Then let's spin our evil tale.
Cryptic stories if you want.
Do you want to hear?
Who did what?
Who went where?
Who did dare?

Meagon Prang, Grade 8
Elkton School, TN

Time Dime

One at a time,
Through the line,
To buy a dime,
That goes through time.

You might get there,
But not come back,
Don't make the choice
You wish you lacked

Emily Faust, Grade 7
Hebron Middle School, KY

Holidays

Thanksgiving comes,
We give thanks;
Surrounded by loved ones,
Precious ones,
Ones we hold dearly to our hearts;
Eating delicious food,
Tantalizing, tender turkey,
Buttery corn
Fluffy mashed potatoes,
Fresh, orange, hot pumpkin pie;
Thanksgiving ends,
Winter on the way,
Snow blanketing the frozen ground;
Bright decorations,
Red, white, and green,
Lights on every block you walk;
Dreams of toys,
Delicious treats,
Giving and receiving,
Loved ones gathered,
Celebrating Christmas.

Abigail Bax, Grade 7
Lewis and Clark Middle School, MO

Hockey

I love to play hockey,
It's my favorite sport.
I love taking slap shots
From the other side of the court.

I love the high speed skating,
The crashes and the pain.
For without those
Coach says we'd have no gain.

David Knotts, Grade 8
Musselman Middle School, WV

Santa

S weet and jolly
A wesome
N orth Pole
T houghtful
A ntlers for reindeer

Samuel Hubbell, Grade 8
Wickliffe Elementary School, OK

Safe Haven

A fertile place
Where thoughts whiz and whir,
And fantasies come to life.
A place where dreams are coined,
And monsters destroyed.

Like the vastness of space
And depths of the oceans,
A place is endless.
With no boundaries to cross,
And no limits to surpass.

Storing the secrets and truths
That baffles all,
And a safe haven.
Which has only one master key.
The truth is to use it or not,
This is the limitless mind.

Karan Bhatia, Grade 7
White Station Middle School, TN

Wonderful Country

The lights of freedom;
we will always see.
In our land,
of the brave;
and home of the free.
Thanks for being the best
through the long year;
to keep our country,
that we hold dear!

Cody Lee Priebe, Grade 8
Rocky Comfort Elementary School, MO

Lost Love

As our dreams met one night
In the twilight mist and dew
One was a dream of old days
One was a dream of the new
We walked along Broadway
Near the midnight tide
As our love charmed the air
Hand and hand, Side by side

lost love — I really miss you, baby
lost love — I can't take it anymore
lost love — Is that all we seem
lost love — Is a dream within a dream

In my heart
Will melt my many tears
We loved to dream of days to come
As days turned to years
So my dreams of you and I
Are neither of our precious dreams.

Alisha Huggins, Grade 7
Asher Middle/High School, OK

Walking

One day I was walking
and was looking around
I looked up I looked down
then I looked at the ground,
my feet were dragging
my thighs were lagging
I ran a few blocks
now I'm home bound.

Stephen Sfakis, Grade 8
Pigeon Forge Middle School, TN

Starnes Alone Across the Room

All night I studied,
more than ever before.
They were multiples of three,
and I was ready to knock it out.
I was anxious, primed to begin.
The paper lands before me
and I flip it without delay.
I'm sent across the room;
no explanation or reason.
My cheeks are now ruby.
Embarrassment overtakes me.
I earn a zero for the day
and the teacher says no more.
That day the rage swarmed,
for I still don't know why
I sat in the back
all alone.

Bryan Starnes, Grade 8
Baylor School, TN

Halloween

Halloween is a fun and scary time.
It is a time for trick-or-treating.
I like to go to my grandfather's and go in his haunted house.
I like to invite friends to come trick-or-treating with me.
I also like to see people in their costumes.
I get scared when I get chased by Jason and Michael Myers.
The candy is the best part.
Every year, my bag gets full.

Oliver Henry, Grade 7
Elkton School, TN

The World's Greatest Sport

Basketball, the world's greatest sport,
Requires a ball, a hoop, and a court
The first things you need to learn
Are to dribble and shoot, pivot and turn.

Also, you need to rebound and pass;
These skills would make you play top class
So, basketball is extremely tough,
But someday you have to show your stuff!

Once you make your middle school team,
It's the first step to anyone's dream
Then, you need to focus for high school
If you're on the team it's just plain cool.

If you then make it to college and the NBA,
Almost anyone you can think of, you can outplay
I hope this lesson really inspired you,
When you become good, no one can argue!

Siddharth Murali, Grade 7
White Station Middle School, TN

Stormy Night

On a stormy night, wind whips through the trees.
I look to see the lightning;
Rain pounds hard against the roof.
I jump with much excitement.

As the night goes on, I can't fall asleep.
The storm keeps me up.
I love the noises; it looks gorgeous.
They excite me, they excite me.

My dog runs and hides.
He hates the loud noises when it lights up the sky.
When the storm is over,
My dog comes out from hiding.

I come back from my window,
Then say my goodnights.
I go to my room, turn out the lights.
Finally I can fall asleep.

Danielle Duffy, Grade 8
Musselman Middle School, WV

A True Friend

A friend is a friend
No matter what they wear
They will always be there
Through the good and the bad
Even when you are mad
You can tell them anything
And you will know that your secret is safe
Even if you are angry at each other
They will still hope that you are happy
They will always have your back
No matter what happens
You will have fights
But fights will just make you closer
No matter what they will always be your friend

Amanda Bolton, Grade 8
Rhea Central Elementary School, TN

Friendship

Friendship is a wonderful thing.
Joy is what it brings.
Having fights and delights,
Is all just a part of life.
Crying and hardship is just one part of friendship.
Friendship is about trust and love,
Never being forsaken, pushed, or shoved.
People who love you all around,
Who pick you up when you have fallen down.

Markeyta Bledsoe, Grade 7
Elkton School, TN

Bobby

He said he loved her as he walked out the front door,
little did she know she would see him no more.
Peacefully driving along with a friend,
very soon the boys life would come to an end.

Just ten minutes longer, a scream and a crash,
he never knew he had even passed.
A stoplight was ran, but it was just too late,
the driver never realized his life she would take.

Lots of phone calls were made on that cold winter night,
millions of hearts were broke as they heard of the sight.
Later on when his wife saw him at the funeral home,
was the first time she felt she was really alone.

He really is gone and he's not coming back,
she knows to be strong, but it's strength that she lacks.
She could just see him now walking through the front door,
but she knows he's not coming, her eyes swollen and sore.

Just a young boy going out for a drive,
just a young man never said his good-byes…

Ginger Wilson, Grade 9
Perkins-Tryon High School, OK

Dracula

Dracula
Creepy, huge, ugly
Related to the vampire bat
Lover of blood, coffins, and darkness
Who feels evil, hungry, and possessed
Who gives screams, wet pants, and terror
Who fears garlic, light, and broken fangs
Who would like to see puddles of blood,
lots of coffins, and creepy caves
Resident of dark basements
Vampire

Rachel Pankau, Grade 8
Avenue City Elementary School, MO

Fall

The leaves are falling,
Every now and then.
Fall is arriving,
But no one knows when.
It's getting chilly,
Like a piece of ice.
Pumpkins are growing,
Like a newborn baby.

It's the middle of fall,
You know what that means.
Thanksgiving is near,
And all the family will be here.
There will be a hot and fresh turkey,
Juicy and tasty.
There will be dressing and cornbread,
No one will leave hungry.
When everyone is gone,
And the house is quiet,
We'll build us a fire,
Until we get tired.

Stephanie Campbell, Grade 7
Nettleton Jr High School, AR

My Name Is Angel

A ngel
N ice
G reat
E xcellent
L oud

A thletic
N eat
D angerous
E ngergetic
R owdy
S assy
O utgoing
N aughty

Angel Anderson, Grade 7
Ketchum Jr High School, OK

What to Do?

What to do on a rainy day?
I could take a much needed nap,
And allow the faint sound
Of rain hitting the roof
Lull me to sleep.

Or tidy up the house; that is always an option.
(But why would I *clean* when I could be doing something else?)

Sit out on the porch and watch the storm develop,
Or for the daring type, sit *in* the rain, becoming one with the storm.

I guess maybe I could watch TV,
Although nothing good is ever on during the day.

But today,
Today I believe I will just relax,
And curl up with a good book
On this peaceful rainy day.

Amy Scott, Grade 8
West Jr High School, MO

34.48 Seconds

The whistle blows.
I adjust my goggles, my cap, my suit
And step onto the big, white block.
I look straight ahead and stare at the opposite end of the pool
Fifty meters away.
35.32 seconds is all it takes to reach that wall.
But I have to get past the water.
The water is my enemy. It slows me down.
"Take your mark," a mechanic voice booms.
I bend over, as still and tense as a hunting lioness ready to pounce and kill.
BEEP.
And I spring off the block and dive into the water in a perfect arc.
Now I'm kicking up a wall of white foam behind me.
I'm sprinting, sprinting, sprinting.
My arms, legs, lungs are burning, burning, burning.
My hand slams into the wall.
The electric timer reacts to my touch and my time flashes on the board.
Now, 34.48 seconds is all it takes.

Suqi Huang, Grade 8
West Jr High School, MO

Love

Love is like when a boy says something to you that means the world to them like
"I love you" that touches you so deeply we feel it inside
We cry when we aren't loved by them
We laugh with them when they say funny stuff
Love is when you get a new pair of jeans you really like them
When they're brand new then they get old
Then you have those jeans you always will like
They are just so cute
Love is not just a word it definitely means a lot to anyone who hears it

Mercedes Gray, Grade 7
Ketchum Jr High School, OK

For This I Am Thankful

I am thankful for
the things on earth
that I can hear and touch
like my sister, brother, my dog
and such;
I sometimes forget to share,
that I love them
and I really do care.

I am thankful for things I cannot see,
for the love and care my parents give to me.

Stephanie Gould, Grade 7
Maury Middle School, TN

Summer

The summer is one of my favorite seasons
I have lots of reasons
I like to be with my best friend
I never want that to end
The summer is really fun
playing games under the sun.
Well that's not all
you could even go to the mall
Sports are in summer, too
I play quite a few
I like to go outside every day
mostly just to play
The other seasons are fun, too
But I prefer summer, how about you?
The summer is one of my favorite seasons
and these are my reasons

Hannah Butler, Grade 8
Lewisburg Middle School, TN

The Birds

There they sit, content together
watching and waiting, they rustle their feathers.
The time is near; that they know,
get ready, get set, Go!
South they fly
Through the pink sky.
They feel the breeze,
they look over the trees.
They pass rolling fields of green and brown.
Look at the city! Look at the town!
The sunrise welcomes the day.
Orange and yellow, every which way.
The turning leaves,
the freshwater seas.
The crisp air,
sailing through the sky without a care.
Watch them go.
They follow the flow.

Casey Gibson, Grade 7
Nettleton Jr High School, AR

Callie

Tail wagging, butt wiggling ball of mischief
Ready to bite toes or ambush the cat,
Stealing cheese puffs from your lips.
Callie rules the house.

Her Sheltie heart is torn between mom and me,
But she obeys no one.
A future agility queen racing from tree to steps,
If she would follow commands.
Barking and growling through the windows,
Callie guards her turf.

A mind of her own, curiosity to get her in trouble
Always fun, never dull
Callie runs the show

Kit Webster, Grade 8
West Jr High School, MO

Boo!

Boo! Said the ghost to the witch
Who frightened, gave a furious twitch
All of the monsters were going out that night
To give little trick-or-treaters an awful fright
They moaned and they growled
They rattled and howled
Until the streets were bare
And all the candy soon would be theirs
They did not want to be mean
But everything goes on this night of Halloween

Kimberly Rhea, Grade 9
Bearden High School, TN

Gone

My world is spinning, confusing.
I'm relenting the time that I spent on you.
Everything is upside down, falling apart.
No time for your lies anymore.
You left me broken, beaten.
I needed something to hold onto, but you ran away.
Lonely is a sad feeling.
Time has kept me within it.
Even when you tried to help me, it was all a lie.
Words cannot describe the hurt, the awesome pain.
that my heart has been going through,
all because you left me.
Staring at a blank stare,
wondering why.
Why I thought you and me.
Sometimes I feel all alone,
in a crowded hall,
trying to reach the end.
Hoping you are there,
waiting for me,
but you are gone.

Kyranna Gilstrap, Grade 8
Owasso 8th Grade Center, OK

Day at the Beach

A day at the beach
is so much fun
playing in the ocean
or just laying in the sun.

Walking on the beach
with sand beneath my feet
I can see the waves pass by
while seagulls soar high in the sky.

A day at the beach
is truly a time to relax
the sound of the ocean
with the sun on my back.

The wind in my hair
and friends by my side
make this day at the beach
such a wonderful time.

Kenzi Vincent, Grade 7
Elkton School, TN

Summer Ends School

bell ringing
teachers fleeing
children screaming
adults yelling
papers flying
summer is here

Seth Blevins, Grade 7
Rocky Comfort Elementary School, MO

Sun

The sun is like a big smiley face.
When it smiles it makes my day happier.
The sun is like a
flashlight
showing
me everything around.
The sun is what gets
me up in the morning.
It's my alarm clock.
The sun is like
God's way of saying he
Loves us.
The warmth of the sun
Shows His love for us.
The sun is what makes
the plants grow.
Without the sun nothing would be living.
The sun is like
Jesus Christ because
Without Jesus we
Would be nothing.

Amanda Muehlbeausler, Grade 9
St John the Baptist High School, MO

My Mahogany Playground

I grasp a piece of history in my hands.
Blowing dust off of covers,
I skim through pages and stories jump.
Witches and wizards duel as spells are thrown
from their worn and wounded wands.
Marching down the Dewey Decimal System
to the beat of the drummer boy, I hear bullets crack.
Gunpowder stings the air as reds and blues collide.
New chapters bring a chained yellow-coated hound, with crazed scarlet eyes.
A brown barrel is raised, but I must look down.
I am unable to gaze upon the despair.
A sudden drop in temperature causes me to lift my head.
A single boat comes into view in an icy underworld.
Why are there no lifeboats for the ones below?
My surroundings blur as a single tear drips down my cheek.
A sudden hush brings its familiar rage.
My stories fade as I find myself on a cold laminate floor.
I am staring into the glasses of my nemesis.
A single finger is poised on her crimson lips telling me: "Hush."
I nod as I place volumes into eerie slots.
Taking dreams of future journeys, I exit my mahogany playground.

Payton Fields, Grade 8
Baylor School, TN

Permit Me to Tell You About Love

Permit me to tell you about love.
The warm, safe feeling inside you when you are around your loved ones,
The burning desire to be with the special someone every waking moment,
The inner drive to be able to do anything for that person,
Feeling the pain in the words "good-bye," but the wonderful sensation
you feel in that first "hello."
But the love I remember the most
Left me feeling confused and scared,
Like if I let go of this feeling I would be swallowed up by pain and misery,
Yet at the same time I still felt wonderful and lighthearted,
Knowing that if I have the strength to keep holding on, my life would be,
at last, one, complete whole.

Clarisse Gunsiorowski, Grade 8
All Saints School, MO

Darkness

Darkness is everywhere
sleeping in the day
waking in the night
darkness brings fear into our lives
children shiver as the darkness creeps its way toward them
the darkness can be found everywhere
darkness is the evil in our lives
The only thing that can destroy darkness is a faint light
This light is known as hope
The darkness is like your soul frozen cold
but hope is the small fire that melts the ice and warms your soul

Justin Robbins, Grade 8
Belle Isle Enterprise Middle School, OK

I Wish

I wish that I could be with you.
I wish that all my wishes came true.
I wish life truly wasn't this way.
I wish...
O, do I wish every single day.
Hoping and praying the same old way.
That I could be with you and not feel so afraid.
I wish I could kiss your tender lips.
While you wrap your arms around my hips.
I wish you knew how much I missed you.
I wish you knew that I was sad and so blue.
But maybe, just maybe!
Someday...
some old fashion way
My wish will come true...
'Cause God knows I want to be with you.
Never letting go
Always saying yes never no
Something is here and it is true.
O God, I WISH you knew!

Evelyn Newman, Grade 9
Gallatin High School, TN

I Am...

I am a questioning and Christian Girl.
I wonder if I will ever go to France.
I hear four-wheeler motors.
I see me beating my brother at a four-wheeler race.
I want to be a Christian girl for the rest of my life.
I am a questioning and Christian Girl.

I pretend to drive awesome cars.
I feel a lot of pressure.
I touch the most beautiful clouds.
I worry I will fall off of a four-wheeler.
I cry when someone I love dies.
I am a questioning and Christian Girl.

I understand who God is.
I say God is real and right.
I dream I will be a pediatrician.
I try to be nice to everyone and be the best I can be.
I hope to go to a good college.
I am a questioning and Christian Girl.

Madison Workman, Grade 7
King City High School, MO

Basketball

Basketball is so much fun.
There's passing dribbling then you run.
Basketball is really intense
Be sure to play good or you'll definitely be benched
Basketball is my favorite sport
That's why I enjoy speeding down the court.

Laura Beth Todd, Grade 7
Highland Rim School, TN

Love Is...

Love is Love
Love is sweet
Love is special and unique,
For everyone that is in love
Like you and I,
Love is powerful, strong and deep,
When you love someone as much as I love you,
Love is perfect and extremely exciting
For everyone like you and I,
Love is creative, special, big,
This love we share is like heaven,
You love me and I love you,
This love we share is for each and every Heartbeat,
We shall keep our love inside as I'll keep your
Love inside,
Love is Love,
Love is sweet,
This love is special to each,
For us to have each other is like a gift from god,
You didn't give me the gift of gold you gave
Your heart and love instead and that's all I need

Jessica Wright, Grade 8
Hebron Middle School, KY

The Life of a Cop

Waking up at five in the morning
Trying not to be late for work after eating breakfast
Heading off to the coffee shop just before work
Trying to get a discount at Krispy Kreme
Yelling at the burger boy for spitting in your hamburger
Getting to an accident as fast as you can
Hand out some tickets for speeding
Having to deal with the same people over and over
Spend part of your weekend at the shooting range
Back to the burger joint for lunch
Bust a couple of people for disturbing the peace
Head back to the highway to pull over a few more people
Go back to your home for your dinner

Charles Edwards, Grade 8
Greenfield Jr/Sr High School, MO

Brandon

Brandon
Funny, active, athletic, and loyal
Sibling of Andrew, Anthony, Josh, and Justin
Lover of games
Who feels happy
Who needs an X-Box 360
Who gives Mrs. Smith a hard time
Who fears having bad grades
Who would like to see cousins
Resident of the baseball field
Little

Brandon Little, Grade 7
Leeton Middle and High School, MO

Spring Is Finally Here

The wind blows high
There are fields full of colorful flowers
The birds are nesting
Calves are dotting the hillside
Baby birds are learning how to fly
Squirrels gathering food
The smell of fresh plowed dirt and
Cut hay is in the air
The light showers are refreshing
Spring is finally here

Katie Sanders, Grade 7
Elkton School, TN

Lovely

I hate to feel sorrow
I hate to feel the pain
To what comes tomorrow
To what makes me insane

My body trembles with fear
My heart skips a beat
I can't help but to care
I can't help but to think

You make me feel crazy
You make me feel like a dove
I have been thinking lately
I am falling in love

Christiana Factory, Grade 8
Belle Isle Enterprise Middle School, OK

Runaway

Running on the snowy ground,
leaving footprints behind.
Nothing they can say or do
will ever change my mind.

Home is far behind me
as I'm shedding a single tear.
I cannot turn back now
for it's the place I fear.

I'm homeless, cold, and heartless
but now I'll never know,
what it feels like to be loved
as I trample through the snow.

Emily Williams, Grade 8
West Middle School, TN

Lake

L ong and deep
A t my grandma's house
K eeps me occupied
E veryone fishes there

John H. Shull, Grade 7
Hartville Jr/Sr High School, MO

Finally

Frosty cars everywhere,
Caroler' voices in the air,
Got some gloves, I need a pair,
Go outside in shorts, I double dare.
Shopping, the worst thing to do,
If I go outside I'll get the flu,
Try and give my parents a little clue,
That I want a car all fresh and new.
Schools are out and everyone leaves, it's cold outside so put on some sleeves,
Playing football, he cocks back and heaves, oh no here comes Mrs. Cleeves.
Kids running down the street, the little ones can't stay on their feet,
The whole family gets to meet relatives, they want to talk so take a seat.
When the snow comes down and piles high,
The kids go sled and claim they can fly,
The teens build ramps they go off and nearly die,
This rhyming is getting hard, you want to try?
Kids claim they see Rudolph but it's only a deer,
All love and happiness no madness or fear,
Yes, it's Christmas, the best time of the year,
So put a smile on, and spread the holiday cheer.

C.J. Ross, Grade 9
West Jr High School, MO

Divorces Are the Worst

Divorces are the worst.
They say it's harder on the parents but you can't prove it by me.
I now they love me but sometimes they can have a hard time showing it.
Sometimes I feel I could just start running and never come back.
Inside I know it's not the right choice.
Divorces are the worst.
Everything changes the way people look and talk to you.
My parents have been divorced for a long time now.
So just know that you're never alone.
And that God has his reasons for everything.

Elizabeth Rhodes, Grade 8
St Mary of the Woods School, KY

Summer

It was stifling hot
The teacher droned on in a boring voice
I could smell the sweat from the class
And the classroom melted around me.
My fingers numbed
The world was white and green
Then zippppp
A skier zoomed by
So I snatched a pair of skis
Zoom, I rocketed down the hill
Unable to stop, I could taste
The snow in my mouth
Briingggggg! The bell woke me from my slumber
The teacher mumbled the last sentence
I moved and dropped into the next class' hard hot sweaty smelling chair
Ready to continue

Josh Garton, Grade 9
West Jr High School, MO

It's Not Fair

It's not fair
How you — with that girl over there
How she gets to make jokes and play with your hair
And how everyone thinks you make a great pair —
It's not fair
How I wish to be in her shoes
How you don't feel the way I do
And how love has restricted me from being with you
It's not fair
How she broke up with you
In the cruelest way one knows how to
And people making fun of you, well just the ones who knew
It's not fair
How you're giving me those looks
How you tell me to meet you in these little nooks
And how you see it like a fairytale in most books
It's not fair
How you like me now
And when you see me you think WOW!
But I think nothing of you
You should have got me while you had the chance…fool

Lauren Milks, Grade 8
Rector A Jones Middle School, KY

Stupid Me

A heart long listened
A heart never seen
A heart that got broken
and buried in me
A teardrop forgotten
A teardrop lost
A teardrop that fell
too much was the cost
Beating pulse that goes so high
Beating pulse that never dies
Beating pulse I'm here, I'm gone
this alone I can't deny
Stupid me no more I swear
Stupid me you're unprepared
Stupid me, not the same me I was back then
Stupid me your heart hurts now,
Never will stupid me fall in love again.

KayDawn Peterson, Grade 9
Grandview Alternative School, MO

When You're Gone

All I have left is the memories,
They never seem to fade away,
Every day they seem to get worse in all different types of ways.
The tears, the nightmares, the freaking out,
All you want to do is SHOUT!
But in the end it's OK,
You weren't worth my time any ways.

Jonell Hester, Grade 9
Jeffersontown High School, KY

Another Day to Ride the TARC

It was pouring down rain this dreary day
Why couldn't I pick another day to ride the TARC
Running, jumping over different sizes and shapes
Sitting, standing, waiting for it to come
Yes it is finally here
It was nice and warm
But just in a flash I was back out in the rain
Running and running for miles it seemed
Finally home
Go up the stairs and jump in my bed all warm and cozy
In my bed
Waiting, dreaming to ride the TARC again.

Nathan Delahanty, Grade 7
Meredith-Dunn School, KY

Kailee Schmidt

Kailee
Sweet, humble, loving, and lost
Sibling of Madeline and Ben Schmidt
Lover of friends, family, and music
Who feels misconstrued, grateful, and indescribable
Who gives happiness, care, and confidence
Who needs order and importance in her life
Who fears loss, being ridiculed, and small spaces
Who would like to see her dad in Iraq, Chris, and Paige
Who lives in Clarksville, TN
Schmidt

Kailee Schmidt, Grade 8
Montgomery Central Middle School, TN

To My Dad

If it weren't for you,
I'd never have anyone to comfort me in time of need.
If it weren't for you,
I'd never have anyone to play basketball with.
If it weren't for you,
I'd have no one to look up to.
If it weren't for you,
I'd never have had shelter.
If it weren't for you,
I'd have no one to help me learn how to play a new sport.
If it weren't for you,
I'd have no one to help me with my homework.

Zach Coffee, Grade 8
All Saints School, MO

The Window in My Life

The window in my life is slightly cracked
Life is rough but its not so bad
Between school, sports and girls life can get pretty tough
But as I said life's not so bad
When things get really, really bad
It seems a slight breeze blows through and
Just like that, I start over and over again

Cody Blanc, Grade 8
Gresham Middle School, TN

Life

As I'm brought to light
I gain my sight
To start a new life
I must fight
I'm older now
And I must begin
To do my chores
Again and again
As I wonder to myself
And start thinking of life
I begin to wonder
How people actually strife
As I lay in bed
I die in my head
And I begin to think
Am I really dead?

Cody Anderson, Grade 9
Grandview Alternative School, MO

Leaves Like Quicksand

Brown leaves as pretty as quicksand
I fall in the leaves,
help me up I need a hand
I'm still stuck
leaves feel like quicksand
Pull, please, pull
Finally,
I stand

D'Andrael Ware, Grade 8
Wilson Middle School, OK

Living Death

The darkness is coming,
my thoughts drifting away.
No more pain, suffering, sadness.
This is my final day.

The darkness is here,
though light still shines through.
There lies the gates,
where I'll be renewed.

I've come to the light.
Taken my final breath.
The doctors have quit
for this is my death.

Cory Smith, Grade 7
St Mary of the Woods School, KY

Navy

N autical
A tomic Powered
V essels Manned By
Y oung Men

Blake Acree, Grade 8
White Station Middle School, TN

Winter

Sitting by the fire, so warm and bright
Crackling and popping like a falling tree
Comforting like a thick blanket
Only to burn out and toss me into the bitter cold to look for more wood

The air is crisp and cool
Like a Sunday shirt freshly starched
The blue sky so clean
And unblemished by any clouds

So still are the trees
Not pestered by the freezing wind
Quiet fills my ears
And nothing moves to destroy it

White fire blinds my eyes
As the now reflects the low sun's light
And icy air enters my lungs
When I breathe in the frosty air

When I exhale all I have in my chest
My breath obscures my vision
I trudge back, toward the warmness of the cabin, arms loaded
And I leave the wint'ry wonderland behind me

Nicholas Poplos, Grade 7
White Station Middle School, TN

Ordinary Day

It's six o'clock in the a.m. and I hear the screaming of my alarm.
I wake up so early it is as if I work on a farm.
I shower and dress in such a hurry,
I put my shirt on backwards, but I must not worry.

I have to get to school on time
If I leave now, I will be just fine.
I grab my unfinished homework that is on my desk,
I hope to God that we do not have a test.

I arrive at school just as the bell is ringing,
A second later and my teacher would be screaming.
My day is filled with confusing lesson after lesson.
This is how my life is wasted when school is in session.

How I long for summer with its many pleasures,
But it is only November, so for now I must only dream of these treasures.
Of sleeping in late and no homework to do,
My life would be complete if only this were true.

My teacher calls on me with my unraised hand,
She has pulled me away from my dream land.
So now I must pay attention and not act like a fool,
So I do not have to go to summer school!

Nick Ross, Grade 8
St Gerard Majella School, MO

Card Captors

Card captors are smart
Capturing cards
And sealing them tight
The cards they capture
Are cards of The Clow
Now I bet you're wondering
Wondering how
First Sakura calls
On her sealing wand
Next she uses another card to
Get the one to
Be captured
Last she calls the card's name
And it is returned
To its original form
Sakura was a card captor
But now she is,
The MASTER of the Clow
As such she must
Transform all the Clow cards into star cards
Using her Star Wand

Isaiah Williams, Grade 7
Independence Charter Middle School, OK

The Dinner on a Cruise

As you walk into the dining room
You can smell the aroma of food
When the waiter brings you the menu
You get to see all the wonderful entrees.
When you get your meal and take a bite
You taste the great delight
After you eat your food
The waiters beckon you to sing and dance.

Cassidy Cross, Grade 8
Highland Rim School, TN

The Real Life

I've been so many places
And seen so many things.
Had people try to come and take away my dreams.
But I didn't let that happen,
I didn't let them see.
And now that I'm gone,
They're wondering, "Where could she be?"
And to tell you the truth I'm still here,
I'm just not showing any more fear.

Brenna Williams, Grade 7
Robidoux Middle School, MO

Dirt Bikes

Dirt bikes are a lot of fun to ride.
Especially in the rain and snow.
You can ride dirt bikes on all kinds of terrain.
A lot of people love to ride dirt bikes.

Will Honea, Grade 7
Highland Rim School, TN

Jesus Our Savior

Christmas comes only once a year
Usually it's about love and cheer
When really it's about Jesus Christ our Savior
Born on Christmas day in a manger
He came to save us from our sins
Nailed to a cross with giant pins
By the Romans, because of their hate towards him
Intimidated by God, cowards all of them
Nowadays Christmas is all about gifts
Yet if we serve God instead he'll lift
Us above the rest for eternity in heaven
Many will face God, but few will be chosen
I want to be one of those few
How about you?
Believe that Jesus is our Lord
Admit your sins, it is foretold
And you will be saved from your sins

Jane Kramer, Grade 8
Chelsea Jr High School, OK

Winter

Every night before I fall asleep I think of snow.
I hope it snows and covers the ground.
When I wake up I go straight to a window.
I look out and see a white blanket all over.
I put on my coat and run outside.
My brother follows soon after.
We grab my snowboard and his sled,
then run to the nearest hill.
We run up and slide down until we can't feel our fingers.
Just before we go in we have a snowball fight.
When we're inside we take our coats off,
then we make mom make hot chocolate.
We spend the day going in and out to play.
The bad thing is school the next day.

Brendan Ross, Grade 7
Maury Middle School, TN

Poetic Leaves

The wind blows fallen colors of
the rainbow drift down the
air rocking them side to side
as they kiss the ground.
Brown leaves luminous as the sun shining in the
eyes of a brown eyed beauty
whisper as they skip along the sidewalk
telling the secrets of Mother Nature's beauty.
Rakes come out shooing the pesky leaves away,
then the children come crushing them as
if disturbing the natural balance of the world.
Sounds of crunched colors rustle above the crust of earth
brilliant colors mixed in a ruined Picasso,
BEAUTY IS IN THE EYE OF THE BEHOLDER.

Faith Abili, Grade 8
Wilson Middle School, OK

Creation

Thank you God for the trees that loom like towers overhead,
For the stars that twinkle like eyes in the night.

Thank you God for birds that sing melodies in the air,
For the crickets that chirp and the owls that hoot throatily throughout the night.

Thank you God for the flowers that perfume the clean, crisp breezes,
For the salty ocean breezes that invigorate my soul.

Thank you God for the refreshingly wet morning dew that sparkles like lights from above,
For the cool breezes that whip around me cooling the hot, dry heat of summer.

Thank you God for the sweet, sweet fruits of tree and of vine that sustain me,
For the honeysuckle that sweetens my mouth on a temperate spring day.

Thank you Lord for all the wonders of your creation
That I have witnessed and I have yet to witness.

Jacob Amsden, Grade 7
Our Lady Catholic School, MO

Cody Jarman

Cody
Who is insane, creative, and intellectual
Brother of Shayna
Who loves to play guitar, listen to music, and read
Who needs music, water, and the sun
Who gives pride to his family, Josh paper, and respect to family
Who feels sorry for the poor, happy for the dead, and content with life
Who fears cat guard slave masters, Baptists, and Republicans
Who would like to see Rob Halford in a church, Led Zeppelin, and an overweight giraffe
Who is a resident of Tennessee
Jarman

Cody Jarman, Grade 8
Montgomery Central Middle School, TN

Expectations

Expectations can be set too high.
By parents and teacher or themselves.
The question must be asked.
Do students do it for themselves or for their parents?
Either way students get stressed.

Their emotions take control.
They cannot handle it.
School turns out to be about everything but their education.
Their education takes the back burner.
Kids should concentrate on academics not fights with friends or their parents' expectations.

Students only get one opportunity to learn.
They should seize it.
School is about students.
Their growth.
Their struggles.
Their education.

Emily Smith, Grade 8
West Jr High School, MO

The Abandoned

He's gone, she's alone,
Not knowing what to do,
Now comes a time,
That she needs help from you.
But now you're gone,
And she's all alone,
All by herself,
She can't go home.
She'd talk without thinking,
Just 'cause she could,
She knew that you'd listen,
Like no one else would.
Now she has to sustain,
Without you there,
To live in a world of darkness,
Without someone who cares.

Alexia Burnette, Grade 8
East Hardy Early/Middle Childhood School, WV

Memories of a Good Friend

I sit here alone on this starry night.
Memories of good times fill my sad mind.
Wishing that you could be here by my side.
How do I move on and leave past behind?

I want to go back and do it again.
Relive each moment, love them once more.
I can't think of you without feeling pain,
But somehow these feelings can't be ignored.

There is some hope on this starry eve.
The stars shimmer down and brighten my heart.
There is a reason why you had to leave.
I now know the cause that we had to part.

You are not here on this starry night,
Yet you cause me to live a better life.

Carin Lagerberg, Grade 9
Bearden High School, TN

Fall

The fall weather is finally here
With these signs so near
Rustle of red, orange, and brown leaves fall
While the flock of crows caw
Through the dense woods, the wind blows
As the children walk to the house in rows
In the house, the fire warm
While the leaves outside storm
The children soon warm, and fast asleep
With blankets piled on in a heap
They dream of lots of fun
Playing in the leaves with everyone!

Jessica Briggs, Grade 7
Skiatook Newman Middle School, OK

Christmastime

Santa Claus is quiet and swift
his purpose, to give a gift
all the toys
for the good girls and boys
The reindeer help him though the night,
to keep him out of sight.
The kids don't see him but they know he is there,
because of their image of the red suit and the white hair.
Finally his job is done but he will be back
with that big red sack.

Michael Baker, Grade 8
Wickliffe Elementary School, OK

The Yellow Mountain

As we walked along the red brick road,
We were shocked to find a big white slope.
We were forced to glide right down it,
Losing some of ourselves — unable to cope.

As we trotted out of some white snow chunks,
We were stunned to see a big green hill.
We were forced to run right up it,
But we had to roll right off of it.
What a false thrill.

As we staggered along the violet path,
We were astonished to find a big yellow mountain.
Pushing our way up this boulder of wrath,
We were gone before we reached the water fountain.
Although we pushed and pulled and worked together,
We didn't have the reasoning to walk around all of this.

Katy Helton, Grade 8
All Saints' Episcopal School, TN

Growing Up

Nine years old without a care in the world
Fifteen years old and so much on my mind
Nine, with many friends
Fifteen, missing those who moved away

Before, in the tree house, like a fortress
Now the tree house remains as I move on
So many days spent in the backyard creek
Now the water is dark and murky with memories

I used to wish for a dog
Now I have one
I used to have no worries or responsibilities
Now I must work much harder

When I was nine, my parents helped me constantly,
Now I am much more independent
When I was nine, I was young
Now I am fifteen, and growing up

Charlie Carson, Grade 9
West Jr High School, MO

The Pitch

at the soccer field
despite the heat
beyond the factory
during all the year
through the trees
beyond the sunset
inside the lines
between the goals
after the week
in peace

Noah Erwin, Grade 8
Heritage Middle School, TN

I Am Me

I'm crazy, I'm silly.
I'm daring, I'm willing.
I'm cute, I'm girly.
I like to have fun and
Get messy, I'm truthful.
I don't care what you
Think of me.
I do it for myself.
I'm not perfect.
I wish for what I'm
Not sometimes, but am
Thankful for what I am,
Because it's those things
That make me who I am,
Because I am me!

Cheyenne Beaver, Grade 9
Glenpool High School, OK

My Cat

Jumping like a frog.
Pouncing as if he were a jungle cat.
Running to the door
To see who's come to visit.
Sleeping all night long.
Napping through the day.
Snoring always.
In his bed.
Purring when he's happy.
Glaring when he's not.
Living like a king because…
He's my cat.

Katie Wimsatt, Grade 7
St Paul the Apostle School, TN

Blue

Waves splashing in the sea,
Reminds me of the bright sky,
Making me feel as happy as I can be,
My life must be flying by.

Craig Bock, Grade 8
St Joseph School, MO

Family Vacation

Have you ever been on vacation
With the family
Going places never been before
Or going to see some relatives
Family vacation
Having fun wherever you are
Whether San Francisco in the west
Or Boston in the east
You'll always have fun
On a family vacation
Because the best of all is
Just spending time with family

Kristian Thompson, Grade 8
Highland Rim School, TN

The Day the World Grew Darker

The day the world grew darker,
Was the day you up and died.
I sat on my bed,
For many hours and cried.
The day the world grew darker,
I went completely insane.
I tried to bring you back,
But soon gave up in pain.
The day the world grew darker,
I could not find a way
To return joy to my life.
While on my bed I lay.
But sleep soon came,
I dreamed the sun out,
From behind a dark cloud,
I no longer felt drought,
And hope it allowed.
Now you come in my dreams.
The flowers bloom on the land,
The animals come out,
You and I watch hand in hand.

Anna Blackbourn, Grade 9
Agra High School, OK

My Favorite Place — The Beach

Toward the ocean
Near the sand
Under the sun
Over the mountains
Out of state
In the water
Through the crowd
Beside the horizon
On the float
Along the sea
The joy of the beach

Halie Sellers, Grade 8
Heritage Middle School, TN

All About Cats!

Cats are cute,
And so cuddly
Cats can claw
you in the jaw
Cats are clumsy
Just like me
But in the heart
They are very smart

Leaping,
Pouncing,
Sleeping,
Hunting,
And havin' fun

Kashaye Powell, Grade 7
Ketchum Jr High School, OK

My Life's Past

I'll never understand that day
Not knowing why he's gone.
It's like a tidal wave crushing my soul
My wounded heart being left to die
The pain and suffering will be eternal.

Having confidence we will meet again
In the gateways of Heaven
Still though in the end
When everything is said and done.
Nothing will repair all the burdens
That you have brought upon me.

Jazmine Skender, Grade 9
Hamburg Jr High School, AR

Dance Camp

Dance Camp,
Third of June,
Meeting our coaches,
Mandy was my favorite,
Sleep,
Miserable camp,
Horrible healthy breakfast,
Miss eating cold pizza and cocoa puffs,
Mandy turned her back on me,
Tired of awake,
Major problem,
Hurt ankle,
Coming home,
Giving up my dream,
Summer was over,
Back to school,
New friends,
Including Mandy.

Courtney Churchwell, Grade 7
Dyer Elementary & Jr High School, TN

American History

American History old and new,
Interesting facts for me and you
From countries near and far.
We learn how things really are
Farmers, minors and fisherman too,
All had important jobs to do
Women cleaned, cooked and sewed
Men chopped wood and panned for gold.
They teach their children all then can.
In hope of raising great young women and men.

Amber Lock, Grade 8
Clarksburg School, TN

Snow Skiing

Snow skiing is hard to do
It is not as easy as tying your shoe
You have to go side to side
When you fall down you start to slide
The best ski resorts are in the west
The Rocky Mountains make the west the best
The trail levels are green, black, and blue
Ski lifts can lift three or four but most lift two
The best ski resort is Steamboat
When you ski you have to wear a heavy coat
You try to do what people do on TV but it is hard to copy
Snow skiing is my favorite hobby

Jackson Wetherington, Grade 8
Highland Rim School, TN

Albert

I've been suffering for awhile,
I've lived a great life,
I know I shouldn't complain to my dear, loving wife.

She tries her hardest to get me what I want and need,
While most of the time I sit in my chair and read.
It's not because I want to, but it's because I have to.

It takes a lot of energy to get up and walk around,
When we have family gatherings I just want to sit down.
It's not easy living life this way,
Having nieces and nephew's who want to play.

It breaks my heart to tell them no,
But it kills me to get from place to place,
To and fro.

I don't want to see those golden gates open,
But God needs an angel,
So some hearts will be broken.

So as I lay here in this hospital bed,
The thought of those golden gates opening,
I dread and dread.

Paige Sutton, Grade 7
Hebron Middle School, KY

Halloween

Halloween is full of children of all ages.
There are ghosts, goblins, pumpkins,
witches, vampires, super heroes, princesses, and much more.
There are lights on every street.
There are children walking on all the roads,
except the dark, spooky ones.
There are haunted houses everywhere.
Halloween lasts all night, but
the candy lasts for about a week.
Last but not least, Halloween is full
of fun and mischief.

Tyler Bergmann, Grade 7
Elkton School, TN

My Saxophone

My saxophone is so cool.
I'm the best saxophone player in school.
I like the way I press the keys and play jazz.
It gives me a very good feeling of pizzazz.

I play my saxophone better than Bill Clinton.
As a matter of fact, maybe better than Eddie Vinson.
When I see everyone dancing to my song,
It gives me a feeling to keep rockin' on.

It takes some people a long time to understand
That I am the man!
So everyone go and spread the word
That Kayson is the best saxophone player you ever heard!

Kayson Latimar, Grade 7
Dunbar Middle School, AR

Friday

Friday is almost over as I sit here in my seat
The clock is ticking, tick, tock, tick, tock
Five more minutes until the whistle blows
I've had a good Friday as I sit here thinking,
Thinking about what I'll do over the weekend
First, I will go home and get my clothes ready
Then I'll go to my grandparents' house
My grandpa will take me to the skating rink
I will skate with my best friend almost all night
My sister will be there, skating with her friends
At ten o'clock pm, my grandpa will pick up my sister and me
WHAM! The teacher slammed a ruler on my desk
She looked at me
I looked down at my paper
I looked at the clock, it read two thirty-eight
TWO MORE MINUTES! I CAN'T WAIT!
After the last three notes on Section One,
The whistle blew
I went home and did everything I wanted to do
I love Fridays.

Kylie Elliott, Grade 7
Highland Rim School, TN

Ten Years

Ten years.
I can remember
The tears
And the fears.

You were never home,
We were always alone.
Our house never
Felt like a home.

You and your awful new wife,
Made us fear for our life.
The parties
And drunk driving.

You thought it was right,
You not in our life.
We took his last name,
And now it's not the same.

Ten years.
I have had a lot of tears.
But dad,
Did you ever miss me over the years?

Krista Campbell, Grade 8
Musselman Middle School, WV

Fall Has Come

The leaves are turning brown,
making their soft touchdown.
The children laugh and play,
going outside every day.
The sky is turning gray,
Ah! What a beautiful fall day!

David Barrera III, Grade 8
Wilson Middle School, OK

Laughter or Tears

Laughter
Happy, joyful
Smiling, joking, cheering
Parties, celebrations — death, tragedies
Crying, mourning, screaming
Sad, dark
Tears

Mackenzie Coffey, Grade 8
Greenfield Jr/Sr High School, MO

The Forest Watchers

Trees
Strong, tall
The forest watchers
Always there and listening
Ancient

Aidan Reap, Grade 8
Belle Isle Enterprise Middle School, OK

Family

My family is loving and caring
Through the good times and the bad.
They help me when I am happy,
And when I am sad.

We enjoy fun vacations throughout the USA,
Taking plane rides and car rides to the destination where we will stay.
There we can enjoy quality family time together
Where we can make memories that will last forever.

We come together on the holidays to share stories and visit,
To watch football games and gather around the table and pray,
To thank God for giving us the beautiful day.

My family supports me when I need them the most,
Especially when I am feeling gross.

Although we may fight sometimes
And may not get along well,
We will always love one another,
And that is very swell!

Nick Yahl, Grade 8
St Gerard Majella School, MO

I Hate Homework

First take a bag of potato chips
Next sit on the couch
Then pinch in a bag of laziness
Add one tablespoon of excuses
Make sure you bake the excuses for a while
Next get all your games out and play with your brother/sister
Then when your parents say it's time for homework say let me finish this game
After that if they say it again then say I got to clean up
Then you serve with doing your boring homework

Thomas Ruez, Grade 7
Meredith-Dunn School, KY

Dust Is Coming

Dust is coming, I can tell.
It gallops across the plains like a million wild horses, reaching to swallow me up.
It runs wild, driven by the howling wind, coming right toward me.
It rattles the windows, clutching at our house.
I try to scream but the thunderous wind grabs the frightened sound and tosses it away.
It's coming closer, the wild horses snorting in rage.
Again I cry out as the wind grabs the fence,
And swallows it into the midst of the angry horses.
It rattles the door and shakes the windows and the stampede is here.
The wind tears at the house, upset that it cannot get to us.
Then it is over.
The stampede is racing off into the distance, gone as quickly as it came,
Leaving the sound of the wind ringing in my ears.
The room is covered in a thick layer of dust,
And the light coming through the broken windows is tinted brown.
I myself am tinted brown, but I am alive and the storm — it is gone, and over.

Aylecia Lattimer, Grade 8
West Jr High School, MO

The Little Mouse

I live in a house with a silly little mouse.
It is stuffed with white fluff.
It lays in the kitchen, it lays on Mom's bed.
It doesn't eat chicken, it is not dead.
When mom comes home, what does she see?
A fake mouse that doesn't roam but she screams!
OMG! OMG! What is that? Mom, it's a toy.
OMG! OMG! Get the cat! Mom, it's the boys'!
Pick it up! Get it out!
That's enough! I'm tired now.
I leave the toy there so I can smile
When someone stares and runs a mile.
And to my surprise, here comes Britt.
It's the sunrise so she has no wits.
When she sees the toy, she yells with no joy.
Ha, ha, ha! I laugh all night!
Ha, ha, ha! So much delight!
But little do I know, little do I see,
My cousin puts the toy on the bed with me.
I wake in the morning. I scream, I scream!
I cry and cry! Why is she so mean?

Kaylynn Tillman, Grade 7
Dunbar Middle School, AR

Love at First Sight

Tonight is the night
I was in such fright
I was going on a date
With one of my mates
He was about 6 feet tall
And always had a basketball
He had the prettiest blue eyes
That matched the fall skies
His name was Blaine
He made me feel like the rain
As the stars float up in the sky
I looked into his beautiful eyes
As he leaned in to give me a kiss
I thought he was going to miss

Taylor Cassinger, Grade 8
Southern Reynolds County R-II School, MO

Fall

I glance out at the open field as the day begins.
I can't help but hear the clucks of the hens.
The day is warm and bright.
Lot of things to see it's a stunning sight.
The wind is blowing and getting cold.
A lot of hay to move, so lots to hold.
The trees are changing colors,
and leaves are starting to fall.
I can't believe they got so tall.
I can hear the rustly rattle of the fall.

Lacey Lovins, Grade 7
Nettleton Jr High School, AR

What I Think of Christmas

Everywhere there is red and green,
For miles and miles that's all that's seen.

Although I hate to get a runny nose,
I love it, if and when it snows.

My mom's Christmas village and gingerbread men,
She has double of everything, but angels, she's got ten.

I love to look at the Christmas tree,
And shake the presents my mom got for me.

My little sister can't wait for Santa Claus,
She hangs a stocking with a pattern of cat paws.

She'll lay out cookies and milk,
And wait for the man in the suit of red silk.

Samantha Keiser, Grade 7
Maury Middle School, TN

Love

Love
is kind
knows no race
wonder, passion, fear, pace
Love knows no race

Molly Kate Campbell, Grade 8
Belle Isle Enterprise Middle School, OK

The Window of My Life

I'm looking out my window,
and no one is around.
The clouds are dark and heavy,
the rain is pouring down.

I'm looking out my window,
something is moving in the distance.
I'm hoping that the clouds will clear,
and that the rain will stop this instant!

I'm looking out my window,
the sun is shining through.
I see my family and my friends,
the sky is now a true blue.

I'm looking out my window,
outside its so beautiful and bright.
I think I'll go outside,
yes, I think I might!

I'm no longer looking out my window,
the birds are all singing.
For now I am a part of the scene outside my window,
and life has a whole new meaning!

Katlyn Watkin, Grade 8
Gresham Middle School, TN

The Dam

Out of bed
In the car
On the road
Through the crowd
Beside the lake
Near the heat
By the tents
Under the fireworks
Off the path
Above the grass
Around all the happiness

Darlene Cardin, Grade 8
Heritage Middle School, TN

Friendly Fellow

Friendly fellow that likes to play,
Squeaks his toy every day.
Likes to run and bark,
And how he likes the park.
He stays beside you all the time,
I wouldn't trade him for a dime.
He's lots of fun to have around,
I'm always glad to hear his sound.

Kathy Bickwermert, Grade 8
St Mary of the Woods School, KY

Scary Movies

Peering over heads
His hand tightly holding mine.
We jump, popcorn spills.

He pulls me closer.
My head buried in his chest
As bad scenes take place

The credits rolling —
Horror, instead of a date...
We exit, still scared.

Julie Shelton, Grade 8
Western Greenbrier Middle School, WV

My Hero

My hero, my hero
only one can be my hero.
Why does each person ask me who
nobody but that one will ever know.
When everything gets complicated
that someone will help me with anything.
If everyone knew who that one is,
everything would get complicated,
and again she would help me.
Oh how I love that someone
Amy you will always be...
My hero

Leslie Bone, Grade 8
Pigeon Forge Middle School, TN

Just One Gift

There are some kids around the world that are different in their own special way
except around Christmas time when they all come together and say:
"Where is the tree?"
Their parents sigh and say, "We don't have one"
and hurt to see that one little tear in that child's eye.
But Christmas morning, it is the same sight when the kids see no presents in their eyes
then the parents cry with that same sigh while their kids say:
"Where are the presents from Santa and his sleigh?"
As you get more than one present under your bought Christmas tree,
remember those kids who don't know that feeling and still have tears in their eyes.

Kaitlyn Sampson, Grade 7
Raytown Middle School, MO

My Childhood

Childhood remembrances are always exciting
If you're as loved as I am
You always remember things like going to Cancun with your family
And spending time with friends
And how good you felt when you were with your family
And somehow you can always love them
And even though you remember some of the hard times
And though you're not perfect
I really hope you are grateful for everything
Because one day you might not have it all
They'll probably talk about my childhood and how loved I was

Ali Stevens, Grade 7
Heritage Hall School, OK

Sally

Sally walks down the hall without care,
John and Neil laugh at her hair.
Susie glares at her tie-dye shirt,
As Molly makes her the subject of the latest dirt.
Neil and Blake laughs at her friends,
As Pat's opinion pends
None of this gets to Sally, she keeps on walking and talking with Calley.

Later on...
Neil gossips about John.
Susie and Molly laugh at Blake's grade in French,
While Neil chuckles about John's time on the bench.
John overhears,
And ends up in tears.
Then Molly tells Blake, Calley thinks you're a fake.

By this time everyone is upset,
Everyone except for Sally, who knows not to fret.
She does not care what other people say,
Because she knows that one day.
People will want to be around Sally,
No Neil, or Blake, or Calley.
Because Sally won't talk smack, not even behind their back.

Mackenzie Schimpf, Grade 8
West Jr High School, MO

Thanksgiving Days

It's that time of year again
When we gather with family and friends
We fill the room with laughter and hugs
As Grandma pours cocoa into our mugs

We say our prayer and take our seat
then we all begin to eat
Ham, potatoes, turkey, and pies
My oh my oh my
I can't believe my eyes

After the meal it's time to play
The kids are hoping for a sunny day
As the footballs zing through the air,
Girls are braiding each other's hair

As the tables begin to clear
Grandpa's stories have grown since last year
When we begin to go our separate ways
We hope for many more Thanksgiving Days

Taylor Hunt, Grade 8
Owasso 8th Grade Center, OK

Mr. Boots

He's soft as a breeze
But he makes mom sneeze

He's cute, fuzzy, and has a new collar
but makes mom's eyes water

He has lots of brothers and sisters
So he never sleeps alone
But mom says
"Free to a good home."

He has paws as white as
Snow and eyes as
Blue as the sky
But as he leaves mom will smile and wave
Good bye

Amber Duvall, Grade 7
Knight Middle School, KY

The Simple Things

It's a splash of colors against a cool blue sky,
A razzle of hues against a quilted white cloud.
It's a frosty white scoop of vanilla ice cream,
A frozen peace of paradise in a rigid cone.
It's a grassy green hill in the middle of a city,
Surrounded by technology yet standing its ground.
It's a tall auburn tree in the middle of the desert,
A towering giant that gives you hope.
Sometimes you need to go back to the simple things,
The quirky features that make life life.

Kirsten Buchanan, Grade 8
West Jr High School, MO

Soccer

Soccer is my favorite sport
Even though it's not played on a court
You try real hard to kick the ball,
But you try even harder not to fall.

The game can be really rough,
But all that does is make you tough.
It sometimes hurts when they foul.
You should hear the wince from the crowd.

Soccer is my favorite sport
Even though it's not played on a court.
So even if you think this poem is cheesy,
Who cares? Play soccer; it's fun and easy!

John Harpool, Grade 7
Dunbar Middle School, AR

Me and My Sister

I have a sister somewhere
But I don't know where
Her mom took her away when she was a baby
I wish I knew where

I know that she's still out there
My daddy even said so
He said she's in Tennessee
But that's a long way from Louisville

I have picture of her as a baby
But she's almost sixteen now
I have dreams that some day, just maybe
I'll meet my sister Meagan

Katie Lawrence, Grade 7
Hebron Middle School, KY

Teenage Stress

I'm tired of this teenage stress.
It's made me a nervous wreck.
The crazy drama, the academic challenge, the cliques,
And even being one of the band geeks.
It always makes it hard to sleep.
I mean, wasn't life easier when the boys had cooties
And the hardest thing to add was 2 + 2?
I guess this is all part of growing up, this teenage stress.
Life will never be the same again, I guess.
Even if all the worries were gone.
Because this teenage stress seems to grow along with me.
It's like a cloud has settled on this teenage world of mine.
And even if I may shine on the outside,
It's still pouring down rain on the inside.
So, what if this teenage stress has made me a nervous wreck?
Today, I think I'll just give up and say "Oh, well."

Rachel Shores, Grade 8
Wilson Middle School, OK

Tomboy or Girly

Tomboy
Redneck, rebel
Hunting, fishing, mudding
Rough rowdy, sweetheart, feminine
Shopping, talking, gossiping
Prissy, stuck-up
Girly.

Rachel Burns, Grade 8
Western Greenbrier Middle School, WV

Love

My mind is racing
and my feet are pacing
100 miles an hour
I don't understand it
Love; why it hurts
It's supposed to be great and awesome
Slowly but surely blossom
but then it's cut and hurt
pulled down made worse and worse
sewed up once more
hoping not to be torn
Oh what shall we think of love?

Jennifer Murphy, Grade 7
Southwest City Elementary School, MO

Summer on the Lake

Kids screaming, water flying;
People fishing, kids swimming.
Everyone laughing, jet skis flying;
Summer on the lake.

Coty Cupples, Grade 7
Rocky Comfort Elementary School, MO

Fall

The birds in the sky,
The leaves in the trees,
They all come together
To put summer to ease.

Goodbye swimming pools
And outside stools.
For the warm air is gone
And now the air cools.

It's quick like a cheetah
And out like a light.
You don't see it coming
Until the air gets light.

When fall is gone
And winter is here,
Then you will know
That spring is near.

Jaqulyn Brantley, Grade 7
Nettleton Jr High School, AR

9/11

A time we stand to fight for our right, wasn't the time we realized we had to unite.
To realize that it wasn't an accident, but just plain mean.

Killing fathers, daughters, mothers, and brothers. And leaving bleeding to the others.
The sight was just a mess…seeing this and this and oh great there goes to rest.
People putting themselves in danger to save others. Now that's a true hero.
To go without a second of knowing what they're in for.
And in the beginning of every day we stand to say,
To all those that were lost, to all those that were free.

To all those that were there that day, who gave and gave or prayed and prayed.
Those who didn't get a say, but those who were remembered that day.
To remember those things they did were wrong, I just say they brought it on.
So I pray, the next time you think or do, just remember who's fighting for you.

They are my heroes, and I pray for all them to come home safely to us all.
So they will be here, to catch us next time we fall.

Brooke Hill, Grade 8
Sherwood Middle School, MO

Geography

G eography is a great thing we learn about our country
E veryone is eligible to learn about geography
O n every continent there is some type of geography
G reat things are discovered with geography
R ivers are also part of geography
A ppreciate the beauty of the world
P eople don't realize what they see when they look around them
H ave you ever realized that you are surround by natural beauty and pure nature
Y ou need to love and appreciate the geography of the world.

Dana Bombe, Grade 7
Clarksburg School, TN

Today's Life

Today you are free.
You can do anything you please.
No one cares about the people in pain,
As long as they are the ones who gain.
No person is treated wrong,
Yet they mistreat everyone else.
The perfect world is just a lie.
The whole world is full of bad guys.
In a perfect world we would consider others feelings,
Instead of worrying only about ourselves.
How would you feel if we weren't free,
Not able to do anything that we please.
We would have to work together just to survive.
All that you would want would be for people to give.
Starving, death, and pain would happen every day.
No one wants it to be this way.
If people understood how it could be,
They would be thankful about their liberties.
May be one day people will know what we have and understand,
Today's life.

Justice Meeks, Grade 8
White Station Middle School, TN

Spaghetti Problems

I visited an Italian restaurant, not knowing what to eat
Then someone pointed out the spaghetti dish
I was so hungry I didn't think how messy it would be
The waitress put the dish in front of me and I smelled the aromas floating towards me
I decided to dig in!
I stuck my fork in the middle of the mound
Spinning, spinning, round, and round
Sauce started splattering other people, but they didn't notice
I shoved the big bite of spaghetti to my mouth waiting for it to "melt"
As soon as I started chewing, it was burning my tongue
I wanted to have good manners but I *had* to get rid of it
I hoped it was like Colton's® where you could spit your peanut shells on the floor, so I
Pretended my spaghetti was peanuts
I let my meal cool and I finished it with the occasional spaghetti sauce on my face
Everyone finished so we left to pay the check
The waiter came up and just so happened to find the "peanuts" with his feet
He slipped, fell and hit the waitress's tray next to him that flipped over onto an upset Chinese man
The Chinese man ran over to that waitress to yell at her, but knocked over another
Waitress, who spilled her water onto another customer
I raced out to the car thinking…we should've left a tip.

Lesley Marie Smith, Grade 8
Alpena High School, AR

Have You Ever

Have you ever wondered what it would be like if there wasn't any fear.
Have you ever wondered what it is like to lose a friend.
Have you ever walked by a little kid in the store and they lost their mom.
Have you ever gave them a hand and helped them find their mom.
Have you ever wondered what it would be like if Eve hadn't talked Adam into eating that Apple.
Well I'm glad they did cause you wouldn't be the way you are now.

Stacie Adams, Grade 8
Ketchum Jr High School, OK

The Words Better Left Unsaid

Why did you have that awful fight?
Remember the one where you hit mom,
Then you left with no good-bye,
Did you even care about the scars left behind?
Miguel never knew what really happened to you,
I've had to grow up so much because of you,
I want you to know that I do blame you,
For all the pain you left behind,
The one thing I miss the most is the one thing I will never have, a dad,
But I can never call you my father, because you are so dead to me,
Why don't you care you hurt us so much, that I can't seem to bare,
Miguel is so old now you won't ever know the amazing boy, who grew up so fast,
Best of all he will never be like you,
There are so many things I wish I could tell you but you're not their to listen,
I will never know a father because of you, you made mom think they were all like you,
The one thing that hurts the most is that you will never know how your kids turned out,
You will never see me graduate or even go on my first date,
I will never become you,
The words better left unsaid.

Angelina Harlow, Grade 8
J Graham Brown High School, KY

September Sky

Where are you my lullaby?
My day and night, my cherry pie
Come with me and you will see
How I feel, what I believe.

Standing here in front of you,
I don't know what else to do.
Come with me my one true friend,
I'll be with you until the end.
Until the hour glass runs out of time,
Take my hand, my September Sky.

Come with me my trouble's gone,
Stand by me from dusk 'til dawn.

Jessica Wheeler, Grade 8
Mayflower Middle School, AR

Fall

Leaves are falling down,
trees are becoming bare.
Kids are running around,
leaves are getting stuck in their hair.

Halloween is coming,
each kid in a scary costume.
Their fingers are numbing,
from house to house they zoom.

Kids are eating candy,
their tummies are getting full.
Telling jokes to get treats,
Halloween is never dull.

Tara Beltrami, Grade 7
St Joseph Institute for the Deaf, MO

Hope

We play along like sunshine dancing
in the face of darkness.
Like two peas in a pod, we laugh
and lie on the beach,
hoping our lives will get easier.
Hope. It fills our hearts with Joy.
Joy. It fills our hearts with Hope.

Tim Hardick, Grade 8
Belle Isle Enterprise Middle School, OK

Christmas

Going shopping
Eating dinner
Being with family
opening gifts
drinking egg nog
putting up lights
waking up early

Kevin Vigano, Grade 7
Rocky Comfort Elementary School, MO

In Loving Memory*

Hold on…
Because this ride goes fast
And before you even know it
Life dims into a faint, distant past

I used to not believe these grand words and their truths
In fact, I regarded them with skepticism
I was frankly quite uncouth

But then the wind began to blow and my grip soon grew tight
I was far too young to set him free
So, I held on with all my might
But alas! My eyes presently overflowed with a deluge of delicate tears
As the sun's fading rays placidly told me his evening was indeed here

"There must be hope. I can't give up."
Thoughts shot through my mind like missiles
So, I still held on as the wind blew harder
Drowning me in its somber whistles

Then suddenly the wind stops —
The morn' brings its pleasant dawn
When I realized I had let go
And forever he was gone…

Victoria F. Chigozie Akah, Grade 8
Germantown Middle School, TN
**In loving memory of Emmanuel Chiedu Akah 1960-1997*

Soccer Stars

Soccer stars are people to look up to,
to aspire to be
Stars are role models,
guiding young players to their full potential

Stars come from all backgrounds,
looking up to the stars before them,
dreaming, hoping, imagining, not knowing they are going to be stars too

But eventually all stars fall,
crashing to the earth in a thud of reality
Eventually someone will grow up to replace them,
you, me, who knows?

Stars are something to want to be,
to work hard to be, but not to lose friends over.
Stars can be an inspiration,
but also a stumbling block

Stars are kind,
but they can also be mean
Soccer stars are people to look up to,
to aspire to be.

Jonas Gassmann, Grade 8
West Jr High School, MO

Oh Christmas Tree

Oh Christmas tree,
You look so good,
You smell so nice,
We cover you with lots of lights,
Then comes ornaments and tinsel too,
Finally a star completes you.

You fill all kids' hearts with joy,
And under you I see a toy,
You stand all day and then all night,
Please oh Christmas tree stay standing bright.

Connor Jordan, Grade 7
Annunciation Elementary School, MO

My Dog Julie

My dog Julie's a good dog
She's a black lab
That's not very tall

When I come home from town
I open up the car door
Julie jumps right in

Julie can be sweet or mean
She kills squirrels and other animals
But she gently plays with kittens

Sometimes Julie plays with me
She runs and jumps and knocks me down
She likes to hunt and roam around

Julie even sleeps with me
She jumps right in and covers her head
She starts to snore and kick

My dog Julie's a good dog
She's more like family than a dog
We're together until the day ends

Zed Barker, Grade 9
Van-Cove High School, AR

A Book

Inside the cover
Among the words
Between the lines
In the story
With the characters
Like a whole different world
Within my mind
Into a different universe
At the end
Beyond the pages, the story continues in my head

Nikki Rooks, Grade 8
Heritage Middle School, TN

I Wonder

I wonder what it was like when dinosaurs roamed
I wonder if I'll have a good future
I wonder what it would be like to have fins instead of feet
I wonder how long I'll live
I wonder if my grades will improve
I wonder why we die
I wonder what it would be like to swim with whales
I just wonder

Brittani Foughty, Grade 7
Newcastle Middle School, OK

Nature

I walk outside just to see
An array of colors that seem just for me.
I look at the red leaves just lying on the ground,
Sitting there peaceful, like small, colorful crowns.
I follow the small stone path that leads toward the stream,
My eyes follow the branches, as if a wondrous dream.
I look at the blue, flowing water, so nice and calm,
It flows so gently as it sings a peaceful song.
I see the trees blowing silently in the wind,
They each are special with their own unique grin.
I look over the horizon to see the sunset,
I smile at the colors that make my heart forget.
And when my day is almost done,
I see the stars shining straight above.

Patricia Jackson, Grade 8
St Gerard Majella School, MO

Cake and Pie

Pie
Tasty, sweet
Crusted, baking, sweetened
Colorful, sweet-smelling, circular, aromatic
Decorated, icing, frosted
Moist, creamy
Cake

Karen M. Mason, Grade 7
Musselman Middle School, WV

Baby

I'm sorry I call you baby.
I know you're getting big.
For me, it's hard to realize
That you are now a big kid.
You can feed yourself and wash your hands,
I don't like it at all.
I cherish all those moments
When you come crying,
Asking to be held in my arms.
I'm sorry I call you baby,
I know you're getting big.
Just remember that I love you,
I love you, my big kid.

Dahyana Arias, Grade 8
Musselman Middle School, WV

Dilip Jag Palanisamy

D isciplined
I ntelligent
L ogical
I ndian
P ractical

J ubilant
A mbitious
G enerous

P rognosticate
A ggressive
L iterate
A ctive
N ice
I mplacable
S alient
A spirant
M ature
Y oung

Dilip Jag Palanisamy, Grade 8
White Station Middle School, TN

Clean Laundry

Around and around
It goes
Tumbling this way
And that
O! how fresh that
Laundry will smell
That sweet clean
Smell
Fills the air
As you take
It out — um'mm
Clean laundry

Taylor Rose Jenkins, Grade 7
Elkton School, TN

Lost Soul

I am a lost soul
hiding in the shadow of your hatred.
Life is no more for me.
I live alone.
Fly through the winter skies alone
Caught by humanity and never to be free.
The sun snowy and sad
just like my blue icy gray eyes
that I have to look through
just to see how horrible it really is.
I am a lost soul
taken from all freedom.

Tia Barker, Grade 7
Odessa Middle School, MO

Monday Morning

Ring ring!
I moan and groan as my alarm goes off.
My mind and body are still asleep.
Reluctantly, I get up.
The agony I feel is worse than
Any other day of the week.
As I waddle downstairs,
My eyes close slowly.
No!
I can't do it!
I have to stay awake.
The rest of the morning is a blur
Of frizzy hair,
Half a piece of toast,
And purses that don't match my shoes.
If only school started at 9.

Grace Delgado, Grade 7
White Station Middle School, TN

Hypocrites

Always watching,
Always waiting,
For another person,
To start hating.
Hypocrites — two-faced liars.
Hypocrites — self-deniers.
I wish that they would disappear —
Their lies are more than I want to hear.
Their words are guns —
Overpowering and dangerous.
Everyone runs.
They pretend their lives are lustrous.
Hypocrites — aggressive non-believers.
Hypocrites — creating non-believers.
I wish they would disappear —
They don't belong anywhere.

Skye Buresh, Grade 9
Alpena High School, AR

Winter Days

Snowy streets with the chill of fears
stories with the end full of tears
Knowing the winter days are near
fills everyone with holiday cheer
presents toys and lots of food
put everyone in a happy mood
Your family stays for many days
because they love you in many ways
They keep you in their heart
and give you that special part
all year around
with the most beautiful sound.

Julia Brockmeier, Grade 8
Hartville Jr/Sr High School, MO

Egg/Duck

Egg
Round, new
Warming, cracking, moving
Duckling, nest — webbed feet, wings
Quacking, waddling, swimming
Feathery, loud
Duck

Sarah Gritton, Grade 8
All Saints School, MO

Advice of an Old, Young Man

Children, learn from my mistakes.
Don't be like me,
Don't dip snuff,
Fight or cuss.
Don't be like me,
Don't fight to fight,
Don't fight to prove a point,
Don't dip snuff,
I've lost friends because
Of fighting and dipping
Don't be like me.
If you become like me
You will lose the one you love
Learn from my mistakes.
Don't be like me.

Blake Thompson, Grade 8
Wainwright Elementary School, OK

Hunting

The morning was cold and clear
While I was waiting to see a deer
Patiently sitting in my stand
Watching the sun rise over the land
Listening closely for any wildlife near

Skyler Barnes, Grade 8
Highland Rim School, TN

United States

U is for unique
N eighborly
I ncredible
T ough
E ducated
D ependable

S astified
T raditional
A dventurous
T alented
E xtraordinary
S ignificant

Kristan Crabtree, Grade 7
Clarksburg School, TN

Rain

Dripping dripping dropped
Splashing splashing splashed
Walking in the pitch dark
Without a care in the world
Lightning strikes the sky
Drip drip drop

Anna Fredericks, Grade 7
Hazelwood Northwest Middle School, MO

My Silent Love

A silent, but sweet love,
Confidence in her smile
With silky smooth hair,
And the face of my wildest fantasy.

Her smell of flowers
leaves a sweet taste in my mouth
As if I was eating my favorite candy.

Her laugh leaves me stunned
And keeps me wondering.
A goddess of beauty
With the soft voice of an angel.

Her wonderful eyes keep me mesmerized
With the colors of black rubies,
Leaving me breathless
And making me believe
I can fly.

Crae Dudley, Grade 8
Lee A Tolbert Community Academy, MO

Just for You…

This is a poem I wrote for you.
I want you to know that I care.
I know that I can have my faults,
Just as you do.
But what I want you to know,
Is that I love you more than everyone else,
In the whole wide world.
I am trying my best to set a good example,
Even though every day I wake up,
Scared you will follow my footsteps.
Make the mistakes I did.
I've always look up to you.
Even though you are 5 years younger.
I have longed to be like you. So perfect.
And even though I may not be the best sometimes,
I am always here for you. No matter what.
And on this day I will let you know something very important.
Friends will come and go throughout our lives.
But what we have will last forever.
We are and always be…
Sisters.

Amanda Grubbs, Grade 8
Adair Middle School, OK

Wonders of the Fall

Happy, hectic yet serene
a busy day of the fall
yet evenings are so peaceful
so calm, so brisk, so quiet
Prancing through the fallen leaves,
twigs and acorns rustling underneath.
Animals scurrying, getting ready for the winter.
No one really knows, what makes this beauty real.
The quiet sunset, like gold all in all
The sweet song of the trees
The colorful flowers and blooms have died away
Only to come later in the spring warmth
Wow! This time of year is simply a delight.

Liz Cossey, Grade 7
Nettleton Jr High School, AR

There Is No Ending!!!

The last fall leaf had hit the ground,
No one dared to make a sound.
They had seen the crash from up the road,
But now they had to stay still and froze.

As mothers wept, and children cried,
They had brought the casket out,
While wiping tears from their eyes.

To this day they still look back, and shudder
On how they try to relive the past.

All they know now is that it's not the end,
It will happen tomorrow, today, and then again.

You gain nothing,
From drinking and driving.
Except a hole in the ground,
And loved ones gathering all around.

Laura Schwarze, Grade 8
Chelsea Jr High School, OK

Skateboards

Lifting off the ground like an air plane
spinning below my feet as a dreidel would on Hanukkah

Nailed the trick roller with joy
1000 pounds of wind blowing against my face

The feeling of a rollercoaster when my hair jumps around
speed increasing as I launch off the quarter pipe
shot in the air like a balloon full of helium

Blasted into a foam pit
soft as a cotton filled pillow

Ryan Pullam, Grade 7
Hazelwood Northwest Middle School, MO

Star with Wings

Sometimes it seems
like all the stars
have fallen
from the skies,
but when I see
the stars have wings,
I know they're fireflies.

Jerry Hayes, Grade 8
Elkton School, TN

Autumn Leaves

Autumn leaves falling, falling, falling,
like snowflakes you can catch
on your tongue.

Autumn leaves falling
through the air
in the mid-October breeze.

Autumn leaves whistling in the
wind as they fall to the
cold, hard ground.

Autumn leaves soaring through
the air until they are caught
by gravity and pulled to the ground.

Geoffrey Bickford, Grade 8
Chelsea Jr High School, OK

Inside the House

Inside the house
around the paintings
up the stairs
in the room
within the closet
like nothing you've ever seen

throughout the house
at the stroke of twelve
since who knows when
during the night
like nothing you've ever heard

above your head
within your heart
nearer than you think
beside you all the way
like nothing you've ever felt

toward your destruction
nearer every second
upon you like never before
from deep inside
you'll never be again

Cherisse Wilkins, Grade 8
Pigeon Forge Middle School, TN

Lacy Lynch

Lacy
Smart, caring, likeable, funny
Sister of Adam and Alisha
Lover of horses, Peyton Manning, Johnny Depp
Who feels energetic, happy, hopeful
Who needs a break from schoolwork
Who fears clowns, heights, and scary movies
Who would like to see movies, Johnny Depp, a real live Indianapolis Colts game
Who lives in Palmyra, Tennessee
Lynch

Lacy Lynch, Grade 8
Montgomery Central Middle School, TN

Delish Carrots

Crunchy orange sticks are delicious snacks.
Make munchies for rabbits
And develop into snacks for squirrels.
Bite on a carrot and you'll hear a satisfying "snap."
Cake becomes healthy — carrot cake!
Chopped up to boil in stews;
Carrots emerge mushy like mashed potatoes.
Growing underground with all the turnips and radishes
Until the head's leaves finally pop out above ground.
Of all the vegetables…
You know that only those carrots will be digested.
Much energy is used yanking giant carrots out of the sun baked soil in your garden.
Buy a bag of cute baby carrots and eat them on road trips;
Before you know it,
They've vanished.
Carrots are that irresistible.

Christina Wang, Grade 8
West Jr High School, MO

Creation

Summer has finally arrived,
The pleasant smell of flowers drift through the air.
The smell of chlorine in swimming pools around the neighborhood.

An apple, freshly picked, tastes as sweet as candy.
Some steak, cooked to perfect,
Was excellent!

The sound of children, praising God that they're out of school,
To see His creation. Birds chirping for this wonderful day
God has brought us.

In the distance, children playing catch and swimming.
The forest flowers, living creatures,
All wonderful things God has created to see.

The warm weather, with a cool breeze felt as nice as
Sitting around a campfire on a cool night. As the evening came,
It became more cold. Then I started to think;
God brought us a beautiful world.

Corey Martin, Grade 7
Our Lady Catholic School, MO

Insights of a Stressed Girl

You wonder who I am.
Well I wonder too.
So many lies have been told,
you can't find the truth.
No one's loyal nor true.
Not me nor you.
Tensions flying by the day.
We are dying in every way.
The end is coming soon if you didn't know.
The news tells us every day our tears show.
Here is my plea.
Send ultimate peace and justice to me.

Olivia Ricks, Grade 9
Hazelwood East High School, MO

A Winter Wonderland

The soft, shining snow is like powder,
A montage of a white, crystal wonderland.

The temperatures are in the negatives,
Below zero which is already very cold.

The grinning snowman newly created,
Sits almost still as a deer.

The warm fire is blazing here inside,
A great feeling floats around this toasty home.

The decorations are now shining brightly,
The beautiful color collages are in harmony with each other.

The winter season is now here to stay,
Just sit back and enjoy the way.

Brendan Kelly, Grade 7
Annunciation Elementary School, MO

A Piece of Me

A gonizing grief of
L osing a piece of your life
O ne day at a time
P retending to be someone you're not
E very day you see it
C oming and going, looking
I n the mirror wondering
A sking yourself, when will it be back again

A nd how different you look now
R ecognizing the girl on the inside but not the out
E very passing day you think
A re you coming back forever
T alking to God, "Please give this piece of me back"
A nd no more alopecia areata

Emily Brawley, Grade 8
Mountain Grove Middle School, MO

A Snow Day to Remember

As the last night of fall comes to an end
There are people sleeping,
Children weeping,
To start a new day that is coming ahead.

As morning approaches,
Of the first day of winter,
When children are waking up,
And getting ready for school,
When to their surprise,
They have the day off,
To relax and play,
for it is a snow day.

Every kid is outside,
Playing with new fallen snow,
With every intention to not waste the day,
Until it is time for them to doze off.

For now it will be a new day for every child to remember,
That remarkable snow day.

Amanda Baghal, Grade 8
West Jr High School, MO

At the Lunch Table

We talk about a lot of things
Like diamond rings.
Who's hot or not.
That's what we talk about at the lunch table.

Ashley Pilkington, Grade 8
Southern Reynolds County R-II School, MO

Seasons of Memories

In winter
I tread to the creek with snowshoes on.
I shield my face from piercing winds.
Skipping pebbles on still water,
I watch snow fall onto rocks in the creek bed.
In spring
I stroll to the creek with blue jeans on.
I observe cardinals in blooming trees.
Sticks, flowers and leaves float down stream.
In summer
I trot to the creek with my raincoat on.
I skip rocks with my granddad while the sky clouds.
We shroud our faces with rain coats
When rain thumps our heads.
In fall
I wander to the creek with my jacket on.
I step through leaves and fallen branches
Observing squirrels stock up for the winter.
As overhead leaves change and fall,
Hoping my memories don't flow away
With the seasons of my childhood.

Jordan Norris, Grade 7
Baylor School, TN

Prairie Wind

The wind in the prairie is subtle,
before the winter snow.

The buffalo wander wherever,
they want to go.

The grass is dry and brittle,
it flows in waves of gold.

Iain Gould, Grade 8
West Jr High School, MO

The Quiet Place

Through the field
After dark
Below the clouds
By the lake
Under the moonlit sky
In the woods where it's full of life
Beyond the fences and houses
By myself
Despite the cold night
This place is beautiful

Kelly Boring, Grade 8
Heritage Middle School, TN

True Love

Looking up at the stars,
She lays her head on his chest.
She hears his heart beating.
He smells her sweet perfume.
She whispers she's cold,
He then wraps his arms around her.
They both kept silent…
Then he bends down to kiss her.
She feels as if she's drunk.
She is, but drunk in love.
Then they look back up at the stars,
She silently drifts to sleep.
Feeling secure,
He bends down to kiss her forehead.
Then he silently says, I love you,
Goodnight…

Nikki Stephenson, Grade 7
Rocky Comfort Elementary School, MO

Our Soldiers

Bombs blowing up,
Soldiers risking their lives to fight.
For the country they love,
Waiting and worried families.
Wanting them home safe and sound,
Not being home for the holidays.
Missing their children,
So they can stay safe.

Janaya Toney, Grade 8
Rocky Comfort Elementary School, MO

Beautiful Thunderstorms

First the wind, calling the clouds to release their tears,
Next, the rain, covering the ground as it pours uncontrollably from the sky
Thunder booms, lightning strikes in the background,
All as if the storm was performing a show,
Then, all is quiet,
The rain ceases,
The wind hushes the trees,
The thunder booms, one last time,
Lightning shows its beauty with one bolt,
The sun pushes through the clouds moving them to the side, out of sight,
A rainbow appears showing the storm is finished,
This is the beauty of a Thunderstorm.

Hannah Early, Grade 8
West Jr High School, MO

Ecology

Lost, lonely monkeys whimper along the foggy, jungle path,
and gaze at the table-flat terrain
wondering how quickly those two-leggers
chop, tie down, and steal the tree houses they call home.
The used-to-be sparkling, swaying sea
twists as it tries to funnel out
each plastic bag, bottle, and oil spill
tossed and blended into its waters.
War persistently rains across the borders
leaving its broken puddles that harden into ice,
and society believes only dancing bullets
can crack this frozen tension.
Indiscriminately and ferociously,
fire wrestles, wrestles, wrestles
and consumes defenseless creatures and their territory,
because flames don't feel; they thrive.
The bystanders' frowns grimace behind their upside-down crescents,
only briefly acknowledging the prickly reality
of our struggling, defiled Earth.
Soon, they revert to their daily smiles
without choosing to alter the world's careless ways.

Paige Elliott, Grade 8
Baylor School, TN

Tennessee Thanksgiving

Eating delicious food
Playing games
Spending time with family old and new
Seeing joyful faces as they shatter the laborous work of the rake
All the colors of leaves flying at your face
Shivering as you go inside to thaw by the fire
The hot chocolate tastes so good as you reminisce with forgotten family
As you curl up and fall asleep dreaming by the fire
Your mother gently carries you to bed
She pulls the blanket high up to your shoulders
Kisses you and wishes that Thanksgiving was not yet over.

Casey Stinnett, Grade 7
Maury Middle School, TN

Confusion

A mix of a thousand feelings
hatred, love, happiness, depression
confusion
A million thoughts running through your head
None of them relevant to the next
With every thought
every feeling
every word
Comes more
confusion
Not sure what to say
or how to feel
or what to do
It takes over every aspect of your life
and steals your thoughts
and feeling
and actions
When a thousand feelings mix to one
when a million thoughts collide
when you're not sure
confusion

Elisabeth Fox, Grade 8
West Jr High School, MO

Someone Help

Will someone help
Will someone help me through the darkness
Will someone just help me up.
There's all these people around me
But no ones here.
All those days of being lonely
Of all those days of being mad
No ones here to help me
I'm all alone in the darkness.
Again and again I fall down
But no ones here to help
I guess that life goes on.
Too bad that life goes on lonely.
Too bad that life goes on with fear
That's just life.

Dallas Moody, Grade 8
White Station Middle School, TN

Friendship

We shared our secrets,
We shared our lives,
We shared our lunches,
We liked the same guys.

Endless friendship for a year and a half,
Endless memories until it all crashed.
Rumors spread, secrets told,
I guess for now this friendship is old,
Never returning, that's what I'm told.

Natalie Tindall, Grade 8
Northwest Valley 7th & 8th Grade Center, MO

Cowgirl Up!

Brush off your jeans
Polish your boots
It's show time baby
You're gonna let loose

You've been preparing all year long
For this one day
When you would prove to all the cowboys
Cowgirls made rodeos what they are today
Full of rough, deadly, and sometimes fatal events

Cowgirls look nice and pretty on the outside
But they have a competitive side
They never turn down a challenge
And never expect to lose.

If the cowgirl gets bucked off
She stands up
Spits out the dirt and brushes off her jeans
Hops back on
And gets the job done

Cowboys made the rodeo
But Cowgirls perfected it!

Ashton Rhine, Grade 8
West Jr High School, MO

Clean Your Own Mirror

A dirty mirror
Can suffice
For shadowy dreams
Or clouded minds

Full of despair
And ruthless ways
Not mirroring truth
On any day

I'll clean your mirror
Once in a while
To clean away sadness
To bring you a smile

But true dreams come
When you dream them yourself
Not when you ask
Someone else for help

So clean your own mirror
Don't let it go to waste
Because there is nothing more inspirational
Than your own face.

Kamyl Harvey, Grade 8
White Station Middle School, TN

Burrito

Burrito
Tasty, yummy
Hot, watering, spicy
Tortilla, meat, beans, onion
Good

Adalberto Esqueda, Grade 8
Belle Isle Enterprise Middle School, OK

Colors

Orange brownish leaves
Fall like paper,
Crunch like ice.
Kids are playing
In the leaves
Running and jumping
Soon the leaves will be gone
But then
Here comes winter.

Madison Robertson, Grade 7
Wilson Middle School, OK

Wolves

Wolves are cool,
white wolves are my favorite,
they hide in the snow,
they eat meat and plants,
they are like dogs,
they see and hear good,
white wolves mostly hunt rabbits,
they run kinda fast,
they live in caves,
packs fight other packs,
white wolves like snow,
they attack each other sometimes,
they fight each other for food,
that is why wolves are cool.

Brandon Warren, Grade 7
Dyer Elementary & Jr High School, TN

My Room

I switch the lights on.
I walk towards my bed.
Without even a thought
I turn the TV on.
Among the many stresses in my life
My room and within it
Calms me down.
Up to right now I don't know what to say.
Except that either night or day
My room takes all my stress away.
So now I turn off the lights
And leave me be.
I love my room
My room of peace.

Cheyenne Miller, Grade 8
Heritage Middle School, TN

My Barn

Down the hill, through the gate
Despite the chill I can feel my heart vibrate
Toward the beautiful home, around the fence
My feet roam, I can't take the suspense
Through the paddock with grass up to my knees
I see my beauty by the lilac, my feet freeze
From the bush my horse walks to me, he puts his nose onto mine
His breath on my face is so cozy, smelling the wonderful pine
I walk inside the barn, under the roof I sit
Along the wall lay his tack
Nearly frostbite, I put on his bit
Past the gate we go, like brother and sister
With love he takes me for a ride

Amy Davis, Grade 8
Heritage Middle School, TN

Roaming Wolves

You do not have to be dominating.
You do not have to rule.
You only have to be free,
free like the roaming wolves
as they roam through the forests trying to find food.
Tell me about your happiness, and I will tell you my sorrow.
The wolves travel in packs to strengthen their odds of survival,
as you must become close and rely on others to strengthen your odds.
Meanwhile the blinding sun on the snow and ice
is crossing their home.
The world treats you like a wolf
proclaiming your freedom.

Evan Hellerstedt, Grade 8
Baylor School, TN

Snake

It resides in abandoned burrows and rock crevices.
From under the rocks,
It emerges during the hot summer day.
Gleaming with its shiny scales,
It hungrily hunts for prey.
Past a tree, it slides across the scorching grassland toward a hole.
Scrutinizing, it uses its forked tongue to track down its prey.
As it hunts for a meal, it is constantly flicking out its tongue.
Slithering fast into the hole, it spots the prey.
Bingo! It's a bunny rabbit, its choice of prey.
It comes up slowly,
Poised to strike.
Frightened, the startled bunny scampers and then pauses.
The snake is gone.
And out the tree, it strikes its prey with uncanny accuracy.
No venom required.
Wrapping around the bunny,
It squeezes.
1st strike.
2nd strike.
3rd strike and the hunting task is complete.

Roger Carter, Grade 7
Baylor School, TN

Fall…

Fall
It's a time of year that I love.
Fall is my favorite season because of all
the things that go on during that time.

Fall
Leaves are turning red, orange, yellow, and brown.
It's the time when Gallatin has their annual Fall Festival.

Fall
As it gets colder we make our selves warmer with
jackets to wear.
It's when kids go trick-or-treating on
Halloween night and come home full of fright.

Teresa Smith, Grade 9
Gallatin High School, TN

I Wonder

I wonder why the grass is green
I wonder why the sky is blue
I wonder where I will be in ten years
I wonder how people can be so judgmental
I wonder what Jesus looks like
I wonder why snowflakes are perfect and pure
I wonder about you
I wonder about me
Why do I wonder?

Meghan Dobbins, Grade 7
Newcastle Middle School, OK

Permit Me to Tell You About Christmas Eve

Permit me to tell you about Christmas Eve.
The twinkling lights on every roof,
The smell of apple pie and warm sugar cookies,
The homemade ornaments on the freshly cut tree,
The excitement of the first snow sighting.
But the Christmas Eve I remember the most
Left my heart feeling warm and fuzzy,
I wanted to jump for joy.
I did something to help others,
I made someone else's Christmas merry and bright,
And that's the best present I could ever receive.

Erin Wachter, Grade 8
All Saints School, MO

The Dark

In the dark are those things you think you hear.
All those hungry creatures roaming closely near.
In the dark I see those things I hope aren't really there.
All those noises and those shadows sure give me a scare.
I hope that I don't get lost in here oh how scared I'd be.
With all those hungry creatures fiercely watching me.

Caye Lowery, Grade 7
Hartville Jr/Sr High School, MO

Heavy Day Dreams

The music is playing, it's rumbling throughout my mind
I don't know how to stop it; it's power is too strong
My ideas are losing track. I need to get them back in place
My mind won't allow it, I can't listen well
The people are talking, I can't read their lips
It's like their voice is on mute, they won't make a sound
But then I gain thought, my mind is plowing with ideas
The music stops, and the heavy day dreams appear.

Chris Hamilton, Grade 7
St Mary of the Woods School, KY

I Wish

I wish
I wish I could relive the days
When you and I
Were together.

I wish
I wish I could go back to
When I saw your beautiful shining face every day,
When you filled my day with merriment
Or when I would rush to be in your arms.

I wish
I wish I could have spent more,
Time with you before you left me.
Now I regret that I didn't take an advantage
Of the time I had to spend with you.
You left quicker than you came.
And I wish you could have stayed.

Oh how I wish
I had you back
With me once again.

Jazmyn Whiteside, Grade 8
Science Hill High School – 8-9 Campus, TN

Hobbies

Skating
fun, exciting
ollies, kickflips, grabs
bone crushing, skull splitting wrecks, broken bones —
tabletops, tailwhips, bunnyhops,
fast, dangerous
Biking.

Kodie Redden, Grade 8
Western Greenbrier Middle School, WV

Fat Mouse

I once saw a tiny fat mouse.
He lived in the walls of my house.
He liked to eat cheese,
But gave us all fleas.
"We're moving," my mom then announced.

Tanner Buschmann, Grade 8
St Joseph School, MO

School

Children laughing,
Teachers yelling.
This is what school is about.

Ashley Taylor, Grade 7
Rocky Comfort Elementary School, MO

Fall Is Coming

Fall is coming
It will be here soon
Now it almost feels like
It is the middle of June

Fall is coming
It brings a breeze
Colder it will turn
With it, fires will burn

Fall is coming
Some smiles will go away
But sooner or later
Everything will be the same

Fall is coming
Get out your coats and jackets
Because you will be as cold as
The midnight breeze

Fall is coming
I've told you enough
Soon you will realize
Why I love it so much

Tanner Ballard, Grade 7
Nettleton Jr High School, AR

Parents

Parents are in your face.
What a big disgrace.
Not everybody loves them
because they ground us.
You may get mad at each of them.
Anybody would say I don't
like either of them.
Another thing about them is
that they are to noisy.
I don't think that a kid
would tell their parents no one
likes you, to them.
Everything about you is weird, either.
Others would say you're annoying.
But there are several of them
in the world so get used to it.
Many of them like to
ground us for fun.
Parents.

Austin Bateman, Grade 8
Pigeon Forge Middle School, TN

How Great Is Our God

As I lie beneath the trees, admiring their beautiful leaves,
All around, falling like snow, glaring at a desert, dry cracked knuckles
Staring at the mountains so tall, so brave,
I thank God for all he has made

Listening to birds chirping, like my brother with a toy
Or the coyote howling, over the moon, as a broken record playing over and over again
When the rushing waves pound the beach
I thank God for all he has made

Chomping into a watermelon, wet as a pool
Sweet as candy apples
Bitter as pickles
Remind me of how great God is

Sniffing the clean laundry,
Rain or the smoke of the fire
And the sweet as pie pine
Remind me of how great is our God

Crunching a leaf in hand, like an eggshell
Petting my cat, soft as grass fur
Or the itty gritty sand reminds me,
How great is our God

Gavin Marmonti, Grade 7
Our Lady Catholic School, MO

A Trip Through Time

The mystical ruins of past civilizations whisper to me as I cross the gentle divide,
separating the past from the present.
Footprints left from those who once lived give a trace of long-ago paths,
that hundreds of years later,
mystify the world.

Unknown markings spell out unfathomable secrets,
Showing how ongoing time locks in secrets of the ages.
Once obvious,
Now deciphered by those with an esoteric knowledge.
Hidden secrets haunt the mysterious lands,
proving cultural ignorance.

Seeming more fictional than fact,
small villages and sandstone homes,
built by sheer human strength,
working together to create structures that modest and silent as they now seem,
once reached toward the heavens.

Looking out from the cliff dwelling of the Spruce Tree House,
a golden sunset silences the outside world,
and listening carefully you can hear glittering voices,
whispering tales of the past,
adding to the mysterious history of a lost civilization.

Kaitlyn Clements, Grade 9
Savannah High School, MO

Miracle Baby

An unexpected miracle, a baby lie
in the womb of my mother.
A new baby boy was born on a June day.
His name is Tenari Noah Vai and
he was a miracle sent from God.

My baby brother is a Christmas gift
that I'll never let go of.
Tenari is like a gift that you will never
want to get rid of even if you have to.
He's my own little comedian.

Born cheerfully, he's always grinning with
others glancing at his cute little smile.
But I'll never give up on him not even for a while.

I can't wait for him to grow, but he'll always
be my little comedian putting on a show.

Tepora Vai, Grade 8
Ervin Middle School, MO

When Summer's Over

When summer is over, we all will know,
by the way the wind will blow.
Hold on to your hat, hold on to your shoes,
for fall has great, big news!

Maylin Harbin, Grade 7
Wilson Middle School, OK

The Greatest Game

There I am a running back playing football
I'm running like a hurricane
In a swimming pool and the strong safety
Coming at me like a bulldozer

There I am spinning around him
Like a tornado
And a stiff arm like a steel arm
With a door hinge for my arm

I'm runnin' in an open field
With my lineman blocking me like a bulldozer
Then the other team comes at me like a wrecking ball
I got tackled

Then my line acted like a brick wall
And theirs a barricade
There I am as if I had a bomb
And blasted their barricade and then I stopped

The crowd as loud as a siren
Their claps as loud as thunder
I did it
I made a touchdown, we won

Gabriel Garcia, Grade 7
St Cecilia Academy, MO

At Last, Fall Is Here

At last, fall is here.
The cold air is coming near.
And the leaves are falling
in a rainbow of color
as the trees become bare
one after another.
There is a fresh crispness in the air,
that feels good to breathe in and out.
Buzzin bees are going away,
as gobbling turkeys are coming out.
The days are getting shorter
and the nights are getting longer.
The nights are getting cooler
as the cool breezes blow through my hair.
At last, fall is here.

Rashelle Williams, Grade 7
Nettleton Jr High School, AR

And It Was a September Morning

Many lives were saved that day
Many more lives lost
Two towers
One Pentagon
Four planes
One field

246 citizens on the planes
246 citizens dead
1/4 of them took control
Deciding the plane shouldn't reach its destination
Four bloody flights that day
One took command

And it was a September morning

Dylan Parker, Grade 8
Benton County School of the Arts, AR

People?

They have their ups, they have their downs,
They reach the sky, they hit the ground.
They never stop moving, around and about,
They just keep going, their own unique route.

They can be different colors, not one is the same,
They can be wild, not one is quite tame.
They can be wrinkly, they can be new,
Some can be stopped, but only a few.

They love the sun, they hate the rain,
Their hearts are restless, they hardly seem sane.
Going with the flow, drifting in the breeze,
Would you believe I'm speaking of leaves?

Michael McLaughlin, Grade 8
St Gerard Majella School, MO

Creations of God

I walked outside to see sunlight twinkle off the stream,
the birds gliding like kites, waiting, just waiting for the bugs to squirm up.

I walked outside to hear birds chirp as they fly away, the howling wind behind them.
I listen to the peaceful melodies of flutes the stream plays,
The frogs playing the drums with their bellowing croaks.
God's creations are truly wonderful.

I walked outside to smell summer air full of the scent of fresh fruit and swaying flowers.
I walked outside to feel spiky emeralds beneath my feet,
While climbing rough bark to pick the smooth fruit from which God has given me.

Tanner Hoog, Grade 7
Our Lady Catholic School, MO

Permit Me to Tell You About Holidays

Permit me to tell you about holidays
The excitement you feel the days before,
The decorations everywhere you look,
The family gatherings so huge, you have to use two different houses,
The smiles on everyone you meet.
But the holiday I always remember the most
Is Christmas
The bright lights and cheerful moods filling the air,
The wonderment in the eyes of young children at the sound of the name, "Santa Claus,"
The goodies tasting as if they were fresh from the bakers,
Enough gifts to go around twice,
And, the One up above who makes it all so special.

Maddie Mendel, Grade 8
All Saints School, MO

Too Many Times

Too many times has my heart been broken. Too many times have I been hurt. Too many times has love been lost. Times have changed, grown darker and true love has been lost. Too many times have I let someone hurt me. Too many times have I let someone break my heart. But never again!

Kylie Brown, Grade 9
Central High School, OK

Speak

In my mind my lips were zipped together.
I afflicted myself by keeping a disgraceful secret, but I didn't have the audacity to speak.
I thought to myself, "Tell anyone? Why should I? No one cares what I have to say."
What I didn't know was that speaking is actually better.
I asked myself, "What led me to my disgraceful, dirty secret? How could I have avoided
feeling torture inside me?" I found but one simple answer: speak.
I didn't want my soul to buildup pain. Whenever pain did build up, I tried relieving it the easy way.
Then I realized that life is precious, and one way for me to conserve it is to speak.
I should've told about my feelings, guiltiness, shame, and humiliation.
Speaking was hard, but it was worth the effort.
Once I spoke I felt better, like being released from a cage.
I was finally able to get that knot out of my stomach.
I realized people love and care about me. Whenever I tortured myself then so did my
Mom and friends, and just about anyone I love.
Someone gave me a little advice, "Speak and release yourself."
So I tried it and it worked. Now I give you advice, "Speak."

Ariana Mauricio, Grade 8
Owasso 8th Grade Center, OK

Love

Love is something
that some may say falls
from the sky, that the wind
will someday blow away.
But in one in a million chances
somebody is blessed to find someone like you.
That is when the wind just
seems to be at a standstill,
and that is when it is safe to say
these three words…I LOVE YOU.

Briana Cherie Jones, Grade 8
Belle Isle Enterprise Middle School, OK

Let Me Go

I'll fight the tears away
Deceptively, I'll sit and pray
Slowly, the ends fray
The same routine every day
Smile; the pain is gone
Gone for now, but not for long
Apathetic when I sing my song
Such a shame, this song does not last long
Please let me go
You don't understand, I just cannot say no
My pain will not longer show
I promise, no one will ever know
From a point of view that is oh so low
Please, just let me go.

Cheyenne Gage, Grade 9
Bearden High School, TN

Why We Like the Weekends

The alarm's shrill scream gets me up because I must,
If I want to frantically rush to catch the bus
And leave it with a tired yawn as I enter school
Hurrying between teacher's gazes and their rules,
To finish the homework yesterday I was too tired to do
Then rush to class before tardiness becomes a problem too
Through cold trailers, jammed lockers, and scorching heat,
Into packed hallways and onto uncomfortable seats
Until at last we're once again unleashed onto the bus
Listening to the others scream and cuss
I finally arrive home, liberated at last
Free to take a nap and visit dreams vast
Only to waken as the family rushes in
Where do they find the energy to make such a din?
Great — Now I have to do my schoolwork again
While wondering if another nap will be a sin
No time for fun
I work till I'm done
Knowing tomorrow will just be today's repeat
You know, the weekend will be a pleasant relief

Allison Wigger, Grade 8
West Jr High School, MO

Love Rocks (If You Know What Love Is)

It's the same thing all the time
always the same never different
waiting to change always wishing
thought about it more than everything
I have ever thought about it's the same,
everything I do or think about it involves you
or something about loving you
wanting you to go away wishing you weren't in my life
though if you left everything would leave with you
somebody thought LOVE ROCKED
until something got in their way
then their love dropped and broke
into a ton of broken glass!!!!

Megan Brooks, Grade 8
Pauls Valley Jr High School, OK

The Night

The night is wondrous
like a pack of wolves
or a barn owl on a soundless flight
maybe a 'coon thieving poultry
it could be the darkness in someone's heart
a black hole also is dark
with the moon glowing
the night is alive

Kenny Walker, Grade 8
Alpena High School, AR

Leaves

The wind blows and the trees shake with fear.
The water on the pond ripples and sloshes.
The leaves gently sail down to the ground, landing quietly.
The colors are changing, the wind is blowing.
Before you know it, the leaves are…gone.

Josh Burns, Grade 8
West Jr High School, MO

Remember April

Don't ever forget the trembling hand,
that reached out for your touch.
And remember that God looked down at us,
and blessed us from above.
Remember the eyes that looked at you,
and cried for your gentle touch.
Remember the arms that held you,
when life was just, "too much."
Remember the lips that said to you,
the words that were so dear.
And remember the heart that bled for you,
so no longer, would you fear.
But most of all, remember April.
Remember the day we met.
Remember April, our hearts were joined,
on that day I shan't forget.

Tyler Burton, Grade 7
Casey County Middle School, KY

I Will Stand

Look through that window
What do you see?
I'm walking right past
But what you see is not me.

I keep to myself
I don't let them know
That they took away my laughter
And for that I hate them so

I thought I knew them
They were once my friends
But now they have hurt me
My memory of that will never end

So I will try to forget them
I won't look at them once more
I don't need their criticism
I've thrown that out the door

Now many years have come and gone
And as I look upon my past
I realize that they were wrong
And I have won at last

Katie Hetlage, Grade 9
Nerinx Hall High School, MO

The Troubled Boy

He has a good life ahead of him
If only he would try.
He has many friends that love him.
They would hate to see him die.

This boy has many issues.
I know he can work them out.
He could deal with his issues
But he would rather do drugs and pout.

I have seen this boy off drugs
And he is as sweet as can be.
I think I love him when he is off drugs.
But does he love me?

I have seen this boy on drugs
And he is nothing like the boy I knew.
I hate him when he is on drugs.
And I know he hates me too.

Why can he not quit?
I miss the old him.
Why will he not quit?
The light between us is starting to dim.

Mariah Harding, Grade 8
Greenfield Jr/Sr High School, MO

Ode to Pickles

Ode to pickles
how you taste so good.
I love your crispy greenness.
When I see I have
eaten all of you I get upset,
but when mom buys me a new jar
my sorrow goes away.
Oh pickle I just love you.

Allyson Parker, Grade 7
Dyer Elementary & Jr High School, TN

A Winter Day

It's snowing outside
a bright blanket covers the ground
you and friends play in the cold
having snowball fights
while a dog lays in the snow
with no reason to care
you see few birds in the air
mom is calling
you are freezing
when you are warm
you go back to play
you sled down the hill
but fall off on the way
now it's dark outside
and mom says you have to come in

Courtland Trent, Grade 7
Maury Middle School, TN

Just Me

My unique name is Mikaya,
I am a cat owner,
Daughter,
And most important, a cousin.
I am a sleeper at most,
But a night owl at times.
I'm a listener to music
And friends.
But mostly iPods.
A shopaholic as some people
Would call me.
I shop at malls across America
Finding clothes to buy.
Swimming is my passion.
But running is amazing.
I'm a licensed boat driver,
But tubing is my favorite.
Photography is what I do
With time on my hands.
My fingernails are red for now,
But will be different tomorrow.

Mikaya Reynolds, Grade 7
Baylor School, TN

ATV's

One day I was riding my ATV
I got a call from my buddy Kevin
He told me that he was
Stuck in the mud

I went over to Kevin's house
And I got a chain
I hooked it onto our 4 wheeler
And I was slinging mud everywhere

Then we just had fun
For the rest of the day
By racing, riding wheelies
And jumping ramps

Christopher Roberts, Grade 7
Van-Cove High School, AR

Open Book

I am an open book.
I feel that throughout my life
When I looked at the sky
I felt as if
Someone was reading
My life, as if it were
An open book.
I felt as though someone
Was looking down on me.
Now as I look at the sky
All I see is an endless
Blue blanket that covers
The tragedy that once was,
And with this I know my
Life is getting better
Never worse.

Robyn Gentry, Grade 8
Bueker Middle School, MO

A True Gift from God

As the baby was born.
A miracle came true.
A little bundle of joy
All dressed in blue.

A mother filled with happiness.
A father filled with pride.
Realize what life has given them.
A true gift of life.

They look up at God.
Thank Him for such a small being.
For the gift that He sent
Was a teeny tiny ME!!

Blake Polly, Grade 7
Elkton School, TN

Winter's Baby Bunnies

I see some fur in her box
And tell my mom so happily.
Out we go to look and see
What little miracles have come to be.
We bring them inside so no one gets cold.
With mommy and babies,
Everything works out like gold.

Alexis Smallwood, Grade 8
Musselman Middle School, WV

My Utopia

In the darkness of night
I will take flight,
I will soar in the sky
About a mile high.

All of my fears
Will surely disappear,
As I feel the wind in my hair
I know I can do what I want without a care.

My pain turns to pleasure
And I feel joy to an extraordinary measure,
As years of inner pain turn to dust,
As I realize the feelings I feel for people
in my life is love, not lust.

Compassion beyond compare
And judgment equally fair,
My little place in the sky,
Is a utopia, about a mile high.

Dominique Ford, Grade 8
Asher High School, OK

Heaven to Me

Safely tucked in my own special world
I dance and drift in my dreams
On my soft mountain pillows and snug blanket meadow
I hear my alarm clock scream

My sleep comes to a screeching halt
That rude ugly noise must cease
It can't be time to wake up yet
Please let me have some peace

I don't want to leave this wonderful place
This soft sleepy world of my bed
Let me sleep longer under my covers
With my pillows beneath my head

I linger beneath my luxurious quilts
They are like a soothing sea
My mind seems to float on the cloud of my pillow
That feels like heaven to me

Rebecca Payton, Grade 7
White Station Middle School, TN

Crae

His face is so confusing it's hard to tell
Like a strong snail stuck in a shell.
When I look in his eyes, dark like tar,
I get lost in his world so dull.
He is way more than a boy,
A bomb exploding with intelligence,
But still as soft as a whisper.
His hair glides like skates on ice,
His lips in a frown, sharp as a knife.
His eyes have so much to tell
About this tough boy.
His jaw structure is sharp and sour,
This boy, a diamond in the dirt.

Monty Tucker, Grade 8
Lee A Tolbert Community Academy, MO

Strength of an Angel

Shed a tear for the dead.
Hold your loved ones close to you.
Pray for the misled.
Do whatever you have to do,
Let go of the hurt and pain.
Be strong for the ones left behind.
Hope that the fog clears from your brain,
Before you completely lose your mind.
Plant love in a Child's heart.
Don't give up on everyone.
Glue the pieces back that were torn apart,
Before your name is wrote in stone.

Sabrina Kennemer, Grade 8
Mayflower Middle School, AR

Aunt Tina

When I look at her
I see a smooth, fragile girl,
An unknown rose.
I hear braveness and confidence
And want to know more
About her unique style.
The way she walks
Only makes me wonder
Could this be the start
Of a true friendship?
Outgoing, outspoken,
Love and courage, but
What is this taste?
I finally open my mouth
And the fruit that is a mystery
Reveals more.
Finally I know what she's about,
The rose that was unknown
is known.

Jourdan Price-Draper, Grade 7
Lee A Tolbert Community Academy, MO

My Family

You have to love them
Spending time with them
You can have lots of fun with them,
Just talking about a lot of stuff.

We go to lots of places,
Like to the store, at the park,
Vacation is heaven, life is a joy
That angels sing in the night.

Some of us love to draw
And write, however,
My sister Sara is like
A flower blooming around.

Some of us love helping.
Our mom cooks good stuff,
Like pancakes, and muffins.
The kittens love to play around,
Like waves dancing.

We should love each other
By showing them that
We really care about them a whole lot.

Tiffany Malone, Grade 9
St John the Baptist High School, MO

Silly Goose

Silly Goose
Diminutive, goofy
Jesting, mocking, chortling
I'm a rebel
San

Indigo Deberry, Grade 8
Belle Isle Enterprise Middle School, OK

Tiny Tot

When I was just a tiny tot,
I remember I used to talk a lot.

I didn't want to be rude,
But I really hated baby food.

I didn't like goodnight time.
When it was time, I began to whine.

I hated getting my diaper changed.
The smell gave me a burning pain.

Learning to walk was such a breeze
Until the time I fell on my knees.

So now you know lots and lots
About the time when I was a tiny tot.

Taylor Thomas, Grade 7
Dunbar Middle School, AR

A Magical Place

Calm and peaceful on the outside,
Bustling with activity on the inside.
Whish of wind brushing coolly over teal blue ocean,
Awakening the sea creatures deep within its depths.
Sharks rising to the surface waiting to pounce on naive prey.
Glowing sun rising from sleep in clear cerulean ocean to light up our world.
Potent waves crashing against defenseless shore like rabid shark catching its dinner.
Seagulls chirping in early morning
Sand swishing beneath my feet
Tides going in and out like eager sea creatures in a coral reef.
It's not always clear and sunny here.
Dark, stormy, destructive hurricanes also fill this magical place,
Destroying wonderful sights as they lay bewildered, not being able to do anything.
How can a place that fills me with peace, joy, and excitement be this violent?
However, as radiant sun retreats into ocean depths, it signals that better days lie ahead.
What a magical place!

Josh Bynum, Grade 8
Barret Traditional Middle School, KY

A Recipe for a Funny Day

1. Begin with a bag-full of hail the size of cannonballs
2. Then add a jug of raining hot dogs
3. Next stir in a pound of jokes
4. Pour in a bowl-full of pranks
5. Meanwhile add a dash of "would you rather" jokes
6. Mix in an ounce of "yo momma" jokes
7. Fold in a pinch of comedians
8. Next pour in a packet of "hillbillies"
9. Meanwhile add a pound of people dressed up in cow costumes
10. Serve with a bag full of the big shiny piece of the sun cheese wheel

Jordan Richards, Grade 7
Meredith-Dunn School, KY

My Little Treasure

"Read me a story!" he would plead,
I always knew what he wanted me to read.
I picked up his pirate book,
If there were pictures I let him look.
When I came to the part of Black Beard's treasure,
His little blue eyes gleamed with pleasure.
"Mommy," he said. "Do you have gold?"
I said "Sure. Your hair and it isn't old."
"Oh, but Mom," he began. "What about sapphires?"
I replied "Your eyes. They glitter like those of squires."
"Okay. What about rubies?" he asked me,
"Your little lips. They're there for you to drink tea."
"What about pearls? How can you have that?"
"Your smile, my dear. I love it when we chat."
"How is it that you have everything?"
"You're my little treasure. Worth more to me than a diamond ring."
"If I'm your treasure, you must be mine."
And with that he hugged me as if he were hugging a pine.
The next day, I heard him sing,
"I'm Mommy's treasure. You can't buy me. I won't ever go Ka-Ching!"

Sarah E. Johnston, Grade 7
Davis Elementary School, MO

Let the Rain Fall

I have seen the rain fall down
Coming out of the gray, sad clouds
I see the melancholy look of the world
When I see the rain fall down.

I have heard a wonderful saying
How I shouldn't just wait for the storm to pass
But that I should learn to dance in the rain
And take my life and let it live.

I have learned to dance in the rain.
To feel the drops land on my cheeks
To throw my hands up into the air,
And to let my life become truly free.

I have felt the rain on my skin
I get shivers from the chill of the drops
I become soaked and cold through my clothes
Yet I still want to dance in the rain.

Allie Blaylock, Grade 9
West Jr High School, MO

Rabbits

I have many rabbits
But few of them like to play.
All of the others love to hop.
I had another white rabbit
but it ran away.
Anyone should know
that rabbits hate people.
I can't do anything with my rabbits,
each of them have sharp claws.
Everybody screams because the rabbit got away.
Either it will be blue or green.
All of a sudden everything stops even the hops.

Lauren Shular, Grade 8
Pigeon Forge Middle School, TN

Cross Country Day

Bull's Eye, busily prancing in the start box
five, four, three, two. one, GO…
power surging through his body
galloping wildly through woods and fields
flying boldly over obstacles solid as bricks
heart beating heavily
breath coming quickly
snorting in anticipation of the next fence
cantering through the water crossing
finally the finish flags
the announcer calls, "clear round"
Cross Country phase
Success!

Hannah Gallagher, Grade 8
St Paul the Apostle School, TN

Blinded

He better ask me before it's too late.
He better ask before I close opportunity's gate.

His mixed signals are confusing me.
If only he knew he held the key.

Why can't he see that to me he is everything?
Am I so blinded that it's all a misunderstanding?

He moves farther and farther from that gate,
Every time he makes me wait.

If he ever reads this poem, I hope he understands,
That all along I was in his hands.

Maegan Dilks, Grade 8
Owasso 8th Grade Center, OK

Virginia Creeper

I am seven, moving through the boulders,
unmindful of thorns and ants,
I move onto the ledge.
I am shivering in the cold weather.
I have my Swiss Army knife
to cut away the plants that impede my amble.
The trees are as tall as a ten story building.
No climbing down the edge of the hundred-foot drop.
I am very close to slipping and dying.
I am seven; I will throw rocks for you if you look away.
No looking back.
I wonder why dogs wag their tails.
There are birds up here that are as big as a cinderblock
and as dark as the night.
I wonder what fear tastes like?
My mama says no exploring near the crag.

James Morgan, Grade 8
Baylor School, TN

Stress

I'm too stressed out to really think about
The work I have to do. There is no way I'll get through.

Where's that meeting at? I have practice after that.
Then off to church I go. Why is she driving so slow?

Homework comes next. My parents are vexed.
That I barely have time to even make this rhyme.

My head might burst! What should I do first?
I have so much to do. I forgot to call Lou.

I don't have extra time that I can call mine.
To relax in a chair and let down my hair.

I would go crazy but I'm already here.

Rachel Witherspoon, Grade 8
West Middle School, TN

Essence of Fall

Breeze
Chilly, shiver
Rustling, shaking, shifting
Laughter, silence, speaking, breathing
Growing, slowing, hushing
Calm, quiet
Stillness

Jay Vance, Grade 8
Musselman Middle School, WV

Era Past

Crystal reflections dance,
inside the painted glass,
I've seen you here before.

Same expression,
same depression.

We have had our differences;
we have had our similarities.
Children of the same era,
both looking for the answers
to the questions we forgot to ask.

Eyes that burn like flames,
words that slash like daggers.
Your love has not been kind…
but then again dearest,
neither have I.

Kiss me as you did in years past,
let your kiss trickle past my waiting lips.
Show me the pain,
show me the anger,
and I will show you my world.

Elizabeth Cantwell, Grade 8
Asher Middle/High School, OK

Good-bye

I remember you said forever.
Oh, what a lie!
Oh, how often you said that
Almost all the time.
Why did I believe you?
Such a fool am I.
I trusted you, believed in you,
Why must that be a crime?
Why did you say such beautiful things?
They always made me cry.
Now there's nothing left of you.
This is where I sigh.
I really believed you
Until you said
Good-bye.

Miranda Basco, Grade 8
Musselman Middle School, WV

What Do They See?

When people look at me what do they see?
Do they see honesty? Do they see courtesy?
When people look at me what do they see?
Do they see a straight "A" student? Do they see someone different?

When I look at me what do I see?
I see someone strong. I see someone that won't give up for long.
When I look at me what do I see?
I see an open book. I see a unique look.

When people look at you what do they see?
Do they see a "Covergirl" do they see the girl next door?
When God looks at you what does He see?
You hope He sees many possibilities.

God may see the things no one else sees.
A heart of gold, or a heart in the cold?

Tammy Knapp, Grade 8
Greeneville Middle School, TN

Loving Hands

You never know how
Special hands are until
Someone passes away.
The things that comfort you
The most a hug, a kiss, or a hand.
A hand to pull you out of the dark night
and into the morning light.
That was how I felt when my great grandma died.
I was stuck in the dark and did not know where to turn.
But then someone reached for me and lent me a loving hand.
That person pulled me out of the dark and into the light.
Next time someone is in that dark place I am going to reach down
And pull them out like they did to me.

Lexie Hatfield, Grade 7
St Mary of the Woods School, KY

Mystifying

You mystify me, ocean
You give throaty growls at night
You have raging winds whipping the sand like it has done wrong
In the morning, you give sun shining smiles
At night, you keep us at bay
Warning us that danger is beneath your dark beautiful waters
But at day you invite us to your waters
But why?
Why at night you tell us to beware of your monstrous waves,
Then at day you tell us to come and play?
Are you forever changing like a butterfly?
Are you more dangerous at night than at day?
But why?
You mystify me, ocean

Darian Wright, Grade 8
Barret Traditional Middle School, KY

Together

One night your eyes met mine. I saw them sparkle like the stars in the sky. I took your hand in mine and goosebumps shivered down my spine. When the silence approached, only soft rustling of air through the leaves, and the crickets chirp could only be heard. We sat there a few minutes and lay in the grass. The soft touch of your arm against mine. Our hands are still clasped together like it was meant to be forever. Finally we talk, but I can hardly pay attention, while looking at your angelic face. All of a sudden from out of the middle of nowhere, your lips touched mine. I blush with eyes still open, but they slowly fall. We break away our hands still together. We don't budge at any given moment. I knew this was meant to be. Oh, how I wished this day to come, when we would kiss, and we would be together forever. Like our hands still together, forever, and ever.

Jordan Crislip, Grade 9
Buckhannon-Upshur High School, WV

Respect

T eachers have a very hard job because,
E ach teacher has to be friendly each day.
A nd it is very hard to be nice having 80 students each day.
C aring is a hard character trait because you have to like people or care for them.
H aving to deal with mean kids is another thing teachers have to deal with.
E veryone has bad and good days but teachers have to change a bad day into a good day.
R espect is a character trait you should show toward teachers.
S tudents should always respect teachers every day.

Elaina Hester, Grade 7
Greenfield Jr/Sr High School, MO

The Night After

When the wind rustles through golden leaves and the mockingbird sings its siren hymn, under the willow reaching with groaning arms outstretched with tears, I shall lay my head and wait.
Silently waiting and watching for enchanted visions and dreams.
Visions of dusty feet and untrodden ways, scarlet hopes and dreams, ashen vessels and crystal tides, of revived reminiscent longings, of romances dancing on faerie wings and songs of elven lords.
My head shall rest in the arms of the willow, of the lonely crying willow, in the breast of the mourning willow I shall lay my head and sleep.

Lily Coleman, Grade 9
Home School, OK

Aria

The old
Radio chirps
Out cheerful jingles
As the tall glasses clink,
Bells performing with the band.
The star on the tree dazzles all who behold it,
Boastfully bringing the multicolored lights to wink.
The presents under the boughs cry out to the squirming children,
"Open me now! I'm exactly what you wrote to jolly Santa Claus for!"
Electric excitement swims in the air, for the party has just commenced,
When all of a sudden, a voice tolls, and the twelfth chime of the
Antique grandfather clock has dictated its final pronouncement, declaring the night over.
I guess that the wheel of time will never stop for me; life's music will never slow down.
But the bliss
Of the season
Will resonate
In my eardrums
Until next Christmas.

Megan Lee, Grade 7
White Station Middle School, TN

My Dreams

Into the meadow
Far from the trees
Under no shade
But covered by leaves

Inside I feel happiness
While among the beautiful wind
A flowing stream of hope
Dances around my skin

Some would call this under minded
But for those that stand beside me
You'll never make it to my place
For this is only in *my* dreams

Carla O'Neal, Grade 8
Heritage Middle School, TN

Grandma

Girl's nights are fun
Homemade food is good
Holidays with family
Sad phone call
Everyone crying
Long days at funeral home boring
Funeral very sad
Family missing Grandma.

Jamie Mattingly, Grade 7
St Mary of the Woods School, KY

When Good Times Go Griffin

A show about family,
A show about dreams,
But this show is ridiculed,
By most public it seems.

Turning one hundred,
Most celebrities probably regret,
That it became this old,
But it will make fun of them yet!

Brian becomes a director,
Peter Griffin as a cop,
Despite all this time,
The insane ideas do not stop

To come from this creator,
This somewhat twisted man.
So, the shows will keep on coming,
He will continue with this plan

Of this crazy Rhode Island family,
And the other weird civilians.
Well, this show may continue forever
Just to mess with the minds of millions!

Britton Black, Grade 8
Greenfield Jr/Sr High School, MO

I am Me

Brianna
Spunky, thoughtful, out-spoken, and loyal
Little sister of Jesse and Danny
Lover of animals, music, creativity, and expression
Who feels like she needs to dance, run, play and create art
Who needs food, free-time, open space, and electronics
Who gives her all, 100% of her heart, and her opinion (even when it isn't asked for)
Who fears the future, pain, and for her loved ones
Who would LOVE to see her favorite band play in concert
Who shares advice, secrets, and her thoughts
Who lives in a state she really doesn't want to live in
Grotts

Brianna Grotts, Grade 8
Montgomery Central Middle School, TN

Missing It All

Sitting, waiting, patiently still
For what they do not know. It will come, he said it would come!
But what they do not know.

Pacing, waiting, impatiently still
For when they do not know. Time is short, it passes them by
When will it ever come?

Sitting, waiting, wondering still
If it would ever come. The old have died, the young have grown
Will it ever come?

Jumping, shouting, angrily still
Why hasn't it ever come? Is it real? Of course it's not real!
That's why it hasn't come!

Racing, playing, happily still
Who cares if it ever comes? Don't bother about that, live life for today!
Who cares if it ever comes?

Flying ever closer still
Look! It has finally come! But nobody sees, so absorbed in their play
And quietly, it passes them by.

Lydia Adams, Grade 9
Bearden High School, TN

Eleven at Night

The hour that things begin to go bump.
The last hour of the day.
The hour that people start filling bars and clubs.
The hour when many people are sleeping.

The chirping of insects disturbs your rest along with the buzzing of the television.
You bury your ears in your pillow to block out the sound.
The covers smell like fabric softener as you toss and turn in them.
You look up at the clock and see that it's the 11 o'clock hour.
The brightness of the television screen makes you squint as it stands in the darkness.
The 11 o'clock hour is the hour of restlessness.

Raticia Manae' Curtis, Grade 9
West Jr High School, MO

My Power My Voice

Outpowered and outspoken
Kicked to the ground like a worthless token
Wondering, were you ever really here
Will you still keep your promise
When your end comes near
A victim of misfortune
My shoulders are burdened
To escape these chains
For my cause to be furthered
I will fight to the end
No matter what the pain
Until my power and voice
are heard again.

Selma Dedovic, Grade 8
Pleasant View School, TN

Ebone

Silky chocolate-skinned
With glistening brown eyes,
Fluffy hair with a flowery ribbon,
Heart diamond earrings,
Colorful shoes with peace and warning signs,
Crispy bright talk
Against dull school uniforms,
Faded Beatles jacket,
Heart of a goddess,
Loud with laughter
And the fragrance of a baby
Right after a bath.

Christian Ruckers, Grade 7
Lee A Tolbert Community Academy, MO

She Puts Me to Sleep

As a waterfall rushing down a mountain slope
So did my tears once forever flow
I twitch and turn
I cannot sleep
Suddenly a gentle touch
A hug, a kiss, a most tender embrace
She rubs her soft cheek against my face
She is my mother
A little click and a clang, a rattle of keys
She drives me around, my restlessness begins to ease
As the wind through the window breathes across my face
I hear the voice of an angel
It is a lullaby to my ears
Where are all my fears?
They have vanished away
I am falling asleep
A soft fuzzy blanket is laid upon me
A sweet still voice whispers its love unto me
My mother has delicately tucked me into my bed
Complaining or fussing, none of these does she do
She only says, it's my mother's love to you

Olivia Grappe, Grade 9
Hamburg Jr High School, AR

Tell Me

What would I do without you?
I wouldn't last a second without you here.
Tell me what I would be like if you weren't in my heart.
Tell me if I'm going to wake up in the morning and be happy.
Tell me that you love me.
Tell me that I'm yours.
I need you with me more than ever.
God, just come into my heart.
I'm a sinner, and you know it.
Come into my heart, God, and cleanse me white as snow.
Thank you for dying on the cross for my sins.
Now tell me that I'm yours.

Lauren Roberts, Grade 8
Family of Faith Christian School, OK

Finding a Path

Taking this road
Just not sure if it's right.
Figured I'd go for it
So I guess as of now I'm all right.
Taking a detour,
The signs seem to no longer be here.
Where do I go?
It seems I'll never know.
I can't just turn back now because the road has disappeared.
I find this lost path
With vines grown up high
Where does it go?
I guess soon I'll know.
First when you'd see it you wouldn't want to enter,
But once inside,
I soon realize
That this inside is much different from the out.
I can see a crack in the road
Where it seems to have just fallen apart
The more I think about it,
I realize this must be our hearts.

Melody Watson, Grade 8
Musselman Middle School, WV

All About Me

Madison
Sweet, smart, caring, loving
Daughter of Howard and Marla Brown
Lover of cats, food, and skateboarding
Who feels mad, happy, upset
Who gives sympathy, care, respect
Who needs a car, a camera, a computer
Who fears hospitals, the ocean, boats
Would like to see Orlando Bloom, Hollywood, Hawaii
Who lives in Tennessee, in a house, Montgomery county area
Brown

Madison Brown, Grade 8
Montgomery Central Middle School, TN

Red

There once was a girl named Red,
Sometimes she didn't use her head.
She never came in last,
She was very fast.
And she always wrote with lead.

Heather Cagle, Grade 7
Rocky Comfort Elementary School, MO

Day at the Pool

At the pool
On the diving board
Into the water
Across the pool
Through the crowd
To the concession stand
By the tables
Under the umbrellas
In the shade
Among the fun

Chelsey Buchanan, Grade 8
Heritage Middle School, TN

Not All on the Paper Yet

I draw.
The pencil soars.
My imagination ignites.
The paint roars.

Curves, shadows, textures, lines
glittering like a thousand mines
beckoning towards the world of art.
I gravitate to it.
I can't resist.

I'm mad, I'm angry, full of indignation
I draw until the point of satiation.
I have homework, I have chores,
but all those will have to wait
for I'm not done, no, not at all —
it's not all on the paper yet.

Daphne McKee, Grade 7
White Station Middle School, TN

Love

Between these walls,
Of inside and out.
Under the stars,
Near the ocean.
Across the beach,
After it turned dark.
In your arms,
Around me so.
During this time,
For I feel LOVE.

Rachel Hurst, Grade 8
Heritage Middle School, TN

I Am Thankful

I am thankful for my dogs,
For some people never have a loving companion
I am thankful for my friends,
For some people don't have someone to lift their spirits
I am thankful for my family,
For some people never have a family to help them in tough times
I am thankful for my cats,
For some people never have a cuddly cat to hold and love.
I am thankful for my sight,
For some people live in the darkness never to see the light of day.
I am thankful for my sense of taste,
For most people would never be able to taste the wonderful flavors of food.

Samantha Allen, Grade 8
Avenue City Elementary School, MO

Basketball

Basketball is my favorite sport.
I like to push myself to hustle down the court,
I love to shot fake and go to the hole.
I like to go between legs, behind the back, and even earl the pearl.
I love the feel of victory after a win,
But I still push myself and hustle if we're down by ten.
I'm a guard on big O.
I'm not a ball hog because I know,
We are a team and we work together.
We all depend on each other,
We are all just links in a basketball chain.
If we work hard and play the game our best,
We will eventually have our claim to fame and soar above the rest.

Amira Squirrel, Grade 8
Ketchum Jr High School, OK

Two Enemies

You laugh at my frustration, I grimace in disgust
At the feeling I get when you look at me
Or even someone else;
I grin at the pain that goes through your body
You smile as I stumble to reach my goal and then fail to reach it at all:
I smirk as you screech from the pain that the guiltiness causes
As it gnaws away at your stomach;
We enjoy each other in pain, and yet,
I love to see you happy; you hate to see me cry;
I hate to see you hurt; you love to see me laugh;
I love it when you smile and you hate it when I'm sad;
We, two enemies, yet friends,
Each an antagonist to the other, but the missing piece to the other's puzzle,
The other's heart;
We hate, yet love each other;
We are not friends, but nor are we enemies;
Not children with crushes, not just teens caught up in lust,
But adults in love maybe;
Whatever it may be we are definitely not just two enemies.

Kaelyn Bittinger, Grade 8
Mayflower Middle School, AR

Personality

Some are sporty, some are prissy
For I tell you, everyone has a personality
Don't hide or be shy, but let it shine
For you are one of a kind
You are special if you're being you
So go out there and show the real you
A true friend is someone
Who loves you for who you are
So show them the things you like to do
Don't be a copy — just be you
For I tell you, you are certainly one of a kind
A star that shines bright

Paris Anderson, Grade 7
Family of Faith Christian School, OK

Princess

Her smile as bright as the morning sun,
She breathes in cool damp air from the November air,
And starts her climb up the long leaf-covered road,
Where a man awaits her arrival,
Whistling a tune to hide his nerves,
She sings songs of sweet summertime,
That she longs to return.
He begins to shake at the beauty of the girl,
When they finally meet,
There is an awkward but loving silence,
The nervous man tells her she is a beautiful princess,
And deserves a king.
They ride off into the crisp cool fall night
In each others arms.

Garrett Andrews, Grade 7
Nettleton Jr High School, AR

Ski Trip

It was just my dad and me.
Father and son
on a trip to go ski.

Getting ready for our vacation,
working without a care.
Driving to the Rockies is quite a sensation.

After ten hours, we are finally there.
It is frightfully cold.
The wind flies through our hair.

"Stay close," I was told,
as we purchased our skis
from the place they are sold.

Walking outside the wind made me sneeze.
Then it started to snow and my nose did freeze!

Jared Gowan, Grade 7
Center Place Restoration School, MO

Peace

Water splashes along the beach
Silence fills the air, not a sound is heard
The sun sets
The people sleep

Birds don't sing, light goes out
You hear the waves as they crash on the beach
Sunrise comes, you take a walk
Let the waves cover your feet

There are so many emotions
You can use to describe this feeling
But only one can truly say what this feeling is
You can make a list, but none can compare to this feeling

The feeling of being the one that we all want
But have trouble
You never know if it's there, you sometimes don't realize it
Sometimes it's right in front of you, but you never see it

Sometimes we need a little bit of faith
And a whole lot of hope
To make it through the days
We all need peace

Rebecca Goldman, Grade 7
Meredith-Dunn School, KY

Aaron

"Bye,"
We all shout as he walks to the gate.
"No Aaron!" I shout
This will be great!
No drumming
Or loud TVs
Or any distractions,
Just me.
Me and my mom and dad together.
Yet, why are they all so sad, I wonder?
Mommy's crying,
Daddy's sighing,
I'm just fine,
Until I realize how empty his room is,
I then remember that I am now the only child.
But, a lonely one at that
At least until semester break.

Rachel Glazer, Grade 7
White Station Middle School, TN

The River

The river carries the fish over herself
It flows from a lazy trickle to a rapid rush
She slowly drags the sly rocks over the river bed
The river fills up the deer that drink from it
It dreams to someday end in the ocean

Kevin Linn, Grade 9
St Charles Homeschool Learning Center, MO

Snow Days

Snow days
Are so fun
Get out of school
Start a snowball fight
Play ice hockey all day long
Watch movies all night
Get some hot cocoa
With something to munch on
I just hope
We don't have a ten car pile-on

Grayson Inman, Grade 7
Maury Middle School, TN

Contrast

At home,
calm, relaxed, quiet,
the boss,
living good,
the man!

Outside,
small, alone inferior
isolated,
search for help,
a bug.

Devon Hamline, Grade 8
Leeton Middle and High School, MO

Disease

Disease spreads like a forest fire
Eating things up uncontrollably
Devouring everything it its path
Passing so easily between its victims
Leaving everything destroyed
Having to start from scratch
Causing hardships
Uncaring

Cameron Solomon, Grade 8
West Jr High School, MO

Fords Rule

One of the first on the road,
Ford trucks can carry heavy loads,
Not only can it get up and go.
It can really tow.
Chevy's are fine, but fords blow my mind.

Fords are sill the best
Even faster than the rest.
go get you a Chevy,
Try beating us to the levy.
Go Fords

Ely Woosley, Grade 8
Chelsea Jr High School, OK

Fear

It is like a distant dream
that haunts unheard souls.
It's the foggy silence
that praises the scarlet war.
When faraway noises ring
it causes panic and dread.
It's like a free fall into oblivion:
the dark abyss of the unknown.

Sammie Pazera, Grade 8
Baylor School, TN

My Lord

You knew me before I was born,
The closer I bring others to You,
The less I feel torn.
Some out there have no clue,
Others just don't care,
And choose not to be with You.
I will always know You are there.
We are together down here,
But soon I won't breathe this air.
When we are in the same place,
We will be a lot closer together,
And I will finally see Your face.

Tyler Wilson, Grade 7
Wainwright Elementary School, OK

Winter Wonderland

Little critters scurry to and fro
Hiding before Winter's snow
In their homes they nest
Until Spring they will rest

The clouds gather in the sky
And soon they will start to cry
Rain soon turns to snow
Burying all the land below

A white blanket covers the ground
Without ever making a sound
The work of God's hand
Creates the Winter Wonderland

Cassie Frailey, Grade 8
Chelsea Jr High School, OK

Far Away

Will she come home,
My cousin I love?
I want her to be safe
And remember we're always here.
I'll be strong and won't shed a tear,
As long as you remember I'm still here.

Rachel DeGrave, Grade 8
Musselman Middle School, WV

It Was a September Morning

We wake up to a sunny day,
Not a cloud up in the sky,
But then it starts to rain.

Our defenses it the ground,
And they shatter all around,
So exposed and destroyed.
We wonder why 19?
Why any at all???
What did we do to deserve this fall??

2,975 Americans found dead,
24 American not found at all!
So what did we do to deserve this fall?

But now we fight a war,
We're not sure what we're fighting for.
3,774 American soldiers dead,
For a crime not yet fed.

They fight for America,
For the people who died that day.
But now we have more and more
People dying every day…

Ciera Wheeler, Grade 8
Benton County School of the Arts, AR

Untold

I stand alone
In a forest of golden
autumn trees,
not seen nor heard.

Seasons change
they grow,
seasons change
I remain untold.

I haven't the courage
to take a stand,
but one day I will
and I will not bend.

Seasons change
they grow,
seasons change
I remain untold.

Through the window of my life
I remain stunted,
but soon, oh very soon,
I too will grow.

Christy Thomas, Grade 8
Gresham Middle School, TN

Charlsie Morrison

Charlsie
Attitude, preppy, speak for myself, I could be your best friend
Sister of Gracie Claire
Lover of golfing, dancing, movies, and music
Who feels excited, loved, and ready to go home
Who needs help, true best friend, and a role model
Who fears, planes, mean teachers, and storms
I would like to see ocean floor, sun, a good boyfriend
Who lives in Clarksville, TN.
Morrison

Charlsie Morrison, Grade 8
Montgomery Central Middle School, TN

Hippopotamus

H uge enormous animals
I ntelligent cool creatures
P owerful strong mammals
P lant eaters
O n some occasions they are called Hippos
P atient and slow
O ddly colored
T hey have very thick skin
A quatic and awesome
M outh is very large
U sually see them at the zoo
S hort legged

McKenzi Divine, Grade 7
Hartville Jr/Sr High School, MO

White Flag

There's a battle goin' on
And my heart's bruised really bad,
Took place on my front lawn,
Biggest argument I ever had.

I give up, don't wanna die.
I give up, don't wanna try.
I give up. I give up.
Make the White Flag fly!

Don't want anyone to be sad.
This is all my fault.
Don't want anyone to be mad.
I spat out those words without a thought.

I surrender. I give up.
It's something I have to stop.
I surrender, don't want to die.
Rifles up, and make the White Flag fly!

This battle's now over, way done.
I've learned my lesson today.
Being in trouble isn't any fun.
So just watch and think about what you say.

Nathan Eaton, Grade 8
Christ at Home Lutheran School, MO

Halloween

Everybody likes to wear costumes,
it's fun to be somebody else.
You can be scary or funny or dress fashionably,
it all depends on your mood.

Because I can't wear a scary costume in school,
I think I will wear something funny.
It is much more fun to be scary,
but if I scare the little kids that's not fun.

I can hardly wait to get home,
because I will go out with my friends.
We run around and get candy,
when the door opens we shout "trick or treat!"

I hope your Halloween is as good as mine.

Kyle Collier, Grade 7
St Joseph Institute for the Deaf, MO

Do You Wonder

Do you ever wonder what the future will be like?
Will we have the same cars?
Will people live on Mars?
Are pigs ever gonna fly?
Are people still gonna lie?

Do you ever wonder what the future will be like?
Will we find alternative fuel?
Will upperclassmen always be so cruel?
Are UFOs gonna become IFOs?
Are BFFs gonna really be forever?

Do you ever wonder what the future will be like?
Will the grass be greener?
Will people be meaner?
What kind of music will they play?
What will be their typical day?

Do you ever wonder what the future will be like?
Don't you think to know would be fun?
Or am I the only one?

Jaclyn Richardson, Grade 9
Southern Boone High School, MO

One with Fire

Someone once told me to stay away from fire.
But nothing could stop me both no one nothing
few things could change my mind.
Something with fire is my desire.
Everybody is afraid of fire, I don't know why.
Much of my desire is fire.
Anything with fire. One with fire.

Matthew Smith, Grade 8
Pigeon Forge Middle School, TN

Thank You

Our hands are so small,
Our feet are too slow
And our favorite word
will always be "no."

We love to get into things,
We hate to eat our veggies,
But we will always love the
way that mommy sings.

Sometimes we annoy you,
Sometimes we're difficult,
But all the time,
we love you!

So thank you for being here,
thank you for being there,
thank you for supporting us
— year after year.

Sierra Peak, Grade 8
Owasso 8th Grade Center, OK

Autumn

Autumn
Cozy, warm
Sleeping, sitting, reading
Relaxed, scents, feeling, seasons
Running, smelling, playing
Breezy, bright
Spring

Blake Hutcheon, Grade 8
Musselman Middle School, WV

Horses with Wings

I hear a stomping,
Oh so loud.
And feel the ground, shaking.
I taste the breeze,
When she flies by,
As I watch them appear.
They are beautiful,
With flowing manes.
These horses with wings
Which they use to soar
Over valleys,
Through the mountains,
Coming ever closer.
I see the lovely patterns
Painted on their skin:
Black, white, blue, gray.
Then I feel the sun
Shining on my face,
As I stand,
Stunned by their beauty and power.

Jesse Campbell, Grade 7
White Station Middle School, TN

Rush

Adrenaline is a rush like blood gushing.
It is the split second at the top of a roller coaster,
when you know your fate is waiting for you two-hundred feet below.
In some ways, it is a surge of power,
in some ways, it is fear of what lies ahead.
Some people are addicted to adrenaline,
some fear it.
It feels like your plane takes off at one hundred-fifty miles per hour.
Adrenaline is falling out of that plane,
but you do have the comfort that when you reach land,
your parachute will have opened, hopefully.
It is raining, and your car slides around a turn.
You start to swerve,
but the car catches itself in the last second.
In the last second you feel a spike of adrenaline.
Adrenaline meets the demands of the top of a roller coaster or free falling.

Sarah Gillman, Grade 8
Baylor School, TN

Timeless Agony

New York city was as alive as ever
When a plane swept overhead in the sky
Screams erupted as the plane crashed
A great fireball spewing flames
Then another plane crashed into the Twin Tower; splintering the glass and walls
Sirens screamed ripping away the silence as people sprinted away
Moaning silently in grief
Firefighters swarmed into the buildings trying to save whoever they could
Office workers threw themselves out the windows of the 40th story and higher
Flailing as if in regret as they fell to their death
The area is clearing as torrents of tears rush down faces
While cracks appear in the Twin Towers
Most are crushed beneath the rubble
Everyone is covered in dust, gravel, and debris
Reports of a plane hitting the Pentagon, leaving it smoldering crackle in on the radio
Then, the first battle against terrorism is won
Passengers crash land the plane in a field, sacrificing their lives for others
Prayers echo in everyone's heads
Time will only heal this monumental disaster and hearts of family and friends
Life must go on, but we must never forget
September 11th

Ty Griggs, Grade 8
West Jr High School, MO

Death

People are afraid of death, but you ask me it is just another phase of life.
You live, you die people get afraid, but God will be at the end.
When you leave this wretched life, you will be in the promise land.
You will dance and rejoice in Heaven.
You will be with the one you love at death and then in the new beginning.
What God says is don't be afraid when you come into the promise land.
You will rejoice in His glory.
Death is just another word for after life, so while you are still living,
Make life the way you want it and don't be afraid of death.

David Eugene Starliper, Grade 9
Vicki Douglas School, WV

Curious Cat

When my cat was small,
He walked down the hall.
At the end was a vent
Which caused him much torment.

He was just too curious.
It made my family furious.
He smelled and sniffed that little vent,
And he fell right "ent."

Then his high pitched little voice
Made a very loud "meoice!"
And when we finally got him out
He was no more curious but had a big old pout!

Keeley Dority, Grade 7
Dunbar Middle School, AR

Fear Not

Fear not the never ending sleep,
For we find comfort in the thought.
Fear not the caressing darkness,
For it cradles us with care.
Fear not the Gates of St. Peter,
For eternal bliss awaits.
Fear not the loss of loved ones,
For you shall meet again.
Fear not the leaving of Earth,
For it is just a shedding of skin.
Fear not the saying of farewells,
For it is just a way of saying hello before you meet.
Fear not the journey that lies ahead,
For you will see a reward, soon.
Fear not death,
For it is a blessing in disguise.

Samantha Comer, Grade 8
Southside Middle School, AR

Spring Day

The flowers grow wide
The babies are here
I see the ocean tide
The waves I can hear

The sights are amazing
The smell of honey
The fire not blazing
No need for money

Under the trees, baskets of apples lay
No need for fear
Children are waiting to get to the roller coasters to ride
Summer is near.

BriAnne Clines, Grade 8
Benton County School of the Arts, AR

Concert

The adrenaline of my blood rushing.
The sweet sound of drums banging.
The shrills and thrills of the fans screaming.
The amazing electric guitar solo.
The best time of your life…
PRICELESS!!

Savannah Rickman, Grade 8
Rocky Comfort Elementary School, MO

Let's Go Play

What shall we play
I really like to play sports
My favorite sport is baseball
So go and get your bat ball and glove
Let's practice first
Then we can go and play it
We can go and play three strikes you're out

Riley McCown, Grade 7
Highland Rim School, TN

Butterfly

What soars through the air without a care,
With ease, beauty, and peace?
Lucky and wonderful is the butterfly.
The beauty of a butterfly can catch
Even the meanest man's eye.
So kind and beautiful is the butterfly,
With love and care without any strife,
The butterfly is a wonderful creature
Which nearly everyone loves.
So loving and gentle is the butterfly.

Joe K., Grade 9
Audubon School, KY

Chocolate Divine

Chocolate, chocolate a woman's quick fix
It's the big hand on the clock that
Speeds up the clock's ticks.
It's an edible soul
It's therapy on the go.
It's an edible heart, a sense to show love.
Chocolate melts in your mouth
It takes the debt out of doubt.
It's the one part of heaven that you can eat.
Chocolate keeps you moving and on both two feet.
It's the perfect conclusion and
Makes the perfect Valentine's
You're sucked into every moment and every savored bite,
Chocolate stays simple and makes life feel good.
Even on a bad day, in a bad mood
Chocolate is magic; it glows on your tongue.
Chocolate doesn't age and keeps us looking young.
Take a piece of chocolate and you will find
Chocolate is fine, chocolate's divine.

Jade Little, Grade 8
Belle Isle Enterprise Middle School, OK

This Is Me

Tanner Hulse is my name.
I am a boy
Who is nice and outgoing.
I am a baseball player
Who will do anything
To stop the ball.
A basketball player
Who dreams of making the shot.
I am an athlete
That has played every sport.
I am a teenager who is funny.
I am a student who will do anything
For good grades.
I am a son
Who makes his parents very proud.
I am a leader that will do anything
For my team to win.
I am a believer
That does everything I can
To make the best of life.
I am me!

Tanner Hulse, Grade 7
Baylor School, TN

Fall

When the weather gets cold
and the leaves start to fall,
All you want to do
is stay behind your walls.

The holidays are coming
they are very near.
There's the one about turkey
and the one about fear.

The bees stop buzzing,
the noises go away
and all that is left
are clouds that are gray.

The world seems asleep
but that's not the truth
though it doesn't seem it,
it's as excited as you.

Deanna Baggett, Grade 7
Nettleton Jr High School, AR

Love

Love is a rose lit with fire
ever burning in our souls.
Changing with every day of life
drifting from the broken soul left behind
Wilting as one more dies
being left behind.

Geneva Crouse, Grade 7
Mountain Pine High School, AR

Go Back

I had been watching from afar
observing the different moves and tricks.
I tried to memorize plays like I would study for a test.
My new Nikes sank into the freshly laid sod.
Coach pointed left and I took off to meet my new soccer team.
I fought for the ball, but it passed my small, unskilled feet.
I turned to try to claim it back, but a girl wouldn't let me past her.
"You don't belong on the soccer field. Go back," she ordered me.
I shuffled my feet towards the playground like they were cement blocks.
Suddenly I was the only person in the world
and I felt so small.

Sara Stockett, Grade 7
Baylor School, TN

David*

I don't care what day of the week it's on it will always be on a Monday
That Monday when my feelings drowned to some secret safer place
To be looked at and remembered many years later
But even with time those memories still have an edge
I still suffer when they appear
I go through agonizing pain with every detail
Every detail about that night is still etched in my brain
And as well as those from many weeks later
But even though the pain's still there I find comfort knowing
That my pain means something special
That for my pain my loved one hasn't lived in vain
That he is somewhere up above watching all those that he loved

Katelyn Maley, Grade 8
Avenue City Elementary School, MO
**In loving memory of David Allen Maley*

God's Wonderful World

In this beautiful world we have today, I see many things
I see the tall grass swaying back and forth in the breeze,
The bright yellow sun that is a giant flashlight on the Earth,
And the pleasant flowers standing tall and proud like any soldier

I hear the water creeping and flowing down a river
And the birds chirping and singing as beautiful as angels

I taste the juicy apples in my mouth that are as sweet as candy,
And the refreshing water that tingles my mouth as I swish it back and forth

I smell the fresh cut grass aroma swaying through the air,
The salty air of a peaceful beach, and the sweet, sweet smell of honeysuckle

In this beautiful world we have today
I feel the ruff bark of a round tree that is a road of rocks,
The dancing wind blowing through my clothes and hair,
And I feel the sun's warmth heating up my body

All these things race through my mind and tell me that God is always there

Alyssa Vechiarella, Grade 7
Our Lady Catholic School, MO

My Life

I live as if a ghost followed me
as if I rode a horse through the grass
I live as if the clouds hid the sun
and peak from behind the mountains…
I live as if today was the last day on Earth.

Blanca Saucedo, Grade 8
Belle Isle Enterprise Middle School, OK

How Long Will This Last?

Groaning in terror
The tree rocks
Like a seasick sailor
Aboard black waves.
At the base of the tree
A sweaty man in an orange vest
Hacks a rhythm with an ax.
Insatiable,
The ax is a tiger.
With each strike, strength and life
Bleed out of the helpless giant.
Trees dedicate their lives offering humans
Oxygen,
Shade,
Beauty
We throw it away
Building roads and houses.
Humans unravel the trees' lives
Leaving a scar on the future of the Earth.

Alice Jones, Grade 7
Baylor School, TN

Imagination

Pine cones falling all around,
their explosions shaking the earth.
Now they are just ignored.

The rapid fire guns take out invisible forces,
the racket piercing the quiet morning.
Sticks have lost their use as weapons.

Secret codes and hand signals meant everything
to become victorious
But all are forgotten.

Special powers:
invulnerability, invisibility, super bullets.
The imagination is not what it was.

Running inside to eat
as we make a treaty,
will never happen again.

Battles had been won
but the war was never over.

Ben Pintel, Grade 9
West Jr High School, MO

Middle School

It's the hardest part of our lives
An adult can never understand
I feel happy when I'm sad and sad when I'm happy
I don't understand it

7th better than 6th but 8th better than 7th
We can't all be equal, of course

The cliques
The drama
It's a vicious never ending cycle
But…after it's all done and you have moved on in your life
You would never give up middle school

Paiten Kelly, Grade 7
Hazelwood Northwest Middle School, MO

Hot House

A death in our family,
The air conditioner has expired,
In the middle of sweaty, sticky, August,
Sleeping in the basement gives no relief.

Lying awake in the motionless, steamy air,
Thinking of cool sheets and early summer breezes,
Ice cold drinks and diving in the swimming pool,
And the soon to come fall winds.

The a/c vent pours life into us,
The gust of cold air on your skin,
Without it, we melt in our own house,
Wishing we could shiver again.

Trapped in the basement, sweat trickles down,
Cold water turns warm in the glass,
Outside or inside we suffer the same,
Couldn't we just move into the car?

Keifer Diamond, Grade 9
West Jr High School, MO

Remembering

I can remember you
Even if you don't remember me
I can still see your face
Even if your eyes can't see mine
I still hear your laugh
Even though mine is now faded in your ear
I still smell your aroma
Even though you can't sniff mine
Your hugs I still hold
Even though my hugs have drifted away from you
Remembering you makes me smile, so much
Will you remember me?

Lauren Phillips, Grade 9
Family of Faith Christian School, OK

Imagination

Above the world
Out of sight
Among all my dreams
Across the seas
Through the rain
Among all my dreams
Below the deepest seas
Above the tallest mountains
Among all my dreams
In the sun
Between reality
In my imagination

Erin Hackney, Grade 8
Heritage Middle School, TN

Monkeys

Everyone loves monkeys,
How could anyone not.
Neither me nor you couldn't,
Many others too.
All monkeys are cool,
Some are big, some are small.
None are man eaters,
But few are ferocious.
Monkeys are cool,
And you won't tell me anything else.

Josh Miller, Grade 8
Pigeon Forge Middle School, TN

Current Journey

The ocean carries me
Its waters are like a train
Its currents are the tracks
The horizon is the weather
The waves greet me as they pass

The horizon changes hearts
It conquers the sun with storms
Fast, furious, ferocious
It becomes a hurling hurricane
Raging, roaring, remarkable

The currents are torn
The waters derail
I fall to horizon's fury
To my surprise I do not crash
On a second current the water lands

The horizon changes now
From hurricane comes sun
Like an ended war
The tensions cease
I travel now so calmly
From Sardinia to Tripoli

Michael Kaminski, Grade 9
St John the Baptist High School, MO

The Rush of Fall

Yellow leaves as bright as the sun.
Brown leaves as brown as chocolate.
I rake the leaves as fast as I can; the excitement is building up.
They're in a pile so I run and jump and the leaves flutter down like snow.
Then I begin to rake again because the excitement I just can't bare it.

Tamra Andrews, Grade 7
Wilson Middle School, OK

All About Me

I was born in Chicago, what a big city!
Lots of tall buildings and very busy streets.
Plenty of strangers you probably don't want to meet.
No need to go through a car wash; you could just stop at a red light.
All kinds of people trying to wash your windows, very scary at night.

But when I was a baby, my mom thought it would be safe
to leave the city and move to a pretty place.
Out in the country, lots of friendly faces.
We aren't scared to talk to strangers
thinking they might have mace.

I might not have a lot, but one thing I know.
We don't stand on corners and wash windows.
We have a home, we have clothes, and we have food to eat.
One day, I know with all my hard work,
there won't be anyone I can't beat.

Just remember these words because one day you'll see.
I got it from my momma, and I'll make her proud of me.
She once had a friend who always said,
"Ooooh weee, I'm straight from Tennessee!"

Marissa Dawson, Grade 7
Elkton School, TN

First Hour of the Night

As the monotonous, dull clock ticks away,
And the crescent moon shines the dark coat of night,
I lie on my soft, cozy bed,
And think about all that has been through my life.

The neighborhood is quiet, as its dwellers merge to sleep,
The whooshing, fresh breeze hustles through the bare leaves,
The tall, shadowy lampposts light the streets,
That lay as empty as the deserted sea.

Somewhere far away, a lonely owl is awake,
Somewhere far away, the endless salty, blue ocean flows with grace,
Someone somewhere may be hopefully gazing at the bright, shining stars
While someone, might just be wishing to go to Mars.

But here within these four walls, I lie on my bed
Wishing these serene moments will never end,
And as the first hour of the night sweeps away,
I drift to sleep with my conscious self.

Farheen Ashrafy, Grade 9
West Jr High School, MO

God Bless

As the Lord covers His grace on this glorious land
The red, white, and blue; the soldiers who took a stand
The freedom the pain is worth fighting for
The future and the children; oh, what they have in store
The courage it took to stand up and fight
The heroes who died, doing what is right
Carrying the flag with pride in their hands
With liberty and justice they demand
Once they're fighting, there's no turning back
At any moment they are ready to attack
Families waiting with a chance of no return
Praying to God with faith and concern
911 hurt us all
But as one nation we still stand tall
The Statue of Liberty proud and true
Without our soldiers what would we do?
The United States of America — the red, white, and blue
May God bless you!

Andrew Aldridge, Grade 9
Comanche High School, OK

Winter

Winter is like a whisper of snow.
I know it is coming, but it seems so slow.
It blankets the ground with bright little crystals.
They glitter and shine and twinkle and blind.
I look out my window and imagine snowball fights.
I look forward to morning and the changes it brings.
I put on my coat, mittens, and other things.
I know the snow won't last for long.
Hurry, hurry or it will be gone.

Alex Hart, Grade 7
St Paul the Apostle School, TN

Time

The tick-tock of the clock,
And engines rumbling in the morning,
People saying "hurry up" and running out the door,
They act like life is a matter of time,
Instead of memories or moments
They rush around to be "on time"
But they don't know what they're missing
LIKE,
A time of laughter to raise you up,
Or a time of sorrow to make you cry,
A time with family that makes you smile,
Or a time when your world is broken into pieces,
And a time of prayer that glues it back together.
The tick-tock of the clock,
Time is of the essence,
Days are racing by them now,
And they don't know what they're missing.

Abby Myers, Grade 7
Dyer Elementary & Jr High School, TN

Deer*

See how he runs
From the field with a flash
See how he sprints
Through the grassy space.
Past grasshoppers and birds
And Evergreen trees
Past piles of
Leaves stirring up from a breeze.
See how he dodges
Small shrubs with ease.
A flash of brown and white
Is all you can see.
See how he goes from point A to B.
He slides to a stop
Only to see a four-legged figure gazing back.

Nick Standefer, Grade 7
Baylor School, TN
**Based on "Seal" by William Jay Smith*

Fall Leaves

Being back to school is like going back to the doctor;
scary and cool.
leaves on a pool look like green snow flakes,
and crunch like corn flakes when I sit on my stool.
Lime green leaves as bright as lemonade.
You'll drool for this lemonade just 50 cents and homemade!

Gloria Bustos, Grade 7
Wilson Middle School, OK

Winter's Christmas

Winter is finally here
and your dad has just caught a deer
"Dinner everyone," your father said
then your family gathers round the table

You pray over the feast
they eat it all up
and hear "present time"
as your excitement becomes unbearable

You open the last one
and it's a little small in size
but size doesn't matter in this case
'cause its a hundred dollar bill from your uncle

Oh, your parents are jealous
but they let it go by
and just hung your uncle anyway
with a sigh and a cry

Winter's Christmas is almost over
but you don't even care
'cause you have a hundred dollar bill to spend
at Wal-Mart or God knows where

Chance Sutton, Grade 7
Maury Middle School, TN

Hunting for Deer

I like to hunt for deer
I usually take a lot of gear
When I am in my chair
I can feel the cool air
But when I am in the timber
I am really limber
So when I see a deer
Nothing can ever interfere

Austin Emery, Grade 7
Greenfield Jr/Sr High School, MO

Ode to Dinky

You birthed before me,
Yet you were my friend.
You were 6 years older,
Yet you protected me.

When I cried you comforted,
When I called you came,
When I was afraid,
I shared your bed.

I'd hide in your fur
When I was sad,
Crying to your blondness,
And you like my tears 'til I slept.

When the large puppies came,
You'd scare them away,
As I hid in your shadow,
Even so close to death and lame.

Kristen Degener, Grade 8
Benton County School of the Arts, AR

Grandpa

My grandpa was my hero
I miss him dearly.
He taught me
The value of work.
When he passed away,
My heart was torn in two.

Aaron Webber, Grade 8
Musselman Middle School, WV

Ocean Waves

I like to go to the ocean.
I like to watch the waves.
I like to look for crabs,
And observe how they behave.

The waves are always coming.
They never seem to slow.
I can't perceive who sent them,
And I guess I'll never know.

Nathan Doss, Grade 7
Benton County School of the Arts, AR

My Dad

My dad and I, we travel lots of places,
All across the U.S. and seeing new faces.
I can't believe I have a dad, who is never mean,
You never know, maybe it's part of his theme.
My dad is like a brother to me,
We always stick together like the roots on a tree.
We always play around making all kind of noises,
Thank you God for giving me him out of all of your other choices.

Martelle McDonald, Grade 8
Mabelvale Magnet Middle School, AR

Take Me as I Am...A Real Young Woman

I may not be perfect but I can only try my best to make you happy.
I may not be a genius but I'm smart.
I may not be 100% nice but not evil enough to play with your heart.
I may not catch your eye at the start but give me a chance.
I may not be the type of girl to give up my body and have sex.
I may not be the girl who does anything without thinking.
And because of this I have been rejected and disappointed in the end.
I can't promise you anything.
It seems like people are all the same in the end
Everyone that says they're different...does different.
I'm not ashamed of who I am and that's what guys look past.
I am Mirhanda Lanaye' Allen people. I'm 15 and have plans for myself.
It doesn't matter anymore, the heart break. I don't have to wait on anyone.
Because I know I mean it when I say you're my friend or I love you.
If you want to leave such a great person behind then go ahead and leave
but look back or come back when you've realized what you had.
Me...A real young woman...So take me as I am.

Mirhanda Allen-Swan, Grade 9
Ritenour Sr High School, MO

Volcán

You make people quake
As you shake and rumble all around
Exploding into air like shooting stars
Soaring across the dark sky
Far away, all hear your sound
Constant booming and cracks as erupting lava and gas implodes
Lava racing down your hillside, conquering anything in its path
Creatures sprinting for their lives as if being chased by the devil himself
Gushing, glowing, gas galore
There is seldom light in this blackened sky
For smoke and ash let little by
Jammed highways of rivers flowing with lava
Dull glow of slowly cooling magma hardening into black rock
Now we're safe from him, as he goes dormant
The wild rampaging monster that exploded inside him has settled down now
Why have you come, what is your purpose?
Maybe one day I will understand your workings
But until then, just keep working your magic
'Cause you must have a purpose

Quinn Barber, Grade 8
Barret Traditional Middle School, KY

'56 Ford

I have a 1956 Ford.
I drive it with my foot to the floor.
When I hit it wide open my tires start smoking.

Brad Price, Grade 8
Southern Reynolds County R-II School, MO

Life in Itself

What is life in itself?
The pain, the love, the happiness.
Is it the unbearable pain life brings?
The unstoppable tears rolling down your cheeks.
Unrevealed scars that are too painful to share.

Or is it love? The wonderful feeling of knowing someone cares.
An encourager, a family member, a lover.
The warm flutter in your heart.
A hug that's right around the corner.
What is love in itself?

Or maybe it's the happiness
The joy of waking up every morning to God's creations.
The way you just can't stop smiling.

The pain, the love, the happiness.
When the pain hits, melt into the arms of Jesus.
When love arrives, accept it into your life.
When the happiness surrounds you, enjoy every minute.
Pain, love, happiness.
That's what life is in itself.

Hollie James, Grade 8
Belle Isle Enterprise Middle School, OK

Here to Guide Me

A small smile creeps over my face,
as I think of you and your thoughtful words.
I wish you were here to guide me,
to talk with me, and give me advice,
You were.
Now you're gone.

You used to be the funny guy,
with jokes, and cracks, and all the laughs.
Then on a dime, you could be the serious one,
bringing us all back.

You knew all the answers,
and no one was afraid to ask you.
We knew you could keep a secret,
we knew you would actually listen.

You taught us how to live,
for the right things and with the right people.
You nursed our gifts and encouraged our dreams.
You taught us how to truly "listen to God."

Aly Tegethoff, Grade 8
Annunciation Elementary School, MO

Of All Things, I Chose to Be Random

Thoughtless, without a clue, feeling bored, write a Haiku!
No, that's not it...
Should I write a poem, or shall I quit?
No, no, no...quitters don't prevail.
I shall not quit!
I will not fail!
Sitting and waiting, not writing at all,
I should be brainstorming and having a ball!
Should I draw,
No way! Mrs. Prater said no, or I will pay!

Shelby Corbett, Grade 7
Meredith-Dunn School, KY

Praise Our God

Flowers that shine very brightly
in the blazing day, animals hopping in the
tall grasses, families having picnics with their
3 or 4 year olds, trees blowing as soft as wind,
footprints in sand at the beach.
Thank you God
Birds singing repeatedly, dogs barking,
kids laughing from jokes like comedians,
frogs hopping, adults jogging.
Thank you God
Fruit to eat from the plants,
peaches to enjoy, grapes to love,
apples to eat from trees, bananas to play with.
Thank you God
Flowers to brighten up the day,
trees to follow around,
clean smell of rain, fresh air in the sky,
food that people enjoy,
Thank you God
The Earth that we live on, fur from animals to love,
grass to play on, rocks to climb,
the breeze in the air.
Thank you God

Tyler Schnurbusch, Grade 7
Our Lady Catholic School, MO

Racetracks

At the racetrack
Going down the backstretch
Start and finish across the finish line
Drive faster than the other person behind you
Don't drive below the yellow line
Wreck and bring out the caution flag
If you spin around and cause the big one
Final lap to go and you start to fear
As you cross the finish line you jump up for joy
Then you go to victory lane
Then you feel like a winner

Rachel Butcher, Grade 8
Heritage Middle School, TN

I Am

I am quiet and mysterious
I wonder about nothing
I hear the sound of the rain dripping on my window sill
I see the mist rising above the mountains turning into clouds
I want to tune the world into nothing and have nothing but oblivion
I am quiet and mysterious.

I pretend the world under my feet is missing and everything is white, and there is no sound
I feel the sudden urge as if I am on a roller coaster and nothing will stay still
I touch the stars and make them move so fast they fall into nothing
I worry about nothing there is no meaning and no time
I cry about what will never be and what can't be but I know it will all turn into dust
and fall into the water like rain into a puddle
I am quiet and mysterious.

I understand that water is everlasting and will never stop like the world
maybe one day it will burst into flames but what I understand
is that what now is now and can never stop
I say what I believe in and what is right
I dream sitting on the moon and fishing with the stars
I try to walk on water and swim in air
I hope all the trees are connected underground in another hidden place where you can find my true face
I am quiet and mysterious.

Felicia Kessler, Grade 8
Western Greenbrier Middle School, WV

The Day of Devastation

Tuesday, September 11, 2001
This was a devastating day for many people in many ways.
Lives were lost, and people were crushed.
The World Trade Center collapsed leaving the area to be now known as ground zero.
Planes were crashed and the Pentagon had been hit.
Thousands of American citizens died.

It seemed so unfair, to why these people were doing this to us; were hurting us for no apparent reason.
Screaming filled the ears of people, and debris covered them.
Fire filled their eyes along with many tears.
No one knew why or what was happening.
This changed drastically within just a short amount of time.
Wives without husbands, husbands without wives, and children without parents.
Everything seemed so unreal.

Tuesday September 11, 2001, also known as 9/11, is one of the worst happenings in the history of the United States.
Loved ones will be missed, and we thank our troops for fighting for our country.
People continue to pray for the ones lost, and for the ones fighting.
It's amazing how everything can be so normal, and in a few hours time be changed then, now, and forever.
September 11th will never be forgotten

Alexis Bumby, Grade 8
West Jr High School, MO

Duck Hunting

When I go to the lake I sit and wait. I sit and wait for the time to come. When the duck flies over me I raise my gun and pull the trigger. He falls to the ground down down he goes. My dog goes to get the duck. He brings him back and drops him on the ground and waits for his treat. Then we go home and after that big day we take a nap.

Michael Mitts, Grade 8
Highland Rim School, TN

Sisters Drive Me Nuts!

I have two sisters who drive me nuts.
To put up with them takes lots of guts.

When it's time for friends to leave, my little sister cries.
And sometimes I catch my big sister telling lies.

It's hard to get little sister out of the game room.
Big sister is easy to scare, as behind her I zoom.

When I found out our family was having another,
I was so happy to learn it would be a brother!

Brandon Burns, Grade 7
St Joseph Institute for the Deaf, MO

A Great Game

The umpire yells "Play Ball,"
And the game begins.
The pitcher looks for the catcher's call
As the batter grins.

The scoreboard shows the teams are tied.
Definitely the teams have battled
But momentum is on the home team's side.
Will the visitors get rattled?

As the 7th inning comes 'round
Fans rise to their feet.
No one makes a sound
To see if the home team is beat.

A walk off homerun
Ends the game.
The home team has won
As the visitors leave in shame.

Logan Phifer, Grade 7
Elkton School, TN

Waterfall

Among my deepest waters.
Around my biggest rocks.
Across me animals love to go.
On those hot summer days.
Until the green grass is gone.
After all the leaves have fallen.
Past me they all will go.
Under me the water will freeze.
Beyond me everything is ice.
Within my ice I'll start to cry.
Before I start to sob, my ice cracks.
As I look around me everything is spring.
Despite the harsh cold winter animals come alas.
Love is everywhere just stop and listen to my roaring waters.

Megan Simerly, Grade 8
Heritage Middle School, TN

Alone Again

alone in her room
a million thoughts racing in her head
she never wanted to be alone
left there with no one to hold
drowning in her sorrow
only in the darkness
does she feel at home
she can feel her life is ending
all the pieces won't fit together
all that's holding her back
all that keeps her awake at night must she find herself
can this all be a dream?
fear is everywhere
falling over her mind
looking through her inside her soul
she can't deny
What she feels inside
she dreams of dying
only to wake up
and find herself alone again

Jennifer Chunn, Grade 8
Lewisburg Middle School, TN

Summertime Beach

The banana hammock sways in the fresh daylight breeze,
held up by powerful tan ropes.
Scratchy sandpaper bark on the trees stands proud,
while pepper green leaves dance in the wind.
Seagulls chirp along with the flow of ocean water.
Soft sand lays untouched on the shore.
White clouds sit in the cotton candy blue sky.
Smells of the open sea just flow through my nose
as the bright sun warms the bluish, greenish water.

Kelly Knierim, Grade 7
Southern Boone Middle School, MO

Time

Tick, Tick, Tick, Gone.
Gone to the middle of nowhere.
In a second you are no more!
Time, you make things in life better and worse,
Happening everywhere.
I cannot get away,
away from you
You are a healer and a killer!
Some come and some go as you pass.
You rip apart people for everything they have,
Ruining the lives of the most innocent.
Tormenting the ones who deserve better.
Always on their minds,
I persevere through you,
Fighting against the currents,
Holding on 'til,
The End!

Chrissy Moore, Grade 8
Boyd County Middle School, KY

The Dragon's Lair

Despite the years of wearing
Among the shops, bland and alike
Down the street filled with people
Against the heat that pains our backs
Beneath the sun high above
Beside the docks with waters green
Near the beach, crowded again
Before the time that we mature
Along the road to growing up
With my friends and family
Until the time it is no more
In my memories, filled with joy

Chelsie Smith, Grade 8
Heritage Middle School, TN

My Favorite Place

At the lake.
Under the sky.
Against the water.
Inside a boat.
Around the land.
Into the water.
Beneath the sun.
During the summer.
With my friends.
Without my sister.
With joy.

Josh Payne, Grade 8
Heritage Middle School, TN

Forever in Time

So, there we sat
your heart next to mine
all I wanted was for it to last
forever in time.
But it was all too good
everything ends.
Hearts are broken
heart will amend.
So now you see me
after it all.
Tears have dried
but more will fall.
You come back
with nothing to lose.
I took you back
with everything lost.
So here we sit
one more time
your heart beating next to mine
all I want is for this to last
forever and always is the task.

Chelsea Perryman, Grade 8
Lewisburg Middle School, TN

Fierce Flyer

Wild, crazy, and fierce
Flying through the sky
Gosh, I hope I don't die
Ripping, tearing, slashing
Flying about, bashing
Scare in the night
A terrible fright
Green, blue, black
Will cause a heart attack
Flying way up high
In the sky
Twirling around
Spinning
Tornado
.

Zachary Jacob Boeckmann, Grade 8
St Joseph School, MO

Impossible Dream

I sat by the window,
Just hoping I would see him.
Does he even think of me?
Am I wasting my life away?
Should I give up?
They are just dreams —
Impossible dreams of mine.

Morgan Sheppard, Grade 8
Musselman Middle School, WV

God's Plan for You

Life,
It's different for everyone
You don't know the places you'll go
Or the things you'll see
But one thing's for sure
No matter where you go
No matter what you see
Don't give up halfway through
Or you'll never see
God's plan for you

Cameron DeSandre, Grade 8
Owasso 8th Grade Center, OK

A Fall Night

I stare at the radiance
Of the moon so late at night
Listening to the howling wind chorus
Flowing through my heart
Trees swaying and shaking
Ripping away the leaves
The moonlight is receding
The night of fall has come

James Rose, Grade 8
Alpena High School, AR

Change

All this
On earth
It falls like rain,
Drenching us with sorrow
So bad,
I'm not sure if we'll make it
'Till tomorrow
So much sorrow
So much pain,
The world
It isn't the same,
So much poverty
So much hate,
I sometimes wonder
If it's too late,
Too late to change the world
And the human race,
The world is changing,
Does that
Have to be the case?

Heidi Vowell, Grade 7
Norris Middle School, TN

The Day You Slipped Away*

I didn't get around to kiss you
Good-bye on the hand.
I wish that I could see you again,
But I know that I can't.
I hope you can hear me
'Cause I remember it clearly,
The day you slipped away.
I found it won't be the same.
It was the day you slipped away.

Tiffany Borggren, Grade 8
Musselman Middle School, WV
**Dedicated to my aunt*

License

I got my license to,
drive a water craft,
by myself I,
drove a houseboat with
a bunch of passengers,
I lost control once,
and hit bottom,
no one got hurt,
I also hit a big wave I,
fell, broke my ankle and arm,
we went to shore,
had trouble loading the boat,
we got it loaded,
we went home.

TJ Gammons, Grade 7
Dyer Elementary & Jr High School, TN

One Last Time

Like a forest fire was my heart
I was not ready for you to part
My heart collapsed, like a burning tree
You were with me only two years
Even when you could barely hear
I still listened to every word you said
The last meeting we had
Before you were buried so deep,
In the cold, dark ground
You laid there like a fresh cut rose
So still and cold, you were
Though I know where you are
It will still be a while before we meet again
Sometimes I look up to say Hi
For I know you can hear me
I only wish you'd answer back
Your memory will always be in my heart
You will be the light of my darkest days
Forever…and always.

Tori Waters, Grade 9
Alpena High School, AR

Recipe for a Perfect Pet

First take a pet
next stir in intelligence
pour in loyalty
add brave with strong
preheat oven to 300,000 degrees Fahrenheit
meanwhile get a jug of play
add fun and loving and mix it all together
then bake for 4 days and that is the recipe for a perfect pet

Shea Ellis, Grade 7
Meredith-Dunn School, KY

Walking in Fall

Stepping out into the brisk air
With the wind blowing through my hair
I see the crunchy pathway
Made like a blanket of colorful leaves

I let go of a bright red leaf
Then see it retrieve
With all of the bright street lights on
Reflecting against the leaves like a mirror

All the kids hanging around the maple tree
Is the wonderful sound of crunching leaves
The chickens clucking around
Making even more of a beautiful sound

The pitter patter of little feet
Running off to school now
I let go of one last leaf
To see it retrieve

Sarah Stevenson, Grade 7
Nettleton Jr High School, AR

The Nature of a Horse

I am a horse, strong and free.
I run as fast as the wind that blows through the trees.
My hoof beats sound like the beating of a drum.
The blood that runs through my vein
is as hot as the evening sun.
The mountains are high.
The valleys are low.
This land is home to the many
animals who roam.
I am wild and carefree.
This is my home and always will be.

Rachel Watson, Grade 8
Elkton School, TN

Dark Girl

Don't look at me,
I am a dark girl.
I am tired of being
The darkest person
In my class.

It seems everybody
Is lighter than me.
I am as dark as Hershey chocolate,
A night without a moon,
A black bear that lives in caves.

I tell myself
Black is beautiful.
I say it to myself,
Black is beautiful.
I am strong
I want peace
I like to dance
I need respect
I am a daughter of God
Look at me,
I am a dark girl.

Melshonn Canada, Grade 8
Lee A Tolbert Community Academy, MO

My Favorite Place

By the desk I am calm
In my world is how I think of it
Around my family is just too crowded
Despite the things I cannot do
At my computer desk I feel at ease
Inside the house is where it stays
Without my computer I am nothing
Among my tasks I make time
To be on my computer
Except for when I have too much homework

Danielle Taylor, Grade 8
Heritage Middle School, TN

Magical

A sunset in the night sky.
A shadow that can't be mad at you.
The snow that falls in the winter.
Or the flowers that pop in the spring.
The moments that make you cry.
Or the laughing that you can't control.
A lone cloud in the sky.
That turns into a storm that you fear.
These moments are magical.

Kristen Clark, Grade 7
Elkton School, TN

Hatred

Hate is evil, Hate is not good,
Hate makes you do things,
You never thought you would.

Hate gets you no where,
Hate stern joy,
Hate is deep within,
The lost hearts of girls and boys.

It holds you back,
Makes life pass you by,
makes you wonder why.
Why do I do this, how could I let this be,
Allowing evil to control me.

Dig deep within,
Understand yourself,
Know how feelings surface,
The root of yourself.

Release evil feelings,
replace them with love;
Let your heart stay pure,
"No hate says the man above."

Chancey Maltsberger, Grade 8
Madisonville Middle School, TN

Someday

I say
Someday
That I shall hunt
In a forest filled with deer
With a gun
Standing still

Shooting many deer
Dressed in camo
I will not fear
In a forest filled with deer
With a gun
Standing still

Benjamin Sobczak, Grade 8
White Station Middle School, TN

My Most Prized Possession

I run my hands up and down her neck so long and smooth.
It feels so right
When I hold her tight
And when I guide her, she sings a lovely tune.
I play all night and day, almost until I swoon.

Her sounds vary upon her moods, in tune with mine.
Every day she gives the greatest advice.
Quite a sight, with her magnificent shades of amber, tan, and auburn,
And since I have started playing her I've learned my guitar is as precious to me as a mother to her daughter.

To me she is more than just a toy,
And possesses a power that many want to employ.
Her music puts people in a magical place.
A song can say much more to a person than words alone.
She is the most precious to me of the things I own.

Shira Grant, Grade 7
White Station Middle School, TN

Sea Turtles

You do not have to be perfect.
You do not have to prance around in the streets,
feeling like you're the royal King Tut.
You only have to be yourself whatever animal that may be,
and explore your gifts.

Tell me about your life, and I'll tell you about mine.
Meanwhile, the world keeps altering through its pedestrian cycles.
Meanwhile, the glimmering sun rises and falls.
The shady trees of the mountains swish, swing, and sway
with each swift breeze.
The oceans curl up and roll out without hesitation.
Each wave crashes onto the shore's sandy surface.
Meanwhile the sea turtles, deep in the clear, turquoise water keep traveling home.
I can taste their excitement.

Whatever kind of person you are, whether jovial or gloomy,
the world can provide you with great opportunities
swimming to you like the sea turtles, slow and sure —
proclaiming what life holds for you.

Mary Collins, Grade 8
Baylor School, TN

Moms

Moms are the ones that tuck us in at night
The one that kisses our head
The one that tells us to go right to bed,
The only one who fixes our macaroni just right without one complaint
Then she will make you a muffin for a snack
And adds the sprinkles you love so much
She even adds her own special touch
There is no secret to being a mom,
Just care and your legacy will go on and on.

Kelsie Henry, Grade 7
Greenfield Jr/Sr High School, MO

You

You call me your best friend, but I can't stand to be around you anymore
You call me your best friend ever, but you talk about me behind my back
You call me your friend, but you tell me one thing and act the complete opposite
You call me your girlfriend, but you say you never liked me
You call me up to go places, then ignore me or don't even come
You call yourselves nice, but all you do is hurt me and everyone else around you
You try and go behind my back, then you deny it ever happened
You wonder why I'm angry at you, but you never really care
You tell me that you care so much about me, but you're too self-absorbed to notice that I'm fading away
You act as if I'm not going anywhere, but I'm already out the door
You assume I'm always going to back you up and always be right behind you, but I'm gone and never coming back
You turn to say good-bye, but all that's left is a distant memory of what used to be
You wonder what happened, but you don't realize that you pushed me away
You try to bring me back, but it's too late and no I can't come back
You forget about me, but I always remember the hurt you caused me
And then there's you...
You tell me that you love me, and I believe you
You talk to me, and I get butterflies
You are the one different person, and you will always be you

Jordan Aikin, Grade 9
Fern Creek Traditional Magnet High School, KY

Darkness

I see the sky so bright and blue and I see the sun a shining yellow basketball and then I see the clouds come so suddenly bringing darkness, sadness, and rain and now I'm lost in the woods and darkness and rain is falling.

I stay in the woods, and darkness overwhelms me and all my senses are filled with darkness.

I stay in the darkness for days, weeks, months and I realize there is light. I slowly find my way out of the woods. The darkness, sadness flows away and I am back to where I was before.

I still see the darkness, but I am rescued by the light, and brought to my happiness. I live in the light.

Jonathan Mills, Grade 7
St Mary of the Woods School, KY

The Songbook of My Life

The songbook of my life is filled with many genres of a vast array.
Most days are like ballads; flowing gently like the strings through the fingers of a harpist.

Other days seem to be syncopated. Nothing is going the right way.
Even though it may be off, I still feel the beat within me.

The songbook of my life is filled with many genres of a vast array.
Whichever one I choose, that is how I will choose my day.

Channing Murphy, Grade 8
Gresham Middle School, TN

Rabbits

Bunny rabbits can be small at birth and not even look like rabbits but look like baby mice. When they grow up I think that they are as cute as can be. They have bushy tails, long ears, and thick coats. They hop everywhere and eat all kinds of food. The colors on rabbits vary. Some can be white or even brown, most wild rabbits are brown. I like rabbits, and I also love to care for them.

Shana Womack, Grade 7
Highland Rim School, TN

Seeing Through Our Eyes

Our eyes are all the same except moms.
Dad, Connor, Sarah, and I all have eyes like the ocean, big and blue.
Bad things can happen when we are angered.
The waves inside of us crash and break against innocent people around us.
Connor's eyes look guilty; always like he has done something wrong or is hiding something.
Sarah's eyes look like a cat; this is her future want-to-be-job.
Yes, she wants to be a cat.
Mom's are sweet and soft, big and brown.
But they can easily correct wrong doings with one stare.
Dad's eyes are smart, they have to be for a financial advisor.
And well, well mine are just big, bright, happy, and blue.
Nothing special.
Some say they seem to pop, differing from the others of my family.
But to me, they are normal, just something to look through.
They say eyes tell a lot about you.
But what do they say about me?
Do they give away my personality?
Guilty, cat-want-to-be, sweet and soft, smart, and big, blue, and happy.
I can see that.

Lauren Sims, Grade 8
Baylor School, TN

Fall

Fall is all around us
Fall is in the brown crunchy leaves on the ground
Fall is also in the fire color leaves falling from the trees
Fall is in the cool crisp breeze
Fall is the time where everything furry will scurry for food
Fall is a time for holidays which is a time for jolly days for me
Fall is a time for wonderful holiday cooking smells in the kitchen
Fall is the time where you get to eat all your favorite foods
Fall is a time to eat so much of our favorite foods that we either have to unsnap our pants or pop a button
Fall is a time for getting the turkey wishbone and hoping you have good luck for the rest of the year
Fall is when those pesky relatives are going to show up
Fall is when you have that big madhouse, crowd crushing holiday sales
Fall is when you start to think about Christmas and start that mile long Christmas Wish List
Fall is a good time for falling asleep on your fall break
Fall is all around us

Tyler Palsgrove, Grade 7
Nettleton Jr High School, AR

Sara Behbahani

Crazy, understanding, caring, and loving.
Sister of Yousef
Lover of listening to music, converses, and soccer.
Who feels bad when people are depressed, feels that harming animals is horrible,
And feels mad when people say they're better than other people.
Who gives love, advice, and care for others.
Who needs happiness, guide to life, and peace.
Who fears loneliness, clowns, and death
Who wants to see peace in the world, to see Australia, and to see that I can make all my goals come true.
Who lives in Tennessee.

Sara Behbahani, Grade 8
Montgomery Central Middle School, TN

Me

Austin
Intellectual, hilarious, kind, and friendly
Brother of Shelby and Ashley
Lover of beauty, family, and friends
Who feels joyful, free willing, and calm
Who needs friends, God, and family
Who gives gifts, love, and friendships
Who fears God's power, feeling unloved, and death
Who wants to see Heaven, the world, and peace
A small house that reminds me of a garden
Dabbs

Austin Dabbs, Grade 8
Montgomery Central Middle School, TN

Music

Music is like a rhyme to me
it lifts my heart
and sets me free
it rocks and rolls
it hips and hops
I never let my music stop
I play it all day
I play it all night
'til the day my boombox
blew up on sight

Alix Montplaisir, Grade 8
Southern Reynolds County R-II School, MO

City Turns to Country

City
Earsplitting, dazzling
Jam-packed, demanding, energetic
Animated, enthusiastic — uncomplicated, breathtaking
Calming, peaceful, soothing
Quiet, spacious
Country

Holly Benbrook, Grade 8
Greenfield Jr/Sr High School, MO

That One Time

Every time she needed him he wasn't there
through all the pain she couldn't bear
that one time she needed him he wasn't there
As she cried on her pillow hoping tomorrow
would be a better day.
She wanted to go far and get away.
Away from the struggle and pain
Happiness was hopefully soon to gain.
She was tired of tears running down her face
She wanted a new dream to chase.
She wanted him to heal the pain she couldn't bear
But that one time she needed him he wasn't there.

Terri Johnson, Grade 8
Belle Isle Enterprise Middle School, OK

Autumn

The wind whistles softly,
leaves crackle loudly.
Autumn sounds are here.
Days are short.
Nights come early.
The weather is cool and pleasant,
leaves change to bright vibrant colors.
They fall gently to ground.
Children jump into cushioning piles of leaves,
delighted that autumn is here.

Gavin Glenn, Grade 7
Maury Middle School, TN

My Stone

I carry a stone in my pocket that says love
love is painful and heartbreaking.
When you love someone you give your life for theirs.
Love is not a token you can't buy love or happiness.

Melissa Vara, Grade 8
Belle Isle Enterprise Middle School, OK

Nana

Your Christmas party is always so great,
with all the family around the tree
You always get the train out for me,
my nana loved by all your grandkids
Since I don't have a Christmas with my mom,
yours fills a little space for it
Cutting your grass in the summer,
then meeting Chris Carpenter
You pick Vallee and I up from school,
then we go do something cool
Once we went to Monkey Joe's,
but mostly we go to Happy Joe's
You also took us to Tower Tee,
I remember you taking Lindsay shopping
Sometimes I would just go to your house to play pool,
I know for a fact that you love us
You are the best Grandma ever,
Vallee thinks so, too

Nicholas Sylvia, Grade 7
Annunciation Elementary School, MO

World Wars

W hen the bombs start falling
O ver a piece of land you call home.
R unning to safety of my safe place
L etting them bomb this place by not paying attention
D oing everything you can to help the injured during this time.

W hen you are hurt, you hope someone will come and help you
A fter the scream of bombs and bullets
R eturning to something you used to call home
S tarting a war isn't easy, but finishing one is even harder.

John Murphy, Grade 7
Clarksburg School, TN

A White Christmas

What a great time of year when
Christ was born.
When you get presents
and hope for snow.
If it snows,
Mom makes snow cream
that melts in
your mouth.
You get iPods and XBox 360's.
All the joyful electronics
of the year.
Just one thing I wish;
please snow on this
wonderful time of year.

Logan Jenkins, Grade 7
Maury Middle School, TN

Fall

As I walk along the street
I hear little animals' feet
They scurry around in the crunchy leaves
Like one of my little puppies.

By the yellow, orange, and red
I can tell it's time for fall.
The leaves are falling on my head.

I feel the crisp of the wind hit my face
I can see my house through the haze
Not too many days until winter.

I see fallen apples on the ground
Maybe a pound
So much to do before you die
So much to do before you die.

Ashley Carter, Grade 7
Nettleton Jr High School, AR

Lost Love

There's not a day goes by
that I stop thinking of you,
But when I stopped thinking,
You stopped caring.
So what I forgot then,
That I'll never forget,
Is that I love you
and I always will.

Joey Smith, Grade 7
Lewis and Clark Middle School, MO

Why?

Why is my question.
The question I ask daily.
The question I hate.

Joel Weston, Grade 7
Rocky Comfort Elementary School, MO

My Aunt

I never thought I'd have to pray every night in my bed,
I never thought her very life might be hanging by a thread.

I never thought that giving birth could cause such a wreck,
I never thought her last words to me would be "I love you Bec."

I never thought my family could be in so much pain,
I never thought we'd fly to Boston on a plane.

So I'm hoping and praying that there's a cure,
And I know that God's love is pure.

Rebecca Franke, Grade 8
Annunciation Elementary School, MO

Thanksgiving

As we wait to eat our big meal, that my uncle went to kill
We talked at the table when my grandma says I know a fable.
It begins by telling about a turkey and a man. But I just couldn't understand.
I could smell the fresh pie almost ready to touch it, when I said Oh My!
As I looked out the window and saw an awful sight, I tried not to cry with all my might.
The colorful feathers on the skin of the turkey were terribly dirty.
I was scared to eat the turkey, 'cause I could see it looking back at me.
Once I saw that face I ran like I was in a race.
Faster, faster right out of the kitchen until ZOOM! and I was in the bathroom.
Once I recovered I felt a little better until I saw all the feathers.
My face was as green as a pear, I just didn't think it was fair.
I'll never forget that one Thanksgiving, when I almost wasn't living.

Claire Case, Grade 7
Nettleton Jr High School, AR

In Darkness and in Silence

She wanders through the streets
Anonymity is her guard.
Never truly seen or heard,
She picks up a green glass shard.
She holds it high above her head and says
"It's the end of the beginning"
No one sees her, no one hears,
Not one of the people passing by.
"Where can I go?" she asks an old man,
But he is deaf and blind.
He can't see her, he can't hear.
He quietly ignores her.
She makes her way back on home,
Disheartened and distraught.
No one saw her, no one heard.
Her dream had once again been ruined.
She opens the door into her house,
No difference, no change.
But someone saw her, someone heard.
Her mother was waiting for her.
Her crying mother's embrace made this memory last for an eternity.

Colleen Roetemeyer, Grade 8
West Jr High School, MO

When the Mockingbird Sings

The hour when the mockingbird sings,
The time, when new fresh air fills my mouth tingling.
The period of the new sun,
The moment of fresh, new start, leaving the past behind.

The hour when the mourning dove mournfully cries,
The time when the moon retires,
The period when new life abounds,
Coming from their deep, dream.
The hour, when children's laughter fills the house with joy.

The time when the warm orange-red sun
Covers me like a feather blanket,
The smell of food, tickling under my nose.
The time when a gentle breeze nudges me,
Waking gently away from the deep, dreamy sleep.
The last sorrowful sound of the mockingbird at
Six o' clock in the morning.

Stephanie Won, Grade 9
West Jr High School, MO

Fear

It grips you
And holds on
It'll take you far
Test your limits, to the beyond

Your heartbeat doubles
You freeze in place
Your eyes go wide
To see a loving face

Be strong and fight
They are there
Look all around
Know that they care

Fear tries to rule your life
Some give in
But there are many
That round the bend

They push through the darkness
They fight through the fright
Head towards the opening
And into the light

Jessica Leuthauser, Grade 8
Northwest Valley 7th & 8th Grade Center, MO

Fall Has Come!

The leaves are beginning to fall,
they look like little firework's in the sky,
they make a big crunch when I step on them,
some are brown but most are golden.

Hailey Iorizzo, Grade 7
Wilson Middle School, OK

Sorrow's Surrender

Though our hearts began to tremble
With the sadness of departure
We shed not a single tear
For hopes of reuniting
Without the obstacle of fear
Long nights were filled with anxious minutes
And the hours doomed my soul
Amidst the dreams of the night
My fears weren't forsaken
But exaggerated into depths of my existence
Without him I suffered
I endured immense depression
And though the torment was hard to bear
My heart triumphed with love for him
So I survived through all the agony
The adoration I have for him
Is so colossal
That the mournfulness matters not
I am consumed within
The lasting endlessness of his soul
Sweet sorrow surrenders its domination

Elizabeth Low, Grade 7
All Saints Catholic School, OK

Determination

You must be determined in life,
to live the way your life plays out.
If you're not determined you'll
lose your step and fall onto despair.
That alone can take your life and break you
until there is nothing else to break.
Be determined for anything you
put your mind to, you can do.
And if you find someone in despair
help them up and let them be determined.

Jonathan Munton, Grade 8
Greenfield Jr/Sr High School, MO

Storms

We live in a world full of fast, destructive storms
They rip through the earth with boundless fury
They strike without warning and in a moment's notice
They strike in a blind rage like nothing but destruction matters
Their gale force winds sweep through the land
The cool rain pelts all that lies beneath it
The storm is full of twists and turns
And you never know what it will do next
When the storm is over the debris is scattered in mounds
It proves nothing can be left standing in a storm's wake
But no storm goes on forever
Then the world returns to its calm, peaceful state
The world keeps spinning and patiently awaits another storm

Charles Carter, Grade 9
Hamburg Jr High School, AR

Picture Perfect

Round and fluffy,
Tall and short,
Smiling, gazing,
Loving enough.

Bald like Bubby,
Little round nose,
Long bendy legs,
Short crooked arms.

Created by a four year old,
Cute as can be,
Round and fluffy,
Picture perfect for all to see.

Shelby Coleman, Grade 7
Hebron Middle School, KY

A Beacon to the Lost

Shining like a beacon to sailors
lost upon the indigo ocean,
like a soothing therapist to those
who cannot find themselves.
Craters stately and subdued
remind us of our imperfections;
blissful beams of bright light beckon us
to recall the time when we first
touched the moon's dull dust.
Far from fiery fights
that rage on Earth,
the hushed, beneficent moon
reminds us of the turquoise peace
that once enveloped
our mystical planet
until our eyes
reach the lasting end,
the eternal bottom
of the living moon
and fall into space.

Lucas Conwell, Grade 8
Baylor School, TN

Love

Love at first sight,
Can always come back to bite,
Suppose he's the one you're looking for,
But you just want more,
You don't know what to do,
That's why you never tell the truth,
You think he loves you,
But does he love you for you,
Love doesn't always stink,
Sometimes you just have to think,
They might not be the one,
But sometimes you just have to have fun.

Keri Wright, Grade 9
Appleton City High School, MO

Grandpa

The night we received the phone call saying you were going to the hospital,
I sensed this would be your last time at home.

You were admitted into ICU, and all we could do was sit and pray.
The smell of sickness lingered through the air.

The sounds of monitors beeping, respirators whooshing, feet scurrying,
and noses sniffling could be heard through the halls.

We all prayed that you would get better, but only seem to fade away
more and more every day.

The last night I saw you, you said to me, "I love you, and come back to see me soon."
You always said that whenever I would leave your house.

I hope I will get to come see you whenever I get to heaven.
I will always remember you. I love you Grandpa!

Brooklyn Gray, Grade 7
St Mary of the Woods School, KY

Where Writing Hides

Writing hides on a bar of soap.
It lingers with the aroma of lilacs,
or even pumpkin pie.
As sudsy soap bubbles float off the bar and flow down the drain,
writing goes along.

It hides its face on a warm, clean cotton shirt in the laundry basket.
It awaits folding and being stuffed into a small drawer,
so it can be worn and the cycle repeated.

Hiding in my history book,
it stands proudly next to the picture of George Washington
or Paul Revere.
It's an American hero,
who would do anything for this country.

Writing hides on the numbers on my cell phone.
It's probably black and blue from texting.
Writing is hidden only if you don't know where to look.

Emily Wildenberg, Grade 8
Baylor School, TN

About Me

Kari
Blonde, funny, crazy, but smart
Sister of Brady, Bailey, and Lexi Alley
Lover of softball, dancing, and singing
Who feels happy for the most part, hyper all the time, and sad occasionally
Who gives unconditional love, great advice, and friendship
Who would like to see Faith Hill and Tim McGraw singing together,
Avril Lavigne in concert, and Miley Cyrus in person
Who lives in Clarksville, TN and loves it there
Alley

Kari Alley, Grade 8
Montgomery Central Middle School, TN

For Jenny and Brittney

I will still be there for you
When the stars refuse to shine,
When the sun forgets to rise someday,
When the moon falls from the sky.

I will still be there for you,
Though we may move away;
When we grow old and the memories fade
The thought of you will stay.

I'll always be there for you
Because you were there for me,
To help me cry or make me smile,
Or to pull me to my feet.

Three peas in a pod, the Three Musketeers,
Three amigas, one plus two;
You two have always been there for me,
So I'll be there for you too.

I'll always be there for you
Until the bitter end;
I love you both with all my heart —
You guys are my best friends.

Christina Palermo, Grade 9
Oak Park High School, MO

Field of Death

I couldn't move,
surprise and astonishment across my face.
Blood everywhere,
life or death was the case.

Loud clings of swords,
and foggy clouds of breath.
There's only one way to describe it,
this is a field of death.

The place smelt of gore,
unfaltering men running towards each other,
you don't see anyone flinching,
or calling for their mother.

Men everywhere around me,
some howling in pain.
Puddles splashing under massive feet,
from all the rain.

Not used to this,
I cringed at the sight,
but I can't hide from it,
I know I have to fight.

Alex Cox, Grade 8
Beebe Jr High School, AR

Different

From different eyes comes a different perspective.
From different perspectives comes a different truth.
From every truth comes a different moral.
From every moral comes a different story.
Every story starts with a dream.
Behind every dream is a different dreamer.
Every dreamer dreams a different dream.
Every dream is made of differences.
But in only one way they are the same…

Kelsey Chafin, Grade 8
Northwest Valley 7th & 8th Grade Center, MO

Past

The past is an evil thing,
Never leaving your side,
Try as you might,
It will take your pride,
Haunting your dreams,
Even when you pray,
You live through it day by day
You try to escape your living hell,
Blocking your memories you live in a shell,
Escape is not an option freedom no longer exist,
Hate overwhelms you for what they did,
You blame yourself,
You don't know why,
They did this to you,
You cry and cry,
The past is an evil thing that's a fact,
Live with it because there is no turning back.

Chasity Gordon, Grade 9
Fern Creek Traditional Magnet High School, KY

United in Their Stories

There is a dragon at my door
with fiery, untamed eyes,
There is a light upon the shore
only just out of reach
There is a knight along the path
merely shining on the outside
There is a girl who waits in the darkness
who stumbles near the light
Bleeding cries of lonely souls
the story of their lives
I see the dragon at my door
feel the heat of his heart
I reach for the light beyond the shore
smell the salt-stained air
I hear the sighs of the knight beyond these woods
find the worth beneath him
I touch the girl with shaking hands
realize her fear of waiting
Broken pieces of a world unknown
united by the truth of stories

Allie Fry, Grade 9
Nerinx Hall High School, MO

Jekyll Island

Across the bridge,
Beside the dunes,
Near the sandbar,
Past the shoreline,
On the sand,
Between the roads,
Against the waves,
Behind all people,
Along the beach we walk,
In the dark,
Without any unwanted sounds.

Gracie Arthur, Grade 8
Heritage Middle School, TN

Bug's Beauty

Creepy
Crawly
Bugs
Unattractive
Slimy
Bugs

With bubbly, buggy eyes.
With scrawny, long legs.
With bumpy, bare backs.

How unpleasant a sight!
How terrible a creature!

Why won't anybody get rid
of these dreadful, horrendous,
revolting, gruesome monsters?

These oily, hideous bugs.

Margo Fitzpatrick, Grade 7
White Station Middle School, TN

Teased

She stands there,
just listening.
Her thoughts disturbed
by the constant teasing
from the ones she loves.
They tear her heart
from limb to limb.
Her confidence dropping
below the rim.
They have no idea
of what goes on inside.
They just look so pleased.
But she's crying,
because they teased.

Bethany Buckner, Grade 7
Madison Middle School, WV

Blind

Look into my eyes
Do you see me,
Or just who I
Pretend to be?
Can you see the
Pain I feel
Every single day?
Are you afraid to look
Or are you
Blind to what's really there?

Each morning I get up
And put on my face
My happy, carefree face
But deep down inside
Behind that face
I'm bleeding and dying
I'm withered and crying
Can you see me,
Can you help me,
Am I alone?

Sarah Garcia, Grade 9
Philip Barbour High School, WV

Life

Life is only worth living
If you're going to live it
To the fullest.
So don't hold back.
Stay on track.
Who knows, one day
You might just snap.
Move forward.
But in the end the past is the past
We all know we will end under grass.
Our soul will be forever
But our body never.
So goodbye forever.

Kody Kiger, Grade 9
St John the Baptist High School, MO

Basketball

B est sport ever
A t Hartville it's popular
S port everyone loves
K now the plays
E veryone plays the sport
T akes it to the basket
B alance
A ttacks the goal
L ots of fans
L ike it more

Austin Arnall, Grade 7
Hartville Jr/Sr High School, MO

Kaylee Nicole Troutman

We all need someone
To talk to in our life
A friend to whom we run
In times of stress or strife

A friend who's always there
Throughout the years
A friend we know will care
And take away our fears

A friend who's always near
Who I love to talk to
Who is always here

A loving friend indeed,
On whom we can depend
To fulfill our every need

Kaylee Nicole Troutman

Justin Tahmassebi, Grade 9
Gallatin High School, TN

My Room

in my room
on my bed
near a window
during the night
without others
beside my TV
under my sheets
with games
inside a book
without noise

Kyle Qualls, Grade 8
Heritage Middle School, TN

Silent Life

Our world seems to be forgotten
The atmosphere is disappearing
That smoke and smog stains the sky
In years time we're gonna die
To stop the pain of our grief
Let's stop polluting, make a leap
Ice caps, glaciers, polar frost
Thanks to you it's kind of lost
Save the planet with your heart
Recycling garbage, that's our part
Give a bright future to our kids
Make them laugh, let them live
Let us all make a choice
So the planet can still live
Or it will have a silent life

Justin Warlick, Grade 8
Chelsea Jr High School, OK

Fall

You walk outside, jacket and jeans
Your nose instantly turns red
There are no more greens
Just yellow and brown

The dry wind hits your flesh
As you step on the crunchy grass
A leaf was blown off of a tree
You know Jack Frost has aced his test

You see a chipmunk scurry across the ground
You wish you could have his furry thick fur
The birds all fly south
You close your eyes and feel yourself fly with them

Halloween costumes are put out
So are all the candy pots
It's the dentists' busy time of year
They just wish kids could eat pears

Bret Sanders, Grade 7
Nettleton Jr High School, AR

My Two Friends

Movement caught my eye
Out the window I gazed
I stare at the whimsical snow
Alas I saw a doe
I watched it scamper away
Stealing a bit of hay
but then it did return
As the snow fiercely churned
Then I watched the doe lead a friend
Through a clearing then over a bend
More hay was stolen then
They moved leery like a startled hen
I quickly realized this friend was a fawn
As the sun was rising nearly dawn
I was hypnotized by an eerie sight
As a brilliant glow grew conquering the night
The snow was lit up immensely bright
I watched the deer disappear with the night
I knew it wasn't the light they fear
It was open season for the deer

Casey Harman, Grade 8
Chelsea Jr High School, OK

Love

What is love?
Love is the writing of one of those corny poems
that always makes you laugh, and starts with:
Roses are red violets are blue
I have a major crush on you do you have one on me too.
It also is a note that happens to get read by Mr. Fred
my first period teacher every day.

Tori Swinford, Grade 8
Highland Rim School, TN

Grandpa

Grandpa is in the hospital,
Everyone is silent.
The family is praying to God,
Hoping that he would give grandpa another chance.
The kids are crying,
The mothers are telling them it's okay.
The doctors came out and said he passes away.
Everybody wished that they could have said goodbye.
My family tried not to cry,
They know that he is in heaven.
Resting in peace.

Johnathan Morris, Grade 7
St Mary of the Woods School, KY

The World

The world is made of many parts, and this is where I'll start.
Asia, Africa Europe too.
These are three parts of the world I've shown you.
North American, South America, Antarctic makes six.
One more
What is it?
Its a place down under and it's hot a lot.
Can you guess what it is?
That's right Australia.
And now to end this prose
A place as sweet as a rose
Clarksburg, Tennessee
A place dear to my heart.

Megan Jarrett, Grade 7
Clarksburg School, TN

Fading Fears

As the day comes to a close,
Fire flies dance like pixies on wing.
Through gathering shadows from leaf to leaf.
The sun in the heavens
Has traveled its course
And slowly sinks from site.
Through gathering night
With deft fingers of light.
Ole Saw paints the clouds of night
With strikes of amber
And shades of pink.
He paints gaily to our delight.
All worries and fears are now
Released and set freely in the sky.
The stars come out and I close my eyes
Breathing in small breaths of the night air.
The wind starts to pick up
Blowing the leaves in the trees.
And as the day has left me with the night,
My soul's troubles have gone with the sun.

Darby Bartlett, Grade 8
Greenfield Jr/Sr High School, MO

Battles

Let us hear the battle cries for the ones who fought and died.
The faithful flag of red, white, and blue led us the way through and through and through.
The ones that survived bear the cross for their horrible tragic loss.
So let us hear the battle cries for the ones who fought and died.

Michelle Hendee, Grade 7
Bigelow High School, AR

Some Things Stay the Same

When I was 6, Mondays were the worst because of the dreaded school week to come.
Now I'm 14, and yet again, on Mondays, I feel like a pig going to the slaughter house.

When I was 6, Friday nights brought the aroma of gooey cheese pizza to the air.
Now I'm 14, and on Friday nights time seems to fly as I savor the mouthwatering slices in my mouth.

When I was 6, Saturday mornings meant kicking the soccer ball, and "Swoosh," into the net for a goal.
Now I'm 14, and the dew on the grass glimmers in the sunlight before the stomping and kicking of feet
destroy the picturesque scene of the untouched soccer field on Saturday morning.

When I was 6, the roar of the vacuum and squeak of the window wiper all came about on Saturday afternoons.
Now I'm 14, and the stench of the bulging trash bag reeks with the smell of week-old garbage.

When I was 6, Sunday afternoons meant the time to hop into bed and doze off with dreams of the previous day's soccer game.
Now I'm 14, and the silky, smooth sheets surround me, and give me relaxation from a hectic week, as my eyes slowly shut
and my body relaxes for a Sunday afternoon nap.

When I was 6, I looked forward to life ahead of me.
Now I'm 14, and I'm still looking in the same direction.

As life goes on, the world changes, but some things stay the same.

Jacob Mingus, Grade 9
West Jr High School, MO

Do You Remember?

Do you remember sitting together at lunch, sharing everything?
Do you remember going everywhere together?
Do you remember telling secrets and staying on the phone until 2 a.m.?
Do you remember talking about anything and everything?
What about having a conversation beyond "I like your shoes?"
Or making best friend bracelets at recess in third grade?
You probably won't talk to me because I'm not popular. It might damage your reputation.
I remember the good times when none of it mattered, do you?

Kayla Bergmann, Grade 7
Annunciation Elementary School, MO

Eric

Eric, Elkie, Eríca, Erie, Mr. What-In-The-World-Do-You-Think-You're-Doing. In German, my name means "the one" and "ever-powerful." Brilliant. I've always admired the whole concept of "ever-powerful:" immense shiny throne, several surreptitious servants somberly serving shimmering silverware, treating me like the president of the United States. There are currently two-hundred seventy-three people in the U.S. whose name is Eric Daniel. Awesome. My mom spelled my name E-R-I-C not E-R-I-K; but everyone just calls me Eric, which sounds like erk. Kind of. And an erk is British slang for an aircraftsman. Cool. Eric could also mean Eric the Red, a famous Viking, or it could mean a normal boy in middle school. My mom called me Elkie, as in there's-my-Elkie. That's not weird at all. Yes, I do have a secret name. If it was a building, it would be a glass skyscraper, shining above all the heavens. If my name was a dragon, it would bellow tenaciously, for everyone to hear. Finally, there is Eric, like Eric the Red, or ericaceous. I like the suppleness of my name, and for that, Eric will do, not just any name.

Eric Daniel, Grade 8
Baylor School, TN

Eighth Grade Graduation

Counting down the days,
The classroom is excited and prepared.
The bell sounds, kids crowd,
"Goodbye, middle school!" a joyful student declared.

No teachers, no papers, no books,
No absents, or tardies each day.
The excitement has come and gone all year,
But now it is here to stay.

We have come a long way from our first day of middle school
Where we started our new lives as the kids we once were.
We have been crafted into the mature teenagers we are today,
But we all still have the little kids inside us we were known for.

People tell us we're crazy;
They tell us we're out of control.
But when it comes to schoolwork,
Good grades are our only goal.

Now it is time for us to part
Where our wonderful lives await.
Look out, high school, here we come,
It's your class of two-thousand and eight.

Shelby Hartman, Grade 8
St Gerard Majella School, MO

I Fell

I wanted to be with you,
You wanted to be with me but also with her!
Finally, you chose, her.

Why did you lead me on?
If you knew you wanted her.
You said you fell,
Fell for me.
Then you said "I can't be with you."

You hurt me!
I would have given anything,
Anything to have you.
I gave up so much, yet gained so little.
I was heartbroken,
I still am.
I'm just good at hiding it.

I just closed my eyes and jumped,
hoping you would catch me.
I jumped and fell.
You didn't catch me.
Don't worry, I'll recover, I always do.
My heart just needs to find a way to forget about you.

Brogan Irvine, Grade 9
Savannah High School, MO

Autumn Leaves

Autumn leaves,
Tumble down, from their place,
In the trees.
Red and orange, purple, too,
Fill the trees with such beauty.

Floating, twirling,
In the wind,
Not quite knowing when the ride will end.
Peacefully, quietly,
Being carried by a breeze,
There's not such a sight as
These autumn leaves.

And even when they reach the ground,
They land silently, without a sound,
And children will enjoy the leaves, too,
But with a loud, grand crunching sound.

Michaela Hart, Grade 7
Nettleton Jr High School, AR

A Distant Solution

Hope is silence amidst stinging war,
the melodious music of the unforgiving ocean,
graceful gulls flying home,
as well as the violent waves breaking on a rocky shoreline.
They pound against the already-eroded cliff.
Hope is the dance of the sunset glimmering in my wide pupils,
like fire radiating through a milky mirror.
It's the feeling of stars looking after me,
it's the blessing of finding an answer.
Hope is not knowing but believing.
It is trusting whatever is beyond the horizon.

Cory Walker, Grade 8
Baylor School, TN

Deer Deer

Deer, deer on my wall,
who's the greatest hunter of them all.
I am, I am the mighty hunter of them all
and I'm ready for next fall.

Michaela D. Chitwood, Grade 8
Southern Reynolds County R-II School, MO

Time

Time is standing still.
The dead not yet lie.
No new baby cry.
The doomed yet not doomed.
What to come not here soon.
It seems as if your life is like that when someone is gone.
The challenge of heartbreak is from dust to dawn.
Time to say good-bye; fate is awake.
It is Time to shred the last shred to take.

Kelsey Matson, Grade 8
Musselman Middle School, WV

Great Hoof Beats of Thunder

So large and majestic
Black, brown, and beige
You cast a giant shadow in luminous moonlight
Yet look like a ghost at midnight
Should I be scared?
Your great hoof beats of thunder
Your magical hoof beats comb through blissful air
As you tease and play like children
You speak in tongues we do not understand
As you run and sparkle in starry light
But I always stop to listen
Great hoof beats of thunder
You stop to beat dew-stained ground
As you start off again
Your coat gleams at sunrise
For the last time I see you
So powerful at sunset
I hear you again
A beautiful wild horse with
Your great hoof beats of thunder

Michaela Craven, Grade 7
Barret Traditional Middle School, KY

Storm

Excitement tears through me like a hurricane in the gulf,
Just like the harsh waves on the shore.
I have to overcome this anxiety and survive.
Just wait until it's over and it will heal like an open sore.
This is just a part of everyone's lives,
But I want it to happen and get it over with.
From this worry and excitement will come happiness,
As long as I wait, sit tight,
Everything will turn out just right.
No more sadness,
Only smiles and heart warming memories,
It will fill our minds with gladness.
All I can do now is wait for that terrible storm to vanish.

Katie Stutler, Grade 8
Musselman Middle School, WV

This Boy

As I looked for a partner
I chose this cool boy.
Tough, smart,
Dark-skinned, dreads.
Deep as a man
In love with football,
The color of blue,
Who fears nothing but God.
If I hadn't been studying him,
I wouldn't know
How great he is.

Brittney Parker, Grade 8
Lee A Tolbert Community Academy, MO

Can You Imagine

Can you imagine a sky without stars
a street without cars
Can you imagine an empty house
a plain white blouse

Can you imagine a school without kids
bottles without lids
Can you imagine Santa without toys
a train without noise
Can you imagine

Alex Robinson, Grade 7
All Saints' Episcopal School, TN

Index

Author Autograph Page

Author Autograph Page

Author Autograph Page

Author Autograph Page

Author Autograph Page

Author Autograph Page